RETHINKING PARTICIPATION IN GLOBAL GOVERNANCE

LAW AND GLOBAL GOVERNANCE SERIES

Editors:
Andrew Hurrell, Benedict Kingsbury, and Richard B. Stewart

Global governance involves the exercise of power, beyond a single state, to influence behaviour, to generate resources, or to allocate authority. Regulatory structures, and law of all kinds, increasingly shape the nature, use, and effects of such power. These dynamic processes of ordering and governance blend the extra-national with the national, the public with the private, the political and economic with the social and cultural. Issues of effectiveness, justice, voice, and inequality in these processes are growing in importance. This series features exceptional works of original research and theory—both sector specific and conceptual—that carry forward the serious understanding and evaluation of these processes of global governance and the role of law and institutions within them. Contributions from all disciplines are welcomed. The series aims especially to deepen scholarship and thinking in international law, international politics, comparative law and politics, and public and private global regulation. A major goal is to study governance globally, and to enrich the literature on law and the nature and effects of global governance beyond the North Atlantic region.

ALSO PUBLISHED IN THE SERIES

Veiled Power
International Law and the Private Corporation 1886–1981
Doreen Lustig

The Rise of China and International Law
Taking Chinese Exceptionalism Seriously
Congyan Cai

Megaregulation Contested
Global Economic Ordering after TPP
Edited by Benedict Kingsbury, David M Malone, Paul Mertenskötter, Richard B Stewart, Thomas Streinz, and Atsushi Sunami

The Design of Competition Law Institutions
Global Norms, Local Choices
Edited by Eleanor M Fox and Michael J Trebilcock

The Rise of the Regulatory State of the South
Infrastructure and Development in Emerging Economies
Edited by Navroz K Dubash and Bronwen Morgan

Balancing Wealth and Health
The Battle over Intellectual Property and Access to Medicines in Latin America
Edited by Rochelle Dreyfuss and César Rodríguez-Garavito

Rethinking Participation in Global Governance

Voice and Influence after Stakeholder Reforms in Global Finance and Health

Edited by
JOOST PAUWELYN, MARTINO MAGGETTI,
TIM BÜTHE, AND AYELET BERMAN

OXFORD
UNIVERSITY PRESS

OXFORD
UNIVERSITY PRESS

Great Clarendon Street, Oxford, OX2 6DP,
United Kingdom

Oxford University Press is a department of the University of Oxford.
It furthers the University's objective of excellence in research, scholarship,
and education by publishing worldwide. Oxford is a registered trade mark of
Oxford University Press in the UK and in certain other countries

First Edition published in 2022

Impression: 1

Published in the United States of America by Oxford University Press
198 Madison Avenue, New York, NY 10016, United States of America

British Library Cataloguing in Publication Data
Data available

Library of Congress Control Number: 2021946952

ISBN 978–0–19–885256–8

DOI: 10.1093/oso/9780198852568.001.0001

Printed and bound by
CPI Group (UK) Ltd, Croydon, CR0 4YY

Praise for *Rethinking Participation in Global Governance*

'Combining rich empirical studies and insightful conceptual frames, this monumental work shows how and why procedural mechanisms to provide traditionally disregarded stakeholders with participation and influence in global administrative bodies have or have not succeeded. A landmark that will define the field for many years to come.'

Richard Stewart, John Edward Sexton Professor of Law, New York University

'This volume offers comprehensive yet careful analyses of participatory reforms in global governance. Its comparative focus on finance and health governance provides rich, compelling evidence that reforms on paper do not always translate into meaningful change in practice. The editors successfully cull powerful insights into the possibilities and barriers to participation in global governance.'

Beth Simmons, Andrea Mitchell University Professor in Law,
University of Pennsylvania

'Contains a truly comprehensive assessment of stakeholder participation in global financial and health institutions. The authors offer a compelling account of these changes and explore their impact on the legitimacy of global governance. A must-read for all who are interested in these critical questions for the future of global governance.'

Michael Zürn, Director of Research Unit Global Governance,
Social Science Center (WZB) Berlin

'This rich volume explores the conditions that allow previously excluded stakeholders, particularly those from the Global South, to influence global decision. This perfectly timed volume provides a nuanced study of how to bring more voices to the table and offers a fresh vision of multi-stakeholder governance.'

Rachel Brewster, Jeffrey and Bettysue Hughes Professor of Law,
Duke University

"An ambitious comparative study that grapples with the salient issues of stakeholder participation, voice and influence, and the continuing democratic deficits in the fast-evolving global governance landscape. The book systematically examines stakeholder participation across two policy domains, six emerging economies and several non-government bodies—and provides us with a conceptual framework for thinking about potential reforms of global institutions. Thoughtful and empirically rich, this is a must read for all who are interest in how representation can be improved in global governance.'

David Coen, Vice Dean and Head of Department,
Department of Political Science, University College London

Acknowledgements

This book would not have come into existence without the help of numerous individuals and institutions, and we are grateful for their support and assistance.

For financial support, we thank, above all, the Swiss Network for International Studies (SNIS), which has generously provided grant support for much of the research presented in this volume, as well as the launch workshop and two authors' workshops of the project. We also thank our own institutions—the Graduate Institute of International and Development Studies in Geneva, the *Hochschule für Politik* at the Technical University of Munich, the Department of Political Science and the Kenan Institute for Ethics at Duke University, the University of Lausanne, and the National University of Singapore—for financial assistance and other support. The Centre for Trade and Economic Integration (CTEI) at the Graduate Institute has taken on the essential role of administering and coordinating this study, with special thanks due to Theresa Carpenter, whose support has been indispensable. Thanks also to Angelica Zanninelli and Jessica Sun for coordinating our workshops. Further, we thank Ernesto Cruz Ruiz, Naomi Koh, Maria Florencia Sarmiento, and especially Yvonne Buckley, all of whom have helped with the preparation of the book at various stages.

We organized three workshops at which we exchanged thoughts and ideas for the project and received valuable feedback and constructive criticisms on earlier versions of the chapters in this volume—two at the Graduate Institute in Geneva (2015 and 2016) and one at the Technical University of Munich's *Akademiezentrum* Raitenhaslach (2017). We thank staff members of global organizations and scholars who provided their insights on these topics. For comments and suggestions at various stages of the project, we thank Thomas Biersteker, Vishnu Calindi, Diana Capone, Francois Degeorge, Camila Duran, Jérôme Duberry, Juan Flores, Daniele Gerundino, Harald Hau, Mark Herkenrath, Tana Johnson, Céline Kauffmann, Nico Krisch, Lida Lhotska, Ching-Fu Lin, Han Wei Liu, Mario Ottiglo, Ugo Panizza, Roxana Radu, Judith Richter, Tobias Rommel, Jean Pierre Roth, Thomas Sommerer, Eelco Szabo, Jonas Tallberg, Michaela Told, Andrea Barrios Villarreal, Charles Wyplosz, and Thomas Zeltner.

We also have benefitted from feedback received from discussants and members of the audience in the context of presentations at numerous international conferences, including the American Political Science Association (2017), the American Society of International Law Research Forum (2017), the OECD International Rule-making by International Organizations meetings (2016–2018), the International Studies Association Annual Convention (2018), the International Society of Public Law (ICON) Annual Conference (2017), the Barcelona Workshop 'Access and Exclusion in Global Governance' (2018), and the ECPR Standing Group on Regulatory Governance Conference (2018), as well as at the International Relations research group meetings at the *Hochschule für Politik* in Munich.

At Oxford University Press, many thanks to Merel Altstein, Jack McNichol, and Matthew Williams for their unwavering support as commissioning and project editors, to Michele Marietta for her excellent copy-editing, and to Mohith Singh and his team for their much appreciated commitment to seeing the production process through to completion despite various challenges with which COVID-19 presented them.

Most of all, we want to express our personal gratitude to our families for their great patience and tremendous support throughout this multi-year project. We dedicate this volume to them and hope that our scholarship may make a small contribution to allowing for productively greater participation in global governance for the generation of our children.

Joost Pauwelyn, Tim Büthe, Martino Maggetti,
and Ayelet Berman
Geneva – Munich and Durham – Lausanne – Singapore
December 2021

Contents

List of Contributors

Kern Alexander is Professor of International Financial Law and Regulation and Chair for Law and Finance at the Faculty of Law, University of Zurich. He is also Director of the Research Network for Sustainable Finance, www.susfin.ch. Online at: https://www.cisl.cam.ac.uk/directory/kern-alexander

Ayelet Berman is Senior Research Fellow at the National University of Singapore's Centre for International Law, where she leads the Global Health Law and Governance program. She is also Adjunct Assistant Professor at the Faculty of Law, National University of Singapore. Email: cilayel@nus.edu.sg

Chris Brummer is a professor of law at Georgetown University Law Center, and the Faculty Director of the Institute of International Economic Law. online at: https://chrisbrummer.org

Gian Luca Burci is Adjunct Professor of International Law at the Graduate Institute of International and Development Studies, Geneva, and Director of the joint Graduate Institute-Georgetown Law LLM on Global Health Law and Governance. He was the World Health Organization Legal Counsel from 2005 to 2016. Email: gian-luca.burci@graduateinstitute.ch; online at: https://www.graduateinstitute.ch/academic-departments/faculty/gian-luca-burci

Tim Büthe is Professor and Chair for International Relations, *Hochschule für Politik*, School of Social Sciences and Technology and TUM School of Management at the Technical University of Munich (TUM), as well as Senior Fellow of the Kenan Institute for Ethics at Duke University. He serves as the corresponding editor for this volume. Email: buthe@hfp.tum.de; online at: http://buthe.net

Sachin Chaturvedi is an Economist and the Director General of the Research and Information System for Developing Countries (RIS), a policy research institute based in New Delhi, India. He also serves on the Board of India's central bank the Reserve Bank of India. Email: sachin@ris.org.in

Cindy Cheng is a Postdoctoral Research Fellow at the *Hochschule für Politik*/School of Governance, Technical University of Munich (TUM). Email: cindy.cheng@hfp.tum.de; online at: http://www.cindyyawencheng.com

Henrique Choer Moraes is a Diplomat, Ministry of Foreign Affairs, Brazil. He is also an associate fellow at the Leuven Centre for Global Governance Studies (KU Leuven, Belgium). He is writing in a personal capacity; the opinions expressed in his contributions to this volume do not necessarily represent the positions of the Brazilian Government. Email: henrique.moraes@itamaraty.gov.br

Mercy Berman DeMenno is Principal of Bosque Advisors, Senior Fellow of the Global Financial Markets Center at Duke University's School of Law, and Affiliate of the Center on Risk at Duke University's Initiative for Science and Society. Email: mercy.demenno@duke.edu

Anh Do is a Data Scientist at The Nielsen Company. She worked on the Rethinking Participation project while completing her PhD in Political Science at Duke University.

David Gartner is a Professor at the Sandra Day O'Connor College of Law at Arizona State University.

Ronald Gindrat is Senior Advisor to the Executive Director for Azerbaijan, Kazakhstan, Kyrgyz Republic, Poland, Serbia, Switzerland, Tajikistan, Turkmenistan, and Uzbekistan at the International Monetary Fund. Email: rogindrat@yahoo.com

K M Gopakumar is Legal Adviser and Senior Researcher with the Third World Network. Email: kmgkumar@gmail.com; online at: https://twn.my/

Paul Inderbinen is Deputy Head of Financial System and Financial Markets at the State Secretariat for International Finance, Swiss Federal Finance Department. Email: paul.inderbinen@sif.admin.ch

Himanshu Jha is a Lecturer and Research Fellow at the Department of Political Science, South Asia Institute, University of Heidelberg. Email: jha@uni-heidelberg.de; online at: http://www.himanshujha.net

Olga Kovarzina is an instructor, as well as an independent scholar of environmental and financial governance, marginalized actor participation, and equitable education. During her work on the Rethinking Participation project, she was a Visiting Researcher at the University of Lausanne, as well as a Research Associate at the Graduate Institute of International and Development Studies, Geneva. Email: olga.kovarzina@graduateinstitute.ch

Martino Maggetti is Associate Professor of Political Science at the Laboratory for the Analysis of Governance and Public Policy in Europe (LAGAPE) and at the Institute of Political Studies (IEP) of the University of Lausanne. Email: Martino.Maggetti@unil.ch online at: https://maggetti.org/

André de Mello e Souza is a Senior Researcher at the Institute for Applied Economic Research (IPEA), Brazil. Email: andre.souza@ipea.gov.br

Suerie Moon is Co-Director of the Global Health Centre and Professor of the Practice of International Relations & Political Science at the Graduate Institute of International and Development Studies, Geneva. She previously was a Lecturer on Global Health at the Harvard T H Chan School of Public Health. Email: suerie.moon@graduateinstitute.ch; online at:https://graduateinstitute.ch/academic-departments/faculty/suerie-moon

Rahul Mukherji is Professor and Head of the Department of Political Science, as well as Director of the South Asia Institute at the University of Heidelberg, where he also serves as Spokesperson for the Centre for Asian and Transcultural Studies. Email: Mukherji@uni-heidelberg.de online at: https://www.uni-heidelberg.de/sai/pol/team/mukherji.html

Gülen Atay Newton is an Independent Scholar-Practitioner with more than two decades of experience as a legal executive in international development finance organizations, including at the Asian Development Bank (ADB) and as General Counsel of The Global Fund to Fight Aids, Tuberculosis and Malaria. Email: gulen.atay@gmail.com

Joost Pauwelyn is Professor of International Law and Head of the International Law Department at the Graduate Institute of International and Development Studies in Geneva, Switzerland, and Murase Visiting Professor of Law at Georgetown Law Center, Georgetown University, USA. Email: joost.pauwelyn@graduateinstitiute.ch

Peter B Payoyo, formerly a Professor of Law at the University of the Philippines, is a Researcher at the Centre for Trade and Economic Integration, Graduate Institute of International and Development Studies, Geneva. Email: payoyo@ziggo.nl

Facundo Pérez Aznar is a Senior Researcher at the Geneva Center for International Dispute Settlement (CIDS), as well as an Associate Professor of International Economic Law at the University of Buenos Aires. Email: facundo.perez@graduateinstitute.ch

Kal Raustiala is Promise Institute Professor of Comparative and International Law at the UCLA School of Law and Director of the UCLA Burkle Center for International Relations. Email: raustiala@law.ucla.edu

Krishna Ravi Srinivas is a Senior Fellow & Consultant at the Research and Information System for Developing Countries (RIS), a policy research institute based in New Delhi, India, as well as Managing Editor of the *Asian Biotechnology and Development Review*. Email: k.ravisrinivas@gmail.com, ravisrinivas@ris.org.in; online at: https://www.researchgate.net/profile/Krishna_Ravi_Srinivas

Weiwei Zhang is International Trade Advisor at Sidley Austin LLP's Geneva office. During her work on the Rethinking Participation project, she was a Research Associate of the Centre for Trade and Economic Integration, Graduate Institute of International and Development Studies in Geneva. Email: weiwei.zhang@graduateinstitute.ch online at: https://www.sidley.com/en/people/z/zhang-weiwei

PART I
INTRODUCTION AND THEORETICAL FRAMEWORK

1
Introduction
Rethinking Stakeholder Participation in Global Governance

Ayelet Berman, Tim Büthe, Martino Maggetti, and Joost Pauwelyn[*]

1.1 Introduction

Technology and public policy have extended what Norbert Elias called the 'chains of interdependence' across the globe.[1] The effectiveness of risk management in financial markets in the United States or Switzerland, for instance, affects the safety of retirement savings in other OECD countries as well as the cost of borrowing for many developing countries. Sanitary conditions in agricultural or fishing communities in Asia or Latin America affect food safety in Europe and North America—with feedback effects for wages and working conditions in developing countries.

Traditionally, governments collaborated through treaty-based intergovernmental organizations (IOs) to deal with the consequences of interdependence. Increasingly, however, governments and non-state actors have turned to a variety of new forms of global governance to address the complex and often rapidly evolving challenges that arise from intensified international interdependence. Sector-specific regulatory authorities collaborate with their counterparts in transgovernmental networks, such as the Basel Committee on Banking Supervision. Government officials collaborate with civil society and business in public–private or multi-stakeholder partnerships, such as the Global Fund to Fight AIDS, Tuberculosis and Malaria. And representatives of industry or non-governmental organizations (NGOs) set standards in transnational private bodies, such as the International Accounting Standards Board or the Forest Stewardship Council.[2]

[*] Authors are listed in alphabetical order.

[1] Norbert Elias, *Über den Prozeß der Zivilisation: Soziogenetische und psychogenetische Untersuchungen. Erster Band: Wandlungen des Verhaltens in den weltlichen Oberschichten des Abendlandes* (Haus zum Falken 1937).

[2] See Kenneth Abbott and Duncan Snidal, 'The Governance Triangle: Regulatory Standards Institutions and the Shadow of the State' in Walter Mattli and Ngaire Woods (eds), *The Politics of Global Regulation* (Princeton University Press 2009) 44-88; Anne-Marie Slaughter, *A New World Order* (Princeton University Press 2004); Benedict Kingsbury, Nico Krisch and Richard B Stewart, 'The Emergence of Global Administrative Law' 68(3/4) *Law and Contemporary Problems* (2005) 15-61; Joost Pauwelyn, Ramses A Wessel and Jan Wouters (eds), *Informal International Lawmaking* (Oxford University Press 2012); Henry Farrell and Abraham L Newman, 'Domestic Institutions Beyond the Nation State: Charting the New Interdependence Approach' 66(2) *World Politics* (2014) 331-363; Klaus Dingwerth, *The New Transnationalism: Transnational Governance and Democratic Legitimacy* (Palgrave Macmillan 2007) 144-185; Kristina Tamm Hallström and Magnus Boström, *Transnational Multi-Stakeholder Standardization* (Edward Elgar 2010); Tim Büthe and Walter Mattli, *The New Global Rulers: The Privatization of Regulation in the World Economy* (Princeton University Press 2011); Graeme Auld and Benjamin Cashore, 'The Forest

Ayelet Berman, Tim Büthe, Martino Maggetti, and Joost Pauwelyn, *Introduction* In: *Rethinking Participation in Global Governance*. Edited by: Joost Pauwelyn, Martino Maggetti, Tim Büthe, and Ayelet Berman, Oxford University Press. © Ayelet Berman, Tim Büthe, Martino Maggetti, and Joost Pauwelyn 2022. DOI: 10.1093/oso/9780198852568.003.0001

Quite often, the actions, decisions, principles, standards, and rules of global governance bodies affect the lives of individuals, groups, and even entire countries, which are not represented in the respective global body, or which do not have any meaningful say in the decision-making process.[3] We focus in this book in particular on the pervasive exclusion of governmental actors from the 'Global South', but also pay attention to the similarly ubiquitous disregard of diffuse, societal interests (including but not only from the South).[4]

With the growing importance of global governance, scholars, policy-makers, and other observers started to pay more attention to such 'stakeholders', which have traditionally been excluded from—or been marginalized within—policy- and decision-making processes.[5] One key issue driving this trend has been the observation that more inclusive governance, while in the short term sometimes less efficient as a way of reaching a decision,[6] can be much more effective because it will be based on better information and might have stronger support among stakeholders who are subsequently called upon to implement the decision.[7] Moreover, expectations regarding the legitimacy of global governance have shifted from the traditional focus on state consent in intergovernmental IOs towards more democratic, participatory forms of legitimation. Allowing those who will be affected by a given rule or decision to participate in the process of rule-making or decision-making is foundational not just for political democracy.

Stewardship Council' in Darryl Reed, Peter Utting and Ananya Mukherjee-Reed (eds), *Business Regulation and Non-State Actors* (Routledge 2012) 134-147.

[3] We use 'global governance body' as a general term for global, international, and transnational bodies and networks that, at a minimum, provide a forum and a set of procedures for drawing up rules, setting standards, articulating principles, developing policies, and making decisions to address issues that (are believed to) require coordinated or maybe even collective actions across borders—and in that sense, if they are effective, 'govern' some part of the global sphere without resort to overt coercive means and beyond the boundaries of a single country. See Thomas G Weiss, *Global Governance: Why? What? Whither?* (Polity Press 2013), who defines global governance as the 'sum of the informal and formal values, norms, procedures, and institutions that help states, intergovernmental organizations, civil society, and transnational corporations identify, understand, and address trans-boundary problems.' For an overview of the diversity of just 'transnational' governance bodies, see Thomas Hale and David Held (eds), *Handbook of Transnational Governance: Institutions and Innovations* (Polity Press 2011). For a discussion of the importance of foregrounding actors and agency in global governance, see Deborah D Avant, Martha Finnemore and Susan K Sell (eds), *Who Governs the Globe?* (Cambridge University Press 2010).

[4] Richard B Stewart, 'Remedying Disregard in Global Regulatory Governance: Accountability, Participation, and Responsiveness' 108(2) *American Journal of International Law* (2014) 211-270.

[5] In putting the emphasis consciously and explicitly on what Pauwelyn *et al.* (n 2) call 'external' stakeholders—i.e. those who are affected by a global governance body's rules and decisions but traditionally excluded from, or marginalized within, the body's rule-making and decision-making—we consciously use the term 'stakeholder' in a strictly analytically and normatively neutral sense. Specifically, we use the term to denote generally *all* those who are affected by—and hence have a stake in—a particular governance body's rules and decisions. Our use of the term explicitly does not imply support for any normative claims, for example, for a 'right' of commercial, private sector stakeholders in public governance.

[6] See, e.g. Cary Coglianese, 'Assessing Consensus: The Promise and Performance of Negotiated Rule-Making' 46(6) *Duke Law Journal* (1997) 1255-1349; Renée A Irvin and John Stansbury, 'Citizen Participation in Decision Making: Is It Worth the Effort?' 64(1) *Public Administration Review* (2004) 55-65.

[7] As the WHO stresses, '[t]he benefit of involving stakeholders is that they are a rich source of practical suggestions, and they are more likely to comply with any requirements they have participated in devising.' (World Health Organization, *Medical Device Regulations: Global Overview and Guiding Principles* (WHO 2003) 25). For a fuller discussion of the pertinent literature, see Mercy B DeMenno and Tim Büthe, 'Voice and Influence in Global Governance: An Analytical Framework.' Chapter 2, this volume.

It is also essential for 'economic democracy',[8] which contributes to the expectation that global governance bodies, too, should provide some practicable form of such participation—even if it might not go as far as Held's proposal for 'cosmopolitan democracy'.[9] In light of such changed norms and expectations, the marginalization and exclusion of stakeholders also undermines the legitimacy of global governance bodies.[10]

Against this background, many global bodies have in recent years reformed decision-making procedures and practices to boost stakeholder participation. They have established a variety of institutional opportunities for developing countries and non-state actors, which had hitherto been excluded from their decision-making processes, to have a voice in such processes. But have these reforms increased the *actual engagement* of previously excluded stakeholders? Have the reforms increased their *influence* in the decision and rule-making processes?

Our primary objective in this book is to examine and explain to what extent such institutional reforms have given voice to previously excluded stakeholders (which motivates our focus on actual engagement, that is, the extent to which such stakeholders have made use of the new voice opportunities) and to what extent they have gained actual influence over outcomes thanks to these opportunities. Normative arguments as to why global bodies should open up to traditionally marginalized stakeholders motivate our inquiry, but we mainly seek to make an empirical and analytical contribution to the understanding of stakeholder participation.

Aside from singular case studies,[11] many of which focus on the WTO, the multilateral development banks, and the International Monetary Fund (IMF),[12] the *empirical* literature on institutional changes that are supposed to address the participation gap of marginalized stakeholders, has been limited.[13] Empirical research has more

[8] Robert A Dahl, *A Preface to Economic Democracy* (University of California Press 1985).

[9] David Held, *Democracy and the Global Order* (Polity Press 1995).

[10] Arthur Benz and Yannis Papadopoulos (eds), *Governance and Democracy: Comparing National, European and International Experiences* (Routledge 2006); Magdalena Bexell, Jonas Tallberg and Anders Uhlin, 'Democracy in Global Governance: The Promises and Pitfalls of Transnational Actors' 16(1) *Global Governance* (2010) 81-101; Michael Zürn, 'Global Governance and Legitimacy Problems' 39(2) *Government and Opposition* (2004) 260-287; Allen Buchanan and Robert O Keohane, 'The Legitimacy of Global Governance Institutions' 20(4) *Ethics & International Affairs* (2006) 405-437.

[11] E.g. Sabino Cassese, Bruno Carotti, Lorenzo Casini, Eleonora Cavalieri and Euan MacDonald (eds), *Global Administrative Law: The Casebook*, 3rd ed. (Institute for International Law and Justice, NYU School of Law and Istituto di Ricerche sulla Pubblica Amministrazione 2012).

[12] Steve Charnovitz, 'The Emergence of Democratic Participation in Global Governance' 10(1) *Indiana Journal of Global Legal Studies* (2003) 45-77; Steve Charnovitz, 'Nongovernmental Organizations and International Law' 100(2) *American Journal of International Law* (2006) 348-372; Steve Charnovitz, 'Opening the WTO to Nongovernmental Interests' 24(1–2) *Fordham International Law Journal* (2000) 173-216; Jeffrey L Dunoff, 'The Misguided Debate over NGO Participation at the WTO' 1(3) *Journal of International Economic Law* (1998) 433-456; Jonathan Fox, 'Transparency for Accountability: Civil Society Monitoring of Multilateral Development Bank Anti-Poverty Projects' 7(2) *Viewpoint: Development in Practice* (1997) 167-178; David Hunter and Nathalie Bernasconi-Osterwalder, 'Democratizing Multilateral Development Banks' in Carl Bruch (ed), *New Public: The Globalization of Public Participation* (Environmental Law Institute 2002) 151-164; Richard G Shell, 'The Trade Stakeholders Model and Participation by Nonstate Parties in the World Trade Organization' 17(1) *University of Pennsylvania Journal of International Economic Law* (1996) 359-381; Jonas Tallberg, Thomas Sommerer, Theresa Squatrito and Christer Jönsson, *The Opening Up of International Organizations: Transnational Access in Global Governance* (Cambridge University Press 2013).

[13] With few exceptions: Tallberg *et al.*, *Opening Up* (n 12); OECD, *International Regulatory Co-Operation: The Role of International Organisations in Fostering Better Rules of Globalisation* (OECD

commonly focused on the factors that influence public opinion regarding the legitimacy of IOs,[14] or the practices that affect such legitimacy.[15] Richard Stewart's lament that there has been 'little careful and sustained analysis' of newer, more informal modes of global governance is therefore still largely valid.[16] Particularly striking is the dearth of analyses of the implications and consequences of such reforms.

We seek to contribute to closing this gap with this volume, which provides a multi- and interdisciplinary international law and international relations perspective[17] as part of what Gregory Shaffer and Tom Ginsburg have identified as the 'empirical turn in international legal scholarship'.[18]

In the remainder of this introduction, we situate the book within the existing literature on global governance, legitimacy, accountability, and participation; highlight the book's key contributions; and provide an overview of the book's structure and chapters.

1.2 The Literature

1.2.1 Evolution of Global Governance

The second half of the twentieth century witnessed an explosion in the rise of treaty-based IOs,[19] some of them fostering their own 'organizational

Publishing 2016), 85; Phillip Y Lipscy, *Renegotiating the World Order: Institutional Change in International Relations* (Cambridge University Press 2017).

[14] Pippa Norris, 'Confidence in the United Nations: Cosmopolitan and Nationalistic Attitudes' in Yilmaz Esmer and Thorleif Pettersson (eds), *The International System, Democracy and Values* (Acta Universitatis Upsaliensis 2009) 17-48; Tana Johnson, 'Guilt by Association: The Link between States' Influence and the Legitimacy of Intergovernmental Organizations' 6 *Review of International Organizations* (2011) 57-84; Lisa Maria Dellmuth and Jonas Tallberg, 'The Social Legitimacy of International Organisations: Interest Representation, Institutional Performance, and Confidence Extrapolation in the United Nations' 41 *Review of International Studies* (2015) 451-475; Bernd Schlipphak, 'Measuring Attitudes toward Regional Organizations outside Europe' 10 *Review of International Organizations* (2015) 351-375.

[15] Martin Binder and Monik Heupel, 'The Legitimacy of the UN Security Council: Evidence from Recent General Assembly Debates' 59(2) *International Studies Quarterly* (2015) 238-250; Dominik Zaum (ed), *Legitimating International Organizations* (Oxford University Press 2013); Steven Bernstein, 'Legitimacy in Intergovernmental and Non-state Global Governance' 18 *Review of International Political Economy* (2011) 17-51; James Brassett and Eleni Tsingou, 'The Politics of Legitimate Global Governance' 18(1) *Review of International Political Economy* (2011) 1-16.

[16] Richard B Stewart, 'Remedying Disregard' (n 4), 244.

[17] See Jeffrey L Dunoff and Mark A Pollack (eds), *Interdisciplinary Perspectives on International Law and International Relations: The State of the Art* (Cambridge University Press 2019).

[18] Gregory Shaffer and Tom Ginsburg, 'The Empirical Turn in International Legal Scholarship' 106 *American Journal of International Law* (2012) 1-46.

[19] Kjell Skjelsbaek, 'The Growth of International Non-Governmental Organizations' 25(3) *International Organization* (1971) 420-442; Oran R Young, 'Political Leadership and Regime Formation: On the Development of Institutions in International Society' 45(3) *International Organization* (1991) 281-308; Cheryl Shanks, Harold K Jacobson and Jeffrey H Kaplan, 'Inertia and Change in the Constellation of International Governmental Organizations, 1981–1992' 50(4) *International Organization* (1996) 593-627; José E Alvarez, *International Organizations as Law-Makers* (Oxford University Press 2005); Ian Hurd, *International Organizations: Politics, Law, Practice* (Cambridge University Press 2011); Jan Klabbers, *Advanced Introduction to the Law of International Organizations* (Edward Elgar Publishing 2015). An insightful critique remains: Guilio M Gallarotti, 'The Limits of International Organization: Systematic Failure in the Management of International Relations' 45(2) *International Organization* (1991) 183-220.

progeny'.[20] Today, global governance increasingly also entails various networks, partnerships, and expert bodies outside formal IOs.[21] These newer global governance bodies include transnational private standard-setting bodies, such as the IASB, which sets rules for corporate financial reporting and disclosure in more than a hundred countries;[22] public–private or multi-stakeholder partnerships,[23] such as the Global Fund to Fight AIDS, Tuberculosis and Malaria; as well as transgovernmental networks,[24] such as the Basel Committee on Banking Supervision, in which

[20] Tana L Johnson, *Organizational Progeny: Why Governments Are Losing Control over the Proliferating Structures of Global Governance* (Oxford University Press 2014).

[21] Pauwelyn *et al.* (eds), *Informal International Lawmaking* (n 2); Ayelet Berman, Sanderijn Duquet, Joost Pauwelyn, Ramses A Wessel and Jan Wouters (eds), *Informal International Lawmaking: Case Studies* (Torkel Opsahl Academic EPublisher 2012) 13-34; Felicity Vabulas and Duncan Snidal, 'Organization without Delegation: Informal Intergovernmental Organizations (IIGOs) and the Spectrum of Intergovernmental Arrangements' 8(2) *Review of International Organizations* (2013) 193-220; Kenneth W Abbott, Jessica F Green and Robert O Keohane, 'Organizational Ecology and Institutional Change in Global Governance' 70(1) International Organization (2016) 247-277; Charles B Roger, *Soft Governance: Why States Create Informal Intergovernmental Organizations, And Why It Matters* (PhD Dissertation, University of British Columbia 2016); Oliver Westerwinter, 'The Politics of Informal Governance' (2017) <https://snis.ch/wp-content/uploads/2017/12/9076_final_wp_working_paper_20072017.pdf>, last accessed 06/12/2019).

[22] Büthe and Mattli, *New Global Rulers* (n 2), esp. chs. 4 and 5; Shawn Donnelly, 'Informal International Lawmaking: Global Financial Market Regulation' in Berman *et al.* (n 21), 179–249; Alan J Richardson and Burkard Eberlein, 'Legitimating Transnational Standard-Setting: The Case of the International Accounting Standards Board' 98(2) *Journal of Business Ethics* (2011) 217–245; Christopher Humphrey and Anne Loft, 'Moving Beyond Nuts and Bolts: The Complexities of Governing a Global Profession through International Standards' in Stefano Ponte, Peter Gibbon and Jakob Vestergaard (eds), *Governing Through Standards* (Palgrave Macmillan 2011) 102–129; Kees Camfferman and Stephen A Zeff, *Aiming for Global Accounting Standards: The International Accounting Standards Board, 2000–2011* (Oxford University Press 2015).

[23] Tanja A Börzel and Thomas Risse, 'Public-Private Partnerships: Effective and Legitimate Tools of Transnational Governance?' in Edgar Grande and Louis W Pauly (eds), *Complex Sovereignty: Reconstituting Political Authority in the Twenty-first Century* (University of Toronto Press 2005) 195-216; Errol Meidinger, 'The Administrative Law of Global Public-Private Regulation: The Case of Forestry' 17 *European Journal of International Law* (2006) 47–87; Marco Schäferhoff, Sabine Campe and Christopher Kaan, 'Transnational Public-Private Partnerships in International Relations: Making Sense of Concepts, Research Frameworks and Results' 11(3) *International Studies Review* (2009) 451–474; Kristina Tamm Hallström and Magnus Boström, *Transnational Multi-Stakeholder Standardization: Organizing Fragile Non-State Authority* (Edward Elgar 2010); Christopher A Whytock, 'Public-Private Interaction in Global Governance: The Case of Transnational Commercial Arbitration' 12(3) *Business and Politics* (2010) 1–27; Tim Büthe and Nathaniel Harris, 'The Codex Alimentarius Commission: A Hybrid Public-Private Regulator' in Thomas Hale and David Held (eds), *Handbook on Innovations in Transnational Governance* (Polity Press 2011) 219-228; Andrea Liese and Marianne Beisheim, 'Transnational Public-Private Partnerships and the Provision of Collective Goods in Developing Countries' in Thomas Risse (ed), *Governance Without a State? Policies and Politics in Areas of Limited Statehood* (Columbia University Press 2011) 115-143; Luc W Fransen, 'Multi-Stakeholder Governance and Voluntary Program Interactions: Legitimation Politics in the Institutional Design of Corporate Social Responsibility' 10(1) *Socio-Economic Review* (2012) 163-192; Graeme Auld, *Constructing Private Governance: The Rise and Evolution of Forest, Coffee and Fisheries Certification* (Yale University Press 2014); Ayelet Berman, 'The Rise of Multistakeholder Global Governance' 111 *Proceedings of the ASIL Annual Meeting* (2017) 205-208.

[24] Kal Raustiala, 'The Architecture of International Cooperation: Transgovernmental Networks and the Future of International Law' 43(1) *Virginia Journal of International Law* (2002) 1-92; Anne-Marie Slaughter, *A New World Order* (Princeton University Press 2004); Francesca E Bignami, 'Transgovernmental Networks vs Democracy: The Case of the European Information Privacy Network' 26(3) *Michigan Journal of International Law* (2005) 807-868; Christopher A Whytock, 'A Rational Design Theory of Transgovernmentalism: The Case of E.U.-U.S. Merger Review Cooperation' 23(1) *Boston University International Law Journal* (2005) 1-53; Abraham L Newman, *Protectors of Privacy: Regulating Personal Data in the Global Economy* (Cornell University Press 2008); David Bach and Abraham L Newman, 'Transgovernmental Networks and Domestic Policy Convergence: Evidence from Insider Trading Regulation' 64(3) *International Organization* (2010) 505-528; Ayelet Berman, *Reining in the*

representatives of twenty-seven countries' central banks set minimum capital requirements for financial institutions and develop best practice standards for banking supervision.[25] Both traditional IOs and these newer modes of governance make up today's global governance.

Substantial literatures in international law, political science, international relations, sociology, and other social sciences have examined these new forms of global governance. A vast number of studies describe the operations of a single international organization or transnational global governance body in depth.[26] A much smaller though fast-growing body of work has been taking a consciously comparative approach to understand and explain the origin, varied forms, and actual practices of inter- and transnational governance, including Abbott and Snidal's work on soft law and transnational new governance, as well as, with Genschel and Zangl, on 'orchestration' in global governance;[27] Bernauer and collaborators' work on the involvement of civil society in global environmental governance;[28] Büthe and Mattli's[29] as well as Cafaggi and collaborators'[30] work on transnational private regulation; Kahler and Lake's work on

Regulators: Transnational Regulatory Networks and Accountability (PhD Dissertation, Graduate Institute of International and Development Studies 2014); Henry Farrell and Abraham L Newman, 'Domestic Institutions Beyond the Nation State: Charting the New Interdependence Approach' 66(2) *World Politics* (2014) 331-363; Sandra Lavenex, 'The Power of Functionalist Extension: How EU Rules Travel' 21(6) *Journal of European Public Policy* (2014) 885-903.

[25] Ben Thirkell-White, 'Private Authority and Legitimacy in the International System' 20(3) *International Relations* (2006) 335-342; David Andrew Singer, *Regulating Capital: Setting Standards for the International Financial System* (Cornell University Press 2007); Pierre-Hugues Verdier, 'US Implementation of Basel II: Lessons for Informal International Lawmaking' in Pauwelyn *et al.* (eds), *Informal International Lawmaking* (n 2), 437-467; Roman Goldbach, *Global Governance and Regulatory Failure: The Political Economy of Banking* (Palgrave Macmillan 2015); Adam William Chalmers, 'When Banks Lobby: The Effects of Organizational Characteristics and Banking Regulations on International Bank Lobbying' 19(1) *Business and Politics* (2017) 107-134.

[26] See, e.g. Kees Camfferman and Stephen A Zeff, *Financial Reporting and Global Capital Markets: A History of the International Accounting Standards Committee, 1973-2000* (Oxford University Press 2007); Lorenzo Casini, 'Global Hybrid Public-Private Bodies: The World Anti-Doping Agency (WADA)' 6 *International Organizations Law Review* (2009) 421-446; Craig N Murphy and JoAnne Yates, *The International Organization for Standardization (ISO): Global Governance through Voluntary Consensus* (Routledge 2008); Marcel Heires, 'The International Organization for Standardization (ISO)' 13(3) *New Political Economy* (2008) 357-367; Elliot Posner, *The Origins of Europe's New Stock Markets* (Harvard University Press 2008); David P Rapkin and Jonathan R Strand, 'Reforming the IMF's Weighted Voting System' 29(3) *The World Economy* (2006) 305-324; James R Vreeland, *The International Monetary Fund: Politics of Conditional Lending* (Routledge 2007).

[27] Abbott and Snidal, 'The Governance Triangle' (n 2); Kenneth Abbott, Philipp Genschel, Duncan Snidal and Bernhard Zangl, 'Orchestration: Global Governance Through Intermediaries' in Kenneth Abbott, Philipp Genschel, Duncan Snidal and Bernhard Zangl (eds), *International Organizations as Orchestrators* (Cambridge University Press 2015) 3-36.

[28] See, e.g. Thomas Bernauer and Carola Betzold, 'Civil Society in Global Environmental Governance' 21(1) *Journal of Environment and Development* (2012) 62-66.

[29] Walter Mattli and Tim Büthe, 'Setting International Standards: Technological Rationality or Primacy of Power?' 56(1) *World Politics* (2003) 1-42; Walter Mattli and Tim Büthe, 'Global Private Governance' 68(3/4) *Law and Contemporary Problems* (2005) 225-262; Tim Büthe and Walter Mattli, 'International Standards and Standard-Setting Bodies' in David Coen, Graham Wilson and Wyn Grant (eds), *Oxford Handbook of Business and Government* (Oxford University Press 2010) 440-471; Büthe and Mattli, *New Global Rulers* (n 2); Tim Büthe, 'Private Regulation in the Global Economy: A (P)Review' 12(3) *Business and Politics* (2010) 1–38.

[30] Fabrizio Cafaggi (ed), *Reframing Self-Regulation in European Private Law* (Kluwer Law International 2006); Colin Scott, Fabrizio Cafaggi, and Linda Senden (eds), *The Challenge of Transnational Private*

political authority in transition;[31] Maggetti's work on regulatory agencies[32] and the effects of governance networks;[33] Pauwelyn and collaborators' work on informal international law-making;[34] Shaffer and Halliday's work on 'transnational legal orders';[35] Kingsbury's, Stewart's, Krisch's, Cassese's and others' work on Global Administrative Law;[36] or von Bogdandy and others' work on International Public Authority.[37]

Jointly, this rich literature demonstrates the growing importance of global governance. Global bodies make consequential decisions across many different issue areas, notwithstanding state and non-state actors' proclivity for resorting to declamatory politics in international just as in domestic politics,[38] as well as the tendency of global bodies to exhibit certain pathologies.[39] The existing literature also reveals tremendous institutional variation in contemporary global governance—with respect to legal status, the mix of public and private authority on which global governance bodies rely, the size and restrictiveness of their membership, decision-making procedures, etc. It is this variation that drew our attention to the question of who actually gets to participate and thus has agency in global governance[40]—and what the consequences are for legitimacy and effectiveness.

Regulation: Conceptual and Constitutional Debates (Wiley-Blackwell 2011); Fabrizio Cafaggi and Andrea Renda, *Measuring the Effectiveness of Transnational Private Regulation* (Strijbis Foundation 2014); Fabrizio Cafaggi, 'The Many Features of Transnational Private Rule-Making: Unexplored Relationships between Custom, Jura Mercatorum, and Global Private Regulation' 36 *University of Pennsylvania Journal of International Law* (2015) 875-938; Fabrizio Cafaggi, 'Transnational Private Regulation: Regulating Global Financial Regulators' in Sabino Cassese (ed), *Research Handbook on Global Administrative Law* (Edward Elgar 2016) 212-241.

31 Miles Kahler and David A Lake (eds), *Governance in a Global Economy: Political Authority in Transition* (Princeton University Press 2003).

32 Martino Maggetti, *Regulation in Practice: The de facto Independence of Regulatory Agencies* (ECPR Press 2012).

33 Martino Maggetti, 'The Rewards of Cooperation: The Effects of Membership in European Regulatory Networks' 53(3) *European Journal of Political Research* (2014) 480-499.

34 Pauwelyn *et al.* (eds), *Informal International Lawmaking* (n 2); Ayelet Berman, 'The Role of Domestic Administrative Law in the Accountability of IN-LAW: The Case of the ICH' in Pauwelyn *et al.*, (eds), *Informal International Lawmaking* (n 2), 468-499; Berman *et al.*, (eds), *Informal International Lawmaking: Case Studies* (n 21).

35 Terence C Halliday and Gregory Shaffer (eds), *Transnational Legal Orders* (Cambridge University Press 2015).

36 Kingsbury *et al.* 'Emergence of Global Administrative Law' (n 2); Cassese *et al.* (eds), *Global Administrative Law* (n 11).

37 Armin Von Bogdandy, Rüdiger Wolfrum, Jochen von Bernsdorff, Philipp Dann, and Matthias Goldmann (eds), *The Exercise of Public Authority by International Institutions* (Springer 2010).

38 See, e.g. Hans Günter Brauch, Czeslaw Mesjasz, and Björn Möller, 'Controlling Weapons in the Quest for Peace' in Chadwick F Alger (ed), *The Future of the United Nations System* (United Nations University Press 1998) 15-53; Stephen D Krasner, *Sovereignty: Organized Hypocrisy* (Princeton University Press 1999); Tim Büthe and Moohyung Cho with Nicholas Becker, Sophie Allen, Daniel Altman, Raisa Chowdhury, Lauren Forman, Evan Glasner, Ateeb Khan, Davis Muthoko, Mark Sater, Chad Vincente, Gregory Vuong, Angela Wang, and Diana Ye, 'Power and Institutionalized International Regulatory Cooperation: A Multi-Method Analysis' 22(s1) *European Affairs Review* (2017) 115-136; Richard M Price (ed), *Moral Limit and Possibility in World Politics* (Cambridge University Press 2008); Catherine E Weaver, *Hypocrisy Trap: The World Bank and Poverty of Reform* (Princeton University Press 2008).

39 See Michael N Barnett and Martha Finnemore, *Rules for the World: International Organizations in Global Politics* (Cornell University Press 2004) and Weaver, *Hypocrisy Trap* (n 38).

40 On the importance of agency in global governance, see also Avant *et al.* (eds), *Who Governs the Globe?* (n 3).

1.2.2 Inclusion, Exclusion, and Legitimacy in Global Governance

The decisions of global bodies are not just consequential for their own members. Many global bodies develop norms, set standards, or make rules that, despite their sometimes private and often legally non-binding nature,[41] govern the behaviour of states, individuals, social groups, and firms across the globe. However, many of those who are affected—the 'stakeholders' of those global governance bodies—have neither formal representation nor any meaningful voice in the decision-making processes. Global governance, in other words, entails the exercise of power and raises questions regarding its legitimacy.[42]

Traditional international law, for which state consent (through ratification of a treaty, accession to a membership-based organization, or compliant behaviour) remains the key source of legitimacy, has little to say about the exercise of power through global governance bodies that are not treaty-based IOs.[43] This approach, however, is increasingly no longer adequate in light of the rapidly growing authority of global institutions and the significant impact global bodies have on states, entities and individuals around the world. To address these shortcomings of traditional *de jure* approaches, scholars of global governance have developed a variety of new approaches for understanding and assessing legitimacy at the international, transnational, and global level.[44] They often draw on political theory and domestic political practice[45]—and much of their work challenges the legitimacy of global governance.[46]

[41] Pauwelyn *et al.* (eds), *Informal International Lawmaking* (n 2); Tim Büthe, 'Private Regulation in the Global Economy' (n 29), esp. 15–20.

[42] Tim Büthe, 'Beyond Supply and Demand: A Political-Economic Conceptual Model' in Kevin Davis, Angelina Fischer, Benedikt Kingsbury, and Sally Engle Merry (eds), *Governance by Indicators: Global Power through Quantification and Rankings* (Oxford University Press 2012) 29-51. See also Bob Reinalda and Bertjan Verbeek (eds), *Decision Making Within International Organizations* (Routledge 2004).

[43] Buchanan and Keohane, 'Legitimacy' (n 10), 405, 406, 412f.

[44] Eyal Benvenisti, 'Sovereigns as Trustees of Humanity: On the Accountability of States to Foreign Stakeholders' 107(2) *American Journal of International Law* (2013) 295-333; Mark Bovens, 'Analysing and Assessing Accountability: A Conceptual Framework' 13(4) *European Law Journal* (2007) 447-468; Nils Brunsson and Bengt Jacobsson (eds), *A World of Standards* (Oxford University Press 2000); Buchanan and Keohane, 'Legitimacy' (n 10), 405; Ruth W Grant and Robert O Keohane, 'Accountability and Abuses of Power in World Politics' 99(1) *American Political Science Review* (2005) 29-43; Yannis Papadopoulos, 'The Challenge of Transnational Private Governance: Evaluating Authorization, Representation and Accountability' *Sciences Po LIEPP Working Paper* No. 8 (2013) <https://www.sciencespo.fr/liepp/sites/sciencespo.fr.liepp/files/WP8.pdf>, last accessed 06/13/2019; Steffen Eckhard and Jörn Ege, 'International Bureaucracies and Their Influence on Policy-Making: A Review of the Empirical Evidence' 23(7) *Journal of European Public Policy* (2016) 960-978.

[45] E.g. Robert A Dahl, 'Can International Organizations be Democratic? A Skeptics View' in Ian Shapiro and Casiano Hacker-Cordon (eds), *Democracy's Edges* (Cambridge University Press 1999) 530-541; Michael Zürn, 'Democratic Governance Beyond the Nation-State: The EU and Other International Institutions' 6(2) *European Journal of International Relations* (2000) 183-221; David Held and Mathias Koenig-Archibugi (eds), *Global Governance and Public Accountability* (Blackwell 2005); Brassett and Tsingou, 'The Politics' (n 15), as well as special issue contributions by Bernstein, Keohane, Scholte, and by Cerutti; M Joseph Colomer, *How Global Institutions Rule the World* (Palgrave Macmillan Press 2014).

[46] E.g. Robert O Keohane and Joseph S Nye, 'Between Centralization and Fragmentation: The Club Model of Multilateral Cooperation and Problems of Democratic Legitimacy', Paper presented at the Annual Meeting of the American Political Science Convention, Washington D.C., 2001 <http://ssrn.com/abstract=262175>, last accessed 06/13/2019; Andrew Moravcsik, 'Is There a Democratic Deficit in World Politics? A Framework for Analysis' 39(2) *Government and Opposition* (2004) 336-363; Zürn, 'Global Governance and Legitimacy Problems' (n 10); Eyal Benvenisti and George Downs, 'Toward Global

The key concern for many contributors to this literature—and most immediately important for our study—is the *input* and *throughput* legitimacy of global institutions.[47] Their main concerns, in other words, are the processes by which decisions and rules are made. Critics of global governance institutions who are motivated by these concerns often focus on exclusionary or opaque procedures, the powerful role of elites and technocrats in those institutions, and the outright exclusion of transnational civil society from many global governance bodies.[48]

Much of this critique of global governance bodies, taking them to task for being closed and undemocratic, has traditionally been targeted at the major multilateral intergovernmental international organizations (IOs), notably the WTO, the World Bank, and the IMF,[49] as well as the UN Security Council.[50] In recent years, however, critics have also targeted newer modes of governance, in diverse policy fields, including transgovernmental networks such as the Basel Committee,[51] but also public–private

Checks and Balances' 20(3/4) *Constitutional Political Economy* (2009) 366-387; Dahl, 'Can International Organizations be Democratic? (n 45); Karl Kaiser, 'Das internationale System der Gegenwart als Faktor der Beeinträchtigung demokratischer Außenpolitik' 10 (Sonderheft 'Die anachronistische Souveränität,' edited by E-O Czempiel) *Politische Vierteljahresschrift* (1969) 340–358; Jan Klabbers, 'Setting the Scene' in Jan Klabbers, Anne Peters and Geir Ulstein (eds), *The Constitutionalization of International Law* (Oxford University Press 2009); Jonathan G S Koppell, *World Rule: Accountability, Legitimacy, and the Design of Global Governance* (University of Chicago Press 2010); Joseph S Nye, 'Globalization's Democratic Deficit: How to Make International Institutions More Accountable' 80(4) *Foreign Affairs* (2011) 2-6; Lori M Wallach, 'Accountable Governance in an Era of Globalization: The WTO, NAFTA and the International Harmonization of Standards' 50(4) *University of Kansas Law Review* (2002) 823-865; Kishore Mahbubani, 'Can Asia Re-Legitimize Global Governance?' 18(1) *Review of International Political Economy* (2011) 131-139; Michael Zürn, *A Theory of Global Governance: Authority, Legitimacy and Contestation* (Oxford University Press 2018); Jonas Tallberg and Michael Zürn, 'The Legitimacy and Legitimation of International Organizations: Introduction and Framework' 14(4) *Review of International Organizations* (2019) 581-606.

47 Key conceptual contributions include Fritz W Scharpf, *Demokratietheorie zwischen Utopie und Anpassung* (Universitätsverlag Konstanz 1970) and *Governing in Europe: Effective and Democratic?* (Oxford University Press 1999); as well as Vivien A Schmidt, 'Democracy and Legitimacy in the European Union Revisited: Input, Output and 'Throughput'' 61(1) *Political Studies* (2013) 2-22. See also Jens Steffek, 'The Output Legitimacy of International Organizations and the Global Public Interest' 7(2) *International Theory* (2015) 263-293; Ingi Iusmen and John Boswell, 'The Dilemmas of Pursuing 'Throughput Legitimacy' through Participatory Mechanisms' 40(2) *West European Politics* (2017) 459-478; and DeMenno and Büthe, 'Voice and Influence' (n 7), esp. Section 2.6.2.

48 Bob Reinalda and Bertjan Verbeek (eds), *Decision Making Within International Organizations* (Routledge 2004); Kingsbury *et al.*, 'Emergence of Global Administrative Law' (n 2); Patrizia Nanz and Jens Steffek, 'Global Governance, Participation and the Public Sphere' 39(2) *Government and Opposition* (2004) 314-335; Anne Peters, 'Membership in the Global Constitutional Community' in Klabbers *et al.* (n 46) 153-179; Sol Picciotto, 'Constitutionalizing Multilevel Governance?' 6 *International Journal of Constitutional Law* (2008) 457-479; Kees Van Kersbergen and Frans Van Waarden, 'Governance as a Bridge between Disciplines: Cross-Disciplinary Inspiration Regarding Shifts in Governance and Problems of Governability, Accountability and Legitimacy' 43 *European Journal of Political Research* (2004) 143-171; Von Bogdandy *et al.* (eds), *Exercise of Public Authority* (n 37).

49 E.g. Robert O'Brien, Anne Marie Goetz, Jan Aart Scholte, and Marc Williams, *Contesting Global Governance: Multilateral Institutions and Global Social Movements* (Cambridge University Press 2000); Donatella della Porta and Sidney Tarrow (eds), *Transnational Protest and Global Activism* (Rowman & Littlefield 2005); Matthew D Stephen and Michael Zürn (eds), *Contested World Orders: Rising Powers, Non-State Actors, and the Politics of Authority Beyond the Nation-State* (Oxford University Press 2019).

50 Ian Hurd, *After Anarchy: Legitimacy and Power in the United Nations Security Council* (Princeton University Press 2007); Binder and Heupel, 'The Legitimacy of the UN Security Council' (n 15).

51 Michael S Barr and Gregory P Miller, 'Global Administrative Law: The View from Basel' 17 *European Journal of International Law* (2006) 15-46.

partnerships, multi-stakeholder governance bodies, or non-state institutions in areas ranging from internet governance[52] to sustainability standard-setting.[53]

Parts of the recent literature also considers output legitimacy by considering the question of *whose interests* global bodies should be expected to take into account, regardless of input. Traditionally, the answer was straightforward: global governance bodies needed to serve the interests of those who had explicitly or implicitly authorized their activities.[54] More recent contributions, often drawing from administrative or public law,[55] emphasize that global governance needs to be 'responsive to the interests of all of those whom their activities impact',[56] that is, the so-called stakeholders.[57]

To make global governance bodies more democratically legitimate, scholars and practitioners alike have been calling for more opportunities for participation—or more precisely, what we in this book call 'voice opportunities'[58]—for traditionally excluded stakeholders.[59] Examples include the Sustainable Development Goals injunction 'to broaden and strengthen the participation of developing countries in the

[52] Ingo Take, 'Regulating the Internet Infrastructure: A Comparative Analysis of the Legitimacy of ICANN, ITU, and the WSIS' 6(4) *Regulation and Governance* (2012) 499-523; Luca Belli, 'A Heterostakeholder Cooperation for Sustainable Internet Policymaking' 4(2) *Internet Policy Review* (2015) 1-21; Madeline Carr, 'Power Plays in Global Internet Governance' 43(2) *Millennium* (2015) 640-659; Berman, 'Rise of Multistakeholder Global Governance' (n 23).

[53] Allison Loconto and Eve Fouilleux, 'Politics of Private Regulation: ISEAL and the Shaping of Transnational Sustainability Governance' 8 *Regulation and Governance* (2014) 166-185; Abdel Alshadafan, 'Energy Efficiency Standards: The Struggle for Legitimacy' 18(1) *International Journal of Standardization Research* (2020), 1-23. More generally, see also Von Bogdandy *et al* (eds), *Exercise of Public Authority* (n 37); Bernstein, 'Legitimacy' (n 15); Pauwelyn *et al.* (eds), *Informal International Lawmaking* (n 2).

[54] Fabrizio Gilardi and Dietmar Braun, 'Delegation aus der Sicht der Prinzipal-Agent-Theorie: Ein Literaturbericht' 43(1) *Politische Vierteljahresschrift* (2002) 147-161; Darren G Hawkins, David A Lake, Daniel Nielson, and Michael J Tierney (eds), *Delegation and Agency in International Organizations* (Cambridge University Press 2006); Roland Vaubel, 'Principal-Agent Problems in International Organizations' 1(2) *Review of International Organizations* (2006) 125-138; Curtis A Bradley and Judith Kelley (eds), 'Special Issue: The Law and Politics of International Delegation' 71(1) *Law and Contemporary Problems* (2008).

[55] Laurence Boisson de Chazournes, Lorenzo Casini, and Benedict Kingsbury (eds), 'Symposium on Global Administrative Law in the Operations of International Organizations' 6 *International Organizations Law Review* (2009) 315-673; Von Bogdandy *et al.* (eds), *Exercise of Public Authority* (n 37); Kingsbury *et al.*, 'Emergence of Global Administrative Law' (n 2); Pauwelyn, Wessel and Wouters (eds), *Informal International Lawmaking* (n 2).

[56] Kingsbury *et al.*, 'Emergence of Global Administrative Law' (n 2).

[57] Kingsbury *et al.*, 'Emergence of Global Administrative Law' (n 2); Grant and Keohane, 'Accountability and Abuses' (n 44); Stewart, 'Remedying Disregard' (n 4); Charles F Sabel, 'Beyond Principal-Agent Governance: Experimentalist Organizations, Learning and Accountability' in Ewald Engelen and Monika Sie Dhian Ho (eds), *De Staat van de Democratie: Democratie voorbij de Staat* (Amsterdam University Press 2004) 173-195; Tim Büthe, *The Dynamics of Principals and Agents: Institutional Persistence and Change in U.S. Financial Regulation, 1934-2003* (Unpublished manuscript, Duke University 2010 <https://ssrn.com/abstract=1796542>, last accessed 06/13/2019; Michael Barnett and Martha Finnemore, *Rules for the World: International Organizations in Global Politics* (Cornell University Press 2014); David Held, Democratic Accountability and Political Effectiveness' in David Held and Mathias Koenig-Archibugi (eds), *Global Governance and Public Accountability* (Blackwell 2005); Keohane and Nye, 'The Club Model of Multilateral Cooperation' (n 46); Mathias Koenig-Archibugi, 'How to Diagnose Democratic Deficits in Global Politics: The Use of the "All-Affected Principle"' 9 *International Theory* (2017) 171-202; Peters, 'Membership' (n 48); Jan Klabbers, 'Law Making and Constitutionalism' in Klabbers *et al.* (n 46); Mathias Koenig-Archibugi, 'Accountability' in Jacob Katz Cogan, Ian Hurd and Ian Johnstone (eds), *The Oxford Handbook of International Organizations* (Oxford University Press 2016) 1146–1169; Eyal Benvenisti, 'Sovereigns as Trustees' (n 44); Tallberg and Zürn, 'Legitimacy and Legitimation' (n 46).

[58] See DeMenno and Büthe, 'Voice and Influence' (n 7), esp. sections 1 and 4.

[59] E.g., Jan Aart Scholte (ed), *Building Global Democracy? Civil Society and Accountable Global Governance* (Cambridge University Press 2011); Terry Macdonald, *Global Stakeholder Democracy: Power and Representation beyond Liberal States* (Oxford University Press 2008); Anne Peters, 'Dual Democracy'

institutions of global governance' and to 'increase the proportion of members and voting rights of developing countries in international organizations',[60] as well as the OECD calling on global bodies to engage stakeholders, so that 'attention is paid to marginalized, disadvantaged or less powerful groups'.[61] A number of observers see such statements as indicative of the emergence of a new international participatory norm.[62] Some even go as far as to argue that the International Covenant on Civil and Political Rights (ICCPR) sets out an international legal right to participate in such international law-making.[63] Such an opening up to external stakeholders ultimately has consequences for a global governance body's input, throughput, and output legitimacy—as explored in greater detail in the next chapter by DeMenno and Büthe.[64]

1.2.3 Marginalized Stakeholders: The Global South and Non-Commercial Actors

The marginalization of the 'Global South' has a long tradition, especially in traditional inter-governmental IOs, where it is often path dependent given colonial legacies and the vast inequality in relative power at the time of many IOs' creation.[65] It is perpetuated or exacerbated by the ability of powerful states to use various mechanisms of 'informal governance' to exercise disproportionate influence when the stakes are high.[66] Under some circumstances, constraining their own freedom of manoeuvre can yield benefits for the less powerful governments in the developing world.[67] But often unequal voice and influence in global governance merely benefit the powerful few in the North at the expense of the many in the South. Joseph Stiglitz, for instance, showed

in Klabbers *et al.* (n 46) 263-341; Claudia Kissling and Jens Steffek, 'CSOs and the Democratization of International Governance: Prospects and Problems' in *Civil Society Participation in European and Global Governance* (Palgrave Macmillan 2008) 208-218; Jan Aart Scholte, 'Civil Society and Democratically Accountable Global Governance' 39(2) *Government and Opposition* (2004) 211-233.

60 United Nations, Goal 16: Sustainable Development Goals, Target 16.8.

61 OECD, *OECD Best Practice Principles on Stakeholder Engagement in Regulatory Policy* (Draft for Public Consultations 2017) 3.

62 Raffaele Marchetti, *Global Strategic Engagement: States and Non-State Actors in Global Governance* (Lexington Books 2016), 132.

63 Nahuel Maisley, 'The International Right of Rights? Article 25(a) of the ICCPR as a Human Right to Take Part in International Law-Making' 28 *European Journal of International Law* (2017) 89-113; Peters, 'Dual Democracy' (n 59).

64 DeMenno and Büthe, 'Voice and Influence' (n 7).

65 See, e.g. Robert W Cox and Harold K Jacobson (eds), *The Anatomy of Influence: Decision-Making in International Organizations* (Yale University Press 1973); Stephen C Schlesinger, *Act of Creation: The Founding of the United Nations. A Story of Superpowers, Secret Agents, Wartime Allies and Enemies, and Their Quest for a Peaceful World* (Westview Press 2004); Thomas G Weiss, David P Forsythe, Roger A Coate, and Kelly-Kate Pease (eds), *The United Nations and Changing World Politics*, 8th ed. (Routledge 2016). See also Jean-Marc Coicaud and Veijo Heiskanen (eds), *The Legitimacy of International Organizations* (United Nations University Press 2001); Daniel W Drezner, *All Politics Is Global* (Princeton University Press 2007); John W McArthur and Eric Werker, 'Developing Countries and International Organizations: Introduction to the Special Issue' 11(2) *Review of International Organizations* (2016) 155-169; Lipscy, *Renegotiating the World Order* (n 13), esp. at 7f.

66 Randall W Stone, *Controlling Institutions: International Organizations and the Global Economy* (Cambridge University Press 2011); Tim Büthe, 'Review of Controlling Institutions' 11 *Perspectives on Politics* (2013) 282-284.

67 Tim Büthe and Helen V Milner, 'Bilateral Investment Treaties and Foreign Direct Investment: A Political Analysis' in Karl P Sauvant and Lisa E Sachs (eds), *The Effect of Treaties on Foreign Direct Investment*

how IMF decisions, taken to stabilize international financial markets and thus minimize economic hardship in high-income countries, have led to job losses and bankruptcies in low-income countries.[68]

The marginalization of developing countries is similarly pervasive—though often much less clearly apparent—in new forms of global governance. The Basel Committee's capital adequacy standards, for instance, have for many years affected banking systems in many countries that were not represented on the Committee, such as Brazil, China, Ghana, India, and Malaysia.[69] Such skewed representation is inherently problematic from an input legitimacy perspective, but also has been shown to result in standards, maladapted to local conditions, that adversely affect and harm the competitiveness of those countries' financial intermediaries, increase the cost and volatility of capital flows to their markets, and negatively affect their credit risk ratings.[70] Similarly, most of the ICH's pharmaceutical standards, traditionally set by the United States, the EU, and Japan, are for commercial reasons followed globally,[71] including in countries such as Brazil, India, and China (BIC).[72] The implementation of these high 'Western' standards has adversely affected the production of essential generic medicines[73] and led to a decline in the development of drugs for neglected diseases

(Oxford University Press 2009) 171-225; Axel Dreher and Stefan Voigt, 'Does Membership in International Organizations Increase Governments' Credibility? Testing the Effect of Delegating Powers' 39(3) *Journal of Comparative Economics* (2011) 326-348; Jack Corbett, Yi-Chong Xu and Patrick Weller, 'Norm Entrepreneurship and Diffusion "From Below" in International Organisations: How the Competent Performance of Vulnerability Generates Benefits for Small States' 45(4) *Review of International Studies* (2019) 647–668. See also Timur Kuran and Jared Rubin, 'The Financial Power of the Powerless: Socio-Economic Status and Interest Rates Under Partial Rule of Law' 128(609) *The Economic Journal* (2018) 758-796.

[68] Joseph E Stiglitz, 'Democratizing the International Monetary Fund and the World Bank: Governance and Accountability' (2003) 16(1) *Governance* 111-139.

[69] Salem H Nasser and Ana Mara F Machado, 'Informal International Lawmaking and Accountability in Brazil' in Berman *et al.* (eds), *Informal International Lawmaking: Case Studies* (n 21), 141-175; Barr and Miller, 'View from Basel' (n 51); Katharina Pistor, 'A Legal Theory of Finance' 41(2) *Journal of Comparative Economics* (2013) 315-330; Emily Jones and Alexandra O Zeitz, 'The Limits of Globalizing Basel Banking Standards' 3 *Journal of Financial Regulation* (2017) 89-124.

[70] Stijn Claessens, Geoffrey R D Underhill and Xiakoe Zhang, 'The Political Economy of Basel II: The Costs for Poor Countries' 31 *World Economy* (2008) 313-344; Stephany Griffith-Jones and Stephen Spratt, 'Will the Proposed New Basel Capital Accord have a Net Negative Effect on Developing Countries?' (Institute of Development Studies University of Sussex 2001) <https://www.bis.org/bcbs/ca/inofdest.pdf>, last accessed 06/13/2019; Giovanni Majnoni, Giovanni Ferri and Liu Li-Gang, 'How the Proposed Basel Guidelines on Rating-Agency Assessments Would Affect Developing Countries' *World Bank Policy Research Working Paper* No. 2369 (2000) <http://documents.worldbank.org/curated/en/841091468767106251/pdf/multi-page.pdf>, last accessed 06/13/2019.

[71] David Bach and Abraham L Newman, 'Governing Lipitor and Lipstick: Capacity, Sequencing, and Power in International Pharmaceutical and Cosmetics Regulation' 17(4) *Review of International Political Economy* (2010) 665-695; David Vogel, *Trading Up: Consumer and Environmental Regulation in a Global Economy* (Harvard University Press 1995).

[72] Berman, 'The Case of the ICH' (n 34).

[73] André de Mello e Souza, 'Patents and Access to Medicines: The Politics of AIDS Treatment in Brazil' in Hans Löfgren (ed), *The Politics of the Pharmaceutical Industry and Access to Medicines* (Social Science Press 2012) 272-299; World Health Organization, 'Report of A WHO Meeting: The Impact of Implementation of ICH Guidelines in Non-ICH Countries', 2001 = Regulatory Support Series No 9 <http://apps.who.int/medicinedocs/pdf/h2993e/h2993e.pdf>, last accessed 06/13/2019.

in developing countries.[74] Similarly, technical standards for medical devices, set by transnational expert bodies to meet the needs of advanced industrialized countries, have resulted in an undersupply of medical devices suitable for the climatic and technical conditions found in many developing countries (such as an unstable supply of electric power).[75]

In the examples mentioned so far, the countries of the Global South appear to be 'accidental' stakeholders. The detrimental consequences of their marginalization are no less real, but for the normative assessment it matters that the effect was unintentional. It is, however, by no means always the case that the excluded or marginalized are unintentionally affected. New forms of global governance and rule-making often primarily and consciously target public policies or private practices in countries in the South. The forty 'Recommendations' for improving detection and prevention of money laundering, drawn up by a by-invitation-only group of Ministry of Finance officials and financial market regulators from the G7 and eight other countries in the OECD-sponsored Financial Action Task Force (FAFT), were designed above all to bring about changes in financial systems and regulations in countries and jurisdictions not invited to participate in the rule-making.[76] Similarly, many food safety standards, developed by the Codex Alimentarius Commission, often with little input from the developing world, seek above all to change farming and basic food processing practices in developing countries—and thereby exclude many Southern farmers from global markets.[77] The same pattern holds for private food safety standards,[78] or for

[74] Trudie Lang, Phaik Yeong Cheah, and Nicholas J White, 'Clinical Research: Time for Sensible Global Guidelines' 377(9777) *The Lancet* (2011) 1553-1555; Yusuf Salim, 'Damage to Important Clinical Trials by Over-Regulation' 7 *Clinical Trials* (2010) 622-625. Since much of the continued marginalization of developing countries is underpinned by resource and capacity constraints, parts of the logic may also apply to small countries, even when they have high income levels, such as Singapore and even Switzerland; see, e.g. Emily Jones, C Deere Birkbeck and Ngaire Woods, *Manoeuvring at the Margins: Constraints Faced by Small States in International Trade Negotiations* (Commonwealth Secretariat 2010).

[75] Robert A Malkin, 'Design of Health Care Technologies for the Developing World' 9 *Annual Review of Biomedical Engineering* (2007) 567-587.

[76] Chris Brummer, *Soft Law and the Global Financial System: Rule Making in the 21st Century* (Cambridge University Press 2012); Stavros Gadinis, 'Three Pathways to Global Standards: Private, Regulator, and Ministry Networks' 109(1) *American Journal of International Law* (2015) 1-57; Kilian J McCarthy, 'Why Do Some States Tolerate Money Laundering? On the Competition for Illegal Money' in Brigitte Unger and Daan van der Linde (eds), *Research Handbook on Money Laundering* (Edward Elgar 2013) 127-142; Jason C Sharman, 'The Bark Is the Bite: International Organizations and Blacklisting' 16(4) *Review of International Political Economy* (2009) 573-596; Concepcion Verdugo, 'International Standards in Anti-Money Laundering and Combating the Terrorist Financing Regulation: Compliance and Strategy Changes' 10 *Global Business and Economics Review* (2008) 353-378; Beth A Simmons, 'International Law and State Behavior: Commitment and Compliance in International Monetary Affairs' 94(4) *American Political Science Review* (2000) 819-835.

[77] Spencer Henson and Rupert Loader, 'Barriers to Agricultural Exports from Developing Countries: The Role of Sanitary and Phytosanitary Requirements' 29(1) *World Development* (2001) 85-102; Büthe and Harris, 'The Codex Alimentarius Commission (n 23).

[78] Jan Wouters, Axel Marx, and Nicolas Hachez, 'Private Standards, Global Governance and Transatlantic Cooperation: The Case of Global Food Safety Governance' [2008] *Leuven Centre for Governance Studies* <https://iis.berkeley.edu/sites/default/files/pdf/woutersmarxhachez_foodsafety.pdf>, last accessed 06/12/2019.

animal drug standards, developed by the VICH.[79] Many technical standards for industrial goods may even be designed to keep developing country competitors out of Northern markets.[80]

The marginalization of stakeholders from the Global South increasingly also calls into question the systemic stability of global governance, because the rise of China, India and Brazil—and more generally the diffusion of economic and political power without a corresponding change in inclusiveness—raises the spectre of multiple alternative, competing regimes, none of which can actually provide truly global governance.[81] China's establishment of the Asian Infrastructure Investment Bank, and the BRICS countries' formation of the New Development Bank,[82] both as alternatives to the World Bank (where these countries feel under-represented), illustrate this tension.

All told, the countries of the Global South are often unintentionally affected or even intentional targeted by global governance, even though they are rarely among the stakeholders who sought the global rules in the first place. Furthermore, they usually have little influence over the rules' contents, that is, they are marginalized or even excluded from the rule- and decision-making.

Another frequently marginalized set of stakeholders consists of the non-commercial, diffuse, and non-expert interests that are often subsumed under the label 'civil society'.[83] As Richard Stewart highlights, many global bodies 'disregard ... the interests of affected but marginalized states, groups, and diffuse economic, environmental or other societal interests'.[84] In traditional IOs, member states' governments are supposed to represent the interests of these stakeholders, but in many 'new' global governance bodies, governments no longer have a 'seat at the table'. And although new

[79] Berman, *Reining in the Regulators* (n 24).

[80] Joseph M Grieco, *Cooperation Among Nations: Europe, America, and Non-Tariff Barriers to Trade* (Cornell University Press 1990); Vinod Rege, Shyam K Gujadhur, and Roswitha Franz, *Influencing and Meeting International Standards: Challenges for Developing Countries* (UNCTAD/WTO International Trade Center and Commonwealth Secretariat 2003); Keith E Maskus, Tsunehiro Otsuki, and John S Wilson, 'The Cost of Compliance with Product Standards for Firms in Developing Countries: An Econometric Study' *World Bank Policy Research Paper* No. 3590 (May 2005); Tim Büthe, 'The Power of Norms; the Norms of Power: Who Governs International Electrical and Electronic Technology?' in Avant *et al.* (eds), *Who Governs the Globe?* (n 3) 292-332.

[81] See also Bruce W Jentleson and Steven Weber, *The End of Arrogance: America in the Global Competition of Ideas* (Harvard University Press 2010); John G Ikenberry, 'The Future of the Liberal World Order' 90(3) *Foreign Affairs* (2011) 56; Christopher A McNally, 'Sino-Capitalism: China's Reemergence and the International Political Economy' 64(3) *World Politics* (2012) 741-776; Bernhard Zangl, Frederick Heußner, Andreas Kruck, and Xenia Lanzendörfer, 'Imperfect Adaptation: How the WTO and the IMF Adjust to Shifting Power Distributions Among Their Members' 11(2) *Review of International Organizations* (2016) 171-196; Sandra Lavenex, Omar Serrano, and Tim Büthe, 'Power Transitions and the Rise of the Regulatory State: Global Market Governance in Flux' 15 *Regulation and Governance* (2021) 445–471.

[82] Deepa M Ollapally, 'India and the International Order: Accommodation and Adjustment' 32(s1) *Ethics & International Affairs* (2018) 61-74, 68.

[83] Other notable external stakeholders are legislatures and public bodies below the nation state and under-represented business interests, for example, small and medium-sized enterprises (SMEs).

[84] Stewart, 'Remedying Disregard' (n 4); Tim Büthe, 'Private Regulation in the Global Economy' (n 29); Büthe, 'Beyond Supply and Demand' (n 42); Joost Pauwelyn, 'Informal International Lawmaking: Framing the Concept and Research Question' in Pauwelyn *et al.* (eds), *Informal International Lawmaking* (n 2) 13-34, esp. 22ff.

forms of global governance are often de jure broadly open to participation by a diverse range of stakeholders, many may be de facto inaccessible to non-commercial, diffuse interests, because participation requires a certain degree of organizational sophistication and resources including time, funding, and technical expertise.[85] Non-commercial and civil society stakeholders sometimes lack the capacity for collective action, often lack the resources, and by definition do not have the ability to recoup expenses by benefitting financially from achieving their preferences. This experience of de facto marginalization is likely to be especially common among civil society groups from the Global South. Participation and hence at least input legitimacy suffer under these conditions; global governance outcomes (and output legitimacy) are also likely to be affected.

In sum, analyses by scholars from a broad range of disciplines identify the countries of the Global South—as well as non-commercial, civil society interests—as the most marginalized stakeholders in many areas of global governance. These deficits in participation not only raise important normative questions concerning input and throughput legitimacy, but also threaten to undermine output legitimacy and hence the regulatory effectiveness of the particular bodies characterized by such deficits. They might even undermine the contemporary system of global governance more broadly.

1.2.4 Stakeholder Participation Reforms

Faced with these challenges to their legitimacy and effectiveness, many global bodies have in recent years broadened their membership, reformed their procedures, and introduced new opportunities for more countries or non-state actors to have a voice in their decision-making processes. The Basel Committee, for example, now includes representatives of the banking supervisory authorities of several emerging countries.[86] The ICH has set up several outreach bodies to improve cooperation with emerging countries.[87] And standard-setting bodies such as the International Organization for Standardization (ISO), the International Electrotechnical Commission (IEC), and the Codex Alimentarius, which used to have few active members from the Global South as recently as the 1990s, today are truly global bodies, with not just a nominal membership roster that spans the world but annual meetings actually attended by representatives from numerous countries from every continent.[88]

[85] Büthe and Mattli, *New Global Rulers* (n 2), ch. 3.

[86] Donnelly, 'Global Financial Market Regulation' (n 22).

[87] Ayelet Berman, 'Harmonization Networks, Informal International Law, and Accountability' 30 *L'Observateur des Nations Unies* (2011) 121-142.

[88] Regarding the evolution of the membership of the ISO, see Murphy and Yates, *The International Organization for Standardization* (n 26); for the IEC, see Tim Büthe, 'Engineering Uncontestedness? The Origins and Institutional Development of the International Electrotechnical Commission (IEC)' 12(3) *Business and Politics* (2010) 1–62; Büthe, 'The Power of Norms' (n 80). Regarding the evolution of the Codex's membership, see Büthe and Harris, 'The Codex Alimentarius Commission (n 23); Cindy Cheng with Anh Do, 'China and Vietnam in Global Health Governance.' Chapter 16, this volume.

Traditional intergovernmental organizations have also become more inclusive.[89] Many have broadened their membership roster, but arguably even more remarkable have been IO reforms to allow for greater participation by non-state actors. As Tallberg, Sommerer, Squatrito, and Jönsson put it, 'one of the most profound changes in global governance in recent decades'[90] has been the opening up of IOs to NGOs. Based on an analysis of NGO participation opportunities in about 300 IOs since 1950, they find that the share of IOs that provide NGOs with opportunities to access rule-making processes has increased from 20% in 1950 to over 70% in 2010.[91] This transformation spans 'all issue areas, policy functions, and world regions'.[92] Today, almost all IOs offer *some* means for non-state stakeholder to have a voice in the IO's decision-making process.[93]

Analyses of changing patterns of 'democratic' participation in IOs moreover suggest a general trend, rather than just the achievement of a new minimum threshold: IOs with no history of allowing NGO participation or a record of very restrictive access for NGOs, such as the World Bank and the WTO,[94] have gradually opened up to these stakeholders, while IOs that already had a tradition of engagement, such as the UN, have become even more open.[95] Tallberg and colleagues point out, for example, that as of 2011, some 3,500 NGOs have consultative status with the United Nations Economic and Social Council (which recognized forty-one NGOs in 1948).[96] Likewise, hundreds of civil society associations now attend the Annual Meetings of the IMF and the World Bank, increasing civil society participation from 21% in 1990 to 72% in 2006.[97] A 2015 OECD survey of fifty global bodies carrying out various regulatory tasks similarly finds that they have almost all increased stakeholder participation opportunities.[98]

While we clearly observe a common trend towards more participation opportunities, the specific institutional changes in global governance that are supposed to

[89] Klaus Dingwerth and Patricia Nanz, 'Participation' in Jacob Katz Cogan, Ian Hurd, and Ian Johnstone (eds), *The Oxford Handbook of International Organizations* (Oxford University Press 2016) 1126-1145.

[90] Jonas Tallberg, Thomas Sommerer, Theresa Squatrito, and Christer Jönsson, 'Explaining the Transnational Design of International Organizations' 68(4) *International Organization* (2014) 741-774, 768.

[91] Tallberg *et al.*, *Opening Up* (n 12).

[92] Tallberg *et al.*, 'Explaining the Transnational Design' (n 90).

[93] Tallberg *et al.*, *Opening Up* (n 12). See also Mark T Buntaine, 'Accountability in Global Governance: Civil Society Claims for Environmental Performance at the World Bank' 59(2) *International Studies Quarterly* (2015) 99-111. When considering the more demanding notion of the delegation of governance functions to non-state actors, Green finds greater variance: Jessica F Green, 'Transnational Delegation in Global Environmental Governance: When Do Non-State Actors Govern?' 12(2) *Regulation & Governance* (2018) 263-274.

[94] E.g. Maria Perez Esteve, 'WTO Rules and Practices for Transparency and Engagement with Civil Society Organizations', Paper presented at the IISD Workshop in Civil Society and WTO Accountability, available at <http://www.iisd.org/pdf/2011/wto_accountability_rules_transparency.pdf>, last accessed 06/11/2019.

[95] See Alexandru Grigorescu, *Democratic International Organizations? Normative Pressures and Decision-Making Rules* (Cambridge University Press 2015).

[96] Tallberg *et al.*, *Opening Up* (n 12).

[97] See also World Bank Group, 'Approach Paper: Engaging Citizens for Better Development Results - An IEG Evaluation of World Bank Group Citizen Engagement', 4 April 2017 <http://documents.worldbank.org/curated/en/752861493760420695/Engaging-citizens-for-better-development-results-An-IEG-evaluation-of-World-Bank-Group-citizen-engagement>, last accessed 12/02/2019.

[98] OECD, *International Regulatory Co-Operation* (n 13), 85.

boost stakeholder participation exhibit tremendous variation. To capture key differences, Richard Stewart has introduced the distinction between decisional and non-decisional participation,[99] and Anne Peters the distinction between vote and voice.[100] Yet, even within these categories, we find varying specific measures, ranging from simply allowing a broader membership to changes in voting weights, setting up outreach bodies for learning about developing countries' preferences, and incentivizing participation by developing countries through subsidies for their participation.[101]

The full range of institutional stakeholder participation reforms is even greater. It includes the introduction of notice-and-comment and other administrative law type procedures; the creation of stakeholder councils, advisory groups, ombudsmen, or other complaint mechanisms (such as the World Bank Inspection Panel); and increased transparency through opening meetings to the public, including online, or the introduction of other corporate social responsibility (CSR)-type mechanisms.[102]

1.2.5 Summary and Gaps in the Existing Literature

In sum, we have witnessed a widespread trend in global governance towards institutional reforms that have the declared goal of increasing the participation of previously marginalized or outright excluded stakeholders, and the fast-growing, empirically rich literature on global governance bodies offers by now several explanations for these reforms. We still know rather little, however, about the consequences of those reforms, including whether attempts to address the marginalization and exclusion of these stakeholders have in fact increased their voice or influence in global governance, nor whether it has increased the legitimacy of the global governance bodies.

This is no small gap in our understanding of global governance: Meaningful reforms, which actually empower previously marginalized interests, are bound to face resistance from established 'insiders'.[103] Yet, although even agreed reforms

[99] Stewart, 'Remedying Disregard' (n 4).

[100] Peters, 'Membership' (n 48).

[101] Patrick Stewart, 'Irresponsible Stakeholders? The Difficulty of Integrating Rising Powers' 89(6) *Foreign Affairs* (2010) 44-53, esp. 49–53.

[102] Cassese *et al.* (eds), *Global Administrative Law: Cases, Materials, Issues* (n 11); Kingsbury *et al.* 'Emergence of Global Administrative Law' (n 2); Berman, 'Reining in the Regulators' (n 24); Von Bogdandy *et al.* (eds), *Exercise of Public Authority* (n 37); David Vogel, *The Market for Virtue: The Potential and Limits of Corporate Social Responsibility* (Brookings Institution Press 2005); Sarah Dadush, 'Profiting in (RED): The Need for Enhanced Transparency in Cause-Related Marketing' 42(4) *NYU Journal of International Law and Politics* (2010) 1269-1336; Stephen Brammer, Gregory Jackson, and Dirk Matten, 'Corporate Social Responsibility and Institutional Theory: New Perspectives on Private Governance' 10(1) *Socio-Economic Review* (2012) 3-28; Wayne Norman, 'Business Ethics as Self-Regulation: Why Principles that Ground Regulations Should Be Used to Ground Beyond-Compliance Norms as Well' 102(s1) *Journal of Business Ethics* (2011) 43-57; Richard Locke, *The Promise and Limits of Private Power: Promoting Labor Standards in the Global Economy* (Cambridge University Press 2013).

[103] See Phillip Y Lipscy, 'Explaining Institutional Change: Policy Areas, Outside Options, and the Bretton Woods Institutions' 59(2) *American Journal of Political Science* (2015) 341-356; Mahbubani, 'Can Asia Re-Legitimize' (n 46). On change and inertia more generally, see Tine Hanrieder, 'Gradual Change in International Organizations: Agency Theory and Historical Institutionalism' 34(4) *Politics* (2014) 324-333; Thomas Rixen, Lora Viola, and Michael Zürn (eds), *Historical Institutionalism and International Relations: Explaining Institutional Development in World Politics* (Oxford University Press 2016).

that redistribute power in global governance bodies tend to remain incomplete, real change is possible.[104] And global governance reforms that result in substantial increases in voice and influence for the Global South (or more generally traditionally marginalized stakeholders) have the potential to be truly transformative. The effectiveness of stakeholder participation reforms in global governance therefore should be neither assumed nor ruled out, but systematically empirically examined—along with other consequences of institutional change, intentional or otherwise.

1.3 Contributions of This Book

Building on the literature reviewed in Section 1.2 and our assessment of the key gaps in the existing literature, this book seeks to make six main contributions.

1.3.1 Mapping the Variety of Stakeholder Participation Reforms

We begin Parts II and III of the book by *mapping* the reforms, which particular global bodies in the realms of finance and health have within the last two decades undertaken with the declared goal of increasing voice opportunities for hitherto marginalized or excluded stakeholders—often with the ostensible larger purpose of boosting the legitimacy of the global governance body.

This mapping seeks to make the considerable variety of such reforms visible and ultimately analytically useful. The reforms include changes that facilitate formal membership (increasing the number of permissible members, reducing barriers such as prerequisites, introducing new membership categories with lower fees for developing countries or advisory bodies for stakeholder categories such as civil society groups traditionally not even recognized) and changes of decision-making or voting rules. Changes range from these reforms of decisional opportunities to the introduction of non-decisional participation options (notice-and-comment; observer status) and merely procedural changes that might nonetheless facilitate participation (such as making meeting agendas public in advance).

While participation of stakeholders may occur at different stages of the governance process, we focus on reforms that are supposed to boost participation at the *rule-making or decision-making stage*. We therefore take a broad approach, not limited to reforms of legally binding rules or agreements. Accordingly, we use the terms decision-making, rule-making, policy-making, or standard-setting interchangeably and loosely.

[104] Zangl *et al.*, 'Imperfect Adaptation' (n 81). For examples of the myriad ways in which change can occur, even in the absence of great power support: Deborah D Avant, 'Pragmatic Networks and Transnational Governance of Private Military and Security Services' 60(2) *International Studies Quarterly* (2016) 330-342.

1.3.2 Comparison between Global Finance Governance and Global Health Governance

We examine changes in global governance within and across two issue areas: finance and health. We chose these two fields for what they have in common, as well as for the variation they exhibit. Both health and finance are intrinsically important; they account for a substantial share of economic activity in most countries and affect economic and human development on a vast scale. Policy-making and decision-making can consequently be highly contentious in both fields. At the same time, there is a strong emphasis on subject matter expertise in both, which may temper (or maybe just disguise?) conflicts of interest. Moreover, economic and political interdependence has created or vastly intensified cross-border governance challenges in both issue areas: a small, localized loophole or failure in global governance can have dramatic systemic effects.

At the same time, the two fields exhibit some notable differences. Analytically most important is that global health governance is widely considered an issue area that has experienced a wealth of institutional innovation in recent years, resulting in numerous opportunities for stakeholder participation. We chose global health as one of the issue areas after having confirmed in preliminary analyses that participation-related institutional changes have indeed been widespread.[105] Preliminary analyses of possible issue areas suggested that the governance of international finance has seen comparatively few and generally only cautious changes; the findings in the chapters on finance governance confirm this initial assessment.[106] The research design of our project uses this combination of commonalities and differences for additional analytical leverage: The separate analyses within each issue area (in Parts II and III, respectively) are followed by an overarching conclusion in Part IV that compares the findings across the two distinctive fields.

1.3.3 Analysis of Various Governmental and Non-Governmental Global Bodies

Comparative empirical analyses of multiple global governance bodies are still rare, including in the literature on accountability and legitimacy in global governance, which tends to be biased towards the few large, well-known, high-visibility global governance bodies.[107] The few studies that examine participation-enhancing reforms in a

[105] See, e.g. Kenneth W Abbott and David Gartner, 'Reimagining Participation in International Institutions' 8(1) *Journal of International Law and International Relations* (2012) 1-35.

[106] See also Layna Mosley, 'Private Governance for the Public Good? Exploring Private Sector Participation in Global Financial Regulation' in Helen V Milner and Andrew Moravcsik (eds), *Power, Interdependence, and Non-State Actors in World Politics* (Princeton University Press 2009) 126-146.

[107] Charnovitz, 'Opening the WTO' (n 12); Charnovitz, 'The Emergence of Democratic Participation' (n 12); Charnovitz, 'Nongovernmental Organizations and International Law' (n 12); Dunoff, 'Misguided Debate' (n 12); Fox, 'Transparency for Accountability' (n 12); Hunter and Bernasconi-Osterwalder, 'Democratizing Multilateral Development Banks' (n 12); Shell, 'The Trade Stakeholders Model' (n 12); Tallberg *et al.*, *Opening Up* (n 12). For discussions of the perils of such a bias towards large, high-visibility entities, see Büthe, 'The Power of Norms' (n 80); Jason C Sharman, 'Small Is Beautiful: The Perils of

large and more comprehensive set of global governance bodies focus on traditional treaty-based IOs, such as the IMF, the World Bank, and the WHO.[108] We seek to avoid both biases by also examining global bodies that are not treaty-based, and as such 'informal' under international law, since these new global governance bodies are playing an increasingly important role alongside IOs.[109] Specifically, we consider four main global governance types (see Table 1.1):

(1) treaty-based IOs;
(2) transgovernmental regulatory networks, understood as networks of public officials or regulators, which set or harmonize standards;
(3) multi-stakeholder partnerships, understood as partnerships between governmental and non-governmental actors, where the latter can be commercial or non-profit actors, or both;[110] and
(4) private (non-governmental) standard-setting bodies.

Table 1.1 Key Governance Bodies in Global Finance and Global Health

Global Governance Type	Global Finance[a]	Global Health[b]
Treaty-based IOs	• International Monetary Fund (IMF) • World Bank	• World Health Organization (WHO) • Codex Alimentarius Commission
Transgovernmental regulatory networks	• G20 • Basel Committee on Banking Supervision (BCBS/BIS) • Financial Action Task Force (FATF) • Financial Stability Board (FSB) • International Organization of Securities Commissions (IOSCO)	• International Council for Harmonization of Technical Requirements for Pharmaceuticals for Human Use (ICH) • International Medical Devices Regulators Forum (IMDRF)

Gigantism and the Pay-offs of Studying Small International Organisations' (Paper presented at the AGORA Workshop on Institutional Diversity in Governance of the Global Economy, Brisbane, January 2011); Jason C Sharman, 'Sovereignty at the Extremes: Micro-States in World Politics' 65(3) *Political Studies* (2017) 559-575. See also Peter J Katzenstein, *Small States in World Markets* (Cornell University Press 1985).

[108] See Tallberg *et al.*, *Opening Up* (n 12); Lipscy, *Renegotiating the World Order* (n 13).

[109] Pauwelyn *et al.* (eds), *Informal International Lawmaking* (n 2); Berman *et al.* (eds), *Informal International Lawmaking: Case Studies* (n 21), 13-34; Halliday and Shaffer (eds), *Transnational Legal Orders* (n 35).

[110] Such arrangements are also known as 'public-private partnerships'. See, e.g. Börzel and Risse 'Public-Private Partnerships' (n 23); Schäferhoff *et al.* 'Transnational Public-Private Partnerships' (n 23); Whytock, 'Public-Private Interaction in Global Governance' (n 23); Liese and Beisheim, 'Transnational Public-Private Partnerships' (n 23); Simon Zadek, 'Will Business Save the World?' in John Mikler (ed), *The Handbook of Global Companies* (Wiley-Blackwell 2013) 474-491.

Table 1.1 Continued

Global Governance Type	Global Finance[a]	Global Health[b]
Multi-stakeholder partnerships	--	• Global Fund to Fight AIDS, Tuberculosis and Malaria • GAVI Alliance
Private standard-setting bodies	International Accounting Standards Board (IASB)	GlobalG.A.P

[a] For details, see Olga Kovarzina and Martino Maggetti, 'Stakeholder Participation Reforms in Global Finance Governance.' Chapter 4, this volume.

[b]See Ayelet Berman, 'Stakeholder Participation Reforms in Global Health Governance.' Chapter 13, this volume.

1.3.4 State and Non-State 'Disregarded' Stakeholders

We focus on stakeholders of global governance who, at least prior to the often quite recent, ostensibly participation-boosting reforms, were de jure or de facto marginalized or excluded from discourses and decision-making in the global governance bodies noted in Table 1.1. Richard Stewart, who subsumes them under the label 'disregarded' stakeholders, points out that these stakeholders tend to be vulnerable and politically weak, and to the extent that their interests are shared by a larger group, they tend to be neither well organized nor well resourced.

These disregarded stakeholders can be states (most commonly: developing countries) as well as non-state entities, especially civil society organizations and other non-commercial groups.[111] While previous analyses usually examine only one or the other, we see their traditional marginalization, as well as recent attempts to boost their participation, as driven by a common logic. We therefore examine both state and non-state stakeholders.

For international legal scholarship,[112] considering non-state actors alongside governmental actors in a common analytical framework for affected stakeholders, irrespective of their formal international legal status, is still rather unusual. It constitutes one of the contributions of this book.[113]

For international relations scholarship, by contrast, it is rather the full consideration of state actors alongside non-state actors that is novel. Not only is there by now

[111] Particularly distinctive in this regard are transnational non-state stakeholders, i.e. groups defined as inherent spread across borders or no longer content with just simply providing inputs into 'their own' government's preference formation process at the national level as imagined by the traditional billiard ball model of international politics. See Alexandru Grigorescu and Çağlayan Başer, 'The Choice Between Intergovernmentalism and Nongovernmentalism: Projecting Domestic Preferences to Global Governance' 71(1) *World Politics* (2019) 88-125.

[112] For recent influential approaches, see Von Bogdandy *et al.* (eds), *Exercise of Public Authority* (n 37). See also Kingsbury *et al.*, 'Emergence of Global Administrative Law' (n 2); Benvenisti, 'Sovereigns as Trustees' (n 44).

[113] An important caveat in this regard is that our ability to empirically trace the experience of previously marginalized non-governmental stakeholders is constrained by their number and diversity.

a long tradition of IR scholarship taking non-state actors seriously,[114] but most of the existing empirical work on deficient or improving participation in global governance actually focuses entirely on NGO participation.[115] Here, our study addresses an important gap by also focusing on developing countries' traditional marginalization and possibly increasing participation.

1.3.5 Comparisons between Large Rising Powers and Smaller/Lower Income Developing Countries

To assess the extent to which the institutional reforms have enabled hitherto excluded stakeholders to participate and/or exert influence, we conduct *comparative analyses of paired country cases*. As explained more fully by Büthe and Cheng,[116] we decided at the outset of the project that it would be important to provide insights into the experience of the three largest 'rising' political and economic powers from the Global South—China, India and Brazil—which are clearly expected to play a greater role in global governance.[117]

At the same time, we sought to provide generalizable insight into the consequences of the ostensibly participation-enhancing reforms undertaken by global governance bodies in recent years, and the exceptional characteristics of the three largest rising powers, which make them intrinsically so important, limit our ability to draw general inferences from their experience. We therefore used 'coarsened exact matching' to systematically match each of them with another country from the same geographic region that is most similar to Brazil, India, or China, respectively, with regard to several theoretically relevant characteristics, such as economic and human development, political regime type, etc., while being dissimilar with regard to size and 'rising power' status.

This case selection method (see Büthe and Cheng)[118] ensures consideration of the experience of otherwise highly comparable countries from the Global South that cannot rely on the political and economic leverage afforded to the BIC countries by their population size and fast-growing vast domestic markets, to gain voice and

[114] For a review of the early literature, see Tim Büthe, 'Governance through Private Authority? Non-State Actors in World Politics' 58(1) *Journal of International Affairs* (2004) 281-290.

[115] Dinah Shelton, 'The Participation of Nongovernmental Organizations in International Judicial Proceedings' 88(4) *American Journal of International Law* (1994) 611-642; Diane Otto, 'Nongovernmental Organizations in the United Nations System: The Emerging Role of International Civil Society' 18(1) *Human Rights Quarterly* (1996) 107-141; Chi Carmody, 'Beyond the Proposals: Public Participation in International Economic Law' 15(6) *American University International Law Review* (2000) 1321-1346; Jens Steffek, Claudia Kissling, and Patrizia Nanz (eds), *Civil Society Participation in European and Global Governance: A Cure for the Democratic Deficit?* (Palgrave Macmillan 2008); Nanz and Steffek, 'Global Governance, Participation and the Public Sphere' (n 48); Tallberg *et al.*, *Opening Up* (n 12). A rare exception to focus on participatory reforms geared towards state actors in IOs is Lipscy, *Renegotiating the World Order* (n 13).

[116] Tim Büthe and Cindy Cheng, 'Analysing the Consequences of Institutional Reforms Using Country Pairs: A Note on the (Coarsened Exact) Matched-Country-Pairs Methodology of the Rethinking Stakeholder Participation Project.' Chapter 3, this volume.

[117] See Lavenex, Serrano, and Büthe, 'Power Transitions' (n 81).

[118] Büthe and Cheng, 'Note on the Matched-Country-Pairs Methodology' (n 116).

influence in global governance. The method yields for the empirical analyses in Parts II and III three country pairs: China and Vietnam; Brazil and Argentina; as well as India and Bangladesh/Philippines.

1.3.6 Towards a General Analytical Framework for Thinking about Stakeholder Participation in Global Governance

Beyond the book's primary empirical contributions, we hope to contribute to a conceptual framework for thinking about stakeholder participation with applicability beyond the particular countries, institutions, and issue areas covered in this book. Starting from (i) each global body's incentives for granting voice opportunities, DeMenno and Büthe theorize (ii) the likelihood that previously marginalized stakeholders make use of such opportunities, and (iii) the conditions under which, given the initial incentives of the global body, participating stakeholders will be able to exercise actual influence over outcomes.[119] This framework informs the empirical analyses in Parts II and III of the book. In Part IV, Berman then compares and contrasts the emphasis on global governance bodies' instrumental pursuit of their organizational self-interest with two ideal-typical alternative or complementary understandings of the patterns and developments observed in the empirical parts of the book.[120]

In our conclusion,[121] we summarize the findings, focusing in particular on the results that have broader implications for current understandings of participation, accountability, and legitimacy in global governance. Across both issue areas and all the countries and global bodies studied in this book, we find that the provision of voice opportunities alone clearly does not ensure actual voice in global governance. Whether marginalized stakeholders take up such opportunities, whether stakeholders who engage can ultimately exert some influence—and whether they even perceive the new voice opportunities as genuine opportunities to participate in global decision-making—depends on a host of other factors. These findings cast a doubt on the widely held view that the introduction of participation and transparency procedures as such is a cure for the democratic deficit in global governance.

1.4 The Book's Structure

We conclude this introduction with an overview of the structure of the book and each chapter's contributions. The book has four parts. Part I sets out the analytical framework. Part II uses the framework to examine global finance governance; Part III uses it to examine global health governance. Part IV covers crosscutting topics and offers an overarching, comparative conclusion.

119 DeMenno and Büthe, 'Voice and Influence' (n 7).

120 Ayelet Berman, 'The Stakeholder Participation Triangle: Trusteeship, Functionality, and Efficiency.' Chapter 23, this volume.

121 Tim Büthe, Joost Pauwelyn, Martino Maggetti, and Ayelet Berman, 'Conclusion: The Participation of Marginalized Stakeholders in Global Governance.' Chapter 25, this volume.

1.4.1 Part I: Analytical Framework

Following this introduction, Mercy DeMenno and Tim Büthe set out a framework for thinking about stakeholder participation in global governance.[122] They start from global bodies' varied incentives regarding stakeholder participation, differentiating between incentives to create de jure voice opportunities and incentives to give stakeholders an opportunity to exercise influence. DeMenno and Büthe also highlight that it is by no means guaranteed that stakeholders (can) make use of de jure voice opportunities—just as citizen in domestic politics do not automatically vote or engage in other forms of political participation 'just' because the political system allows for it. Instead, actual engagement—that is, making use of de jure voice opportunities—depends on the stakeholders' positive incentives (importance of the issue area and availability of alternative avenues for influencing outcomes[123]) as well as their financial, analytical, and political resource constraints, including their capacity for collective action.[124] Finally, DeMenno and Büthe develop a set of hypotheses about the conditions under which we should expect the use of voice opportunities to result in actual influence in global governance bodies.

Tim Büthe and Cindy Cheng then explain the methodological rationale for the coarsened-exact-matching-based country pairs research design for the empirical analyses in Parts II and III of the book.[125]

1.4.2 Part II: Global Finance Governance

Part II is devoted to stakeholder (non)participation in the governance of global finance. In the first two chapters of this part, Olga Kovarzina and Martino Maggetti map stakeholder participation reforms across a range of formal and informal bodies for the governance of international finance,[126] while Kern Alexander examines the reforms adopted in the G20 and the Basel Committee in response to the 2008 financial crisis—followed by a general assessment of how successful those reforms were in integrating hitherto marginalized countries and broader societal interests.[127]

The second section of Part II contains the three pairs of comparative country case studies. Henrique Choer Moraes and Facundo Pérez Aznar analyse Brazil's and Argentina's enhanced participation opportunities in global finance governance and examine to what extent their participation and influence has actually increased. They also identify the factors that have undermined the two countries' capacity to take full

[122] DeMenno and Büthe, 'Voice and Influence' (n 7).

[123] See also Büthe and Mattli's discussion of institutional focal points for regulatory governance in *New Global Rulers* (n 2).

[124] For a further overview of the broad range of reasons why actual participation of developing countries in global governance may differ, see also Hongying Wang and Erik French, 'Middle Range Powers in Global Governance' 34(6) *Third World Quarterly* (2013) 985-999.

[125] Büthe and Cheng, 'Note on the Matched-Country-Pairs Methodology' (n 116).

[126] Kovarzina and Maggetti, 'Stakeholder Participation Reforms' (n 111).

[127] Kern Alexander, 'Global Financial Governance and Banking Regulation: Redesigning Regulation to Promote Stakeholder Interests.' Chapter 5, this volume.

advantage of their participation opportunities.[128] In her comparative case study of China's and Vietnam's participation in several key global financial institutions, Weiwei Zhang traces the evolution of these countries' participation and influence over the years. She analyses the factors that have driven increased participation as well as the factors that have contributed to (and limited) the extent of their influence in global governance.[129] Tracking India's and Bangladesh's participation in bodies such as the Global Environment Facility and the Green Climate Fund (focusing thus on climate finance bodies), Rahul Mukherji and Himanshu Jha document these two countries' active participation and growing influence on global norms.[130]

The chapters in the third section of Part II assess the consequences of the reforms and the findings, beginning with Martino Maggetti and Olga Kovarzina, who identify commonalities and variations across the case studies and highlight the unevenness of reforms across the global financial institutions, and their selectiveness with respect to the stakeholders that have been given an opportunity to participate.[131] Their analysis is followed by responses to the comparative case studies and more generally reflections on the underlying developments in global finance governance from practitioners. Comparing between reforms in traditional IOs (such as the IMF) and newer forms of global finance governance such as the G20 and FSB, Ronald Gindrat of the IMF and Paul Inderbinen of the Swiss Federal Department of Finance suggest that informal inter- and transgovernmental bodies do not yield inferior participation outcomes than formal IOs.[132] Focusing on the FATF and FSB, Brazilian diplomat Henrique Choer Moraes highlights the role of regional consultative mechanisms in creating a bridge between the global body and non-member states and demonstrates that such mechanisms allow some room for exerting influence. Nevertheless, due to capacity gaps, participation in such mechanisms remains uneven, as is the degree of influence exerted.[133] Finally, Chris Brummer offers some critical reflections about the questions that remain open regarding stakeholder participation in global finance governance and suggests avenues for further research.[134]

1.4.3 Part III: Global Health Governance

Part III is devoted to global health governance. Similar to Part II, it begins with two chapters mapping the participation reforms: Distinguishing between participation

[128] Henrique Choer Moraes and Facundo Pérez Aznar, 'Brazil and Argentina in Global Finance Governance.' Chapter 6, this volume.

[129] Weiwei Zhang, 'China and Vietnam in Global Finance Governance.' Chapter 7, this volume.

[130] Rahul Mukherji and Himanshu Jha, 'India and Bangladesh in Global Finance Governance: From Structural Conflict to Embedded Liberalism in the Climate Finance Regime.' Chapter 8, this volume.

[131] Martino Maggetti and Olga Kovarzina, 'Assessing Stakeholder Participation Reforms in Global Finance Governance.' Chapter 9, this volume.

[132] Ronald Gindrat and Paul Inderbinen, 'Comparing Formal and Informal Bodies in International Finance: A Policy-Making Perspective.' Chapter 11, this volume.

[133] Henrique Choer Moraes, 'Can Regional Institutions Increase the Legitimacy of Global Governance? The Cases of the Regional Branches of the FATF and of the FSB.' Chapter 12, this volume.

[134] Christopher J Brummer, 'On Expanding the Theory of Stakeholder Participation.' Chapter 10, this volume.

reforms that grant an opportunity to participate, and reforms that seek to advance balanced and fair decision-making, Ayelet Berman surveys the main reforms in the WHO, the Codex Alimentarius Commission, International Council on Harmonization, International Medical Devices Regulators Forum, Global Fund to Fight AIDS, Tuberculosis and Malaria, GAVI Alliance, and the GlobalG.A.P.[135] David Gartner traces the evolution of stakeholder participation in the World Bank, the World Health Organization, GAVI, and the Global Fund to Fight AIDS, Tuberculosis and Malaria. Based on the impact of stakeholder participation on the institutional effectiveness of these leading global health institutions, he offers his insights into how stakeholder participation might be structured in order to optimize engagement and to foster institutional effectiveness.[136]

The chapters in the second section of Part III present the paired comparative country case studies of participation in global health governance. Comparing Brazil's and Argentina's experiences in global health governance, André de Mello e Souza and Facundo Pérez Aznar find that Brazil has benefitted more from the institutional reforms in terms of both participation and influence, which they attribute to contrasting patterns of economic growth, different foreign policy positions, as well as gaps in human and material resources.[137] Cindy Cheng and Anh Do analyse China's and Vietnam's participation in the Codex and several other global health bodies, focusing on issue salience, participant resources, and institutional specificity as conditioning participation. Based on a rigorous multi-method empirical analysis, including a computer-assisted textual analysis of the meeting minutes of several decades of Codex meetings, they show that China's engagement (and by all indications also its influence) tends to be much more substantial than Vietnam's, consistent with differences in resources and, across global governance bodies, in institutional specificity.[138] The final empirical chapter offers a synthesis of the key findings from Sachin Chaturvedi and Krishna Ravi Srinivas's detailed case study of India and Peter Payoyo's detailed case study of the Philippines in global health governance. Büthe, Chaturvedi, Payoyo, and Srinivas demonstrate that India and the Philippines have both experienced similarly notable increases in participation and even some influence in organizations such as the WHO, the Global Fund, and the Codex Alimentarius Commission—but often in quite different ways. The reforms undertaken by the ICH, by contrast, have left both countries with only very limited participation opportunities and no real influence.[139]

The papers in the third section of Part III assess the consequences of the reforms of global health governance in light of the comparative country studies. Based on the paired-country case studies of global health governance, Ayelet Berman and Joost Pauwelyn point out that, notwithstanding a general trend towards greater participation opportunities for previously excluded and marginalized stakeholders across all forms of global health governance, IOs are most inclusive of developing countries,

[135] Berman, 'Stakeholder Participation Reforms' (Table 1.1, note 'b').

[136] David Gartner, 'Global Health Governance and Stakeholder Participation.' Chapter 14, this volume.

[137] André de Mello e Souza and Facundo Pérez Aznar, 'Brazil and Argentina in Global Health Governance.' Chapter 15, this volume.

[138] Cheng with Do, 'China and Vietnam' (n 88).

[139] Tim Büthe, Sachin Chaturvedi, Peter B Payoyo, and Krishna Ravi Srinivas, 'India and the Philippines in Global Health Governance.' Chapter 17, this volume.

followed by multi-stakeholder partnerships, and then by standard-setting bodies. They also highlight that stakeholder and issue or institutional characteristics, such as salience, resources or capacity play a critical role in determining whether and to what extent stakeholders actually take advantage of their participation opportunities. These factors provide a powerful explanation for variations in participation between large emerging economies and smaller developing countries.[140]

Global health practitioners also respond, providing a practitioners' perspective. Former Legal Counsel of the WHO Gian Luca Burci points out that participatory reforms might make less of a difference than some had expected, because technical knowledge, the tactical use of WHO procedures, and the strategic formation of alliances are bound to give certain states influence well beyond their political and economic importance. He further argues that participation and influence is driven by complex power dynamics, with some previously neglected stakeholders participating indirectly through regional organizations and groupings.[141] Suerie Moon, Co-Director of Research at the Graduate Institute's Global Health Centre, argues that even after years of reforms, governments and non-state actors from middle-income or smaller/poorer countries wield only sporadic rather than systematic influence—with rare exceptions due to skilled leaders. Further, governmental and private sector economic actors exhibit much greater capacity to make use of participation opportunities than public interest non-state actors from the Global South, which still seem largely absent.[142] Gülen Atay Newton, previously chief legal counsel at the Global Fund, points out that, despite their inclusive nature, multi-stakeholder partnerships are also plagued by power asymmetries. Weaker stakeholders often lack the capacity, funds, or interest to participate effectively, though capacity building efforts can empower weaker stakeholders over the medium to long term.[143] Finally, K M Gopakumar of the advocacy NGO Third World Network critically assesses the WHO Framework of Engagement with Non-State Actors (FENSA). Sceptical about FENSA's ability to limit undue influence of the private sector, Gopakumar warns that, rather than prevent undue private sector influence, FENSA might ultimately legitimize it.[144]

1.4.4 Part IV: Cross Cutting Topics

Part IV contains two cross-cutting chapters on stakeholder participation in global governance.

Ayelet Berman presents the stakeholder participation triangle, visualizing three prescriptively ideal-typical ways in which a global body may view its own role, with

[140] Ayelet Berman and Joost Pauwelyn, 'Assessing Stakeholder Participation Reforms in Global Health Governance.' Chapter 18, this volume. See also DeMenno and Büthe, 'Voice and Influence' (n 7).

[141] Gian Luca Burci, 'The Effects of Stakeholder Reforms on Global Health Governance: A Response.' Chapter 19, this volume.

[142] Suerie Moon, 'How Much Do Health Actors from the Global South Influence Global Health Governance? A Response.' Chapter 20, this volume.

[143] Gülen Atay Newton, 'Evolving Norms and Objectives Regarding Stakeholder Participation: The Global Fund to Fight AIDS, Tuberculosis and Malaria.' Chapter 21, this volume.

[144] K M Gopakumar, 'The World Health Organization's Engagement with Non-State Actors: The Risk of Corporate Influence.' Chapter 22, this volume.

important implications for its engagement with stakeholders: trusteeship, functionality, and efficiency. The trusteeship approach, building on the work of Eyal Benvenisti, suggests that a global body should take into account the interests of anyone affected by its decisions, whereas under the functionality approach a global body should engage only stakeholders who can contribute to the body's performance. While trusteeship or functionality call for engaging stakeholders, concerns over efficiency may act as a counterforce, given widespread concern that increases in participation generally lead to a decrease in efficiency. To test these concepts in practice, Berman examines whether or how these concepts might explain participation in four global health organizations: the WHO, Codex, the Global Fund, and GAVI.[145]

Drawing on examples from across multiple policy fields, Kal Raustiala demonstrates that multi-stakeholder governance increasingly characterizes twenty-first century governance. He argues that private power need not and has not come at the expense of public actors, but instead often works to the political benefit of those public actors. This symbiotic relationship between public and private actors is insufficiently appreciated and helps to explain the striking rise of multi-stakeholderism in global governance and the increase in stakeholder participation.[146]

In the last chapter, we draw together the main findings of the book, reflect on the implications of those findings for the hypotheses developed in chapter 2, and sketch an agenda for future research.[147]

[145] Berman, 'The Stakeholder Participation Triangle' (n 120).
[146] Kal Raustiala, 'Public Power and Private Stakeholders.' Chapter 24, this volume.
[147] Büthe *et al.*, 'Conclusion' (n 121).

2

Voice and Influence in Global Governance

An Analytical Framework

*Mercy Berman DeMenno and Tim Büthe**

2.1 Introduction

This book aims to advance our understanding of global governance by examining the consequences of institutional reforms in global governance bodies, which have the declared purpose of boosting the participation of previously marginalized or even entirely excluded (disregarded) stakeholders.[1] This requires us to think about the incentives and opportunities of, at a minimum, two sets of actors: (i) the stakeholders of the particular global governance body and (ii) the global governance body itself as an organization with agency.[2]

* The authors are listed in reverse alphabetical order; both have contributed equally to the paper. For comments and suggestions on earlier drafts, we are grateful to Abdel Alshadafan, Ayelet Berman, Cindy Cheng, Ernesto Cruz Ruiz, Tana Johnson, Zlatina Georgieva, Joost Pauwelyn, Martino Maggetti, Tobias Rommel, Thomas Sommerer, Jonas Tallberg, Nora von Ingersleben-Seip, as well as the contributors to this volume and other attendees of presentations at the SNIS authors' workshops at the Graduate Institute Geneva and the Technical University of Munich (TUM) *Akademiezentrum* Raitenhaslach, the 2017 American Political Science Association meeting, the 2018 ECPR Regulatory Governance meeting, and in the IR Research Group meetings at the *Hochschule für Politik*/TUM School of Governance.

[1] See Richard B Stewart, 'Remedying Disregard in Global Regulatory Governance: Accountability, Participation, and Responsiveness' 108(2) *American Journal of International Law* (2014) 211-270 and Joost Pauwelyn, 'Informal International Lawmaking: Framing the Concept and Research Question' in Joost Pauwelyn, Ramses A Wessel and Jan Wouters (eds), *Informal International Lawmaking* (Oxford University Press 2012) 13-34, respectively. We use the term 'global' broadly for any cross-border activities, actors, and institutions, without presuming that these phenomena necessarily span the globe, making 'global', for purposes of this chapter, essentially a synonym for 'international'.

[2] We recognize—but do not separately model in this chapter—that (the lack of) opportunities for participation may in some cases be dictated by global governance bodies' political principals, i.e. stakeholders who are already well entrenched and powerful within the global governance body and who might have distinct preferences regarding stakeholder participation, which may diverge from the global governance body's preferences. We nonetheless focus our model on the global governance bodies as 'governors' in the sense of Debora D Avant, Martha Finnemore and Susan K Sell (eds), *Who Governs the Globe?* (Cambridge University Press 2010) to underscore their potential for autonomous agency (see e.g. Tana L Johnson, *Organizational Progeny: Why Governments Are Losing Control over the Proliferating Structures of Global Governance* (Oxford University Press 2014); Jeffrey M Chwieroth, *Capital Ideas: The IMF and the Rise of Financial Liberalization* (Princeton University Press 2009); Christoph Knill and Martin W Bauer 'Policy-Making by International Public Administrations: Concepts, Causes and Consequences' 23(7) *Journal of European Public Policy* (2016 special issue) 949-959; Johan Christensen and Kutsal Yesilkagit, 'International Public Administration: A Critique' 26(6) *Journal of European Public Policy* (2019) 946-961). This still allows us to take entrenched stakeholders (and their possible opposition) into account, since the governance body's organizational self-interest in effectiveness and legitimacy should include keeping those established stakeholders on board. Of course, those entrenched stakeholders might themselves have instrumental reasons for wanting to see the global governance body integrate—selectively—certain previously excluded

Mercy Berman DeMenno and Tim Büthe, *Voice and Influence in Global Governance* In: *Rethinking Participation in Global Governance*. Edited by: Joost Pauwelyn, Martino Maggetti, Tim Büthe, and Ayelet Berman, Oxford University Press.
 DOI: 10.1093/oso/9780198852568.003.0002

Specifically, we address three related but analytically separable core questions to understand participation in global governance:[3]

1. Under what conditions should we expect a given global governance body to expand the opportunities for voice (participation) in rule- and decision-making for previously disregarded stakeholders?
2. Under what conditions should we expect previously disregarded stakeholders to increase their level of actual engagement with a given global governance body (making use of expanded voice opportunities)?
3. Under what conditions should we expect previously disregarded stakeholders to gain actual *influence* over rule- and decision-making in a given global governance body?

Reforms with the declared purpose of expanding stakeholder participation have been undertaken by many global governance bodies in recent years. In the realm of global finance, for instance, the Basel Committee on Banking Supervision, in a series of reforms between 2009 and 2014, extended its membership from the original eleven to twenty-eight member countries, and it added three observers;[4] the International Monetary Fund (IMF) between 2008 and 2010 redistributed the weights for the weighted voting in the IMF, substantially increasing the weights of Brazil, China, and India among its 188 member countries.[5] In the realm of global health, the universalist (194 member states) World Health Organization in 2003 opened the meetings of its exclusive Executive Board (EB) to observers from beyond the thirty-four EB members, and in the years since has undertaken a series of further reforms to increase voice opportunities for non-commercial, civil society stakeholders; the Codex Alimentarius Commission in 2004 (and again in 2016) established a 'Trust Fund' for developing country delegations whose participation might have been constrained by a lack of financial resources.[6]

Such reforms are puzzling, since inclusiveness vis-a-vis the full range of stakeholder interests has generally not been a key concern of global governance. The unequal distribution of power has been a characteristic of international affairs seemingly forever, and the injustice of the detrimental consequences for the weak has been lamented to little avail since at least the Melian dialogue in Thucydides' *Peloponnesian War*.[7]

members, as Ayelet Berman has argued in 'Accordion Governance' 13(3) *Vienna Journal of International Constitutional Law* (2020) 203–236.

[3] The primary focus is on questions 2 and 3, but the answer to question 1 may condition the answers to 2 and 3. See also the conceptual discussion of participation in Tim Büthe, Joost Pauwelyn, Martino Maggetti and Ayelet Berman, 'Conclusion: The Participation of Marginalized Stakeholders in Global Governance.' Chapter 25, this volume.

[4] Spain already had been added as a twelfth member in 2001.

[5] For details, see Olga Kovarzina and Martino Maggetti, 'Stakeholder Participation Reforms in Global Finance Governance.' Chapter 4, this volume.

[6] For details, see Ayelet Berman, 'Stakeholder Participation Reforms in Global Health Governance.' Chapter 13, this volume.

[7] Seemingly much less powerful actors do of course sometimes succeed against powerful opposition, but when they do, it is rarely about changing the system (see e.g. Robert O Keohane, 'Big Influence of Small Allies 2 (Spring) *Foreign Policy* (1971) 161–182; James C Scott, *Weapons of the Weak: Every-day Forms of Peasant Resistance* (Yale University Press 1985); Jack Corbett, Yi-Chong Xu and Patrick Weller, 'Norm Entrepreneurship and Diffusion "From Below" in International Organisations: How the Competent

The principle of sovereign equality at the core of modern international law may seem to remedy such inequality to some extent.[8] But although the principle was foundational to the institutionalization of world politics after the Second World War,[9] even the United Nations with its five 'permanent members' of the security council in fact enshrined George Orwell's dictum in *Animal Farm* that 'some are more equal than others'.

International Law and International Relations (IR) scholarship offers a number of functional reasons for disregarding a wide range of stakeholders in order to make or keep global governance feasible: Many global bodies traditionally take decisions by consensus rather than by voting,[10] such that expanding stakeholder participation may undermine a global governance body as means for 'choosing in groups'.[11] For simple coordination tasks, the costs might 'only' be a loss of efficiency—with compensating gains in legitimacy from the inclusion of more of the Global South.[12] For the governance of more complex issues or issues with distributional conflicts, expanding participation might reduce the probability of achieving international cooperation and thus meaningful governance at all,[13] unless greater inclusiveness is accompanied by procedural changes towards majoritarian decision-making, possibly involving unequal members, weighted votes, etc.[14] And if the terms of international cooperation reflect the lowest common denominator, then more inclusive global governance might come at the cost of the depth of whatever cooperation still occurs.[15] Even if the same rules or decisions are adopted in the end, the transactions costs (that is, the time and effort

Performance of Vulnerability Generates Benefits for Small States' 45(4) *Review of International Studies* (2019) 647-668.

[8] F H Hinsley, *Sovereignty* (Basic Books 1966); Stephen D Krasner (ed), *Problematic Sovereignty* (Columbia University Press 2001); Ulrich K Preuß, 'Equality of States: Its Meaning in a Constitutionalized Global Order' 9(1) *Chicago Journal of International Law* (2008) 17-49; Alia M Matanock, 'Governance Delegation Agreements: Shared Sovereignty as a Substitute for Limited Statehood' 27(4) *Governance* (2014) 589-612; and Lora Anne Viola, Duncan Snidal and Michael Zürn, 'Sovereign (In)Equality in the Evolution of the International System' in Stephan Leibfried, Evelyne Huber, Matthew Lange, Jonah D Levy, and John D Stephens (eds), *Oxford Handbook of Transformations of the State* (Oxford University Press 2015) 221-236, esp. 225f.

[9] Hans Kelsen, 'The Principle of Sovereign Equality of States as a Basis for International Organization' 53(2) *Yale Law Journal* (1944) 207-220.

[10] Where consensus need not mean strict unanimity but requires support that goes far beyond a minimum winning coalition under the existing voting rules and usually at least acquiescence from the non-supporters, even if sustained only through side-payments. Still insightful in this regard is C Wilfred Jenks, 'Unanimity, the Veto, Weighted Voting, Special and Simple Majorities and Consensus as Modes of Decision in International Organizations' in *Cambridge Essays in International Law* (Stevens & Sons 1965), 48-63.

[11] Michael C Munger and Kevin M Munger, *Choosing in Groups: Analytical Politics Revisited* (Cambridge University Press 2015).

[12] Kishore Mahbubani, 'Can Asia Re-Legitimize Global Governance?' 18(February) *Review of International Political Economy* (2011) 131-139, esp. 133f.

[13] Robert O Keohane and Joseph S Nye, 'Between Centralization and Fragmentation: The Club Model of Multilateral Cooperation and Problems of Democratic Legitimacy' *Kennedy School of Government Working Paper* no. 01-004 (February 2001).

[14] Josep M Colomer, *How Global Institutions Rule the World* (Palgrave Macmillan Press 2014).

[15] George W Downs, David M Rocke, and Peter N Barsoom, 'Managing the Evolution of Multilateralism' 52(2) *International Organization* (1998) 397-419. The argument assumes that more inclusive (participatory) governance means giving voice and vote to stakeholders with weaker preferences for cooperation.

required) to identify possible compromises will be greater with a larger, more inclusive group of participants than with a small group.[16]

IR scholars who are focused on the distributional implications of political institutions offer yet a different explanation. They suggest that marginalization, exclusion, and disregard of large parts of the Global South (and most non-commercial civil society stakeholders) exist and persist because they are a means to maintain distributions of power and benefits that are highly beneficial to the established powers.[17] Such distributional benefits have been found even in the realm of transnational 'private' governance, and even when they might not have been intended. The creation of the International Electrotechnical Commission by the leading European and American physicists, engineers, and entrepreneurs of the 1890s and 1900s—in ways that de facto excluded participants from the (largely colonized) developing world—had the effect that developing countries' concerns were not on the agenda whereas issues with commercial potential in Northern industrializing countries were prioritized.[18] In other words, expanding previously disregarded stakeholders' opportunities for participation—especially if it gives those stakeholders a chance to exert real influence over decisions—is likely to have distributional consequences. This makes participation-boosting institutional reforms all the more puzzling.

One possible explanation for why participation reforms nonetheless have occurred could be a shift in the norms governing global governance. As Robert Dahl argued, the validity of the fundamental principle of liberal democracy—that everyone who is affected by a decision should have the opportunity to participate in making that decision—is not restricted to national-level political institutions.[19] And as Alexandru Grigorescu shows, the 'normative pressure' on international organizations to become more inclusive and more 'democratic' in their decision-making—both with regard to smaller and poorer states and with regard to transnational non-governmental actors—has substantially increased over the past century.[20] Global governance bodies

[16] Lisa Martin, 'Interests, Power, and Multilateralism' 46(4) *International Organization* (1992) 765-792. Johns and Pelc even suggests that the recognition of the greater challenge (i.e. the greater likelihood of failure) will prompt some stakeholders to forego opportunities to participate (Leslie Johns and Krzysztof J Pelc, 'Fear of Crowds in World Trade Organization Disputes: Why Don't More Countries Participate?' 78(1) *Journal of Politics* (2016) 88-104).

[17] See e.g. Miles Kahler, 'Multilateralism with Small and Large Numbers' 46(3) *International Organization* (1992) 681-708; Richard H Steinberg, 'In the Shadow of Law or Power? Consensus-Based Bargaining and Outcomes in the GATT/WTO' 56(2) *International Organization* (2002) 339-374; Walter Mattli and Tim Büthe, 'Global Private Governance: Lessons from a National Model of Setting Standards in Accounting' 68(3/4) *Law and Contemporary Problems* (2005) 225-262.

[18] Tim Büthe, 'The Power of Norms; the Norms of Power: Who Governs International Electrical and Electronic Technology?' in Avant *et al.* (eds), *Who Governs?* (n 2) 292-332, esp. 299-302.

[19] Robert A Dahl, *A Preface to Economic Democracy* (University of California Press 1985). With regard to international organizations, Dahl later expressed an explicitly sceptical view in 'Can International Organizations Be Democratic?' in Ian Shapiro and Casiano Hacker-Cordón (eds), *Democracy's Edges* (Cambridge University Press 1999) 19-36.

[20] Alexandru Grigorescu, *Democratic International Organizations? Normative Pressures and Decision-Making Rules* (Cambridge University Press 2015), esp. 22–29, 51–75, 181-202. See also e.g. Jonas Tallberg, Thomas Sommerer, Theresa Squatrito and Christer Jönsson, *The Opening Up of International Organizations* (Cambridge University Press 2013); Klaus Dingwerth and Patrizia Nanz, 'Participation' in Jacob Katz Cogan, Ian Hurd and Ian Johnstone (eds), *Oxford Handbook of International Organizations* (Oxford University Press 2015) 1126-1145.

might therefore provide previously marginalized stakeholders with opportunities to add their voice to the chorus (and even to exert influence) because they have come to recognize it as 'the right thing to do', following the logic of appropriateness often emphasized by sociological institutionalists.[21] Relatedly yet distinctly, the stakeholder reforms of global governance bodies might be explained by their understanding of their role as something like a trusteeship.[22] In either case, to explain variation across issue areas and across global governance bodies within the same issue area, the actual contents of the discourse through which the pertinent social norms are constructed and maintained,[23] or the pushback against institutional change from well-entrenched stakeholders with a privileged power position under the status, which IR Realists are prone to emphasize,[24] would need to differ across issue areas or particular global governance bodies.[25]

While our personal normative commitment to participatory democracy was among our motivations for undertaking this research, we bracket the discussion of the explanatory power, the desirability, and the practical feasibility of extending democratic

[21] See James G March and Johan P Olsen, 'The New Institutionalism: Organizational Factors in Political Life' 78(3) *American Political Science Review* (1984) 734-749 and 'The Institutional Dynamics of International Political Orders' 52(4) *International Organization* (1998) 943-969; Martha Finnemore and Kathryn Sikkink, 'International Norm Dynamics and Political Change' 52(4) *International Organization* (1998) 887-917; Steven Bernstein and Benjamin Cashore, 'Can Non-State Global Governance Be Legitimate? An Analytical Framework' 1(4) *Regulation & Governance* (2007) 347-371.

[22] For the trusteeship notion, see Giandomenico Majone, 'Regulatory Legitimacy' in *Regulating Europe* (Routledge 1996) 284-301 and 'Two Logics of Delegation: Agency and Fiduciary Relations in EU Governance' 2(1) *European Union Politics* (2001) 103-122; as well as Eyal Benvenisti, 'Sovereigns as Trustees of Humanity' 107 *American Journal of International Law* (2013) 295-333. Note, however, that the paternalistic connotations of trusteeship might lead to a greater emphasis on taking marginalized and excluded stakeholders' interests into account (thus possibly boosting output legitimacy, only) rather than increasing opportunities for actual voice and influence for such traditionally disregarded stakeholders. See e.g. Steven Brint, *In an Age of Experts: The Changing Role of Professionals in Politics and Public Life* (Princeton University Press 1994) and JoAnne Yates and Craig N Murphy, *Engineering Rules: Global Standard Setting since 1880* (Johns Hopkins University Press 2019).

[23] Thomas Risse, 'Let's Argue: Communicative Action in World Politics' 54(1) *International Organization* (Winter 2000) 1-39. For an example of an analysis showing the actual contents for transnational bodies dominated by non-governmental versus state actors, see Tim Büthe, Solomon Major and André de Mello e Souza, 'The Politics of Private Foreign Aid: Humanitarian Principles, Economic Development Objectives, and Organizational Interests in the Allocation of Private Aid by NGOs' 66(4) *International Organization* (Fall 2012) 571-607.

[24] See e.g. Stephen D Krasner, 'Power Politics, Institutions, and Transnational Relations' in Thomas Risse-Kappen (ed), *Bringing Transnational Relations Back In: Non-State Actors, Domestic Structures and International Institutions* (Cambridge University Press 1995) 257-279.

[25] Grigorescu, *Normative Pressures* (n 20), esp. 29–38. See also Phillip Lipscy, *Renegotiating the World Order: Institutional Change in International Relations* (Cambridge University Press 2017), esp. 23ff, 246ff. This leads to the expectation, which historical institutionalists have often articulated in other contexts, that institutional change is difficult and often incomplete, resulting in suboptimal outcomes because the status quo ante, due to feedback loops, tends to generate its own supporting coalition; see e.g. Theda Skocpol, *Protecting Soldiers and Mothers: The Political Origins of Social Policy in the United States* (Harvard University Press 1992); Paul Pierson, *Dismantling the Welfare State* (Cambridge University Press 1994); Tim Büthe, 'Taking Temporality Seriously: Modeling History and the Use of Narratives as Evidence' 96(3) *American Political Science Review* (2002) 481-494; and Kathleen Thelen, 'How Institutions Evolve: Insights from Comparative Historical Analysis' in James Mahoney and Dietrich Rueschemeyer (ed), *Comparative-Historical Analysis* (Cambridge University Press 2003) 208-240.

norms to the international sphere.[26] We take a different approach in developing the analytical framework here.

Following Ngaire Woods' call for a rejection of the trade-off between participation-based legitimacy and effectiveness in global governance as a 'false dichotomy',[27] we take a positive political economy approach.[28] It relies, at its core, upon only the minimalist assumptions that global governance bodies need to exhibit policy effectiveness and that they will expand stakeholder participation to the extent that it helps them achieve this goal. Specifically, our approach assumes that (at least some) stakeholders can help a given governance body by providing what Peter Haas has called 'usable knowledge'[29] or by contributing to the global governance body's democratic legitimacy[30]—and that those stakeholders will be willing to do so as long as the expected benefits of doing so exceed the costs.

Our conceptual and analytical framework for understanding the incentives of, and interactions among, global governance bodies and their stakeholders builds upon Albert Hirschman's seminal *Exit, Voice, and Loyalty*, which distinguishes two ideal-typical responses to dissatisfaction with the status quo: Socio-political actors may attempt to bring about changes by articulating their dissatisfaction and engaging with(in) the governance institutions in which they are currently embedded ('voice'), or they may disengage and leave those institutions ('exit').[31] Given the distinctive *political* logic of regulatory governance, we define exit more narrowly as removing oneself from the jurisdiction of the global governance body (see discussion in Sections 2.2.3 and 2.5.1). Exit thus implies losing stakeholder status and hence the basis for having a legitimate claim to participation. Note, however, that being passive vis-à-vis a particular global governance body (that is, not engaging) does not as such shield the stakeholder from being affected by the body's policy- or decision-making.

Note also that we treat the question of how much *influence* a participating stakeholder is able to exert as analytically separable from the logically prior questions of what explains voice opportunities and a stakeholder's use of existing voice opportunities (to which we also refer as 'engagement' in global governance). Importantly,

[26] Ayelet Berman, 'The Stakeholder Participation Triangle: Trusteeship, Functionality, and Efficiency.' Chapter 23, this volume.

[27] Ngaire Woods, 'Multilateralism and Building Stronger International Institutions' in Alnoor Ebrahim and Edward Weisband (eds), *Global Accountabilities: Participation, Pluralism, and Public Ethics* (Cambridge University Press 2007) 27-44, esp. 31ff.

[28] See James E Alt and Kenneth A Shepsle, *Perspectives on Positive Political Economy* (Cambridge University Press 1990).

[29] Peter M Haas, 'When Does Power Listen to Truth?' 11(4) *Journal of European Public Policy* (2004) 569-592.

[30] For an insightful discussion of such dynamics, foreshadowing the emphasis on 'throughput legitimacy' discussed in Section 2.6.2, see Jens Steffek, 'Sources of Legitimacy Beyond the State: A View from International Relations' in Christian Joerges, Inger-Johanne Sand, and Gunther Teubner (eds), *Transnational Governance and Constitutionalism* (Hart Publishing 2004) 81-101. For details, see Section 2.4.2 and Section 2.6.2.

[31] Albert O Hirschman, *Exit, Voice, and Loyalty: Responses to Decline in Firms, Organizations, and States* (Harvard University Press 1970).

voice-only forms of participation are inherently what Richard Stewart has called 'non-decisional',[32] whereas influence requires, in addition, either a 'decisional' role, defined as 'the right to vote or otherwise exercise a role in the making of decisions',[33] or voluntary responsiveness by the global governance body, for instance in pursuit of greater output legitimacy. At the same time, we posit that understanding influence in the aftermath of global governance reforms requires us to consider why reforms that increase voice opportunities were undertaken in the first place (even though the reasons for the reforms are not otherwise a focus of this book).

The remainder of this chapter lays out the analytical framework for the empirical chapters in Part II and Part III of this book (focused on governance of global finance and global health, respectively). To help clarify the distinctive challenges of stakeholder participation in global governance, we contrast in Section 2.2 global and domestic rule- and decision-making with regard to three key aspects of stakeholder participation. In Section 2.3, we briefly explain our positive political economy approach to modelling the global governance body's and the stakeholders' decisions. The resulting analytical framework is summarized in Figure 2.1.

In Section 2.4, we develop our conceptual and theoretical model of the decision to expand participation opportunities for traditionally disregarded stakeholders, which we treat as being controlled by the governance body as a 'global governor'.[34] In Section 2.5, we model stakeholders' propensity to exercise their voice once the opportunity has opened up. We posit that stakeholders' incentives to actually engage in a given global governance body's rule- and decision-making are a function of the importance of that particular forum for the stakeholders and of the stakeholders' capabilities, including material, analytical, and political resources.

Actual engagement makes it possible—but does not in itself guarantee—that a stakeholder will get to exert influence over policy outcomes, that is, the rules and decisions of the global governance body. In Section 2.6 we develop a conceptual and theoretical model for thinking about why (or under what conditions) voice opportunities result not only in stakeholder voice but also in stakeholder influence over global rules and decisions.

The theoretical discussion in this chapter yields a number of tentative answers to the question under which conditions we should expect previously marginalized stakeholders to gain voice opportunities, actually engage, and exercise influence, which we spell out as hypotheses—to be critically empirically examined for the governance of global finance and global health in Part II and Part III of this volume, respectively.

[32] Defined as opportunities 'to make submissions on proposed decisions or otherwise provide input to the decision makers' (Stewart, 'Remedying Disregard' (n 1), 214).

[33] Stewart, 'Remedying Disregard' (n 1), 213.

[34] See Avant, Finnemore and Sell, *Who Governs?* and related works (n 2).

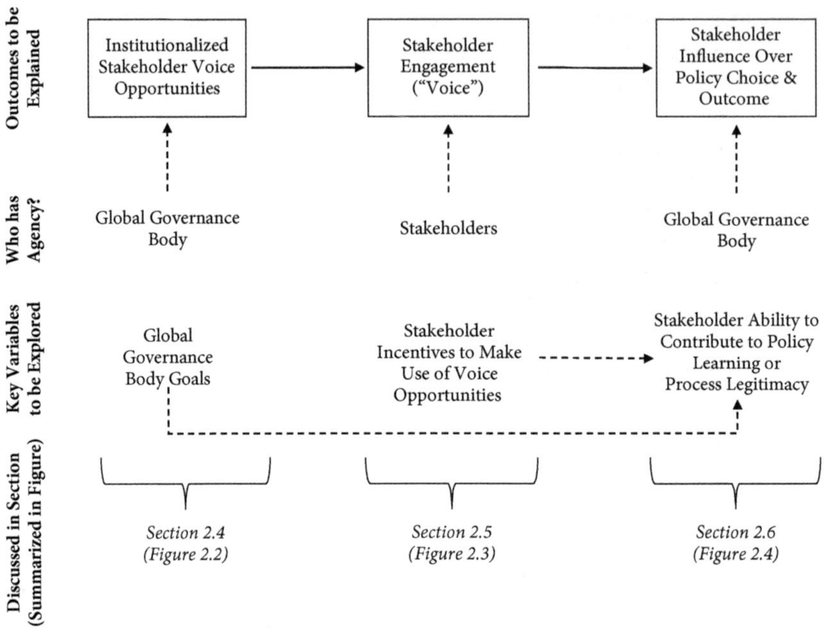

Figure 2.1 Overview of the Analytical Framework

2.2 Stakeholder Participation in Domestic and Global Governance

We begin with a brief discussion of similarities and contrasts between domestic and global regulatory governance, both to avoid reinventing the wheel and to gain a clearer understanding of what is distinctive about stakeholder participation in global governance. Many of the governance issues that arise at the international level are familiar and have been well theorized and empirically examined in domestic regulatory politics. The fruitfulness of focusing on those similarities is illustrated by the 'global administrative law' literature, which started from the observation that many forms of institutionalized participation in global governance reflect institutionalized participation in domestic administrative processes.[35]

[35] Kingsbury, Benedict, Nico Krisch, and Richard B Stewart, 'The Emergence of Global Administrative Law' 68(3/4) *Law and Contemporary Problems* (2005) 15-61; Michael S Barr and Geoffrey P Miller, 'Global Administrative Law: The View from Basel' 17(1) *European Journal of International Law* (2006) 15-46. In addition, understanding stakeholder (non)participation at the domestic level is important for thinking about accountability at the international level: Stakeholders who are marginalized at the international level are often assumed and supposed to be represented by national governments; see Anne-Marie Slaughter, *A New World Order* (Princeton University Press 2004); Ruth W Grant and Robert O Keohane, 'Accountability and Abuses of Power in World Politics' 99(1) *American Political Science Review* (2005) 29-43; Ayelet Berman, 'The Role of Domestic Administrative Law in the Accountability of Informal International Lawmaking: The Case of the ICH' in Pauwelyn *et al.* (eds), *Informal International Lawmaking* (n 1) 468-499; Tallberg *et al.*, *Opening Up* (n 20)—though Alexander Libman and Anastassia Obydenkova caution that more democratic countries appear to be less active in global governance, see 'Informal Governance and Participation in Non-Democratic International Organizations' 8(2) *Review of International Organizations* (2013)

At the same time, there are ways in which global governance systematically differs from domestic governance, starting with the fact that, *in global governance, the traditionally disregarded stakeholders include states—until recently virtually all states of the Global South*. Therefore, supposedly participation-boosting reforms often target states, whereas in domestic governance, the state is inherently present, even when it remains largely out of sight[36] or is severely deficient and thus only exist as a 'shadow'.[37] Our discussion of similarities and differences between domestic and global governance focuses on possible modes of participation, the stages of the policy-making process during which stakeholder participation may occur, and the availability of the exit option.

2.2.1 Participation Modes

Stakeholder participation in domestic regulatory processes can take myriad specific forms. These 'modes' of participation include notice-and-comment procedures (providing stakeholders with opportunities to provide written comments on draft rules), hearings and public meetings (where stakeholders can ask questions and provide information about proposed or draft rules), and advisory committees (through which stakeholders with specialized knowledge or positions provide feedback on rule development or draft rules).

Many of the modes employed in global governance mirror those employed in domestic regulatory processes. For example, a recent OECD analysis of fifty international organizations with regulatory governance functions finds that 46% (twenty-three) of these organizations provide opportunities for the general public, that is, anyone, to comment on proposed actions; 94% (forty-seven) have procedures to allow recognized stakeholder groups to provide comments on proposed rules or policies; and 64% (thirty-two) have stakeholder advisory committees.[38] These proportions are comparable to what we find in the domestic regulatory processes of liberal democracies,

221-243. For recent surveys of the literature on participation in domestic (mostly U.S.) rule-making, see Cary Coglianese, 'Citizen Participation in Rulemaking: Past, Present, and Future' 55(5) *Duke Law Journal* (2006) 943-968; Cornelius Kerwin, Scott R Furlong and William West, 'Interest Groups, Rulemaking, and American Bureaucracy' in Robert F Durant (ed), *The Oxford Handbook of American Bureaucracy* (Oxford University Press 2010) 590-611; David Levi-Faur (ed), *The Oxford Handbook of Governance* (Oxford University Press 2012); Alberto Alemanno, 'Chapter 3: Stakeholder Engagement in Regulatory Policy' in *Regulatory Policy in Perspective: A Reader's Companion to the OECD Regulatory Policy Outlook 2015* (OECD Publishing) 115-158; Mercy B DeMenno, *Rethinking Stakeholder Participation in Regulatory Governance: A Historical-Institutional Analysis and Causal Process Model of Participatory Effectiveness* (Unpublished manuscript, Duke University, 2021).

[36] Adrienne Héritier and Sandra Eckert, 'New Modes of Governance in the Shadow of Hierarchy: Self-Regulation by Industry in Europe' 28(1) *Journal of Public Policy* (2008) 113-138.

[37] Tanja A. Börzel and Thomas Risse, 'Governance Without a State: Can It Work?' 4(2) *Regulation and Governance* (2010) 113-134 and 'Dysfunctional State Institutions, Trust, and Governance in Areas of Limited Statehood' 10(2) *Regulation and Governance* (2016) 149-160; Thomas Risse, Tanja A. Börzel, and Anke Draude (eds), *The Oxford Handbook of Governance and Limited Statehood* (Oxford University Press 2018).

[38] OECD, *International Regulatory Co-Operation* (OECD Publishing, 2016), 85. Percentages reported are for the sum of IO practices reported as 'systematic', 'frequent', and 'occasional'.

although public consultation is much more widespread at the domestic level. Among the thirty-four OECD member countries and the European Union, 94% (thirty-three) jurisdictions post proposed rules on the internet for public comment, 97% (thirty-four) conduct informal consultations with selected groups, and 94% (thirty-three) have stakeholder advisory committees.[39]

Notwithstanding striking similarities between domestic and global governance processes, certain modes appear to be distinct to global governance. For example, international organizations (IOs) and many other global governance bodies have designated 'members' with voting rights and thus exclusive decisional authority, but then engage in making rules and decisions that are also binding on other, excluded stakeholders.[40] Here, institutional reforms to boost participation might consist of broadening the membership (as occurred in the International Council for Harmonisation of Technical Requirements for Pharmaceuticals for Human Use, ICH, and the International Medical Device Regulators Forum, IMDRF)[41], possibly by changing the fee structure for members or creating additional membership categories, for instance for poorer countries or for non-commercial interests in a multi-stakeholder body.

Recent studies suggest that global regulatory bodies also differ from their domestic counterparts in that they rely to a greater extent on targeted stakeholder engagement with specific groups, rather than the general public.[42] This observation may be unsurprising, given the lack of a global 'demos'.[43] It implies, however, that global governance bodies may suffer from more severe political inequity between stakeholders that are recognized or even embedded in the governance body (for example, as members) and the traditionally marginalized stakeholders with which we are primarily concerned in this book.

2.2.2 Participation across the Stages of the Governance Sequence

We also compare domestic and global governance with respect to the stages of the governance sequence at which opportunities for stakeholder participation arise. Büthe distinguishes five stages of the 'governance sequence': (1) agenda-setting, (2) rule-making, (3) adoption-implementation-compliance, (4) monitoring (of rule-compliant implementation), and (5) enforcement (when compliance is required).[44] These

[39] OECD, *OECD Regulatory Policy Outlook 2018* (OECD Publishing 2018), 55.

[40] For an insightful survey of transnational bodies with membership structure, including sometime unequal voting rights among those members, see Peter Kotzian and Jens Steffek, 'Do Members Make a Difference? A Study of Transnational Civil Society Organizations' 5(1) *European Political Science Review* (2013) 55-81. Such an institutional structure is, at least in liberal democracies, not found in domestic public governance and relatively rare in private governance at the domestic level.

[41] See Berman, 'Stakeholder Participation Reforms' (n 6).

[42] OECD, *OECD Regulatory Policy Outlook 2015* (OECD Publishing 2015); OECD, *Regulatory Co-Operation* (n 38); OECD, *Regulatory Policy Outlook 2018* (n 39). The studies are based on samples that are not perfectly comparable, but the tendency is unmistakable.

[43] Compare to David Held, *Democracy and the Global Order* (Polity Press 1995) and Michael Zürn, 'Democratic Governance Beyond the Nation-State' 6(2) *European Journal of International Relations* (2000) 183-221.

[44] Büthe, 'Who Governs?' (n 18), 315-330. Similarly: Kenneth W Abbott and Duncan Snidal, 'The Governance Triangle: Regulatory Standards Institutions and the Shadow of the State' in Walter Mattli and Ngaire Woods (eds), *The Politics of Global Regulation* (Princeton University Press 2009) 44-88, esp. 63 and *OECD, Regulatory Policy Outlook 2018* (n 39), 158.

five stages comprise—and help us distinguish—the key phases of most governance processes, at both the domestic and international level. Opportunities for stakeholder participation, however, may vary between domestic and global governance across the five stages.

In domestic regulatory processes, there are (at least in liberal democracies) myriad opportunities to participate across all five stages. Stakeholders may participate during the agenda-setting stage[45] as well as during the (iterative) rule-making stage.[46] Stakeholders who are the intended implementers or users of the rules (the 'targets' of governance) are inherently participants during the context-specific implementation of a given rule and may also participate in the *ex post* evaluation of existing rules.[47] In

[45] For studies of participation in agenda-setting at the U.S. federal level see: Keith Naughton, Celeste Schmid, Susan Webb Yackee, and Xueyong Zhan, 'Understanding Commenter Influence During Agency Rule Development' 28(2) *Journal of Policy Analysis and Management* (2009) 258-277; William F West and Connor Raso, 'Who Shapes the Rulemaking Agenda? Implications for Bureaucratic Responsiveness and Bureaucratic Control' 23(3) *Journal of Public Administration Research and Theory* (2013) 495-519; Susan Webb Yackee, 'The Politics of Ex Parte Lobbying: Pre-Proposal Agenda Building and Blocking During Agency Rulemaking' 22(2) *Journal of Public Administration Research and Theory* (2012) 373-393. For comparative and transnational examples, see e.g. Anne Binderkrantz, 'Interest Group Strategies: Navigating Between Privileged Access and Strategies of Pressure' 53(4) *Political Studies* (2005) 694-715; Adriana Bunea and Robert Thomson, 'Consultations with Interest Groups and the Empowerment of Executives: Evidence from the European Union' 28(4) *Governance* (2015) 517-531; Jenna R Jambeck and Kyle Johnsen, 'Citizen-Based Litter and Marine Debris Data Collection and Mapping' 17(4) *Computing in Science and Engineering* (2015) 20-26; and Joanna Vince and Britta Denise Hardesty, 'Plastic Pollution Challenges in Marine and Coastal Environments: From Local to Global Governance' 25(1) *Restoration Ecology* (2017) 123-128, esp. 125.

[46] For studies of participation in rule-making at the U.S. federal level, see Marissa Martino Golden, 'Interest Groups in the Rule-Making Process: Who Participates? Whose Voices Get Heard?' 8(2) *Journal of Public Administration Research and Theory* (1998) 245-270; William F West, 'Formal Procedures, Informal Processes, Accountability, and Responsiveness in Bureaucratic Policy Making: An Institutional Policy Analysis' 64(1) *Public Administration Review* (2004) 66-80; Mariano-Florentino Cuéllar, 'Rethinking Regulatory Democracy' 57(2) *Administrative Law Review* (2005) 412-497; Scott R Furlong and Cornelius M Kerwin, 'Interest Group Participation in Rule Making: A Decade of Change' 15(3) *Journal of Public Administration Research and Theory* (2005) 353-370; and Susan Webb Yackee, 'Sweet-Talking the Fourth Branch: The Influence of Interest Group Comments on Federal Agency Rulemaking' 16(1) *Journal of Public Administration Research and Theory* (2006) 103-124; for examples from other countries and global governance, see Binderkrantz, 'Interest Group Strategies' (n 45); Claudia Kissling and Jens Steffek, 'CSOs and the Democratization of International Governance: Prospects and Problems' in Jens Steffek, Claudia Kissling and Patrizia Nanz (eds), *Civil Society Participation in European and Global Governance: A Cure for the Democratic Deficit?* (Palgrave Macmillan, 2008) 208-218, esp. 211f; Tobias Böhmelt, Vally Koubi, and Thomas Bernauer, 'Civil Society Participation in Global Governance: Insights from Climate Politics' 53(1) *European Journal of Political Research* (2014) 18-36; Thamy Pogrebinschi and Matt Ryan, 'Moving Beyond Input Legitimacy: When Do Democratic Innovations Affect Policymaking?' 57(1) *European Journal of Political Research* (2018) 135-152.

[47] Regarding retrospective review in regulatory rule- and decision-making, see: Cary Coglianese, 'Moving Forward with Regulatory Lookback' 30 *Yale Journal on Regulation* (2013) 57-66; Cass R Sunstein, 'The Regulatory Lookback' 94(2) *Boston University Law Review* (2014) 579-602; Yurij A Rakhmanin, G N Krasovsky, N A Egorova, and R I Mikhailova, [100 Years of Drinking Water Regulation. Retrospective Review, Current Situation and Prospects] Mar–Apr(2) *Gigiena i sanitariia* (2014) 5-18; Jonathan Wiener, 'Comparing Regulatory Oversight Bodies: the US Office of Information and Regulatory Affairs and the EU Regulatory Scrutiny Board' in Susan Rose-Ackerman, Peter L. Lindseth, and Blake Emerson (eds), *Comparative Administrative Law* (Edward Elgar 2017) 333-351. Regarding stakeholder participation in retrospective review, see Mercy B DeMenno, 'Banking on Burden Reduction: How the Global Financial Crisis Shaped the Political Economy of Banking Regulation' 21 *Journal of Banking Regulation* (2020) 315–342 and 'Technocracy, Democracy, and Public Policy: An Evaluation of Public Participation in Retrospective Regulatory Review' 13(3) *Regulation & Governance* (2019) 362-383.

some cases private, bottom-up civil society initiative also contributes to implementation by undertaking local or transnational efforts to solve problems identified but not yet effectively addressed in global governance.[48] Stakeholders who have often had little or no voice in the first three stages of the governance sequence can play a critical role during the monitoring stage, including dispersed, seemingly 'powerless' stakeholders who are 'on the ground' locally and thus possess (or can gain access to) information about compliance that would be hard or impossible to obtain for the seemingly powerful regulatory body.[49] Finally, various stakeholders may participate at the enforcement stage, including otherwise marginalized ones. Such an enforcement role is in fact implicitly assigned to otherwise 'disregarded'[50] stakeholders, whenever laws or meta-regulations grant the right to seek damages to those who can claim to have been harmed (such as when the law allows class actions against the producers of consumer goods that do not meet established safety standards).[51]

In global governance processes, participation is (in principle) also possible at all five stages for a wide variety of stakeholders—including states or governments, as well as local, national, and transnational groups or affected individuals. At the same time, deductive logic as well as empirical observation suggests much greater and systematic unevenness in opportunities for participation across the stages of global governance.

In the domestic context, agenda-setting, for instance, often occurs through the adoption of primary legislation, which typically establishes a regulatory body, delegates regulatory authority to that body, and allocates funding for ongoing regulatory and programmatic implementation activities. Importantly, the budget allocation is usually for a limited amount of time[52] and hence requires periodic renewals, for example, in the form of regular appropriations bills. This important element of the

[48] See e.g. Vince and Hardesty, 'Plastic Pollution' (n 45), esp. 125. The civil society groups that get involved in such problem-solving efforts need not even be targets of global rule- or decision-making bodies.

[49] For studies of participation in monitoring and enforcement in the United States, see John T Scholz, 'Cooperative Regulatory Enforcement and the Politics of Administrative Effectiveness' 85(1) *American Political Science Review* (1991) 115-136; David L Markell and Tom R Tyler, 'Using Empirical Research to Design Government Citizen Participation Processes: A Case Study of Citizens' Roles in Environmental Compliance and Enforcement' 57(1) *The University of Kansas Law Review* (2008) 1-38; Jonathan H Adler, 'Stand or Deliver: Citizen Suits, Standing, and Environmental Protection' 12 *Duke Environmental Law & Policy Forum* (2001) 39-84; John C Coffee, *Entrepreneurial Litigation: Its Rise, Fall, and Future* (Harvard University Press 2015). For studies of participation in monitoring and enforcement in other countries, see e.g. Colin Scott, 'Private Regulation of the Public Sector: A Neglected Facet of Contemporary Governance' 29(1) *Journal of Law and Society* (2002) 56-76; Elizabeth Chrun, Daniel Berliner, and Aseem Prakash, 'Stakeholder Scrutiny, Urban Bias, and the Private Provision of Public Goods' 20(2) *Business and Politics* (2018) 273-300.

[50] Stewart, 'Remedying Disregard' (n 1).

[51] See in general Cass R Sustein and Richard B Stewart, 'Public Programs and Private Rights' 95 *Harvard Law Review* (1982) 1193-1322; Barak D Richman, 'Firms, Courts, and Reputation Mechanisms: Towards a Positive Theory of Private Ordering' 104(8) *Columbia Law Review* (2004) 2328-2367; Fabrizio Cafaggi and Agnieszka Janczuk, 'Private Regulation and Legal Integration' 12(3) *Business and Politics* (2010); and J Maria Glover, 'The Structural Role of Private Enforcement Mechanisms in Public Law' 53 *William and Mary Law Review* (2012) 1137-1217. As well as in application to antitrust/competition law and policy: Kai Hüschelrath and Sebastian Peyer, 'Public and Private Enforcement of Competition Law' *ZEW Discussion Paper* no.13-029 (April 2013) and Daniel A. Crane, Keith Klovers, and Adam Speegle, 'Private Antitrust Enforcement: Comparative and Policy Considerations' in John Duns, Arlen Duke, and Brendan Sweeney (eds), *Comparative Competition Law* (Edward Elgar 2015) 384-412.

[52] Even the delegation of authority sometimes has sunset clauses.

agenda-setting stage therefore is recurring. Stakeholders thus have an opportunity during every reauthorization and budget appropriation to affect the structure and substantive content of governance at a fundamental level through engagement with political principals (for example, members of legislatures/parliaments).[53]

This avenue for stakeholder participation is much less promising at the international level. While traditionally disregarded stakeholders certainly sometimes succeed with their agenda-setting efforts,[54] opportunities for agenda-setting through regular recontracting is much less likely for transnational or global bodies, once they have been established, due to the multiple-principals problem.[55] Stakeholder voice opportunities during the critical agenda-setting stage are therefore more limited.

Turning to empirics, the most comprehensive recent comparative analysis, Tallberg and colleagues' study of fifty international organizations and 289 sub-bodies from 1950 and 2010, finds considerable variation in opportunities for transnational actors' access and participation across the stages of the policy-making process—in addition to variation across organization type, time, and issue area.[56] Specifically, consistent with our theoretical expectations about the more limited voice opportunities during the agenda-setting stage, they find that stakeholder access to global governance bodies is less common during the 'policy formulation' (that is, agenda-setting) stage than during monitoring and enforcement.[57] They also find that stakeholder participation

[53] Among the thirty-four OECD countries and the European Commission, 94% have requirements to engage stakeholders in the development of at least some primary laws compared to 97% with requirements to engage stakeholders in the development of at least some subordinate regulations (OECD, *Regulatory Policy Outlook 2018* (n 39)).

[54] See e.g. Jutta Joachim, 'Framing Issues and Seizing Opportunities: The UN, NGOs, and Women's Rights' 47(2) *International Studies Quarterly* (2003) 247-274; R Charli Carpenter, 'Setting the Advocacy Agenda: Theorizing Issue Emergence and Nonemergence in Transnational Advocacy Networks' 51(1) *International Studies Quarterly* (2007) 99-120; Wendy H. Wong, *Internal Affairs: How the Structure of NGOs Transforms Human Rights* (Cornell University Press 2012); and Helen Margetts, Peter John, Scott Hale, and Taha Yasseri, *Political Turbulence: How Social Media Shape Collective Action* (Princeton University Press 2016).

[55] Tim Büthe, *The Dynamics of Principals and Agents: Institutional Persistence and Change in U.S. Financial Regulation, 1934-2003.* (Manuscript, Duke University 2005) online at https://ssrn.com/abstract=1796542, last accessed 11/11/2019; Mattli and Büthe, 'Global Private Governance' (n 17); Daniel L Nielson, Michael J Tierney and Catherine E Weaver, 'Bridging the Rationalist-Constructivist Divide: Re-Engineering the Culture of the World Bank' 9(2) *Journal of International Relations and Development* (2006) 107-139; Leslie Johns, 'A Servant of Two Masters: Communication and the Selection of International Bureaucrats' 61(2) *International Organization* (2007) 245-275.

[56] Tallberg *et al.*, *Opening Up* (n 20), esp. 75–82. Note that prior studies find that finance (along with national security) is one of the two policy issue areas where stakeholder participation is least prevalent (Layna Mosley, 'Private Governance for the Public Good? Exploring Private Sector Participation in Global Financial Regulation' in Helen V Milner and Andrew Moravcsik (eds), *Power, Interdependence, and Non-State Actors in World Politics* (Princeton University Press 2009) 126-146; Christer Jönsson and Jonas Tallberg (eds), *Transnational Actors in Global Governance* (Palgrave Macmillan, 2010)). For an even greater historical sweep, Steve Charnovitz's essay 'Two Centuries of Participation: NGOs and International Governance' 18(2) *Michigan Journal of International Law* (1997) 183-286) remains insightful.

[57] This finding from their large-N comparative analysis confirms the emphasis put on stakeholder contributions to monitoring in a wealth of previous single-issue studies. See e.g. Chi Carmody, 'Beyond the Proposals: Public Participation in International Economic Law' 15 *American University International Law Review* (2000) 1321–1346); Ann Marie Clark, *Diplomacy of Conscience: Amnesty International and Changing Human Rights Norms* (Princeton University Press 2001); Xinyuan Dai, 'Information Systems in Treaty Regimes' 54(4) *World Politics* (2002) 405-436; Tim Bartley, 'Certifying Forests and Factories' 31(3) *Politics & Society* (2003) 433-464; Benjamin Cashore, Graeme Auld and Deanna Newsom, 'The United States' Race to Certify Sustainable Forestry: Non-State Environmental Governance and the Competition

appears less common during the adoption–implementation–compliance stage and, surprisingly, least common during the 'decision-making' (that is, rule-making) stage.[58]

In what follows, we focus on the rule-making stage, notwithstanding the finding by Tallberg and colleagues that opportunities for participation are relatively rare at this stage. We do so for two reasons. First, given the constraints during the agenda-setting stage of global governance, the first direct interaction between rule-makers and stakeholders often occurs in the context of rule development, analysis, drafting, and promulgation. Second, recent studies suggest that opportunities for participation tend to be well institutionalized during the rule-making stage, whereas opportunities for participation during agenda-setting, implementation, and *ex post* evaluation are less systematic.[59]

2.2.3 The Exit Option

Another notable difference between domestic and global regulatory governance concerns the availability of the exit option: Firms generally have opportunities to 'exit' from any particular national-level jurisdiction's regulatory policy, though this option may be limited to re-locating to another jurisdiction, closing/selling the business, or—in federal systems, if they allow it—venue-shopping between different sub-national regulatory regimes.[60] Other stakeholders—citizens, consumers, civil society organizations—usually have no realistic exit option.

for Policy-Making Authority' 5(3) *Business and Politics* (2003) 219-259; Olga Avdeyeva, 'When Do States Comply with International Treaties? Policies on Violence against Women in Post-Communist Countries' 51(4) *International Studies Quarterly* (2007) 877-900; Luc W Fransen and Ans Kolk, 'Global Rule-Setting for Business: A Critical Analysis of Multi-Stakeholder Standards' 14(5) *Organization* (2007) 667-684, esp. 669f, 677f; Laurence R Helfer, 'Monitoring Compliance with Unratified Treaties: The ILO Experience' 71(1) *Law and Contemporary Problems* (2008) 193-217; Magnus Boström and Kristina Tamm Hallström, 'NGO Power in Global Social and Environmental Standard-Setting' 10(4) *Global Environmental Politics* (2010) 39-59; Devesh Kapur and Dennis Whittle, 'Can the Privatization of Foreign Aid Enhance Accountability?' 42(4) *NYU Journal of International Law and Politics* (2010) 1143-1180; Judith G Kelley, *Monitoring Democracy: When International Election Observations Works, and Why It Often Fails* (Princeton University Press 2012); Jessica F Green, *Rethinking Private Authority: Agents and Entrepreneurs in Global Environmental Governance* (Princeton University Press 2014); Timothy D Lytton, 'Competitive Third Party Regulation: How Private Certification Can Overcome Constraints that Frustrate Government Regulation' 15(2) *Theoretical Inquiries in Law* (2014) 539-571; Tim Bartley, *Rules Without Rights: Land, Labor, and Private Authority in the Global Economy* (Oxford University Press 2018).

[58] Other studies also find variation across policy areas and thus implicitly across the stages of the policy process, given the often issue area-specific different foci of the bodies. Steffek *et al.* (eds), *Civil Society Participation* (n 46), for instance, find variation in participation opportunities by policy area in a study of thirty-two cases of civil society participation (access, transparency, responsiveness, and inclusion). Similarly, a recent OECD survey of fifty international organizations that are engaged in regulatory governance suggests that the mode of participation varies by the type of international organization activity (e.g. production of technical standards vs. pure exchange of information); see OECD, *Regulatory Co-Operation* (n 38).

[59] OECD, *Regulatory Policy Outlook 2015* (n 42) and *Regulatory Policy Outlook 2018* (n 39).

[60] Federal or quasi-federal systems might even intentionally offer (some) choice between different policymaking regimes to encourage experimentation, as the EU has done in allowing corporations above a certain size threshold to choose between national and European supranational models of incorporation (Orfeo Fioretos, 'The European Company Statute and the Governance Dilemma' in Sophie Meunier and

In global governance, the 'exit' option can be more or less easily available than in national-level governance, depending on the comprehensiveness and effectiveness of efforts to build truly global governance institutions. Where the institutional structure at the global level is 'unitary', resulting in a single, globally encompassing (and effective) set of rules, the 'exit' option is less available than in national-level governance. By contrast, where the institutional structure is 'plural', that is, when two or more international bodies compete to establish the rules in a given issue area without clear pre-eminence or hierarchy or an agreed division of labour among them,[61] states and at least some non-state actors may decide to 'exit' from a particular set of rules and the global governance body underpinning it. Specifically, they may disengage (or not make any use of voice opportunities offered to them) *and address the issue in an alternative international forum.*[62] Such an option rarely exists in domestic regulatory regimes, except for federal systems, whereas it is quite common at the international level—though highly unevenly.[63]

In light of such variation, we follow Hirschman in treating the availability of exit as a variable, which enters into the overarching conceptual model through its inverse proportional relationship with the importance of the global governance body for the stakeholder—as discussed in Section 2.5.1.

2.3 Towards a Theory of Stakeholder Participation in Global Rule- and Decision-Making

We are now ready to address the central analytical questions this book seeks to answer. To begin, why would a global governance body expand voice opportunities for previously disregarded stakeholders? Under what conditions should we expect such stakeholders to make use of the new opportunities and actually engage in the process?

Kathleen McNamara (eds), *Making History* (Oxford University Press 2007) 157-173 and 'The Regulation of International Corporate Identity' 42(9) *Comparative Political Studies* (2009) 1167-1192).

[61] Tim Büthe and Walter Mattli, *The New Global Rulers: The Privatization of Regulation in the World Economy* (Princeton University Press 2011), esp. 23–29, 33.

[62] Laurence R Helfer, 'Regime Shifting: The TRIPS Agreement and New Dynamics of International Intellectual Property Lawmaking' 29(1) *Yale Journal of International Law* (2004) 26-45; Josh Lerner and Jean Tirole, 'A Model of Forum Shopping' 96(4) *American Economic Review* (2006) 1091-1113; Marc L Busch, 'Overlapping Institutions, Forum Shopping, and Dispute Settlement in International Trade' 61(4) *International Organization* (2007) 735–761; Karen J Alter and Sophie Meunier, 'Symposium: The Politics of International Regime Complexity' 7(1) *Perspectives on Politics* (2009) 13–70; Joseph Jupille, Walter Mattli, and Duncan Snidal, *Institutional Choice and Global Commerce* (Cambridge University Press 2013). Errol Meidinger points out that such a plural structure might make global governance more democratic in 'Competitive Supranational Regulation: How Could It Be Democratic?' 8(2) *Chicago Journal of International Law* (2008) 513-534, though we do not anticipate the conditions to be met in contemporary global health and global finance governance.

[63] Powerful states might even, by threatening to exit (and thus act as spoilers) force changes in existing global regulatory regimes, see Lipscy, *Renegotiating the World Order* (n 25); Joost Pauwelyn and Rebecca Hamilton, 'Exit from International Tribunals' 9(4) *Journal of International Dispute Settlement* (2018) 679-690; Sandra Lavenex, Omar Serrano, and Tim Büthe, 'Power Transitions and the Rise of the Regulatory State: Global Market Governance in Flux (Introduction to the Special Issue)' 15(3) *Regulation and Governance* (2021) 445–471.

And under what conditions would we expect the increased participation to result in an actual increase in the level of *influence* of these stakeholders in global governance?

Assuming instrumental and strategic behaviour, we might expect a global governance body to expand opportunities for participation for previously marginalized or excluded stakeholders if those stakeholders can help the global governance body become or remain 'influential'. But what makes inter- and transnational bodies influential? Scholarship on global governance appears not to have converged on a clear answer to this question yet. Knill and Bauer, for instance, suggest that a governance body's influence is largely a function of the 'governmental resources' it has at its disposal.[64] In other words, Hood's notion of governmental [power] resources—nodality, authority, treasure, and organization[65]—derived from the study of domestic public administrations[66] may be equally applicable to global governance bodies. Eckhard and Ege, by contrast, suggest that expertise, authority, and entrepreneurial leadership are the key drivers of an organization's influence.[67] Studies of the influence of global bodies in various particular issue areas suggest a multitude of additional factors. As Christensen and Yeslikagit summarize the current state of affairs: 'What determines [international administrative bodies'] influence is poorly understood and defined.'[68]

In light of this assessment, we develop in the next three sections three interlinked sequential models of participation in global governance, which are based on a more minimalist yet common set of positive political economy assumptions about global governance bodies and their stakeholders, building on both the global governance literature[69] and the literature on stakeholder participation in domestic regulatory rule- and decision-making.[70] The combination of those models allows us to develop one integrated analytical framework for the analysis of voice opportunities (Section 2.4) and stakeholder influence (Section 2.6)—with the stakeholder decision of whether to make use of the voice opportunities explicitly theorized as an intermediate step (Section 2.5). Moreover, we carefully spell out the causal processes and mechanisms for each step—and propose the notion of 'input ∩ throughput legitimacy', that is, the intersection of input and throughput legitimacy, as introduced more fully in Section 2.6.2.

[64] Knill and Bauer, 'International Public Administrations' (n 2), esp. 952–956.

[65] Nodality refers to an actor's centrality within its social network, conditional on the extent and density of that network; authority refers to the perceived legitimacy of the exercise of power; treasure here means literally the financial resources (not the bases of power in the broader Dahlian sense adopted later); and organization refers to the efficiency and effectiveness of the governance body's administrative routines and standard operating procedures.

[66] See Christopher C Hood, *The Tools of Government: Public Policy and Politics* (Palgrave Macmillan Publishers Ltd 1986); Christopher C Hood and Helen Z Margetts, *The Tools of Government in the Digital Age* (Palgrave Macmillan 2007).

[67] Stefan Eckhard and Jörn Ege, 'International Bureaucracies and Their Influence on Policy-Making: A Review of the Empirical Evidence' 23(7) *Journal of European Public Policy* (2016) 960-978.

[68] Christensen and Yeslikagit, 'International Public Administration' (n 2), esp. 6.

[69] We note, in particular, that we agree with Tallberg and colleagues and their emphasis on governance bodies' 'functional demand' for external resources to solve governance problems and 'strategic legitimation' to mitigate opposition and legitimacy challenges.

[70] In particular, our argument builds (in Sections 2.4 and 2.6) on DeMenno, 'Rethinking Stakeholder Participation' (n 35).

2.4 Opportunities for Stakeholder Voice

Rule- and decision-making processes are often black-boxed or, even when transparent, allow only very limited input from stakeholders who do not already have an assigned role in the rule- and decision-making process. The analyses in this book focus on global governance bodies that have undertaken reforms with the declared purpose of boosting the participation of stakeholders who have traditionally been marginalized or excluded. While we are primarily interested in the consequences of these reforms, we also investigate the global bodies' reasons for undertaking the reforms, on the assumption that understanding the drivers of the expanded opportunities for stakeholder participation is necessary for understanding the likelihood of actual engagement and influence in the aftermath of these reforms.

So why would inter- or transnational bodies undertake reforms that increase opportunities for participation by previously disregarded stakeholders? We start from the assumption that global governance bodies, as socio-political actors with agency, aim to be effective.[71] We stipulate that being effective requires, first, to develop or choose policies that are well suited to address the issues at hand, which in turn requires substantial 'expertise' (as discussed in greater detail in Section 2.4.1). Global governance bodies might have all the requisite expertise; if they do not, they might strategically create or expand stakeholder voice opportunities in the hopes of gaining access to the expertise they do not have. Regardless of whether a global governance body has all the requisite expertise 'in house' or not, being effective also requires implementation (and acceptance) of those policies by stakeholders, which in turn requires policy-making processes that are perceived as 'democratically legitimate'.[72] In domestic contexts, administrative law seeks to ensure democratic accountability and legitimacy.[73] In recent years, elements of administrative law have become increasingly common in the design of global governance institutions, often creating new opportunities for stakeholder

[71] This assumption is compatible both with Haas's notion of 'international organizations as problem solvers' (Ernst B Haas, *When Knowledge is Power: Three Models of Change in International Organizations* (University of California Press 1990), esp. 18ff) and with the notion that they seek to be influential as policy-makers (see Tallberg *et al.*, *Opening Up* (n 20). Of course, the goal of a given global governance body might in a particular instance be to achieve nothing more than declamatory politics; we suggest that giving the appearance of addressing a policy problem without actually changing anything is merely a (cynical) special case of 'effectiveness'.

[72] On the importance of expertise for the authority of 'global governors', see Avant, Finnemore and Sell, 'Who Governs the Globe?' in Avant *et al.* (n 2), 1–31, esp.12f; Sigrid Quack, 'Law, Expertise and Legitimacy in Transnational Economic Governance' 8(1) *Socio-Economic Review* (2010) 3-16; and Annabelle Littoz-Monnet (ed), *The Politics of Expertise in International Organizations: How International Bureaucracies Use and Produce Knowledge* (Routledge 2017). If there is a direct trade-off between expertise and democracy, rule-makers need to balance the two, both at the domestic level; see DeMenno, 'Rethinking Stakeholder Participation' (n 35) and internationally; see Joost Pauwelyn, Ramses Wessel and Jan Wouters, 'Informal International Lawmaking: An Assessment and Template to Keep It Both Effective and Accountable' in Pauwelyn *et al.* (eds), *Informal International Lawmaking* (n 1) 500-537, esp. 517f). On the complex relationship between expertise and democracy, see esp. Frank Fischer, *Democracy and Expertise: Reorienting Policy Inquiry* (Oxford University Press 2009).

[73] Richard B Stewart, 'The Reformation of American Administrative Law' 88(8) *Harvard Law Review* (1975) 1667-1813.

participation in unelected global bodies akin to domestic regulatory agencies.[74] More generally, then, the need for greater legitimacy to mitigate implementation challenges is a second reason why global governance bodies in pursuit of effectiveness might strategically create or extend stakeholder voice opportunities (as discussed in greater detail in Section 2.4.2).

The concern with democratic legitimacy warrants a brief discussion of the debate over whether (and which) models of domestic democracy (for example, deliberative, participatory, or direct) can be meaningfully extrapolated to the global level. A key challenge for this debate is to define the 'demos' for global governance. For domestic governance, this question can arguably be treated as answered (however imperfectly) by the established national-level political institutions under which domestic governance takes place. For some democratic theorists, this implies that transnational democracy is impossible because there is no comparable transnational 'demos'; for others, it implies that the conscious formation or construction of a transnational demos must precede any attempt to establish transnational democracy.[75] Yet others either argue that something like a transnational demos already sufficiently exists or suggest that deepening democracy at the transnational level is meaningfully possible without it.[76] Still others contest the premise upon which seeking further democratization of international institutions is based—namely, that there is a 'democracy deficit'[77]—while some argue that democracy should not be presupposed as the basis for assessing legitimacy in global governance but rather the basis should be constructed by those affected by the policies of a given global governance body.[78]

To cut through this Gordian knot, Bexell, Tallberg, and Uhlin suggest that we instead consider how key principles of democracy, which are shared across the various models of democracy, might be applicable globally.[79] In particular, they identify participation as a means to increase external accountability and hence democratic legitimacy. Furthermore, as Grant and Keohane note, the legitimacy of international organizations is evaluated based upon 'some combination of conformity to shared norms and to established law', and there is 'increased agreement that many normative

[74] Kingsbury, Krisch and Stewart, 'The Emergence' (n 35); Richard B Stewart, 'U.S. Administrative Law: A Model for Global Administrative Law?' 68(3) *Law and Contemporary Problems* (2005) 63-108; Barr and Miller, 'Global Administrative Law' (n 35); and Laurence Boisson de Chazournes, Lorenzo Cassidi, and Benedikt Kingsbury (eds), Symposium on 'Global Administrative Law in the Operations of International Organizations' 6(2) *International Organizations Law Review* (2009) 319-666.

[75] Dahl, 'Can International Organizations Be Democratic?' (n 19); Fritz W Scharpf, *Governing in Europe: Effective and Democratic?* (Oxford University Press 1999).

[76] David Held, 'The Transformation of Political Community: Rethinking Democracy in the Context of Globalization' in Ian Shapiro and Casiano Hacker-Cordón (eds), *Democracy's Edges* (Cambridge University Press 1999) 64-84; Jan Aart Scholte, 'Civil Society and Democracy in Global Governance' 8 *Global Governance* (2002) 281-304; Patrizia Nanz and Jens Steffek, 'Global Governance, Participation and the Public Sphere' 39(2) *Government and Opposition* (2004) 314-335.

[77] Andrew Moravcsik, 'Is There a 'Democratic Deficit' in World Politics? A Framework for Analysis' 39(2) *Government and Opposition* (2004) 336-363; Slaughter, *New World Order* (n 35).

[78] Steven Bernstein, 'Legitimacy in Intergovernmental and Non-State Global Governance' 18(1) *Review of International Political Economy* (2011) 17-51.

[79] Magdalena Bexell, Jonas Tallberg and Anders Uhlin, 'Democracy in Global Governance' 16(1) *Global Governance* (2010) 81-101.

principles inherent in democracy are applicable at the global level'.[80] Indeed, Grant and Keohane identify the 'right to exercise voice' as one of those 'normative principles inherent in democracy' applicable at the global level.[81]

Figure 2.2 shows our causal process model of the creation of opportunities for voice in global rule- and decision-making, which takes into account the dual need for technocratic expertise *and* democratic legitimacy. We hypothesize that a global governance body's goal of policy effectiveness (X) leads to the creation of opportunities for stakeholder voice (Y) through either or both of two causal mechanisms: choosing/designing better policies (A) and mitigating implementation challenges (B).

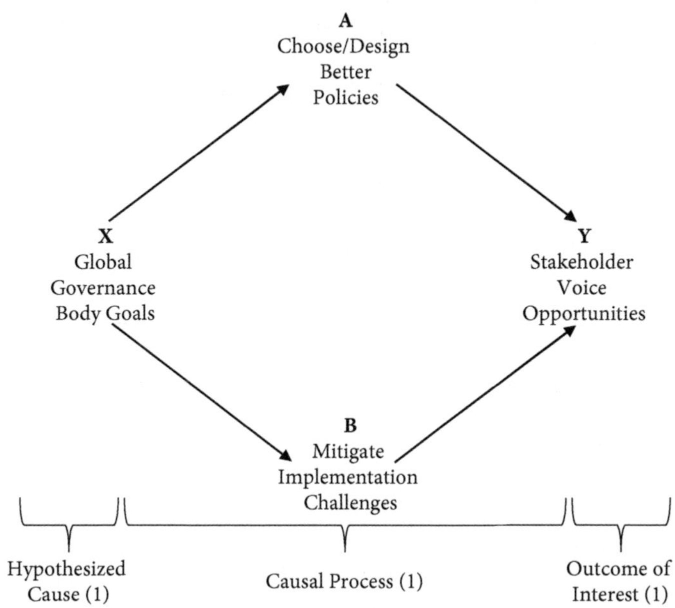

Figure 2.2 Why Global Governance Bodies Create Stakeholder Voice Opportunities

2.4.1 Choose/Design Better Policies

A governance body's ability to choose or design effective policies is a function of its expertise, including the quality or quantity of the underlying information. While the nature of the expertise needed for effective policy-making is highly context-dependent, we generally expect global governance bodies to possess a high degree of 'technocratic', analytical expertise by design. At the same time, stakeholders often are best positioned to provide

[80] Grant and Keohane, 'Accountability' (n 35), 34f. The authors refer specifically to international organizations empowered through delegation, but the same criteria should in principle also be applicable when the global governance body's role is not due to a formal act of delegation.

[81] Grant and Keohane, 'Accountability' (n 35), 35.

key evidence required to put the technocratic expertise to good use. For example, specific information about stakeholder needs and what is working (or not) is a critical input for choosing better, more effective policies. Indeed, some global governance bodies claim to have adopted mechanisms for greater participation, especially participation by previously marginalized civil society stakeholders, precisely for this reason.[82]

We therefore expect global governance bodies, when faced with a possible information deficit, to create opportunities for voice, hoping that engagement with previously disregarded stakeholders will allow them to bolster their internal technocratic expertise and thus choose/design better policies. In keeping with the bureaucracy literature, we refer to the needed expertise as 'technocratic', but acknowledge that such expertise need not be 'technical' in nature and might encompass a range of political, economic, or social considerations.[83] Therefore, choosing/designing better policies (A) is one mechanism through which the global governance body's goal of policy effectiveness (X) might lead to the creation of stakeholder voice opportunities (Y).

2.4.2 Mitigate Implementation Challenges

Policy effectiveness is not just a function of selecting and designing theoretically optimal policies; it also is a function of the willingness of the governed to actually implement those rules and policies.[84] As Pauwelyn and colleagues note, deficits in accountability and legitimacy of global governance organizations 'not only raise important normative questions but also threaten to undermine the[ir] regulatory effectiveness'.[85] Legitimacy (as we discuss in greater detail in Section 2.6) matters for effectiveness because, as Max Weber taught us, when decision are accepted as authoritative and the authority that is exercised in making the decision is recognized as appropriate and justified, the 'targets' of the rule- and decision-making[86] implement and comply voluntarily.[87] Strikingly, this suggests that fostering stakeholder voice to increase legitimacy might have elements of both the 'logic of consequences' and the 'logic of appropriateness',[88] because it is simultaneously normatively appealing and has instrumental value to global governance bodies.

[82] Dingwerth and Nanz, 'Participation' (n 20), 1128; Berman, 'Accordion Governance' (n 2).

[83] In fact, Neshkova finds in an analysis of EU regulatory policymaking, that the more important strictly technical knowledge is, the less responsive is the EU to stakeholder input: Milena I Neshkova, 'Salience and Complexity in Supranational Policymaking: The Case of Subnational Interests' 27(1) *Governance* (2014) 9-36.

[84] There may be an interaction here with policy design in that the best policy is ultimately the one that performs well in actual implementation rather than only in theory or in the 'laboratory', but we do not attempt to model this interaction for the sake of parsimony.

[85] Joost Pauwelyn, Tim Büthe, Martino Maggetti and Ayelet Berman, 'Rethinking Stakeholder Participation in Global Governance' (Framing Paper for the Launch Workshop for the SNIS Project on Rethinking Stakeholder Participation in Global Governance: What are the Issues? What Works?' Graduate Institute, Geneva, 26–27 February 2015) 5.

[86] Tim Büthe, 'Beyond Supply and Demand: A Political-Economic Conceptual Model' in Kevin Davis, Angelina Fischer, Benedikt Kingsbury and Sally Engle Merry (eds), *Governance by Indicators: Global Power through Quantification and Rankings* (Oxford University Press 2012) 29-51, esp. 43–45.

[87] Max Weber, Wirtschaft und Gesellschaft: Grundriß der verstehenden Soziologie, 5th rev and extended edn, edited by Johannes Winckelmann (J.C.B. Mohr 1972, first published 1921/1922), esp. 122-124.

[88] March and Olsen, 'The New Institutionalism' (n 21) and 'Institutional Dynamics' (n 21).

Focusing on the instrumental aspect here, we posit that a global governance body's perceived legitimacy impacts policy effectiveness by affecting the likelihood and quality of rule adoption or compliance expected at the implementation stage.[89] Stakeholder participation as the 'pragmatic and normative' basis of organizational legitimacy[90] may thus help with policy effectiveness. Therefore, mitigating implementation challenges (B) is the other mechanism through which a global governance body's goal of policy effectiveness (X) might lead to the creation of stakeholder voice opportunities (Y).

2.4.3 Operationalizing the Argument: Two Hypotheses about Stakeholder Voice Opportunities

Figure 2.2 summarizes the argument thus far. Note that, in this model, A or B is individually sufficient to lead to Y.[91] From this causal process model, we derive two operationalized hypotheses related to the incentives of global finance/health governance bodies to create opportunities for voice (which we further build upon in Section 2.6):

> H_{1A}: *A given global governance body will create or expand stakeholder voice opportunities if it needs stakeholder input to choose/design better policies.*

For H_{1A}, we assume that uncertainty about the effects of a given policy may lead to the creation of opportunities for voice as a means to choose/design better policies. As a consequence, a more complex policy issue might result in a greater concern about policy choice/design than a relatively simple policy issue, for which the impact can be more easily forecast. In contrast, it may also be the nature of the global finance/health governance body, rather than a policy issue, that gives rise to concerns about policy choice or design. For example, a global governance body facing resource constraints, such as limited internal data gathering or analysis capabilities, might be more likely to seek external input to address deficits in its internal information gathering and analysis resources.

> H_{1B}: *A given global governance body will create or expand stakeholder voice opportunities if it needs stakeholder input to mitigate implementation challenges.*

For H_{1B}, we assume that potential challenges in implementing a given policy—which, no matter how efficacious, cannot be effective unless implemented—may lead to the creation of opportunities for voice. A high degree of uncertainty about the processes of implementation or high implementer discretion might lead global finance/health

[89] E.g. Virginia Haufler, *The Public Role of the Private Sector: Industry Self-Regulation in a Global Economy* (Carnegie Endowment for International Peace 2001); Bernstein and Cashore, 'Can Non-State Global Governance Be Legitimate?' (n 21); Tim Büthe, 'Private Regulation in the Global Economy: A (P)Review' 12(3) *Business and Politics* (October 2010) 19f. But compare with David Vogel, 'Private Global Business Regulation' 11 *Annual Review of Political Science* (2008): 261-282, esp. 268f.

[90] Julia Black, 'Constructing and Contesting Legitimacy and Accountability in Polycentric Regulatory Regimes' 2(1) *Regulation & Governance* (2008) 137-164, 147.

[91] For a fuller discussion of such alternative causal pathways and their importance for policy analysis, see Tim Büthe, 'Causal Process Tracing in Multi-Methods Research: Three Provocations' (Unpublished manuscript, Duke University, 2014).

governance bodies to create opportunities for voice to build consensus and enhance democratic legitimacy, in the expectation that it will increase support for implementation prospectively.[92]

2.4.4 From Voice Opportunities to the Exercise of Voice

Stakeholder participation may be constrained not just by a lack of voice opportunities provided by the global governance body but also by the stakeholder's own limitations. Some traditionally disregarded stakeholders surely face few resource and capacity constraints. And some institutional reforms to boost participation might also boost stakeholders' incentives or lower their resource constraints at the same time as they introduce new voice opportunities. Under those conditions, creating, for instance, new modes of participation, may be fully sufficient for a marked increase in actual stakeholder engagement in global governance. Under more common conditions, however, explaining why some reforms lead to an increase in actual engagement—while others do not—requires asking whether the new voice opportunities sufficiently help overcome the obstacles and constraints faced by the stakeholders whose voice the 'global governors'[93] now supposedly want to hear. Therefore, in Section 2.5 we first examine stakeholders' desire and ability to make use of the new opportunities, before turning to the issue of stakeholder influence in Section 2.6.

2.5 Stakeholder Incentives to Participate

Consistent with the positive political economy approach that we have adopted, we assume that political-economic actors want to participate in rule- or decision-making processes that affect them, provided that the expected benefits exceed the costs of doing so. The fruitfulness of this assumption has been shown, for instance, in the literature on the governance of finance, by analyses of why firms lobby financial reporting standard-setters.[94] It begs the question, however, what explains the differences in perceived/expected costs and benefits. In Section 2.4, we discussed one source of costs: limited

[92] Note that it is also possible that the creation of voice opportunities occurs as a retrospective response to existing legitimacy challenges, i.e. such opportunities might get disproportionately created where legitimacy is low.

[93] Avant, Finnemore and Sell, *Who Governs?* (n 2).

[94] See Sutton's early study of lobbying vis-à-vis financial reporting standard-setting bodies by firms that are required to implement the standards (Timothy G Sutton, 'Lobbying of Accounting Standard-Setting Bodies in the U.K. and the U.S.A.: A Downsian Analysis' 9(1) *Accounting, Organizations and Society* (1984) 81-95), but also numerous later studies: Robert J Walker and Peter Robinson, 'A Critical Assessment of the Literature on Political Activity and Accounting Regulation' 7(1) *Research in Accounting Regulation* (1993) 3-40; Stephen A Zeff, 'Political Lobbying on Proposed Standards' 16(1) *Accounting Horizons* (2002) 43-54; Roland Königsgruber, 'Lobbying bei der Rechnungslegungsstandardsetzung: Ein Literaturüberblick' 79(11) *Zeitschrift für Betriebswirtschaft* (2009) 1309-1329; George Georgiou, 'The IASB Standard-Setting Process: Participation and Perception of Financial Statement Users' 42(2) *British Accounting Review* (2010) 103-118; and Wei Chern Koh, 'What Drives Firms' Decision to Lobby and Determinants of their Lobbying Positions: Evidence from Firms' Comment Letter Submissions during FASB's Stock Option Expensing Proposal in 2004' 46(1) *International Journal of Accounting* (2011) 1-24.

or foreclosed *opportunities for voice*, which arise from the institutional structure and procedures of the global governance body (such as membership requirements, non-transparent processes, and decision-making procedures that do not allow for input from external stakeholders). To understand why stakeholder voice in global governance might vary *even when global governance bodies and processes provide opportunities for it*, we focus on a stakeholder's incentives to make use of voice opportunities—and specifically the importance of the global governance body for the stakeholder and the stakeholder's capabilities (or lack of capabilities, which may act as constraints).[95] We discuss these two determinants of stakeholder *incentives to participate* in turn.

2.5.1 Importance of the Global Governance Body

A major determinant of a stakeholder's incentives to engage in any particular global governance body's governance process is necessarily the salience of the issue(s) governed by this body, which may vary even among those who see themselves as stakeholders. Private sector firms, business associations, and civil society groups tend to have more limited, issue-specific concerns than governments that are supposed to concern themselves with the interests of everyone in their respective countries.[96] At the same time, on any particular issue, the stakes might be greater for more narrowly defined stakeholder groups. Confirming our straightforward intuition about this motivation for exercising voice, existing research on non-participating as well as participating stakeholders in various governance processes shows that a stakeholder's expectation that a particular decision will have few or small effects for the stakeholder is the strongest determinant of non-participation, whereas expecting dearly held interests to be affected is an effective predictor of participation.[97] But even large developing countries, most of which until recently were among the excluded or marginalized stakeholders in most global governance bodies, tend to prioritize some issues over others. In the main international technical standard-setting bodies, the International Organization for Standardization (ISO) and International Electrotechnical Commission (IEC), for instance, many developing countries choose a lower-cost membership category that gives them voting membership in only a handful of the hundreds of issue-area-specific technical committees where most technical rule-making takes place, rather than full membership that would give them voting membership in all technical committees.[98] And the stakeholder representatives from countries whose membership

[95] The rather intuitive assumption that participation is, at least in substantial part, a function of these factors is supported by previous research, such as Klaus Dingwerth, *The New Transnationalism: Transnational Governance and Democratic Legitimacy* (Palgrave Macmillan 2007); Tallberg *et al.*, *Opening Up* (n 20); Tim Büthe, 'Distributional Consequences of Transnational Private Regulation' Duke University Rethinking Regulation Working Paper no. 6 (2013) <http://dx.doi.org/10.2139/ssrn.2238100>, last accessed 6/30/2020.

[96] Accordingly, the proper names of the non-governmental stakeholders tend to differ from one specific issue to the next.

[97] See e.g. Christine M Schalow, 'Participation Choice: The Exposure Draft for Postretirement Benefits Other than Pensions' 9(1) *Accounting Horizons* (1995) 27-41; Walter Mattli and Tim Büthe, 'Setting International Standards: Technological Rationality or Primacy of Power?' 56(1) *World Politics* (2003) 1-42.

[98] Tim Büthe, 'Engineering Uncontestedness? The Origins and Institutional Development of the International Electrotechnical Commission (IEC)' 12(3) *Business and Politics* (2010) 1–62.

category would allow them to exercise the voice option in all committees tend to be regular participants only in a subset thereof, though in the fora they prioritize even medium-sized developing countries' representatives can become important contributors to the rule-making process.[99]

The importance of a given global governance body for any particular stakeholder, however, is not just a function of the salience of the issue(s) governed by that body but also should be a function of the structure of global governance for that issue. Particularly important in this regard should be the availability of alternative ways of influencing the pertinent global rules, norms, and practices in a given issue area.[100] When alternatives are available, stakeholders might be able to engage in regulatory (or more generally governance) 'forum-' or 'venue-shopping' where stakeholders exit from one governance body to address the issue in another—the focus of an entire literature in recent years.[101] In the context of achieving a theoretical understanding of a stakeholder's incentives with respect to any one particular global governance body, however, this might be better understood as opportunities for 'exit' in Hirschman's sense.[102] We therefore elaborate here on the earlier brief discussion of exit.

Büthe and Mattli's distinction between a 'unitary' and a 'plural' institutional structure of rule- and decision-making at the international level is key for understanding the role of exit (options) in this context.[103] When the institutional structure at the global level is unitary, that is, when there is a single, globally encompassing (and effective) set of rules or a clear institutional focal point for adopting or changing the rules, where alternative fora are clearly secondary or subordinated to it, 'exit' does not entail an option to switch to an alternative global governance body since such alternatives are by definition not available. For most stakeholders, this effectively takes the exit option off the table. Only powerful stakeholders can (credibly) threaten exit and thus try to force changes in existing global bodies if their non-participation has the kind of negative externalities for global governance of the issue that their exit would effectively make them spoilers.[104] For all others, the more the institutional structure of

[99] See Büthe, 'Distributional Consequences' (n 95).

[100] Lipscy, *Renegotiating the World Order* (n 25) puts this characteristic of global governance—the extent to which there is, for the governance of a given issue, competition among international organization—at the core of his account of why some IOs adapt rapidly to shifts in the global distribution of power while others IOs change very little.

[101] See Helfer, 'Regime Shifting' (n 62); Lerner and Tirole, 'Forum Shopping' (n 62); Alter and Meunier, Symposium' (n 62); Busch, 'Overlapping Institutions' (n 62); Jupille *et al.*, *Institutional Choice* (n 62).

[102] See Hirschman, *Exit, Voice, and Loyalty* (n 31), esp. 21–29.

[103] Büthe and Mattli, *New Global Rulers* (n 61), esp. 23–29, 33; Tim Büthe, 'A Typology of Global Rule-Making' (Manuscript, Duke Law School, October 2011); Büthe, 'Distributional Consequences' (n 95).

[104] Beth A Simmons, 'The International Politics of Harmonization: The Case of Capital Market Regulation' 55(3) *International Organization* (2001) 589-620; David A Singer, *Regulating Capital: Setting Standards for the International Financial System* (Cornell University Press 2007); Lipscy, *Renegotiating the World Order* (n 25); Pauwelyn and Hamilton, 'Exit' (n 63); Lavenex *et al.*, 'Power Transitions' (n 63). Entrepreneurial stakeholders might even set up alternative governance arrangements, as regional powers have at times attempted; see e.g. Ruth Ben-Artzi, *Regional Development Banks in Comparison: Banking Strategies versus Development Goals* (Cambridge University Press 2016)) and transnational civil society and business actors have demonstrated for issues ranging from sustainable forestry to corporate social responsibility (CSR); see Green, *Private Authority* (n 57). If successful, such new bodies might ultimately become competitors to the primary body in an existing, unitary global order. Much of the concern about the 'rise of China' in global governance is precisely about such attempts to transform a unitary structure of global governance into a plural one (see e.g. David Shambaugh, *China Goes Global: The Partial*

global governance is unitary and thus devoid of alternative ways to influence an issue area—the more a particular body is the 'institutional focal point'[105] for global governance in the issue area—the more important should be this particular, focal global governance body, and the greater are the stakeholder's incentives to participate.

Conversely, the more the institutional structure is 'plural', that is, the more international bodies compete to establish the rules in a given issue area without clear preeminence of one or a hierarchy or an agreed division of labour among them, the more readily does it provide stakeholders with alternative ways of influencing the issue. And the greater the availability of alternative means of influencing the prevalent global norms and rules in a given issue area, the lower is the importance of any one particular global governance body in that issue area and the lesser are the stakeholder's incentives to participate in that particular body's rule-making process.

2.5.2 Stakeholders' (Cap)Ability to Participate

Wanting to participate may not suffice. Participation in global governance also requires material, analytical, and political resources.[106] In other words, the incentives to participate in a given global governance body should also be a function of the stakeholder's 'capabilities' in the sense of Nussbaum and Sen, that is, access to what stakeholders need to recognize, articulate, and pursue their own interests.[107] Constraints on a stakeholder's capabilities reduce its incentives to participate.

A wealth of existing research underscores the need for material resources to participate in inter- and transnational governance. While the government of a wealthy country can readily allocate material resources to ensure participation of national representatives in any forum it considers important to the national interest,[108] the lack of material

Power (Oxford University Press 2013); Michael Mastanduno, 'Order and Change in World Politics: The Financial Crisis and the Breakdown of the US-China Grand Bargain' in G John Ikenberry (ed), *Power, Order and Change in World Politics* (Cambridge University Press 2014) 162-191; Daniel C Lynch, *China's Futures: PRC Elites Debate Economics, Politics and Foreign Policy* (Stanford University Press 2015), esp. 155-198; Oliver Stuenkel, *The BRICS and the Future of Global Order* (Lexington Books 2015); Tomas Casas i Klett and Omar R Serrano Oswald, 'Free Trade Agreements as BRI's Stepping-Stone to Multilateralism: Is the Sino–Swiss FTA the Gold Standard?' in Wenxian Zhang, Ilan Alon, and Christoph Lattemann (eds), *China's Belt and Road Initiative: Changing the Rules of Globalization* (Palgrave Macmillan 2018) 75-93; Laura Mahrenbach, 'Conceptualizing Emerging Powers' in Timothy Shaw, Laura C Mahrenbach, Renu Modi, and Xu Yi-chong (eds), *The Palgrave Handbook of Contemporary International Political Economy* (Palgrave Macmillan 2019) 217-231; Omar R Serrano Oswald, 'The New Architects: Brazil, China, and Innovation in Multilateral Development Lending' 39(4–5) Public Administration and Development (2019) 203–214. This option to transform the structure of global governance, however, would seem to be open only to the most powerful states.

105 Büthe and Mattli, *New Global Rulers* (n 61).

106 Büthe and Mattli, *New Global Rulers* (n 61), esp. ch. 3.

107 See Amartya K Sen, *Commodities and Capabilities* (Elsevier Science Publishers 1985) and Development as Freedom (Knopf 1999); Martha Nussbaum, *Women and Human Development: The Capabilities Approach* (Cambridge University Press 2000) and *Creating Capabilities: The Human Development Approach* (Harvard-Belknap Press 2011); see also Fabrizio Cafaggi and Katharina Pistor, 'Regulatory Capabilities: A Normative Framework for Assessing the Distributional Effects of Regulation 9(2) *Regulation and Governance* (2015) 95–107.

108 Daniel W Drezner, *All Politics Is Global: Explaining International Regulatory Regimes* (Princeton University Press 2007). Indeed, a recent paper suggests that states and non-state actors who are

resources is a serious constraint for many stakeholders. For developing countries' governments, retaining the requisite expertise and sending multiple experts to participate in negotiations is sufficiently costly that participation in global governance requires prioritization and trade-offs.[109] For non-governmental stakeholders, the resource constraints might be prohibitive. Boström and Tamm Hallström, for instance, show financial resources to be an important determinant of NGO participation in the transnational governance of social and environmental issues.[110] Büthe and Mattli find firm size (a widely used proxy for available material resources) to be one of the most consistent predictors of company involvement in processes of setting standards for global product and financial markets.[111] Similar findings in other realms of non-state governance[112] contribute to Mayer and Gereffi's concerns about power inequities in global private politics.[113]

Resource constraints are not just a matter of a shortage of financial resources, though financial resources are arguably usable to acquire or otherwise compensate for a shortage of critical resources. Weetman and colleagues find lack of time to be an important reason for non-participation in financial reporting governance.[114] This resource constraint is also often mentioned in interviews and surveys by smaller organizations, including small and medium-sized firms that cannot afford (or for other reasons do not have) a designated standards manager, government relations officer, etc.[115]

Analytical resources likewise are key for participation in global governance.[116] As discussed by Cafaggi and Pistor,[117] having (or being able to gain) an expert understanding of the issue is often critical to the empowering *capabilities*—in the sense of Sen and Nussbaum. Those analytical resources allow stakeholders to recognize what's

willing to offer financial resources to global bodies may be able to gain substantial influence over their agenda and decisions: Cecilia Cannon and Thomas Biersteker, 'Losing Control of International Organizations: When Member States Refuse to Put Their Money Where Their Mouth Is' (Paper presented at ECPR, September 2019).

109 Büthe, 'Engineering Uncontestedness?' (n 98). Direct costs of participation are all the more constraining the more 'participation in negotiations' requires regular in-person attendance at a series of meetings, often held all over the globe over several years. Under those conditions, offering (for instance) a financially constrained stakeholder 'free' observer status for committee meetings may be good declamatory politics but bad for boosting actual participation; see Abdel Alshadafan, 'Energy Efficiency Standards: The Struggle for Legitimacy' 18(1) *International Journal of Standardization Research* (2020), 1–23. Some global governance bodies have attempted to address such constraints, for instance by introducing the option to hold virtual meetings of technical committees to reduce the travel expenses associated with participation, which lowers organizationally controlled barriers to participation and stakeholder resource constraints at the same time. Scheduling committee-level negotiations as extensions to major meetings already attended by many resource-constrained stakeholders is another option. But there appear to be limits to such 'technological' and logistic solutions, most of which are too recent to allow conclusive assessments.

110 Magnus Boström and Kristina Tamm Hallström, 'NGO Power in Global Social and Environmental Standard-Setting' (November 2010) 19(4) *Global Environmental Politics* 39-59.

111 Mattli and Büthe, 'Setting International Standards' (n 97); Büthe and Mattli, *New Global Rulers* (n 61).

112 See e.g. Robert K Larson, 'Corporate Lobbying of the International Accounting Standards Committee' 8(3) *Journal of International Financial Management and Accounting* (1997) 175-203.

113 Frederick W Mayer and Gary Gereffi, 'Regulation and Economic Globalization: Prospects and Limits of Private Governance' 12(3) *Business and Politics* (October 2010) 1–25.

114 Pauline Weetman, Elizabeth S Davie, and William Collins, 'Lobbying on Accounting Issues: Preparer/User Imbalance in the Case of the Operating and Financial Review' 9(1) *Accounting, Auditing & Accountability Journal* (1996) 59-76.

115 E.g. Büthe and Mattli, *New Global Rulers* (n 61).

116 Haas, *When Knowledge is Power* (n 71); A Claire Cutler, Virginia Haufler, and Tony Porter (eds), *Private Authority and International Affairs* (State University of New York Press 1999).

117 Cafaggi and Pistor, 'Regulatory Capabilities' (n 107).

at stake, articulate their self-interests in global governance, and devise a strategy to pursue those interests. Without such expertise-based capabilities, stakeholders are not really in a position to make use of voice opportunities—or engage in other forms of political behaviour.[118] In regulatory governance, moreover, expertise is not only an important source of authority, but also often literally required to have a voice in the process, because much of the discussion is conducted in very technical language, as shown in empirical analyses across numerous specific issue areas.[119]

Finally, there is the issue of political resources: Major states (and maybe a few very large multinational firms), which control a large share of the global market for a particular product or a large share of a particular type of activity, might be able to get others to pay attention to them merely because the risk that their unilateral norm-deviant behaviour would pose to global rules for the given issue area.[120] All others—that is, almost everyone, most of the time—need collective action capacity to be credible in the political sphere. The capacity to undertake collective action has of course been long known as an important enabler or constraint in domestic politics and domestic governance.[121] The ability to overcome collective action problems is likely to be even more important in global governance, where the number of individual stakeholders is often much larger, the value of being able to credibly speak for many is even greater, and the

[118] Here again, reforms *can* boost stakeholder's (cap)ability at the same time, for instance, by combining a rule-change that has the stated purpose of facilitating input from non-technical-expert stakeholders with the introduction of a technical assistance program for previously marginalized stakeholders. We would expect such a program to make a real difference (increasing actual stakeholder voice) if it helps the non-expert stakeholders more fully understand the structure and standard operating procedures of the organization or allows them to gain technical background information for the items on the agenda.

[119] Magnus Boström and Kristina Tamm Hallström, 'Organising the Process of Standardization' in Nils Brunsson (ed), *A World of Standards* (Oxford University Press 2000) 85-99; Leonardo Martinez-Diaz, *Private Expertise and Global Economic Governance: The Case of International Accounting Standards 1972-2001* (M.Phil. Thesis, Oxford University 2001); Mattli and Büthe, 'Setting International Standards' (n 97); Frédérique Déjean, Jean-Pascal Gond, and Bernhard Leca, 'Measuring the Unmeasured: An Institutional Entrepreneur Strategy in an Emerging Industry' 57(6) *Human Relations* (2004) 741-764; Sebastian Botzem and Sigrid Quack, 'Contested Rules and Shifting Boundaries: International Standard-Setting in Accounting' in Marie-Laure Djelic and Kerstin Sahlin-Andersson (eds), *Transnational Governance: Institutional Dynamics of Regulation* (Cambridge University Press 2006) 266-286; Ben Thirkell-White, 'Private Authority and Legitimacy in the International System' 20(3) *International Relations* (2006) 335-342; Pavel Castka and Michaela A Balzarowa, 'The Impact of ISO 9000 and ISO 14000 on Standardization of Social Responsibility: An Insider Perspective' 113(1) *International Journal of Production Economics* (2008) 74-87; Abbott and Snidal, 'Governance Triangle' (n 44); Büthe, 'Engineering Uncontestedness?' (n 98); Christopher Humphrey and Anne Loft, 'Moving Beyond Nuts and Bolts: The Complexities of Governing a Global Profession through International Standards' in Stefano Ponte, Peter Gibbon and Jakob Vestergaard (eds), *Governing Through Standards: Origins, Drivers and Limitations* (Palgrave Macmillan 2011) 102-129; Yates and Murphy, *Engineering Rules* (n 22). Note that expertise can also shield the regulator from being criticized for deviating from prescriptions of democratic governance for input and throughput legitimacy, which might be functionally useful but of course can also be problematic without strong mechanisms to hold the expert body accountable if it fails to achieve or maintain output legitimacy.

[120] David Vogel, *Trading Up: Consumer and Environmental Regulation in a Global Economy* (Harvard University Press 1995); Lloyd Gruber, *Ruling the World: Power Politics and the Rise of Supranational Institutions* (Princeton University Press 2000); Simmons, 'Politics of Harmonization' (n 104); Lavenex *et al.*, 'Power Transitions' (n 63).

[121] Mancur Olson, *The Logic of Collective Action*, 2nd ed. (Harvard University Press 1971); Tim Büthe, 'The State as Facilitator of Collective Action' (Unpublished manuscript, Columbia University, May 1998); Jay Tate, 'National Varieties of Standardization' in Peter A Hall and David Soskice (eds), *Varieties of Capitalism* (Oxford University Press 2001) 442-473; Abraham L Newman and David Bach, 'Self-Regulatory Trajectories in the Shadow of Public Power: Resolving Digital Dilemmas in Europe and the United States' 17(3) *Governance* (2004) 387-413.

expenses that may need to be shared are likely even higher (requiring collective action just to be politically sustainable).[122] At the same time, traditionally marginalized stakeholders likely face more severe collective action problems in global governance, although those problems can arguably be overcome with the help of suitable institutional arrangements.[123] In sum, we would expect the capacity to engage in collective action to be an important enabler of (and the absence of such capacity an important constraint on) participation in global governance.

2.5.3 Operationalizing the Argument: Five Hypotheses about Stakeholder Participation

We summarize the above discussion in Figure 2.3.

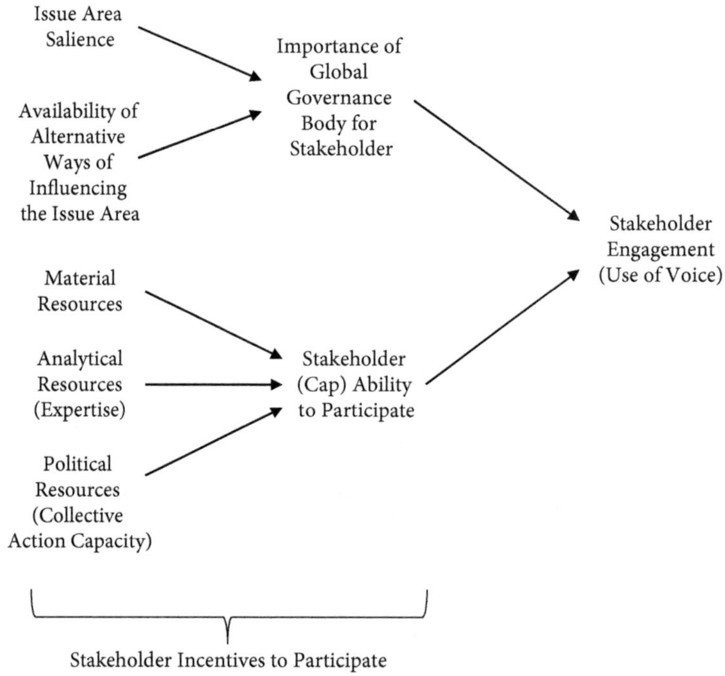

Figure 2.3 Stakeholder Incentives to Make Use of Voice Opportunities

[122] Adrienne Héritier and Sandra Eckert, 'Self-Regulation by Associations: Collective Action Problems in European Environmental Regulation' 11(1) *Business and Politics* (2009) 1–22; Pierre-Hugues Verdier, 'The Political Economy of International Financial Regulation' 88(4) *Indiana Law Journal* (2013) 1405-1474; Matthew D Stephen and Michal Parízek, 'New Powers and the Distribution of Preferences in Global Trade Governance: From Deadlock and Drift to Fragmentation' 24(6) *New Political Economy* (2019) 735-758.

[123] See e.g. Katharina Holzinger, 'Common Goods, Matrix Games and Institutional Response' 9(2) *European Journal of International Relations* (2003) 173-212; Burkard Eberlein and Abraham L Newman, 'Escaping the International Governance Dilemma? Incorporated Transgovernmental Networks in the European Union' 21(1) *Governance* (2008) 25-52; Matthew Potoski and Aseem Prakash (eds), *Voluntary Programs: A Club Theory Approach* (MIT Press 2009); Andrea Liese and Marianne Beisheim, 'Transnational Public-Private Partnerships

From the discussion, we can derive five operationalized hypotheses about the conditions under which we would expect a stakeholder to want to make use of the voice opportunities provided by a given global governance body:

H_{2i}: *The greater the salience of the issue area for a stakeholder, the more likely is the stakeholder's actual engagement.*

H_{2ii}: *The greater a stakeholder's access to alternative ways of influencing the issue area, the less likely is the stakeholder's actual engagement.*

H_{2iii}: *The scarcer the stakeholder's material resource (especially financial resources and time), the less likely is the stakeholder's actual engagement.*

H_{2iv}: *The scarcer the stakeholder's analytical resources (especially pertinent expertise), the less likely is the stakeholder's actual engagement.*

H_{2v}: *The scarcer the stakeholder's political resources (especially collective action capacity), the less likely is the stakeholder's actual engagement.*

2.6 Stakeholder Influence

Having established the conditions under which global governance bodies might expand voice opportunities—and the conditions under which we would expect traditionally disregarded stakeholders to make use of those voice opportunities, resulting in an actual increase in stakeholder participation—we can now consider the conditions under which stakeholders might not just exercise voice but also influence in global governance.[124]

It is by no means a given that stakeholders, especially long excluded or marginalized stakeholders, can leverage having gained a 'voice' or a 'seat at the table' into influence. Theoretically, we would expect entrenched interests to resist changes that diminish their privileged position—in global governance,[125] just as in other spheres of world politics.[126] Empirically, representatives of developing countries in various global governance bodies have reported finding it difficult to gain traction, even after they start to participate regularly.[127] And Kwok and Sharp's study of rule-making in the International Accounting Standards Committee/Board suggests that among private interests, too, gaining recognition as a stakeholder and even regularly

and the Provision of Collective Goods in Developing Countries' in Thomas Risse (ed), *Governance Without a State? Policies and Politics in Areas of Limited Statehood* (Columbia University Press 2011) 115-143.

[124] We use influence here in the broad sense of affecting the outcome, not necessarily achieving an outcome that fully satisfies a stakeholder, given its preferences.

[125] E.g. Grigorescu, *Normative Pressures* (n 20); Lipscy, *Renegotiating the World Order* (n 25).

[126] The classic study here is Robert Gilpin, *War and Change in World Politics* (Cambridge University Press 1981).

[127] See e.g. Vinod Rege, Shyam K Gujadhur, and Roswitha Franz, *Influencing and Meeting International Standards: Challenges for Developing Countries* (UNCTAD/WTO International Trade Center and Commonwealth Secretariat 2003); Spencer Henson, Rupert Loader, Alan Swinbank, and Maury Bredahl, 'How Developing Countries View the Impact of Sanitary and Phytosanitary Measures on Agricultural Exports' in Merlinda D Ingco and L Alan Winters (eds), *Agriculture and the New Trade Agenda* (Cambridge

participating in the transnational rule-making body's meetings, is no guarantee that the stakeholder's interests will be considered.[128] Dür and de Bièvre likewise report: 'A survey of NGOs and business groups as well as two in-depth case studies on the negotiations concerning the EU's Economic Partnership Agreements and the EU's policy on access to medicines in developing countries [...] show that although NGOs have gained access to policy-makers, they have largely failed to shift policy outcomes in their favour.'[129]

Why some stakeholders appear to be at times quite unable to exert any influence in global governance whereas others seem to gain considerable leverage is still an under-researched question. As Tallberg and colleagues summarize it: 'Why are NGOs sometimes successful in influencing political decisions in global governance and sometimes not? [...] Existing research on this topic offers anything but a conclusive answer ... The literature is rich in hypothesis-generating case studies ... but poor in comparative assessments of influence across different types of [stakeholders], IOs and issue areas.'[130]

To advance our understanding of the aftermath of global governance reforms, we develop a causal process of model of possible stakeholder influence, conditional on their actual participation.[131] This model, building on the model developed in Section 2.4 and extending DeMenno's model of participation in domestic rule-making,[132] assumes that stakeholders prefer a policy choice and outcome (Y′) more in line with their preferences, relative to the baseline outcome that would have obtained absent engagement and influence. As shown in Figure 2.4, for a global governance body seeking to enhance or maintain policy effectiveness, the preferred policy choice and outcome (Y′) embodies technocratic expertise and is reached through processes that are perceived to be legitimate. We hypothesize that the causal mechanisms, through which stakeholder participation-with-influence can enhance a global governance body's technocratic expertise and democratic credentials, and in turn influence policy choices and outcome (Y′), are policy learning (A′) and process legitimacy (B′), respectively.

University Press 2004) 359-375; John S Wilson and Tsunehiro Otsuki, *Standards and Technical Regulations and Firms in Developing Countries* (Preliminary World Bank Working Paper, June 2004); HeeJin Lee and Sangjo Oh, 'The Political Economy of Standards Setting by Newcomers: China's WAPI and South Korea's WIPI' 32(9–10) *Telecommunications Policy* (2008) 662-671.

[128] Winston Chee Chiu Kwok, and David Sharp, 'Power and International Accounting Standard Setting' 18(1) *Accounting, Auditing & Accountability Journal* (2005) 74-99.

[129] Andreas Dür and Dirk de Bièvre, 'Inclusion without Influence? NGOs in European Trade Policy' 27(1) *Journal of Public Policy* (2007) 79-101, 79. Similarly, see Robert K Larson and Sara York Kenny, 'Developing Countries' Involvement in the IASC's Standard-Setting Process' 11(s1) *Advances in International Accounting* (1998) 17-41; Khursheed Omer and Darshan Wadhwa, 'International Financial Reporting Standards: A Cautionary Note from Emerging Economies' 6(1) *Business Review* (2011) 9-25.

[130] Jonas Tallberg, Lisa M. Dellmuth, Hans Agné, and Andreas Duit, 'NGO Influence in International Organizations: Information, Access and Exchange' 48(1) *British Journal of Political Science* (2018) 213-238, 214f.

[131] The outcome of the political process depicted in Figure 2.2 thus becomes the initial causal trigger for the process depicted in Figure 2.4.

[132] DeMenno, 'Rethinking Stakeholder Participation' (n 35).

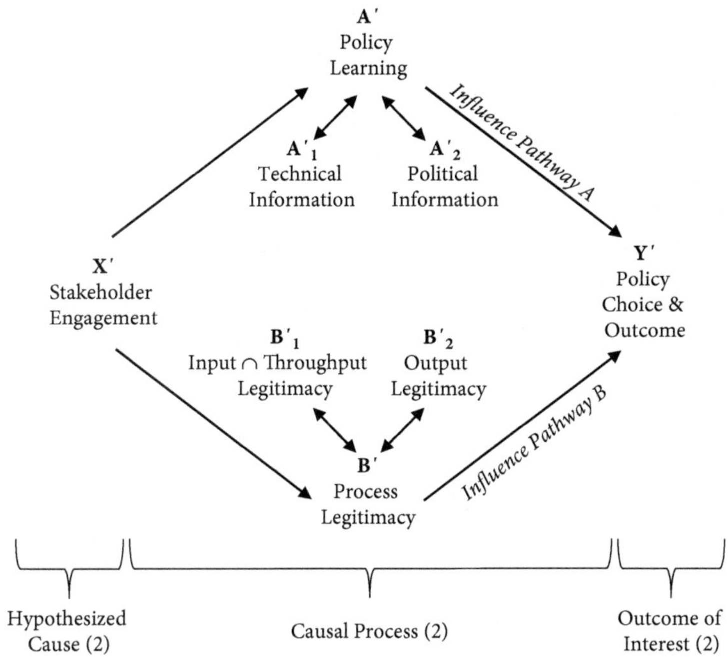

Figure 2.4 Why Global Governance Bodies may Allow Stakeholder Influence

2.6.1 Policy Learning

Stakeholder voice can enable policy learning—understood here as a 'change in [policy-relevant] beliefs […] or the development of new beliefs, skills or procedures as the result of the observation and interpretation of experience'[133]—if the stakeholder provides technical or political information that the global governance body would not otherwise have. Specifically, stakeholders' specialized expertise can mitigate uncertainty regarding the substantive and distributional effects of available policy choices. Providing opportunities for stakeholder voice, to which stakeholders respond with increased engagement in global governance, creates a mechanism to collect this otherwise highly diffuse information from stakeholders, motivating Stevenson's claim about the 'epistemic superiority' of participatory governance that promotes diversity of input.[134] Such epistemic superiority, however, is conditional on global governance

[133] Jack S Levy, 'Learning and Foreign Policy: Sweeping a Conceptual Minefield' 48(2) *International Organization* (1994) 279-312, 283.

[134] Hayley Stevenson, 'The Wisdom of the Many in Global Governance: An Epistemic-Democratic Defense of Diversity and Inclusion' 60(3) *International Studies Quarterly* (2016) 400-412. Similar observations have also been made concerning domestic public administration and regulatory governance, for instance by, Archon Fung, 'Varieties of Participation in Complex Governance' 66(s1) *Public Administration Review* (2006) 66-75.

bodies' ability to recognize it. As Haas and Haas put it: 'The capacity to learn is based on the willingness to make use of available (or obtainable) knowledge.'[135]

While it is frequently observed that a 'symbiotic' relationship exists between resource-constrained regulatory agencies and technically-expert and/or well-resourced interest groups,[136] some have noted that it is especially the historically under-voiced stakeholders that may be able to provide critical 'situated' or 'local' knowledge.[137] This includes, critically, 'information about impacts, problems, enforceability, contributory causes, unintended consequences, etc.', based upon 'lived experience in the complex reality' into which policies are implemented.[138] Such information is often highly diffused among diverse stakeholders, and it may therefore be exactly the traditionally disregarded stakeholders who are best positioned to provide such knowledge.[139]

The second form of policy learning involves the provision of political information, mitigating uncertainty regarding the distributional effects of policy choices. This kind of policy learning is concerned with both information about who the stakeholders are, which ones would be impacted by the policy (non)decision, and which stakeholders are most likely to support or oppose any particular policy choice, given

135 Peter M Haas and Ernst B Haas, 'Learning to Learn: Improving International Governance' 1(3) *Global Governance* (1995) 255-285, 259.

136 See e.g. including for critical discussions of the undue influence it may allow for well-resourced—usually commercial private-sector stakeholders: Stacy Williams, 'A Billion Dollar Donation: Should the United Nations Look a Gift Horse in the Mouth?' 27(2) *Georgia Journal of International and Comparative Law* (1999) 425-455; Peter Utting, 'UN-Business Partnerships: Whose Agenda Counts?' Paper presented at seminar on 'Partnerships for Development or Privatization of the Multilateral System?', organized by the North–South Coalition, Oslo, 8 December 2000; Lawrence O Gostin and Emily A Mok, 'Grand Challenges in Global Health Governance' 90 *British Medical Bulletin* (2009) 7-18; Mayer and Gereffi, 'Private Governance' (n 113); Kerwin, Furlong, and West, 'Interest Groups' (n 35), 593; Büthe and Mattli, *New Global Rulers* (n 61); Devi Sridhar, 'Who Sets the Global Health Research Agenda? The Challenge of Multi-Bi Financing' 9(9) *PLOS Medicine* (2012): e1001312; Anne Emanuelle Birn, 'Philanthrocapitalism, Past and Present: The Rockefeller Foundation, the Gates Foundation, and the Setting(s) of the International/Global Health Agenda' 12(1) *Hypothesis* (2014) 1-27; Kenneth W Abbott, Philipp Genschel, Duncan Snidal, and Bernhard Zangl, *International Organizations as Orchestrators* (Cambridge University Press 2015); Sophie Harman, 'The Bill and Melinda Gates Foundation and Legitimacy in Global Health Governance' 22(3) *Global Governance* (2016) 349-368; and Sandra Eckert, *Corporate Power and Regulation: Consumers and the Environment in the European Union* (Palgrave Macmillan 2019).

137 See also Harry M Collins and Robert Evans, *Rethinking Expertise* (University of Chicago Press 2007).

138 Cynthia R Farina, Mary Newhart, and Josiah Heidt, 'Rulemaking vs. Democracy: Judging and Nudging Public Participation That Counts' 2(1) *Michigan Journal of Environmental & Administrative Law* (2012) 123-172, 148.

139 Ronnie D Lipschutz, 'From Place to Planet: Local Knowledge and Global Environmental Governance' 3(1) *Global Governance* (1997) 83-102; Franklin Daniel Rothman and Pamela E Oliver, 'From Local to Global: The Anti-Dam Movement in Southern Brazil, 1979–1992' in Jackie Smith and Hank Johnston (eds), *Globalization and Resistance: Transnational Dimensions of Social Movements* (Rowman & Littlefield 2002) 115-132; Vince and Hardesty, 'Plastic Pollution' (n 45), esp. 126. The diversity of local knowledge, needed for governance effectiveness, is also central to De Búrca, Keohane, and Sabel's notion of 'global experimentalist governance', which, however, assumes a non-hierarchical structure, which we do not assume (and rarely find) in this book; see Gráinne De Búrca, Robert O Keohane, and Charles Sabel, 'Global Experimentalist Governance' 44(3) *British Journal of Political Science* (2014) 477-486. It is the tendency to ignore such local differences, which motivates much of the resistance to the use of indicators such as ranking and ratings (where this tendency is common though not strictly necessary); see Kevin Davis, Angelina Fischer, Benedict Kingsbury, and Sally Engle Marry (eds), *Governance by Indicators: Global Power through Quantification and Rankings* (Oxford University Press 2012); Judith Kelley and Beth Simmons, 'Politics by Numbers: Indicators as Social Pressure in International Relations' 59(1) *American Journal of Political Science* (2015) 55-70.

how preferences are distributed among those stakeholders. Stakeholders provide political information by identifying the relevant actors[140] and by signalling the degree of opposition or support for a proposed action or inaction.[141]

Technical and political information might in fact reinforce each other in allowing the global governance body to achieve greater policy effectiveness through learning. Political information enables global governance bodies to engage in hedging strategies and place different relative weights on the technical information received from different stakeholders if there is genuine uncertainty (that is, wide confidence intervals) versus technical information received from different stakeholders in cases where there are conflicts over scientific or technical aspects of the issue.

In sum, policy learning (A′) enhances technocratic expertise by reducing technical and political uncertainty. Specifically, technical information (A'_1) enhances technocratic expertise by mitigating uncertainty regarding the substantive effects of a policy while political information (A'_2) mitigates uncertainty regarding the distributional effects of a policy. In this model, the provision of technical information (A'_1) and/or political information (A'_2) may enable policy learning (A′) The relative importance of A'_1 and A'_2 is dependent upon the baseline of the global governance body.

2.6.2 Process Legitimacy

We use the term 'process legitimacy' to refer to stakeholders' assessment of the legitimacy of an entire rule- and decision-making process. We assume that, to meet the expectations of 'democratic legitimacy', a global governance body must allow for a certain level and quality of stakeholder participation, though it need not go as far as achieving the ideal of 'deliberative democracy' (and it rarely if ever does at the global level).[142] To gain a better understanding and make process legitimacy analytically tractable, we distinguish between input, output, and throughput legitimacy.

Recent scholarship on the democratic legitimacy of governance processes has emphasized what Schmidt has called 'throughput legitimacy', that is, the legitimacy of 'what goes on between the input and output'.[143] As Schmidt notes, throughput

[140] Mathew D McCubbins, Roger G Noll, and Barry R Weingast, 'Administrative Procedures as Instruments of Political Control' 3(2) *Journal of Law, Economics & Organization* (1987) 243-277.

[141] Cary Coglianese, 'Assessing Consensus: The Promise and Performance of Negotiated Rulemaking' 46(6) *Duke Law Journal* (1997)1255-1347.

[142] See Diana C Mutz, *Hearing the Other Side: Deliberative versus Participatory Democracy* (Cambridge University Press 2006); Charlotte Dany, 'Civil Society Participation under Most Favorable Conditions: Assessing the Deliberative Quality of the WSIS' in Steffek *et al.* (eds), *Civil Society Participation* (n 58): 53-70; Kissling and Steffek, 'CSOs' (n 46); James Fishkin, *When the People Speak: Deliberative Democracy and Public Consultation* (Oxford University Press 2009); Antonio Floridia, 'Beyond Participatory Democracy, Toward Deliberative Democracy: Elements of a Possible Theoretical Genealogy' 44(3) *Rivista Italiana Di Scienza Politica* (2014) 299-326; Stephen Elstub, 'Deliberative and Participatory Democracy' in André Bächtiger, John S Dryzek, and Jane Mansbridge (eds), *Oxford Handbook of Deliberative Democracy* (Oxford University Press 2019) 187-202.

[143] Vivien A Schmidt, 'Democracy and Legitimacy in the European Union Revisited: Input, Output and Throughput' 61(1) *Political Studies* (2013) 2-22, 14.

legitimacy comes in 'many guises',[144] and many of its elements have been previously discussed, though without having been recognized in their conceptual unity until she introduced the notion of throughput legitimacy. In the literature on global governance, the notion of throughput legitimacy may be said to have its most direct predecessors in Kingbury, Krisch, and Stewart's (overwhelming procedurally focused) work on 'global administrative law'[145] and in Zürn's discussion of the interest mediation elements of different 'negotiation systems' in 'democratic governance beyond the nation state',[146] as well as his analyses of the mechanisms of decision-making through which international institutions—often very effectively—solve problems of international collisions of law and regulations in a highly interdependent world.[147]

In democratic contexts, throughput legitimacy refers to the democratic qualities of the procedures through which the various inputs into a rule- or decision-making process are transformed into the ultimate policy choice or outcome. Specifically, high throughput legitimacy is generally thought to require that (i) the full range of voices that provide input are given serious consideration during the decision-making process, for instance in an iterative process of 'engagement *with* stakeholders',[148] and (ii) the process of drafting and adopting rules and decisions is transparent or 'open' to scrutiny by stakeholders, so as to allow them to hold their representatives and the decision-makers accountable,[149] all the while (iii) assuring efficacy in the sense that the governance body must still be able to arrive at decisions that are jointly binding.[150] Throughput legitimacy is thus closely related to the notion of 'procedural justice', that is, the perceived justness of the processes that generate a given rule or decision.[151]

Schmidt, as well as democratic theorists such as Merkel,[152] emphasize the distinctiveness and analytical separability of throughput legitimacy from input legitimacy, defined by Scharpf as 'government *by* the people'.[153] Emphasizing the distinctiveness is surely important for clarity in the development of a new concept,[154] but we see throughput legitimacy as necessarily linked to input legitimacy.

[144] Schmidt, 'Democracy and Legitimacy' (n 143), 3.

[145] Kingsbury, Krisch, and Stewart, 'The Emergence' (n 35).

[146] Michael Zürn, 'Democratic Governance Beyond the Nation State' 6(2) *European Journal of International Relations* (2000) 183-221, esp. 192-195, 202ff.

[147] As Zürn points out, in doing so, international institutions might create new legitimacy problems ('Global Governance and Legitimacy Problems' 39(2) *Government and Opposition* (2004) 260-287, esp. 272-274), resulting in his call for moving 'from executive to societally backed multilateralism' (Zürn, 'Global Governance', 285ff).

[148] Schmidt, 'Democracy and Legitimacy' (n 143), esp. 3, 14f.

[149] Schmidt, 'Democracy and Legitimacy' (n 143), 15f. This requires stakeholders to be well informed (or at least have ready access to information) about the rule- and decision-making processes; see Adrienne Héritier, 'Composite Democracy in Europe: The Role of Transparency and Access to Information' 10(5) *Journal of European Public Policy* (2003) 814-833.

[150] Schmidt, 'Democracy and Legitimacy' (n 143), 6, 16f.

[151] Tom R Tyler, *Why People Obey the Law* (Princeton University Press 2006), 5.

[152] See e.g. Sascha Kneip and Wolfgang Merkel, 'Demokratische Legitimität: Ein theoretisches Konzept in empirisch-analytischer Absicht' ('The Idea of Democratic Legitimacy') in Sascha Kneip, Wolfgang Merkel, and Bernhard Wessels (eds), *Legitimationsprobleme der Demokratie in Deutschland* (Springer 2020) 25-55.

[153] Scharpf, *Governing in Europe* (n 75), 6; emphasis added.

[154] Giovanni Sartori, 'Concept Misformation in Comparative Politics' 64(4) *American Political Science Review* (1970) 1033-1053; David Collier and Steven Levitsky, 'Democracy With Adjectives: Conceptual Innovation in Comparative Research' 49(3) *World Politics* (1997) 430-451; Robert Adcock and David

Input legitimacy refers to how well the institutional mechanisms for providing input into public policy-making reflect the full range of stakeholders' genuine preferences.[155] When scholars who focus on politics and policy-making at the national level seek to assess input legitimacy, they often start by examining the means through which citizens grant (or consent to the exercise of) authority to the legislative and executive branch of government—assuming a logic of representative democracy that seems predestined to portray global governance as less legitimate.[156] A more meaningful approach for the comparative assessment of policy-making at different levels of aggregation may be to focus on the full range of means available to stakeholders to articulate and communicate their preferences, that is, to provide input into the rule- and decision-making process.[157] Ensuring that a (more) comprehensive set of stakeholders has the opportunity to participate—by expanding their voice opportunities—is supposed to address exactly this understanding of input legitimacy.[158]

We label this element of our model 'input ∩ throughput legitimacy' to convey that we see input and throughput legitimacy not as additive but as inherently linked in such a way that it is mathematically the lesser of the two which determines their joint effect. Inclusive, transparent, accountability-assuring, and highly efficacious procedures, which as such should result in high throughput legitimacy, are worthless for overall democratic legitimacy if input into the process is, for instance, restricted to a privileged few. On the flipside, input without throughput amounts to 'non-decisional participation',[159] that is, voice without influence.[160] Moreover, corrupt, power-abusing, and oppressive/coercive practices that violate throughput expectations delegitimize governance—no matter how high the input legitimacy of the governance institutions.[161]

Collier, 'Measurement Validity' 95(3) *American Political Science Review* (2001) 529-546; Gary Goertz, *Social Science Concepts: A User's Guide* (Princeton University Press 2006). See also Mark Bevir and Asaf Kedar, 'Concept Formation in Political Science: An Anti-Naturalist Critique of Qualitative Methodology' 6(3) *Perspectives on Politics* (2008) 503-517.

155 Fritz W Scharpf, *Demokratietheorie zwischen Utopie und Anpassung* (Universitätsverlag Konstanz 1970); Scharpf, *Governing in Europe* (n 75).

156 Key questions then are: How free, fair, and contestable are the elections? How well does the electoral system ensure that the full range of citizen preferences are represented in the legislature? Is the government (executive) subject to regular confirmation or change by citizen in an orderly majoritarian, non-violent process? See Kneip and Merkel, 'Democratic Legitimacy' (n 152), 30–33.

157 This approach might result in most global governance bodies appearing deficient but such an assessment is not a foregone conclusion (i.e. it is not necessarily so).

158 See e.g. the discussion of transnational civil society consultation as generating input legitimacy in Steffek *et al.* (eds), *Civil Society Participation* 46.

159 Stewart, 'Remedying Disregard' (n 1), 214.

160 The distinction matters for the analyses in this book, inter alia, because non-decisional participation may suffice if the goal is only to solicit information so as to allow policy learning, but it is insufficient if the goal is to boost legitimacy.

161 Schmidt, 'Democracy and Legitimacy' (n 143), 3, 9. Some studies suggest that input legitimacy is sufficient to achieve legitimacy for the entire policymaking process; see e.g. Chris Ansell and Alison Gash, 'Collaborative Governance in Theory and Practice' 18(4) *Journal of Public Administration Research and Theory* (2008) 543-571; Ian Ayres and John Braithwaite, *Responsive Regulation* (Oxford University Press 1992); Cary Coglianese, Heather Kilmartin, and Evan Mendelson, 'Transparency and Public Participation in the Federal Rulemaking Process: Recommendations for the New Administration' 77(4) *George Washington Law Review* (2009) 924-972. Even these studies, however, suggest that it is necessary for such input to be inclusive of the full range of affected stakeholders and not just at the moment when preferences are first 'voiced', thus implicitly incorporating an element of throughput legitimacy, consistent with

And they reduce 'input ∩ throughput legitimacy' even if the policy outcome does not notably suffer.[162]

The third distinct form of legitimacy is output legitimacy, defined by Scharpf as 'government *for* the people'.[163] It is a function of whether policy choices and outcomes are perceived to be in the interest of those whom they affect, that is, whether the effect of rules or policies is in the public interest. In a domestic democratic context, this is generally understood to require at a minimum serving the interests of the majority without violating basic rights of any minority and maybe while also meeting certain requirements of distributive justice. Determining what output legitimacy would 'objectively' require in global governance is much harder,[164] but since we are here not concerned with what Buchanan and Keohane call the [objective] 'normative legitimacy' but rather *perceived legitimacy*,[165] it may suffice to simply ask whether the policy choices and their consequences are *perceived* by stakeholders as addressing their problems and serving their needs.

Stakeholder participation promotes output legitimacy if it involves not only providing opportunities to voice one's concerns and preferences, but also enables stakeholders to influence policy (resulting in participation-with-influence). Thus, output legitimacy can be achieved through 'decisional participation'[166], that is, having 'a role in the making of decisions by an organization', for example, by having a vote—though a governance body might be responsive to a stakeholders' preferences without granting them a decisional role. Output legitimacy also relates to 'distributive justice', that is, the perceived justness of a rule or decision, as contrasted with procedural justice, that is, the perceived justness of the process that generates the rule or decision.[167]

Although not an explicit focus of our model, it should be noted that several feedback loops may exist in the causal process depicted in Figure 2.4. For example, participation may enable the participating stakeholders to better understand, and possibly appreciate, the global body's policy objectives, thereby making it easier for them to implement or work with the resulting rules or decisions.[168] Thus, participating stakeholders might also engage in a form of 'policy learning' that mitigates implementation challenges via improved compliance. Similarly, rule- and decision-making processes

the notion that legitimacy is constituted by those affected by a given organization (Bernstein and Cashore, 'Can Non-State Global Governance Be Legitimate?' (n 21); Bernstein, 'Legitimacy' (n 78)).

[162] Policy choice and outcomes might not discernibly suffer because, for instance, an individual politician personally enriching themself as such tends to have little discernible effect on the overall government budget.

[163] Scharpf, *Governing in Europe* (n 75), 6.

[164] For a discussion of the feasibility of a 'global public interest', see Jens Steffek, 'The Output Legitimacy of International Organizations and the Global Public Interest' 7(2) *International Theory* (2015) 263-293.

[165] Allen Buchanan and Robert O Keohane, 'The Legitimacy of Global Governance Institutions' 20(4) *Ethics & International Affairs* (2006) 405-437, esp. 405. Buchanan and Keohane discuss what we here call perceived legitimacy under the label 'sociological legitimacy'.

[166] Stewart, 'Remedying Disregard' (n 1), 213.

[167] Tyler, *Why People Obey* (n 151), 5.

[168] Thomas C Beierle and Jerry Cayford, *Democracy in Practice: Public Participation in Environmental Decisions* (Resources for the Future Press 2002); Steven P Croley, *Regulation and Public Interests: The Possibility of Good Regulatory Government* (Princeton University Press 2008); Haufler, *Industry Self-Regulation* (n 89); John J Kirton and Michael J Trebilcock (eds), *Hard Choices, Soft Law: Voluntary Standards in Global Trade, Environment and Social Governance* (Ashgate 2004); Susan L Moffitt, *Making Policy Public: Participatory Bureaucracy in American Democracy* (Cambridge University Press 2014).

deemed legitimate may engender greater support for derivative policies.[169] Improved perceptions of output legitimacy, in turn, may both enhance the likelihood of compliance (mitigating implementation challenges) and affect the distribution of preferences among stakeholders (that is, political information).

In sum, input ∩ throughput legitimacy (B'_1), enhances perceived democratic legitimacy by assuring stakeholders that they have a real opportunity to access the rule- and decision-making process. Output legitimacy (B'_2) enhances perceived democratic legitimacy by assuring stakeholders of bureaucratic responsiveness. For any single interaction, we hypothesize that input ∩ throughput legitimacy (B'_1) and/or output legitimacy (B'_2) may enable process legitimation (B'). However, across multiple interactions, we hypothesize that output legitimacy (B'_2) becomes a necessary condition, as the perceived legitimacy associated with the opportunity to exercise voice is eroded by evidence of a persistent inability to have any influence over policy.

2.6.3 Operationalizing the Argument: Two Hypotheses about Stakeholder Influence

Figure 2.5 brings together the two causal process models presented in Figures 2.2 and 2.4, that is, the stages of our analytical framework during which primary agency rests with the global governance body. Both models are based on the claim that policy effectiveness is a function of the design (or choice) as well as the implementation of a given policy. The figure then depicts how a global governance body's pursuit of policy effectiveness can lead to the creation of voice opportunities and how stakeholder exercise of voice (that is, actual engagement), in turn, can lead to influence through policy learning and/or process legitimacy. The left-hand side of Figure 2.5 addresses the first question (discussed in greater detail in Section 2.4) about the conditions under which we should expect increased voice opportunities for previously disregarded stakeholders in a given global governance body. The right-hand side of Figure 2.5 addresses the third question (discussed in greater detail in Section 2.6): Given actual engagement by those traditionally marginalized or excluded stakeholders (making use of the increased voice opportunities), under what conditions should we expect those stakeholders to have *influence* in the global governance body?

This conceptualization of how stakeholder participation can promote technocratic expertise and perceived democratic legitimacy in global rule- and decision-making processes results in the following operationalized hypotheses about stakeholder influence in global rule- and decision-making processes:

> H_{3A}: *Assuming* H_{1A}, *a participating stakeholder will be able to influence policy choices and outcomes if the stakeholder can enable policy learning through the provision of technical and/or political information.*

For H_{3A}, we assume that the global governance body has expanded stakeholder voice opportunities in rule- and decision-making to promote technocratic expertise through

[169] Eric Biber and Berry Brosi, 'Officious Intermeddlers or Citizen Experts-Petitions and Public Production of Information in Environmental Law' 58 *UCLA Law Review* (2010) 322-395.

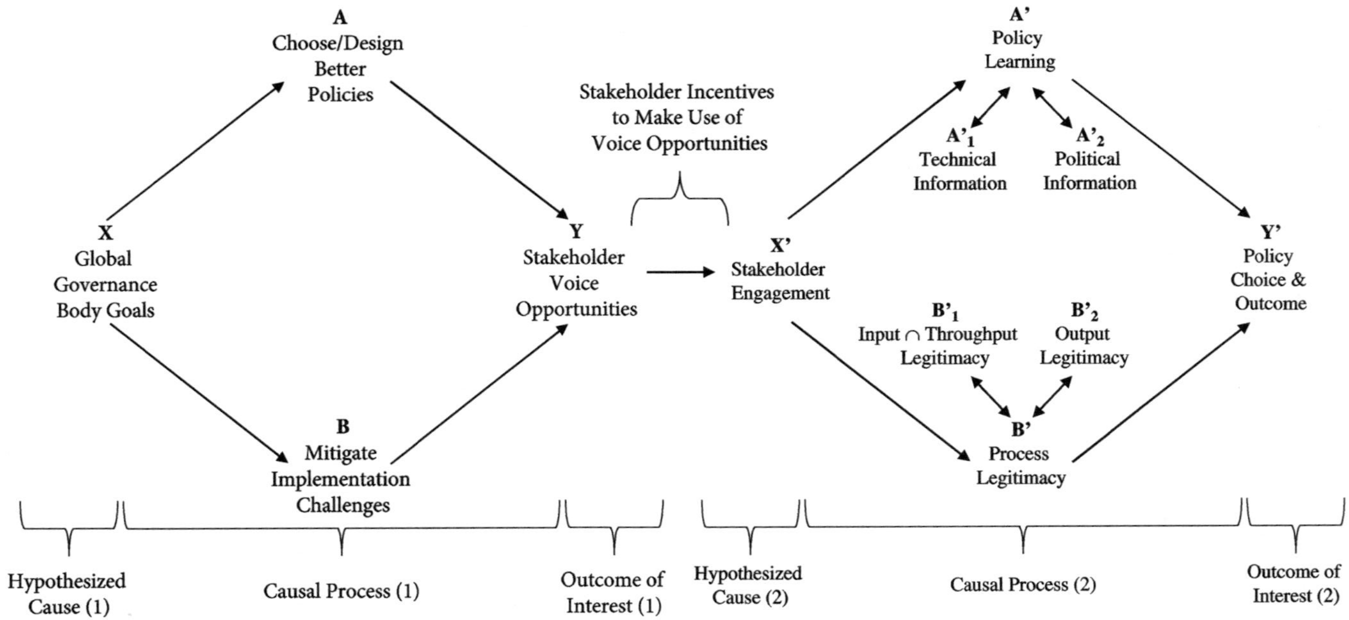

Figure 2.5 Integrated Causal Process Model for Global Governance Body

policy learning. It follows from A'_1 that the provision of what we have called technical information, particularly information that is novel, should enable participating stakeholders to be influential. Alternatively (following the logic of A'_2), the ability to provide political information should enable the participating stakeholders to exercise influence. The ability to provide such information, in turn, might be a function of the identity of the participant, for instance due to a stakeholder's situational importance or knowledge.

> *H_{3B}: Assuming H_{1B}, a participating stakeholder will be able to influence policy choices and outcomes if its participation promotes process legitimation through increased input ∩ throughput legitimacy and/or increased output legitimacy.*

For H_{3B}, we assume that the global governance body has expanded stakeholder voice opportunities in rule- and decision-making to promote democratic legitimacy through enhanced process legitimacy. Participation may be particularly likely to influence policy choices and outcomes when it results in more balanced interest representation, thereby improving/increasing input legitimacy. Raising input ∩ throughput legitimacy, moreover, may require creating decisional participation opportunities, which, by granting leverage, increases the likelihood of influence. Finally, to shift perceptions of output legitimacy, participation needs to enhance bureaucratic responsiveness and thus give the stakeholder a chance to influence policy choices and outcomes, without necessarily giving the stakeholder a decisional role.

2.7 Conclusion

Stakeholder participation requires global governance bodies to make such participation possible and meaningful, as well as stakeholder ability and willingness to participate. In this chapter, we have developed a conceptual and theoretical positive political economy model of the conditions under which a global governance body might allow and possibly even seek expanded participation, *even if the global governance body has no intrinsic normative commitment to stakeholder participation*. The model also identifies stakeholder incentives (and constraints) to participate. This model serves as the analytical framework for the empirical analyses in Part II and Part III of the book, which focus on global finance and global health governance, respectively.

In developing the model, we have distinguished between two ideal-typical components of participation: voice (opportunities) and influence. The distinction is important for understanding the political dynamics of recent and ongoing changes in global governance. Many institutional reforms in global governance, for instance, provide traditionally disregarded stakeholders with opportunities to have a strictly non-decisional role. Seemingly designed to allow stakeholders to articulate their preferences and objections, these voice-only opportunities may be good declamatory politics but are unlikely to result in any changes in policy choices or outcomes—*unless* the global governance body also seeks to increase its democratic legitimacy through enhanced responsiveness-based output legitimacy.

Our model posits, specifically, that global governance bodies will expand opportunities for participation in order to choose or design better policies and/or to mitigate implementation challenges, thereby ensuring policy effectiveness.[170] All forms of participation must offer participants at least a voice opportunity in Hirschman's sense. Whenever voice opportunities arise, stakeholders to whom those opportunities apply must decide whether in fact to engage with the global governance body. We have modelled this decision as a function of the importance of the particular global governance body for any given stakeholder and of stakeholders' material, analytical, and political resources, which enable or constrain stakeholders' participation capabilities. Actual stakeholder participation, in turn, will be influential when the stakeholders are able to contribute to policy learning or process legitimacy.

The empirical chapters in Part II and Part III of the book allow the reader to evaluate the hypotheses derived from our analytical framework with regard to specific governance bodies in global finance and global health, respectively, and with regard to traditionally disregarded state and non-state stakeholders. These empirical analyses are presented in a series of paired-case studies, which therefore also offer a comparative perspective, for which the methodological rationale is laid out more systematically in Chapter 3.[171]

Some chapters also address what we have not spelled out systematically here in order not to make the model overly complex: interactions and possible feedback effects. For instance, reforms that have the declared purpose of creating new voice opportunities but do not help overcome stakeholder resource constraints, which can be readily predicted to prevent any increase in the exercise of stakeholder voice, are little more than simply participation cheap talk—but such reforms therefore also can, nominally, be far reaching. If the legitimacy challenge to prior governance arrangements focuses on insufficient output legitimacy only (for instance, due to strong deference to highly specialized expertise), then one might expect non-decisional, voice-only opportunities to be the primary or sole interest of the global governance body in its reforms, making real influence unlikely. And if, to give a final example, participants are prevented from exercising influence (for instance because they are restricted to voice-only roles) this would seem likely to have a feedback effect on their incentives for engagement.[172] Conversely, if participants are assured to have influence, it raises the political costs of expanding voice opportunities.

While the empirical chapters address aspects of the stakeholder participation that go beyond this analytical framework, chapter authors also had to be selective, not least due to resource and length constraints. Consequently, not every chapter addresses every hypothesis with regard to both state and non-state actors and every one of the global governance bodies identified for each of the two issue areas in the introductions to Part II and Part III, respectively.[173]

[170] Across both the creation of opportunities for voice and the stakeholder participation processes, balancing technocratic expertise and democratic legitimacy is identified as a key goal.

[171] Tim Büthe and Cindy Cheng, 'Analysing the Consequences of Institutional Reforms Using Country Pairs: A Note on the (Coarsened Exact) Matched-Country-Pairs Methodology of the Rethinking Stakeholder Participation Project.' Chapter 3, this volume.

[172] Such a feedback effect might explain why Agné, Dellmuth, and Tallberg find that IOs offering 'opportunities for involvement' does not (by itself) result in stakeholder groups believing 'most people significantly affected by' the IO's decisions to have been represented or even listened-to during the organization's decision-making (see Hans Agné, Lisa Maria Dellmuth, and Jonas Tallberg, 'Does Stakeholder Involvement Foster Democratic Legitimacy in International Organizations? An Empirical Assessment' 10(4) *Review of International Organizations* (2015) 465-488, esp. 476f).

[173] Kovarzina and Maggetti, 'Stakeholder Participation Reforms' (n 5), and Berman, 'Stakeholder Participation Reforms' (n 6).

3

Analysing the Consequences of Institutional Reforms Using Country Pairs

A Note on the (Coarsened Exact) Matched-Country-Pairs Methodology of the Rethinking Stakeholder Participation Project

Tim Büthe and Cindy Cheng[*]

3.1 A Note on Methodology

Many international organizations and transnational governance bodies have in recent years undertaken institutional reforms with the stated goal of increasing the participation of previously marginalized or excluded stakeholders. This volume examines the consequences of those reforms: Have those reforms indeed increased previously marginalized stakeholders' opportunities to have a voice in global governance? Which of those stakeholders have actually utilized the new opportunities? Which haven't and why? And have any of those traditionally marginalized stakeholders gained actual *influence* in global governance? If so, which reforms (or which contextual factors) make greater inclusiveness of global governance most likely?

To answer these questions, DeMenno and Büthe have developed a series of theoretical propositions about the consequences of global governance reforms.[1] The answers suggested by their theoretical framework must now be subjected to empirical scrutiny; that is, the hypotheses must be compared to the observable experience of previously marginalized stakeholders. These empirical assessments are undertaken in Parts II and III of the volume in the form of in-depth case studies of the global governance of finance and health, respectively. The contributors to this project opted for mostly qualitative case studies, building on Büthe and Mattli's[2] call for analysing institutional features of global governance as part of institutional configurations with greater or lesser complementarity of their parts (rather than independent 'variables'), which makes it critical to consider and present contextual factors as part of

[*] The authors are listed alphabetically; both have contributed equally to this chapter.

[1] See Mercy DeMenno and Tim Büthe, 'Voice and Influence in Global Governance: An Analytical Framework.' Chapter 2, this volume. See also Ayelet Berman, Tim Büthe, Martino Maggetti, and Joost Pauwelyn, 'Introduction: Rethinking Stakeholder Participation in Global Governance.' Chapter 1, this volume.

[2] Tim Büthe and Walter Mattli, *The New Global Rulers: The Privatization of Regulation in the World Economy* (Princeton University Press 2011).

Tim Büthe and Cindy Cheng, *Analysing the Consequences of Institutional Reforms Using Country Pairs* In: *Rethinking Participation in Global Governance*. Edited by: Joost Pauwelyn, Martino Maggetti, Tim Büthe, and Ayelet Berman, Oxford University Press. © Tim Büthe and Cindy Cheng 2022. DOI: 10.1093/oso/9780198852568.003.0003

the analysis. But which traditionally marginalized stakeholders should be selected for such in-depth analysis?

At the inception of the project, Büthe and Pauwelyn decided that the project should provide insights into how institutional reforms in global governance have affected the ability of Brazil, India, and China ('BIC') to participate in global governance—and how the reforms have affected interests from within those countries. These three countries were chosen for their intrinsic importance: China and India, with more than 1.3 billion people each, together account for a third of the world's population; all three have, over the last thirty years, gone from being relatively marginal players in the world economy to being among the twenty largest economies, highly integrated into global value chains.[3] To assess the experience of these three countries, the main empirical chapters of this book (Chapters 6, 7, 8, and 15, 16, and 17) contain in-depth analyses of the changing experiences of Brazil, India, and China, respectively, in the key bodies for the governance of global finance and global health.[4]

We did not, however, want our empirical analyses to 'just' yield insights into the potentially idiosyncratic experiences of Brazil, India and China. We also—and quite importantly, given the normative concerns that have driven the legitimacy challenges to global governance—wanted to learn something about the experience of stakeholders from developing countries more generally. The BIC countries are so intrinsically important precisely because they have atypically large populations and have experienced sustained, very high levels of economic growth for most of the past twenty to thirty years. And changes in opportunities to participate and exert influence may be correlated with, and even causally related to, the atypical characteristics of the three countries.

We therefore sought to combine the case studies of Brazil, India, and China with case studies of suitably comparable developing countries that are not as atypically large, both demographically and economically. The remainder of this chapter explains the matching approach we used to select our country pairs.

3.2 Why Matching? A Non-Technical Introduction

In conventional statistical analyses, the inclusion of certain observable characteristics (which might affect the observed outcome) as 'control variables' allows the analyst to incorporate those characteristics into the *ceteris paribus* disclaimer when reporting the statistical findings for the main variable(s) of interest, even if some observations may be atypical with regard to those characteristics.

[3] See Sandra Lavenex, Omar Serrano and Tim Büthe, 'Power Transitions and the Rise of the Regulatory State: Global Market Governance in Flux' 15(3) *Regulation and Governance* (2021) 445–471; Gary Gereffi, *Global Value Chains and Development: Redefining the Contours of 21st Century Capitalism* (Oxford University Press 2019).

[4] For overviews of the key global governance bodies (and the key stakeholder participation reforms) in the two issue areas, see the introduction to Part II (Olga Kovarzina and Martino Maggetti, 'Stakeholder Participation Reforms in Global Finance Governance.' Chapter 4, this volume) and the introduction to Part III (Ayelet Berman, 'Stakeholder Participation Reforms in Global Health Governance.' Chapter 13, this volume).

But as Don Rubin points out,[5] this approach will not (fully) work if the characteristic measured by a 'control variable' is correlated with the variable of interest. Such correlation leads to biased estimates of the effect of the variable of interest (for us: institutional change in global governance and stakeholder characteristics on which its effectiveness may depend) on the outcome (for us: voice or influence in global governance). And if all the observations that score very high (or very low) on a particular control variable are clustered at one end of the range of possible values of the main variable of interest (such that the two variables are substantially correlated), then the observable cases do not allow us to assess the effect of the main variable of interest independently of the characteristic that makes some cases 'atypical.'

Statistical 'matching' refers to a set of techniques to remove or avoid such bias. Using the language of experimental 'treatment' to refer to the main variable of interest, matching aims to find, for every treated observation, a non-treated observation that is maximally comparable to the treated observation *except for the treatment*. If highly comparable matches can be found, the average effect of the treatment can be statistically assessed without confounders.

Exact 'one-to-one' matching involves only using treated–untreated pairs of observations that are literally identical on all the observable characteristics on which they have been matched for the analysis, establishing what is known as unit homogeneity. A full set of matched pairs should consequently be statistically equivalent to random assignment of the experimental treatment in an experimental setting.

If there are, however, multiple characteristics on which a researcher needs to match, or if characteristics are continuous rather than dichotomous or categorical, exact matching tends to leave prohibitively few observations for analysis. This practical limitation on the usability of exact matching has led to the development of variants such as Mahalanobis nearest-neighbour matching and propensity score matching.[6] These newer matching techniques circumvent the problem of not having enough exactly matched observations by aiming for an approximation of unit homogeneity rather than demanding perfection.

Unfortunately, however, many methods that establish proximity may re-introduce the problem matching was supposed to solve, and it may even make it worse. Recent work also shows that some of the matching approaches (especially propensity score matching) result in quite unstable matches.[7]

A simpler approach, which depends on fewer assumptions, is 'coarsened exact matching' (CEM), introduced by Iacus, King, and Porro.[8] CEM essentially uses substantive knowledge or information about the distribution of each variable to turn continuous variables into categorical ones, which then allows the application of exact

[5] Donald B Rubin, 'Estimating Causal Effects of Treatment in Randomized and Nonrandomized Studies' 66(5) *Journal of Educational Psychology* (1974) 688-701.

[6] For a recent overview, see Shenyang Guo and Mark W Fraser, *Propensity Score Analysis: Statistical Methods and Applications* (Sage 2010).

[7] Stefano M Iacus, Gary King, and Guiseppe Porro, 'Causal Inference Without Balance Checking: Coarsened Exact Matching' 20(1) *Political Analysis* (2012) 1–20, esp. 4-7; Gary King and Richard Nielsen, 'Why Propensity Scores Should Not Be Used for Matching' 27(4) *Political Analysis* (2019) 435-454.

[8] Iacus, King and Porro, 'Casual Inference' (n 7), 8ff.

matching to identify pairs of observations (= cases)—as well as identify observations that lack a match.

3.3 Applicability of Matching to Case Study Research

While the use of 'control variables' in the statistical sense is naturally not possible in qualitative case studies, the fundamental challenge that has motivated the turn to matching in statistical analyses is equally (or maybe even more severely) present in case study research. Two cases that differ with respect to one particular characteristic (or a particular 'variable') of interest often also differ in other consequential ways, turning seemingly highly comparable cases into possibly highly problematic cases for case study research.

As an example, suppose we are interested in how a country's political institutions affect its experience in global governance, and we have theoretical reasons to believe that the experiences of democratic and non-democratic countries differ significantly. This might suggest that, for an empirical study of the stipulated effect of democratic domestic institutions on a country's experience in global governance, Taiwan, which underwent a far-reaching democratization process in the 1980s and 1990s, would be a great comparative case for China, which exhibits tremendous cultural similarities with Taiwan but has experienced little democratization. But if a country's experience in post-reform global governance is also very significantly a function of its size, Taiwan would actually be a highly problematic match for China, because the difference in size is highly (inversely) correlated with the difference in democratization.[9]

In some respects, case study researchers have been aware of this issue for a long time. Qualitative methodologists writing about case selection and the comparative method[10] have long emphasized the importance of comparing cases that differ on the key variable of interest, but otherwise are as similar as possible.[11] We therefore might say that the best work on case selection already calls on researchers to undertake comparisons of closely 'matched' cases without invoking the language of matching.

[9] The inferential problem might be circumvented by having sufficiently detailed causal process information—for both the Chinese and the Taiwanese case—to allow us to differentiate between elements of the outcome that are attributable to one causal factor and elements of the outcome attributable to the other. In-depth case studies might yield such information but making a compelling argument that a readily available alternative explanation does *not* hold in a particular case is very challenging.

[10] E.g. Alexander L George, 'Case Studies and Theory Development: The Method of Structured, Focused Comparison' in Paul Gordon Lauren (ed), *Diplomacy: New Approaches in History, Theory, and Policy* (Free Press 1979) 43-68; Barbara Geddes, 'How the Cases You Choose Affect the Answers You Get: Selection Bias in Comparative Politics' 2 *Political Analysis* (1990) 131-150; Gary King, Robert O Keohane, and Sidney Verba, *Designing Social Inquiry: Scientific Inference in Qualitative Research* (Princeton University Press 1994) esp. 43–63, 128–149. See also David Collier and James Mahoney, 'Insights and Pitfalls: Selection Bias in Qualitative Research' 49(1) *World Politics* (1996) 56–91; W Phillips Shively, 'Case Selection: Insights from Rethinking Social Inquiry' 14(3) *Political Analysis* (2006) 344-347.

[11] Case study researchers also have used other research designs, but Sekhon cautions that they may be based on misunderstood assumptions about the applicability of Mill's methods to the social sciences, and those alternative designs are not at issue here (see Jasjeet Sekhon, 'Quality Meets Quantity: Case Studies, Conditional Probability, and Counterfactuals' 2(2) *Perspectives on Politics* (2004) 281-293).

As long as a small number of dichotomous variables can capture the possibly confounding characteristics of the potential cases, exact matching can be readily implemented in the case selection process—often entirely informally. Finding the best way to avoid or at least minimize the bias identified by advocates of statistical matching, however, becomes much more challenging when possible cases must be compared on several dimensions or when the measures are continuous (such as per capita GDP or the Human Development Index), which renders exact matching virtually impossible. To put it simply: If countries A and B are a very close match on variables 1 and 2 but a very poor match on variable 3, whereas countries A and C are a mediocre match on all three variables, is it better to compare country A with country B or with country C? And at what point are the differences sufficiently great that we should conclude that there is no match, such that the country in question should be dropped from the comparative analysis? The use of formal matching methods can help, as they provide a systematic way to answer these questions for *qualitative* case study research.

One of the major recent developments has been a shift towards explicit multimethod research designs. In the realm of case selection, this has been driven by strong arguments for the benefits of using available statistical information about the full range of possible cases to select a small number of observations to be examined in detail.[12] This approach allows the researcher to more systematically (and reliably) select specific individual cases for any of the major types long distinguished in the case study literature, such as a deviant case, a case with an extreme value on any particular variable, or a case that is typical of the relationship between X and Y in the larger population of cases.[13] And since metrics for statistically matching cases, such as propensity scores, can be extracted and examined without actually carrying out the regression analysis for which they are typically generated,[14] quantitatively assisted selection of cases for qualitative analysis can be used to select matched pairs of cases, so as to make comparisons within each pair more meaningful.

Gerring and Seawright,[15] Levy,[16] and Tarrow[17] thus variously advocate using propensity scores or similar approximate-matching metrics to choose case pairs. As Nielsen points out, the benefit of this approach is that '"most-similar" cases are in fact most similar ... [It] make[s] scope conditions, assumptions, and measurement

[12] See Evan S Lieberman, 'Nested Analysis as a Mixed-Method Strategy for Comparative Research' 99(3) *American Political Science Review* (2005) 435-452.

[13] E.g. Alexander L George and Andrew Bennett, *Case Studies and Theory Development in the Social Sciences* (MIT Press 2004); Harry Eckstein, 'Case Study and Theory in Political Science' in Fred I Greenstein and Nelson W Polsby (eds), *Handbook of Political Science* (Addison-Wesley 1975) 79-137; Arend Lijphart, 'Comparative Politics and the Comparative Method' 65(3) *American Political Science Review* (1971) 682-693; Stephen Van Evera, 'What Are Case Studies? How Should They Be Performed?' in *Guide to Methodology for Students of Political Science* (Cornell University Press 1997) 48-88.

[14] See Daniel Ho, Kosuke Imai, Gary King, and Elizabeth A Stuart, 'Matching as Nonparametric Preprocessing for Reducing Model Dependence in Parametric Causal Inference' 15(3) *Political Analysis* (2007) 199-236.

[15] John Gerring and Jason Seawright, 'Techniques for Choosing Cases' in John Gerring (ed), *Case Study Research: Principles and Practices* (Cambridge University Press 2007) 86-150.

[16] Jack S Levy, 'Case Studies: Types, Designs, and Logics of Inference' 25(1) *Conflict Management and Peace Science* (2008) 1-18.

[17] Sidney Tarrow, 'The Strategy of Paired Comparison: Toward a Theory of Practice' 43(2) *Comparative Political Studies* (2010) 230-259.

explicit, and [it] make[s] case selection transparent and replicable.'[18] It has at least on two occasions been used to good effect.[19]

3.4 Using Coarsened Exact Matching (CEM) to Select Country Pairs

While CEM is fairly straightforward, it requires the analyst to make a number of decisions in advance, some of which are a matter of assumptions (as for any case selection procedure). The two most crucial decisions are: (1) which variables to consider in the CEM procedure and (2) which protocol to use to coarsen the variables (i.e. how to turn continuous variables into dichotomous or categorical measures). In what follows, we first discuss the rationale for including certain variables before discussing the coarsening protocols we use for each of them. Note that we use average values for the time period between 2000 and 2012,[20] since we are concerned with institutional reforms in global governance in quite recent years.

3.4.1 Variable Selection

3.4.1.1 Treatment variable

The characteristic that makes Brazil, India and China unlike most other countries in the world is their very large population size. To find out to what extent any changes in their participation in global governance is caused by this characteristic (rather than, for instance, institutional reforms adopted by global governance bodies) we want to match each of the three countries with another country that *differs* from the respective BIC country with respect to population size but is otherwise as similar as possible. In the tradition of the Neyman-Rubin causal model, the matching literature calls the variable on which the cases are supposed to differ the 'treatment variable'.[21]

Specifically, we encoded a dichotomous (and thus coarsened) 'treatment variable.' coded 1 for the largest countries in the world; 0 otherwise.[22] The CEM procedure is

[18] Richard A Nielsen, 'Case Selection via Matching' 45(3) *Sociological Methods & Research* (2016) 569-597, 569.

[19] Surely more instances exist, but as of the beginning of the Rethinking Participation project, we readily found two examples of an actual implementation of the approach: Róger Madrigal, Francisco Alpízar, and Achim Schlüter, 'Determinants of Performance of Community-Based Drinking Water Organizations' 39(9) *World Development* (2011) 1663-1675; Tim Büthe and Helen V. Milner, 'Institutional Diversity in Trade Agreements and Their Effects on Foreign Direct Investment: Credibility, Commitment, and Economic Flows in the Developing World, 1971–2007' 66(1) *World Politics* (2014) 88-122.

[20] 2012 was the most recent year for which reasonably comprehensive data was available as of Nov/Dec 2015, which was when we started these analyses.

[21] Successfully matching each of the units of interest with at least one highly similar unit that *differs* on this variable, then allows the quasi-experimental interpretation of statistical analyses of the resulting dataset, for which this variable can then be considered the 'treatment'. Hence the label 'treatment variable'. We, however, do not intend to conduct any subsequent statistical analyses but simply use the matching method for case selection.

[22] Specifically, for the baseline models, the treatment dummy takes a value of 1 for China, India, Indonesia, Pakistan, and Brazil, thus ruling out these countries as possible matches for each other; missing data resulted in changes to the group of countries encoded with a 1 for some of the matching with health- or

then used to find for China, Brazil, and India, respectively, one or more countries that differ on the population dummy but match on the other variables identified for the theoretical reasons discussed in Sections 3.4.1.2 and 3.4.1.3, below.

3.4.1.2 Variables considered for matching

Aside from having a notably smaller population size, we wanted the other country in each pair to be maximally comparable to Brazil, India, or China, respectively. We focused, first, on three dimensions that we considered highly likely to shape how previously marginalized or excluded actors might engage with global governance institutions: region, level of economic development, and political institutions (regime type). We use these variables as our baseline in each CEM analysis that we run.

3.4.1.3 Baseline control variables

3.4.1.3.1 Region

History and culture are widely believed to be important drivers of a country's 'civic culture,' including common forms of political behaviour and foreign policy styles—which in many respects tend to exhibit similarities within and differences across geographic regions, notwithstanding distinct national cultures within regions.[23] Countries from a given region also tend to have access to shared regional institutions, if any. Consequently, how previously marginalized or excluded actors respond to changes in global governance is likely to be informed by characteristics that are particular to each region of the world. For example, many diseases are specific to—yet common within—certain geographic and climatic regions (e.g. tropical diseases), which we would expect to have consequences for stakeholder participation from those countries in global health governance.[24]

3.4.1.3.2 Economic development

There are several reasons why economic development is important for comparability. National governments, as well as stakeholders from within countries, are often marginalized or excluded in global governance, in large part, because their lack of financial and human resources prevents participation in international meetings and fruitfully engaging with other participants. A country's level of economic development may also affect the types of issues and concerns that such actors bring to the table. We measure economic development using GDP per capita in constant 2005 dollars.[25]

finance-specific variables. The supplemental material for this chapter (available via the Oxford University Press website for this volume) includes the dataset used as well as the code for the CEM procedure.

[23] See Gabriel Almond and Sidney A Verba, *The Civic Culture* (Princeton University Press 1963) and The Civic Culture Revisited (Sage 1989), and a wealth of literature since then.

[24] For specific measures used, see Section 3.4.2.

[25] The data was collected from: World Bank, *World Development Indicators 2016* <http://documents.worldbank.org/curated/en/805371467990952829/World-development-indicators-2016>, last accessed 11/12/2015.

3.4.1.3.3 Political institutions

We also expect the structure and quality of domestic institutions to affect how countries interact with international bodies. In particular, democracies differ from autocracies in whose preferences matter and how to aggregate them. This is likely to affect what issues these countries raise in global governance bodies and how they engage with other actors. We use the 'polity2' measure from the Correlates of War Polity dataset as our measure of political institutions.[26]

3.4.1.4 Additional control variables

Region, economic development, and political institutions form an important baseline for comparing how countries engage in global governance. Given our interest in assessing previously marginalized or excluded actors' ability to participate in international health and finance governance, we additionally evaluate comparability with respect to key health and finance variables.

3.4.1.4.1 Health variables

We use two health-related measures to assess how comparable countries are. The first measure, 'Health Expenditures Per Capita,' evaluates how much effort the country's government has devoted to prioritizing public health. The second, 'Immunization, DPT (% of children ages 12–23 months)' evaluates how successful a country is in achieving good health outcomes through implementing a medical procedure that has a high success rate in preventing disease but requires little in the way of infrastructure and equipment to implement. Furthermore, DPT immunization can be accomplished quickly and generally without the need for further follow-up. Unlike many other health outcome measures, it also benefits from relatively good data coverage. Both of these measures are provided by the World Bank.[27]

3.4.1.4.2 Finance variables

Similarly, to assess the comparability of different countries in the realm of finance, we use 'FDI (% GDP)' as a measure of how much contact a particular country has with foreign investment, which should correspond to the relevance of international financial rules for that country.[28] We also use 'Bank nonperforming loans, % of total gross loans' as a measure of how healthy a country's domestic financial system is and how well the government is able to regulate it. These measures are also taken from the World Bank.[29]

[26] Monty G Marshall, Keith Jaggers, and Ted Robert Gurr, 'Polity IV Annual Time-Series, 1800–2013.' Website for the Polity project. College Park: *University of Maryland Center for International Development and Conflict Management* 2014: <http://www.systemicpeace.org/inscrdata.html> (1800–2013 dataset, last accessed 12/09/2015).

[27] Data collected from: *World Development Indicators* (n 25). DPT stands for diphtheria, pertussis (whooping cough), and tetanus.

[28] Aseem Prakash and Matthew Potoski, 'Investing Up: FDI and the Cross-Country Diffusion of ISO 14001 Management Systems' 51(3) *International Studies Quarterly* (2007) 723-744; William Judge, Shaomin Li, and Robert Pinsker, 'National Adoption of International Accounting Standards: An Institutional Perspective' 18(3) *Corporate Governance: An International Review* (2010) 161-174.

[29] Data collected from: *World Development Indicators* (n 25).

3.4.2 Coarsening Protocol

The second, quite important decision for conducting a CEM analysis is how to 'coarsen' different variables. Deciding on the cut points for turning continuous measures into categorical or dichotomous ones is very important for how the CEM algorithm subsequently decides to group countries and, consequently, which countries are deemed to be maximally comparable. These decisions should be maximally theoretically informed.

3.4.2.1 Regions

We used the World Bank definition of regions and required possible matches to come from the same region as Brazil, India and China, respectively. The three World Bank regions of specific relevance are:

- LATIN AMERICA & CARRIBBEAN (31 countries): Antigua & Barbuda, Argentina, Barbados, Belize, Bolivia, Brazil, Chile, Colombia, Costa Rica, Cuba, Dominica, Dominican Republic, Ecuador, El Salvador, Grenada, Guatemala, Guyana, Haiti, Honduras, Jamaica, Mexico, Nicaragua, Panama, Paraguay, Peru, St. Kitts & Nevis, St. Lucia, St. Vincent & the Grenadines, Suriname, Trinidad & Tobago, Uruguay.
- SOUTH ASIA (8 countries): Afghanistan, Bangladesh, Bhutan, India, Maldives, Nepal, Pakistan, Sri Lanka.
- EAST ASIA AND PACIFIC (21 countries): Australia, Cambodia, China, Fiji, Indonesia, Japan, Kiribati, Malaysia, Mongolia, Myanmar, New Zealand, Palau, Papua New Guinea, Philippines, Samoa, Singapore, Thailand, Tonga, Tuvalu, Vanuatu, Vietnam.

Due to the small number of countries in the World Bank's South Asia category, we also allowed India to match on the pooled set of countries from the East Asia/Pacific and South Asia regions (see Figure 3.4 and accompanying discussion).

For the Polity variable, we followed the Polity project's recommendation to define four broad categories: −10 to −6 [autocracy]; −5 to 0 [closed autocracy]; 1–5 [open anocracy]; 6–10 [democracy and full democracy].[30] As robustness checks, we further coarsened this variable to differentiate just two categories. First, we differentiated between 'more autocratic-than-democratic' countries (with polity scores between −10 and 0) and 'more democratic-than-autocratic' countries (1–10). Second, we differentiated between 'democracies' (6–10, using the customary cut-off of a polity score of at least 6 for democracies) and non-democracies (−10 to 5). Except where noted, these changes did not result in substantively different findings.

[30] See Monty G Marshall and Ted Robert Gurr, Polity IV Project: Political Regime Characteristics and Transitions, 1800–2013. Dataset description page of the Polity IV Project for the 1800–2013 dataset (6 June 2014): <https://www.systemicpeace.org/polity/polity4.htm>, last accessed 11/23/2018.

For continuous variables for which there is, a priori, no theoretical rationale for using particular cut-offs, there are a number of algorithms that one can use to empirically establish different cut points:

- Freedman–Diaconis rule (FD): uses the interquartile range to determine cut points for continuous data
- Sturges: uses the range to determine cut points for continuous data
- Scott: uses the underlying normal distribution to determine cut points for continuous data
- Shimazaki–Shinomoto's rule (SS): calculates cut points based on minimizing the mean integrated square error of a histogram of the data.

Since we had no strong prior as to which of these rules should be applied, we allowed each continuous variable to be subject to each of these cut-off rules. This resulted in $2 \times (p-1)^4$ ways to conduct a CEM analysis,[31] where p is the number of control variables, not including the region variable.

3.4.3 Results

The CEM procedure does not guarantee one unique match for each country of interest; it can also produce multiple matches or no match. For example, when using the FD criterion for choosing the cut-off for the economic development variable, the Polity project's four-category criteria for choosing cut-offs for the Polity variable, and the Sturges criteria for choosing the cut-off for health outcomes as measured by health expenditures, the CEM analysis identifies both Argentina and Panama as equally best matches for Brazil. To arrive at a case selection decision, we therefore calculated—separately for Brazil, India, and China—how frequently each country in the same region was selected as a match across all of the different combinations of control variables and cut point algorithms.

Figures 3.1 (China), 3.2 (Brazil), as well as 3.3 and 3.4 (India) provide visual summaries of the results. Noted above each subfigure are the variables included in the CEM analysis. The y-axis indicates the frequency with which each country was selected as a match for the particular country of interest.

3.4.3.1 Results of the CEM analysis for China

The CEM analysis suggests Vietnam as the best match for China when considering only the baseline variables (region, level of economic development, and regime type), as well as across five combinations of the baseline variables with additional controls (see Figure 3.1). Only when non-performing loans (NPL) are included among the matching variables did the CEM analyses not suggest Vietnam as the best match, though for CEM with NPL, there generally appears to be no good regional match for China. Across all the combinations of the variables that we considered for CEM matching, the only other country that comes up as a good match for China is Fiji, but

[31] If we had allowed the polity variable to be coarsened like the other variables (using the FD, Sturges, Scott, and SS cut point criterion), the CEM analysis would have been conducted $p4$ possible number of ways.

much more rarely than Vietnam.[32] The combination of CEM analyses thus strongly suggests Vietnam as the match for China in our matched-country-pairs case studies of participation in global finance and health governance.

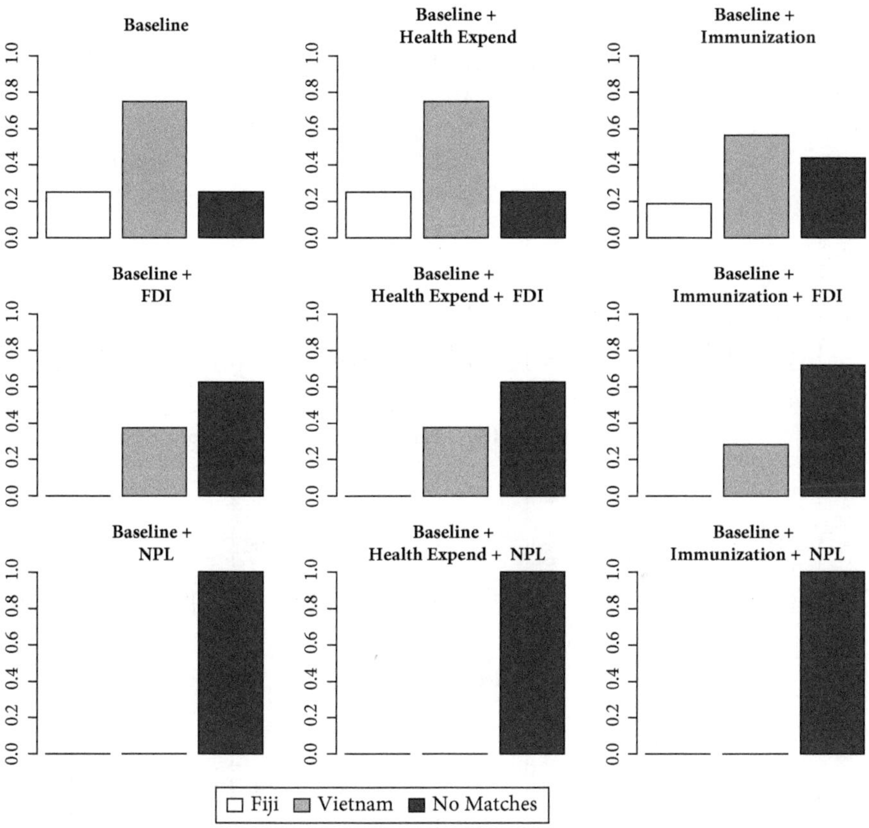

Figure 3.1 CEM Country Matches for China

The Y-axis indicates the frequency with which a particular country was selected as a match for China over the universe of CEM analyses conducted with all the different cut-point criteria for a given set of variables. Baseline [variables] = Region + Economic Development (GDP per capita) + Political Institutions (Polity 2). Health Expend = health expenditures per capita; Immunization = percentage of children ages 12-23 months immunized against DPT; FDI = FDI as a percentage of GDP; NPL = bank nonperforming loans, as a % of total gross loans.

3.4.3.2 Results of the CEM analysis for Brazil

Figure 3.2 shows that Uruguay is the most frequently matched country for Brazil when considering four combinations ('sets') of matching variables,[33] whereas Costa

[32] The same finding holds when dichotomizing polity, except when we dichotomize democracies vs. non-democracies with a polity2 cut point score of 6, in which case—and only with this particular combination of matching variables—Malaysia also emerges as a match for China. Overall, Vietnam is clearly the best match under the broadest range of conditions.

[33] Uruguay: Baseline; Baseline + Immunization, Baseline + FDI, Baseline + Immunization + FDI.

Rica is the most commonly matched when considering another four combinations.[34] To complicate matters further, across five combinations of variables, Panama is also very commonly matched—and under some conditions more frequently than Costa Rica and Uruguay—but Panama drops out completely for three combinations.[35] A few other countries, including Argentina, are suggested as a match across all of the combinations of matching variables, though not particularly frequently for any of them. The CEM analysis for Brazil thus does not leave us with a clearly optimal selection, an issue to which we return later.

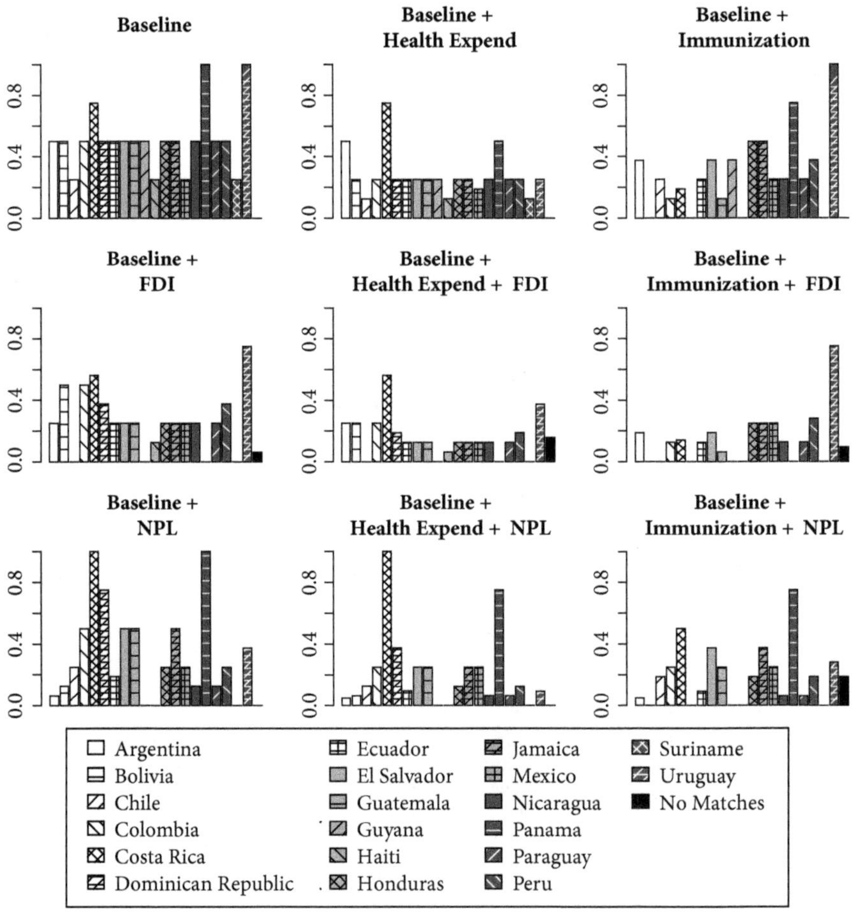

Figure 3.2 CEM Country Matches for Brazil

The Y-axis indicates the frequency with which a particular country was selected as a match for Brazil over the universe of CEM analyses conducted with all the different cut-point criteria for a given set of variables. Labels and matching variables used are defined as for Figure 3.1.

[34] Costa Rica: Baseline + Health Expend, Baseline + Health Expend + FDI, Baseline + NPL, Baseline + Health Expend + NPL.

[35] Panama most frequently matches in the analysis considering Baseline + Immunization + NPL; it is tied with Costa Rica in the Baseline + NPL analysis and with Uruguay in the Baseline analysis. It appears as the second-best choice after Costa Rica in the analyses based on Baseline + Health Expenditure and after Uruguay in the Baseline + Immunization analysis.

3.4.3.3 Results of the CEM analysis for India

Finally, with regards to India, when we restrict the matching analysis to the South Asian group of countries (see Section 3.4.2), Bangladesh and Sri Lanka are most frequently chosen by the CEM analysis as matches for India across four combinations of matching variables. However, for the remaining five of the nine combinations, CEM suggests that there is, for India, no suitable match at all in this region (see Figure 3.3).[36]

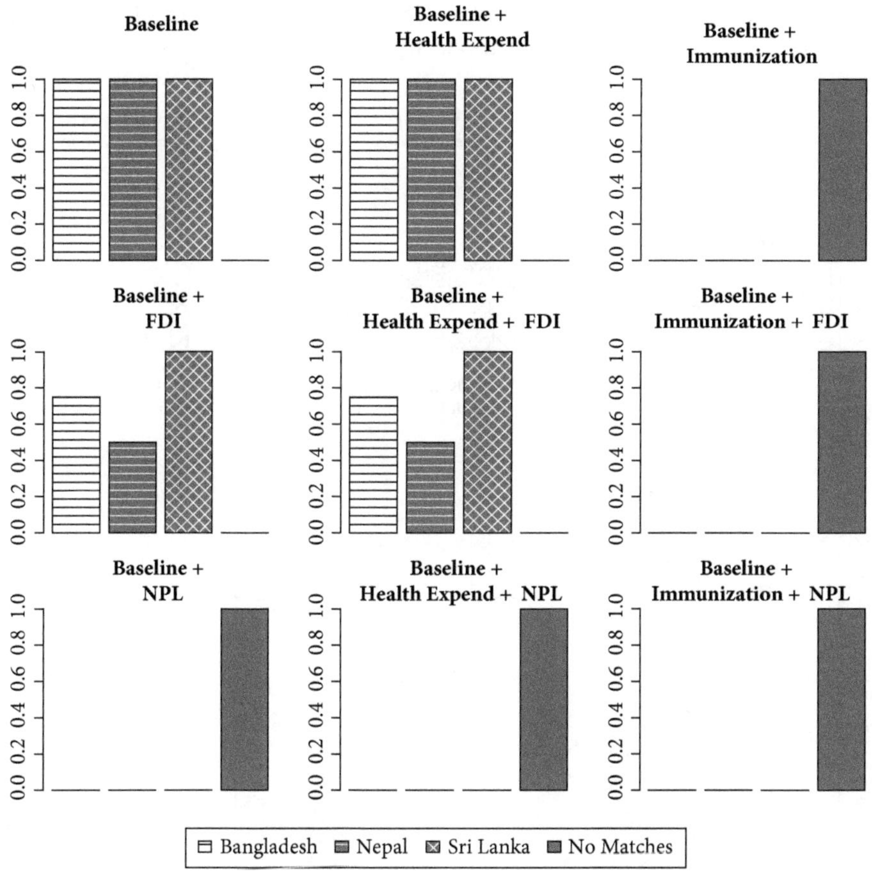

Figure 3.3 CEM Country Matches for India, South Asia Only

The Y-axis indicates the frequency with which a particular country was selected as a match for India over the universe of CEM analyses conducted with different combinations of cut-offs for a given set of variables and considering only South Asian countries as possible matches. Labels and matching variables used are defined as for Figure 3.1

When we broaden the analysis to allow India to be matched with countries in South or East Asia (in one combined analysis), CEM now identifies Indonesia, Mongolia, and the Philippines as best matches for India across two combinations of matching variables; the Philippines and Indonesia are identified as best matches across four sets of variables.[37] For the five combinations, for which the South Asia-only analysis yielded

[36] These results persist in all of the robustness checks.

[37] Baseline; Baseline + Health Expend; Baseline + FDI; Baseline + Health Expend + FDI.

no match at all, Indonesia, Thailand,[38] and Malaysia[39] sometimes are identified as a match, but there is for these combinations still no country that is chosen as a match with higher frequency than 0.3. When allowing for a broader conceptualization of the pertinent region, we thus find that Indonesia and the Philippines are the best matches for India, which implies two possible matched pairs for the Indo-Pacific region (see Figure 3.4)—though Indonesia is ruled out by its large population size. Overall, then, considering both the more restrictive and the broader conceptualizations of the pertinent region, Bangladesh, Sri Lanka, and the Philippines appear to be suitable matches for India, with none of the possible pairs clearly superior to the others.

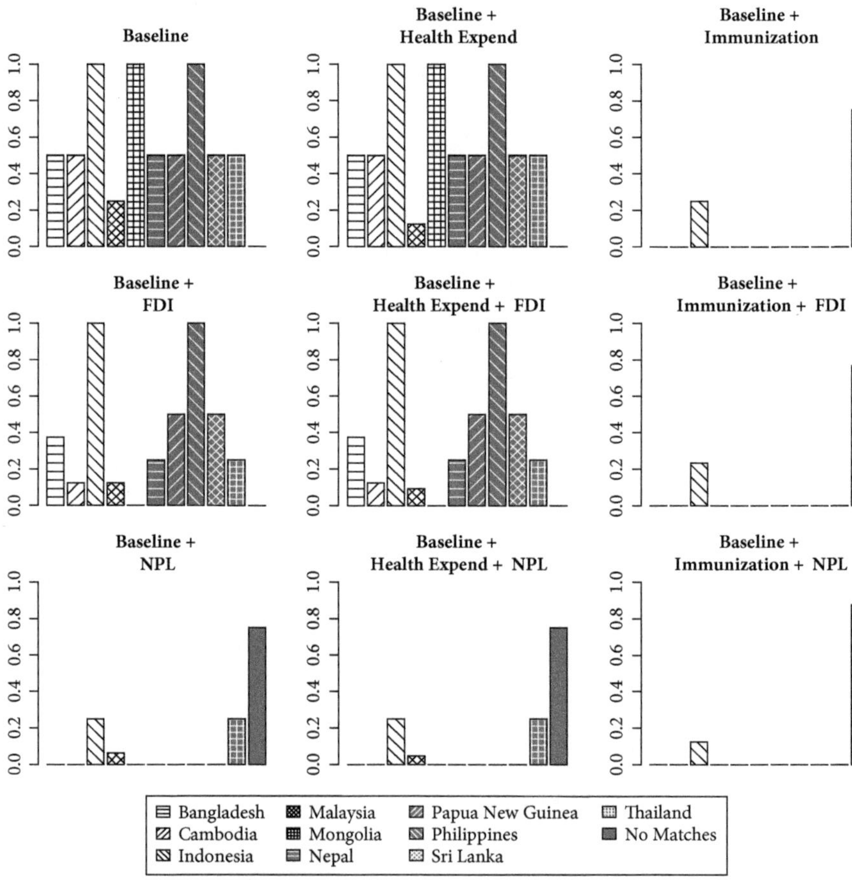

Figure 3.4 CEM Country Matches for India, South/East Asia

The Y-axis is the percentage of times a particular country was selected as a match for India over the universe of CEM analyses conducted with all the different cutpoint criteria for a given set of variables, considering the full set of South/East Asian countries as possible matches. Labels and matching variables used are defined as for Figure 3.1.

[38] Thailand: Baseline + NPL; Baseline + Health Expend + NPL.
[39] Malaysia: Baseline + NPL; Baseline + Health Exp + NPL.

3.5 Conclusion

The natural strength of in-depth case studies is that, by allowing for careful process-tracing, they promise to give us greater confidence that our explanation of the particular case is valid (high internal validity). Efforts to generalize from such case studies, however, are inherently more challenging. Coarsened Exact Matching analysis provides a way to boost the chances of increasing external validity through the more systematic selection of cases for in-depth comparative analysis.

This chapter has discussed the rationale and illustrated both the promise and the limitations of using CEM to choose maximally comparable cases (given that BIC were of intrinsic interests), using as few assumptions as possible.

The CEM analysis has yielded one unambiguous 'best' pair: China–Vietnam. Accordingly, Cheng and Do explore how the participation of stakeholders from these two countries in global health governance has been similarly and differently affected by supposedly participation-boosting reforms of health governance bodies,[40] whereas Zhang examines China's and Vietnam's respective participation in global finance institutions in response to the (more limited) institutional reforms for the governance of global finance.[41]

For India, Mukherji and Jha analyse the Indian experience with trying to exercise greater voice in the governance of global finance in a matched comparison with the experience of Bangladesh—one of the two countries suggested by the CEM analysis for India when restricting the analysis to the countries of the South Asia region.[42] In light of the substantial practical challenges of gathering data on the experience of Bangladeshi interests, we drew for the analysis of global health governance on the CEM matching analysis for the broader South/East Asian/Indo-Pacific regional group and paired Chaturvedi and Srinivas's analysis of how India has responded to changes in global health institutions with Payoyo's analysis of the same question for the Philippines.[43]

Finally, for Brazil, for which the CEM analysis had yielded ambiguous results, the case selection was ultimately allowed to be guided, in part, by criteria beyond the matching analysis. Argentina, which in the CEM analyses had come up *sometimes* for *all* combinations of variables, is another relatively large Latin American country,[44] but one that has been on a very different economic and developmental trajectory: Whereas Brazil has, for most of the last three decades sustained phenomenal rates of economic growth, Argentina—historically the most economically advanced South American

[40] Cindy Cheng with Anh Do, 'China and Vietnam in Global Health Governance.' Chapter 16, this volume.

[41] Weiwei Zhang, 'China and Vietnam in Global Finance Governance.' Chapter 7, this volume.

[42] Rahul Mukherji and Himanshu Jha, 'India and Bangladesh in Global Finance Governance.' Chapter 8, this volume.

[43] Tim Büthe, Sachin Chaturvedi, Peter Payoyo, and Krishna Ravi Srinivas, 'India and the Philippines in Global Health Governance.' Chapter 17, this volume.

[44] Brazil with a population of about 210 million is here compared with Argentina with 45 million; the other most likely comparisons would have been Costa Rica (5 million) or Uruguay (approximately 3.4 million).

country—has experienced stagnation or even decline in recent decades. Accordingly, Mello e Souza and Pérez Aznar[45] examine how reforms in international health governance bodies have affected Brazil's and Argentina's ability to participate and exercise influence in global health, while Moraes and Pérez Aznar[46] compare and contrast how institutional reforms in global financial institutions have affected Brazil's and Argentina's subsequent participation in global finance.

[45] André de Mello e Souza and Facundo Pérez Aznar, 'Brazil and Argentina in Global Health Governance.' Chapter 15, this volume.

[46] Henrique Choer Moraes and Facundo Pérez Aznar, 'Brazil and Argentina in Global Finance Governance.' Chapter 6, this volume.

PART II
INSTITUTIONS AND REFORMS IN GLOBAL FINANCE GOVERNANCE

A. MAPPING THE REFORMS

4
Stakeholder Participation Reforms in Global Finance Governance

Olga Kovarzina and Martino Maggetti

4.1 Introduction

This chapter provides an overview of reforms that aimed at increasing participation in the main global finance governance institutions. It focuses specifically on the inclusion of previously marginalized stakeholders, which could be either state or non-state actors. In line with our overarching framework, we examine whether or not these institutions underwent participation reforms and what types of reforms have been introduced, if any. We also look at the magnitude of these reforms, and how they affect the governance of these institutions. To do so, we first concentrate on the main organizational features that characterize the governance structure of these institutions and, respectively, on the measures taken in the last decades to improve the participation of previously marginalized stakeholders. To account for the existing variation in organizational features, we selected institutions with different organizational forms: intergovernmental organizations like the International Monetary Fund (IMF) and the World Bank (WB), transgovernmental/transnational bodies like the Financial Action Task Force (FATF) and the Financial Stability Board (FSB), and private standard-setters like the International Accounting Standards Board (IASB; see Table 4.1). The measures taken to improve stakeholder participation typically consist of reforms such as expanding the membership base, re-allocating voting and quota rights, opening regional offices in marginalized countries, or reforming governance structures (adding new bodies or agencies, changing their size or composition, etc.).

Before continuing, two important features concerning stakeholder participation in global finance governance institutions require a brief gloss. On the one hand, the governance of global finance typically relies on institutions that are relatively opaque, secluded, and inward-looking. Global finance is indeed usually framed as a highly technical subject whose governance is conducted by a narrow community of experts aiming to establish and maintain a financial system that should deliver financial stability and economic efficiency at the same time.[1] Global finance governance institutions are best understood as 'club-like' technocratic institutions that tend to operate quite autonomously from national elected politicians and attract little attention from the public.[2] In this context, business interests have traditionally

[1] Elizabeth Friesen, *Challenging Global Finance: Civil Society and Transnational Networks* (Springer 2012).

[2] Robert Keohane and Joseph S Nye Jr, 'Between Centralization and Fragmentation: The Club Model of Multilateral Cooperation and Problems of Democratic Legitimacy' *Harvard, John F. Kennedy School of Government Faculty Research Working Paper Series* (2001).

Olga Kovarzina and Martino Maggetti, *Stakeholder Participation Reforms in Global Finance Governance* In: *Rethinking Participation in Global Governance*. Edited by: Joost Pauwelyn, Martino Maggetti, Tim Büthe, and Ayelet Berman, Oxford University Press. DOI: 10.1093/oso/9780198852568.003.0004

had access to the rule-making process, while NGOs and representatives of the global South have been systematically side-lined.[3] On the other hand, reforms to improve stakeholder participation in global finance took place in a crisis moment and initially emerged as relatively open-ended reforms. The 2007–2008 financial crisis prompted a sizeable change in the international regulatory regime in this area, namely, by expanding the scope of international regulation, reinforcing its institutional architecture, and putting into question the attribution of regulatory powers to private actors, such as rating agencies.[4] Against this background, the next section presents and describes the core reforms experienced by the main global finance governance institutions.

Table 4.1 Main Global Finance Governance Institutions (selection)

Bank for International Settlements (BIS)
Basel Committee on Banking Supervision (BCBS)
Financial Action Task Force (FATF)
Financial Stability Board (FSB)
Group of Twenty (G20)
International Accounting Standards Board (IASB)
International Monetary Fund (IMF)
International Organization of Securities Commissions (IOSCO)
World Bank (WB)

4.2 Overview and Major Reforms in the Main Institutions

This section offers an overview of the governance structure of each institution, followed by a description of the main reforms to improve stakeholder participation.

4.2.1 Bank for International Settlements (BIS)

The Bank for International Settlements (BIS) is the world's oldest international financial organization, set up in May 1930 and headquartered in Basel, Switzerland. BIS is a treaty-based organization with its own secretariat, a convention, charter, statutes, Brussels protocol, and a series of formal agreements.[5] Its purposes are to act as a bank for central banks, to promote monetary and financial stability, and to foster international cooperation in banking matters.

[3] Susanne Soederberg, *The Politics of the New International Financial Architecture: Reimposing Neoliberal Domination in the Global South* (Zed Books 2004).

[4] Eric Helleiner, Stefano Pagliari, and Hubert Zimmermann (eds), *Global Finance in Crisis: The Politics of International Regulatory Change* (Routledge 2010).

[5] Bank for International Settlements (BIS), 'About BIS: Legal Information–Overview' <https://www.bis.org/about/legal.htm>, last accessed 02/01/2017.

4.2.1.1 Governance structure

BIS members are around sixty countries represented by their central banks, which together make up around 95% of world's GDP. Some international organizations are also included as participants. As regards our list of previously marginalized stakeholders, these sixty countries represented include Argentina, Brazil, India, China (BIC), but neither Vietnam nor Bangladesh.[6] The right of representation and voting is proportional to the number of shares subscribed in each country.[7] Decision-making in the board occurs generally by simple majority of those present or represented by proxy.[8] Decisions affecting the structure or functioning of the Bank (such as its regulations or reforms) requires two-thirds supermajority and the approval by majority of the general meeting.[9] Representation is proportional and based on the amount of shares a holder subscribes to, similar to the special drawing rights (SDR) system of the IMF (see Section 4.2.6).[10]

4.2.1.2 Main reforms

Most of the—quite limited—reforms to improve stakeholder participation included building other 'off-shoot' organizations, namely the Committee on the Global Financial System (CGFS), the Committee on Payments and Market Infrastructures (CPMI), and the Markets Committee (MC).[11] The BIS also progressively expanded the number of its members, but it did so only incrementally and to a limited extent Finally, BIS established Representative Offices for Asia and the Pacific (in 1998), for the Americas (in 2002), an Asian Consultative Council (in 2001), and a Consultative Council for the Americas (in 2008).

4.2.2 Basel Committee on Banking Supervision (BCBS)

The headquarters and Secretariat of the Basel Committee on Banking Supervision (BCBS) are located at the BIS in Basel. The BCBS was established in 1974, after the financial market turmoil following the Bretton Woods breakdown in 1973. It shares similar functions with the BIS, as it focuses on the promotion of financial stability, standard-setting, cooperation, soft law, monitoring, and supervision. It therefore does not produce any directly enforceable law; rather, it generates guidelines and recommended practices for individual national authorities to be taken up according to their discretion.

6 BIS, 'Member Central Banks', <http://www.bis.org/about/member_cb.htm>.

7 Statutes of the Bank for International Settlements, 20 January 1930, amended 27 June 2005), Chapter II, Art. 14; Bank for International Settlements, 'About BIS: Legal Information' <https://www.bis.org/about/legal.htm>, last accessed 02/01/2017.

8 Statutes of the Bank for International Settlements.

9 Statutes of the Bank for International Settlements.

10 Statutes of the Bank for International Settlements.

11 BIS, 'About BIS: History—Overview', <https://www.bis.org/about/history_5new_fin_architecture.htm>, last accessed 02/01/2017.

4.2.2.1 Governance structure

Formal members include banking institutions of each member state, as well as regulatory authorities and international organizations. Each member has a vote, and decision-making takes place by consensus. The original BCBS members were Belgium, Canada, France, Germany, Italy, Japan, the Netherlands, Sweden, Switzerland, United Kingdom, and the United States (the so-called G10 countries), plus Luxembourg. In 2001, Spain was invited to join.[12] In March 2009, membership was extended to Australia, Brazil, India, China, Korea, Mexico, and Russia.[13] Further, in June of the same year, several additional countries were invited: Argentina, Indonesia, Saudi Arabia, South Africa, Turkey, Hong Kong SAR, and Singapore.[14] In 2014, Chile, Malaysia, and the United Arab Emirates were invited as observers.[15] The current membership structure of BCBS relies upon three categories. Full members correspond to a total of twenty-eight, whereby the previously marginalized countries examined in our volume are included with the exception of Vietnam and Bangladesh. As mentioned, the central banking institutions of Chile, Malaysia, and United Arab Emirates are included as observers. Finally, several supervisory groups, international agencies, and other bodies are taking part to the meeting, such as the BIS itself, the Basel Consultative Group, the European Banking Authority, the European Commission, and the IMF.

4.2.2.2 Main reforms

The transformation of the two original governance groups—the Core Principles Liaison Group and the Core Principles Consultation Group—can be seen as an indirect change of participation mechanisms. Their mission was to bring together supervisors from G10 and non-G10 countries (along with the IMF and the World Bank) for discussions on the work of the Basel Committee.[16] Core Principles Liaison Group members include all the previously marginalized countries examined in this volume except Vietnam and Bangladesh. Consultative Group members corresponded to twenty-one members in total, none of which are from our sample, but many otherwise small and/or peripheral countries are included. These two groups no longer exist and in 2009, in view of the expansion reforms, they were replaced by the Basel Consultative Group.[17] Additionally, the Basel Committee started the International Conference of Banking Supervisors (ICBS) serving as a forum for discussions and information-sharing among senior supervisors from many countries—over 100 in 2004, and which convenes every other year.[18] The joint establishment of the Financial

[12] As per correspondence with Karl Cordewener, BCBS Deputy Secretary General, 24 November 2015.

[13] BIS, 'Expansion of membership announced by the Basel Committee', 13 March 2009, <http://www.bis.org/press/p090313.htm>, last accessed 02/01/2017.

[14] As per correspondence with Karl Cordewener (n 12).

[15] As per correspondence with Karl Cordewener (n 12).

[16] Basel Committee on Banking Supervision, *Promoting Financial Stability*, Submission for the G-7 Heads of Government at the 1999 Köln Summit, March 1999, 3, 13, <http://www.bis.org/publ/bcbs48a.htm>; Basel Committee on Banking Supervision, *Report for the G7 Summit*, May 2005, 8, <http://www.bis.org/publ/bcbs113a.htm>, last accessed 02/01/2017.

[17] As per correspondence with Karl Cordewener, (n 12).

[18] BIS, 'Report for the G7 Summit', May 2005, <http://www.bis.org/publ/bcbs113a.htm>, 8, last accessed 02/01/2017.

Stability Institute (FSI) in 1999 by the BIS and the Basel Committee could possibly be considered as an opportunity for increased participation and access, given that it serves as a cross-border communication and collaboration forum among participants from different countries. It is, however, an informal channel.[19]

As for the non-state input, some progress can be observed over time, for instance, in the preparation of the Basel Accords, a crucial set of regulations in the banking industry. The preparation of Basel I (1988) took place as a closed meeting with limited transparency and no public input. Basel II (2004), instead, was developed with the use of notice-and-comment procedure allowing for public input. The Basel III framework was agreed in 2010–2011 and also included such participation opportunities. For instance, when the proposal for the reform was first issued in 2009, incorporated comments from a variety of stakeholders, and drew participation from a wide number of them. As a result, the revised proposal significantly differed from the original.[20]

4.2.3 FATF

The FATF was established in 1989 to set and implement standards against money laundering and terrorism financing. The FATF developed a set of recommendations for its members to follow, issued in 1990, and then revised in 1996, 2001, 2003, and 2012. The organization also monitors the implementation progress of its members, their anti-money laundering (AML) and counter-terrorist financing (CTF) techniques and measures, and it promotes the adoption and implementation of such measures internationally. FATF also collaborates with other international actors to prevent financial crime and to protect the international financial system.

4.2.3.1 Governance structure

The FATF plenary meets three times a year[21] and appoints a president (a senior official) and a vice-president from among its members once a year.[22] FATF also has a secretariat that supports the task force and the president; this service is provided by the Organization for Economic Co-operation and Development (OECD) in Paris. Its functions comprise supporting FATF activities, including its working groups; facilitating cooperation between the three types of members; facilitating communication to members and others; and managing and administration. FATF secretariat is funded by an annual budget supported by the member contributions according to the OECD scales, with the OECD channelling these services.[23] In addition to its AML and CTF activities, FATF also focuses on financial inclusion—defined as 'ensuring access to financial services at an affordable cost in a fair and transparent manner'[24]—and releases

[19] BIS, 'Report for the G7 Summit' (n 18), 9.

[20] Chris Brummer, *Soft Law and the Global Financial System: Rule Making in the 21st Century* (Cambridge University Press 2015), 203f.

[21] FATF, 'Who we are' <http://www.fatf-gafi.org/about/>, last accessed 02//201017.

[22] FATF, 'FATF Presidency' <http://www.fatf-gafi.org/about/fatfpresidency/>, last accessed 02/01/2017.

[23] FATF, 'FATF Secretariat' <http://www.fatf-gafi.org/about/fatfsecretariat/>, last accessed 02/01/2017.

[24] FATF, Topic: Financial Inclusion, 8 Financial Inclusion Publications, <http://www.fatf-gafi.org/publications/financialinclusion/?hf=10&b=0&s=desc(fatf_releasedate)>, last accessed 02/01/2017.

a number of reports on this topic.[25] Actors at risk of such financial exclusion are identified as emerging markets and developing countries.[26]

There were sixteen original 'full' FATF members; currently there are thirty-seven members.[27] From among the countries considered in this volume, BIC and Argentina are current members, but not Vietnam and Bangladesh. In addition, nine related organizations serve as associate members; and twenty-two organizations are involved as observers.[28] The former are mostly various regional groups, such as the Asia/Pacific Group on Money Laundering (APG) and the Caribbean FATF (CFATF). The latter tend to include regional development or central banks, as well as organizations such as Europol, Interpol, United Nations Office on Drugs and Crime (UNODC), Organization for Security and Co-operation in Europe (OSCE), and the like.[29] Not every or any country can become a FATF member. There are specific requirements of strategic importance to be met, which are assessed through quantitative and qualitative indicators. Quantitative indicators include their GDP; the size of the banking, insurance, and securities sectors; and population size. Qualitative indicators comprise their impact on the global financial system (including the degree of openness of the financial sector and its interaction with international markets); active participation in a FATF-Style Regional Body (FSRB) and regional prominence in and commitment to AML/CFT efforts; level of AML/CFT risks; and efforts to fight those risks. Other indicators relate to the level of compliance with financial sector standards and participation in the relevant international organizations.[30]

4.2.3.2 Main reforms

Reforms concerned first and foremost participation criteria. In 1991–1992, FATF expanded its nation-state membership from the original sixteen to twenty-eight members. This was followed by another expansion in 2000 to thirty-one members, with yet another expansion to its current thirty-seven members.[31] As regards non-state actors, a variety of organizations participate in FATF in the quality of observers; those are mostly intergovernmental organizations or large banks. These include the European Bank for Reconstruction and Development (EBRD), Europol, Eurojust, and the IMF. Regional banks from less-developed regions are included as well, for example, the African Development Bank and the Asian Development Bank.[32] As regards

[25] Asia/Pacific Group on Money Laundering, World Bank, Financial Action Task Force, *FATF Guidance: Anti-money laundering and counter-terrorist financing measures and Financial Inclusion*, June 2011, http://www.fatf-gafi.org/media/fatf/content/images/AML%20CFT%20measures%20and%20financial%20inclusion.pdf, last accessed 10/20/2021.

[26] Asia/Pacific Group on Money Laundering, *FATF Guidance* (n 25).

[27] FATF, 'History of the FATF' <http://www.fatf-gafi.org/about/historyofthefatf/>, last accessed 02/01/2017.

[28] FATF, 'The 36 Members of the FATF' <http://www.fatf-gafi.org/about/membersandobservers/>, last accessed 02/01/2017.

[29] FATF, 'The 36 Members of the FATF' (n 28).

[30] FATF, 'FATF Membership Policy' <http://www.fatf-gafi.org/about/membersandobservers/fatfmembershippolicy.html>, last accessed 02/01/2017.

[31] FATF, 'History of the FATF' <http://www.fatf-gafi.org/about/historyofthefatf/>, last accessed 02/01/2017.

[32] FATF, 'FATF Members and Observers' <http://www.fatf-gafi.org/about/membersandobservers/>, last accessed 02/01/2017.

civil society representatives or other non-profit participation, the 2002 Best Practices Paper on Combating the Abuse of Non-Profit Organisations publication, also known as Recommendation 8, can be seen as an indirect form of such inclusion. It requires a review of laws and regulations in order to protect the non-profit sector and prevent financial crime and establishes best practices. The paper was updated in June 2013, and further revised in 2014 with input from governments and private sector (including non-profit organizations).[33] Another and more direct development included a Consultation and Dialogue Meeting with Non-Profit Organisations (NPOs) in March 2015 in Brussels. The main purpose of the meeting was specifically to increase communication with non-state actor representatives on the relevant FATF work. Some specific issues discussed concerned Recommendation 8; the roles of states and the non-profit sector in protecting them against terrorist financing, as well as the ways in which to protect them against such abuse; assessing compliance with the FATF standards, including the standards concerning non-profit organizations; and the non-profit organizations' access to financial services. The meeting itself included twenty-one attending non-profit organizations, the representatives of which were able to engage in the discussions directly.[34]

4.2.4 FSF-FSB

The Financial Stability Forum (FSF) was founded in 1999 by the G7 finance ministers and central bank governors following recommendations by the president of the Deutsche Bundesbank, who was commissioned to suggest new structures to improve the international coordination among supervisory bodies and financial institutions with the goal of promoting financial stability. The Forum was very informal in nature and its purpose was to bring together the following actors: national authorities responsible for financial stability in treasuries, central banks, and supervisory agencies; sector-specific international groupings of standard-developing regulators and supervisors; international financial institutions engaged in surveillance, monitoring, and implementation of standards; and central bank expert committees concerned with market infrastructure and functioning.[35] Then, the FSB was established in 2009 to take over from the FSF upon the same structures with a broader mandate in the wake of the financial crisis. More ambitious than its predecessor, FSB is an international body that monitors and makes recommendations regarding various aspects of the global financial system. Its secretariat is located in Basel, hosted by the BIS.[36] In terms of legal framework, FSB was recognized as a not-for-profit association in 2013 under Swiss law.[37] The FSB functions include advising, coordination, standard-setting and soft law (in the form of guidelines), and monitoring.[38]

[33] FATF, 'Best Practices on Combating the Abuse of Non-Profit Organisations' <http://www.fatf-gafi.org/documents/documents/bpp-combating-abuse-npo.html>, last accessed 02/01/2017.

[34] FATF, 'Consultation and Dialogue with Non-Profit Organisations' <http://www.fatf-gafi.org/publications/fatfrecommendations/documents/npo-consultation-march-2015.html>, last accessed 02/01/2017.

[35] FSB, 'Our History' <http://www.fsb.org/about/history/>, last accessed 02/01/2017.

[36] FSB, 'Contact' <http://www.financialstabilityboard.org/contact/>, last accessed 02/01/2017.

[37] FSB, 'Our History' <http://www.fsb.org/about/history/>, last accessed 02/01/2017.

[38] FSB, 'About the FSB' <http://www.fsb.org/about/>, last accessed 02/01/2017.

4.2.4.1 Governance structure

The FSB organizational structure includes the plenary, the steering committee, standing committees, working groups, the regional consultative groups, the chair, and the secretariat. The plenary is the only decision-making body of the FSB.[39] Decisions by the plenary are taken by consensus.[40] There are now twenty-five member jurisdictions, including four of the originally marginalized stakeholders examined in this book (BIC and Argentina), but not Vietnam and Bangladesh, which remain non-members.[41] Membership also includes some international organizations, such as the BIS, IMF, OECD, and World Bank; international standard-setting and other more informal bodies, namely, the BCBS; CGFS; CPMI; International Association of Insurance Supervisors (IAIS); IASB; and the International Organization of Securities Commissions (IOSCO).[42] Members are represented by a quota system, with the number of seats reflecting financial and economic indicators.[43]

Thus, formal membership includes governments, which are represented by their finance ministry, plus a central bank or a financial regulator representative, and the main international financial institutions. Representatives of the private sector are informally included in the discussions, but they are not formal members. Similarly, there are no civil society representatives as full members. FSB nevertheless incorporates into its charter Article 3, which concerns external consultation in decision-making, involving consulting non-members and other external stakeholders. It also states a need for a structured process for public consultation on policy proposals; and for periodical reporting to its members and beyond for accountability purposes.[44]

4.2.4.2 Main reforms

In November 2008, the leaders of the G20 countries called to expand the FSF membership in order to strengthen its effectiveness and to develop and implement stronger regulatory and supervisory standards.[45] This membership expansion and formalization of the organization into the FSB has been the main type of reform across the organization's history, given its otherwise quite short timeline. There have also been some reforms in the participation process and structure, against the background of an upper limit of seventy plenary seats. Many emerging markets and developing economies countries only had one each, but now several of them (Argentina, Indonesia, Saudi Arabia, South Africa, and Turkey) hold two seats each (at the cost of the international financial institutions members reducing theirs from two to one).[46] As regards

[39] FSB, *Charter of the Financial Stability Board*, June 2012, 4 <http://www.fsb.org/wp-content/uploads/FSB-Charter-with-revised-Annex-FINAL.pdf>, last accessed 02/01/2017.

[40] FSB, About the FSB, Charter of the FSB, June 2012, <http://www.fsb.org/about/>, last accessed 02/01/2017.

[41] FBS, 'FSB Members' <http://www.financialstabilityboard.org/about/fsb-members/>, last accessed 02/01/2017.

[42] FBS, 'FSB Members' (n 41).

[43] FBS, 'FSB Members' (n 41), Art. 11.

[44] FSB, 'About the FSB', Charter of the FSB, June 2012, Arts. 3, 4 http://www.fsb.org/about/>, last accessed 02/01/2017.

[45] FSB, 'Our History' (n 37).

[46] FSB, 'Report to the G20 Brisbane Summit on the FSB's Review of the Structure of Its Representation, 15–16 November 2014' <http://www.financialstabilityboard.org/wp-content/uploads/Report-to-the-G20-Brisb

external participation, it appears that non-member authorities refer to finance regulators or ministries that are not from the member jurisdictions. This does not include NGOs or third-sector organizations, but it is apparent that some informal engagement with them does occur as well.[47]

4.2.5 G20

The Group of Twenty (G20) was established in 1999 for the purposes of bringing some of the key economies in the world to cooperate on global economic and financial matters. It was meant to expand from the similar goals of the G7 (created in 1976) to reflect the interests of a broader range of key nation-state participants so as to include emerging market economies' goals and perspectives.

4.2.5.1 Governance structure

There is no particular headquarters for G20. The members generally meet once a year (more often in case of special circumstances such as a deep crisis or recession) in various locations.[48] In terms of its legal framework, G20 is an informal forum and does not have a permanent bureaucracy, but instead has a temporary secretariat set up by the country that holds the presidency at the time. It does have a president, and the presidency rotates annually, with regional balance in mind. The presidential rotation proceeds in form of a 'troika' pattern, whereby the current president is supported by the preceding and future host country.[49] Moreover, the 'troika' rotation occurs according to regional groupings, so that a member from each group gets an equitable turn to participate.[50] The current members of G20 are: Argentina, Australia, Brazil, Canada, China, France, Germany, India, Indonesia, Italy, Japan, Mexico, Republic of Korea, Russia, Saudi Arabia, South Africa, Turkey, the United Kingdom, the United States, and the European Union (EU),[51] therefore including nineteen nation-states and the EU. The 'previously marginalized countries' examined in this book are thus included, except for Bangladesh and Vietnam.

The members—heads of state or government, finance ministers and central bank—are represented each with one vote; however, since the organization is highly informal, the decision-making process is more similar to consensus-building as a result of discussions. There is no charter nor legally binding decisions.[52] Other countries—and

ane-Summit-on-the-FSB%E2%80%99s-Review-of-the-Structure-of-its-Representation.pdf>, last accessed 02/01/2017.

[47] Correspondence with Joe Perry, Member of Secretariat, Financial Stability Board (FSB), 5–26 October 2015.

[48] Correspondence with Joe Perry (n 47).

[49] B20 Coalition, 'About G20' <http://www.b20coalition.org/about-g20.php>, last accessed 02/01/2017.

[50] CIGI, 'The Future of the G20 Process' <https://www.cigionline.org/publications/2010/11/future-g20-process>, last accessed 02/01/2017.

[51] G20, 'About G20' <http://g20.org/English/aboutg20/AboutG20/201511/t20151127_1609.html>, last accessed 02/01/2017.

[52] *The Group of Twenty: A History* <www.g20.utoronto.ca/docs/g20history.pdf>, 24, last accessed 02/01/2017.

international organizations—can be invited to participate in summits and ministerial meetings at the discretion of the host country.[53] Other opportunities for participation are obtained by international organizations. The G20 has been particularly close to the Bretton Woods institutions due to having been designed as part of their framework from its inception.[54] Other organizations include the FSB, the ILO, the OECD, the UN and its bodies, and the WTO, among others. Such international organizations are typically invited to attend some of the most important of the G20 meetings.[55] There is also a variety of committees and groups that provide advice to these institutions (so, their participation is thus very indirect).[56] Further in terms of non-state participation, there are a number of official engagement groups: B20, C20, L20, T20 and Y20, which include business, civil society, organized labour, academia, and youth as participants. Such groups collaborate externally with G20.[57]

4.2.5.2 Main reforms

Given the nature and the structure of the organization, there have been no membership reforms as such, only expansion over G7 to G8 and to G20 in terms of the member numbers, accordingly. The formal composition of the group remains unchanged since its inception.

4.2.6 The IMF

The IMF is a treaty-based body created in 1945 following the Bretton Woods conference to build an international framework for economic cooperation. The organization's primary official goal is to ensure the stability of the international monetary system, namely, with respect to exchange rates and international payments for transactions. The IMF seeks to accomplish this goal via surveilling the member-states' relevant activities and by advising them. Other functions include facilitating trade, research and analysis, adjudication, and enforcement (including sanctions). It also provides the members with (conditional) financial and technical assistance.[58]

4.2.6.1 Governance structure

As regards its governance, the highest decision-making body is its board of governors, where all members have a vote. The board has a governor and an alternate governor per each member-state. The governor is appointed by the member-state and is usually either a finance minister or a major bank head. The board's powers include approving quota increases, allocating SDRs, admitting or withdrawing members, changing articles of agreement and by-laws, electing and appointing executive directors, and

[53] G20 Information Centre, G20 Members <http://www.g20.utoronto.ca/members.html>, last accessed 02/01/2017.

[54] *The Group of Twenty: A History* (n 52), 43.

[55] G20, Turkey 2015, 'About G20' http://g20.org.tr/about-g20/, last accessed 02/01/2017.

[56] *The Group of Twenty: A History* (n 52), 42.

[57] *The Group of Twenty: A History* (n 52), 42.

[58] IMF, Factsheet, 'The IMF at a Glance', 16 September 2015 <http://www.imf.org/external/np/exr/facts/glance.htm>, last accessed 02/01/2017.

resolving issues pertinent to articles of agreement.[59] The board of governors is advised by two ministerial committees: International Monetary and Financial Committee (IMFC, composed of twenty-four members from the pool of 187 governors) and the Joint IMF–WB Development Committee (composed of twenty-four ministers of finance or development). Another important IMF decision-making body is the executive board, which handles daily business of the organization, including discussions of member-states' economies and global financial and economic policy issues. It is composed of twenty-four members that are meant to represent all member-states. Certain large economies, such as the US and China, have their own seats, while most others are grouped by four or more countries, with the largest constituency consisting of as many as twenty-four member-states. The board makes decisions via informal discussions (especially for preliminary analysis of complex issues). It also uses consensus mechanism or formal voting (often followed by summing up the views). It may also be useful to note that the IMF (namely, its boards of governors) usually meets with the World Bank group on an annual basis for any common discussions relating to their work. The IMF is currently governed by and accountable to 188 member-states. The representation is comprised of basic votes (the importance of which receded over the years) and the quota votes based on the aforementioned SDRs, which is based on a country's perceived contributions to the global economy. The membership is near-universal, thereby it also includes the countries designated as previously marginalized in this volume. Non-state actors, for example, individual civil society members or NGOs, are able to participate only informally.

4.2.6.2 Main reforms

The first thirty member-states acceded in 1945, with China and India among them. Brazil joined in 1946, Argentina and Vietnam both joined in 1956, and Bangladesh in 1972.[60] Nonetheless, the IMF has been criticized with respect to its problems of governance and accountability, along with those experienced by the World Bank. According to some commentators, the IMF has left much to be desired in its institutional structure, representation, and accountability issues.[61] In particular, it has been pointed out that the majority of the IMF votes and most of its power were in the hands of the richer countries (the minority), and specifically, that the US is the only country with an individual veto power. What is more, governments are represented in the IMF solely via finance ministers and central bankers, whereby these actors are only accountable to specific groups while possibly neglecting and under-representing the interests of other groups. Against this backdrop, a number of important reforms took place in 2008 and 2010.[62] Table 4.2 presents the

[59] IMF, 'Governance Structure' <http://www.imf.org/external/about/govstruct.htm>, last accessed 02/01/2017.

[60] IMF, 'List of Members', last updated 13 June 2012, <https://www.imf.org/external/np/sec/memdir/memdate.htm>, last accessed 02/01/2017.

[61] Joseph E Stiglitz, 'Democratizing the International Monetary Fund and the World Bank: Governance and Accountability' 16(1) *Governance* (2003) 111–139.

[62] IMF, The IMF's 2008 Quota and Voice Reforms Take Effect, Press Release No. 11/64, 3 March, 2011, <http://www.imf.org/external/np/sec/pr/2011/pr1164.htm>, last accessed 02/01/2017.

distribution of quotas (in millions of SDRs) by comparing the data from 2007 with those of 2017.[63]

Table 4.2 Quotas of IMF Members in 2007 and 2017

Member	Quotas in 2007	Quotas in 2017
Argentina	2,117.1	3,187.3
Bangladesh	533.3	1,066.6
Brazil	3,036.1	11,042.0
China	8,090.1	30,482.9
India	4,158.2	13,114.4
Vietnam	329.1	1,153.1

All quotas of the investigated countries increased—some spectacularly, namely those of Brazil, India, and China (BIC). The IMF Executive Board promoted these reforms in order to improve the effectiveness of governance, as well as to enhance the transparency and credibility of the institution. The work started with some initial preparations and deliberations in 2006 aiming to redistribute members' quota shares with their respective economic weight. It has been also planned to make quota and voting shares more flexible and responsive to any changes in the global economy, and to give more voice to low-income countries, especially when the IMF plays an important advisory and financial role in them.[64] The 2008 quota and voice reforms were quite significant in scale and amended the IMF's articles of agreement.[65] The results included an increased quota for fifty-four member countries (up to 20.8 billion SDRs), and nearly tripling basic votes (each member has an equal number of them). They also comprised a mechanism for keeping constant the ratio of basic votes to total votes and allowed executive directors (representing seven or more members) to appoint a second alternate executive director (after 2012 elections of executive directors).[66] Another result was to simplify members' relative positions and to increase transparency.[67] Although some members expressed reservations regarding the 2008 reform package, it was said to be a significant improvement of the status quo. According to the executive board, more work needed to be done on measuring openness on value added, intra-currency union flows treatment, financial openness assessment, and measuring variability. Some of this, in turn, required improvements in data availability.[68]

[63] <https://www.imf.org/external/np/fin/tad/query.aspx>, last updated 20/01/2017, last accessed 02/01/2017.

[64] IMF, *Report of the Executive Board to the Board of Governors, Quota and Voice Reform in the International Monetary Fund, 31 August 2006*, <https://www.imf.org/external/np/pp/eng/2006/083106.pdf>, last accessed 02/01/2017.

[65] IMF, *Report of the Executive Board* (n 64).

[66] IMF, 'The IMF's 2008 Quota and Voice Reforms Take Effect' (n 62).

[67] IMF, *Reform of Quota and Voice in the International Monetary Fund—Report of the Executive Board to the Board of Governors, 28 March 2008*, <https://www.imf.org/external/np/pp/eng/2008/032108.pdf>, last accessed 02/01/2017.

[68] IMF, *Reform of Quota and Voice* (n 67).

The 2010 reform package brought about changes in two main areas: quota shares and governance in terms of the executive board size and composition.[69] The reform consists of several components. To begin with, all quotas were doubled, and the New Arrangements to Borrow (NAB) rolled back to preserve relative shares.[70] Most importantly for the purposes of our study, there has been a significant shift of voting powers to emerging markets and developing economies countries (over 6%).[71] As a result, the top ten shareholders really represent the top ten countries in the world in terms of economic contribution (the countries include the US, Japan, four main European countries, and the four BRICs (Brazil, Russia, India, and China)). Thereby, 80% of the shift comes from advanced countries and oil producers, with 20% coming from other emerging countries.[72] In terms of governance structure, the executive board member size is to be held at twenty-four. However, it is now all-elected, there are two fewer seats for advanced European countries, and its composition is to be reviewed every eight years.[73] What is more, following Dennis and Robert Leech in their analysis of the IMF voting procedures, it is important to distinguish between a member-state's voting power and its weight.[74] They define power as the ability to make a difference to the outcome, and weight as simply the number of votes allocated by the rules. The authors claim that combining the provision of capital with voting rights does not necessarily result in a democratic and accountable system. It also results in gaps between a member's power and weight: for instance, the US has much more power than its weight. The authors use voting power analysis to examine the power relations of the IMF governance structures, as well as the effects of the membership and governance reforms. They also look at the two-level voting procedures, where member-states are placed into groups and each group's executive director (of the executive board) casts the vote *en bloc*, rather than each member-state casting it individually. This also has understandable implications for marginalizing some stakeholders. By being a part of such groups, some stakeholders give up their independent votes for the membership. On the other hand, being part of a particular group may strengthen it if members' goals can be satisfied.

Table 4.3 presents the changes in the executive directors resulting from the reforms.[75] As evident from the table, while some countries in our sample (BIC) benefitted from the quota reforms, others (Argentina) declined both in their weight and power. Bangladesh and Vietnam are not reported in their study because they did not feature among the most prominent countries. More specifically, the biggest gainers in the Executive Board are China, India, Mexico, Brazil, and the South East

[69] IMF, *IMF Quota and Governance Reform—Elements of an Agreement, 31 October 2010* <https://www.imf.org/external/np/pp/eng/2010/103110.pdf>, 1, last accessed 02/01/2017.

[70] IMF, *IMF Quota and Governance Reform* (n 69).

[71] IMF, *IMF Quota and Governance Reform* (n 69).

[72] IMF, *IMF Survey Magazine: In the News*, IMF Governance Reform, IMF Board Approves Far-Reaching Governance Reforms, 5 November 2010, <http://www.imf.org/external/pubs/ft/survey/so/2010/NEW110510B.htm>, last accessed: 02/01/2017.

[73] IMF, *IMF Quota and Governance Reform* (n 69).

[74] Dennis Leech and Robert Leech, 'A New Analysis of *a priori* Voting Power in the IMF: Recent Quota Reforms Give Little Cause for Celebration' in Manfred J Holler and Hannu Nurmi (eds), *Power, Voting, and Voting Power: 30 Years After* (Springer 2013) 389–410.

[75] Leech and Leech, 'A New Analysis' (n 74) 30–33.

Asian constituency; the biggest losers are industrialized countries, including the US. However, following Leach and Leach, the effects of the reforms upon the executive board power relations exist, but are small. The US voting power share remains much larger than its weight; all other members' voting power shares are a little lower than their weights; and many emerging markets and developing economies countries are still seriously under-represented, even despite the reforms (which yielded positive yet modest results). Even for the biggest gainer in the board of governors (China), the increase amounts to less than 1% of total voting power. Buckley joins Leach and Leach in criticizing even the 'historic' 2010 quota reforms as insufficient. Indeed, while the BRICs now have 14.17% (which is near the 15% needed for a veto), the US continues to be the only member with a veto power, and with by far the greatest power in the institution.[76] Buckley posits that such small reforms, while 'better than nothing', did not resolve the lack of balance of power.

Table 4.3 Executive Directors' Reforms

Country	2006			2012		
	Rank	Weight (%)	Power (%)	Rank	Weight (%)	Power (%)
Argentina	23	1.99	1.89	23	1.84	1.75
Brazil	21	2.47	2.33	18	2.81	2.67
China	17	2.94	2.78	11	3.82	3.63
India	22	2.40	2.27	17	2.81	2.67

To conclude, the IMF has developed some provisions for non-state actor participation, namely, to include civil society organizations (CSOs). The IMF definition of civil society includes 'business forums, faith-based associations, labour unions, local community groups, nongovernmental organizations (NGOs), philanthropic foundations, and think tanks' and excludes anything governmental, media, or individual businesses.[77] At the global level, CSOs are involved via communication with the IMF management, in meetings and forums. The public is formally allowed to participate in consultations with the IMF papers; it can also participate in meetings and seminars on specific policy or country issues, or to review its existing policies. CSOs can also attend seminars and provide comments. Additionally, the IMF and the World Bank together organized a civil society policy forum occurring alongside the annual and spring meetings of the organizations. CSOs can participate, as well as organize their own sessions. There is also a CSO fellowship programme during those meetings. The Independent Evaluations Office (IEO) has collaboration platform with CSOs[78]. At the country level, the involvement occurs via the IMF Managing Director or surveillance mission meetings with CSOs, for instance, at country visits. When dealing with

[76] Ross P Buckley, 'Reforming the International Monetary Fund' 3(1) *Global Policy* (2012) 102–107.

[77] IMF, 'Factsheet: The IMF and Civil Society Organizations, 5 April 2016, <http://www.imf.org/external/np/exr/facts/civ.htm>, last accessed 02/01/2017.

[78] IMF, 'Factsheet' (n 77).

developing countries on issues of poverty reduction, such meeting options also exist, notably for consultation purposes when designing the programmes. Finally, the resident representatives of the Fund interact with the local CSOs[79].

4.2.7 IASB

The IASB was set up for the purposes of ensuring transparency, accountability, and efficiency in global financial markets.[80]

4.2.7.1 Governance structure

IASB is an independent, private-sector body that operates in the framework developed by the International Financial Reporting Standards (IFRS) Foundation. More specifically, IFRS oversees the IASB in terms of its governance and support operations, namely through IFRS trustees, while the IASB itself functions as a standard-setting body that includes technical, as well as advisory and sector-specific, expert staff.[81] This structure also includes the monitoring board that serves as a link between the IFRS trustees and public authorities. Finally, the IFRS advisory council serves as a formal expert body to advise the IASB and the IFRS Trustees.[82]

Members are individuals, not countries, with occasional and very general 'geographical allocation', which is referred to by continental areas or regions rather than nation-states. IASB statutes mention: '(a) six trustees appointed from the Asia/Oceania region; (b) six trustees appointed from Europe; (c) six trustees appointed from North America; (d) one trustee appointed from Africa; (e) one trustee appointed from South America; and (f) two trustees appointed from any area, subject to maintaining overall geographical balance.'[83] Membership is, however, non-representative in the sense that the so-called independent experts are selected according to their professional competence and practical experience, rather than as delegates of a particular government, bank, or other institution. According to the organization's constitution, each expert has one vote.[84]

4.2.7.2 Main reforms

Since their establishment in 2001, the IFRS and IASB conducted a number of reforms. Few of them aimed at modifying stakeholder participation in a direct way, but some affected participation indirectly. As regards state actors, the establishment of new groups, boards, and offices can indicate an increase in indirect participation.

79 IMF, 'Factsheet' (n 77).

80 IFRS, 'About Us, Mission Statement' <http://www.ifrs.org/About-us/Pages/IFRS-Foundation-and-IASB.aspx>, last accessed 02/01/2017.

81 Tim Büthe and Walter Mattli, *The New Global Rulers: The Privatization of Regulation in the World Economy* (Princeton University Press, 2011).

82 IFRS, 'About Us: Mission Statement' (n 80).

83 IFRS Foundation, *Constitution, Revised and Approved by the Trustees, January 2013* <http://www.ifrs.org/The-organisation/Governance-and-accountability/Constitution/Documents/IFRS-Foundation-Constitution-January-2013.pdf>, last accessed 02/01/2017.

84 IFRS, 'Process for IASB Member Appointments' <http://www.ifrs.org/About-us/IASB/Members/Pages/Process-for-IASB-Member-Appointments.aspx>, last accessed 02/01/2017.

In 2011, the IASB emerging economies group was created, and in 2012, the Asia-Oceanic office.[85] There are also a number of recent developments in the IASB and the IFRS viewed as reforms towards a greater inclusion of non-state actors. Some of these developments reflect a fairly substantive review process, one of which is the creation in 2009 of the IFRS monitoring board, consisting of capital market authorities, whose main purpose of this board is to increase public accountability of the entire foundation.[86] The board reviewed the IFRS governance in 2010–2011 (including the issues of structure and representation) and published the review along with an action plan in 2012. The results contained a decision to include up to four more emerging markets representatives and to increase collaboration with IOSCO. Importantly, it introduced a periodic evaluation for existing members every three years.[87] The review itself was conducted jointly by the monitoring board and the trustees, and a global public consultation took place with a two-month comment period and a number of subsequent public stakeholder meetings in Asia, Europe, and North America. In total, a few hundred comments were received and considered when producing the resulting action plan.[88]

4.2.8 IOSCO

The International Organization of Securities Commissions (IOSCO) is an association that brings together securities regulators in over 115 jurisdictions, with regulators in emerging markets accounting for 75% of its membership. IOSCO serves as a standard setter for the international securities sector, thus promoting, developing, and implementing such standards. It also collaborates with the G20 and the FSB on the global regulatory reform agenda. The principles and objectives of IOSCO also provide a basis for evaluation of the securities sector by the IMF and the World Bank.[89]

4.2.8.1 Governance structure

There are several bodies within the IOSCO structure: presidents committee, IOSCO board, growth and emerging markets committee, regional committees, and affiliate members consultative committee. Currently, ordinary members of the presidents committee are the financial or securities' representatives of 126 countries or jurisdictions, wherein the six countries considered as previously marginalized for the purposes of this research (Argentina, Bangladesh, Brazil, China, India, and Vietnam) are all included. Associate members of the president's committee are the financial or securities' representatives of seventeen countries, regions, or organizations, such as

[85] IFRS, 'Process for IASB Member Appointments' (n 84).

[86] *Charter of the IFRSF Monitoring Board*, <http://www.ifrs.org/About-us/Documents/CHARTER-OF-THE-IFRSF-MONITORING-BOARD_rev_Feb_2016.pdf>, last accessed 02/01/2017.

[87] *Charter of the IFRSF Monitoring Board* (n 86).

[88] IFRS, 'Monitoring Board and the Trustees of the IFRS Foundation Announce Conclusions of Their Governance and Strategy Reviews, 9 February 2012' <http://www.ifrs.org/Alerts/PressRelease/Pages/Strategy-review-Feb-2012.aspx>, last accessed 02/01/2017.

[89] OICU-IOSCO, 'About IOSCO' <https://www.iosco.org/about/?subsection=about_iosco>, last accessed 02/01/2017.

the European Commission, European Securities and Markets Authority, OECD, IMF, etc.[90] The IOSCO board is a governing and standard-setting body composed of thirty-three to thirty-four securities regulators, with a chair and two vice-chairs.[91]

4.2.8.2 Main reforms

There were a number of smaller administrative reforms and some more important ones that relate to participation. The smaller reforms address the changes in by-laws and concern a variety of IOSCO's functions and governance procedures, namely, the 1996 reformed by-laws introduced decision-making through consensus in its preamble.[92] The 1996 reformed by-laws allow self-regulatory organizations (SROs) from countries with no governmental securities regulator to become ordinary members.[93] Also, derivatives regulators with supervisory responsibilities from countries where the national body is an ordinary member are now eligible to join IOSCO as associate members. Prior to the amendment, ordinary membership applicants had to state the dates and cities of the conferences they had previously attended; the 1996 reform makes it no longer mandatory. Although a rather symbolic change, 1996 by-laws make a greater mention of the technical and emerging markets committees and set out some rules for their functioning.[94] Further, as per section 17, the executive committee was reformed to consist of nineteen members, rather than eighteen. This includes the chairperson of the technical, emerging markets, and regional committees and thirteen elected ordinary members (including one by each regional committee). This expands the membership slightly and increases regional representation.[95] Voting allocations were modified for a number of members by appendix 4.[96] More important participation reforms, however, stem from the expansions of their numbers to the current inclusion of most of the world's capital markets—a series of expansions that occurred since 1999.[97]

4.2.9 The World Bank

Similar to the IMF, the World Bank (WB) started its history in 1944 at the Bretton Woods conference.[98] It is headquartered in Washington, D.C. and has over 120 offices worldwide, with two main official goals that have evolved into what they are

[90] OICU-IOSCO, 'About IOSCO' (n 89).
[91] OICU-IOSCO, 'IOSCO Board', <https://www.iosco.org/about/?subsection=display_committee&cmtid=11>, last accessed 02/01/2017.
[92] OICU-IOSCO, International Organization of Securities Commissions, Reformed By-Laws, <https://www.iosco.org/about/?subsection=by-laws>, 2, last accessed 02/01/2017.
[93] OICU-IOSCO, 'Reformed By-Laws' (n 92), 4.
[94] OICU-IOSCO, 'Reformed By-Laws' (n 92), 5.
[95] OICU-IOSCO, 'Reformed By-Laws' (n 92), 5–6.
[96] OICU-IOSCO, International Organization of Securities Commissions, Appendix 4—Voting arrangements under by-law 28.1 and 28.2, <https://www.iosco.org/about/?subsection=by-laws>, last accessed 02/01/2017.
[97] Tony Porter and Duncan Wood, 'Reform Without Representation? The International and Transnational Dialogue on the Global Financial Architecture' in Leslie Elliott Armijo (ed), *Debating the Global Financial Architecture* (SUNY Press 2002) 236–256.
[98] The World Bank, 'History' <http://www.worldbank.org/en/about/archives/history>.

today: ending extreme poverty and promoting shared prosperity by fostering income growth. More specifically, the Bank's tasks include international development projects, research and analysis, monitoring and surveillance, enforcement (including sanctions), and adjudication.[99]

4.2.9.1 Governance structure

Over time, the World Bank came to comprise five institutions in one: the International Bank for Reconstruction and Development (IBRD), International Development Association (IDA), the International Finance Corporation (IFC), the Multilateral Guarantee Agency (MIGA), and the International Centre for the Settlement of Investment Disputes (ICSID)[100]. The WB is a treaty-based organization with 188 member countries. The WB has two main organizational units: the executive directorate and the boards of governors. The executive directors consist of the WB president and twenty-five directors.[101] The boards of governors is the WB's senior decision-making unit, even if it delegated most of its powers to the executive directors.[102] In terms of its organization, the boards of governors includes one governor and one alternate governor appointed by each member country. Those individuals are typically the country's minister of finance, governor of its central bank, or a similar senior official. They serve for terms of five years and can be reappointed.[103]

Membership in the World Bank is open to all members of the IMF.[104] The membership is also slightly different for each of the WB Group (WBG) organizations. With regards to the IBRD, the assignment of the voting quota occurs on the basis of the country's quota in the IMF, in a similar fashion.[105] Full membership is limited to governments.[106] CSOs can participate informally by being involved in discussions, consultations, and information exchange. Such participation includes CSOs at global, regional, and country levels, trade unions, faith-based organizations, indigenous movements, foundations, and so on. Participation also includes monitoring the WB's activities and collaborating in operational activities in various fields of the WB's work. Some examples of CSO interlocutors with the WB include the Access Initiative, Action Aid, Environmental Defense, and others.[107] This collaboration results in a wide variety and a high number of publications and reports.[108] The WB and CSOs also

[99] The World Bank, 'What We Do' <http://www.worldbank.org/en/about/what-we-do>, last accessed 02/01/2017.

[100] The World Bank, 'History' (n 98).

[101] The World Bank, 'Boards of Directors' <http://www.worldbank.org/en/about/leadership/directors>, last accessed 02/01/2017.

[102] The World Bank, 'Boards of Governors' <http://www.worldbank.org/en/about/leadership/governors>, last accessed 02/01/2017.

[103] The World Bank, 'Boards of Governors' (n 102), last accessed 02/01/2017.

[104] The World Bank, 'Member Countries' <http://www.worldbank.org/en/about/leadership/members>, last accessed 02/01/2017.

[105] The World Bank, 'Board of Directors' (n 101).

[106] The World Bank, 'Member Countries' (n 104).

[107] The World Bank, 'Civil Society Organizations' <http://web.worldbank.org/WBSITE/EXTERNAL/TOPICS/CSO/0,,contentMDK:20127718~menuPK:288622~pagePK:220503~piPK:220476~theSitePK:228717,00.html>, last accessed 02/01/2017.

[108] The World Bank, 'Civil Society Publications on the World Bank' <http://web.worldbank.org/WBSITE/EXTERNAL/TOPICS/CSO/0,,contentMDK:20127029~pagePK:220503~piPK:220476~theSitePK:228717,00.html>, last accessed 02/01/2017.

collaborate extensively for consulting purposes on matters such as governance, access to information, climate change, the WB's strategies (including sector strategies such as agriculture or health), research, and studies such as the annual World Development Reports.[109] The WB manages its collaboration with the CSOs via 120 civil society focal points across the institution in over eighty countries and in its D.C. office, as well as regionally and in its operational and departmental units. The Civil Society Team (CST) facilitates coordination, formulates institutional strategy, advises senior management, provides research, and disseminates information.[110]

4.2.9.2 Main reforms

One of the main types of reforms that took place gradually over the years pertains to the expansion of the number of member states. Since the World Bank also includes four other sub-organizations, Table 4.4 summarizes membership years for the members on our 'previously marginalized countries' list in the respective organizations.[111]

Table 4.4 The WB Organizations Membership: Entry Years of 'Marginalized' Countries

Country	IBRD	IDA	IFC	MIGA	ICSID
Argentina	1956	1962	1959	1992	1994
Bangladesh	1972	1972	1976	1988	1980
Brazil	1946	1963	1956	1993	Not a member
China	1945	1960	1969	1988	1993
India	1945	1960	1956	1994	Not a member
Vietnam	1956	1960	1967	1994	Not a member

In 2010, the WB also underwent a reform of its quota allocations, similarly to the IMF. At same time, over the past two decades, the WB established funding mechanisms to facilitate non-state actor participation in its development activities. It provides grants either indirectly via governments, or directly via specialized mechanisms. Currently, about 10% of the WB's annual funding portfolio ($2 billion US dollars) is given to government-operated community-driven development projects or social funds.[112] The WBG established two semi-independent compliance mechanisms for its financed projects. The first mechanism is the Inspection Panel, established in 1993 as an independent forum for private citizens who may have concerns of their interests being harmed by a WB-funded project. The second mechanism is the Compliance Advisor/Ombudsman Office (CAO) established jointly by the IFC and the MIGA in

[109] The World Bank, 'Frequently Asked Questions' <http://web.worldbank.org/WBSITE/EXTERNAL/TOPICS/CSO/0,,contentMDK:20093224~menuPK:225318~pagePK:220503~piPK:220476~theSitePK:228717,00.html>, last accessed 02/01/2017.

[110] The World Bank, 'World Bank Staff Working with Civil Society' <http://web.worldbank.org/WBSITE/EXTERNAL/TOPICS/CSO/0,,contentMDK:20093777~menuPK:225317~pagePK:220503~piPK:220476~theSitePK:228717,00.html>, last accessed 02/01/2017.

[111] The World Bank, 'Member Countries' (n 104).

[112] The World Bank, 'Frequently Asked Questions' (n 109).

2000. The CAO audits IFC's and MIGA's compliance with environmental and social safeguard policies and plays a role of an ombudsman mediating disputes between companies, governments, and CSOs.[113] Additionally, and to promote a greater level of transparency and accountability, the WB expanded its information disclosure policy in 1994, and further updated it in 2001 and 2005. Further, in 2009, it adopted a new access to information policy with a 'presumption of disclosure', meaning that all WB documents are presumed to be public unless they are on a 'positive list' of exceptions. This 2009 information reform also includes an appeals mechanism for stakeholders searching unavailable documents.[114]

4.3 Concluding Remarks

This overview has shown that even in global finance governance—a hard case for stakeholder inclusiveness—there have been a number of institutional reforms to enhance the participation of previously marginalized stakeholders, corresponding to both state and non-state actors. Specifically, we identified four major types of reforms: reforms that relate to membership rule, namely to the extension of the membership base or quotas; voting reforms, that is, reforms entailing the modification of voting rights to empower previously marginalized stakeholders; the rearrangement of organizational structures to include previously marginalized stakeholders in boards of directors and the like; and informal changes to support participation, such as consultation and disclosure practices. At the same time, we observed that the scope of these reforms is relatively limited, as radical reforms are rare, many of them correspond to minor changes that do not fundamentally alter the logic of participation and representation, and the overall intensity of reform activity is moderate. What is the emerging picture with respect to the participation of previously marginalized stakeholders? Do reforms make a difference? First of all, an in-depth examination is required, as reforms appears to differ considerably across institutions and with respect to the concerned stakeholders. Then, after the case studies, a comparative chapter focusing on this policy area will provide a systematic examination of these patterns to bring together cross-case and within-case insights.

[113] The World Bank, The Inspection Panel, About Us, <http://ewebapps.worldbank.org/apps/ip/Pages/AboutUs.aspx>; Compliance Advisor Ombudsman, About the CAO <http://www.cao-ombudsman.org/about/>, last accessed 02/01/2017.

[114] The World Bank, Frequently Asked Questions (n 109).

5
Global Financial Governance and Banking Regulation
Redesigning Regulation to Promote Stakeholder Interests

Kern Alexander[*]

5.1 Introduction

The global financial crisis of 2007–2008 demonstrated serious weaknesses in global financial governance and led to comprehensive reforms of international financial regulation. The Group of 20 (G20) and the Financial Stability Board (FSB) have taken the lead post-crisis with efforts to make setting international financial standards more accountable and legitimate by involving more countries in the standard-setting process and by making deliberations more transparent and reflecting the views of a broader number of stakeholders. Moreover, at the Heads of State Summit in September 2009 the G20 initiated an extensive reform of international financial regulation with the overall aim 'to generate strong, sustainable and balanced global growth'. An important feature of the international regulatory reforms is the G20's stated objective to make financial regulation more 'macro-prudential', that is, to address risks and vulnerabilities across the financial system and broader economy that might threaten the stability of the financial system—and hence imperil the stability and sustainability of the economy. The crisis demonstrated the need to adopt a more holistic approach to financial regulation and supervision that involves linking micro-prudential supervision of individual institutions with broader oversight of the financial system and to macroeconomic policy. This chapter makes the novel contention that the crisis was the result not only of inadequate international regulatory standards (for example, Basel II), but also that it resulted from flawed international decision-making structures that failed to incorporate the views and perspectives of most countries and many non-state actors that represent societal stakeholders whose interests were not taken into account in the international financial standard-setting process.

As is highlighted throughout this book, the process of spreading and implementing effective regulation represents a central challenge in the governance of today's global financial system. This chapter contributes to the overall theme of this volume by attempting to shed more light on the decision-making processes in international financial standard-setting bodies such as the Basel Committee on Banking Supervision

[*] I am grateful to Bruce Pollock, Dr. Xenia Karametaxas, and Leonardo Gelli for research assistance.

Kern Alexander, *Global Financial Governance and Banking Regulation* In: *Rethinking Participation in Global Governance*. Edited by: Joost Pauwelyn, Martino Maggetti, Tim Büthe, and Ayelet Berman, Oxford University Press.
DOI: 10.1093/oso/9780198852568.003.0005

and to analyse critically whether or not the views and interests of other countries and stakeholder groups outside the Basel Committee are adequately taken into account in the development of international banking supervisory standards. Other chapters in this volume analyse the extent to which stakeholder groups contribute to, and have a voice in, international decision-making and standard setting in important areas of global public policy. After critiquing pre-crisis international financial standard setting, the chapter discusses how post-crisis international regulatory reforms have increased the number of countries involved in international standard setting from the small number of advanced industrialized countries pre-crisis to a much broader grouping that includes large emerging market and developing countries and representatives from regional trading blocs. This chapter submits that, although significant progress has been made in increasing the number of countries involved in international financial decision-making, these bodies still do not meaningfully involve other countries (outside of the G20) in decision-making, nor do they adequately involve non-state actors representing a large number of societal stakeholder groups in such decision-making. This is particularly the case with international financial bodies, such as the Basel Committee, which still do not adequately consult nor involve societal stakeholder groups, for example, environmental and social governance representatives, in their decision-making processes and institutional structures.

This chapter suggests that the inclusion of more countries and societal stakeholder groups in global financial governance will enhance the efficacy, accountability, and legitimacy of international financial regulatory norms. This is because stakeholder engagement is driven most often by enlightened self-interest, in which the effectiveness of decision-making depends crucially on the expertise and resources of societal stakeholders, who, as strategic actors, are in a position to influence more effective governance and because of their incentives, expertise, and resources are able more effectively to diffuse policies globally.[1]

The chapter first considers how decision-making has evolved in the most important international financial sector bodies, namely, the Group of 10 (G10) central banks with particular focus on how they have influenced the development of international standards of banking supervision. Second, the chapter considers the case of the Basel Committee on Banking Supervision and its role pre-crisis in setting international banking supervisory standards for all countries with market-based banking systems, but without the involvement or participation of countries who were not members of the Basel Committee or of non-governmental organizations (NGOs) that represent societal stakeholder groups affected by the standards. The crisis of 2007–2008 demonstrated how the Basel Committee's supervisory standards failed to estimate and manage the risks that toppled the global banking system. The section suggests that had decision-making been more accountable and legitimate in involving more countries and stakeholder groups from outside the G10 advanced economies, then the harshest aspects of the crisis could have been mitigated. Third, the chapter discusses how the post-crisis international regulatory reforms have expanded the number of countries involved in international standard setting, particularly the Basel Committee which now has close to thirty members in contrast to thirteen pre-crisis. Although

[1] Tim Büthe, Joost Pauwelyn, Martino Maggetti, and Ayelet Berman, 'Conclusion: The Participation of Marginalized Stakeholders in Global Governance' Chapter 25, this volume.

international financial committees are now consulting a broader number of countries, stakeholder groups that represent broader economic and societal interests are under-represented and often not consulted in international financial standard-setting activities, particularly regarding environmental and social sustainability concerns.

Further, Section 5.4 discusses the emergence of informal bodies of standard setters consisting of representatives from the financial sector, regulatory community, and stakeholder groups, which act outside of international financial standard-setting bodies. These new international bodies are beginning to influence the content of international norms in environmental and social governance. These initiatives, however, are limited and suggest that more should be done to integrate a broader array of international bodies and stakeholder groups into international financial standard-setting processes.

5.2 Global Financial Governance and the Rise of G10 Committees

In international finance, the globalization of financial services has necessitated that central banks and financial regulators develop cooperative relations to facilitate their oversight and regulation of banking and financial services. Beginning in 1962, the central banks of the ten leading industrialized nations began to meet regularly at the Bank for International Settlements[2] and other venues to coordinate central bank policy and to organize lending to each other through the General Arrangements to Borrow.[3] From the 1960s until 1990s, the G10 central bank governors represented the world's most advanced industrialized countries and were responsible for setting the regulatory agenda of other international financial standard setting bodies.

In the early 1970s, the International Monetary Fund (IMF) fixed exchange rate regime collapsed, leading many countries to delink the value of their own currencies to the value of the US dollar, thereby resulting in increased volatility in foreign exchange rates and considerable instability in global banking and financial markets. The ensuing volatility resulted in a clear and present threat to financial stability when the German bank *Herstatt Bankhaus* of Cologne Germany collapsed into insolvency in 1974 because of mismanaged foreign exchange exposures and the collapse of the Franklin National Bank of New York—a systemically important US bank—because of mismanaged foreign exchange exposures. This led G10 central bank governors to create the Basel Committee on Banking Regulation and Supervisory Practices (Basel Committee) in December 1974 to address cross-border coordination issues and to enhance cooperation between central banks and bank supervisors in overseeing cross-border banking activity.[4]

[2] The Bank for International Settlement (BIS) is an international organization created under the Hague Agreements of 1930 and the Constituent Charter of the Bank for International Settlements of 1930. See James C Baker, *History of the Bank for International Settlements* (Cambridge University Press 2002), 32. See Kern Alexander, 'Bank for International Settlements' in Christian Tietje and Alan Brouder (eds), *Handbook of Transnational Economic Governance Regimes* (Brill), 305-318.

[3] See Kern Alexander, 'The Fund's Role in Sovereign Liquidity Crises' in *Current Issues in Monetary and Financial Law*, Volume 5 (International Monetary Fund 2008) 131-190, 140-146.

[4] Charles A E Goodhart, *A History of the Basel Committee on Banking Supervision* (Cambridge University Press 2011), chapter 14.

Since the 1970s, the three main G10 (also known as 'BIS') committees—the Basel Committee, the Committee on Payment and Market Infrastructure, and the Committee on the Global Financial System—have become the most influential international financial standard setting bodies by exercising either direct or indirect influence over the development of banking, currency, market, and payment system regulation for all developed countries and most developing countries. The Committees have examined many important central banking and financial regulatory issues, as well as attempted to elaborate and promulgate best practices in supervision and regulation, the functioning of payment and settlement systems, and the overall operation of financial markets. They are usually chaired by senior officials of member central banks and are composed of experts from central banks, regulatory authorities, and finance ministries. In the case of the Basel Committee, members also include non-central bank supervisory authorities and other regulatory and economic policy experts. Members of the Committees have voting power and decision-making authority, while non-G10 country representatives are often consulted for their views on a variety of regulatory and economic issues. Frequently, special initiatives are undertaken to share experience with, and invite the opinions of, those not directly involved in the work of the Committees.

In promoting cooperation in their respective areas, the Committees determine their own agenda and follow their respective mandates to operate independently from their host organization, the BIS, which only provides its good offices for meetings as well as administrative and research support. Significantly, these Committees have resolved not to adopt legally binding international standards in a public international law sense, but rather to influence domestic regulatory practices and standards by adopting what has become known as 'international soft law'.[5] This practice is also observed in global health standard setting, where soft law is used as a tool to achieve compliance with global standards.[6]

Although international soft law standards have been praised as allowing international standard setters to respond flexibly to rapidly changing developments in financial markets and to diffuse standards to a wider number of countries,[7] they began to attract much criticism in the early 2000s after the Basel Committee proposed amendments (known as Basel II) to the 1988 Capital Accord, which were intended to apply to the G10 countries and indirectly to all countries that were members at the time of the IMF and World Bank (WB). This attracted significant critical comment—especially later after the crisis began in 2007 when Basel II's capital and risk management standards were shown to have failed to protect the banking system. This brought the work of the Basel Committee under close scrutiny by leading policymakers and regulators.

[5] See Kern Alexander, Rahul Dhumale, and John Eatwell, *Global Governance of Financial Systems: The International Regulation of Systemic Risk* (Oxford University Press 2006), chapter 3 (discussing international soft law).

[6] See Büthe *et al.*, 'Conclusion' (n 1).

[7] George Alexander Walker, *International Banking Regulation: Law, Policy, and Practice* (Kluwer 2001), preface, xxiii; see also Büthe *et al.*, 'Conclusion' (n 1).

5.3 The Basel Committee on Banking Supervision: A Case Study of Inadequate Stakeholder Participation

The Basel Committee has been the most influential of the G10 committees with respect to its impact on developing legally non-binding international financial norms of banking regulation, especially through the adoption of the *Capital Accord, the Concordat*, and *the Core Principles for Effective Banking Supervision (revised 2012)* and their impact on domestic regulatory and supervisory practices. The Basel Committee's most famous international standards agreement was the 1988 Capital Accord. The Capital Accord established a minimum 8% capital adequacy requirement on internationally active banks with headquarters in G10 countries.[8] Between 1999 and 2004, the Committee engaged in a lengthy and radical revision of the Accord known as 'Basel II'. Basel II was concluded and text finalized in June 2004.

Although the revision of the Accord involved non-members of the Basel Committee offering their views on the new capital framework, final decision-making and deliberation was controlled by the G10 countries (thirteen countries as of 2004) and decisions were taken in opaquely operated committees consisting of G10 members without consultation or involvement of countries outside the G10 or of civil society groups who represent societal stakeholder interests affected by the Committee's decision-making. The flawed decision-making structure of the Basel Committee not only produced inadequate regulatory standards for the countries that had adopted them (because the bank supervisors were under tremendous influence by the global banking interest groups), but also produced particularly pernicious standards for the many countries of the world not on the Basel Committee but who were subject to its standards—particularly developing and emerging market countries.

The financial crisis of 2007–2008 revealed that banks were exposed to significant liquidity risks, especially in their off-balance sheet exposures, and that they should have been holding more loss-absorbent capital.[9] The flawed decision-making structure of the Basel Committee contributed to the final agreement (Basel II) failing to incorporate realistic assessments of credit, market, and liquidity risks into bank capital models. Another major flaw in Basel II was that it allowed banks to rely excessively on risk-weightings of bank assets to calculate regulatory capital, resulting in procyclicality, which meant that banks were holding too little capital during market upturns and too much capital during downturns.[10] The procyclicality of Basel II also had pernicious effects on countries whose economies were more prone to volatility and booms and busts—specifically, developing and emerging market countries. Basel II also favoured

[8] See the 'International Convergence of Capital Measurement and Capital Standards' and their application based on the principle of home country control to banks based in G10 countries with international operations: Committee on Banking Regulations and Supervisory Practices (1988). *International Convergence of Capital Measurement and Capital Standards* (Basel, Switzerland).

[9] G20 Summit Communique, (September 2009, Pittsburgh), par. 13f.

[10] Kern Alexander, John Eatwell, Avinash Persaud, and Robert Reoch, 'Financial Supervision and Crisis Management in the EU' (Commissioned Report for the EU Parliament Committee on Economic and Monetary Affairs, EU Parliament 2007) < https://www.europarl.europa.eu/thinktank/en/document.html?reference=IPOL-ECON_ET(2007)400992(last accessed 23.10.2021).

large banks with sophisticated data management systems over small banks (mainly in developing and emerging economies) with less data in that it allowed banks with large amounts of credit default and loss data to input that data into their regulatory capital calculation models, while banks without the data (mainly smaller banks and most banks from developing countries) had to hold higher capital amounts based on the regulator's standardized model. The imbalance in how regulatory requirements apply between developed economies and smaller developing and emerging economies unfortunately persists in other areas of international financial regulation and in other areas of global governance outside of finance, which is repeatedly reflected in other chapters of this book.[11]

As discussed, the Basel Committee and other international standard-setting bodies have been characterized as 'networks' of international technical experts, which are not concerned with broader public policy or international political economy issues. Rather, they are at the 'coal face' of technical and regulatory standard setting. They form a type of epistemic community concerned with the stable and efficient operation of the global financial system and share common views and philosophies regarding the role of regulation and central banks in overseeing the operations of the banking and financial system.[12] The goal of these regulatory technicians in international bodies is to coordinate and cooperate with each other regarding the cross-border operations of banks and financial conglomerates with operations across financial sectors. These networks are composed of national regulators and supervisors—mainly from developed countries—who have established several international bodies to coordinate communication and the exchange of ideas among regulators on common issues of concern. These regulatory networks play an important role in disseminating information among regulators across financial sectors in different jurisdictions and, as is the case with other global standard setting bodies, serve as the principal diffusion mechanism of global standards.[13]

Before the 2007–2008 crisis, non-state actors that constituted industry-lobbying bodies (that is, the Institute of International Finance) for the banking and financial services sector played a role in international financial standard setting by sending representatives to participate in the deliberations of the Financial Stability Forum (FSF) and other international financial bodies, such as the Joint Forum on Financial Conglomerates, which consisted of representatives of the Basel Committee, the International Organization of Securities Commissions, and the International Association of Insurance Supervisors. Crucially, the FSF and the Joint Forum involved representatives of the banking and financial services industry in their deliberations, and it is commonly known that the major global banks were recruiting regulators who were involved in the Basel II deliberations to come to work for the banks after the Basel II agreement was concluded. The major banks were the only representatives from so-called stakeholder groups who were permitted to participate in international financial standard setting on the grounds that the deliberations were addressing merely technical issues of risk management and bank corporate governance and therefore were

[11] See Büthe *et al.*, 'Conclusion' (n 1).
[12] See, e.g. Büthe *et al.*, 'Conclusion' (n 1).
[13] See, e.g. Büthe *et al.*, 'Conclusion' (n 1).

not the concern of other societal groups not directly involved in the financial services industry. Despite the criticism of involvement by industry-funded stakeholder bodies in international standard setting because of their parochial interests that do not reflect broader societal concerns, it is submitted that their involvement can be seen as a positive development in enhancing stakeholder participation as long as it is based on transparent decision-making structures and sound accountability mechanisms that involve other non-state stakeholder groups on an equal basis.[14]

5.3.1 Decision-Making and Legitimacy of International Financial Standard Setting

The international financial bodies lack the formal requisites of international organizations, namely, that they are not subject to international law, and insofar as these bodies are neither composed of States nor founded upon an international treaty, they are typically not subject to minimum rules of transparency regarding, for example, the keeping of meeting minutes and other records concerning decision-making and deliberations. It is argued in some quarters that this lack of accountability in decision-making and operational processes can potentially undermine the effectiveness and legitimacy of the IFIs. Achieving legitimacy is another theme that resonates throughout this book and is an essential criticism of international financial bodies as well as standard setters in other fields.[15]

On the other hand, other commentators suggest it is precisely because these international standard-setting bodies are devoid of legal personality and excluded from the potential discipline of international law that they gain in flexibility and enhanced coordination benefits, by not being subject to formalistic rules of decision-making process and consultation, and therefore are in a position to devise international norms that turn out to be more effective in influencing state practice than traditional methods and procedures of public international law-making.[16] This flexibility offers the benefit of enhancing effectiveness and accelerating the process of influencing the creation of law, but simultaneously risks drawing criticism, since this process lacks accountability and traditional control mechanisms.[17] For these exact reasons outlined, the worldwide financial crisis called the efficacy of this flexible and unstructured decision-making framework into question and in particular has raised concerns regarding the accountability, effectiveness, and legitimacy of the IFI standard-setting processes.

The case of the Basel Committee and its adoption of Basel II is a case in point about how limited input from stakeholder groups—including the great majority of countries who were expected and pressured to comply with Basel II by the IMF and World Bank—can result in flawed and detrimental standards of regulation. To improve

[14] Büthe *et al.*, 'Conclusion' (n 1).
[15] Büthe *et al.*, 'Conclusion' (n 1).
[16] See Christopher Brummer, *Soft Law and the Global Financial System*, 2nd ed. (Cambridge University Press 2015), 338f.
[17] Büthe *et al.*, 'Conclusion' (n 1).

standard setting, it must be based on the principles of accountability and legitimacy. In assessing whether the Basel Committee's standard setting process complies with the principle of legitimacy, a closer look at the Basel Committee's deliberation and decision-making process is necessary.

The Basel Committee addresses issues that are of global concern to regulators and supervisors through a set of committees established to address particular issues of concern to bank regulators. After committees deliberate, they issue recommendations to the Basel Committee Secretary General and Deputy Secretary General, who are in position to table recommendations or issues of concern (including reports by external bodies) to the Committee. The Basel Committee's decision-making operates on a consensus basis. Although the Committee's decision-making has traditionally been secretive and substantially relied on personal contacts, it has become more formalized in recent years because of the considerable attention given to the deliberations over Basel II.[18] The Committee's decision-making places a great deal of emphasis on decentralized implementation and informal monitoring of member compliance. The Committee has sought to extend its informal network with banking regulators outside the G10 through various consultation groups. For example, the Core Principles Liaison Group remains the most important forum for dialogue between the Committee and systemically relevant non-G10 countries. Most recently, it has conducted seminars and conferences with many countries outside of the G20 through the BIS Financial Stability Institute that addresses implementation issues concerning international financial standards.

As mentioned, monitoring non-compliance has generally been a decentralized task that is the responsibility of Member States themselves, not international organizations like the BIS, or other international bodies. Nonetheless, the Committee monitors and reviews the Basel framework with a view to achieving greater uniformity in its implementation and convergence in substantive standards. To ensure that its standards are adopted, the Committee expects the IMF and World Bank to play a surveillance role in overseeing Member State adherence through its various conditionality and economic restructuring programmes. This extended application of the Basel Committee's standards to non-G10 countries has raised questions regarding the accountability of its decision-making structure and its suitability for application in developing and emerging market economies. In addition, because most G10 countries are members of the European Union, they are required by EU law to implement the Capital Accord into domestic law.[19]

[18] For instance, during the Basel II negotiations, the Committee put a number of issues for consultation and engaged in a public dialogue on its website through the publication of its quantitative impact studies, which measured the impact of Basel II on a hypothetical basis on bank capital levels, based on the reports of a number of banks in both G10 and non-G10 countries. See Basel Committee on Banking Supervision, QIS 3: Third Quantitative Impact Study (2003) <https://www.bis.org/bcbs/qis/qis3results.pdf>, last accessed 7/30/2020. Results regarding G10 and non-G10 countries are pinpointed on pages 3ff. and 13ff.

[19] See Capital Requirements Directive (CRD) IV, which consists of the Directive 2013/36/EU of the European Parliament and of the Council of 26 June 2013 on access to the activity of credit institutions and the prudential supervision of credit institutions and investment firms, and Regulation (EU) No 575/2013 of the European Parliament and of the Council of 26 June 2013 on prudential requirements for credit institutions and investment firms and amending Regulation (EU) No 648/2012 [2013] OJ L176/1.

5.3.2 Ineffective Standard Setting

Although the flexible and secretive manner in which the Basel Committee conducted its deliberations and standard setting was generally considered a strength in the effectiveness of its governance structures and decision-making processes, it also had the unfortunate result of insulating the Committee from outside public scrutiny that could have legitimately been carried out by a wider array of non-state actors representing stakeholder interests concerned with the development of banking and other financial regulatory standards. Indeed, the risk of regulatory capture and conflict of interests resulted from an opaque decision-making process in which only a few stakeholder groups (banks and their lobbying organizations) were allowed to influence Basel Committee standard setting. This is the main danger that exists in non-state actor participation in international standard setting. The pressure by special interest groups, as it occurred in the context of Basel II, was the manifestation of these risks that arose because of the asymmetric involvement of a few stakeholder groups (in this case, the banking industry) in the decision-making process in the absence of any involvement of broader societal stakeholder groups while decision-making itself lacked transparency and was not adequately scrutinized by the public.[20]

The implications for global financial governance of the international financial standards produced by the Basel Committee and other international financial bodies discussed above have raised important questions regarding the accountability, and legitimacy, of global financial governance. The growing importance of international financial standards and their acceptance by most countries for their domestic regulatory systems demonstrates the influence of international financial standard setting in its current guise. Nevertheless, international financial standard setting and related global governance structures failed in part to produce effective regulations and supervisory standards because the countries and the banking industry that developed the standards did not consult countries outside of the G10 industrial countries and did not (with the exception of the financial services industry) consult non-state actor organizations that represent broader stakeholder groups directly affected by international financial decision-making. Unfortunately, the exclusion of countries that were not members of the Basel Committee and neglecting the interests of other stakeholders is indicative of a more general trend in stakeholder participation and integration in the creation and implementation of international standards that, despite some improvement, that still persists. Other chapters of this book reflect this.[21]

5.4 Post-Crisis International Institutional Reforms

The global financial crisis of 2007–2008 resulted in the largest global economic slowdown since the 1930s and demonstrated serious weaknesses in global financial governance. The post-crisis international regulatory reforms have centred around the

[20] Büthe *et al.*, 'Conclusion' (n 1).
[21] Büthe *et al.*, 'Conclusion' (n 1).

international policy initiatives of the G20 and the implementation efforts led by the FSB.

5.4.1 The G20 Response

The financial crisis has triggered intense efforts internationally, nationally, and regionally to enhance the monitoring of systemic stability and to strengthen the links between macro- and micro-prudential oversight, supervision, and regulation. One such response is the widening of the international forum in which worldwide economic and financial policy issues are discussed from G8, the group of eight leading industrialized countries, to G20 in 2008. The transition from G8 to G20/ FSB is of great importance because at all G20 meetings 2008–2010, notably those in London (2009), Pittsburgh (2009), and Seoul (2010), the dominant topics were the financial crisis and the international response to it. And it was indeed decisions taken by the assembled twenty heads of state that kick-started many of the national and regional responses to the crisis discussed in this section. For instance, in motivating the steps it has taken to avoid a repetition of the crisis (or at least to mitigate the negative effects that a new financial crisis might have), the EU authorities regularly referred to commitments made at G20 meetings.

Since the crisis, the philosophy of prudential financial regulation has shifted away from a sole focus on micro-prudential regulation and supervision—the regulation of individual banks and financial firms—to a broader focus on the whole financial system and how it relates with the broader economy. This is called macro-prudential regulation. The redesign of international financial regulation—and the main objective of global financial governance—posed by the financial crisis will be how regulators and central bankers can strike the right balance between micro-prudential regulation and supervision with macro-prudential controls on the broader financial system and economy. The overriding theme of the international financial reform initiatives (for example, the G20, the FSB, and Basel Committee) that began with the G20 Summits in Washington D.C. in November 2008 and London in April 2009 has been how to devise effective regulatory frameworks that durably link micro-prudential supervision with broader macro-prudential systemic risk concerns.

5.4.2 The Financial Stability Board

The FSB is the international body that was given the responsibility by the G20 Heads of State to develop international financial standards that control systemic risk and provide more effective oversight of the global financial system.[22] The FSB was created at the G20 London Summit in April 2009 and was later established with legal personality by the G20 in the Cannes 2010 Summit Communique that stated that the FSB will have 'legal personality', which could potentially change the present system of legally

[22] See G20, 'London Statement' (4/2/2009), par.15.

non-binding international financial soft law standards. The Cannes Communique also provided for enhanced G20's/FSB's coordination with the International Monetary Fund on macro-prudential financial regulation and oversight of the global financial system. This raises important issues regarding the reach of FSB/G20/IMF decision-making and standard setting to countries outside the FSB and G20 and their impact on the broader economy, environment, and society. The G20 has addressed this concern partially by expanding the membership of the FSB and other international standard setting bodies such as the Basel Committee to include twenty-six member countries, the European Central Bank, and IMF. This expansion mirrors the more general tendency of incorporating emerging economies into international financial committees, which this book expands on in other chapters.[23]

The FSB has adopted twelve key standards for sound financial systems, all of which are legally non-binding soft law, but nevertheless are expected to be incorporated into the national regulatory regimes of all countries.[24] Since its establishment, the FSB has addressed a diverse range of regulatory issues, for example, it adopted key 'attributes' or principles governing effective bank resolution regimes in 2009 that allow banks experiencing financial distress to be taken into resolution without causing a systemic crisis. Also, banks were required under Basel III to 'move expeditiously' to raise the level and quality of capital, but in a manner that 'promotes stability of national banking systems'.

It has taken some of the work of the FSF forward by overseeing reviews of the system of supervisory colleges to monitor each of the largest international financial services firms.[25] It has developed guidance notes and drafted bank recovery and resolution plans to assist with its advice to national authorities for implementing the FSB *Principles for Cross-Border Cooperation on Crisis Management*.[26] It has established *Principles for Sound Compensation Practices*,[27] and has coordinated with other international financial bodies, for example, IOSCO, to develop a consistent regulatory framework for the oversight of hedge funds.[28] It also oversees the emergence of national and regional frameworks for the registration, regulation, and oversight of credit rating agencies and encouraging countries to engage in bilateral dialogues to resolve

[23] See Büthe *et al.*, 'Conclusion' (n 1). The same trend of including emerging economies can be seen, inter alia, in organizations such as the BIS, BCBS, FATF, IMF, and WB.

[24] Financial Stability Board, 'Key Standards' <http://www.financialstabilityboard.org/cos/key_standards.htm>, last accessed 6/18/2018.

[25] See the FSB protocol to establish colleges of supervisors for all major cross-border financial institutions. Financial Stability Board (2009) 'Overview of Progress in Implementing the London Summit Recommendations for Strengthening Financial Stability' (Report of the Financial Stability Board to G-20 Leaders), 2-3; and Financial Stability Board (2009), 'Guidance to Assess the Systemic Importance of Financial Institutions, Markets and Instruments: Initial Considerations' (Report to G20 Finance Ministers and Governors, International Monetary Fund, Bank for International Settlements, Financial Stability Board), 13. Other FSB initiatives include the Financial Stability Board, see Financial Stability Forum (2009). 'Principles for Cross-Border Cooperation on Crisis Management' <http://www.financialstabilityboard.org/2009/04/principles-for-cross-border-cooperation-on-crisis%2Dmanagement/>, last accessed 1/15/2015.

[26] Financial Stability Board (2009) 'Overview of Progress' (n 25).

[27] Financial Stability Board, 'Principles for Sound Compensation Practices: Implementation Standards' (25 September 2009) 14, <http://www.financialstabilityboard.org/wp-content/uploads/r_090925c.pdf?page_moved=1>, last accessed 1/15/2015.

[28] FSB, *Principles for Cross-Border Cooperation* (n 25), 11f.

home-host country issues involving inconsistencies and disagreements that may arise because of different regulatory approaches.

To enhance the legitimacy of the FSB standard setting, the G20 and FSB increased their membership to include twelve additional member countries, compared to the previous membership of the FSF and the G10 standard setting committees. The additional membership includes large developing and emerging market countries, such as China, South Africa, India, and Brazil.

5.4.3 Consequences of Global Financial Governance Reform

As discussed, the G20 and the FSB have adopted the overall objective of reconstructing financial regulation to address broader system-wide macroprudential economic and financial risks. This requires not only stricter capital and liquidity requirements for individual institutions, but also monitoring risk exposures across the financial system and the inter-connections with the broader economy. For example, the G20/FSB objective of requiring systemically significant financial instruments (that is, OTC derivatives) to be traded on exchanges and centrally cleared with central counterparties is an important regulatory innovation to control systemic risk in wholesale securities markets. Also, systemically important financial institutions are subjected to more intensive prudential regulatory requirements, including higher capital requirements and more scrutiny of their cross-border operations.

5.5 The Role of Non-State Actor Stakeholder Groups

The global financial standard-setting bodies discussed earlier have failed to interact with and coordinate their standard-setting activities with other relevant non-state actors that represent stakeholder interests on the international stage. An important question arises whether international financial regulation adequately addresses environmental and social risks—for example, the economic risks associated with the financial sector's exposure to high carbon assets and other environmental and social sustainability challenges.[29] Recent research suggests that international financial standard-setting bodies are not being used to their full capacity to address systemic environmental and social risks and that such risks are in the 'collective blind spot of bank supervisors'.[30] Despite history demonstrating direct and indirect links between systemic environmental risks and financial sector stability, evidence suggests this trend will continue to become more pronounced and complex as environmental sustainability risks grow for the global economy. For example, the Basel Committee has yet to take explicit account of, and therefore only marginally addresses, the environmental and social risks that could threaten banking sector stability. Nevertheless, some

[29] The challenge of addressing environmental systemic risks was first introduced in the literature by an empirical report, see Kern Alexander *Stability and Sustainability in Banking Reform: Are Environmental Risks Missing in Basel III?* (UNEP/Cambridge University Press 2014).

[30] Alexander, *Stability and Sustainability in Banking Reform* (n 29), 2.

international standard-setting groups are taking the lead in addressing environmental and social risks in the banking and other financial sectors. There have been a number of initiatives undertaken by industry groups consisting of financial institutions and investment firms to improve their management of environmental and social risks. For instance, the largest banks, financial institutions, and other multi-national firms involved in large-scale infrastructure development have adopted the Equator Principles, which apply to risk management 'for determining, assessing and managing environmental and social risk in projects'.[31] The Equator Principles are primarily intended to provide minimum standards for due diligence and monitoring to support responsible risk management decision-making regarding lending and investing in largescale infrastructure projects. They apply globally to all industry sectors and specifically pertain to four financial products: 1) Project Finance Advisory Services; 2) Project Finance; 3) Project-Related Corporate Loans; and 4) Bridge Loans. Different stakeholder groups provide guidance to financial institutions and other multi-national enterprises that have signed up to the Equator Principles (EPFIs) on issues such as biodiversity and ecosystem services, climate change, and social risks.

Similarly, the Global Sustainable Investment Alliance (GSIA) is a collaboration of the seven largest sustainable investment organizations in the world.[32] The GSIA's mission is to deepen the impact and visibility of sustainable investment organizations at the global level. The GSIA aims to influence investment firms, insurance, and asset management companies to 'integrate into financial systems and the investment chain' in order to 'represent and advance the sustainable investment community'.[33]

The Global Reporting Initiative (GRI) is another important non-state actor representing stakeholder interests affected by disclosure and reporting of the risk associated with unsustainable economic activity. The GRI helps businesses and governments worldwide to understand and communicate their impact on critical sustainability issues such as climate change, human rights, governance, and social well-being. The GRI Sustainability Reporting Standards are developed with multi-stakeholder contributions and rooted in the public interest.[34] The GRI mission aims '[t]o empower decisions that create social, environmental and economic benefits for everyone'.[35] It focuses on creating standards and guidance to advance sustainable development and providing the market with leadership on consistent sustainability disclosures, including engaging with stakeholders on emerging sustainability issues. The GRI also attempts to promote efficient and effective sustainability reporting by improving the quality of disclosures made using the GRI Standards, reducing reporting burden, and exploring reporting processes that aid decision-making. It also liaises with policymakers, stock

[31] See Equator Principles <https://equator-principles.com/>, last accessed 7/30/2020.

[32] See Global Sustainability Alliance <http://www.gsi-alliance.org/aboutus/>, last accessed 12/3/2019. These organizations are the Association for Sustainable & Responsible Investment in Asia (ASrIA), European Sustainable Investment Forum (Eurosif), Responsible Investment Association Australasia (RIAA), Responsible Investment Association (RIA) in Canada, UK Sustainable Investment and Finance Association (UKSIF), US Forum for Sustainable and Responsible Investment (US SIF), and Vereniging van Beleggers voor Duurzame Ontwikkeling (VBDO) in the Netherlands.

[33] See GRI, 'About GRI' <https://www.globalreporting.org/information/about-gri/Pages/default.aspx>, last accessed 1/15/2019.

[34] See GRI, 'About GRI' (n 33).

[35] See GRI, 'About GRI' (n 33).

exchanges, regulators, and investors to promote transparency and enable effective reporting of sustainability risks. The GRI produces the Sustainable Reporting Standards, which represent global best practice for reporting on economic, environmental, and social risks and challenges. In addition, GRI advises governments, stock exchanges, and market regulators in their policy development to help create a more conducive environment for sustainability reporting.[36]

Of relevance as a non-state international actor in global financial policy is the International Institute for Sustainable Development (IISD).[37] The IISD is a research institute based in Canada that influences the development of standards and understanding of sustainability issues. This independent and research-focused institute analyses many different kinds of sustainable development issues. The IISD's work is organized around five programmes: economic law and policy, energy, resilience of communities and ecosystems, water, and sustainable development governance knowledge. It produces reports that inform policymakers on areas of economic and financial policy essential to sustainable development, including investment, trade, public procurement and infrastructure finance, and sustainability standards. It also conducts research on the effect of financial regulation on the economy and has argued for the reform of the financial regulatory system in order to improve transparency of climate-related financial risks.

Other important stakeholder groups that consist of both state and non-state actors include the Sustainable Banking Network (SBN) of the International Finance Corporation—consisting of bank regulators of developing and emerging market countries, China, Brazil, and Peru, and a number of large banking groups and financial institutions and other stakeholder groups. These groups have adopted standards of bank corporate governance that incorporate environmental and social risk controls into the institution's risk governance strategy.[38] The SBN consults not only a wide number of countries that are normally involved in international financial standard setting, but also involves other non-governmental stakeholder bodies in their deliberations and outreach.

Under the SBN guidelines, bank supervisors in participating jurisdictions have engaged in a variety of innovative regulatory and market practices to control environmental systemic risks and to adopt practices that mitigate the banking sector's exposure to environmentally unsustainable activity and related social risks. A defining feature of the SBN is that its membership largely consists of regulatory officials and financial institution representatives from developing and emerging market countries and that none of their members are from central banks or other regulatory authorities of the G10 advanced industrial countries. This has allowed the SBN to define itself in a unique way by emphasizing innovative and forward-looking regulatory approaches

[36] See GRI, 'About GRI' (n 33).

[37] See International Institute for Sustainable Development <https://www.iisd.org/>, last accessed 7/30/2020.

[38] See Sustainable Banking Network <https://www.ifc.org/wps/wcm/connect/topics_ext_content/ifc_external_corporate_site/sustainability-at-ifc/company-resources/sustainable-finance/sbn>, last accessed 7/30/2020, and the Global Progress Report of the Sustainable Banking Network, October 2019, <https://www.ifc.org/wps/wcm/connect/topics_ext_content/ifc_external_corporate_site/sustainability-at-ifc/publications/publications_report_sbnglobalprogress2019>, last accessed 7/30/2020, 5ff.

that address (in many instances) broader stakeholder interests related to the environmental and social drivers of risk in the financial sector and the relationship with financial stability and sustainability.

SBN regulatory members—including Bangladesh, Brazil, India, Peru and China—have been concerned with how prudential bank regulation affects the green economy and inequality in society. Their regulatory initiatives have been based on existing regulatory mandates in Basel III to promote financial stability by identifying, monitoring, and managing banking risks both at the transaction specific level and at the broader portfolio level. What is significant about these various country and market practices is that the regulatory approaches used to enhance the bank's risk assessment fall into two areas: 1) greater interaction between the regulator and the bank in assessing wider portfolio level financial, social, and political risks, and 2) banks' enhanced disclosure to the market regarding their exposures to systemic environmental risks. These innovative regulatory approaches and market practices are the result of pro-active policymakers and regulators adjusting to a changing world. Other international bodies, such as the United Nations Finance Initiative, have sought to promote further dialogue between practitioners and regulators on environmental sustainability issues and to encourage a better understanding of these issues by financial regulators.[39] Although the Basel Committee has formed a committee to address certain areas of social risks, such as financial inclusion, it (and other international financial bodies) has not addressed broader environmental and social risk governance concerns. In 2017, a study[40] commissioned by the United Nations Environment Programme suggested that international financial standard setting could be made more effective and legitimate by recognizing some of the synergies that could be achieved by linking up the financial regulatory reform agenda with international reforms undertaken in the area of sustainable development, particularly regarding climate and environmental protection, financial inclusion, and related cultural sustainability issues. The UN report, however, stressed that none of the international financial standards it reviewed has an explicit reference to sustainable development. It argues that integrating sustainable development into the global financial governance agenda is crucial for ensuring a more robust, efficient, and sustainable financial system. Despite some efforts to this end, approaches are still uncoordinated and fragmented.

Accordingly, the UNEP report proposes to consider five pillars, or 'entry points', that might enhance the consideration and incorporation of sustainable development into international financial standard setting. The five pillars are systemic risk, transparency, governance, materiality, and culture.[41] Some countries have already begun to link financial regulatory objectives to sustainable development policies and practices. Acting under the guidance of the SBN, China, Brazil, and non-governmental actors,

[39] See United Nations Environment Programme Finance Initiative, 'Inquiry into the Design of a Sustainable Financial System', 23 January 2014; <http://www.unep.org/inquiry/portals/50215/Inquiry_expanded.pdf>, last accessed 1/15/2015.

[40] See Toby A A Heaps and Danyelle Guyatt, 'A Review of International Financial Standards as they Relate to Sustainable Development' (United Nations Environment Programme: Inquiry into the Design of a Sustainable Financial System, February 2017) <http://unepinquiry.org/wp-content/uploads/2017/02/A_Review_of_International_Financial_Standards_as_They_Relate_to_Sustainable_Development.pdf>.

[41] Heaps and Guyatt, 'A Review' (n 40), 5f.

for example, the GSIA, GRI, and IISD, have embarked on innovative risk-assessment programmes to assess financial stability risks associated with environmental and social sustainability concerns. These international initiatives spearheaded by important emerging market countries and non-governmental actors are beginning to influence state practice internationally and should be linked to and coordinated with the work of the traditional international financial standard setting bodies, for example, the Basel Committee.

5.6 Conclusion

The global financial crisis of 2007–2008 called into question the efficacy of the traditional global financial governance model's flexible and unstructured decision-making framework and in particular has raised concerns regarding the accountability and legitimacy of the IFI standard-setting processes. The discussion of the international financial standard-setting bodies' efforts in this area and the need for them to be more inclusive in their membership and to include more non-governmental stakeholder groups suggests that global financial governance should be more inclusive in who they involve in their decision-making processes. This point is also emphasized as one of the core conclusions of this book.[42] The case of the Basel Committee's adoption of the flawed Basel II agreement based on a loosely organized decision-making framework (which did not adequately incorporate the perspectives of non-G10 countries or of the relevant non-governmental civil society groups) demonstrated the failure of global financial governance prior to the crisis to address the risks that had imperilled the international financial system.

Although the number of countries involved in standard setting after the crisis has increased under the aegis of the G20, there remains inadequate involvement in the FSB and other international financial bodies by non-G20 countries. Moreover, non-state stakeholder groups should be consulted more and involved in international financial standard setting. For example, the international bodies concerned with sustainability issues should be expressly included in international standard setting. This would enhance the quality of the standards adopted by international bodies by providing the opportunity to address the broader economic and societal risks—particularly environmental and social risks—that can have a significant effect on financial stability, thereby contributing to more sustainable economic growth and financial development for all countries and stakeholder groups. The overall message, welcomed in many reform circles, is that economic policymakers should consider building institutional mechanisms to transcend national borders, which establish solidarity between the financial sector and all parts of society that are affected by financial risk-taking.

[42] Büthe *et al.*, 'Conclusion' (n 1).

B. DEVELOPING COUNTRIES' PARTICIPATION IN COMPARISON

6
Brazil and Argentina in Global Finance Governance

Henrique Choer Moraes and Facundo Pérez Aznar[*]

6.1 Introduction

The participatory status enjoyed by Argentina and Brazil in global financial institutions was upgraded in recent years, when both countries were recognized with a seat at the decision-making table as a result of institutional reforms for global finance governance. These reforms have, in a number of ways, been inspired by the pragmatic perception that some actors—excluded until then—should now be allowed in, so as to enhance the effectiveness of global finance governance. At the same time, some of these reforms—particularly those implemented in the aftermath of the 2008 financial crisis—have also responded to a call for increased legitimacy, with a view to granting voice to actors that had been at the receiving end of decisions taken by others.[1]

This chapter studies the interaction between the current position of Argentina and Brazil as participants in global finance governance and reforms adopted by institutions that give shape to such governance. In particular, it presents elements to discuss the extent to which Argentina and Brazil advocated for reforms to render global finance governance more open to excluded stakeholders. It asks if they considered themselves excluded stakeholders, and in the cases where—and to the extent that—reforms have been implemented, if these reforms contributed to increase in participation by Argentina and Brazil.

In order to address these issues, the chapter focuses on the following institutional changes to global finance governance: (a) the establishment of the G20 at the level of leaders, of which Argentina and Brazil have been original members; (b) the quota and governance reform of the International Monetary Fund (IMF), adopted in 2010; (c) the creation of the Financial Stability Board (FSB), an overhaul of the former Financial Stability Forum (FSF) with an expanded competence and membership,

[*] Henrique Choer Moraes is grateful for the suggestions and useful information collected from interviews with Lucio Capelletto, Carlos Marcio Cozendey, Paulo Elias Moraes, Norberto Moretti, Isabella Rosa Silva, David Salles Valente, and Carolina von der Weid. Facundo Pérez Aznar is grateful for the suggestions and useful information collected from interviews with Ayelén Amigo, Carlos Bianco, Ariana Destefanis, María Victoria Ferrari, Sebastián Kaufman, and Ariel Martins. The author is extremely grateful for the collaboration of Magdalena Bulit Goñi in the preparation of this research. This chapter covers developments through early 2018.

[1] For an overview of the reforms, see Olga Kovarzina and Martino Maggetti, 'Stakeholder Participation Reforms in Global Finance Governance' Chapter 4, this volume. Our analysis is informed by Mercy B DeMenno and Tim Büthe, 'Voice and Influence in Global Governance: An Analytical Framework' Chapter 2, this volume.

Henrique Choer Moraes and Facundo Pérez Aznar, *Brazil and Argentina in Global Finance Governance* In: *Rethinking Participation in Global Governance*. Edited by: Joost Pauwelyn, Martino Maggetti, Tim Büthe, and Ayelet Berman, Oxford University Press.
 DOI: 10.1093/oso/9780198852568.003.0006

which included Argentina and Brazil from its inception; and (d) the first enlargement of the Financial Action Task Force (FATF) to include Argentina and Brazil.

As a general assessment, which is elaborated in the rest of the chapter, we argue that Argentina and Brazil have traditionally taken a critical stance with respect to the structure and functioning of global finance governance. This approach has been in many ways influenced by their trajectories vis-à-vis the IMF, a key element in understanding how Argentina and Brazil shaped their views about the deficiencies of global finance governance as well as their proposals for improving this system. As traditional 'clients' of the Fund for most of their histories, the two countries unsurprisingly saw these discussions from the position of excluded stakeholders. But also in the case of the FATF—where the criticisms, if existing, were not so acute—Argentina and Brazil moved from a position of excluded stakeholders to full members.

The reforms examined in this chapter have certainly enabled an increased participation of Argentina and Brazil, but there are differences in the extent to which the two countries have taken advantage of these new opportunities.

Following this introduction, we take a closer look at the four institutions selected and the reforms they implemented, and we examine specific details and examples with a view to flesh out the argument that, in general, Argentina and Brazil have been given more participatory capacities and have taken advantage thereof. Section 6.3 discusses the main takeaway points emerging from the comparison of Argentina and Brazil, so as to provide an overview of how much (or if) reforms have enabled an increased participation of the two countries on global finance governance. The conclusion assesses the evolution of the participation of Argentina and Brazil and offers some reflections on the interplay between legitimacy and effectiveness behind the reforms undertaken in the cases studied.

6.2 The Participation of Argentina and Brazil in Global Finance Governance: Assessing the Impacts of Reforms

6.2.1 G20 Leaders' Summits

6.2.1.1 Background

The establishment of the G20 at the level of leaders of the largest world economies is one of the main reforms undertaken in global finance governance in the aftermath of the 2008 financial crisis. The competences of the G20 encompass areas that extend beyond finance and, although not setting standards, provide for a unique venue to coordinate policies at the highest political level as well as to oversee and steer the work of a number of international institutions. Brazil and Argentina have been participants since the first G20 summit, held in Washington, in November 2008.

When US President George W Bush invited leaders for what came to be the inaugural G20 Summit,[2] Brazil was holding the presidency of the G20 forum of ministers

[2] Statement by Press Secretary Dana Perino (G20 Washington Summit, 22 October 2008) <http://www.g20.utoronto.ca/2008/2008announcement.html>, last accessed 12/18/2019.

and governors. In this capacity, shortly before the Washington Summit, Brazil convened a ministerial meeting (São Paulo, November 2008) in which it sketched its views on measures required to deal with the crisis and its consequences. One of these views was the need to elevate the 'current G20 status to a forum composed by Heads of Government'.[3]

6.2.1.2 Importance of the agenda of the G20 for Argentina and Brazil/Alternative fora for influencing topics covered by the mandate of the G20.

The agenda of the G20 was initially set up with a view to responding to the challenges emerging from the 2008 financial crisis. The set of topics moving this agenda dovetailed with the interest of Argentina and Brazil to see a reform of global finance governance, so as to better reflect the reality of the world economy. The G20 provided both countries with a global forum to voice their criticisms and proposals for updating the global finance governance. Because the claims for reform were not coming across as effectively in other international financial settings, the G20 was viewed as the main forum to advance the views of Argentina and Brazil.

The agenda of the G20 has been broadening since the Washington summit from topics more related to financial regulation and macroeconomic management to areas more directly concerned with development.[4] The 2010 Seoul Summit marks a moment when development issues gained more prominence in the G20 agenda with the adoption of the Seoul development consensus for shared growth.[5]

For Brazil, the financial and non-financial issues in the G20 leaders' agenda find resonance on a number of its domestic policies as well as in positions advocated by Brazil on international fora. Participation of Brazil in the G20 has served to showcase at a global venue some of its successful experiences. This is the case with the G20 agenda items on food security—where Brazil has developed a number of internationally acclaimed solutions—and on the costs of international remittances.

Similarly, for Argentina, many of the topics discussed within the G20 have relevance mainly because of the financial aspects of the Argentine economic crisis of 1998–2003. As shown later, a number of initiatives submitted by Argentina stem directly from its own experience with a financial crisis. Perhaps the most evident sign of the importance Argentina ascribes to the G20 was its decision to take the rotating presidency of this forum, beginning in the end of 2017.[6]

[3] Brazilian Ministry of Finance, 'Global Financial Governance: Brazilian Proposal to the G20 Leaders Meeting on Financial Markets and Global Economy' (Washington, 15 November 2008) <http://www.g20.utoronto.ca/2008/2008proposals.html>, last accessed 12/18/2019.

[4] John Kirton, 'The G20, the G8, the G5 and the Role of Ascending Powers' (27 December 2010) 14 <www.g20.utoronto.ca/biblio/kirton-g20-g8-g5.pdf>, last accessed 12/18/2019.

[5] Tony Payne (2014), 'The Global Governance of Global Crisis: Why the G20 Summit was Created and What We Still Need it to Do' University of Sheffield, SPERI Paper No 17, 4 <http://speri.dept.shef.ac.uk/wp-content/uploads/2015/02/Paper-17-Global-Goverance-G20-Summit.pdf>, last accessed 12/18/2019; Lee Dong-hwi, 'G20 Seoul Summit: Assessment and Future Prospects' (IFANS, 12/13/2010) <http://www.g20.utoronto.ca/biblio/LEE-5-20101213-en.pdf>, last accessed 12/18/2019.

[6] Argentinian Ministry of Foreign Affairs, 'Argentina presidirá el G20 en 2018' <http://echin.cancilleria.gov.ar/content/argentina-presidirá-el-g20-en-2018>, last accessed 12/18/2019.

6.2.1.3 The establishment of the G20 and changes in the level of involvement and influence of Argentina and Brazil

Because of its particularly broad mandate, with implications for the work of other international institutions, the elevation of status of the G20 to a high-level political setting saw a clear increase in the involvement of Argentina and Brazil—not only in the forum itself, but also in global finance governance more generally. Participation as members in the G20 gave the two countries a voice on topics about which they previously had little or no opportunity to express their views; it also allowed them to raise the political profile of a number of topics that were either covered chiefly by a technical perspective at the finance ministers' G20, or not covered at all.

Brazil is an active member of the G20, although its engagement has shown a varying degree of influence over decision-making and agenda setting. The country was to a great extent successful in its efforts to strive for a reform of global economic governance, although Brazil was not alone in these efforts. While not always taking the lead in putting forward initiatives in the summits, Brazil is actively involved in advancing a number of items tabled by other members that converge with domestic experiences in Brazil or that give expression to Brazilian views and aspirations regarding the global agenda.

This type of engagement is illustrated by the following examples. First, as regards the global economic governance reform, from the Brazilian perspective the financial crisis gave credence to its views that global economic governance needed to be overhauled, in particular to bring emerging countries into decision-making in this area. Brazil was active in expressing this position.

Subsequently, already in the summits, Brazil took advantage of the visibility provided by the G20 leaders' meetings to reinforce—now to a higher-level audience—the claim that the Bretton Woods Institutions 'must adjust to the new status of developing countries as indispensable actors in an increasingly interdependent world'.[7] This claim was in fact not new, since it had been in the agenda of the ministerial G20 since at least 2005.[8] But it was then formulated openly as a political claim.

In what concerns the IMF, for instance, the Brazilian claim translated into a commitment adopted by the G20 leaders, in Pittsburgh, to 'a shift in quota share to dynamic emerging market and developing countries of at least five percent from over-represented to under-represented countries'.[9]

Participation of Brazil in the G20 has also enabled it to effectively voice its concerns—often along with other members—with respect to some proposals tabled in the context of measures to combat the crisis. For example, Brazil was one of the G20 members not to support the proposal to implement a bank levy.[10]

[7] Luiz Inácio Lula da Silva, 'The G20 in the Midst of the Crisis', G20 London Summit 2009.

[8] In 2005, the Ministers of Finance and Central Bank Governors had adopted the G20 Statement on Reforming the Bretton Woods Institutions (BWI), where it was recognized that the governance structure of the BWIs—both quotas and representation—should reflect the shifting changes in economic weight of countries. See G20 Statement on Reforming the Bretton Woods Institutions (Meeting of Finance Ministers and Central Bank Governors, 16 October 2005) <http://www.g20.utoronto.ca/2005/2005bwi.html>, last accessed 12/18/2019.

[9] G20 Leaders Statement: The Pittsburgh Summit (Pittsburgh Summit, 24–25 September 2009) para 20 <http://www.g20.utoronto.ca/2009/2009communique0925.html>, last accessed 12/20/2019.

[10] Katharina Gnath and Claudia Schmucker (2011), 'The Role of the Emerging Countries in the G20: Agenda-setter, Veto Player or Spectator?' Bruges Regional Integration & Global Governance Papers

Since the creation of the G20 Argentina has sought to have an important role on issues related to the financial sector, many of them drawing on its own experience.

Some of the positions voiced by Argentina gave expression to lessons it drew from its provision of assistance from the IMF. Thus, during the summit of 2008 Argentina warned about the risk of exacerbation of the international economic crisis and claimed for the regulation of the international financial markets and the reform of multilateral lending institutions. Argentina also suggested that the IMF should provide financial assistance to member countries to reverse the effects of the global crisis *without imposing policy demands*—a criticism many developing countries, not only Argentina, had with respect to the assistance provided by the IMF.

Aside from using the G20 to channel concerns regarding the practices of the IMF, Argentina also turned into proposals at the G20 a number of other aspects deriving from its experience with the 1998–2003 financial crisis. First, during the summit of 2011, Argentina raised criticism against the role played by credit rating agencies in the financial crisis. Second, Argentina sought to introduce the debate on sovereign debt and holdout bondholders at the G20, since there was a resistance to debate this topic at the IMF and the World Bank (WB), particularly the Argentinian proposal to implement an international system for sovereign debt restructuring. Third, in 2015, before the G20, Argentina supported the need to safeguard countries from vulture funds.

Another important issue of the agenda of the G20 was the debate on 'base erosion and profit shifting' (BEPS), whose inclusion in the agenda of the 2014 summit, in Brisbane—and the result obtained therein—were perceived as a success for the Argentine government. This topic reflected a particular domestic concern in Argentina, in view of tax avoidance strategies implemented in the country. However, it was also perceived as a stepping stone to enable Argentina to participate in the corresponding committee of the Organization for Economic Cooperation and Development (OCDE) and to amplify its presence in that organization.

6.2.1.4 Governance/policy-making of G20-related issues in Argentina and Brazil

Both in Argentina and in Brazil, policy-making regarding G20-related issues is done across the government.

The work of coordination and follow-up of Brazil's participation in the G20 leaders' summits is shared by the Ministry of Foreign Affairs—responsible for the agenda not belonging to the 'financial track'—and the Ministry of Finance. The Brazilian 'Sherpa', the representative of the leader in the intersessional period, is a high-ranking diplomat from the Ministry of Foreign Affairs.[11] In the performance of its role as coordinator for non-financial topics, the Ministry of Foreign Affairs interacts with other government agencies that may be relevant for Brazil's participation in the G20.

2/2011, 8 <https://www.coleurope.eu/sites/default/files/research-paper/brigg_2-2011_gnath_schmucker.pdf>, last accessed 12/20/2019; John Kirton, 'Brazil's Contribution to G20 and Global Governance' (18 May 2011) <http://www.g20.utoronto.ca/biblio/kirton-eneri-110518.html>, last accessed 12/20/2019.

[11] Brazilian Ministry of Foreign Affairs, 'O Brasil no G-20' <http://www.itamaraty.gov.br/pt-BR/politica-externa/diplomacia-economica-comercial-e-financeira/15586-brasil-g20>, last accessed 12/20/2019.

In the case of Argentina, this work is shared by the Ministry of Foreign Affairs and the Ministry of Finance, which also liaise with other government agencies such as the ministries of Agroindustry, Labour, Employment, and Social Security.

6.2.2 The IMF

6.2.2.1 Background

The case of the IMF, particularly the reform undertaken therein, shows a clear difference between the approaches taken by Argentina and Brazil. The factor that accounts for this difference is the break-up of Argentina with the IMF (until 2015) in pursuance of its view that the Fund held responsibility for leading the country to the severe 1998–2003 crisis.

In September 2003, refusing to make concessions to seal a three-year aid package from the IMF, Argentina defaulted on a $3 billion loan payment to the IMF. On January 2006, after years of an openly hostile relationship with the IMF, Argentina cleared its entire $9.81 billion debt with the institution. When announcing this decision, then-President Néstor Kirchner called the debt 'a constant vehicle for meddling, because it is subject to periodic reviews and was the source of requirements that contradicted each other and were opposed to the objective of sustainable development'.[12]

While Argentina opted for a strategy of 'non-participation' at the IMF following its financial crisis, Brazil sought to strengthen its financial position in the institution in order to claim more voice. When the IMF agreed the quota and governance reform of 2010—the main institutional change operated in the Fund in the past years—Brazil was seeing the materialization of a process in which it had been actively involved.[13]

Interestingly, rather than being the cause of an increased engagement of Brazil vis-à-vis the IMF, the 2010 reform is the culmination of a process marked by a drastic change in Brazil's role in the IMF, from a decades-long position of debtor to one of a provider of resources. Irrespective of whether the 2010 reform will yield more influence to Brazil—something that remains to be seen, since it entered into force in January 2016—the very fact that it was agreed is the result of an increased influence of Brazil in the IMF.

Under the 2010 reform, a realignment in the decision-making power was produced to the effect that more than 6% of quota shares in the IMF have shifted to 'dynamic emerging market and developing countries'. This means that Brazil, China, India, and Russia now rank among the ten largest members of the IMF. Before the reform took effect, Brazil was the fourteenth largest member; it is now the tenth largest. Brazil's quota shares moved from 1.782% to 2.315% of the total. Its voting power increased

[12] Alex Van Schaic, 'Argentina: Government Pays Back IMF Debt' (*Nacla*, 25 September 2007) <https://nacla.org/article/argentina-government-pays-back-imf-debt>, last accessed 12/20/2019.

[13] International Monetary Fund, 'IMF Board of Governors Approves Major Quota and Governance Reforms' (Press Release No 10/477, 16 December 2010) <https://www.imf.org/en/News/Articles/2015/09/14/01/49/pr10477>, last accessed 12/20/2019.

from 1.713% to 2.217%.[14] In contrast, the reform brought about a decrease in the formal participatory rights of Argentina.[15]

In December 2015 the change of government in Argentina made a radical transformation in the nature of the relationship with the IMF. Argentina expressed its intention to normalize its relations with the institution. On 9 November 2016, the Executive Board of the IMF concluded the first Article IV Consultation with Argentina after ten years where it praised the changes undertaken by the new government.[16] On the same date the IMF Executive Board lifted the censure on Argentina's official data.[17]

6.2.2.2 Importance of the agenda/issues governed by the IMF for Argentina and Brazil

As with many developing countries, the IMF has been a relevant actor in the debates of economic policies in Brazil and Argentina. Although the importance of the IMF has become less salient in the past years, it is still a reality.

From its accession in 1946 until mid-2000s, Brazil had been a client of the International Monetary Fund. In varying amounts, the country signed agreements with the IMF in 1958, 1961, 1965, 1966, 1967, 1968, 1969, 1970, 1971, 1972, 1983, 1988, 1992, 1998, 2001 and 2002.[18]

The year of 2005, though, saw a change in the relation between Brazil and the IMF. In March of that year, the Brazilian authorities informed the IMF that they would not need a new extension of the credit arrangement due to expire then.[19] Later, in July 2005, Brazil decided to an early repayment of some of its dues to the IMF.[20] Then, in December, Brazil announced that it was repaying all of its outstanding obligations to the IMF, which were not due before 2007.[21]

[14] International Monetary Fund, 'Quota and Voting Shares Before and After Implementation of Reforms Agreed in 2008 and 2010' <https://www.imf.org/external/np/sec/pr/2011/pdfs/quota_tbl.pdf>, last accessed 12/20/2019.

[15] 'Impact of 2010 IMF Quota Reform: Winners, Losers and Realignments' (*New Rules for Global Finance*, 24 July 2012) <http://www.new-rules.org/storage/documents/imf_reform/impact%20of%202010%20imf%20reforms.pdf>, last accessed 12/20/2019.

[16] International Monetary Fund, 'IMF Executive Board Concludes Article IV Consultation with Argentina' (Press Release No 16/500, 10 November 2016) <https://www.imf.org/en/News/Articles/2016/11/10/PR16500-IMF-Executive-Board-Concludes-Article-Consultation-with-Argentina>, last accessed 12/20/2019.

[17] International Monetary Fund, 'IMF Executive Board Removes Declaration of Censure on Argentina' (Press Release No 16/497, 9 November 2016) <https://www.imf.org/en/News/Articles/2016/11/09/PR16497-Argentina-IMF-Executive-Board-Removes-Declaration-of-Censure>, last accessed 12/20/2019.

[18] International Monetary Fund, 'Brazil: History of Lending Arrangements as of August 31, 2013' <https://www.imf.org/external/np/fin/tad/extarr2.aspx?memberKey1=90&date1key=2013-08-31>, last accessed 12/20/2019.

[19] International Monetary Fund, 'Statement by IMF Managing Director Rodrigo de Rato on Brazil' (Press Release No 05/67, 28 March 2005) <https://www.imf.org/external/np/sec/pr/2005/pr0567.htm>, last accessed 12/20/2019.

[20] International Monetary Fund, 'IMF Welcomes Brazil's Intention to Make an Early Repayment of its Outstanding Supplemental Reserve Facility Obligations to the IMF' (Press Release No 05/164, 14 July 2005) <https://www.imf.org/external/np/sec/pr/2005/pr05164.htm>, last accessed 12/20/2019.

[21] International Monetary Fund, 'Brazil Announces Intention to Complete Early Repayment of Entire Outstanding Obligations to the IMF' (Press Release No 05/275, 13 December 2005) <https://www.imf.org/external/np/sec/pr/2005/pr05275.htm>, last accessed 12/20/2019.

In 2009, in order to increase its capacity to support members affected by the financial crisis, the IMF adopted a new mechanism whereby its members were allowed to purchase notes issued by the Fund. Brazil agreed in 2010 to buy US$10 billion in notes issued in the framework of this operation.[22]

With respect to Argentina, from its accession in 1946 until mid-2000s, Argentina has also been a client of the IMF. In varying amounts, the country signed 18 standby agreements and 2 extended fund facility agreements with the IMF between 1958 and 2003.[23]

6.2.2.3 Alternatives to the IMF for influencing global finance governance

As highlighted, the emergence of the G20 as a high-level forum added more space to influence the work of the IMF. Argentina has taken advantage of its membership in the G20 to compensate for its strategy of 'non-participation' in the IMF, and examples in this sense are presented earlier. Thus, while not a participant in the process that led to the reform at the IMF, Argentina harnessed another reform—the creation of the G20 at the level of leaders—to pursue a strategy that arguably would fall within the competences of the IMF.

Brazil also used the G20 to influence the work of the IMF. One example where the G20 sought to steer debates in a direction not so aligned with the position of the IMF was in the area of capital controls/management of capital flows. This discussion gained prominence at a moment when the Brazilian currency was experiencing a significant appreciation due to an upsurge in inflow of foreign capital.

At the G20 Seoul summit (November 2010), the leaders acknowledged that under certain circumstances, 'emerging market economies with adequate reserves and increasingly overvalued flexible exchange rates' may resort to 'carefully designed macro-prudential measures'.[24] Brazil was one of the countries that supported inclusion of language to that effect in the final communiqué of the summit. Subsequently, Brazil was among the G20 countries pushing for a follow-up deliverable that would spell out the understanding expressed by the leaders, in particular, one that would endorse the idea that countries could resort to measures targeting the management of capital flows according to their specific circumstances.

By that time, the IMF was working on guidelines recommending measures designed to manage capital flows. Countries such as Brazil welcomed the fact that the IMF was more openly recognizing that capital controls may be needed in certain cases.[25] Still, developing countries were concerned with the IMF documents since they were viewed as possible constraints on the flexibility those countries enjoyed to make use of

[22] International Monetary Fund, 'IMF Signs US$10 Billion Note Purchase Agreement with Brazil' (Press Release No 10/14, 22 January 2010) <https://www.imf.org/external/np/sec/pr/2010/pr1014.htm>, last accessed 12/20/2019.

[23] International Monetary Fund, 'IMF Lending Arrangements' <https://www.imf.org/external/np/fin/tad/extarr2.aspx?=30&date1key=2005-05-31>, last accessed 12/20/2019.

[24] The Seoul Summit Document (G20 Seoul Summit, 12 November 2010) para 6 <http://www.g20.utoronto.ca/2010/g20seoul-doc.pdf>, last accessed 12/20/2019.

[25] Statement by Guido Mantega, Minister of Finance, Brazil (International Monetary and Financial Committee, Twenty-First Meeting, 24 April 2010), welcoming that the Fund was increasingly recognizing capital management measures as part of the tool-kit countries can resort to when facing surges of capital flows <https://www.imf.org/External/spring/2010/imfc/statement/eng/bra.pdf>, last accessed 12/20/2019.

capital controls.[26] Brazil was among those criticizing the fact that—following the push by some developed countries, which held a majority of the voting power—the Fund was used 'to impose their [developed countries'] agenda on developing countries that are not willing to face any restrictions on the liberty to manage the capital account', according to the then Brazilian Executive Director at the IMF.[27]

Discussions in the G20 led to the adoption in October 2011 of the Coherent Conclusions for the Management of Capital Flows. Among others, the document recognizes that '[c]apital flow management measures may constitute part of a broader approach to protect economies from shocks'.[28] The Coherent Conclusions also underscored that there 'is no one-size-fits-all approach or rigid definition of conditions for the use of capital flow management measures'.[29] This safeguards the understanding of countries such as Brazil with respect to the possible reduction of its leeway by operation of the IMF guidelines.

6.2.2.4 Change in the level of involvement and influence of Argentina and Brazil in the IMF

Since the 2010 IMF reform entered into force in January 2016, its consequences on the involvement and influence on the work of the IMF are still not clear.

But even in the case of Brazil, as argued earlier, the main angle to approach the 2010 reform is the process that led to its approval, particularly the changes in the participation of Brazil at the IMF that were taking place during this process. In fact, the evolution of Brazil's position in the IMF—from client to supplier of resources—corresponded also to a more engaged attitude with respect to the agenda of the IMF.

The more active role coincided in part with the moment when the initial waves of the crisis were becoming visible. At the IMF debates during this period, Brazil presented the crisis as a historical moment that called for addressing the legitimacy deficit of the IMF as well as for updating its working instruments and methods. The following examples show how Brazil translated these claims into concrete proposals.

First, as regards the quota and voice reforms, already in the years immediately preceding the financial crisis, Brazil was voicing the position that the distribution of IMF decision-making power in place at the time jeopardized the IMF's legitimacy.[30] For Brazil, it was urgent that the allocation of decision-making power in the IMF reflected

[26] Kevin P Gallagher (2012), 'The Global Governance of Capital Flows: New Opportunities, Enduring Challenges' University of Massachusetts Amherst, Working Paper Series No 283, 17 <https://www.peri.umass.edu/fileadmin/pdf/working_papers/working_papers_251-300/WP283.pdf>, last accessed 12/20/2019.

[27] Paulo Nogueira Batista Jr, 'The IMF, Capital Account Regulation, and Emerging Market Economies' in *Regulating Global Capital Flows for Long-Run Development* (Pardee Center Task Force Report 2012) 100 <http://stephanygj.net/papers/RegulatingGlobalCapitalFlowsForLongRunDevelopment2012.pdf>, last accessed 12/20/2019.

[28] G20, Coherent Conclusions for the Management of Capital Flows Drawing on Country Experiences (15 October 2011) <http://www.g20.utoronto.ca/2011/2011-finance-capital-flows-111015-en.pdf >, last accessed 12/23/2019.

[29] G20, 'Coherent Conclusions' (n 29).

[30] See Statement by Guido Mantega, Minister of Finance, Brazil (International Monetary and Financial Committee, Sixteenth Meeting, 20 October 2007) <https://www.imf.org/External/AM/2007/imfc/statement/eng/bra.pdf>, last accessed 12/23/2019.

the new economic realities, where developing countries had more influence than in the past.

This position would be articulated in more detail as the debates over the financial crisis evolved in the IMF as well as in the G20. Brazil advocated strongly in favour of a 'significant quota realignment [...] in order to better reflect the economic weight of member countries and to increase the quota and voting shares of developing countries'.[31] This claim was reinforced by Brazil at the IMF following the decision of the G20 Leaders (Pittsburgh, September 2009) that there should be a shift in the IMF quota-share 'of at least five percent' from over-represented to under-represented members.[32]

Brazil remained active in its efforts to see adopted the realignment of quota shares—the centrepiece[33] of IMF reform—until a decision to realign over 6% of quota-shares was finally agreed by the Board of Governors of the IMF and endorsed by the G20 leaders (Seoul, November 2010).[34]

Second, with respect to innovative lending instruments, since the initial debates about the role of the IMF in the financial crisis, Brazil was a leading proponent of new lending instruments.[35] In Brazil's view, these instruments: (i) should be able of quick deployment to economies in need; (ii) would do away with the unnecessary 'conditionalities' that had made the IMF a notorious institution in many developing countries; and (iii) should be designed so as to avoid or at least mitigate the 'stigma' often attached to countries signing up for IMF support.

A type of instrument with these 'innovative' features would contribute to renewing the importance of the Fund, aside from signalling that the IMF was capable of reacting swiftly and adequately to the crisis.

These discussions led to the creation of the Flexible Credit Line (FCL) in 2009, an instrument that 'provides large upfront support with no conditionality' whose access is 'quick and almost automatic'.[36] One of the innovative elements in the FCL is the concept of ex-ante conditionality, where eligible countries are those that meet pre-set qualification criteria, instead of ex-post conditions as under the traditional IMF programs.

Third, Brazil also took issue with working methods at the IMF. At the outbreak of the financial crisis, Brazil denounced what it believed to be a double standard between the IMF's approach to developing countries in the recent past and the way it was dealing with the crisis that was springing from developed countries. According

[31] Statement by Guido Mantega, Minister of Finance, Brazil (International Monetary and Financial Committee, Nineteenth Meeting, 25 April 2009) <https://www.imf.org/External/spring/2009/imfc/statement/eng/bra.pdf>, last accessed 12/20/2019.

[32] G20 Leaders Statement: The Pittsburgh Summit (Pittsburgh Summit, 24–25 September 2009) para 20 <http://www.g20.utoronto.ca/2009/2009communique0925.html>, last accessed 12/20/2019.

[33] Statement by Guido Mantega, Minister of Finance, Brazil (International Monetary and Financial Committee, Twenty-Second Meeting, 9 October 2010) <https://www.imf.org/External/AM/2010/imfc/statement/eng/bra.pdf>, last accessed 12/20/2019.

[34] Seoul Summit Document (n 24) para 16.

[35] Statement by Guido Mantega Minister of Finance, Brazil (International Monetary and Financial Committee, Seventeenth Meeting, 12 April 2008), when the topic was raised by Brazil as 'an idea that is still not on the agenda but is worth exploring ... ' <https://www.imf.org/External/spring/2008/imfc/statement/eng/bra.pdf>, last accessed 12/20/2019; see also Carlos Márcio Cozendey, *Instituições de Bretton Woods* (FUNAG 2013) 126.

[36] Statement by Guido Mantega (n 31).

to Brazil, '[u]ntil recently, the IMF had been focusing on problems in emerging market and developing countries. It seems to have devoted insufficient attention to major financial centers .... There is a clear need to strengthen the monitoring of these markets.'[37]

From Brazil's perspective, the narrow scope of attention that led the IMF to overlook the systemic vulnerabilities coming from developed countries was a symptom of an institutional bias. This bias, in turn, was the expression of an 'insularity of perspectives' that stemmed, among others, from the fact that the 'most important positions in the Management and staff continue to be held by nationals of a few advanced countries'. Unbalanced geographic representation in the staff affected the surveillance performed by the IMF. For Brazil, '[s]taff diversity needs to be at the forefront of efforts to strengthen surveillance and improve governance.'[38] Brazil associated the solution to this question to a redistribution of quotas and voting power in favour of developing countries.

6.2.2.5 Domestic policy-making concerning IMF issues in Brazil and Argentina

The Ministry of Finance is the main agency responsible for Brazil's participation in the IMF. An important actor in shaping Brazilian foreign policy in this area is the International Advisor to the Minister of Finance, a position often held by a senior diplomat from the Ministry of Foreign Affairs.

In the case of Argentina, the Ministry of Finance is in charge of the relationship with the IMF. The Central Bank of Argentina also intervenes in those issues that fall under its competence.

6.2.3 The FSB

6.2.3.1 Background

The creation of the FSB was a major institutional development that led to an increased participation of Argentina and Brazil in this forum, and it was established in 2009 by the G20 leaders as a 'successor' of the FSF.[39] One of the main differences between the two institutions is that the FSB was established with a wider membership than its predecessor. While Brazil and Argentina are among the twenty-five member jurisdictions of the FSB, they were not members of the FSF, whose membership comprised only the G7 countries, plus Australia, Hong Kong, the Netherlands, Singapore, and Switzerland.

[37] Statement by Guido Mantega, Minister of Finance, Brazil (International Monetary and Financial Committee, Eighteenth Meeting, 11 October 2008) <https://www.imf.org/External/AM/2008/imfc/statement/eng/bra.pdf>, last accessed 12/20/2019.

[38] Statement by Guido Mantega, Minister of Finance, Brazil (International Monetary and Financial Committee, Twenty-Fourth Meeting, 24 September 2011) <https://www.imf.org/External/AM/2011/imfc/statement/eng/bra.pdf>, last accessed 12/20/2019.

[39] Statement by G20 Leaders, 'Global Plan for Recovery and Reform' (G20 London Summit, 2 April 2009) section 15 <http://www.g20.utoronto.ca/2009/2009communique0402.html>, last accessed 12/23/2019.

6.2.3.2 Importance of the FSB issues/agenda for Argentina and Brazil

With a track record of financial crises in the 1980s and the late 1990s, Argentina and Brazil learned the hard way the importance of ensuring the stability of their financial systems.[40] The legal and institutional framework put in place in Brazil to avert the recurrence of these shocks helped it to weather the 2008 financial crisis to a great extent, at least in its initial stages.[41]

Despite the satisfactory domestic regulatory and institutional environment, Brazil's traditionally critical assessment of the legitimacy deficit in global finance governance extended also to the area of financial stability. In the initial stages of the 2008 financial crisis, Brazil advocated for an expansion of the FSF 'so that emerging countries' representation is considerably strengthened'.[42]

6.2.3.3 The creation of the FSB and the evolution in the level of involvement/influence of Argentina and Brazil

As a full member of the FSB, Brazil has used its participation at different levels. First, Brazil has been active in the FSB Regional Consultative Group of the Americas (RCGA), of which it held the presidency 2013–2015. Second, Brazil has also appointed officials to work on peer-reviews carried out by the FSB. Third, as is the case with other global financial institutions that Brazil has joined, its participation in the FSB has served as an opportunity to promote at the global level successful domestic experiences in the area of financial stability.

A case in point is the discussion on the reporting of financial transactions to trade repositories. The Brazilian legislation grants national authorities access to a comprehensive range of information regarding financial transactions. This 'granularity' enables Brazilian regulators to assess the risks of instability to its financial system in a more precise manner. What the regulators see is very close to what happens in the reality of the market. The murky, incomplete picture of the domestic financial system that emerged to the dismay of some countries' authorities during the financial crisis was not a problem faced by Brazil.

Brazil has drawn on this experience to promote the 'best practice' of adopting regulation that requires reporting not only 'over-the-counter' transactions with derivatives, but also other types of financial transactions. In its capacity as president of the RCGA, Brazil coordinated a stock-taking report on the practices of jurisdictions in its region on this topic. It was a study that deliberately focused on national reporting

[40] Luiz Awazu Pereira da Silva, 'Some Lessons of the Global Financial Crisis from an EME and a Brazilian Perspective' (IMF Conference: Rethinking macro policy III: Progress or confusion?, Washington, 14–15 April 2015) <http://www.bcb.gov.br/pec/appron/apres/Discurso_Luiz_Pereira_IMF_Wash_Conf_Rethinking_%2015-04-2105.pdf>, last accessed 06/23/2019.

[41] According to Nelson Barbosa, then Deputy Finance Minister, 'Brazil was frequently criticized for its interventionist and heavy financial regulation up until the 2008-09 world financial crisis. […] Part of Brazil's success in dealing with 2008-09 crisis came from the country's pre-existing financial regulation.' See Nelson Barbosa, 'A Note on Financial Regulation and the Brazilian Response to the 2008-09 Financial Crisis' (Workshop Financial Stability and Financial Governance, Brazil, 21 March 2011) <http://cnd.fgv.br/sites/cnd.fgv.br/files/Panel%203%20-%20Nelson%20Barbosa.pdf>, last accessed 12/23/2019.

[42] Brazilian Ministry of Finance, 'Global Financial Governance: Brazilian Proposal to the G20 Leaders Meeting on Financial Markets and Global Economy' (9 November 2008) <http://www.g20.utoronto.ca/2008/2008proposals.html>, last accessed 12/23/2019.

practices of financial transactions extending beyond the OTC derivative contracts.[43] It was a descriptive report, but a 'G20-plus' report as far as its scope is concerned. The recommendations of the report endorse the view promoted by Brazil that '[o]ne of the best practices observed in the Americas is that the reporting of an array of financial transactions allows for a more comprehensive monitoring of activities by financial authorities and may also facilitate the measurement of the interconnectedness between financial institutions.'[44]

The involvement of Argentina in the FSB might also be increased. In 2014 the FSB reviewed the structure of its representation and adopted measures that seek in particular to strengthen the voice of emerging market and developing economies (EMDEs). The measures included allocating an additional seat to the five EMDE jurisdictions that had a single seat each in the Plenary—Argentina, Indonesia, Saudi Arabia, South Africa, and Turkey.[45]

6.2.3.4 Governance/policy-making of FSB-related issues in Argentina and Brazil

Brazil holds three seats at the FSB, which are distributed to the Ministry of Finance, the Central Bank, and the Securities and Exchange Commission. Coordination to support Brazilian participation in the FSB is fluid especially because topics in the FSB agenda do not overlap significantly across these agencies. It is recognized, though, that most topics in the agenda fall under the authority of the Central Bank.[46]

Argentina holds two seats in the FSB: one for the Minister of Economy and Public Finances and the other for the Governor of the Central Bank of Argentina.[47]

6.2.4 Financial Action Task Force

6.2.4.1 Background

As far as the participation of Brazil and Argentina in the FATF is concerned, the major institutional change was the expansion of its membership in 2000. Until their accession, Argentina and Brazil had little (or no) say over deliberations by the FATF. The motivation of the two countries to apply for membership is in a way associated to the

[43] 'The RCGA [Regional Consultative Group of the Americas] survey covered the reporting of a wide array of financial transactions to TRs [trade repositories] in the Americas, expanding the approach adopted by international bodies on the G20 Leaders' statements on reporting OTC derivatives to TRs.' See Financial Stability Board Regional Consultative Group for the Americas, 'Reporting Financial Transactions to Trade Repositories in the Americas' (9 October 2015) 47 <http://www.fsb.org/wp-content/uploads/Reporting-Financial-Transactions-to-Trade-Repositories-in-the-Americas.pdf>, last accessed 12/23/2019.

[44] Financial Stability Board RCGA, 'Reporting Financial Transactions' (n 44), 47.

[45] Financial Stability Board, 'Report to the G20 Brisbane Summit on the FSB's review of the structure of its representation' (15–16 November 2014) <http://www.fsb.org/wp-content/uploads/Report-to-the-G20-Brisbane-Summit-on-the-FSB%E2%80%99s-Review-of-the-Structure-of-its-Representation.pdf>, last accessed 12/23/2019.

[46] Brazilian Ministry of Finance, 'Conselho de Estabilidade Financeira – FSB: A participação brasileira na regulação financeira internacional' <http://www.fazenda.gov.br/assuntos/atuacao-internacional/cooperacao-internacional/conselho-de-estabilidade-financeira-2013-fsb>, last accessed 12/23/2019.

[47] Financial Stability Board, '3rd Annual Report, 1 April 2015–31 March 2016' (25 July 2016) <http://www.fsb.org/wp-content/uploads/FSB-3rd-Annual-Report.pdf>, last accessed 12/23/2019.

perception that it would be in their interest to endorse the commitments governed by the FATF.

6.2.4.2 Importance of the FATF issues/agenda for Argentina and Brazil

The accession of Brazil and Argentina to the FATF was a key component in raising the importance of anti-money-laundering (AML) measures in the agenda of these two countries, both among public authorities and the private sector.

Brazil enacted its first legislation dedicated to anti-money laundering in 1998, shortly before being admitted as a member to the FATF. The adoption of the legislation was part of a package of measures promoted at the time with a view to better position the country in a globalized economy, measures that focused mainly on modernizing relevant laws and institutions.[48]

As for Argentina, the first record of a legislation related to anti-money laundering—even marginally—was in 1988 through the ratification of the United Nations Convention on psychotropic substances, which incorporates the concept of money laundering. The accession to the FATF—as well as a negative evaluation of Argentina in 2009—resulted in the 2011 reform of the anti-money-laundering norms.[49]

The increased importance of FATF-related issues in the Brazilian agenda was the result of a deliberate political option made by Brazilian authorities to embrace the obligations stemming from the FATF membership.[50] One of the reasons for this emphasis is the link between money laundering and corruption,[51] an area that has ranked as a priority in the agenda of law enforcement authorities in Brazil.

Furthermore, from an international perspective, domestic legislation on AML-CFT is one of the international financial standards assessed by the IMF and the WB under the Financial Sector Assessment Program (FSAP) and the Report on the Observance of Standards and Codes (ROSC). This element serves as an additional stimulus for the implementation of FATF standards.

6.2.4.3 Alternative settings to FATF for influencing global governance in the areas of anti-money laundering/counter-terrorism financing

In the course of more than twenty-five years since its establishment, the FATF has managed to position itself as an important institution in the landscape of global finance governance.[52] The solid status enjoyed by the FATF as the standard-setter on AML and CFT is partially due to the collaboration it has forged with international settings such as the United Nations Security Council (UNSC) and the IMF.

[48] Luiz Maria Corrêa, *O Grupo de Ação Financeira Internacional (GAFI): Organizações internacionais e crime transnacional* (FUNAG 2013) 171.

[49] Law No 26.683: Criminal Code Amendment 2011 (Modificación del Código Penal, Argentina).

[50] In a study comparing Brazilian and Argentinian measures adopted subsequently to their accessions to the FATF, Maira Machado argues that Brazil has equipped itself with a satisfactory domestic regime to implement the FATF obligations as a result of a clear political commitment. In contrast, in Argentina the domestic regime has advanced reluctantly, and in some instances not much at all. See Maira Machado (2011), 'Similar in Their Differences: Transnational Legal Processes Addressing Money Laundering in Brazil and Argentina' 37(2) *Law & Social Inquiry* 330–366.

[51] Machado, 'Similar in their Differences' (n 50), 358.

[52] Kenneth Blazejewski (2008), 'The FATF and its Institutional Partners: Improving the Effectiveness and Accountability of Transgovernmental Networks' 22(1) *Temple International Law Journal* 1–61.

Although the FATF Recommendations nominally rank as soft law, they certainly acquired a different pedigree when the UNSC strongly urged UN members to implement them, for example, in Resolutions 1617 (2005) and 2083 (2012). The UNSC also acknowledged the importance of guidance prepared by the FATF on the implementation of financial aspects of Resolution 1737, which imposed sanctions on Iran.[53]

The FATF recommendations also received an important boost when they were recognized, as mentioned earlier, as one of the international standards assessed by the IMF—and the WB, in some cases—under the FSAP and the ROSC, first on a pilot basis starting in 2001, later, in 2004, in the regular assessment work of the IMF.[54]

In an interesting manner, the collaboration the FATF managed to forge with the UNSC and the IMF opens the possibility that the latter settings may be used as venues to influence the FATF.

This is what occurred in the IMF in 2001, when a number of developing countries led by Brazil raised concerns regarding the 'blacklisting' process the FATF was pursuing against non-members. Aware of the interest of the FATF to have its standards incorporated into the FSAP and the ROSCs, Brazil brought the concern of developing countries to the attention of the IMF expressing the position that '[a] n approach based on international cooperation is preferable to one based on confrontation.'[55] Later, in 2002, the Boards of the Fund and the Bank conditionally endorsed a pilot-program to consider the FATF standards in the ROSCs. One of the conditions was that the FATF did not perform the 'blacklist' procedures at least for the period during which the pilot-program was carried out.[56]

Another institutional avenue that has been used to affect the work of the FATF is the G20, particularly through the FSB. One of the topics the G20 mandated the FSB to focus on is the decline in correspondent banking, an area that affects money-laundering discussions. In November 2015 the FSB prepared a report that takes stock of the situation of this issue across international institutions, including the FATF.[57]

6.2.4.4 Change in the level of involvement and influence of Argentina and Brazil in the FATF

Soon after joining the FATF, Brazil and Argentina led the efforts to create a South American FATF-Style Regional Body (FSRB),[58] which came to be the GAFISUD (now

[53] UNSC Resolution 1803 (3 March 2008) UN Doc S/RES/1803, para 10.

[54] International Monetary Fund, 'Review of the Fund's Strategy on Anti-Money Laundering and Combating the Financing of Terrorism' (IMF Policy Paper 2014) 7.76 <https://www.imf.org/external/np/pp/eng/2014/022014a.pdf>, last accessed 12/23/2019.

[55] Statement by Pedro Malan, Minister of Finance, Brazil (International Monetary and Financial Committee, Third Meeting, 29 April 2001) para 30 <https://www.imf.org/external/spring/2001/imfc/bra.htm>, last accessed 12/23/2019.

[56] International Monetary Fund and the World Bank, 'Intensified Work on Anti-Money Laundering and Combating the Financing of Terrorism (AML/CFT)—Joint Progress Report on the Work of the IMF and World Bank' (25 September 2002) <https://www.imf.org/external/np/mae/aml/2002/eng/092502.htm>, last accessed 12/23/2019.

[57] Financial Stability Board, 'Report to the G20 on actions taken to assess and address the decline in correspondent banking' (6 November 2015) <http://www.fsb.org/wp-content/uploads/Correspondent-banking-report-to-G20-Summit.pdf>, last accessed 12/23/2019.

[58] Financial Action Task Force, 'Annual Report 1999–2000' (June 2000) 16.

GAFILAT). The FSRBs are a key component of the institutional network the FATF employs to disseminate and enforce its standards to non-members.

Brazil chaired the GAFISUD in 2006 during which period it sought to share with its neighbours the Brazilian experience in implementing the FATF recommendations.[59] In 2008– 2009 Brazil held the presidency of the FATF. One of the priorities of the Brazilian presidency was to reach out to non-members and to the private sector.[60]

Brazilian authorities have also become providers of capacity building in the area of money laundering, in particular to South American countries and to Portuguese-speaking African countries.[61] Brazil has also been providing experts to perform mutual assessments of national AML/CFT regimes.[62]

As for Argentina, its participation at the FATF has been affected in recent years by assessments carried out by the FATF whereby a number of recommendations have been found unimplemented in the country. The FATF included Argentina in a list of countries with strategic deficiencies in their anti-money-laundering system and it also subjected it to an intensive follow-up by the plenary of the FATF. In 2010, Argentina proposed a plan of action to address the issues identified, which was accepted by the FATF. In 2011 the FATF expressed specific concerns with persistent shortcomings in the criminalization of money laundering.[63] It was not before 2014 that Argentina was excluded from the FATF's ongoing Global AML/CFT Compliance Process.[64]

6.2.4.5 Governance/policy-making of FATF-related issues in Argentina and Brazil

Domestic policy-making is well-institutionalized in the AML/CFT areas in Brazil. Since 2003, public and private entities meet annually to define the National Strategy Against Corruption and Money Laundering (ENCCLA, in the Portuguese acronym). The ENCCLA is the 'primary policy-co-ordination mechanism in Brazil with respect to ML, FT and corruption'.[65] Currently, more than sixty entities participate in the ENCCLA Plenary.[66]

[59] Luiz Maria Corrêa, *O Grupo de Ação Financeira Internacional* (n 48) 199.

[60] Financial Action Task Force, 'Annual Report 2008 -2009' (July 2009) 5.

[61] See, for example, the 2008 Report of the Brazilian Council for Financial Activities Control (COAF) for 2008. Conselho de Controle de Atividades Financeiras, Relatório de Atividades 2008, 41 <http://www.fazenda.gov.br/centrais-de-conteudos/publicacoes/relatorio-de-atividades/arquivos/relatorio-de-atividades-coaf-2008.pdf/view>, last accessed 12/23/2019.

[62] COAF, 'Relatório de Atividades' (n 62), 36.

[63] Hugo Alconada Mon, 'Argentina, en la lista gris y con una alerta por lavado' *La Nación* 4 June 2011 <http://www.lanacion.com.ar/1384243-argentina-en-la-lista-gris-y-con-una-alerta-por-lavadoargentina-en-la-lista-gris-y-con-una-alerta-por-lavado?TB_iframe=true&height=650&width=850>, last accessed 12/23/2019.

[64] Financial Action Task Force, 'High-risk and non-cooperative jurisdictions: Improving global AML/CFT compliance: on-going process' (24 October 2014) <http://www.fatf-gafi.org/media/fatf/documents/statements/Compliance-24-October-2014.pdf>, last accessed 12/23/2019.

[65] Financial Action Task Force and Financial Action Task Force Task Force on Money Laundering in South America (GAFISUD), 'Mutual Evaluation Report - Anti-Money Laundering and Combating the Financing of Terrorism - Federative Republic of Brazil' (2010) 221 <http://www.fatf-gafi.org/media/fatf/documents/reports/mer/MER%20Brazil%20full.pdf>, last accessed 12/23/2019.

[66] Estratégia Nacional de Combate à Corrupção e à Lavagem de Dinheiro (ENCCLA), 'Quem somos' <http://enccla.camara.leg.br/quem-somos>, last accessed 12/23/2019.

Governance and day-to-day management of FATF-related measures in Brazil is under the responsibility of the Council for Financial Activities Control (COAF, in the Portuguese acronym). Among tasks related to the flow of relevant financial information between the private sector and state agencies, the COAF is also the forum for multi-agency coordination of various aspects relating to the participation of Brazil in the FATF, including foreign policy-making in this area.[67]

In the case of Argentina, the Law on Concealment and Laundering of Proceeds of Crime of 2002, sets the Financial Information Unit (UIF for its acronym in Spanish) in the preventive level, making it responsible for analysing, handling, and disclosing information for the purpose of preventing and deterring the laundering of assets arising from crime.[68] The Law on Terrorist Criminal Associations and Financing of Terrorism of 2007 extends the mandate of the UIF to the analysis of suspicious terrorist financing transactions.[69]

Furthermore the FATF has been consulted in the implementation of some recent laws such as the Tax Amnesty law (*Régimen de Sinceramiento Fiscal*, in the original in Spanish) adopted in July 2016. The FATF has also had an impact on the domestic regulation through its recommendations that are somehow translated by resolutions and other norms of the different agencies that have an impact on the finance system, such as the Central Bank and the National Securities Commission.

6.3 What Lessons Emerge from the Experiences of Argentina and Brazil?

The experiences of Argentina and Brazil as new participants—or participants with reinforced status—in global finance governance raises the following set of insights about reforms in this area.

a) *The effect of reforms in enabling more participation by excluded stakeholders might be more visible when approached from a systemic perspective than from focusing on each individual institution.*

This might be a peculiarity of global finance governance, where reforms undertaken in the aftermath of the 2008 crisis led to a relevant degree of rearrangement in the architecture of the system. Of particular importance is the fact that the G20 leaders' forum, a new institution established at that period, came to share a number of competences with other financial institutions, such as the IMF. Participation of Argentina as a member of the G20 is a case in point. Until the end of 2015, while the country opted for an 'exit' strategy with respect to the IMF, in view of its unique experience with the Fund, it was promoting an agenda at the G20—thanks to its participation

[67] Conselho de Controle de Atividades Financeiras (COAF), 'A participação brasileira' <http://www.coaf.fazenda.gov.br/menu/atuacao-internacional/atuacao-do-coaf-no-ambito-internacional>, last accessed 02/11/2020.

[68] Law No 25.246: Concealment and Laundering of Assets Derived from Criminal Activities 2000 (Encubrimiento y Lavado de Activos de Origen Delictivo, Argentina).

[69] Law No 26.268: Illegal Terrorist Associations and Terrorism Financing 2007 (Asociaciones Ilícitas Terroristas y Financiación del Terrorismo, Argentina).

therein—that to a great extent overlapped with that of the IMF. Argentina thus used its participation at the G20 to advance initiatives that it could not have done if not a member of the G20, and since it had decided to reduce its participation in the IMF. The case of Brazil also provides examples in this direction, but to a lesser extent. This type of insight would perhaps not be captured if one would focus only on the reforms at the IMF.

b) *Argentina and Brazil were advocating for more participation within global finance governance. Reforms granted them more participation and they made active use of it—with impact on the legitimacy of the institutions. Participation led to some degree of influence.*

With the sole exception of the case of Argentina vis-à-vis the IMF, the previous assertion, by and large, summarizes the examples studied in this chapter, even the one of the FATF. Argentina and Brazil have long held the position of rule-takers in global finance, in many cases due to the fact that these countries did not participate at decision-making within this policy area. The enlargement of the FATF, the first ever, with the accession of the two countries as full members, enabled them to take a step in changing this traditional role. However, it was the reforms following the 2008 crisis that gave Argentina and Brazil the opportunity to influence agenda-setting. As the examples in this chapter show, as they sought to exert such influence, Argentina and Brazil drew on their previous experiences as clients of the system. It could be argued that, by enabling these perspectives to be brought to the fore, the reforms in question increased the legitimacy of the institutions where they took place—a claim that could perhaps apply more strongly to the G20.

c) *There does not seem to be a hierarchy ranking of different types of reforms (creation of new institutions, enlargement of memberships or redistribution of formal decision-making power) according to how much participation is enabled.*

This chapter surveys the following types of reforms with the purpose of assessing the participation of Argentina and Brazil: (i) creation of a new institution/reengineering of a previous institution to endow it with increased competences (G20) and membership (FSB); (ii) reallocation of decision-making power across the membership, to the benefit of some members (IMF); and (iii) enlargement of membership (FATF). There does not seem to be any indication—in the cases studied in this chapter—that any reform type was more conducive to increased participation than the other. Rather, the instances of more active participation, for example, the claim of Brazil for more balanced representation of emerging economies in global finance governance, made both at the G20 and the IMF, seem to be more a function of the agenda of the institution than a result of any institutional reform. In contrast, Brazil has not been equally vocal in the FSB—certainly not with the same visibility that it attracted at the G20.

d) *Participation reforms might be the formalization of a pre-existing factual situation*

Examining the 2010 quota and governance reform of the IMF (in force since 2016) might not be as instructive—in the attempt to grasp its effect on stakeholder participation—as a closer look at the political process that led to it. The experience of Brazil in this episode reveals that, irrespective of the concrete consequences the reform might yield in terms of participation, the very fact that the reform materialized in the way it did is in part a function of an increased participation of Brazil in the Fund—which, in turn, was driven by a radical shift in the profile of Brazil from a 'client' to a creditor of the IMF.

e) *Assessing the importance of a given institution to a country is a matter of perspective*

All global financial institutions researched in this chapter are relevant for Argentina and Brazil, although just *how relevant* is subject to variation. Clearly, the IMF *as an institution* lost, for Argentina, a significant amount of importance, no matter how much the IMF agenda continued to matter to Argentina. But even in the case of Brazil, it could not be claimed that the four institutions have a similar degree of relevance. They do not, and it could be reasonably claimed that the G20 and the IMF are placed at the top of priorities. This does not mean, though, that the FATF and the FSB are less relevant since they are relevant to the issue-areas in which they are embedded. The point seems to be that, while the G20 and the IMF—but especially the G20—focus on a larger number of topics, the FATF and the FSB do not. And this might provide an incomplete assessment of their importance to the countries.

6.4 Concluding Remarks: Reforms and Participation, Legitimacy, and Effectiveness

In general, it can be argued that the reforms in global finance governance studied in this chapter have enabled Argentina and Brazil to voice their views, concerns, and initiatives to a global audience not previously available. Additionally, they have sought to take advantage of this new capacity to exert influence. Furthermore, in some cases Argentina and Brazil have also had some degree of influence on decisions or in setting the agenda of global finance, thus confirming the findings in this respect by the editors.[70]

This assertion is not applicable to all cases, nor to the same extent to all the cases. Obviously, the IMF 2010 reform has done exactly the opposite to Argentina. As the chapter highlighted, the peculiarity of the Argentinian situation vis-à-vis the IMF until 2015 is a fundamental element to take into account when examining the participation of the country at global finance institutions. But even here it is interesting to underscore how another reform—the establishment of the G20 at the level of leaders—has given Argentina a new forum to effectively express its views in replacement to the IMF. This development confirms that reforms have also improved legitimacy.[71]

How much the reforms studied in this chapter have owed to concerns for effectiveness or legitimacy is a question open to debate. The cases of the G20 and the FSB—two new institutions—seem to be inspired by both elements. They give expression to

[70] Tim Büthe, Joost Pauwelyn, Martino Maggetti, and Ayelet Berman, 'Conclusion: The Participation of Marginalized Stakeholders in Global Governance' Chapter 25, this volume. See also DeMenno and Büthe, 'Voice and Influence' (n 1).

[71] Büthe *et al.*, 'Conclusion' (n 70).

the perception that new actors should be included in decision-making, or else the effectiveness of decisions risks being negatively affected. At the same time, being a by-product of the 2008 financial crisis, an episode that shook the credibility of established economic powers as guarantors of global economic stability, the G20 and the FSB have also been driven by a desire to inject legitimacy into global finance governance.

The IMF 2010 reform also seems to owe partially to both elements, although there is a strong dimension in it of a formalization of an underlying concrete reality. Also, one could debate the extent to which the reform appeased the demand for more legitimacy in the IMF.

In contrast, the reforms undertaken by the FATF have been oriented by the goal of ensuring the effectiveness of the system centred around this forum, as has been argued elsewhere in this volume.[72]

The reforms studied in this chapter are the product of the particular moment in history when they took place—an assertion especially valid to those reforms implemented after the 2008 crisis. Argentina and Brazil, in varying degrees, benefitted by and large from these reforms at that time. But they did so for reasons that are particular to each of their individual circumstances, including their capacity to harness these opportunities, following the pattern described by Büthe *et al.*[73] The question then should be posed as to whether, and to what extent, these reforms could also serve other stakeholders to good effect.

[72] Martino Maggetti and Olga Kovarzina, 'Assessing Stakeholder Participation Reforms in Global Finance Governance' Chapter 9, this volume.

[73] See Büthe *et al.*, 'Conclusion' (n 70).

7
China and Vietnam in Global Finance Governance

Weiwei Zhang

7.1 Introduction

China and Vietnam[1] share many similarities. Both countries were heavily dominated by planned economies for decades; both countries embarked on ambitious economic reforms in the 1980s aiming to transfer from a centralized planned economy to a market-oriented economy; both countries made significant reform efforts before their accession into the World Trade Organization (WTO); and both have benefited from participation in the global trading system and achieved impressive economic development in the past two decades. On the one hand, as both countries' importance in the global economy grows, the rest of the world seeks their more active participation in global governance in monetary coordination and financial supervision. On the other hand, as both countries' economies are more integrated in the world economy, each faces greater challenges in macro-economic policy-making and supervision of financial markets. Thus, they desire to be more engaged in global governance as regards their own interests. Meanwhile, China and Vietnam are fundamentally different, especially in terms of their stage of economic development and the size of the economy. These similarities and differences may influence their respective participation in the global financial architecture.

This chapter compares China's and Vietnam's participation in four key global financial institutions: the International Monetary Fund (IMF), the Basel Committee on Banking Supervision (BCBS), the International Organization of Securities Commissions (IOSCO), and the Financial Action Task Force (FATF).[2] It traces their participation from the beginnings of their respective economic reform and presents an evolutionary picture of their participation over the years. It explores whether China's and Vietnam's level of participation in these institutions have changed over time, and if so, what the factors are that enabled such change. Finally, it investigates if each country's influence in global finance governance has changed over time, and if so, whether this influence is related to their increased participation in these four institutions. The G20, as well as the Financial Stability Board (FSB) and the Asian

[1] See Tim Büthe and Cindy Cheng, 'Analysing the Consequences of Institutional Reforms Using Country Pairs: A Note on the (Coarsened Exact) Matched-Country-Pairs Methodology of the Rethinking Stakeholder Participation Project.' Chapter 3, this volume.

[2] For more detailed background information regarding these major institutions for global finance governance, see Olga Kovarzina and Martino Maggetti, 'Stakeholder Participation Reforms in Global Finance Governance.' Chapter 4, this volume.

Weiwei Zhang, *China and Vietnam in Global Finance Governance* In: *Rethinking Participation in Global Governance.* Edited by: Joost Pauwelyn, Martino Maggetti, Tim Büthe, and Ayelet Berman, Oxford University Press. © Weiwei Zhang 2022.
DOI: 10.1093/oso/9780198852568.003.0007

Infrastructure Development Bank, are presented as instruments or institutions that supplement the traditional global financial architecture centred around the IMF. Overall, this chapter assesses whether China and Vietnam are able to have their voices heard in global finance governance.[3]

Section 7.2 and Section 7.3 present China's and Vietnam's role, respectively, in global finance governance. Each section covers the institutions identified in the chapter, introduces the relevance of the particular regulatory issue covered by that institution in the country concerned, and how each issue was organized domestically. It then discusses the country's participation in that institution to identify changes in the level of participation, if any. After that, it assesses any change of that country's influence on the specific regulatory issue in global governance, and if so, the factors enabling that change. Vietnam is not yet a member of BCBS or FATF. For BCBS and FATF, Section 7.3 therefore explores the reasons behind non-membership and how the situation may change. Finally, Section 7.4 summarizes how the similarities and differences between China and Vietnam affect their respective participation in global finance governance.

7.2 China's Participation in Global Finance Governance

7.2.1 IMF and China

7.2.1.1 Introduction

China joined the IMF and the World Bank (WB) in 1980. Upon accession, it committed that it would eventually accept the obligations of Article VIII, Sections 2, 3, and 4 ('Article VIII obligations') of the Agreement of Articles of the IMF in 1996, including avoidance of restrictions on current payments, avoidance of discriminatory currency practices, and convertibility of foreign-held balances. The sixteen years between 1980 and 1996 marked the most important period in China's economic reform. As the country moved from a planned economy to a market economy, its financial sector underwent fundamental institutional adjustments, including establishing commercial banks and reforming the foreign exchange rate management system. These changes were needed for China's domestic economic reforms and were crucial for China to engage in global trade. Indeed, the issue of current account convertibility was discussed extensively during China's bid to the General Agreement on Tariffs and Trade (GATT, the predecessor of the World Trade Organization, WTO).[4] Eventually, a unified, managed floating foreign exchange rate regime was introduced; the foreign exchange retention system was replaced by a system of exchange settlement and sale; a foreign exchange market through commercial banks was established; and the administrative

[3] In distinguishing between participation and influence, the analysis builds on Mercy B DeMenno and Tim Büthe, 'Voice and Influence in Global Governance: An Analytical Framework.' Chapter 2, this volume. See also Ayelet Berman, Tim Büthe, Martino Maggetti, and Joost Pauwelyn, 'Introduction: Rethinking Stakeholder Participation in Global Governance.' Chapter 1, this volume.

[4] Report of the Working Party on China's Accession to the WTO, WT/ACC/CHN/49, Section 3 'Foreign Exchange and Payments'.

order of allocation of foreign exchanges was abolished. A new foreign exchange management system was thus established in 1994, leading to China's acceptance of Article VIII in 1996.

China witnessed unprecedented economic growth following its domestic economic reform and trade liberalization. Figure 7.1 shows how China's GDP on a purchasing-power-parity (PPP) basis as share of the world increased from less than 5% in the early 1990s to 17.2% in 2015. Despite its economic growth, China's voting share in the IMF was less than 4% until the end of 2015. In comparison, while the United States' share of the world GDP dropped to 15.7% in 2015, its voting share in the IMF remained at 16.73%. The United States thus remained not only the biggest shareholder, but also the only country that can veto all major decisions at the IMF. In 2010, the IMF proposed a reform package to increase the voice and vote of many under-represented emerging and developing countries, including China, but the package was put on hold by the US Congress until the end of 2015. This delay made China feel frustrated and under-represented.[5] Even though the reform eventually passed, leading to an increase in China's voting share—from 3.81% to 6.16%—this share still does not represent a voice relative to its size in the world economy.[6]

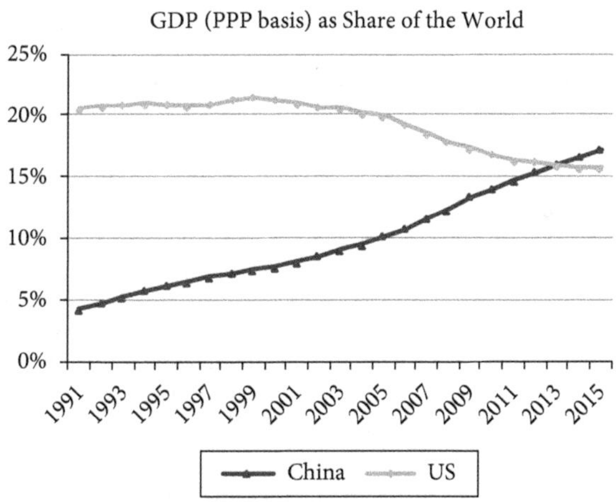

Figure 7.1 China's Increasing Share of World GDP
(source: World Bank)

[5] Statement by the Hon. Jiwei Lou, Governor of the Bank for the People's Republic of China at the 2015 Lima Annual Meetings of the World Bank Group and the International Monetary Fund, 9 October 2015: 'As a quota-based institution, the IMF needs adequate representativeness and sufficient resources to safeguard global financial stability. We are deeply disappointed that the 2010 quota and governance reforms were not ratified by the extended deadline of September 15, 2015, which further undermines the credibility, legitimacy, and effectiveness of the Fund. Besides, the gap between calculated and existing quota shares for emerging market and developing economies has been widening . . . '.

[6] See Henrique Choer Moraes and Facundo Pérez Aznar, 'Brazil and Argentina in Global Finance Governance.' Chapter 6, and Ronald Gindrat and Paul Inderbinen, 'Comparing Formal and Informal Bodies in International Finance: A Policy-Making Perspective.' Chapter 11, both this volume.

7.2.1.2 Institutional changes and involvement
As mentioned, China participated in the IMF and the World Bank since 1980 and accepted the Article VIII obligations in 1996. Table 7.1 summarizes China's positions made at the IMF annual meetings since 1996.[7] Before the Asian Financial Crisis in 1997, China supported the IMF's jurisdiction to cover current account convertibility. On the governance level, while China noticed the declining voting share of developing countries, its criticism was gentle. However, following the 1997 crisis, China's position on the current account convertibility changed. China became critical on issues like capital account liberalization, as well as the standards and codes developed by the IMF. In the 2000s, China became increasingly concerned with the IMF's surveillance function. China requested that the focus be put on the surveillance of major developed countries, especially those issuing major reserve currencies. It also opposed the 2007 Surveillance Decision. In the meantime, China took a strong position that the IMF should not intervene in its members' choice of the level of exchange rates. It also became more assertive in pushing for governance reform in the IMF. In 2006, China highlighted that the distribution of quotas should better reflect changes in members' economic positions. Thus, China's participation in the IMF, although increased over the years, is still characterized by the lack of representation and inability to influence key decision-making due to its limited voting share.

Table 7.1 China's Interventions at the Annual Meetings of IMF and the World Bank Group

	Assistance to developing countries	**Policy-related Issues**	**Quotas/Institutional issues**
1997	Support ESAF	Support the inclusion of capital account convertibility in the IMF's purposes, but IMF should respect the sovereignty and allow members to proceed 'in an orderly and healthy manner'	Brought attention of the declining quota share of developing countries and requested to address the issue at an early date
1997 Asian Financial Crisis			
1998	Support ESAF and HIPC Initiative; Called on the IMF to pay more attention to the specific circumstances of the countries concerned	Blame premature liberalization for the financial crisis; Capital account convertibility should be carried out in 'an orderly and well sequenced manner'; Called on the Fund to be vigilant to the risks posed by international capital flows	Urged the Eleventh General Quota increase and the NAB can take effect as soon as possible

[7] The table is summarized from the speeches made by China in IMF and the World Bank's annual meetings.

Table 7.1 Continued

	Assistance to developing countries	Policy-related Issues	Quotas/Institutional issues
1999	Insisted economic development is a precondition to solutions to poverty alleviation and social issues (in response to the increased emphasis put on social sector issues by the IMF and the WB)	Proposed the IMF's role should be helping developing countries put into place the necessary conditions for liberalizing capital account, rather than pushing with the speed of liberalization only; Oppose the mandatory enforcement of transparency as China did not believe lack of transparency was the main cause of the financial crisis; Article IV consultation should not be linked with transparency assessment	Strongly request that the representation of developing countries be safeguarded in the newly named International Monetary and Financial Committee
2000	Heavily criticize the WB's increasingly evident political orientation; In implementing its assistance strategies, the WB should not unduly emphasize those issues that should be addressed by developing countries themselves, such as governance and institutional reform	Standards and codes of the WB and the IMF should be disseminated and implemented based on voluntary and progressive principles; Called on to enhance the transparency of the private sector, and strengthen the supervision and regulation of highly leveraged institutions;	
2002	Stated country should enjoy ownership in designing development policy	The IMF and the WB should confine their operations to their mandate (that is, not to step on other issues such as AML/CFT)	
2003		Welcomed the decision to implement Monterrey Consensus, enhancing the voice and participation of developing and transition countries, opening up markets to developing countries, and promoting infrastructure development to accelerate poverty reduction	

(continued)

Table 7.1 Continued

	Assistance to developing countries	Policy-related Issues	Quotas/Institutional issues
2004		Proposed the IMF should place greater focus on surveillance of the major developed countries that have a significant impact on the global economy; Standards and codes should be introduced on a voluntary basis; In developing these standards and codes, the IMF should listen more to developing countries	
2005	Concrete proposals were made to improve global development financing; Proposed the WB and the IMF should strengthen Middle Income Countries strategy	Concrete proposals to better guide the economic globalization	Proposed reform of their governance structure
2006		Surveillance should always adhere to its purposes of promoting global exchange and macro-economic stability, and respect the autonomy of member countries in choosing their own exchange rate regime; it also should focus its surveillance on the systemically important countries issuing major reserve currencies	Support governance reform aimed at to make the distribution of quotas better reflect changes in members' economic positions in the world economy; to enhance the voice of low-income countries continue to call for the establishment of a more transparent procedure for the selection of the Managing Director.
2007		Continue to emphasize that the IMF should enhance its surveillance over countries issuing major reserve currencies so as to play an effective role in promoting financial stability and economic prosperity. Opposed the 2007 Decision; Opposed IMF's intervention on the *level* of interest rate	Should continue to improve their own governance and ensure the rights of the developing countries to effectively participate in the decision-making of the institutions

Table 7.1 Continued

	Assistance to developing countries	Policy-related Issues	Quotas/Institutional issues
2008 US Financial Crisis			
2008		Called on the surveillance priority to be given to the ongoing financial turmoil; 2007 Surveillance Decision should be reviewed and revised	
2009			Called upon the IMF to speed up quota reform; Continue that the selection of the head should be open, transparent and merit-based.
2010		Suggested the IMF adjust its focus of surveillance and pay more attention to the macro-economic policies of major reserve currency-issuing economies, the financial sector, and the cross-border capital flows; Refine the international monetary system, keeping the exchange rates of the major reserve currencies relatively stable, while diversifying and rationalizing the system	Call for understanding, support, and contribution to the governance reform
2011		Suggested the IMF should seek the root cause of the crisis and adjust the monitoring framework and transform monitoring priorities accordingly; Should further study the inherent defects of the international monetary system, promote diversification of the international reserve currency system, and build the international reserve currency system into one with stable value, rule-based issuance, and manageable supply; Welcome the adoption of the Integrated Surveillance Decision by the IMF	Should continue to improve its quota and governance structure

(continued)

Table 7.1 Continued

	Assistance to developing countries	Policy-related Issues	Quotas/Institutional issues
2012			Call on member countries to conclude the 2010 quota and governance reforms by completing the domestic approval process by the agreed deadline; All parties to call on all parties to complete the review of the quota formula by January 2013 in the spirit of cooperation.
2013		Continue upgrading its knowledge and expertise in order to respond effectively to new trends and challenges; Cooperation between the IMF and other international organizations remains crucial	Urged IMF to complete the 2010 quota and governance reform
2014	Should continue to provide strong support to low-income countries	Called on to continue to enhance its crisis prevention capacity in the face of the increasingly complex and interconnected global macro-financial environment; To further enhance the resilience of the international monetary system, the IMF should continue to promote reforms of crisis resolution frameworks, in addition to strengthening the global financial safety net and cooperating with regional financing arrangements	'Deeply disappointed' with the lack of progress in implementing the 2010 quota and governance reforms
2015		Continue to upgrade its crisis prevention capacity; Further deepen its analysis on social and financial inclusions, while leveraging other multilateral institutions' expertise on other issues of importance	'Deeply disappointed' that the 2010 quota and governance reforms were not ratified by the extended deadline of 15 September 2015, which further undermines the credibility, legitimacy, and effectiveness of the IMF

Table 7.1 Continued

	Assistance to developing countries	Policy-related Issues	Quotas/Institutional issues
2016		IMF should continue to improve its surveillance, strengthen its research and analytical work on key common challenges in economic transitions across countries, and provide risk alerts in a timely manner; Should press ahead with international monetary system reforms	The IMF should continue its quota and governance reforms and ensure that the IMF is strong, quota-based, and adequately-resourced

7.2.1.3 Institutional changes and influence

China's growing economic importance in the world led to increase its presence in global finance governance, especially after two financial crises. Despite its under-representation in the IMF, China participates in global governance in finance—also via other channels, including the Group of 20 (G20) and the recently established Asian Infrastructure Investment Bank (AIIB).

The G20 is a group of key advanced and emerging market economies. After the 2008 global financial crisis, this forum was promoted because it comprised heads of state and government; it was designated as 'the premier forum for our international economic cooperation' during their Pittsburgh Summit in 2009. In response to the G20 declaration in Pittsburgh, the IMF has worked closely with the G20. As the IMF itself acknowledged, '[t]he IMF's work often provides a platform for G20 deliberations, and vice versa, agreements reached at the G20 level are taken into consideration in the IMF's decision-making process, even though such agreements have no legal status or binding effects at the IMF.'[8] As an important member of the G20, China could influence the IMF and the World Bank agenda by increasing its voice in the G20.

Another way for China to directly participate in global finance governance is through its membership in the FSB. The FSB, created in April 2009, represents the G20 leaders' first major international institutional innovation following the 2007–2008 global financial crisis. It was established to promote international financial stability by coordinating national financial authorities and international standard-setting bodies.[9] All G20 countries, including China, are members of the FSB. All members are entitled to participate in the Plenary, the FSB's sole decision-making body. The Plenary adopts a wide range of decisions on matters of policy respecting the regulation of the financial sector and on jurisdictions' observance of international financial standards on consensus basis. Thus, by being a member, China can effectively participate in decision-making on issues pertinent to the governance of global finance.

[8] See <http://www.imf.org/en/About/Factsheets/A-Guide-to-Committees-Groups-and-Clubs#G7>, last accessed 04/13/2020.

[9] See <http://www.fsb.org/about/>, last accessed 04/13/2020.

China also sought to influence the global financial architecture by setting up the AIIB. The AIIB is a new multilateral financial institution founded in late 2014 to address the daunting infrastructure needs across Asia. The AIIB was signed by China and twenty-one other Asian countries, but its membership is not limited to regional partners. Out-of-region countries such as the UK, Switzerland, France, Germany, and Italy also joined the AIIB.

7.2.1.4 Domestic organization and impact

As mentioned, IMF membership helped China's liberalization of the current account and commitment to capital account convertibility. However, as the financial crisis unfolded and given the lack of internal reform in the IMF, its standards and codes became less suitable for China's development needs.

7.2.2 BCBS and China

7.2.2.1 Introduction

China's financial sector is characterized by the predominance of banks over other types of financial institutions. The banking sector also plays an important role in financing other sectors of the economy. China adopted a sectoral approach to financial regulation and supervision. The China Banking Regulatory Commission (CBRC), the China Securities Regulatory Commission (CSRC), and the China Insurance Regulatory Commission (CIRC) supervise banks, securities firms, and insurance companies, respectively.

As a general rule, China takes a cautious and incremental approach in liberalizing its financial services sector, including permitting private participation, foreign participation, and cross-border capital flows. The government's philosophy is that innovative financial products are important, but that they should be introduced at a pace at which appropriate controls can be instituted. In this way, supervisory bodies could learn over time, and the market would develop in an orderly manner. This philosophy also explains China's approach towards prudential regulation when the CBRC was first established.

First, CBRC took a step-by-step approach in the implementation of the Basel capital framework. One of the driving forces of the Basel capital framework is to stay ahead of financial innovation and ensure that bank capital is commensurate with bank risk. With its cautious, proscriptive approach to bank risk-taking, especially with regard to financial innovation, China initially felt no urgency to adopt the latest version of the capital framework. Indeed, the February 2004 CBRC *Rules Governing Capital Adequacy of Commercial Banks* (revised in July 2007) were based on the 1998 Basel Capital Accord (Basel I). Basel II was only implemented gradually afterwards. In April 2011, the CBRC issued a Guideline for Implementation of New Regulatory Standards (CBRC Circular 2011/44) and requested the implementation of Basel III as of 1 January 2012.

Second, as Chinese commercial banks rely heavily on deposits with limited use of securitizations, liabilities tend to be more stable and more amenable to direct measurement, compared to many other global banks that are reliant on wholesale funding. Thus, liquidity is less of an issue for China than for many other countries; it could readily establish the liquidity standard proposed by the BCBS. However, Chinese banks may find liquidity risk management to become more challenging as they embark on a wider variety of products and compete in oversea markets.

Third, China adopted prudential measures to tackle systemic risks, for example, non-performing loans and real estate assets bubbles, and recently reinforced prudential regulations to comply with the Basel Committee recommendations. In addition, China's WTO accession further opened up China's financial market to foreign banks. When they entered the market with innovative financial products, it prompted CBRC to update its regulatory approach and seek more cooperation with banking supervisors in other countries. Furthermore, as Chinese commercial banks increasingly went abroad to compete internationally, the CBRC became increasingly interested in participating in the standard-setting work in the Basel Committee.

7.2.2.2 Institutional changes and involvement

China was invited to join the BCBS in March 2009, when the Committee decided to expand its membership to include Australia, Brazil, China, India, Korea, Mexico, and Russia. The Chairman of the Committee noted that this step was to follow the call from G20 leaders for major standard-setting bodies to review their membership.[10] China's change from non-member to member status was driven both by the G20 call and China's cooperation and contribution during the period following the financial crisis.[11]

Nevertheless, by the time China joined the BCBS, the Committee had already completed a number of critical reforms to the Basel II framework. Thus, China had limited involvement in constructing Basel III, and its role in the ongoing revisions of the Basel III framework remains to be seen. In 2016, the CBRC called on the banking industry in China to actively participate in the new round of revisions.[12] The China

[10] BCBS press release, Expansion of membership announced by the Basel Committee, 13 March 2009, <http://www.bis.org/press/p090313.htm>, last accessed 04/13/2020.

[11] See opening speech by Mr Stefan Ingves, Chairman of the Basel Committee on Banking Supervision and Governor of Sveriges Riksbank, at the 18th International Conference of Banking Supervisors, Tianjin, China, 24 September 2014: 'China joined the Basel Committee in March 2009 in the midst of what turned out to be a prolonged, far-reaching, and complex financial crisis. Since then, the CBRC and the People's Bank of China have become active members of the Basel Committee and have made valuable contributions during an extremely busy and critical period. When I think about what the Committee has achieved since the financial crisis, I don't think it would have been possible without the support of the Chinese authorities and the other members that joined the Committee in 2009. The new members have brought an important new dimension to the Committee table—drawing, of course, on their own experience and perspective as emerging economies.'

[12] See Xi Chao, 'From Rule-Taker to Rule-Maker: China's Changing Roles in Global Banking Regulation', in Friedl Weiss and Armin J Kammel, *The Changing Landscape of Global Financial Governance and the Role of Soft Law* (Brill Nijhoff 2015, 312–336).

Banking Association has been active in providing comments to the revisions proposed by the BCBS.[13]

7.2.2.3 Institutional changes and influence

Given the relatively late development of China's banking industry and the precautionary regulatory approach, the influence of the CBRC and the industry's impact on global standard setting remains low. Thus far, Chinese industry has largely been a standard taker. As Chinese banks gradually undertake business abroad, they may seek greater involvement in standard-setting.

7.2.2.4 Domestic organization and impact

As a formal member of the Committee, China had the compliance of its domestic rules with the international Basel capital adequacy standards assessed as part of the Committee's Regulatory Consistency Assessment Programme (RCAP). This process alone has led to higher compliance. The Committee noted during its assessment that the CBRC issued four new regulatory documents rectifying a number of provisions initially identified as deviations from the Basel framework. According to the Committee, these additional regulatory documents considerably improved the level of compliance with the Basel standards. Overall, China's implementation of the Basel capital framework is closely aligned with the Basel III global standards, which shows China's membership in the BCBS resulted in a higher level of prudential regulation in China.

7.2.3 IOSCO and China

7.2.3.1 Introduction

China adopted a sectoral approach to financial regulation and supervision, and the CSRC supervises securities and futures market. The CSRC was established in late 1992. In 1995, CSRC joined the IOSCO.

7.2.3.2 Institutional changes and involvement

China was elected as a member of the Executive Committee in 1998. In 2009 it also was invited to join the IOSCO Technical Committee, a specialized working group established by the Executive Committee. The Technical Committee led most standard-setting activity and therefore was effectively the IOSCO's powerhouse. The Chairman of the Technical Committee noted:

> The changing landscape of the international financial system in this time of crisis demands that organizations, such as ours, reflect such changes in the composition of its membership. It is quite proper that the Technical Committee now should include the members from Brazil, the People's Republic of China and India within its ranks.[14]

[13] See, for example, the CBA provided comments in BCBS Consultation on Revisions to the Standardised Approach for Credit Risk on 7 March 2016.

[14] IOSCO Media Release IOSCO/MR/002/2009, 'IOSCO Technical Committee invites Brazil, China and India to join its membership', 19 February 2009, Madrid.

According to the IOSCO, the new members 'were chosen on the basis of the size of their capital markets, the international nature of their markets and the development of their regulatory system and authority'.[15] Similar to China's membership in BCBS in the same year, China's presence in the Technical Committee also reflected the call from the G20 to broaden emerging countries' membership in standard-setting bodies.[16]

7.2.3.3 Institutional changes and influence

Since the IOSCO and BCBS work together in developing financial standards, China's participation in IOSCO is similar to its participation in BCBS described in Section 7.2.2.

7.2.3.4 Domestic organization and impact

As acknowledged by IOSCO assessment in 2012, the Chinese securities and futures industry and its regulation has undergone 'considerable development' since the establishment of the CSRC in 1992.[17] These reforms have been carefully planned and implemented and have been welcomed by market participants. The Report also pointed out a few areas, in which the regulatory framework had not met the IOSCO standards, which require improvement.

7.2.4 FATF and China

7.2.4.1 Introduction

China is increasingly concerned about its vulnerability to money laundering as the economy grows. Criminal cases handled by the public security organs indicate that the predicate crimes for money laundering continue to expand in scope. In addition to drug crimes, smuggling, and crimes against property, other types of criminal activities, for example, economic crime, is increasing. Additionally, money laundering was connected to a large number of corruption cases. China openly acknowledged that corruption was a serious problem and posed a serious threat to China. Against this background, China signed the United Nations Convention against Corruption in 2003 and ratified it in 2006. As a result, anti-money-laundering (AML) initiatives, as an indispensable part of the anti-corruption campaign, have been high on China's policy agenda.

Between 2003 and 2007, a comprehensive framework to tackle money laundering was built from scratch.[18] An AML Bureau was set up in the central bank in 2003 to coordinate all matters relating to AML; the China Anti-money Laundering Monitoring & Analysis Center (CAMLMAC) was subsequently instituted under the central bank to collect, analyse, and monitor AML intelligence and an AML Joint-ministerial

[15] IOSCO Media Release IOSCO/MR/002/2009 (n 14).

[16] Following the governance reform in 2012, the functions of the Technical Committee, Executive Committee and Emerging Market Committee Advisory Board was subsumed by the Board of the IOSCO. Today the IOSCO Board is the governing and standard-setting body of IOSCO and is made up of thirty-four securities regulators, including China.

[17] People's Republic of China: Detailed Assessment Report: IOSCO Objectives and Principles of Securities Regulation, IMF Country Report No. 12/80, April 2012.

[18] See *2007 China Anti-Money Laundering Report*, People's Bank of China, August 2008. See also *Summary of the First Mutual Evaluation Report on Anti-Money Laundering and Combating the Financing of Terrorism: People's Republic of China*, FATF/ME(2007)2/ADD, 29 June 2007.

Conference of twenty-three ministries or agencies was instituted to coordinate on AML work. Furthermore, the Criminal Law was amended to bring the definition of money laundering into line with international practice, and the first ever Chinese AML law was promulgated in 2006 to set up an administrative framework to tackle ML and obligate the financial institutions to undertake AML activities.

In the meantime, China became a member of the Eurasian group on combating money laundering and financing of terrorism (EAG) in 2004, resumed its participation in Asia/Pacific Group on Money Laundering (APG) in 2009, and joined FATF in 2007. It has also signed bilateral memoranda of understandings (MOUs) to seek AML/CFT cooperation and intelligence exchanges.

7.2.4.2 Institutional changes and involvement

7.2.4.2.1 China's accession in 2007

In 2007 China became a member of the FATF. Not every country can become a FATF member. First, to be considered a *potential* candidate, the FATF must be satisfied that it is strategically important according to certain quantitative as well as qualitative criteria.[19] Quantitative criteria include the size of GDP, size of the banking, insurance, and securities sectors, and population. Qualitative criteria include its impact on the global financial system (including the degree of openness of the financial sector and its interaction with international markets); its active participation in an FSRB and regional prominence in AML/CFT efforts; its level of commitment to AML/CFT effort; and the level of AML/CFT risks faced and efforts to combat the risks. Equally important is the FATF's geographic balance. Table 7.2 illustrates how China satisfies these criteria. Indeed, China's rapid economic growth and its fast expansion and liberalization of its financial services sector had made it undoubtedly 'strategically important' for FATF issues.[20]

Table 7.2 Assessing China against FATF's quantitative and qualitative membership criteria

Criteria	China's performance by 2005
Quantitative criteria	
GDP	>18 trillion RMB, 9.9% growth rate
Size of the financial sectors	30,195 entities; 39,852 billion RMB assets[a]
Population	1.3 billion (the most populous)
Qualitative criteria	
Impact on the global financial system	Integrated as a result of its liberalization following its WTO accession
participation in an FSRB	Member of EAG in 2004
level of commitment to AML/CFT effort	Intensively implementing AML measures

[a] *First Mutual Evaluation Report on Anti-Money Laundering and Combating the Financing of Terrorism: People's Republic of China*, FATF, 29 June 2007, 12.

[19] For the current version of membership policy, see <http://www.fatf-gafi.org/about/membersandobservers/fatfmembershippolicy.html>, last accessed 04/13/2020.

[20] Size of the economy also matters in other areas of global governance, as covered by DeMenno and Büthe, 'Voice and Influence' (n 3).

The candidate then embarks on a mutual evaluation process. Membership is granted if the evaluation is satisfactory in that it finds the country to have reached certain levels of compliance with the FATF-recommended standards for combating money laundering and terrorist financing.[21] China's adoption of the AML/CFT measures since 2003 resulted in a decent level of compliance with the FAFT's recommendations.

7.2.4.2.2 FATF's decision to expand membership

As a result of the review of the FATF's future in 1998, the organization was required to promote AML initiatives in all continents and regions of the globe and to build a world-wide anti-money-laundering network.[22] First and foremost, the FATF decided to foster the establishment of a world-wide anti-money laundering network 'based on <u>an adequate expansion of the FATF membership to strategically important countries</u> which already have certain key anti-money laundering measures in place . . ., and which are politically determined to make a full commitment towards the implementation of the forty Recommendations, and which could play a major role in their regions in the process of combating money laundering.'[23] FATF thus developed a membership policy.[24] In particular, rather than waiting for applications, 'it was believed that FATF should take a more proactive approach.'[25] This institutional change led to the inclusion of six new members before China joined.[26]

In sum, China's accession into the FATF was a result of FATF's strategic decision to expand its membership in 1998 and China's political willingness to embark on serious AML initiatives since 2003.

7.2.4.3 Institutional changes and influence

Even though China joined the FATF in 2007, it was required to participate in an enhanced follow-up process as a result of partially compliant and non-compliant ratings in certain areas of the Core and Key Recommendations in its mutual evaluation report in 2007. Thus, in the first years of its FATF membership China focused on addressing these deficiencies. In 2008, the FATF Plenary agreed to place China on the regular follow-up process and in 2012 China was taken off the regular follow-up process.[27] In 2013 the FATF established a temporary committee of seven

[21] For details, see <http://www.fatf-gafi.org/about/historyofthefatf/#d.en.3157>, last accessed 04/13/2020.

[22] On 28 April 1998, FATF Ministers and the European Commissioner for Financial Services endorsed the report prepared by the FATF which defines a five-year plan (1999–2004) to spread the anti-money-laundering message to all continents and regions of the globe. For an introduction to the FATF membership, see Kern Alexander, 'Global Financial Governance and Banking Regulation: Redesigning Regulation to Promote Stakeholder Interests.' Chapter 5, this volume.

[23] See FATF Annual Report 1997–1998 (emphasis mine).

[24] See FATF Annual Report 1998–1999, para. 151. For the current version of membership policy, see <http://www.fatf-gafi.org/about/membersandobservers/fatfmembershippolicy.html>, last accessed 04/13/2020.

[25] FATF Annual Report 1998–1999 (n 24), para. 152.

[26] The six new members are Argentina, Brazil, China, Mexico, South Africa, and the Russian Federation. During 1991 and 1992, the FATF expanded its membership from the original sixteen to twenty-eight members. In 2000 the FATF expanded to thirty-one members and has since expanded to its current thirty-seven members.

[27] See <http://www.fatf-gafi.org/countries/a-c/china/documents/follow-upreporttothemutualevaluationreportofchina.html>, last accessed 04/13/2020.

members, including China, to conduct research into developing and accepting new members.[28] In 2014, China was invited to join the FATF guiding committee of ten members.[29] The People's Bank of China stated in its annual report in 2015 that China was using the platform of the guiding committee to play a key role in the global CFT strategy-making, FATF's internal governance, and acceptance of new members.[30] China has also assumed a more active role in regional and global AML activities.[31]

China also influences the FATF's activities through its G20 membership as the FATF's activities follow the G20 agenda. For example, in 2009, the G20 specifically called for the FATF to reinvigorate its process for assessing countries' compliance with international AML/CFT standards and to publicly identify high-risk jurisdictions. In the same year, the G20 called on the FATF to address corruption by finding ways to create greater transparency of the financial system.[32] As China plays an increasingly important role in driving the G20 agenda, its influence on the FATF's work will grow.

7.2.4.4 Domestic organization and impact

China's FATF membership directly impacts the legal framework and the institution-building of the AML. As explained, candidate countries must go through strict mutual evaluation processes. After China's accession, it was put on (enhanced) follow-up process to address deficiencies. As a result, China's domestic AML system significantly improved.

7.3 Vietnam's Participation in Global Finance Governance

7.3.1 IMF and Vietnam

7.3.1.1 Introduction

Vietnam initiated its socio-economic renewal reform, known as 'doi moi', in 1986. This marks the beginning of a grand initiative to shift from a centrally-planned economic system to a market-oriented mechanism.[33] Vietnam normalized its financial relations with the IMF, the WB, and the Asian Development Bank (ADB) in

[28] See *2013 China Anti-Money Laundering Report*, People's Bank of China, 12.

[29] See *2014 China Anti-Money Laundering Report*, People's Bank of China, 12.

[30] *2015 China Anti-Money Laundering Report*, People's Bank of China, 12.

[31] For example, China hosted EAG Plenary meetings in 2009 and 2011; its representative served as Deputy Chairman of the EAG from December 2010 to November 2012. At the APG, China resumed its involvement as a member and held the rotating APG Co-Chair appointment from 2012 to 2014. In July 2013, it held the 16th Plenary meeting in Shanghai and took the opportunity to expand its bilateral and multi-lateral cooperation and through the APG getting more engaged in FATF's rule-making.

[32] FATF Annual Report 2010–2011, 20. See <http://www.fatf-gafi.org/media/fatf/documents/reports/FORMATTED%20ANNUAL%20REPORT%20FOR%20PRINTING.pdf>, last accessed 04/13/2020.

[33] WTO document WT/ACC/VNM/2, 'Accession of Vietnam: Memorandum on the Foreign Trade Regime', 24 September 1996, 1.

October 1993. Like China, Vietnam could not immediately meet the requirements of Article VIII of the IMF's Articles of Agreement.[34] After a decade of reform, Vietnam finally accepted these obligations in 2005.[35] Like China, the acceptance of Article VIII obligations facilitated its accession into the WTO in 2007.[36]

7.3.1.2 Institutional changes and involvement

7.3.1.2.1 Vietnam's participation in the IMF

A country may influence the IMF's decision-making through representation in the Board of Governors, the appointment or election to the IMF's executive board, indirectly through the IMFC, or through country groups like the G20.

As any other member of the IMF, Vietnam is represented by one governor and one alternate governor in the Board of Directors. However, in the Executive Board, which is responsible for conducting the day-to-day business of the IMF, Vietnam is represented by a director elected to represent a group of thirteen countries consisting of Brunei, Cambodia, Fiji, Indonesia, Laos, Malaysia, Myanmar, Nepal, Philippines, Singapore, Thailand, Tonga, and Vietnam. This group is called the Southeast Asia Voting Group (SEAVG). It is represented by the same group of countries in the International Monetary and Financial Committee (IMFC), which advises and reports to the IMF Board of Governors on the supervision and management of the international monetary and financial system and considers proposals by the Executive Board to amend the Articles of Agreement and advises on any other matters that may be referred to it by the Board of Governors.[37]

Table 7.3 summarizes Vietnam's interventions at the annual meetings of IMF since 1997. The summary is grouped into three categories, corresponding to the IMF's three functions. Vietnam's request to the IMF was primarily focused on IMF assistance to developing countries. This is in line with its status as an assistance recipient. Topics of concern have included the availability of sufficient funding, the conditionality of the assistance programmes, and the cooperation between the Fund and the Bank on assistance programmes. In 2016 Vietnam expressed satisfaction with the current IMF approach in assisting countries, describing it as 'a flexible, comprehensive policy framework with focus on individual country's characteristics'.[38]

[34] See Articles of Agreement of the International Monetary Fund.

[35] IMF Press Release, 'Vietnam accepts IMF's Article VIII obligations', 5 January 2006. For an introduction on the reforms undertaken, see WTO document WT/ACC/SPEC/VNM/5, Working Party Report on the Accession of Viet Nam, 22 November 2004, paras. 15–22.

[36] WTO document WT/ACC/SPEC/VNM/5, Working Party Report on the Accession of Viet Nam, 22 November 2004.

[37] IMF, 'A Guide to Committees Groups and Clubs', 19 April 2017.

[38] Statement by the Hon. Nguyen Dong Tien, Governor of the Bank of Vietnam, at the 2016 Annual Meetings of IMF and the World Bank Group, 7 October 2016.

Table 7.3 Vietnam's interventions at the annual meetings of IMF and the World Bank Group

	Assistance to developing countries	Policy-related issues	Quotas/institutional issues
1997	Express gratitude for the support and assistance provided	–	–
1997 Asian Financial Crisis			
1998	Increase concessionary funding and provide technical assistance in a more timely and more practical fashion in implementing economic reform and structural adjustment; Urge reaching agreement on a SAC and an ESAF programme	External advice and assistance must take into account the positive impact of globalization while minimizing the negative effects for the economy of each country	Urged to complete the 11th quota review and the IDA Fund contributions, as well as allocate additional SDR to the Fund
1999	Call upon to make more efforts in ensuring adequate financing for assistance through SAC and ESAF programme; Call for expedited multilateral and bilateral contributions to the HIPC funds	–	–
2000	Conditionality of the assistance programmes be closely associated with the specific circumstances of the host countries		Called for further efforts to reform the organization and working procedures to build a sound financial world and to facilitate developing countries to face challenges
2003			Called upon the Independent Evaluation Office to reflect their voice to the IMF Management in order to have necessary adjustments and thus making the assistance programs of the IMF and associated conditionality more in line with the actual situation of the beneficiary countries reflecting differences in their economic, cultural, political, and legal conditions.

Table 7.3 Continued

	Assistance to developing countries	Policy-related issues	Quotas/institutional issues
2004	–	–	–
2005	Initiative to support the developing countries in the process of trade liberalization and integration should cover not only the WTO members but also those countries seeking membership in this organization, like Vietnam		
2006	Urged the WB to respect recipient countries' sovereignty Further cooperation between the WB and the IMF is needed		Speed up the implementation of the main substances of the Medium-Term Strategy, especially the Quotas and Voice Reform
2007		Adoption of revised 1977 Decision on Surveillance: Fund surveillance activities under the revised framework should take into account of country-specific socio-economic conditions while refraining from putting further obligations on member countries	Quota and Voice reform: new quota distribution should be better aligned to recognize the increasing role of developing countries in the global economy
2008 US Financial Crisis			
2008	Cost sharing in TA provision: the priority should be given towards developing countries, facilitating them to maintain their access and utilization of the IMF's assistance		IMF priorities: play the coordination role to organize a global response to weaknesses in the global financial system; review its lending instruments; Look forward to further advances of the IMF's governance agenda, including the next step beyond strengthening membership representation through quotas and voice improvements
2009			Initiate reform of international financial architecture and governance, in which quota and voice is a focal component and of great importance

(continued)

Table 7.3 Continued

	Assistance to developing countries	Policy-related issues	Quotas/institutional issues
2011		To adapt itself to focus more on serving member countries with the same extent as focusing on the international monetary system; To have more comprehensive surveillance, not only looking at the traditional macroeconomic measures, but also other factors, including social and political issues; To keep track of the global interconnectedness and improve the IMF's credibility	Urge to continue reforms, especially in quota and voice issues, including the protection of quotas shares of poorest countries, as well as strengthened voices of dynamic and developing countries at the IMF
2012	Develop new lending instruments with higher flexibilities and in line with the situation, conditions, and accessibilities of all member countries	Enhance its capacity in monitoring, analysing, and forecasting the world, regional, and member economies	
2014	Further strengthen its technical assistance to improve macro-economic policy management capacity, strengthen regional and international collaboration, to better assist member countries.		Hope to see notable progress in reforming governance such as quota formula, budget, and income reviews with a commitment to increase the representation of dynamic economies and strengthen the voice of low-income countries
2015	No IMF-specific comments		
2016	Expressed satisfaction with the current IMF approach in assisting countries		

Vietnam occasionally touched upon surveillance issues. Even though it was also concerned about the adoption of revised 1977 Decision on Surveillance in 2007, its criticism was milder than that of China. Vietnam only requested the IMF surveillance activities to take into account country-specific socio-economic conditions and refrain from putting further obligations on member countries.[39] In 2016 Vietnam expressed satisfaction with the Fund's surveillance activities in the recent years: '[m]acroeconomic surveillance followed by policy advices and assistance to address current and future challenges has shown appropriation, helped to strengthen Fund's position as a global economic surveillance and ensure global financial stability'.[40] In general, the Vietnam governor commented, '[i]nitiatives generated by the Fund particularly fit emerging economies, including Vietnam.'[41]

Vietnam is also concerned about its representation in the IMF. Its interventions in the annual meetings on the quota-related reform are two pronged. On the one hand, it wants the new quota distribution to be more aligned with developing countries' increasing role in the world economy; on the other hand, it aims to preserve the quota share of low-income developing countries like itself.

Overall, it appears that by 2016, Vietnam was fairly content with its IMF membership.

7.3.1.2.2 Institutional changes and the impact on Vietnam

The 2008 Quota and Voice reform package provided an additional increase, or 'booster', to ensure a minimum increase in quota or quota share for dynamic under-represented emerging market and developing economies. Vietnam benefited from the booster and its quota share increased by 40%. The 2010 reform led to a more significant increase from 0.15% to 0.24%.[42] However, since the overall weight of Vietnam's economy in the world remains rather small, the increase did not lead to any significant change in Vietnam's ability to participate in the IMF decision-making processes.

7.3.1.3 Institutional changes and influence

Vietnam's influence in the IMF cannot be assessed without taking into consideration the joint efforts of the group of countries to which it belongs. Vietnam's main interest in participating the IMF is to have access to assistance to facilitate its domestic economic reform. For that purpose, it is concerned with the sufficiency of financing, the conditionality of the assistance, and the soundness of the policy advice. Connected with that, it hopes the governance reform could generate more representation of developing countries. These goals of Vietnam are no different than the goals of many other developing countries, most of which are also assistance recipient countries.

As a result of the two quota and voice reforms, the voting share of developing countries increased. More specifically, the voting share of emerging market and developing countries increased from 40.5% as of March 2011 to 44.8% post-2010 reform.[43] The increase is most significant for Asian developing countries—from 11.6% to

[39] Statement by the Hon. Nguyen Van Giau, Governor of the Fund for Vietnam at the Joint Annual Discussion, 22 October 2007.

[40] Statement by the Hon. Nguyen Dong Tien, Governor of the Bank of Vietnam, at the 2016 Annual Meetings of IMF and the World Bank Group, 7 October 2016.

[41] Statement by the Hon. Nguyen Dong Tien (n 40).

[42] IMF statistics.

[43] IMF, 'Quota and Voting Shares Before and After Implementation of Reforms Agreed in 2008 and 2010 (In percentage shares of total IMF quota)'.

16.1%—which reflects the recognition of the Asian countries' dynamic economic development, including Vietnam's.[44] In addition, the establishment of the Independent Evaluation Office (IEO) in 2001 also helped developing countries' needs being heard by the IMF management.[45] All these developments contributed to the general satisfaction of Vietnam with the IMF.

Beyond the IMF, Vietnam also sought to enhance its participation in global financial architecture by joining the Asian Infrastructure Investment Bank in April 2016.[46] As a board member, Vietnam works with the AIIB to arrange lending for projects.[47]

7.3.1.4 Domestic organization and impact

Vietnam has benefited from the assistance provided by the IMF and the World Bank in terms of policy advice, financing medium-term economic programmes, infrastructure and socio-economic projects, and a range of technical assistance programmes.[48] Benefits include highly concessional loans from the Enhanced Structural Adjustment Facility (ESAF) and Structural Adjustment Credit (SAC). In 1999, Vietnam was chosen from a dozen pilot cases for a Comprehensive Development Framework.[49] Vietnam acknowledged that this assistance has significantly benefited the country's economic reform, especially in the field of monetary policy, effectiveness improvement, statistics and forecast, foreign exchange reserve management, and macro-economic management.[50]

7.3.2 IOSCO and Vietnam

The State Securities Commission (SSC), Vietnam's securities market regulator, was established in 1997. The first stock exchange—the Ho Chi Minh City Stock Exchange—launched in July 2000, and the second one—the Hanoi Stock Exchange—launched in March 2005. The Vietnam securities depository centre officially launched operations in May 2006.[51]

The SCC was first admitted to Appendix B of the Memorandum of Understanding (MMoU) of the IOSCO in 2011. The MMoU provides for a global framework to enhance cooperation between securities regulators, thereby helping to ensure effective regulation and to preserve the strength of securities markets. Prior to signing the MMoU, applicant regulators must demonstrate their ability to provide assistance to other regulators in enforcement investigations, which includes being able to obtain

[44] IMF, 'Quota and Voting Shares (n 43).

[45] See <http://www.ieo-imf.org/>, last accessed 04/13/2020.

[46] See <https://www.aiib.org/en/about-aiib/governance/members-of-bank/index.html>, last accessed 04/13/2020.

[47] See <https://asia.nikkei.com/magazine/20170504/THE-FUTURE-OF-ASIA-S-INFRASTRUCTURE/Vietnam-can-leverage-the-ADB-and-AIIB-to-its-advantage>, last accessed 04/13/2020.

[48] See, for example, Statement by Hon. Le Duc Thuy, Alternate Governor of Vietnam at the 1997 World Bank/IMF Annual Meetings, Hong Kong, 23–25 September 1997.

[49] See Statement by Vietnam at the 1999 World Bank/IMF Annual Meetings.

[50] See Statement by Vietnam at the 2015 World Bank/IMF Annual Meetings.

[51] Hoang Phu Cuong, Overview of Vietnam Securities Market, available at: <http://www.asiasecuritiesforum.org/pdf/2015/HoangPhuCuong_s.pdf>, last accessed 04/13/2020.

specific forms of information and disclose that information to overseas regulators. Applicants are required to undergo a rigorous screening process, during which their capacity for cooperation is examined in detail by a group of experts. IOSCO members who have previously applied unsuccessfully to become signatories, but who have formally expressed their commitment to take the steps necessary to achieve MMoU compliance, are listed on Appendix B to the MMoU.[52] The SCC made major efforts to comply with the MMoU since its admission to Appendix B. Finally, on 18 September 2013, Vietnam signed Appendix A and became a full signatory of the IOSCO MMoU.[53]

Since Vietnam is a relatively new signatory of the IOSCO MMoU, and the major institutional changes happened years before 2013, it is difficult to evaluate the impact of the institutional change on Vietnam's participation. Clearly, though, acceding to the IOSCO has enabled the development of Vietnam's capital market.[54]

7.3.3 Vietnam in Other Organizations

Vietnam is not yet a member of the other organizations in the global financial architecture examined in this book (BCBS and FATF). This section briefly addresses how the issues covered by these organizations are organized domestically in Vietnam and explores the potential for further participation in these organizations.

7.3.3.1 BCBS

The development of Vietnam's banking sector shares many similarities to China's in that its move from a centralized system towards a modern banking system is part of the broad market-oriented economic reform that began in 1986. The State Bank of Vietnam (SBV) functioned as the central bank as well as a commercial bank before 1990. The 1990 Ordinance on the State Bank of Vietnam removed the commercial functions from the SBV and bestowed them upon four newly created state-owned commercial banks. The conclusion of the Vietnam–US bilateral trade agreement (BTA) in 2000 and the conclusion of its accession negotiations into the WTO in 2006 resulted in further liberalization of its banking sector. The presence of foreign banks has increased, and under the pressure of competition, domestic state-owned banks underwent reforms. Meanwhile, Vietnam progressively brought its regulatory regime for foreign bank branches, including minimum capital requirements, into alignment with commonly accepted international practice. The same legal capital requirements for foreign and domestic bank branches were set in 2008, and revised 2010 and again at the end of 2011.[55] Regarding Basel capital standards, Vietnam

[52] See <https://www.iosco.org/about/?subSection=mmou&subSection1=2013_list>, last accessed 04/13/2020.

[53] SCC, 'SSC Becomes Full Signatory to IOSCO MMoU—a Milestone in International Integration of Vietnamese Capital Market', 27 September 2013.

[54] See <http://vietnamnews.vn/economy/245611/ssc-deepens-links-to-international-markets.html#Zsrq0rAI4rfHpOP1.97>, last accessed 04/13/2020.

[55] WTO, Trade Policy Review Report, November 2013, Section 4.6.4.1. See also, Federal Reserve Bank of San Francisco, 'Banking Reform in Vietnam', June 2011.

currently applies Basel I to the banking industry. However, SBV started in 2017 to apply Basel II standards to a selected group of the ten largest and most prestigious domestic commercial banks; the application of Basel II to other commercial banks in the country is underway.[56]

Despite rapid development, Vietnam's banking sector remains underdeveloped and faces many challenges in risk management. However, with the further liberalization of the industry, Vietnam sees increasing need to implement Basel standards.[57] As the industry grows and the supervisory authority is more experienced, the expectation is that Vietnam will be more active in participating in Basel Committee standard-setting.[58]

7.3.3.2 FATF

Vietnam is not a member of the FATF but is a member of the Asia/Pacific Group on Money Laundering (APG), one of the regional transgovernmental bodies with Associate membership in the FATF. As Vietnam's economy became increasingly integrated with regional and global economies, international money-laundering crimes increased. In 2010, the FATF identified Vietnam as a jurisdiction with strategic AML/CFT deficiencies. Vietnam built up necessary legal and regulatory framework to address these deficiencies. Since February 2014, Vietnam is no longer subject to the FATF's monitoring process under the global AML/CFT compliance process. Currently, Vietnam is working with the APG as it continues to address the full range of AML/CFT issues identified in the mutual evaluation report.

7.4 Comparing China and Vietnam

7.4.1 Trade Liberalization: A Catalyst for Participation in Global Finance Governance

Both China and Vietnam have experienced economic reforms of a similar nature, that is, from a centralized planned economy to a market economy. Importantly, both countries employed trade liberalization to further reform. For China, its WTO accession led to a more open and competitive domestic financial market. Competition brought about innovation, the need for the authority to seek more regulatory cooperation from other jurisdictions, and the need for further reform of domestic banks—specifically to incorporate key principles of the Basel Accord into the regulatory framework. A similar pattern can be identified in Vietnam, where trade liberalization is stimulated by the Vietnam–US BTA , as well as the WTO accession. With

[56] See *Viet Nam News*, 'New Regulation Prepares for Basel II', 17 January 2017. <http://vietnamnews.vn/economy/349833/new-regulation-prepares-for-basel-ii.html#CfVzMpiRvWaefH3k.97>, last accessed 04/13/2020.

[57] *Viet Nam News*, 'New Regulation Prepares for Basel II' (n 56).

[58] As identified in the other chapters of the book, expertise in certain policy area drives participation. See Henrique Choer Moraes, 'Can Regional Institutions Increase the Legitimacy of Global Governance? The Cases of the Regional Branches of the FATF and of the FSB.' Chapter 12, this volume.

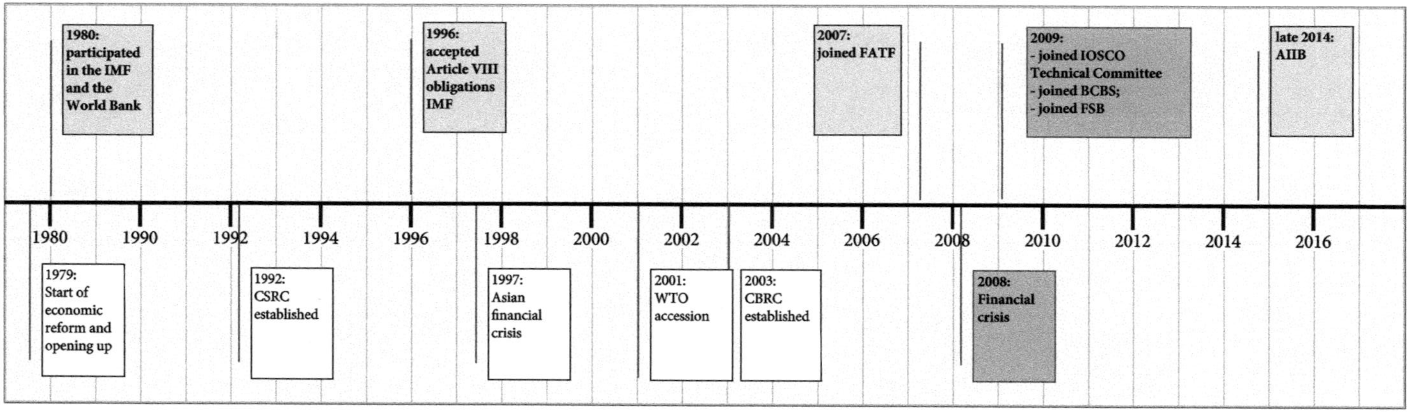

Figure 7.2 Timeline of China's Participation in the Global Financial Architecture

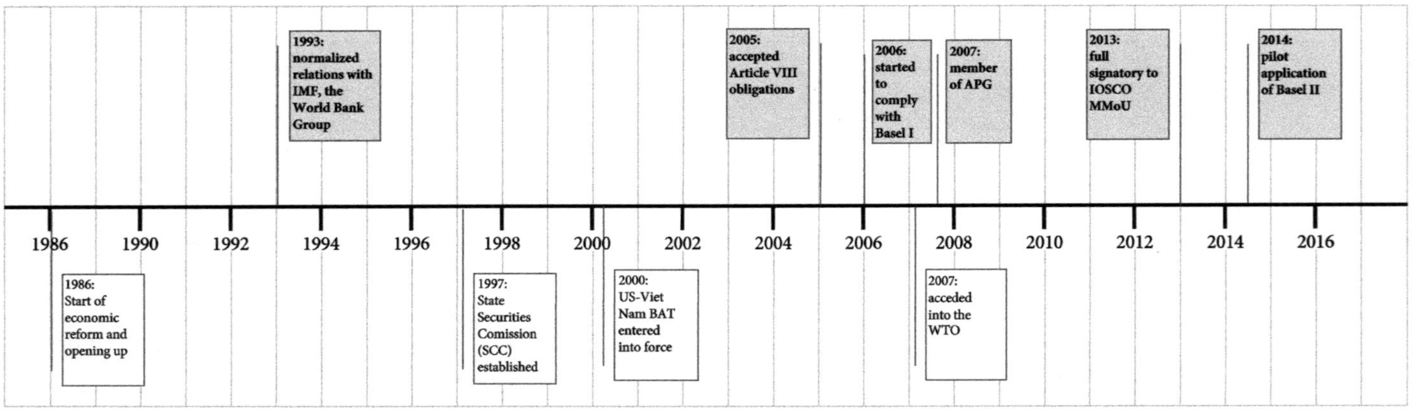

Figure 7.3 Timeline of Vietnam's Participation in the Global Financial Architecture

increased foreign participation and therefore more fierce competition, the SBV felt the need to fully implement Basel II. Meanwhile, a more open financial market also brought about concern about money laundering. Both countries are therefore motivated to participate in global AML initiatives. As regards monetary issues, the acceptance of Article VIII's obligation of the IMF is a prerequisite to enable ambitious trade liberalization. Indeed, both countries undertook Article VIII obligations before joining the WTO.

The close relationship between the market liberalization process and the participation in international financial institutions can be best illustrated by the following two timelines. They place China's and Vietnam's participation in global financial architecture against their respective economic reform process. Active participation in the IMF enabled both countries to liberalize their trade policy, which inevitably increased both countries' interest in issues like minimum capital requirement for financial institutions, cooperation with foreign capital market regulators, and anti-money laundering. Thus, for both China and Vietnam, the need to participate in global finance governance goes hand in hand with the liberalization of their economies.

7.5 Size Matters, but Opportunities Lie Ahead

Even though both China and Vietnam have followed similar paths to market liberalization (and therefore experienced similar needs to participate in global finance governance), their levels of participation and their ability to influence various regulatory issues differ. These differences can be, at least, partly explained by their different economic sizes. While Vietnam has achieved impressive economic growth since the reform, its overall weight in global economy remains small. While China's GDP in PPP terms accounts for 17.2% of the world economy, Vietnam's is only 0.48%. The resulting difference in their systematic impact on the world economy explains China's membership in institutions from which Vietnam remains absent. The global financial crisis in 2008 made China's systemic importance in finance governance even more prominent and such prominence was reflected in its increasingly larger voice in the G20. China's membership in the FSB, the BCBS, and the former Technical Committee of the IOSCO are all the result of the implementation of the G20 agenda. Such importance is also reflected in IMF and FATF, the mandates of which are directly impacted by the G20 decisions after 2008. Furthermore, China has created a competing institution for development finance—the AIIB—to influence global finance governance.

Even though Vietnam remains behind China in terms of its economic development, it can benefit from the growing voice of developing countries, or groups of developing countries. As metioned, Vietnam's concerns in organizations such as the IMF are similar to other developing countries. Furthermore, its position on various issues is similar to that of large developing countries like China, due to the similarity in the transitional nature of their economies. The increasing influence of the G20 in global finance governance offers an opportunity for Vietnam to cooperate with other developing countries to participate in decision-making more effectively. The recent active participation in the AIIB is another way for Vietnam to be more involved in global finance governance for its own benefits.

In short, China and Vietnam's participation in the emerging global finance architecture is a tale of two cities. For the two countries the rapidly evolving tale is similar, but its pattern is different.

8

India and Bangladesh in Global Finance Governance

From Structural Conflict to Embedded Liberalism in the Climate Finance Regime

*Rahul Mukherji and Himanshu Jha**

8.1 Introduction

In this chapter, we argue that India and Bangladesh have transformed their respective engagements with the global climate finance architecture from a relationship that can be conceptualized as 'structural conflict' within the emerging international regime to support for 'embedded liberalism'.[1] Central to understanding why and how this shift has occurred is the idea of 'legitimate social purpose' that defines the way a state thinks. We first engage the idea of 'legitimate social purpose' as a way of understanding how power gets converted into interest and consequently contributes to global order. We then argue how India's and Bangladesh's legitimate social purpose transformed itself from North South structural conflicts to embracing an embedded liberal order. We first conceptualize this transition using the idea of legitimate social purpose as a way of defining global order. We then explore the issue of legitimate social purpose of the state in India and Bangladesh, respectively. Finally, we demonstrate how this transition works for India and Bangladesh through climate finance.

We employ a comparative case analysis of India and Bangladesh despite the obvious difference in size, following the methodological rationale spelled out by Büthe and Cheng.[2] India is much larger than Bangladesh in terms of population (1.3 billion vs. 160 million) and area (2.9 million vs. 130,170 km^2). However, the countries are

* The authors thank and acknowledge A S M Mostafizur Rahman (Meah Mostafiz) and Tanvi Deshpande, doctoral candidates at the Department of Political Science, South Asia Institute, Universität Heidelberg for their valuable research support. Comments by Tim Büthe, Martino Maggetti, Kern Alexander and colleagues at the SNIS authors' workshop for the Stakeholder Participation project at the TUM *Akademiezentrum* Raitenhaslach-Burghausen were useful to develop this paper.

[1] See Stephen D Krasner, *Structural Conflict: The Third World Against Global Liberalism* (University of California Press 1985); John G Ruggie, 'International Regimes, Transactions, and Change: Embedded Liberalism in the Postwar Economic Order' 36(2) *International Organization* (1982), 379-415; Rahul Mukherji, 'India and Global Economic Governance: From Structural Conflict to Embedded Liberalism' 16(3) *International Studies Review* (2014) 460-466.

[2] For details, see Tim Büthe and Cindy Cheng, 'Analysing the Consequences of Institutional Reforms Using Country Pairs: A Note on the (Coarsened Exact) Matched-Country-Pairs Methodology of the Rethinking Stakeholder Participation Project.' Chapter 3, this volume.

Rahul Mukherji and Himanshu Jha, *India and Bangladesh in Global Finance Governance* In: *Rethinking Participation in Global Governance*. Edited by: Joost Pauwelyn, Martino Maggetti, Tim Büthe, and Ayelet Berman, Oxford University Press.
 DOI: 10.1093/oso/9780198852568.003.0008

among the most comparable on the Human Development Index (rank 130 and 142; only Bhutan at 132 is closer to India among the countries of South Asia).[3] Moreover, Bangladesh is very similar to India among the South Asian countries with regard to per capita gross development product (GDP)—USD 1,212 vs. USD 1,598[4]—most similar with regard to infant mortality (31 vs. 38 per 1,000 births), very similar with regard to life expectancy at birth (72 vs. 68 years),[5] and second-most similar with regard to the literacy rate (83.2% vs. 89.7%).[6] Additionally, both countries have grown rapidly and consistently at a rate greater than 6% per annum during the last decade. The two countries also exhibit a high and rapidly increasing integration into the global economy, as is evident from Bangladesh's garment exports and India's prowess in information technology.

We explore whether the differences in size (as a proxy for the power differential between India and Bangladesh) makes a difference for these two traditionally marginalized countries' opportunities to participate, actual participation, and influence in the global governance of climate change financing. Climate finance thus is our entry point to explore stakeholder participation in the emerging global financial architecture. Despite the size variable, we find that Bangladesh and India have both embraced the embedded liberal order. We contend that ideas embraced by the state are central to our explanation.

8.2 Legitimate Social Purpose and Global Order

We argue that power is combined with what John Ruggie called 'legitimate social purpose' to understand the nature of India's rise. India's globalism has transformed itself from 'structural conflict' to 'embedded liberalism'. Both 'structural conflict' between the global North and the South, and an order based on 'embedded liberalism' require us to think deeply about the concept of 'legitimate social purpose'.[7] Opposition to economic liberalism in North-South conflict was clearly derived from domestic level factors such as ideational milieu and state capacity. The 'embedded liberal' order emphasizes a liberal multilateral setting where states have the sovereign right to pursue domestic prerogatives, even though they pay respect to the multilateral system (Table 8.1). Ruggie argued persuasively that the embedded liberal order was the product of the 'legitimate social purpose' of the post Second World War world led by the United States.

[3] The comparisons presented here are based on open data for 2015 from the World Bank, 'World Bank Open Data' <http://data.worldbank.org/>; United Nations Educational, Scientific and Cultural Organization, 'Education: Literacy Rate' <http://data.uis.unesco.org/Index.aspx?queryid=166>; and the United Nations Development Programme, 'Human Development Data (1990–2018)' <http://hdr.undp.org/en/data>; all last accessed 8/14/2017.

[4] Source: World Bank; the amounts shown are not ppp-adjusted. Only Pakistan was in 2015 more similar to India, with 1,435; all other South Asian countries differ much more notably from India.

[5] Only Bhutan and Nepal were in 2015 more similar to India, with a life expectancy of 69 and 70.

[6] Only Nepal was, with 89.9% more similar to India.

[7] Krasner, *Structural Conflict* (n 1), 379–415.

Table 8.1 The nature of globalization

Legitimate social purpose	Engagement with globalization
Autarkic industrialization	Structural conflict
Globalization	Embedded liberalism

Source: Authors

What then is legitimate social purpose driving global order? Legitimate social purpose or the moral purpose of the state has to do with the way a state thinks. For Ruggie, hegemony in international relations did not automatically produce a free trade order, as many hegemonic stability theorists would argue. Comprehending the nature of global order needed a good understanding of both interests and the dominant ideas of the day. To give a few examples: Dutch hegemony in the seventeenth century produced a mercantilist order. Thereafter, an open trading system could evolve when the idea of free trade was articulated under a single market by the British state. *Laissez-faire* was planned in such a way that the balance between authority and the market shifted in favour of the market. According to this narrative, Great Britain played a leadership role in maintaining the gold standard and other states respected the authority of the single market and subjected themselves to its discipline.

The legitimate social purpose of Britain in the nineteenth and the early twentieth centuries was not shared by the US till the end of the Second World War. The US, for a long time, even when it had surpassed Britain in the twentieth century, remained a mercantilist state. Protectionism had roots in the ideas of thinkers like the first treasury secretary of the US Alexander Hamilton, who argued in favour of import substitution. He had opined in the eighteenth century that the US will have to manufacture its own goods and services till it possessed a strong Navy and until such times that its goods could compete with those of Great Britain. He was certain that the US would one day assume that role.[8]

The First World War disrupted the British dominated *laissez-faire* order. Domestic economic considerations such as social stability became the salient guiding force driving the global economy. States were no longer willing to make adjustments dictated by a *laissez-faire* order. Domestic imperatives began to impede international economic coordination. Protectionism became the order of the day. This was the time when domestic social policy rather than adjusting to the global market became the dominant theme.

The post-Second World War consensus, for Ruggie, was the compromise of 'embedded liberalism'—a position between market-led adjustments in the global economy and total subservience to domestic imperatives. This compromise reflected a battle of ideas within the US and between US and European states. The chief negotiators of the Bretton Woods system, Harry Dexter White of the US and John Maynard Keynes of the UK, both believed in the need for state intervention. According to Albert

[8] Edward Mead Earle, 'Adam Smith, Alexander Hamilton, Friedrich List: The Economic Foundations of Military Power' in Peter Paret, Gordon A Craig and Felix Gilbert (eds), *The Makers of Modern Strategy: From Machiavelli to the Nuclear Age* (Princeton University Press 1986), 217-261.

Hirschman, the spread of Keynesianism to Europe had much to do with the American victory and its faith in deploying Keynesian policies to revive Europe. Keynesian ideas triumphed at the end of the Second World War when the US sought fashion the global economic order.[9]

The rise of Keynesianism in the US had much to do with the manner in which the state came to embrace that world view. Mark Blyth tells the story of why Keynesian ideas came to dominate US policy. The great depression created circumstances that spoke directly to the concerns that Keynes's work was seeking to address. There were no clear alternative paths to resolve this problem when Keynes seemed to provide a succinct answer to the problem of the great depression. Keynes was accepted not because business lobbies or interest groups supported it but because this seemed to be the only way out to deal with a substantial social problem. Thus a policy paradigm was born out of the US's legitimate social purpose.[10]

Legitimate social purpose enshrined in the compromise of 'embedded liberalism' ran counter to the *laissez-faire* demands of Wall Street. States were allowed to run deficits and these deficits could be financed with surplus from other states. Moreover, the global trading system enshrined in the General Agreement on Trade and Tariffs (GATT) came up with the most favoured trading nation rule—every GATT member would accord the most-favoured nation tariffs to every other member. But states were allowed to violate these principles through a variety of escape clauses. Autonomy for the domestic realm was enshrined in the Bretton Woods institutions in a number of ways.[11]

These approaches to hegemony in international relations stress two important facts regarding stakeholder participation. First, hegemony mattered. Second, hegemony did not automatically produce a liberal economic order. What mattered was the ideational logics of appropriateness within the hegemonic state that gave rise to mercantilism, *laissez-faire*, and embedded liberalism. The non-hegemonic and less-endowed countries played a relatively marginal role here. We now turn to the issue of how North–South relations made an impact on the global order.

8.3 North–South Relations and Global Order

We now consider the issue of North–South relations to understand legitimate social purpose in a different way. India and China, today's emerging powers, were until recently considered a part of developing countries or the global South. Steven Krasner's conceptualization of 'structural conflict' was a powerful explanation for North-South conflicts in the post-Second World War era. Read differently, the legitimate social purpose of the Third World, according to Krasner, was to lock its horns with the First. Third-World countries wanted to reduce their vulnerability with respect to

[9] Ruggie, 'International Regimes' (n 1), and Albert O Hirschman, 'How the Keynesian Revolution was Exported from the United States, and Other Comments' in Peter A Hall (ed), *The Political Power of Economic Ideas: Keynesianism Across Nations* (Princeton University Press 1989), 347-359.

[10] Mark Blyth, *Great Transformations: Economic Ideas and Institutional Change in the Twentieth Century* (Cambridge University Press 2002).

[11] Ruggie, 'International Regimes' (n 1); see also John G Ruggie (ed), *The Antinomies of Interdependence: National Welfare and the International Division of Labor* (Columbia University Press 1983).

the industrialized world. Krasner found that developing countries have weak state capacity to tax and create infrastructure, and for making market-led adjustments. Devoid of this capacity, Third-World countries would not be competitive with respect to the industrialized West. This would engender structural conflict between the North and the South.

Structural conflict would be facilitated by two factors. First was the principle of sovereign equality, central to the embedded liberal order. Sovereign equality ensured that all states large and small had the same number of votes in the United Nations. Second, was the powerful ideology of dependency theory that had its lineage in Lenin's imperialism? These theories argued persuasively that the wealth of the industrialized countries depended largely on the poverty of the developing world. Wallerstein's classic application of Lenin to the post-colonial world, the theory of World Systems reasoned why industrialized countries needed to exploit the less industrialized ones for raw materials and markets. These structural pre-conditions material and ideational, argued Krasner, enabled the Third-World state to define its social purpose in terms of neo-colonial dependency narratives.[12]

The result: the countries of the South refused to cooperate with the multilateral order. They opposed market adjustments and kept demanding compensation for the historic exploitation from colonial times. This was clearly the case regarding India's views within the Group of 77 nations, which worked as a powerful lobby in many international arenas. This chapter clearly shows that India and Bangladesh desired exceptions in arenas such as trade and the environment. These exceptions would allow them to deviate from market rationality. Furthermore, these deviations also sought resources from Northern countries for adjustment to the global order. Consistent with the Krasner's logic, the Third World did get embroiled in structural conflict with the developed world in the 1970s and the 1980s. This was clearly evident during the oil shock inspired by the Organization of Petroleum Exporting Countries (OPEC).

We find that India and Bangladesh have both shifted gears from structural conflict to embedded liberalism, in their quest to adjust to emerging climate finance order. Adjustment to the embedded liberal order would require these countries to make adjustments while respecting domestic social concerns. We explore how and why this shift has occurred. In the next section, we propose a way to think beyond Krasner to explain why emerging economies such as India and Bangladesh successfully made this shift.

8.4 India and Bangladesh: Structural Conflict to Embedded Liberalism

If the global order requires us to think about the legitimate social purpose of the leading power, the nature of India's emergence or the interests of smaller countries

[12] Krasner, *Structural Conflict* (n 1); see Immanuel Wallerstein, *The Modern World-System I: Capitalist Agriculture and the Origins of the European World-Economy in the Sixteenth Century* (Academic Press 1974); Immanuel Wallerstein, *The Modern World-System II: Mercantilism and the Consolidation of the European World-Economy, 1600-1750* (Academic Press 1980); Immanuel Wallerstein, *The Modern World-System III: The Second Era of Great Expansion of the Capitalist World-Economy, 1730-1840s* (Academic Press 1989).

like Bangladesh in relation to the multilateral order prods us to think about how this idea of legitimate social purpose can be applied to other states as well. As argued elsewhere, states become rational in relation to the logics of appropriateness they pursue.[13] The Indian state began as a votary of autarkic industrialization since independence since 1947. The idea that the global economic realm is exploitative was driven both by the experience of colonialism and by how Indian policy-makers were eyeing development paradigms such as import substitution, and Soviet and Chinese communism. We narrate briefly how India's autarkic import substitution was transformed by an embrace of globalization that engendered the demand of maintaining an embedded liberal order. We establish a connection between India's tryst with embedded liberalism in climate change negotiations as well. We conduct a similar exploration for Bangladesh, even though the literature on Bangladesh's globalization is substantially sparser.

First, India defined its legitimate social purpose in a rather autarkic way from 1950 till about 1975. It's trade to GDP ratio rose consistently only after 1991. The period between 1975 and 1991 is a period when the social purpose shifted in the direction of change through a tipping point rather than a punctuated equilibrium model. The tipping point model is a gradual model of economic change where change seems abrupt and cataclysmic like an earthquake. However, it is largely an endogenous model of economic change when abrupt change occurs when ideas reach a threshold. The tipping model persuades us to explore how the social purpose of a state undergoes change.[14]

India adopted an autarkic model. Its trade-to-GDP ratio was in the range of 10–15% in the early 1970s. This model consolidated itself over a period time. The First Prime Minister Jawaharlal Nehru was one of the key architects influenced by technocrats who favoured import substituting industrialization. India's Second Five-Year Plan was considered a model plan. It impressed both the communists in the USSR and the Keynesians economists in the US, where import substituting industrialization was an important idea in development theory. The plan's execution earned resources both from the US and the USSR in the early years until about the mid-1960s.[15]

The import substituting consensus was reinforced over time. In 1966, India faced a severe balance of payments crisis. The US wanted India to devalue its currency and promote both exports and private sector production. India did devalue its currency owing to severe pressure from the US and the World Bank (WB) only to adopt an even more autarkic and state-guided system after 1967.[16]

[13] Rahul Mukherji, *Globalization and Deregulation: Ideas, Interests and Institutional Change in India* (Oxford University Press 2014).

[14] For tipping point see Mukherji, *Globalization and Deregulation* (n 13); Himanshu Jha, 'State Processes, Ideas an Institutional Change: The Case of the Right to Information Act in India' 91(2) *Pacific Affairs* (2018) 309-328; Peter A Hall, 'Politics as a Process Structured in Space and Time' in Orfeo Fioretos, Tulia G Falleti, and Adam Sheingate (eds), *The Oxford Handbook of Historical Institutionalism* (Oxford University Press 2016), 31-50.

[15] See I G Patel, *Glimpses of Indian Economic Policy: An Insider's View* (Oxford University Press 2003); Medha M Kudaisya, *The Life and Times of G. D. Birla* (Oxford University Press 2003); Jagdish N Bhagwati and Padma Desai, *India: Planning for Industrialization* (Oxford University Press 1970).

[16] Rahul Mukherji, *Political Economy of Reforms in India: Oxford India Short Introductions* (Oxford University Press 2014); Francine R Frankel, *India's Political Economy: The Gradual Revolution (1947-2004)* (Oxford University Press 2005).

This was also the time when India was locked in 'structural conflict' with the West. It became a leader of the Group of 77 (G77) that demanded authoritative and redistributive transfers rather than market-driven allocations. India spearheaded the move to remove textiles trade from GATT—a project that led to the creation of the Multi-Fibre Agreement. Even though the oil price hike during the two oil shocks hurt the Indian economy, India did not object to it. It argued for allocating resources for the development of poor countries.

If India was locked in structural conflict and did not acquiesce to adjustment to the market in other realms, we would expect India to demand authoritative international resource allocations in its favour rather than market-led adjustments during this period. In a subsequent section, we demonstrate how India demanded systematic redistributive transfers in international environmental regimes ranging from ozone negotiations to climate change.

India's tryst with import substitution changed gradually, mostly due to how the legitimate social purpose of the state changed to critiquing autarky from 1975. Substantial reports of the Government of India discussed the need for exports, foreign investment, and resources to fund India's development. Additionally, some technocrats clearly saw the limits of this economic model. However, import substitution found powerful support base in what economist Pranab Bardhan called the dominant coalition. It would therefore be tough to revolutionize the import substitution order, even in the presence of a sceptical technocratic elite.[17]

India's policy paradigm favouring embedded liberalism tipped in July 1991, when in response to a severe balance of payments crisis, India revolutionized its economic policies in relation to private sector participation, trade, and foreign investment. July 1991 was a tipping point rather than a response to an exogenous shock. The shock was largely due to internal reasons—substantially because of how the policy-makers thought about the problems of the time. They had a clear plan and good arguments, and Washington largely respected the consensus in Delhi. Moreover, Delhi used the crisis to push reforms in a manner that would be politically impossible in the absence of a crisis. The reforms were of a heterodox nature. Heterodox reforms subsequently engendered home-grown adjustment to globalization and private sector orientation in the IMF's most successful tryst with a developing country. India's adjustment deviated from orthodox IMF programmes.[18]

The nature of India's engagement with globalization subsequently transformed itself from 'structural conflict' to 'embedded liberalism'. Decades of persisting with import substitution driven structural conflict in the global economy persuaded the technocrats to embrace an embedded liberal order that allowed for a heterodox home-grown adjustment plan. The legitimate social purpose within the Indian state had shifted towards the promotion of an embedded liberal order. India was now willing to play the game of globalization, albeit after paying due respect to domestic considerations. We characterize the period 1970–2001 as a period when India opposed the liberal order and demanded merely redistributive transfers and exceptions in global environmental

[17] Mukherji, *Globalization and Deregulation* (n 13); see also Pranab K Bardhan, *Political Economy of Development in India* (Oxford University Press 1998).

[18] Mukherji, *Globalization and Deregulation* (n 13); Bardhan, *Political Economy* (n 17).

regimes. Thereafter, we find a clear shift in India's approach. India was willing to abide by liberal principles, after giving due consideration to domestic imperatives. We code this behavioural principle as the shift to embedded liberalism.

Bangladesh, too, has begun playing the 'embedded liberal' game in climate negotiations in the new millennium. The country has embraced globalization and made a mark in garment exports. The country's early years beyond independence from 1971 till the end of the decade were a socialist period inspired by founding father Sheikh Mujibur Rehman. The 1980s increasingly took the country in the private sector direction. The post-1990 period for Bangladesh, like the one in India, witnessed the embrace of globalization. The success of Bangladesh's globalization is reflected in the rise of its garment sector, fisheries, ship recycling, and remittances.[19] We find that Bangladesh engaged in structural conflict with respect to global environmental regimes between 1980 and 2006. Thereafter, Bangladesh moved towards favouring an embedded liberal order. It is willing to make investments that make it a player in the investment regime.

For countries like India and Bangladesh, the shift from 'structural conflict' to 'embedded liberalism' in climate finance negotiations has much to do with the legitimate social purpose guiding these states. Both are developing countries that are vulnerable to climate change. Each has a long coastline, and Bangladesh is home to the world's largest delta. If these state structures were wedded to the idea of autarkic industrialization, they would be locked in structural conflict. The reason for this lock in would be the inability of these states to rationalize the benefits of market-led adjustments. However, when these states began engaging globalization, they were willing to make adjustments, but not necessarily in a manner subservient to the Washington consensus. Then these states would push for an embedded liberal order where they would be able to make adjustments after paying due consideration to domestic concerns. They could then not be viewed as states merely demanding redistributive transfers.

8.5 Institutions of Climate Finance

From the standpoint of stakeholder participation in global governance this section examines two global institutions involved with climate finance: the Global Environment Facility (GEF) and the Green Climate Fund (GCF). These institutions are the arena for exploring Bangladesh and India's tryst with embedded liberalism. The GEF is the longest-serving climate finance mechanism in operation since 1991. After the launch of pilot programmes in 1991, the GEF was restructured as a unique climate funding entity and managed trilaterally by the WB, the United Nations Environment Programme (UNEP), and the United Nations Development Programme (UNDP), where the WB was the dominant partner.[20]

[19] See Rehman Sobhan, *Bangladesh: Problems of Governance* (Konark Publishers 1993); David Lewis, *Bangladesh: Politics, Economy and Civil Society* (Cambridge University Press 2011), 136-166.

[20] Shalendra Sharma, 'The World Bank and The Global Environment Facility: Challenges and Prospect for Sustainable Development' 3(2) *The Brown Journal of World Affairs* (1996) 275-287. See also Helen S K Sjöberg, 'Restructuring the Global Environment Facility (Working Paper 13 September 1999)' <http://documents.worldbank.org/curated/en/335511487673481446/pdf/109668-NWP-13-Box396324B-PUBLIC.pdf>, last accessed 08/14/2017.

The GCF is the newest funding mechanism at the global level. The WB is the interim trustee of the GCF. A need to have an alternate financial mechanism beyond the framework of grants and assistance was expressed jointly by developing countries. Against this backdrop, the GCF was first proposed in the Conference of Parties (Cop) 15 in 2009 and established in Cop 16 (2010). This funding mechanism was supposed to be in line with country programmes and domestic needs. GCF's governing instrument was formally adopted at Cop 17 (2011) primarily on the initiative of developing countries to have a financial mechanism for both climate adaptation and mitigation. Departing from the funding framework of the GEF, the unique feature of this fund was equal weightage given to funds for both adaptation and mitigation.[21] The funding through GCF comes in form of grants and concessional loans,[22] although this is a source of confusion because developing countries expect the flow of climate funds primarily in form of grants.[23]

Both these institutions of global climate finance are located at the unique intersection of major institutions of global governance. For example, the GEF has eighteen implementing partners, including the WB, the Asian Development Bank, and the UNEP. GCF's interim trustee is the WB. This demonstrates the cross-cutting nature of climate finance with direct engagement with institutions of global governance.

8.6 India and Climate Finance

8.6.1 The Structural Conflict Phase (1970–2001)

In this phase India's stance can be located directly within the North–South divide. This was the period of 'structural conflict', where the country's development needs were the priority, and climate finance was the responsibility of the developed world. India's position was characterized by a paradox: at one level India acknowledged the threat of climate change, and at another level priority was accorded to the developmental needs of the country. Distinction was made between the 'survival emissions' of the poor and 'luxury emissions' of the rich,[24] meaning that India would not make any adjustment from its internal resources without redistributive transfers from the rich countries. There would either be redistribution or conflict—Krasner's classic position in arguing for structural conflict.

'Structural conflict' shaped the domestic climate finance imperatives around three areas: untied aid, technology transfer, and varying degree of commitments and responsibilities. Therefore, the initial response was more around developmental needs

[21] Climate adaptation has to do with how citizens can cope with climate-related disasters.

[22] Green Climate Fund, 'Financial Terms and Conditions of Grants and Concessional Loans' <https://www.greenclimate.fund/documents/20182/24940/GCF_B.06_16_-_Financial_Terms_and_Conditions_of_Grants_and_Concessional_Loans.pdf/9a5584c0-a1e4-42da-8ce3-2424a725b6ab>, last accessed 02/14/2017.

[23] Saleemul Huq, 'Loans or Grants for Climate Finance?' <https://www.climatechangenews.com/2015/10/19/loans-or-grants-for-climate-finance/>, last accessed 02/10/2017.

[24] Huq, 'Loans or Grants' (n 23).

rather than the climate related commitments. Climate, after all, was a global public good. This was evident in India's stance in the early climate discourse, finding concrete expression in the statement of Minister for environment Maneka Gandhi in 1989, who declared 'CFC issues as irrelevant' and that 'India's reforestation is important, but it competes with roads and electricity'.[25] Consequently, climate finance was primarily dependent on aid. For example, in the 1980s, India was the second-largest recipient of the environmental aid from the WB, receiving 1.5 billion USD (Brazil was the largest, receiving 2 billion USD).[26]

Without compromising its stance on the flow of funds from developed to the developing world, India was not averse even in the early years to make domestic adjustments where it felt the need. These had to do more with domestic environmental commons issues than global commons.[27]

8.6.2 From Structural Conflict to Embedded Liberalism (2001–2016)

In the second phase we find a transition from 'structural conflict' to 'embedded liberalism'. It took a decade beyond India's market adjustments around 1991 for the country to become a player rather than a disruptive force for the multilateral order. India's engagement with climate negotiations is one of embedded liberalism characterized by a deeper global engagement. However, this global engagement required the multilateral system to be aware of India's special developmental needs. To demonstrate the embedded liberal engagement here, we link India's positions in the global governance of climate discourse with climate finance. The embedded liberal approach is evident from two emerging patterns. First, from 2001 onwards we find a shift in both the content and form of engagement,[28] evident in the role India played in the codification of the Kyoto protocol in 2001, emphasizing the technology transfer, financial resources, and the clean development mechanism. Second, India's engagement was largely contingent on the domestic discourse. Climate change negotiations became a political issue, shifting from the realms of bureaucratic wonks to that of political policy leaders.[29] The politicization of climate change is evident from debates in both

[25] United Nations General Assembly, 18 December 1989. See, Theron A Mehr, 'International Technology Transfer: Constructing and Financing an Environmental Program' 15(3) *Loyola of Los Angeles International and Comparative Law Review* (1993) 731-760.

[26] Robert L Hicks, Bradley C Parks, J Timmons Roberts, and Michael J Tierney, *Greening Aid?: Understanding the Environmental Impact of Development Assistance* (Oxford University Press 2008), 194.

[27] For example, legal and regulatory steps were taken such as the Wildlife (Protection) Act 1972, Water (Prevention and Control of Pollution) Act 1974, Forest Conversation Act 1980 to name a few. Government of India also instituted the department of Environment in 1980, expanded as the Union Ministry of Environment and Forests in 1985.

[28] This was also the period when the geopolitics of the world was undergoing a change characterized by the emergence of China, India, or Brazil. The North–South divide was not as stark as before. See D Raghunandan, 'India's Official Position: A Critical View Based on Science' in Navroz K Dubash (ed), *Handbook of Climate Change and India: Development, Politics and Governance* (Routledge 2012), 170-179.

[29] See Aaron Atteridge, Manish Kumar Shrivastava, Neha Pahuja, and Himani Upadhyay, 'Climate Policy in India: What Shapes International, National and State Policy?' 41(1 Supplement) *Ambio* (2012) 68-77.

the houses of parliament raising questions such as, 'what is the non-negotiable minimum of India' in the climate negotiations?'[30]

8.7 Climate Finance

We examine India's position on climate finance against this backdrop. India's embedded liberal position was officially articulated during Cop 8, hosted by India in 2002, where developing countries stressed the significance of technology transfer, financial resources, and capacity building.[31] Concern was also expressed regarding the accessibility of funds available under the GEF.

Additionally, issues ranging from domestic challenges to climate finance received substantial attention. Climate finance entered the government's domestic discourse for the first time in 2011–2012 in the Economic Survey of India, which had a section on climate change and sustainable development.[32] The survey recognized climate change as both an 'environmental issue' as well as an 'economic issue' and 'lack of funding was a large impediment to adaptation plans'.[33] The economic survey emphasized that India needed access to finance and technology to meet its adaptation and mitigation challenges. This was in the immediate aftermath of the Durban Cop in 2011, which launched the programme for long-term finance. The Minister of Environment and Forests (MOEF) on the occasion of the 2017 Cop reflected this concern, saying 'developed country parties who have commitment to provide resources should agree to capitalize the fund, its legal status and to the structure of long-term sources of the finance for the Green Climate Fund'.[34]

In this light, the climate finance architecture has to be understood at two levels: domestic and global. At the global level India's source for climate finance can be divided into four categories: i) grants from the bi-lateral assistance; ii) multilateral grants under the GEF managed by the United Nations and the WB; iii) multilateral loans and technical assistance; and iv) soft loans and technical assistance. India engages with international climate change finance through the GEF, Special Climate Change Fund (SCCF),[35] Adaptation Fund (AF), and the Clean Technology Fund

[30] Suresh Prabhu, 'Climate Change and Parliament: Excerpts from the Lok Sabha and Rajya Sabha Debates' in Navroz K Dubash (ed), *Handbook of Climate Change and India: Development, Politics and Governance* (Routledge 2012), 230-245

[31] United Nations Framework Convention on Climate Change (UNFCCC), The Delhi Ministerial Declaration on Climate Change and Sustainable Development (No. FCCC/CP/2002/L.6/Rev.1, 1 November 2002) <https://unfccc.int/resource/docs/cop8/l06r01.pdf>, last accessed 01/22/2017 .

[32] See chapter 12, page 293 of Government of India (GOI), 'Economic Survey of India 2011–12' <https://www.indiabudget.gov.in/budget2012-2013/survey.asp>, last accessed 12/27/2016 . Also see pages 6–7 of the report by Vyoma Jha, 'The Coordination of Climate Finance in India (Overseas Development Institute/Centre for Policy Research)' <https://www.odi.org/sites/odi.org.uk/files/odi-assets/publications-opinion-files/9329.pdf>, last accessed 12/27/2016.

[33] GOI, 'Economic 2011–12' (n 32), 293–329.

[34] Statement by Jayanthi Natarajan, Minister of Environment and Forests, Government of India, Durban, 7 December 2011. United Nations Framework Convention on Climate Change (UNFCCC), 'Statement by India at the High-level Segment of COP17/CMP7' < https://unfccc.int/files/meetings/durban_nov_2011/statements/application/pdf/111207_cop17_hls_india.pdf >, last accessed 03/1/2017.

[35] The SCCF was established under the Convention in 2001 to finance projects relating to: adaptation; technology transfer and capacity building; energy, transport, industry, agriculture, forestry, and waste management; and economic diversification. United Nations Framework Convention on Climate Change

(CTF).[36] In the subsequent sections we discuss two main institutions of climate finance: the GEF and GCF.

8.7.1 The GEF

Following seven rounds of intense negotiations between 1991–1994 the GEF was accepted as a funding mechanism with not only universal participation but also greater transparency and accountability in global governance.[37] India played a significant role in these negotiations, which can be ascertained from the fact that India's representative, Nand Kishore Singh was the chairman of the core group for negotiations. GEF was to provide grants incrementally to the developing countries to fulfil their commitments made in the international conventions.[38] Significantly, in line with India's policy priorities, it has raised questions about the imbalance in the GEF structure between adaptation and mitigation related funds: 'India has received very little funds for adaptation ... this imbalance needs to be addressed by the GEF as adaptation is a higher priority area for us.'[39]

India began contributing to the climate finance architecture rather than just demanding resources. This acknowledged that the global order of climate finance was one to which India could profitably contribute. The structural conflict described in the previous section was thus replaced with an embedded liberal approach to funding projects. India began its journey as a net recipient. Between 1991 and April 2012, India received USD 340 million as grants under the GEF for forty-nine approved projects.[40] By 2015 the same figure had risen to USD 477.3 million, of which USD 284.2 million was utilized for mitigation projects and USD 10 million were for adaptation.[41] India was also a contributor to GEF. In the GEF pilot phase (1991–1994) India had contributed USD 6 billion to its core funding. By 2012, the same figure had risen substantially to USD 48.75 billion.[42]

India's contributions required the country's own approach to monitoring and evaluation of projects. The GEF's Office for Monitoring and Evaluation evaluates the use

(UNFCCC), 'The Special Climate Change Fund (SCCF)' <http://unfccc.int/cooperation_and_support/financial_mechanism/special_climate_change_fund/items/3657.php>, last accessed 08/14/2017.

[36] Jha, 'The Coordination' (n 32), 13.

[37] For instance, developed and the developing countries were divided on the issue of whether to use the UN system (based on one vote one country) or the Bretton woods system of voting rights on the basis of economic strength. See Nicholas Van Praag, 'Introductory Note. The Global Environment Facility: Instrument Establishing' 33(5) *International Legal Materials* (1994) 1273-1308.

[38] GEF India: Enabling Transformations (GOI, MOEF&CC 2015) <http://moef.gov.in/wp-content/uploads/2017/10/GEF-India-Enabling-Transformation.pdf>, last accessed 03/12/2017.

[39] This was expressed by the special secretary MOEF&CC in operational charge of GEF. See, *GEF India: Enabling Transformations* (n 38).

[40] GEF Independent Evaluation Office (GEFIEO), 'GEF Country Portfolio Evaluation (CFE) India (1991–2012)', <http://www.gefieo.org/evaluations/country-portfolio-evaluation-cpe-india>, last accessed 08/14/2017.

[41] See GOI, 'Economic Survey of India 2014-15', 126 <https://www.indiabudget.gov.in/budget2015-2016/survey.asp>, last accessed 01/20/2017.

[42] Department of Economic Affairs | MoF | GOI, 'India and Global Environmental Facility (GEF)' <http://dea.gov.in/sites/default/files/India_GEF_0.pdf>, last accessed 01/22/2017.

of funds and recommends an increase or decrease in a country's allocation according to the country's performance.[43] Within India, the GEF evaluation is operationalized through two domestic focal points—a political focal point located in the Department of Economic Affairs in the Ministry of Finance, and an operational focal point in the Ministry of Environment, Forest and Climate Change (MOEF&CC).[44] Additionally, a GEF-empowered committee located within the MOEF&CC determines the national priorities, approves projects, and monitors the progress.[45] A domestic framework is essential as the GEF primarily co-funds only a quarter of the total project costs, the rest of the funding stems from the government and other partner organizations (see Figure 8.1).[46]

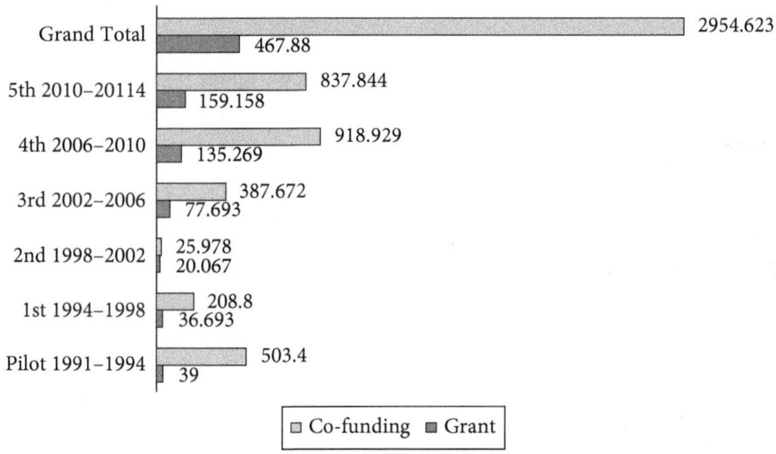

Figure 8.1 GEF: India Share of Grants and Co-funding (in Millions of USD)
Source: Ministry of Environment, Forest and Climate Change, Government of India, 2015

8.7.2 The GCF

India's 'embedded liberal' position took a sharper turn with the formation of the GCF for three reasons. First, India aggressively raised the issue of the quantum of international financial assistance after the formation of the GCF. It deployed considerable

[43] Answer to Unstarred Question No: 70, 26 February 2007. Lok Sabha (the lower house), Parliament of India, GOI.

[44] In 2014, Ministry of Environment and Forests was renamed Ministry of Environment, Forest and Climate Change. So far, the GEF has provided USD 13.5 billion in grants, leveraged USD 65 billion in co-financing for 3,900 plus projects in more than 165 developing countries. Through its Small Grants Programme (SGP), the GEF has made more than 20,000 grants to civil society- and community-based organizations for a total of USD 1 billion.

[45] See 'How GEF India is Governed', Ministry of Environment. Forest and Climate Change, Govt. of India <http://moef.gov.in/division/establishment-divisions/international-cooperation-ic/gef-india/about-gef/> last accessed 04/14/2020.

[46] See 'Funding of GEF', MOEF&CC, <http://moef.gov.in/division/establishment-divisions/international-cooperation-ic/gef-india/funding/> last accessed 04/14/2020.

weight on the need to fulfilling the pledge of the developed countries to raise USD 100 billion by 2020. The official view asserted that '... it can be from a variety of sources, but the goal agreed to was $ 100 billion per year by 2020 ... the fact of the matter is that we are nowhere near it'.[47]

The second issue raised was the type of finance available for adaptation measures, underlining the significance of public finance for adaptation as private actors were not coming forward: 'the primacy of public resources is very important in this scheme of things. For instance, do we expect private investment for adaptation, which is a dire need of the developing countries? [...] Public resources will have to address these concerns.'[48]

India's third point continued from its earlier question on who will pay:

> ... every Climate Action has a cost and the world must think, who would pay the cost. Instead of making the polluters to pay, we should not end up with a formula where we make the poor pay ... all the principles and provisions of the Convention should apply to the new architecture of 2015 Agreement.[49]

The expectation from GCF was a continuation of India's persisting position on 'equity and Common but Differentiated Responsibilities (CBDR)', specifically focusing on access to finance and technology transfer to the developing world: 'India, like other developing countries, can do more, if finance and technology development and transfer and capacity building support are ensured as per the convention and its Paris Agreement.'[50] Developing countries such as India and China played a leading role in operationalizing this fund.[51] This was a culmination of a continuous collaboration between the two countries on climate finance-related issues.[52]

Notably, India, along with China and Saudi Arabia from the Asia Pacific region, was represented on the GCF board since its inception[53] and played a significant role. For example, in 2013 during the early years of the GCF's existence India's representative

[47] See Press Information Bureau | Government of India | Ministry of Environment, Forest and Climate Change (PIB), 'India Will Work with International Community to Find Practical and Equitable Solutions to Climate Change: Javdekar' <http://pib.nic.in/newsite/PrintRelease.aspx?relid=121858>, last accessed 02/18/2017.

[48] PIB, 'India Will Work' (n 47).

[49] PIB, 'India Will Work' (n 47).

[50] Harsh Vardhan, Minister of Environment, Forest and Climate Change, GOI (Keynote Speech on the occasion of the signing of Accreditation Master Agreement (AMA) between GCF and NABARD, New Delhi, 11 August 2015). Press Information Bureau | Government of India | Ministry of Environment, Forest and Climate Change (PIB), 'Green Climate Fund' <https://pib.gov.in/newsite/PrintRelease.aspx?relid=124811>, last accessed 08/14/2017.

[51] Arabinda Mishra and Neha Pahuja, 'Cooperation on Climate Change Mitigation: An Indian Perspective' in Kanti Bajpai, Jing Huang, and Kishore Mahbubani (eds), *China-India Relations: Cooperation and Conflict* (Routledge 2016), 108-129.

[52] For example, in 2009 prior to the Copenhagen COP India and China signed an agreement of cooperation on climate change which established two bilateral mechanisms—one of India–China partnership for combating climate change and India–China working group on climate change. This entailed regular dialogue, exchange of views, and cooperation on both mitigation and adaptation. See Mishra *et al.*, 'Cooperation on Climate' (n 51), 111.

[53] Currently, Dinesh Kumar, an Additional Secretary at the Department of Economic Affairs, Ministry of Finance, GOI is India's representative on the GCF board.

Dipak Dasgupta prepared the vision and resource mobilization document matching the fund's instruments with outcomes.[54] India's representative even played a key role in designing the logo for the fund.

The reforms within the institutions of global governance are reflected in operationalization of the GCF.[55] The GCF required national governments to set up institutional mechanisms at the domestic level to access funds. India selected the MOEF&CC as Nationally Designated Authority (NDA) for operationalizing the GCF, which has two tracks of funds access. The first is the direct access for regional, national, and sub-national institutions, which are accredited by the NDAs. The second is the international access track for international institutions like the United Nations, multilateral banks, international financial institutions, and regional banks. The MOEF&CC initiated steps to have accreditation for three organizations: the National Bank for Agriculture and Rural Development (NABARD), Small Industries Development Bank of India (SIDBI), and the Infrastructure Development Finance Company Limited (IDFC). In 2015, NABARD was accredited as the National Implementing Entity (NIE) for the GCF in India.[56] Similar to its view in the CoP negotiations, India's 'embeddedness' was visible in its engagement with the GCF as well, where India's developmental needs were stressed: 'we need to take cognisance of our population size and income inequality, and cannot ignore the basic requirement of electricity, housing, and food for the poor. We expect GCF to partner with us on these issues and prioritize their work to overcome these challenges.'[57] Significantly, the central government has organized capacity-building programmes for the sub-national governments to directly access the funds available under the GCF.[58]

In 2017 India directly accessed USD 34.4 million for a project on 'groundwater recharge and solar micro irrigation' in the state of Odisha.[59] An additional USD 132 million are to be co-financed by a loan from the International Bank for Reconstruction and Development (IBRD) and the state convergence fund and community. The total project investment is USD 166.3 million, out of which 79.3% is co-financed in the form of loans, and the rest is grant from the GCF.[60]

Two points emerge from these discussions. First, we note a transition in the nature and flow of climate finance from an aid oriented to a participatory framework. This is evident in matching grants provided by the national government, which shows an institutional evolution where, on one hand, the domestic imperatives

[54] Green Climate Fund (GCF), 'Report of the Second Meeting of the Board, 18–20 October 2012' <https://www.greenclimate.fund/documents/20182/24928/GCF_B.02-12_13_-_Report_of_the_Second_Meeting_of_the_Board__18-20_October_2012.pdf/3c610794-e76f-4403-9bda-fd816e15a85a>, last accessed 08/14/2017.

[55] WB is the interim trustee of the GCF.

[56] PIB, 'Green Climate' (n 50).

[57] Harsh Vardhan, Minister of Environment, Forest and Climate Change, GOI (Keynote Speech on the occasion of the signing of Accreditation Master Agreement (AMA) between GCF and NABARD, New Delhi, 11August 2015). PIB, 'Green Climate' (n 50).

[58] Press Information Bureau | Government of India | Ministry of Environment, Forest and Climate Change (PIB), 'Environment Ministry Holds Third Regional Workshop with State Governments' <http://pib.nic.in/newsite/PrintRelease.aspx?relid=138781>, last accessed 02/20/2017.

[59] Direct access is to receive funds without any financial intermediaries such as the WB.

[60] Green Climate Fund (GCF), 'Projects & Programmes' <http://www.greenclimate.fund>, last accessed 08/14/2017.

demand greater participation, and on the other, reform process within international institutions also facilitated stakeholder participation. India is now a stakeholder in the institutions of climate finance representing a classic 'embedded liberal' order. This is evident from the crucial role that India played in the operationalization of the GCF.

Second, institutional mechanisms are in place at the domestic level often calibrated with its engagement with the global institutions. For example, while at the global level India has demanded greater flow of finances towards both adaptation and mitigation, institutional mechanisms that are in line with the developmental needs of the country have been put in place at the domestic level.[61] In 2009, as part of India's National Action Plan on Climate Change (NAPCC), the central government directed the state governments to prepare State Action Plan for Climate Change (SAPCC); by March 2015, thirty-one states had prepared their SAPCCs.[62] A Climate Change Finance Unit (CCFU) was also established in the Department of Economic Affairs located in the Ministry of Finance in 2011.[63]

This section highlighted the embedded liberal nature of India's response since the early years of the 2000s. India has transitioned from structural conflict, where poverty was deemed to be the greatest polluter to a regime where it has made commitments towards cutting emissions. These commitments, however, are contingent on finances available to developing countries. India has also put in place a domestic financial and implementation architecture to deal with climate issues. In the next section, we explore Bangladesh's transition from structural conflict to embedded liberalism.

8.8 Bangladesh and Climate Finance

Bangladesh's initial engagement with climate change can be discerned in two phases as well. The first phase of structural conflict runs from 1980–2006, and the second embedded liberal phase runs from 2006 onwards. In the first phase, Bangladesh was quick to realize the problem of climate change and was demanding redistributive transfers. These demands changed during the second phase, when Bangladesh not only led the demand emanating from least-developed countries but also devoted substantial resources for domestic adjustments.

[61] For example, domestic climate finance mechanisms such as the National Clean Energy Fund (NCEF); National Adaptation Fund (NAF); Compensatory Afforestation Fund (CAF) and National Disaster Response Fund (NDRF) are funded through public finance. In addition, the provisions for funding of national adaptation and mitigation missions under National Action Plan on Climate Change (NAPCC) are endowed in the national budget. See, Centre for Budget and Governance Accountability, 2017. *Climate Finance Architecture in India*. New Delhi: Centre for Budget and Governance Accountability (CBGA).

[62] Answer to Unstarred Question No.1230, by Minister of State of Environment, Forests and Climate Change, Lok Sabha Questions, Parliament of India, 3 March 2015. Parliament of India Lok Sabha House of the People (POI), 'Unstarred Question No: 1230: State Action Plan on Climate Change' <http://164.100.47.194/Loksabha/Questions/QResult15.aspx?qref=12547&lsno=16>, last accessed 08/14/2017.

[63] Jha, 'The Coordination' (n 32), 7. The key function of this unit was to provide policy advice to the government on climate finance, provide inputs to the designing of the GCF and closely follow the pledges and commitments made by other countries in the UNFCCC.

8.8.1 Structural Conflict Phase (1980–2006)

The first phase was a period of 'structural conflict', when Bangladesh's quickly understood the challenge of climate change and demanded redistributive transfers. This is evident from the early acknowledgment of climate risk during the 1995 Berlin negotiations, when chief negotiator Atiq Rahman declared that 'If climate change makes our country uninhabitable, we will march with our wet feet into your living rooms.'[64] This realization coincided with the formation of alliances among the scientists to think collaboratively on the issue of climate change.

Even though Bangladesh was early to acknowledge the problem of climate change, it was a part of the global South that was in structural conflict with the North. It deemed climate change to be the responsibility of the developed world, viewing both the problem and solution with the industrialized countries.[65] Meanwhile, at the domestic level an epistemic network of stakeholders continued their scientific interventions through publications.[66] These interventions often found their way in the global climate change discourse. For instance, some of these scientists were the lead authors of some sections of IPCC's third assessment report (2001) and the fourth assessment report (2008).

8.8.2 Embedded Liberal Phase (2006–2017)

Around 2006 there was a shift from 'structural conflict' to 'embedded liberalism'. It is important to point out that the continued domestic demands provided a platform for Bangladesh's climate engagement. At the same time, we find shifts in Bangladesh's global position. This shift often followed the domestic imperatives pointing towards an 'embedded liberal' approach. For example, domestic imperatives were paramount in the policy papers such as the national paper on climate change and the first Bangladesh Climate Change Strategy and Action plan (BCCSA 2008). Significantly, in September 2008 Bangladesh and the United Kingdom (UK) jointly organized the London Climate Change Conference. Bangladesh's Minister for Environment and Forests C S Karim insisted that Bangladesh should produce its own national paper without any support from the UK's Department for International Development (DFID). The next section discusses how Bangladesh's interaction with globalization is influenced substantially by its domestic needs.

8.8.2.1 Bangladesh and the GEF

Since its inception in 1991, Bangladesh has engaged with the GEF primarily for adaptation projects. Bangladesh undertook thirty-eight projects with total grants of USD

[64] Bradley C Parks and J Timmons Roberts, 'Inequality and the Global Climate Regime: Breaking the North-South Impasse' 21(4) *Cambridge Review of International Affairs* (2008) 621-648.

[65] Manoj Roy, David Hulme and Joseph Hanlon, *Bangladesh Confronts Climate Change: Keeping Our Heads Above Water* (Anthem Press 2016), 30.

[66] Roy *et al., Heads Above Water* (n 65), 30f.

138.52 million. This was matched by an additional co-financing of USD 845.83 million. The GEF was operationalized through two focal points. National level operations were undertaken by the Ministry of Environment and Forests. The Economic Relations Division of the Ministry of Finance served as the political focal point. In addition, Bangladesh received climate finance from the Least Developed Countries Fund (LDCF), which is managed by the GEF. The LDCF is aimed at financing the most immediate needs of the least developed countries (LDCs) and supports them to prepare, prioritize, and implement National Adaptation Programme of Action (NAPA). Bangladesh was one of the first countries to prepare its NAPA in 2005.[67]

Bangladesh's approach to engage with targeted sources of climate finance such as the LDCF should be viewed in light of a strategic shift in its stance in the global climate negotiations. Moving beyond the G77, Bangladesh strategically aligned with smaller groups to make a bigger impact in the climate negotiations. This would also give it greater clout for respecting its domestic imperatives at the international level. Bangladesh is part of the LDCs, Most Vulnerable Nations (MVN), coalition of rain forest nations,[68] and the Cartagena group.

Bangladesh has played a leadership role within these groups. For instance, in 2008 Bangladesh delivered a statement on behalf of the LDC to the UN general assembly. This statement demanded specific attention to the LDC's especially in the realm of resource mobilization, 'we have noted with concern that the resources mobilized under different international mechanisms for the purpose of adaptation are grossly inadequate'[69]. Moreover, Bangladesh stresses that the clean development mechanism is not suitable for the LDC's because they are not getting any projects. The 'lion's share of resources earmarked for climate change is deployed for clean development mechanism'.[70]

Keenness to have a dedicated pool of fund for vulnerable and least developed countries is reflected in the minister for MOEF's statement in Cop 18 (2003) expressing vulnerability in concrete terms of 'loss and damage', 'a reality for Bangladesh', which, 'could not be addressed only by adaptation activities'. The minister urged that 'a separate international mechanism be established to address loss and damage that could be done through disaster risk reduction, compensation, rehabilitation and other approaches'.[71] A clear message was also delivered on the issue of finance: 'Finance is

[67] The preparation of NAPA was supported by the GEF. In line with the decision made during Cop 7, the GEF council in December 2001 authorized the GEF to provide financial support to the LDCs for the preparation of NAPA through a dedicated fund. See GEF, 'Operational Guidelines for Expedited Funding for the Preparation of National Adaptation Programs of Action by Least Developed Countries' <http://unfccc.int/files/cooperation_and_support/capacity_building/application/pdf/gefsecnapaguideeng.pdf>, last accessed 08/14/2017.

[68] The group's focus is on protecting rainforests. This group was instrumental in pushing for 'reducing emissions from deforestation and degradation (REDD)'. See Joyeeta Gupta, *The History of Global Climate Governance* (Cambridge University Press 2014), 153-154.

[69] Statement by Bangladesh on the Behalf of the LDC, Delivered by Secretary, Ministry of Environment and Forests, Government of the People's Republic of Bangladesh. UNGA Thematic Debate on Climate Change, New York, 12 February 2008.

[70] Statement by Bangladesh (n 69).

[71] Hasan Mahmud, 'Statement QNCC Doha, 5 December 2012' <http://unfccc.int/resource/docs/cop18_cmp8_hl_statements/Statement%20by%20Bangladesh%20(COP).pdf>, last accessed 08/14/2017.

linked to all issues we are negotiating; to ensure sustained flow of resources in the future, decisions on how the finance gap in post 2012 period shall be addressed.'[72]

8.8.2.2 Bangladesh's engagement with the GCF

Bangladesh has a grant of USD 40 million from the GCF for an adaptation project on 'Climate-Resilient Infrastructure Mainstreaming in Bangladesh'. Another USD 15 million is co-financed from a bilateral loan of USD 15 million from Germany and USD 25 million from the Bangladesh Ministry of Local Government. The primacy of Bangladesh's domestic imperatives was evident when the country demanded access to climate finance in form of a grant instead of the proposed soft loan during the Paris summit because of its aversion to loan conditions.

Like India, Bangladesh has a National Designated Authority (NDA) and a National Implementing Authority (NIA) to give shape to its domestic concerns within the GCF. The Economic Resource Division within the Ministry of Finance was appointed the NDA for administering Bangladesh's actions within the GCF. A secretary at the Economic Resources Division serves as the focal point. The two NIAs are the Infrastructure Development Company Limited (IDCOL) and the Palli Karma Sahayak Foundation (PKSF).[73]

Bangladesh even initiated policy reforms within the GCF. A three-day workshop for the NDAs and NIAs of developing countries was organized by the Government of Bangladesh (GOB) to discuss the issues in the process of accreditation. Two representatives of the GCF were invited in the meeting. NIAs and NDAs from South Asian countries shared their experiences of applying for accreditation and unanimously agreed that the process of accreditation needs to be streamlined, accompanied by the capacity building within the NDA's. Three issues were pointed out: first, the voluminous documents to be submitted to prove the fiduciary capacity of the NIA's; second, the lack of clarity on showing the transformational impact of the proposed projects; and third, ambivalence about the need to differentiate between climate and development projects.[74] This workshop turned out to be instructive on two counts. It demonstrated that the process of reform in an international body like GCF can be initiated by the small and poor participating member states like Bangladesh. Second, the suggested policy reforms were prescribed in the context of the domestic imperatives. This points towards an 'embedded liberal' nature of the reforms within the GCF.

The case of Bangladesh demonstrates that countries in the global South were willing to make their own adjustments, given their domestic imperatives. India and Bangladesh are both vulnerable. They are no longer using climate as a tool for redistributive transfers from the rich countries. Bangladesh's smaller size and scientific awareness of vulnerability has created its own imperatives. The country has not only embraced globalization through its readymade garments industry, but it also has made substantial allocations for climate adaptation climate mitigation. Its strategies

[72] Mahmud, 'Statement QNCC' (n 71).

[73] See Green Climate Fund (GCF), 'Bangladesh: Country Profiles' <https://www.greenclimate.fund/countries/-/country-profiles/bangladesh>, last accessed 04/18/2018.

[74] Saleemul Huq, 'Green Climate Fund: Still a Work in Progress' <https://www.thedailystar.net/opinion/politics-climate-change/green-climate-fund-still-work-progress-1580005>, last accessed 06/01/2018.

for adaptation and mitigation are self-conscious. These strategies are even wary of blindly exposing the country to conditions of the WB that come tied with funding.

Due to the uncertain and inadequate nature climate finance from the multilateral and bilateral sources, Bangladesh like India has established domestic institutional mechanisms to manage climate finance.[75] For instance, in 2008 along with BCCSA, the National Climate Change Trust Fund (NCCTF) was established. BDT 3 billion (USD 35 million approximately) were allocated towards this fund in 2008 and this was increased to BDT 7 billion (USD 82 million approximately) when the new government assumed power in 2009.[76] Subsequently in 2010, the Climate Change Trust Act was passed by the Parliament for guiding Bangladesh Climate Change Trust Fund (BCCTF) to manage domestic funds made available through national budgets.[77]

8.8.2.3 Bangladesh Climate Change Resilience Fund (BCCRF)

Moreover, domestic institutional mechanisms were also designed to manage multilateral and bilateral funds originating from foreign sources. Significantly, the WB and the International Monetary Fund were unacceptable funding organizations. This need to establish a funding mechanism to manage bilateral funds for climate change was expressed in the first United Kingdom (UK)–Bangladesh Conference held in April 2008. Following this conference, at the London Climate Change Conference, the UK pledged a grant of GBP 75 million to Bangladesh towards Bangladesh Climate Change Strategy and Action Plan (BCCSAP) launched at this conference. Since this grant could not be directly disbursed to Bangladesh, a multi-donor trust fund (MDTF) was established to manage this resource.[78] Bangladesh had refused to accept this grant from the UK government if it were channelled through WB because it would come with strings attached: 'If this money is channeled through the World Bank and the IMF it will attract strings and conditions which are not favorable to Bangladesh.'[79]

Such was the importance of domestic considerations that the MDTF was expanded into the Bangladesh Climate Change Resilience Fund (BCCRF) in May 2010 to manage bilateral and multilateral funds from the developed countries and the WB. Like BCCTF, this fund provided resources to operationalize BCCSAP. A three-tier

[75] S M Munjurul Hannan Khan *et al.*, 'The Bangladesh National Climate Funds', LDC Paper Series, DFID and Institute for Environment and Development (IIED), 2012 <https://www.ldc-climate.org/wp-content/uploads/2018/02/LDC-paper-series-18.pdf>, last accessed 04/14/2020; S M Munjurul Hannan Khan, Saleemul Huq, and Md Shamsuddoha, 'The Bangladesh National Climate Funds: A Brief History and Description of the Bangladesh Climate Change Trust Fund and the Bangladesh Climate Change Resilience Fund' <https://www.ldc-climate.org/wp-content/uploads/2018/02/LDC-paper-series-18.pdf>, last accessed 05/17/2017.

[76] Khurshid Alam, Md Shamsuddoha, Thomas Tanner, Moshahida Sultana, Muhammad Jahedul Huq, and Sumaiya S Kabir, 'Planning Exceptionalism? Political Economy of Climate Resilient Development in Bangladesh' <https://www.ids.ac.uk/files/dmfile/BangladeshPECCMainReportFinal2.pdf>, last accessed 08/14/2017, 11–12.

[77] BCCTF is first national climate fund established by an LDC. See Md Kamruzzaman Aman, 'Introduction to the Bangladesh Climate Change Trust Fund', *Dhaka Tribune*, 13 June 2015 <https://www.dhakatribune.com/uncategorized/2015/06/13/introduction-to-the-bangladesh-climate-change-trust-fund>, last accessed 11/29/2016.

[78] Khan *et al.*, 'Bangladesh National' (n 75).

[79] Representative from the Bangladesh government was quoted in a news story. See *The Guardian*, 'Bangladesh Rejects Terms for £60m of Climate Aid from UK' <https://www.theguardian.com/environment/2010/feb/15/bangladesh-world-bank-climate-finance>, last accessed 08/14/2017.

governance structure was established to manage BCCRF, which also represented well the domestic interests. The chairperson of the governing council was the Minister of Environments and Forests (MOEF), and the Secretary to the MOEF served as the secretary general providing strategic direction and guidance. The Prime Minister's Office, the Planning Commission, and the ministers of Finance, Food and Disaster Management, Foreign Affairs, Agriculture, and Women and Children Affairs were also included as members of the governing council. Two representatives from development partners and civil society (nominated by the government) were also included. The WB was granted only an observer status without voting rights. A joint secretary of the MOEF managed the BCCRF's secretariat. Amidst much protest by the GOB and the civil society, the WB was made the trustee of the fund for the first five years, because donors were not ready to transfer funds directly to the GOB. Eight development partners, primarily developed countries, pledged USD 188.2 million (see Table 8.2).

Table 8.2 Contributions for BCCRF (up to 2012)

Countries	Contributions (in USD Millions) for year 2012
United Kingdom	96.9
EU	37.6
Sweden	19.3
USAID	13
Switzerland	12.5
Ausaid	7.1
Denmark	1.8
Total	188.2

Source: Bangladesh Climate Fiscal Framework, 2014.
Finance Division, Ministry of Finance, GOB: 28

Despite Bangladesh's acceptance of multilateral and bilateral funds, climate finance architecture was primarily dictated by the domestic imperatives evident in the governance architecture of BCCRF. Domestic interests were overwhelmingly represented in the way global climate finance was administered in the country. Such a governance structure of BCCRF was finalized after long drawn negotiations between the GOB and the global financiers.[80] The tension between the WB and the GOB resurfaced in 2016 when the WB declined to continue the trusteeship of the fund. The GOB was in the process of lobbying with the donors to directly transfer the funds without the involvement of the WB, but the Department for International Development (DFID) refused to release the money to the BCCRF. However, the donors, along with the WB, discontinued the BCCRF in 2017.[81] UK Aid's unfavourable report on the progress of

[80] See Khan *et al.*, 'Bangladesh National' (n 75).

[81] *The Daily Star*, 'Dhaka Loses £13m Climate Funds' <http://www.thedailystar.net/backpage/dhaka-loses-£13m-climate-funds-1312921>, last accessed 08/14/2017.

the BCCRF provided the backdrop. Global–domestic antagonism was cited as one of the reasons why the 'delivery was hampered' due to 'competition from the nationally owned BCCTF'.[82] Therefore, as things stand, more than 80% of the climate projects are financed from domestic sources. One-third of the foreign finance is in form of grants, while the remaining two-thirds is loans.

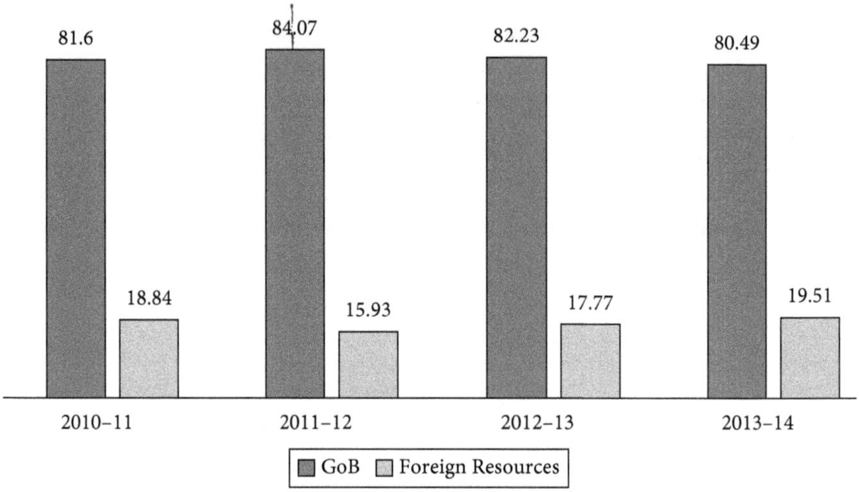

Figure 8.2 Funding Proportion (%) of Climate Budget
Source: Bangladesh Climate Fiscal Framework, 2014 (Finance Division, Ministry of Finance, GoB: 20)

8.9 Conclusion

India and Bangladesh are both comparable countries. Even though they differ in terms of size, they look quite similar in terms of human development and per capita income. Both countries have democratic regimes and are faced with the challenge of climate change. They have long coastlines and deltas. Both countries have also made the transition to globalization as a development strategy after an initial period of import substitution. They are part of South Asia's rapid economic growth story.

Our strong conjecture is that autarkic industrialization would generate the demand for transferring resources to the developing world, consistent with Steven Krasner's structural conflict. We find that India led the way among the G77 nations in its quest for transferring resources from rich to poor countries. Poverty for India was the biggest polluter in the pre-globalization world. Bangladesh also participated in this Third World strategy. The country was early to note the problem of climate change but

[82] Annual Review, Department for International Development UK, 30 April 2015 <http://iati.dfid.gov.uk/iati_documents/5005829.odt> last accessed 04/14/2020. Also see, 'Climate finance dispute prompts Bangladesh to return £13m of UK aid', *The Guardian*, 10 November 2016. <https://www.theguardian.com/global-development/2016/nov/10/climate-finance-dispute-bangladesh-returns-13-million-uk-aid-world-bank> last accessed 04/14/2020.

argued that the way out was redistribution of resources from the North to the South. In the early years, these countries exploited the environment to garner resources from the developing world rather than finding means to collectively make adjustments to the challenges posed by climate change.

These countries have embraced globalization since the 1990s. The embrace of globalization in poverty-stricken parts of the world necessitates that adjustments can only be made consistent with domestic social commitments. This is what Ruggie (following Polanyi) called 'embedded liberalism'. India and Bangladesh have made the transition from 'structural conflict' to 'embedded liberalism'. They are now making adjustments that are not contingent on the transfer of resources from rich countries. However, they need resources from the global North and need their own pace and methodology to make these adjustments. The embedded liberal behaviour is evident in tapping resources from domestic sources, as well as, from organizations such as the GEF and the GCF on their own terms. India has played a leading role within the GEF, and Bangladesh is proactive within the least developed country coalitions. Both countries have been proactive in regard to national plans for adaptation and mitigation and have begun the quest for garnering resources for it. They have nationally designated implementing and monitoring authorities. Figures 8.1 and 8.2 demonstrate how the national commitments far outstrip the resources mobilized from abroad.

We find that India and Bangladesh are comparable. Both the states have made the transition from promoting North–South structural conflict to engaging the world in an embedded liberal way. They are actively participating in global negotiations, demanding resources as well as contributing substantially to domestically driven adjustment. Bangladesh and India are also actively contributing to global norms—India as an emerging power, and Bangladesh as a leader among least-developed nations.

C. CONSEQUENCES OF AND RESPONSES TO THE REFORMS

9

Assessing Stakeholder Participation Reforms in Global Finance Governance

Martino Maggetti and Olga Kovarzina

9.1 Introduction

This chapter provides a concise comparative discussion of the type and intensity of stakeholder reforms in global finance governance institutions. We identified these reforms in Chapter 4 and further elaborated in the subsequent paired country case studies.[1] Furthermore, a number of comparative lessons are distilled from the paired case studies presented in the previous chapters, concerning Brazil–Argentina, China–Vietnam, and India–Bangladesh. On the one hand, we highlight cross-country patterns of commonalities and variations in the representation of previously marginalized stakeholders, for example, by checking whether larger developing countries are more systematically integrated in global finance governance institutions than smaller and/or lower income counterparts. On the other hand, we look at the demand-side of participation by previously marginalized stakeholders, that is, at the country-level factors that shape participation patterns. Overall, this chapter shows that, in the realm of global finance, there were overall moderate but non-negligible institutional reforms geared towards the inclusion of these stakeholders. However, these reforms were uneven across institutions and selective with respect to stakeholders. They mostly concerned the largest emerging countries, to the detriment of other stakeholders, that is, of smaller and/or lower income countries, and, above all, with respect to non-state actors, which are largely excluded from the governance of these institutions. In particular, representatives of non-commercial interest remain outsiders with little voice and scarce influence. This is a finding that partly contrast with the developments in global health, analysed in Part III of this book, confirming the peculiar nature of global finance governance, whereby the international policy community tends to organize its interactions according to a narrow club-like model.[2] Beyond country-specific factors, the organizational form of the specific global finance governance institutions appears to matter considerably for the scope and consequences of stakeholder reforms. Formal, treaty-based institutions, such as the IMF and the World Bank (WB), experienced some significant

[1] Olga Kovarzina and Martino Maggetti, 'Stakeholder Participation Reforms in Global Finance Governance.' Chapter 4, this volume.

[2] Eleni Tsingou, 'Club Governance and the Making of Global Financial Rules' 22(2) *Review of International Political Economy* (2015) 225-256.

Martino Maggetti and Olga Kovarzina, *Assessing Stakeholder Participation Reforms in Global Finance Governance* In: *Rethinking Participation in Global Governance*. Edited by: Joost Pauwelyn, Martino Maggetti, Tim Büthe, and Ayelet Berman, Oxford University Press. © Martino Maggetti and Olga Kovarzina 2022. DOI: 10.1093/oso/9780198852568.003.0009

reforms, especially regarding participation and voting rights. However, these reforms mostly concerned the participation of larger emerging countries, and, above all, they did not fundamentally alter (yet) the historical balance of power. By contrast, softer and more flexible organizational forms—first and foremost the G20—gave an authoritative voice to the largest emerging countries (such as Brazil and China) and were instrumental in securing a voice for these countries in other, more narrowly issue-specific, institutions for governing global finance. This is the case of the FATF, which deals specifically with money laundering, and the FSB. At the same time, these more informal institutions remained even more restrictive with respect to the other (more) marginalized stakeholders.

9.2 Types and Intensity of Reforms

In Chapter 4, we provided an overview of the governance structure and main reforms in the Bank for International Settlements (BIS), the Basel Committee on Banking Supervision (BCBS), the Financial Action Task Force (FATF), the Financial Stability Board (FSB), the Group of Twenty (G20), the International Accounting Standards Board (IASB), the International Monetary Fund (IMF), the International Organization of Securities Commissions (IOSCO), and the World Bank (WB). In doing so, we identified four major types of reforms enacted by global finance governance institutions. First, we observed a number of reforms that relate to membership, and more specifically to the extension of the membership base (that is, the number of stakeholders that are entitled to be a member) or members quotas (which are broadly—and only imperfectly—based on each member's relative position in the world economy and determine crucial rights and duties such as financial commitment, access to financing, and voting power). Second, there have been voting rights reforms, whose main goal was to enhance the decision-making capacity of (some) previously marginalized stakeholders that were already formal members of the investigated institutions. An instance of this type of reforms is the increase in the voting share attributed to China in the IMF, which doubled in the years under consideration. Third, organizational structures have been rearranged and widened to further include previously marginalized stakeholders in the governance of global finance governance institutions. Last, we identified a fourth category, which one might call 'consultation/disclosure changes', that is, changes that increase the actual opportunities for participation by non-member stakeholders.

By systematizing the data collected in our overview and the case studies, we obtain a measure of the relative frequency of each type of reform at aggregate level. Those frequencies differ substantially, depending on whether we consider reforms pertaining to state actors or, respectively, reforms pertaining to non-state actors. As regards state actors, the most common type of reform has been the expansion of membership to include government representatives, high-level officials, diplomats, regulators from previously excluded emerging and developing countries (Figure 9.1). By contrast, consultation/disclosure changes were the predominant type of reform aiming at the inclusion of non-state actors, and most of those reforms aimed only at providing input opportunities to representatives of large financial institutions, accountant firms, and audit and consulting services (Figure 9.2).

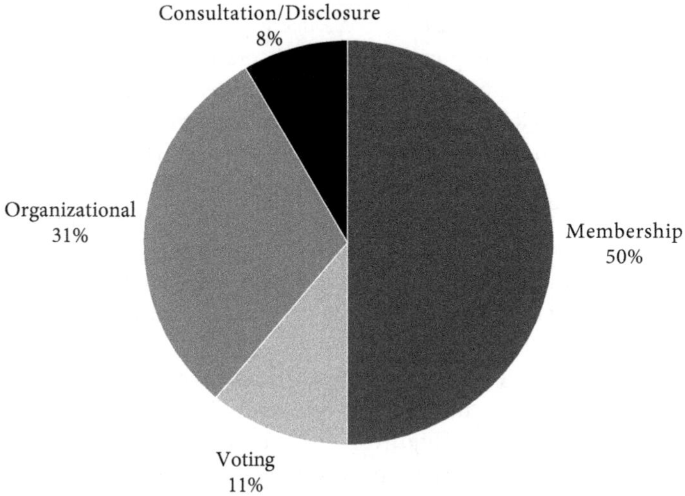

Figure 9.1 Types of Reforms to Increase Stakeholder Participation in Selected Organizations (State Actors)

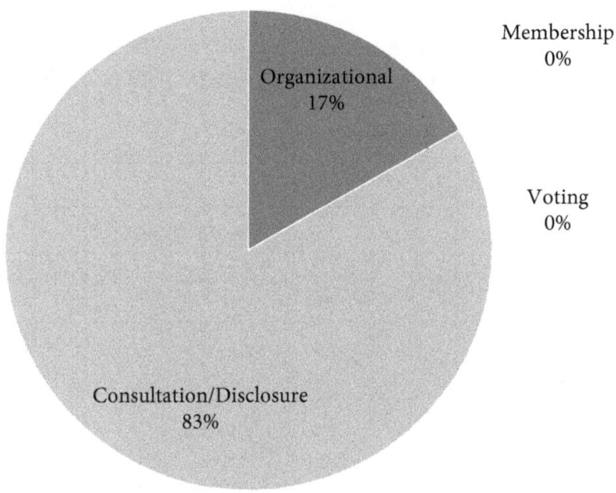

Figure 9.2 Types of Reforms to Increase Stakeholder Participation in Selected Organizations (Non-State Actors)

To gain a better sense of the depth of these reforms, we then coded the intensity of each type of reforms in the investigated organizations with a three-point scale, accounting for 'none', 'minor', or 'substantial' reforms. The first category simply accounts for the status quo (no reform of that type in the time period under investigation; these instances correspond to 'negative cases' that are not included in the tables reported earlier). Minor reforms are marginal or merely formalistic changes that do not fundamentally alter the logic of participation and representation. Substantial ones are those that imply a sizeable redistribution of participation and/or representation rights (which might or might not affect the real influence of stakeholders; this is a separate issue, examined later). We used qualitative information from the overview and from the country case-study chapters to distinguish between these two latter categories. For example, the extension of the membership of FATF can be considered substantial as it involved the gradual expansion from the sixteen original members to thirty-seven members, resulting in a post-reform membership that included Argentina, Brazil, China, and India (though not Vietnam nor Bangladesh). At the same time, IOSCO organizational reforms with respect to state actors primarily entailed procedural measures with no direct implications for the involvement of previously marginalized stakeholders—for example, a more explicit mention of the technical and emerging markets committees in the organization chart—so that they were qualified as minor.

As an additional step, we aggregated the different types of reforms to produce two overall indicators of the intensity of reforms (Table 9.1), one for state- and the other for non-state actors (Figure 9.3). According to this measure, the aggregated level of reform intensity seems moderate but still quite substantial with respect to state actors (an average of about 2 out of 4 points), while it is decidedly low as regards non-state actors (an average of less than 1 point on the same four-point scale).

Table 9.1 Intensity of reforms to increase stakeholder participation in selected organizations (disaggregated)

	Intensity of reform by type of actor							
	State actors				**Non-state actors**			
	Membership	**Voting**	**Organizational**	**Consultation/ Disclosure**	**Membership**	**Voting**	**Organizational**	**Consultation/ Disclosure**
BIS	●	⊗	●	⊗	⊗	⊗	⊗	⊗
BCBS	●	⊗	●	●	⊗	⊗	⊗	●
FATF	●	⊗	⊗	⊗	⊗	⊗	⊗	●
FSF-FSB	●	•	●	⊗	⊗	⊗	⊗	•
G20	●	⊗	⊗	⊗	⊗	⊗	⊗	⊗
IASB	●	⊗	●	⊗	⊗	⊗	•	●
IMF	●	•	•	⊗	⊗	⊗	⊗	•
IOSCO	●	•	•	•	⊗	⊗	⊗	⊗
WB	●	•	•	⊗	⊗	⊗	•	●

Membership reforms correspond to the extension of membership base or quota. Voting reforms relate to the modification of voting rights to empower selected actors. Organizational reforms consist of the re-arrangement of organizational structures to include previously marginalized actors. Consultation/disclosure reforms involve means to enhance participation in a procedural way. Each category has been coded with respect to the intensity of reform: none (0), minor (0.5), or substantial (1). These categories are represented in the table with: none (⊗), minor (•), and substantial (●).

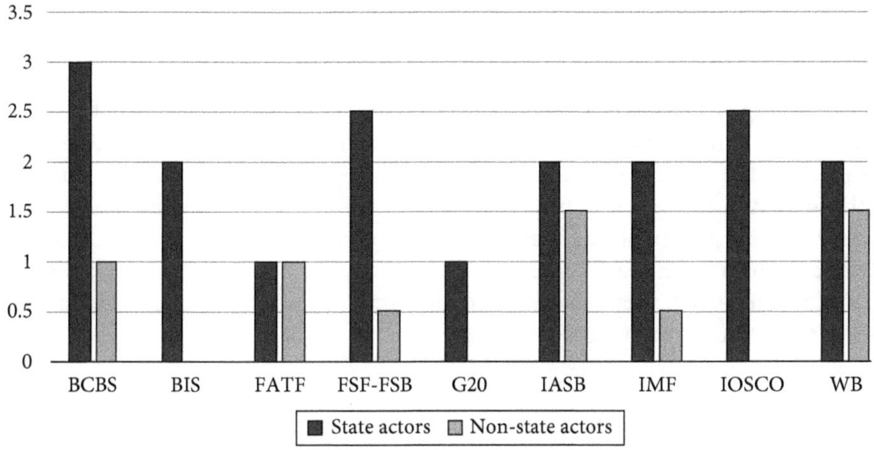

Figure 9.3 Intensity of Reforms to Increase Stakeholder Participation in Selected Organizations (Aggregated)

Turning to specific organizations, some of the more informal transnational bodies, for example, the BCBS, the FSF-FSB, and the IOSCO, clearly outperform traditional international organizations (for example, the IMF and the WB) in terms of overall reform intensity. At the same time, smaller and/or narrower organizations—such as FATF—tend to stay somewhat restrictive and club-like. Larger organizations, no matter their organizational form, engage in reform activity and orient their reforms primarily towards increasing the number of members, striving to include more emerging and developing countries. Specifically, organizations like the IMF and the WB—but also BIS, possibly due to their size and prominence—produce a mixture of participation reforms that include expanding the number of members geographically, reforming and restructuring their governance bodies—for example, the representation on the executive board of the IMF. They also engage in reforming the number of votes or the amount of quota rights attributed to each member. While the latter type of organization produces visible reforms, the effectiveness of those reforms has been called in question. For instance, as noted in Chapter 4, the IMF received a number of criticisms pointing to insufficient and superficial changes in opportunities for participation. While a number of developing countries benefit from an increase in their quotas (that is, the building blocks of the IMF's financial and governance structure that should approximately reflect each country's position in the world economy), industrialized European countries and the United States continue to bear a disproportionally high amount of voting power.

The IASB is another example of controversial reform efforts. While the One World Trust gave the IASB a top ranking in accountability and participation performance, a number of critics disagreed, claiming, for instance, that some stakeholder organizations' representatives were not allowed to speak at IASB meetings.[3] What is more,

[3] Klaus Dingwerth, 'Global Democracy and the Democratic Minimum: Why a Procedural Account Alone is Insufficient' 20(4) *European Journal of International Relations* (2014) 1124-1147; CFO, Global Accounting Board Cheered, Jeered on Transparency, 11 December 2007, http://ww2.cfo.com/accounting-tax/2007/12/global-accounting-board-cheered-jeered-on-transparency/.

certain IASB accounting standards, such as IFRS8, are seen as very opaque and have been criticized for decreasing transparency, reducing stakeholders' ability to analyse companies' performance. The IASB thus stands accused of diluting accountability and impeding any possible agreement on globally-accepted international accounting standards.[4] With regards to non-state actor participation, many organizations made some effort, but in most cases, improvements have been marginal and very indirect, with the partial exception of the Basel Committee notice-and-comment procedure. Indeed, a clear pattern shows that reforms to include previously marginalized non-state actors have been less frequent than those concerning state actors. Furthermore, when they occurred, they have been softer, that is, mostly geared towards informal means to sustain participation.

9.3 From Participation Opportunities to Actual Involvement and Influence: Lessons from the Case Studies

We now turn to a short comparative discussion of the country case studies presented in the previous global finance chapters, focusing on the consequences of the observed reforms for actual stakeholder participation and influence. Comparing across the paired case studies allows us to examine the pattern of commonalities and variations in the representation of previously marginalized stakeholders. To begin with, the case studies confirm that global finance governance institutions have reformed their governance structures to provide opportunities for inclusion of *some* previously marginalized stakeholders. However, all in all, these reforms have increased actual participation only to a very limited extent and they have made little difference to the pattern of influence. Developed countries remain largely predominant. For instance, even though the United States and China are now approximately equal as the largest economies in the world, with about the same share of the world's GDP, the former retains a dominant position in the IMF with a veto-wielding voting share of 16.73%. Conversely, the latter has seen only a limited vote share increase (from 3.81% to 6.16%). Moreover, the paired case studies show that the larger emerging economies (Brazil, China, and India) have gained much more influence than the corresponding countries displaying similar contextual conditions except for their relative smallness and/or lower national income (Argentina, Vietnam, and Bangladesh). As an example, following the 2010 reforms of the IMF, the voting power of Brazil increased from 1.713% to 2.217%. By contrast, Argentina lost as much as 31% of its voting rights.

Finally, it appears that non-state actors are still marginalized in global finance governance institutions. In the residual cases where they have also been concerned by sizeable participation reforms, the included actors mostly correspond to business representatives, while the non-profit sector remains weakly integrated. A telling example are IOSCO's consultations to widen stakeholder representation, which are primarily geared towards including investors, professionals, and audit firms, along with regulators and public sector organizations, while NGOs have less influence on the process.

[4] CFO, Global Accounting Board Cheered, 2007.

A closer look at the paired comparisons allows some further insights regarding the role of domestic factors in shaping the intensity of reforms and their effectiveness. To begin with, Chapter 6, written by Choer Moraes and Aznar deals with two countries—Brazil and Argentina—that have adopted a critical stance towards existing global finance governance structures and have been differentially able to achieve more participation in finance governance institutions.[5] They have been able to exploit the 2007–2008 financial crisis as a trigger creating a window of opportunity for reform. They took advantage of the rising importance of the most recent, informal, and flexible governance bodies, such as FATF and, above all, the G20. Indeed, the G20 provided Brazil and Argentina with an authoritative channel to voice their concern on issues for which they were mostly confined to the role of rule-takers in the past. However, as mentioned above, there are crucial differences in the way these two countries have able to bring their stakes to the forefront. Brazil exploited the G20 as a key player to raise concerns about existing institutions, for example, the IMF, wherein this country gained prominence following the shift in its position from a long-term debtor to a provider of resources. Conversely, Argentina has embraced its own exit from the IMF with the attendant decline in participation rights in the view of its differences with the Fund in the context of the economic crisis experienced in the late 1990s–early 2000s. Another difference is the activism of Brazil within focused governance bodies. Brazil is now extensively represented in the FATF and the FSB. What is more, it can make use the recent regional branches of these institutions to exert a wider influence and try to pursue its strategy of bringing into being a more multipolar order (see Chapter 12 on the role of these regional branches).[6]

Zhang (Chapter 7) shows that China is being involved more extensively in global finance governance institutions as a consequence of its growing importance in the world economy—albeit the latter remains only partially reflected in the former.[7] For instance, China was invited to join the BCBS in March 2009, but by the time China joined the BCBS, the Basel Committee had already completed a number of crucial reforms that consequently remained beyond the reach of China's representatives. Furthermore, China's vote shares at the IMF doubled over the last few years. However, its vote share remains rather limited in comparison with developed countries and does not allow China to effectively influence the IMF's decision-making. Informal bodies seem to grant more influence to the largest emerging economy. On the one hand, the implementation of the G20 agenda after 2008 resulted in China's participation in the FSB, the BCBS, and IOSCO. On the other hand, China has established AIIB as a competitor to challenge the traditional global finance governance institutions. Vietnam, by comparison, benefitted from a similar extension of its vote shares at the IMF following the 2008 and 2010 quota and voice reform packages aiming at ensuring a minimum increase in quota or share for dynamic under-represented emerging market and

[5] Henrique Choer Moraes and Facundo Pérez Aznar, 'Brazil and Argentina in Global Finance Governance.' Chapter 6, this volume.

[6] Henrique Choer Moraes, 'Can Regional Institutions Increase the Legitimacy of Global Governance? The Cases of the Regional Branches of the FATF and of the FSB.' Chapter 12, this volume.

[7] Weiwei Zhang, 'China and Vietnam in Global Finance Governance.' Chapter 7, this volume.

developing economies. However, even more clearly than for China, this increase did not lead to significant change in involvement and influence for Vietnam in the IMF. Moreover, contrary to China, Vietnam, whose size of economy and role in the global financial system is still relatively minor, is not yet a member of other key institutions in the global financial architecture (BCBS, FATF, and FSB). Therefore, its participation in finance governance institutions remains relatively marginal.

Mukherji and Jha's contribution on India and Bangladesh (Chapter 8) focuses on climate finance as an entry point to examine the participation of these previously marginalized stakeholders in the global finance governance architecture.[8] Despite the different size of their economy and population, in the last decades both countries have experienced quite consistent economic growth and globalization as a development strategy. In doing so, they have transitioned from structural conflict to an embedded liberal approach to North–South relations. As a consequence, they became active participants in global negotiations and also contributors to the elaboration of global financial norms. For instance, similarly to the trajectory of Brazil, India departed from the long-standing passivity role of large aide recipient and acquired a leading position within the Global Environmental Facility (GEF) managed by the United Nations and the WB. In this capacity, India has been able to shape climate finance negotiations at the highest level while also creating domestic financial and implementation arrangements to deal with climate issues. Bangladesh also moved towards a more active stance with respect to climate finance negotiations but following a quite different strategy, that is, by playing a leading—and somewhat more confrontational—role among the subgroup of the least developed countries. This way it has been able to put forward its domestic interests within international institutions, namely by arguing that, besides bilateral and multilateral engagements, a key issue relates to the redistribution of resources from the North to the South. However, while India is becoming increasingly integrated within the architecture of global finance governance, Bangladesh strives to exert its influence from a more peripheral position.

9.4 Concluding Remarks

This chapter has shown that reforms concerning the participation of stakeholders were, overall, of moderate but non-negligible intensity. These participation reforms provide a number of opportunities to (some) previously marginalized stakeholders but do not directly translate into much more influence. What is more, the scope of these reforms was uneven across institutions and selective with respect to stakeholders. State representatives of larger developing countries (Brazil, China, and India) have become more systematically integrated in global finance governance institutions than their counterparts from smaller and/or lower income counterparts (Argentina, Vietnam, and Bangladesh). Non-state actors (especially non-commercial ones)—from large and small countries alike—remain even procedurally marginalized. This result partly contrasts with the case of global health (see Part III, this volume), where global institution

[8] Rahul Mukherji and Himanshu Jha, 'India and Bangladesh in Global Finance Governance: From Structural Conflict to Embedded Liberalism in the Climate Finance Regime.' Chapter 8, this volume.

opened up to non-state actors to a considerable extent. What is more, the organizational form of the investigated institutions shaped the implications and consequences of stakeholder reforms. Treaty-based institutions such as the IMF and the WB underwent formal changes in term of membership rules and voting rights. However, these reforms did not fundamentally alter the existing balance of power—at least not yet. Conversely, more informal networked organizations such as the G20 brought the concerns of the largest emerging countries such as Brazil and China to prominence, and allowed them to promote reforms in other, more focused institutions such as FATF and FSB, or to develop alternatives. Gindrat and Inderbinen (Chapter 11) show that these informal arrangements entail more flexibility and facilitate the acceptance of reforms.[9] At the same time, some of these institutions remained even more restrictive with respect to the other (more) marginalized stakeholders.

To conclude, it is worth remembering that the 2007–2008 financial crisis provided a crucial window of opportunity for reform. No counterfactual is readily available at the global level, but it is plausible to hold that without the crisis we would have witnessed a much lower reform intensity and, thereby, an even more restrictive participation of previously marginalized stakeholders. Indeed, according to Alexander (Chapter 5), the crisis brought a specific lesson to the insiders—that a more inclusive global finance governance architecture would also contribute to the legitimization of the system.[10]

[9] Ronald Gindrat and Paul Inderbinen, 'Comparing Formal and Informal Bodies in International Finance: A Policy-Making Perspective.' Chapter 11, this volume.

[10] Kern Alexander, 'Global Financial Governance and Banking Regulation.' Chapter 5, this volume.

10
On Expanding the Theory of Stakeholder Participation

Christopher J Brummer

In this collection of highly informative chapters, the authors try to tackle core questions of soft law legitimacy and efficacy while pushing the discourse further in light of evolutionary changes in the makeup and organizational governance of key financial and standard-setting institutions. Up to this point, theoretical questions have typically centred on the enforceability and effectiveness of informal rules that do not inherently carry the weight of international law. The questions in this series of chapters go a step deeper, and take a much needed, and incisive, look at the organizational mechanisms, and governance reforms, which are intermediating the very provision of informal standards and best practices. With this in mind, this chapter provides a collective framing of these must-read contributions and offers additional developments that could bolster—or complicate—their conclusions.

Serving as the basis of the substantive analysis for financial regulation are 'Assessing Stakeholder Participation Reforms in Global Finance Governance' (hereinafter *Effects*) by Martino Maggetti and Olga Kovarzina, as well as 'Stakeholder Participation Reforms in Global Finance Governance' by Olga Kovarzina and Martino Maggetti (hereinafter *Overview*).[1] Both operate in tandem to take an empirical look at a number of reforms that relate to membership rule, and more specifically to the extension of membership base or members quotas.

In *Overview*, Kovarzina and Maggetti undertake an institutional analysis of the individual changes wrought since the financial crisis in key international standard setting bodies and global financial institutions. Together, they observe and helpfully document how reforms have been adopted to modify voting rights. In doing so, they aim to enhance the influence of (some) previously marginalized stakeholders that were already formal members of the investigated institutions. Additionally, they note that organizational structures have been rearranged and their membership widened to include previously excluded or marginalized stakeholders. Finally, they note the mechanisms devised to enhance the participation of non-state stakeholders, such as the BIS paper consultation on their website, and the incorporation of cost benefit analysis into notice and comment procedures. *Overview* and the paired country case studies chapters[2] are then followed by the *Effects* chapter, which asserts that many of

[1] Olga Kovarzina and Martino Maggetti, 'Stakeholder Participation Reforms' [here: Overview]. Chapter 4, and Martino Maggetti and Olga Kovarzina, 'Assessing' [here: Effects]. Chapter 9, both this volume.

[2] Henrique Choer Moraes and Facundo Pérez Aznar, 'Brazil and Argentina in Global Finance Governance.' Chapter 6, this volume; Weiwei Zhang, 'China and Vietnam in Global Finance Governance.'

Christopher J Brummer, *On Expanding the Theory of Stakeholder Participation* In: *Rethinking Participation in Global Governance.* Edited by: Joost Pauwelyn, Martino Maggetti, Tim Büthe, and Ayelet Berman, Oxford University Press. © Christopher J Brummer 2022. DOI: 10.1093/oso/9780198852568.003.0010

these changes came about through the ability of actors to leverage the reform moment (or, more precisely 'exploit' the moment) as a window of opportunity for more progressive changes in governance.

It is worth noting that the sample size of the investigation is ambitious and assesses a variety of international institutions: International Monetary Fund (IMF), World Bank (WB), Bank for International Settlements (BIS), Basel Committee on Banking Supervision (BCBS), Financial Action Task Force (FATF), Financial Stability Board (FSB), International Organization of Securities Commissions (IOSCO), Group of Twenty (G20), and International Accounting Standards Board (IASB). Notably, they do not all occupy the same legal status, a point I've mentioned elsewhere.[3] Some institutions, like the International Monetary Fund are formal international organizations. As such, changes to their structure and membership and operations often require the amendment of underlying treaty-like obligations (in this case, the fund's Articles of Agreement). Meanwhile other organizations, like the G20, are not based on any formal agreements. And because they are not formal international organizations, amending or upgrading their governance and even membership can be as easy as updating the entity's webpage.[4]

Nonetheless, in every instance there will be friction. Many soft law organizations operate around systems of consensus. In such circumstances, for policies to move forward, all members have to agree—or at a minimum, there has to be the absence of a vociferous dissent.[5] Thus from a practical standpoint, reform of some soft law organizations could be even trickier than that which might be required from institutions requiring supermajorities for reforms (though still less onerous than formal institutions that require unanimity for core governance changes). As a result, in some instances, governance changes may embed certain prerogatives—like veto powers—for incumbents or dismantle altogether consensus mechanisms in favour of majoritarian (or super-majoritarian) governance.

What might be the push and pull factors for change? For one, changes in governance impact the utility of investing in international organizations. Governments can be viewed as self-interested players in a chaotic, no holds barred world, seeking to maximize their own welfare. And certainly, cooperating on issues of international financial cooperation may serve as means to that end. However, it also implies costs, not only in terms of sovereignty and the limits and constraints that are imposed on actors bound by consensual and cooperative relationships, but also in terms of the time and effort required in coordinating. Increasing the membership of the body can likewise increase the negotiation and information gathering costs. Furthermore, changes in governance structures can make reaching a deal or

Chapter 7, this volume; and Rahul Mukherji and Himanshu Jha, 'India and Bangladesh in Global Finance Governance.' Chapter 8, this volume.

[3] See generally, Chris Brummer, *Soft Law and the Global Financial System*, 2nd ed. (Cambridge University Press 2015).

[4] In such circumstances, the most critical restraints will be those found in the charters of the organization. However, in most instances the charters are themselves 'soft law' products, and thus reforming the charters themselves can be a relatively expeditious exercise.

[5] Brummer, *Soft Law* (n 3), 98f.

a desired policy less likely, and by consequence dis-incentivize negotiation on the front end.

Nonetheless, the authors ingeniously identify other factors that can be very important in informing just how and in what ways organizations undertake governance changes. Among them is the possibility that media attention can impact reforms—which can bring attention to the legitimacy of international standards and the bodies that produce them. Just how strong the causality is remains nonetheless unclear. For one, as the authors note, media attention may not necessarily be directed to stakeholder reforms. As a result, institutions may not necessarily be internalizing the costs or benefits of undertaking more accommodating governance structures. It also seems questionable as to whether or not the reforms undertaken by these institutions are of such a nature that, even when reported, readers of the financial press can adequately recognize the value brought by the governance changes.

In some ways, this problem is a twist on the traditional notions of 'compliance' theories for international standard setting. The standard line of theory holds that reputational costs can incentivize international organizations to adopt rules, and enforce them, even where they may not be bound to do so under international law. This is because nonconformity can generate an impression that the relevant financial institutions may be undercapitalized or subject to undue risks of fraud and by implication incentivize the market to charge a higher risk premium for transactions with those institutions. For this to be effective, there must be adequate surveillance of compliance, along with a sufficient understanding of the nature of the underlying rule against which compliance is being judged. Here however, surveillance acts in a way so as to determine what reputational costs should be incurred where institutions do not adopt regulatory changes, and thus do not take on the kinds of traditional reputational costs conventionally associated in the literature.

One takeaway that the editors of this volume identify is that larger, more powerful countries are most likely to benefit from reforms than smaller countries.[6] This is, in many ways, to be expected. Larger countries typically have bigger economies and can, as a result, exert more pressure on member states to include them in discussions. Yet even there, a number of other factors can impact the ability for a state to participate effectively. The authors identify six factors, including foreign policy, importance, resources, capacity, policy learning and teaching, and availability of domestic processes.

Still, administrative theory holds that there are many ways to participate. To be sure, the most common forms of participation involve situations where actors that are potentially impacted by a rule or regulation are availed the opportunity to participate in the discussions and voting concerning those rules and regulations. But other avenues are also available. One is the introduction of notice and comment rule-making. As the articles briefly observe, some international standard-setting bodies including the Basel Committee and Financial Stability Board allow individuals and firms—and even

[6] Tim Büthe, Joost Pauwelyn, Martino Maggetti and Ayelet Berman, 'Conclusion: The Participation of Marginalized Stakeholders in Global Governance.' Chapter 25, this volume. See also Ayelet Berman, Tim Büthe, Martino Maggetti and Joost Pauwelyn, 'Introduction: Rethinking Stakeholder Participation in Global Governance.' Chapter 1, this volume, and Mercy B DeMenno and Tim Büthe, 'Voice and Influence in Global Governance: An Analytical Framework.' Chapter 2, this volume.

other countries, a point worth noting—to provide their views on pending rules with especially important valence. IOSCO, similarly, has executed a number of public consultative processes geared to harvest public input on a number of issues.[7] And though beyond the scope of the articles, the International Accounting Standards Board, the entity responsible for promulgating international accounting rules, has perhaps adopted the most radical post-crisis changes. Among them: the introduction of a slew of formal due process reforms that include new rules for agenda-setting, project planning, developing and publishing international financial reporting standards, and reviewing such standards after they are published.[8] As part of this reform process, it has a permanent web portal open for notice and comment rule-making. The agency invites public comments on all proposals that are published as discussion papers, exposure drafts, draft interpretations, draft amendments two interpretations.[9]

I think these innovations, which emphasize 'voice' over 'voting', deserve a bit of attention, especially where one seeks to ultimately draw conclusions about the legitimacy of international standard setting in lieu of post-crisis reforms.[10] On the one hand, voice-based reforms do not achieve full or robust levels of organizational legitimacy insofar as countries and governments impacted by international standard setting are not able to directly exercise power over the organization's promulgation of new rules. However, on more basic level, these kinds of reforms do improve the legitimacy of the information that is presumably taking into consideration for the promulgation of these rules. It also preserves a degree of operational efficiency that could be lost with more extensive organizational reforms, especially were memberships are enlarged and super-majoritarian and consensus decision-making are preserved.

Many of today's international sentencing bodies also have established regional consultative bodies to assist them in their work. Outreach is not haphazard or by chance, and indeed can also be empirically assessed. The post-crisis FSB Charter, for example, declares that the organization 'should have a structured process for public consultation on policy proposals', indicating a formal process by which the organization will engage in, in the words of the *High Level Report*, 'dialogue with market participants and other stakeholders, including through round-tables, hearings and other appropriate events'.[11] Furthermore, the Charter explicitly references regional consultative groups as part of the FSB architecture, broadening the range of participants beyond G20, as well as working groups, which can be constituted by representatives of countries beyond the FSB's membership.[12]

The FSB, likewise, has six Regional Consultative Groups (RCGs), established under its (post-financial crisis) FSB Charter, to connect member governments with non-member countries to exchange views on vulnerabilities affecting financial systems and

[7] Brummer, *Soft Law* (n 3), 204.

[8] Brummer, *Soft Law* (n 3), 204.

[9] Brummer, *Soft Law* (n 3), 204.

[10] Chris Brummer, *Minilateralism: How Trade Alliances, Soft Law and Financial Engineering are Redefining Economic Statecraft* (Cambridge University Press 2014), 186.

[11] Financial Stability Board, 'Report to the G20 Los Cabos Summit on Strengthening FSB Capacity, Resources, and Governance', 12 June 2012 <http://www.financialstabilityboard.org/publications/r_1206 19c.pdf>, last accessed 11/24/2019.

[12] Chris Brummer, 'Introductory Note to the Financial Stability Board Charter' 51(4) *International Legal Materials* (2012) 828-839.

on initiatives to promote financial stability.[13] The RCGs have been identified as comprising the Americas, Asia, Commonwealth of Independent States, Europe, Middle East and North Africa, and Sub-Saharan Africa—and each RCG meets twice each year.

Along similar lines, the Basel Committee's Charter emphasizes consultation, and establishes a Basel Consultative Group (BCG) to a facilitate broad supervisory dialogue with non-member authorities on new Committee initiatives.[14] The BCG comprises the main outreach organ for the Basel Committee and is an active organ for consultations regarding the Basel III reforms instituted after the crisis to enhance the capitalization of internationally active banks.[15]

As noted, both models stand as important examples of the role 'voice' can play—and has played—especially since the financial crisis—in enhancing stakeholder participation in global governance. Both allow a means of providing input. And neither relies on a country's availability of large travel budgets to meet members in far-flung locales in Europe.

But even here, there are key differences. In one model, decision makers are brought into direct contact with their counterparts, presumably on a more even playing field, and as peers. Although non-members are not permitted to necessarily participate in voting, they are able to provide direct and unfettered input to key officials who are involved in decision-making. And in optimal circumstances, the regional body could itself promulgate suggestions and rules for consideration by primary decision-making organs.[16] However, many of these discussions will be private. As a result, there may be weak surveillance of whether members have taken into consideration the specific policy preferences or needs of non-participants.

By contrast, public notice and comment tools allow for explicit articulations of policy preferences, as well as an opportunity to explain the basis for the recommendations and suggestions that are made. Furthermore, depending on the institution, there may be organizational norms that require the international standard-setting body to respond, either formally or informally to the suggestions. However, notice and comment does not involve a reiterative back and forth between regulators as seen in regional consultations, and instead comprises a one-shot forum for policy influence.

In the end, these observations, which place more emphasis on certain observations routinely noted in passing, may offer a more optimistic interpretation of the reforms identified by the authors, both in their volume and substance. At a minimum, they suggest that, in addition to membership reforms and the increasing openness to non-state actors, a number of administrative reforms are designed—much like membership reforms—to enhance stakeholder participation, whatever the decision rules of an entity. It also suggests that whatever the disproportionate gains enjoyed by larger,

[13] Financial Stability Board, 'Charter of the Financial Stability Board', June 2012 <http://www.fsb.org/wp-content/uploads/r_120809.pdf>, last accessed 11/24/2019.

[14] Bank for International Settlements, 'Basel Committee Charter', 5 June 2018 update <https://www.bis.org/bcbs/charter.htm>, last accessed 11/24/2019.

[15] See, e.g. Basel Consultative Group, 'Impact and Implementation Challenges of the Basel Framework for Emerging Market, Developing and Small Economies' *Basel Committee Working Paper* No. 27, November 2014 <https://www.bis.org/bcbs/publ/wp27.pdf>, last accessed 11/24/2019.

[16] See Base. Consultative Group, 'Impact and Implementation Challenges' (n 15), providing advice for the Basel-based committees concerning the implementation of Basel III standards.

formerly marginalized or excluded countries, smaller countries, too, may yet be able to wield a surprising amount of influence. At the same time, administrative piecemeal reforms like regional consultations and notice-and-comment mechanisms *do* at least implicitly underscore the fact that such stakeholder participation remains highly diluted. Control ultimately remains in the hands of incumbents and those countries most economically significant or integral to the mission of the organization.

With such contrast, Henrique Moraes and Facundo Aznar's observation in their case study of Brazil and Argentina rings especially true, that 'the effect of reforms in enabling more participation by excluded stakeholders might be more visible when approached from a systemic perspective than from focusing on each individual institution'.[17] As I have offered in a similar context, 'the entire regulatory ecosystem has to be taken into account—the forest, in short, can't be overlooked for the trees'.[18] Reforms concerning organizational membership or voting power should be viewed in conjunction with other changes, where appropriate—from the inclusion of heads of state to administrative and procedural innovations aimed at enhancing the influence of nonmembers. To be sure, many of these innovations are themselves inherent with their own trade-offs—like allowing voice while undermining direct participation—but they illuminate a more qualitatively complex regulatory ecosystem than scholars have traditionally recognized.

[17] Choer Moraes and Pérez Aznar, 'Brazil and Argentina' (n 2).
[18] Brummer, *Minilateralism* (n 10), 193.

11
Comparing Formal and Informal Bodies in International Finance
A Policy-Making Perspective

Ronald Gindrat and Paul Inderbinen[*]

11.1 Introduction

Governance is generally needed to ensure collective action in the provision of public goods, such as securing property rights or maintaining financial stability, and in controlling public bads, for example, the externalities arising from monetary and financial crises. In the case of the international monetary and financial system, the significant mobility of financial activity and capital flows and the associated movements of exchange rates and asset prices require a governance structure that allows for coordinated approaches at the international level to ensure stability, as well as swift responses to crises.

In an integrated world, countries have an interest in being attractive for financial and economic activity, avoiding the build-up of domestic vulnerabilities, and having in place safeguards that preserve their economies from negative monetary and financial externalities. To a certain degree, this provides an incentive to coordinate policies and regulation. Whereas at distinct historical moments, a stronger alignment of incentives allowed the establishment of governance institutions endowed with a formal status and elements of an enforcement apparatus, such instances are rare. The current levelling out of the relative weights among the largest economies makes the chance of creating such moments even less likely, with consensus harder to reach. As noted by Helleiner and Pagliari: '[…] the diffusion of power may increase competition among great powers, and generate more possible focal points around which convergence could take place'.[1] However, as suggested by Pauwelyn *et al.*, this tendency does not mean '[…] that cross-border agreement can no longer be found. It is simply that it takes different forms and involves a different constellation of actors and processes, outside the traditional confines of international law'.[2] Against this backdrop, the global

[*] The views expressed in this article are solely those of the authors and not of the Swiss authorities or the IMF.

[1] Eric Helleiner and Stefano Pagliari, 'The End of an Era in International Financial Regulation? A Postcrisis Research Agenda' 65(1) *International Organization* (2011) 169-200, 185. See also Eric Helleiner, *The Status Quo Crisis: Global Financial Governance After the 2008 Meltdown* (Oxford University Press 2014).

[2] Joost Pauwelyn, Ramses A Wessel, and Jan Wouters, 'When Structure becomes Shackles: Stagnation and Dynamics in International Lawmaking' 25(3) *European Journal of International Law* (2014) 733-763, 738.

Ronald Gindrat and Paul Inderbinen, *Comparing Formal and Informal Bodies in International Finance* In: *Rethinking Participation in Global Governance.* Edited by: Joost Pauwelyn, Martino Maggetti, Tim Büthe, and Ayelet Berman, Oxford University Press.
 DOI: 10.1093/oso/9780198852568.003.0011

financial crisis of 2008–2009 acted as a catalyst for the establishment of new and less formal forms of international monetary and financial cooperation.

Are formal cooperation and enforcement rules preferable? By observing that higher-income countries generally have a more formal domestic governance structure and stronger enforcement rules than middle- and lower-income countries, one might infer that formal governance generally leads to better results and that the same might apply, by extension, to international governance. However, as pointed out by Pauwelyn *et al.*, '[N]o inherent or automatic benefits come with being part of international law. Yet, to conclude a treaty, in particular a multilateral one within a formal international organization requires huge transaction costs and once concluded [it] is hard to adapt to changing circumstances.'[3] Conversely, informal governance structures represent a minimal common denominator on which participating countries can develop a core of agreed policies and standards. The weaker enforcement power allows for flexibility in implementation at the domestic level, increasing the acceptance of what was agreed internationally.

In the context of the international monetary and financial system, the G20 and the FSB are the expression of an alternative way of shaping international cooperation and policy coordination, based on the search of an informal consensus around a common denominator of policies and standards rather than a formal set of rights and obligations. However, the emergence of such forms of global governance bodies raises the question of their legitimacy. The informal character of the agreements underlying such bodies, and also the fact that their membership is far from universal, may speak against their legitimacy. In order to look at this question, we base our arguments on the benefits and drawbacks that such governance bodies have generated, both for their members and non-members. We attempt to analyse these governance forms from the angle of the *stability* of these agreements, that is the recognition of such governance bodies' right to rule by members, their *accountability* vis-à-vis non-members, and their *efficiency*, that is, their ability to achieve the objectives for which they were brought to life in the first place.

We argue that—in the context of the international financial architecture—informal governance does not lead to inferior solutions when compared to bodies with formal statutes. Of course, any form of governance is a 'second best' at most, subject to constraints of information, incentives, commitment, and rules of the political game. Whereas formal governance may—perhaps—offer a better response to some of these constraints, it is generally better to have a reasonably well implemented informal norm rather than a badly applied formal rule. To give an illustration, you may consider the analogy with traffic light signals (a formal rule).[4]

To illustrate our point, we will focus on some elements of the international financial architecture: the G20, the FSB, and the IMF. This selection spans the spectrum of governance formality and inclusiveness, from the very informally structured and exclusive G20 to the IMF with its Articles of Agreement and By-laws, formally detailing rights and obligations of its near-universal membership.

[3] Pauwelyn *et al.*, 'Stagnation' (n 2), 750.

[4] Avinash Dixit, 'Governance Institutions and Economic Activity' 99(1) *American Economic Review* (2009) 5-24.

The paper is organized as follows. Section 11.2 discusses the notion of legitimacy as a composite of stability, accountability, and efficiency. Sections 11.3 to 11.5 apply the concepts developed in Section 11.2 to the case of the G20, the FSB and the IMF. Section 11.6 concludes.

11.2 A Definition of Legitimacy

This section defines the concepts of *efficiency*, *stability*, and *accountability* mentioned in the introduction. We consider these elements as key characteristics of a legitimate agreement. Formally, an agreement is a couple (g,t), where g is a set of *participants*, that is, a *coalition*, and t is the *type* of agreement detailing rights and obligations. Each agreement is associated with a *value*, which aggregates the individual *outcomes* for the involved parties. For instance, the value of an agreement could be the sum of the GDP changes in involved countries. Involved parties are not only agreement participants, but also *outsiders*. The outcome of an agreement for an outsider results from the non-excludability property of the public good underlying the agreement.

An agreement generating the maximal value is said to be *efficient*. However, given the two dimensions of an agreement (coalition and type), efficiency has to be qualified.

DEFINITION 1. (A) Agreement (g,t) is *coalition-efficient* if, for the same type of agreement, there is no other agreement with a different coalition that yields a larger value.

(B) Agreement (g,t) is *type-efficient* if, holding the coalition fixed, there is no other type of agreement that yields a larger value.

Efficiency *per se* does not imply that the coalition members are willing to participate in that agreement. To take account of the incentives of (potential) participants, we consider a *stability* condition.

CONDITION 1. (A) Coalition g of agreement (g,t) is *stable* if, holding the type of agreement fixed, no participant could achieve a better outcome under a different coalition.

(B) The type t of agreement (g,t) is *stable* if, holding the coalition fixed, no participant could achieve a better outcome under a different type of agreement.

Stability ensures that an agreement is worth of support in the eyes of the participants. This overlooks, however, the position of outsiders. To take account of the impact of an agreement on outsiders, we consider an *accountability* condition.

CONDITION 2. (A) Coalition g of agreement (g,t) is *accountable to outsiders* if, holding the type of agreement fixed, no outsider could achieve a better outcome under a different coalition.

(B) Type t of agreement (g,t) is *accountable to outsiders* if, holding the coalition fixed, no outsider could achieve a better outcome under a different type of agreement.

C2 implies that being an outsider does not mean being disregarded. C2 is close to the notion of *trusteeship* that Benvenisti sees as appropriate to ground accountability obligations of global governance bodies.[5] C2 could also be seen as imposing to the agreement a certain degree of conformity to universally shared norms (for example, human rights, or financial stability). If an agreement were not aligned with such norms, it would be hard to think that none of the outsiders could be better off under a different agreement. Note that C2 could also be seen as a 'complementary' stability condition: if C2 is satisfied, no outsider would have an interest in participating in the agreement.

With *stability* and *accountability*, we define legitimacy with respect to the two agreement dimensions.

DEFINITION 2. (A) Agreement (g,t) is *legitimate relative to g* if it satisfies C1A and C2A.
(B) Agreement (g,t) is *legitimate relative to t* if it satisfies C1B and C2B.

Legitimacy is seen here from the standpoint of the agreement's potential to best serve the individual needs of participants (stability) and the notion that the policies derived from the agreement should at least not cause harm to outsiders relative to all alternatives (accountability).

Note that if an agreement satisfies C1 and C2, it is efficient (D1). Legitimacy implies efficiency, but efficiency cannot imply legitimacy because it considers only the value generated by an agreement and not the outcomes for every involved party. That is, an agreement is legitimate, if there is *unanimity* among the involved parties about how to achieve an efficient outcome.

D2 depicts legitimacy as a solution maximizing individual outcomes, which in reality may be too strict. Global governance institutions are normally the result of compromises and, as such, likely to be second-best solutions. A way to relax D2 would be to admit as legitimate agreements that yield *sufficient* degrees of stability and accountability.

According to C1, legitimate agreements are those that are consistent with the *self-interest* of the participants. However, as argued by Buchanan and Keohane, legitimacy 'is a moral notion that cannot be reduced to rational self-interest. To say that an institution is legitimate implies that it has the right to rule even if it does not act in accordance with the rational self-interest of everyone who is subject to its rule.'[6] They argue that 'there are advantages in achieving coordinated support for institutions on the basis of moral reasons'.[7] The interplay between self-interest and moral reasons can reasonably lead to *reservation outcomes*, above which potential participants are willing to participate. C1 can be relaxed accordingly.

[5] Eyal Benvenisti, 'Sovereigns as Trustees of Humanity: On the Accountability of States to Foreign Stakeholders' 107 *American Journal of International Law* (2013) 295-333.

[6] Alan Buchanan and Robert O Keohane, 'The Legitimacy of Global Governance Institutions' 20(4) *Ethics and International Affairs* (2006) 405-437, 410.

[7] Buchanan and Keohane (n 6), 410.

CONDITION 1′. (A) Coalition g of agreement (g,t) is *sufficiently stable*, if, holding the type of agreement fixed, each participant achieves an outcome that at least equals its reservation outcome.

(B) Type t of agreement (g,t) is *sufficiently stable*, if, holding the coalition fixed, each participant achieves an outcome that at least equals its reservation outcome.

Analogously, accountability towards outsiders may be relaxed by considering *minimum positive externalities*, above which outsiders can tolerate being excluded by an agreement.

CONDITION 2′. (A) Coalition g of agreement (g,t) is *sufficiently accountable* to outsiders if, holding the type of agreement fixed, each outsider benefits from an outcome that at least equals its minimum externality.

(B) Type t of agreement (g,t) is *sufficiently accountable* to outsiders, if, holding the coalition fixed, each outsider benefits from an outcome that at least equals its minimum externality.

Note that by relaxing in this way C1 and C2, the legitimate agreements need not be efficient. However, it is reasonable to think that to be legitimate an agreement must also achieve a *sufficient* degree of efficiency to fulfil the objectives for which the agreement was conceived in the first place.

CONDITION 3′. (A) Agreement (g,t) is *sufficiently coalition-efficient* if it generates a value above an efficiency threshold.

(B) Agreement (g,t) is *sufficiently type-efficient* if it generates a value above an efficiency threshold.

Condition C3′ is consistent with Buchanan and Keohane, who suggest that 'legitimacy is not to be confused with optimal efficacy and efficiency'.[8] By replacing C1 and C2 with C1′ and C2′ and adding C3′ in D2, we enlarge the set of legitimate agreements. This modification of D2 would still embody a notion of *unanimity* that is closer to the one considered by Nagel.[9]

The concepts discussed in this section are applied to the cases of the G20, the FSB, and the IMF.

11.3 The G20

The G20 summit mechanism was established at the height of the global financial crisis in 2008. It was born of the necessity to act quickly and in a coordinated manner. The G20 has since become central to economic cooperation and global partnership. From the beginning, the G20 has been broad in scope, including development and climate change.

[8] Buchanan and Keohane (n 6), 422.

[9] Thomas Nagel, *Equality and Partiality* (Oxford University Press 1991).

Members' obligations are codified in Communiqués. As such, commitments are the result of a 'rolling consensus' that continuously adjusts to the evolving context. The informal setting and the relevance of the topics render the agreement sufficiently stable in the sense of the previous section. Nevertheless, the set of members is restricted, which raises issues of accountability. A key question is whether a larger grouping could achieve a more satisfactory result. Given the weight of the G20 (80% of the global GDP, 75% of the global trade, and close to two-thirds of world population) and the aggregate impact that coordinated policy actions can generate, it can be reasoned that the inclusion of further participants could improve the overall result by a little margin at best. More likely, it could have a negative impact. A larger set of participants would imply that a broader range of opinions would have to converge, potentially reducing the forcefulness of the G20. The lack of inclusiveness is partially mitigated by the participation of international organizations. It should also be underscored that policies endorsed by the G20 are often prepared by international organizations, which (in many cases) have been submitted to their respective memberships.

Nonetheless, and although the decisions of the G20 are not binding, it should be underscored that non-members can hardly escape their consequences. For instance, the G20 Seoul summit largely determined the outcome of the 2010 IMF governance reform.

The question of whether the G20 is sufficiently accountable should, however, also be assessed with respect to the positive externalities. Also, the costs of participation that non-members would incur should be taken into account. Exclusion of some countries may be possible without impinging on the legitimacy of a multilateral agreement, if the resource mobilization entailed by participation is disproportionately higher than the benefits of participating or arising from externalities. This may be especially the case for small economies.

Interesting accountability issues may, nevertheless, arise for countries that are significant enough on a global scale in some particular respect (for example, the financial sector), but lack the overall weight of a G20 country. Examples of such 'outer boundary' countries are the Netherlands, Spain, Switzerland, and Singapore. The G20 mechanism is, however, flexible enough to accommodate such cases, allowing G20 presidencies to invite additional countries to part of the G20 work streams on an ad hoc basis.

It is questionable whether a more formal setting could bring about the same or better dynamics. It is likely that a formal agreement would be less appealing for participating countries, with the risk of ultimately not being sufficiently stable by requiring too strict commitments, or not being sufficiently efficient by limiting cooperation to topics of marginal relevance. Also, it is reasonable to argue that the decision procedures within the UN or the IMF would have not allowed the same speed of action that was instrumental in avoiding a global economic depression in 2008–2009.

Taking all this into account, we consider the G20 mechanism as sufficiently legitimate.

11.4 The Financial Stability Board (FSB)

The FSB was established in 2009 as the successor to the Financial Stability Forum (FSF), with an enlarged membership and a broadened mandate. The 2009 Charter of the FSB lays down its mandate, including its role in coordinating the work of national financial authorities and the standard setting bodies, detecting vulnerabilities, and in promoting the implementation of supervisory and regulatory standards.

The FSB member jurisdictions are represented by their finance ministries, central banks, and supervisory authorities. The European Commission, the ECB, international financial institutions, and standard-setting bodies are also represented. FSB members commit to pursue the maintenance of financial stability, the openness of financial sectors, implementation of standards, and periodic peer reviews.

In 2013, the institutionalization of the FSB was taken a step further by establishing it as an association under Swiss law. While the founding documents of the FSB convey a certain degree of formality, the FSB Charter and its Articles of Association are not comparable to the founding documents of a formal international organization. In particular, they have not been formally approved by any legislature and ratified by the member jurisdictions.

Besides a plenary, the FSB has standing committees, including on regulatory cooperation and standards implementation, as well as working groups on derivatives reform, data gaps, and other issues. To promote interaction with non-members, the FSB has created six Regional Consultative Groups (RCG).

Its Articles state that the FSB's activities 'shall not be binding or give rise to any legal rights or obligations'.[10] The consensual approach to decision-making and the lack of enforcement have given rise to doubts about the ability of the FSB to ensure adherence to sufficiently strong standards.[11] This could suggest that the FSB may not be *sufficiently efficient*.

However, despite the lack of enforcement power, FSB member countries strive to be good 'international citizens'. Lack of compliance means losing credibility and influence. Compliance with international standards is assessed in peer reviews. It can be argued that peer reviews encourage members to be strategically benevolent when assessing their peers, expecting to be treated the same way themselves. However, it should be noted that the reviewer may well have the incentive to deviate from such an equilibrium. By receiving a strict review, an insufficiently compliant member would lose credibility and weight in the decision process to the advantage of other members, including the reviewer. In anticipation of this deviating strategy, all other members may also decide to be strict reviewers. In turn, being a strict reviewer has also a disciplining effect on the reviewer himself. If the reviewer were not sufficiently compliant, there would be an inconsistency and a loss of credibility.

Note that the consensus-based governance of the FSB ensures that all participants are held accountable for the results. Moreover, the interest in maintaining competition and openness and avoiding the negative externalities of inadequate rules of foreign jurisdictions induce a willingness to cooperate at least on a core set of agreed standards. Also, a soft law approach gives member countries additional flexibility on regulatory design. Besides accommodating potentially heterogeneous preferences for financial regulation, differences in the level of financial development across member

[10] Eric Helleiner, 'Did the Financial Crisis Generate a Fourth Pillar of Global Economic Architecture?' 19(4) *Swiss Political Science Review* (2013) 558-563, 561.

[11] Helleiner, 'Did the Financial Crisis' (n 10).

countries can also be taken into account. Indeed, Helleiner and Pagliari note that 'the greater diversity in domestic political arrangements and regulatory preferences represented in international standard-setting bodies may hinder the capacity to commit to detailed harmonized international standards, lead to increasingly uneven levels of implementation of international regulatory initiatives, and trigger unilateral moves to preserve distinctive domestic arrangements'.[12] Informal governance and softer enforcement rules can strike a reasonably good balance between a typically technocratic and knowledge-based process, that is, standard setting, and the political need for tailoring international norms to national circumstances. For all these reasons, we tend to consider the FSB as a *sufficiently efficient* and *stable* governance body.

Like the G20, the FSB has quite a narrow membership, and its work, by its very nature, affects countries outside its membership. This raises the issue of *accountability* to outsiders. At the same time, the lack of inclusiveness is mitigated by the outreach activities in the RCGs. Choer Moraes finds that 'RCGs can effectively bring their concerns into the workstream of [the FSB]'.[13] Moreover, accountability is also expressed through the acceptance of the objectives and mandate of the FSB. The key standards cover areas that are relevant independently of the jurisdiction concerned and are broadly accepted as minimum requirements beyond the FSB membership. The soft law approach allows the adaptation of regulations to the specific country contexts, which increases the acceptance of standards in non-members. Since international financial stability is a public good, non-member countries stand to benefit from the implementation of international standards in FSB members. It is also questionable whether extending the FSB's membership to an even larger set of jurisdictions would have been practicable. The complexity of the issue, combined with a larger heterogeneity in financial market structures, could have slowed down discussions and impeded swiftly addressing the major vulnerabilities that had originated in countries with highly developed financial markets. Thus, it can be argued that the FSB largely conforms to legitimacy in the sense of Section 11.2.

11.5 The International Monetary Fund (IMF)

The IMF can be viewed as a mutual insurance mechanism for its members against the risk of facing balance of payment difficulties. The relationship between the IMF and its members is formally regulated by the Articles of Agreement. The great majority of the IMF's activities are published, and much of its work is critically reviewed by its independent evaluation office. While these characteristics suggest legitimacy, the formal governance structure favours the preservation of a status quo, which, in a changing environment, can prevent the IMF from rapidly adapting. An example is the long-delayed implementation of the 2010 governance reforms.

The discussions on the jurisdiction of the IMF over capital flows provide another example. Curiously, given the mandate of the IMF to ensure the stability of

[12] Helleiner and Pagliari, 'The End of an Era' (n 1).

[13] Henrique Choer Moraes, 'Can Regional Institutions Increase the Legitimacy of Global Governance?' Chapter 12, this volume.

the international monetary system the IMF has no formal mandate on capital movements. Despite the integration of global financial markets in the course of the past half century, the IMF's formal jurisdiction remains limited to avoiding restrictions and discriminatory practices of members on current account transactions. What would be required is a multilateral setting in which countries would formally commit to the liberalization of transactions on their capital accounts, and a mechanism to monitor these commitments.

Interestingly, in the late 1990s the international community came close to adapting the mandate of the IMF to cover capital movements. These discussions took place within the relatively short window of opportunity that offered itself in the interim between the 1994 financial crisis of Mexico and the Asian crisis of the late 1990s. These crises demonstrated how the risks inherent in exchange rate mismatches, macroeconomic instability, and insufficiently regulated and supervised financial sectors are compounded in an environment of free cross-border financial flows.

With the onslaught of the crisis in Asia, the discussion was terminated. In the aftermath of the crises, the focus of the international community shifted to increased scrutiny of countries' financial sectors (via the Financial Sector Assessment Program, launched in 1999), addressing gaps in economic and financial data compilation and dissemination, and the development of a set of key standards for macro-economic and financial sector policies.

Capital movements, and their relation to IMF policy, again came to the fore following the global financial crisis of 2008–2009. When emerging markets took recourse to protective measures to limit the appreciation of their currencies against the US dollar, discussions led to the adoption by the IMF's Executive Board in 2012 of an 'Institutional View' on the liberalization and management of capital flows. While the Institutional View provides a framework for advising members and for exercising surveillance over their policies, it is far from the original aim of extending the IMF's formal mandate to capital flows.

Thus, although the global integration of financial markets is likely the most salient development of the international monetary and financial system over the past decades, and although this integration has paralleled a marked increase in the magnitude and costs of financial crises, the international institution charged with preserving the stability of the system lacks a formal mandate to promote and oversee the liberalization of capital movements. As it stands, members are, in Article VI of the IMF's Articles of Agreement, explicitly given license to 'exercise such controls as are necessary to regulate international capital movements [. . .]'. The IMF can also request a member to implement capital controls to prevent the use of its resources by members facing 'a large or sustained outflow of capital [. . .]'.[14]

And yet, members remain committed to financing the IMF, and they willingly subject themselves to regular assessments of the macro-economic and financial policies by the IMF's staff. They accept the incomplete—and somewhat contradictory—formal mandate of the institution as a second best, rather than having no such multilateral framework at all. While the type of agreement underlying the IMF can thus be

[14] International Monetary Fund, *Articles of Agreement* (1944).

regarded as *sufficiently stable*, it could, in light of the above, be questioned whether it remains *sufficiently type-efficient* and, hence, legitimate.

The question also arises whether a superior solution might be possible in a more informal setting. One very onerous aspect of adapting the mandate of an international institution is that it typically entails changes to the members' obligations—the portion of sovereign rights to be ceded to the multilateral level. This entails fixed costs. An informal setting generally entails lower costs and thus provides an environment that is more amenable to change. The introduction of membership obligations in the course of the transformation of the FSF into the FSB in the aftermath of the global financial crisis serves as a case in point. The introduction of these obligations, together with the expansion of its membership, fundamentally altered the FSB. Both the type and the coalition of the agreement were significantly altered. This was achieved without lengthy discussions at the technical and ministerial level that typically precede changes to formal international institutions.

Thus, the incentive to preserve the representation structure of a formal international institution can serve to ensure that the benefits of the institution are maintained, although certain important aspects of the particular setting no longer conform to all the members' preferences. This is accepted because the costs of adapting the setting are prohibitively high. Such a second-best setting will be sufficiently stable, and thus legitimate, in the sense of Section 11.2, as long as the benefits of membership exceed the reservation outcomes of the members. Conversely, a more informal setting allows for far-reaching changes to the mandate and governance of an international body when necessary. Informal settings are thus more likely to fulfil the strict stability condition, and thus for legitimacy, in the sense of the framework in Section 11.2.

It is, however, important to recall that the institutional form that best facilitates international cooperation is not independent of the 'content' of cooperation. In the case of the IMF, given the significant provision of funding by its members, a formal framework with clearly defined rights and obligations seems warranted.

11.6 Conclusion

Alternative forms of global governance have emerged since the financial crises of 2008–2009. The limited memberships of the G20 and the FSB, and the informality of the agreements upon which they are based, give rise to questions about their legitimacy. By analysing these forms of governance from the angle of stability, accountability, and efficiency, we find that informal settings do not yield inferior outcomes compared with traditional bodies with formal statutes.

As far as the G20 is concerned, we find that a more inclusive membership would likely improve outcomes by a small margin only. The G20 has proven flexible in accommodating non-members that, while lacking the overall weight of a G20 member, have a significant position in the international financial system. A more formal setting would likely be less appealing to members, and thus be less effective.

We argue that the FSB comes close to a legitimate organization. While the FSB lacks enforcement power, the soft-law approach underlying international financial standards offers flexibility to member countries and facilitates acceptance by non-members.

Non-members benefit from international financial stability. The latter can be viewed as a public good supplied by the adoption of key financial standards that the FSB membership is committed to.

We have argued that the IMF's formal governance structure favours conservation. This has prevented the institution from adapting its governance structure and from including the jurisdiction over capital flows in its mandate. Adapting the mandate of a formal international organization entails fixed costs that are significantly higher than in the case of less-formal arrangements. Informality more readily allows for far-reaching changes to the mandate and governance of an international body; informal settings are more likely to fulfil a condition for stability, and thus, legitimacy.

Overall, however, for the governance of the international monetary and financial system, coexistence of formal and informal bodies serving different purposes would seem reasonable.

12

Can Regional Institutions Increase the Legitimacy of Global Governance?

The Cases of the Regional Branches of the FATF and of the FSB

*Henrique Choer Moraes**

12.1 Introduction

This chapter focuses on two key actors in global finance governance—the Financial Action Task Force (FATF) and the Financial Stability Board (FSB). It examines the policy adopted by both institutions of creating or stimulating the creation of regional 'branches' with a view to bringing non-member states closer to their work.

In particular, this chapter seeks to provide elements to assess to which extent the creation of such regional branches represents an effective solution to enable increased participation of excluded stakeholders, in this case of non-members of the 'core' institutions.

Section 12.2 explores the FATF-Style Regional Bodies (FSRBs). It deliberately begins with the FATF because it is a forerunner to many global governance institutions. Many features now widespread in other fora have been tried before by the FATF,[1] and the FATF trajectory may thus suggest time-tested lessons. Section 12.3 examines the Regional Consultative Groups (RCGs) of the FSB, a more recent experience that seems to draw on the FATF precedent while at the same time points to more room for regional inputs. Based on these two cases, Section 12.4 discusses whether regional branches are a viable alternative to grant non-member states voice in decision-making processes that ultimately affect them.

* I am grateful for the input and useful information collected from interviews with Carolina Barbosa, Lucio Capelletto, Carlos Marcio Cozendey, Helio Franchini Neto, Bernardo Mota, Marcus Vinícius Ramalho, and David Salles Valente. This chapter reflects developments through the end of 2016.

[1] Andrew Walter, 'Can the FSB Achieve Effective Surveillance of Systemically Important Countries?' in Stephany Griffith-Jones, Eric Helleiner, and Ngaire Woods (eds), *The Financial Stability Board: An Effective Fourth Pillar of Global Economic Governance?* (CIGI 2010) 32-35.

Henrique Choer Moraes, *Can Regional Institutions Increase the Legitimacy of Global Governance?* In: *Rethinking Participation in Global Governance*. Edited by: Joost Pauwelyn, Martino Maggetti, Tim Büthe, and Ayelet Berman, Oxford University Press.
 DOI: 10.1093/oso/9780198852568.003.0012

12.2 The FATF-Style Regional Bodies (FSRBs) of the Financial Action Task Force

In many respects, the FATF is the ultimate example of the club-like institution: its reduced membership sets globally valid standards, it subjects members and non-members alike to intense peer reviews and coerces non-members to compliance by threatening with the possibility of countermeasures. Not all global financial institutions combine all these features.

Essentially, the tasks performed by the FATF fall into three categories: (i) setting standards to counter money laundering and terrorism financing; (ii) monitoring compliance with the standards through mutual evaluations (peer reviews); and (iii) enforcing the standards by means of measures that include warning financial institutions of the risks of operating with a non-compliant country or jurisdiction.[2]

Throughout its existence, the FATF has remained faithful to the goal of 'spread[ing] the FATF's message to all continents and regions of the globe'[3] while keeping a lid on the expansion of its membership.[4] The crucial element that enabled the FATF to reconcile these seemingly opposite objectives is the network of FSRBs. The FSRBs are regional settings that gather FATF members and non-members and where the latter are submitted to 'the same peer pressure which encourages FATF members to improve their anti-money laundering systems'.[5] There currently exist nine FSRBs covering virtually all the regions of the world.[6]

The wide geographic span of the FSRBs certainly contributes to 'spread the FATF message' to significant distances. But to what extent does it also help bringing the FSRB members' 'message' into the work of the FATF? How much was the creation of the FSRBs inspired by the intent to respond to the legitimacy challenge faced by the FATF?

The experience of the FATF does not bear out the notion that the FSRBs have been conceived to increase the legitimacy of the FATF. Rather, the push for the dissemination of FSRBs around the world was primarily targeted at ensuring the effectiveness of the FATF system. From the perspective of the FATF, the FSRBs play a very specific role: 'FATF relies on its co-operation with the […] FSRBs to promote effective global implementation of the FATF Recommendations'.[7] Or, in the words of a president of the FATF, 'it seems impossible to envisage an FATF as effective as it is today without

[2] FATF, *Annual Report 2004–2005*, 6f.

[3] FATF, *Annual Report 1997–1998*, 7.

[4] FATF, *Annual Report 1993–1994*, 7.

[5] FATF, *Annual Report 1999–2000*, 14.

[6] The FSRBs are: *Asia*: Asia/Pacific Group on Money Laundering (APG) and Eurasian Group (EAG); *Western Hemisphere*: Caribbean Financial Action Task Force (CFATF) and Financial Action Task Force of Latin America (GAFILAT); *Africa*: Eastern and Southern Africa Anti-Money Laundering Group (ESAAMLG), Task Force on Money-Laundering in Central Africa (GABAC); Intergovernmental Action Group Against Money Laundering in West Africa (GIABA), Middle East & North Africa Financial Action Task Force (MENAFATF); *Europe*: Committee of Experts on the Evaluation of Anti-Money Laundering Measures and the Financing of Terrorism (MONEYVAL).

[7] FATF, *Annual Report 2012–2013*, 32.

FSRBs'.[8] 'Effectiveness', not 'legitimacy', is the term more frequently associated with the creation and diffusion of the FSRBs[9]—consistent with DeMenno and Büthe's hypothesis H_{1B} rather than H_{1A}.[10]

12.2.1 Evolution of the FATF-FSRBs Relations

The record of the FATF–FSRB relations reveals an evolutionary process marked by a tension between, on the one hand, the push for global implementation of FATF standards and, on the other hand, the recognition of an increasing role to the FSRBs within the network centred around the FATF.

The strategy of 'world-wide implementation of the FATF program'[11] was at first pursued by seminar diplomacy activities in the shape of regional conferences. These events were at the time understood as 'an effective means of introducing the issue of money laundering around the world'.[12]

The experience with the first round of FATF outreach towards third countries led to the recognition that the expansion of regional entities in the FSRB format could provide an adequate platform to engage non-members while keeping them outside of the FATF membership.[13] This element marks the second stage of the FATF–FSRB relations, when the FATF was mandated to promote the establishment of FSRBs in as many regions as possible.[14]

However, by this period, the FATF was introducing a 'blacklist' targeted at non-members ranked as 'Non-Cooperative Countries and Territories' (NCCT) for failing to 'provide effective international administrative and judicial co-operation in money laundering cases'.[15] Countries and territories thus labelled pursuant to the FATF procedures could be subject to countermeasures with palpable impact on their financial sectors.[16]

The NCCT procedure strained the FATF–FSRB relations[17] for many reasons, predominantly that the FATF unilaterally invested itself with the capacity to recommend the imposition of restrictive measures on third countries that were excluded from its decision-making process.

[8] 'The Essential Role of the FATF Style Regional Bodies (FSRBs) in the Fight Against Money Laundering and Terrorist Financing', Remarks by the FATF President, Brisbane, 7 July 2009 <https://amarbheenick.blogspot.be/2009/07/essential-role-of-fatf-style-regional.html>, last accessed 06/24/2017.

[9] It thus does not seem convincing to argue that the FSRBs are the product of a strategy to 'buy back' the legitimacy of the FATF from non-members, as suggested by Jonathan Koppell, *World Rule: Accountability, Legitimacy, and the Design of Global Governance* (University of Chicago Press 2010) 175.

[10] Mercy B DeMenno and Tim Büthe, 'Voice and Influence in Global Governance: An Analytical Framework.' Chapter 2, this volume.

[11] FATF, *Annual Report 1990–1991*, 15.

[12] FATF, *Annual Report 1991–1992*, 17.

[13] FATF, *1993–1994* (n 4).

[14] FATF, *1997–1998* (n 3), 4.

[15] FATF, *Annual Report 1998–1999*, 35.

[16] FATF, *1999–2000* (n 5), 12 (Annex A).

[17] FATF, *Annual Report 2000–2001*, 11.

The NCCT experience opened way to a new stage in the FATF–FSRB relations, in which the FATF sought to '*improve*' and '*enhance*' the way it worked with the FSRBs.[18] Steps were attempted to bring the FSRBs closer to the FATF. Perhaps the most significant measure in this sense was taken during the review process that led to the 2003 version of the FATF Recommendations, in which the FSRBs were invited to provide input and to participate.[19] The desire to improve working relations with the FSRBs was also inspired by the goal of seeking consistency across regions in the way standards compliance was assessed and monitored.[20] The FATF has for a long time focused on levelling the expertise of the FSRBs to perform assessments.

Additionally, these developments culminated in the upgrading of the status enjoyed by the FSRBs, from observers to associated members of the FATF. This recognition meant the FATF had decided to grant the FSRBs 'much greater participation in the processes within the FATF',[21] such as by 'giving the eligible FSRBs full access to FATF work and to FATF discussions' and also 'direct access to Plenary meetings'.[22]

The current stage in the FATF–FSRBs relations (Figure 12.1) represents a sophistication of the recognition of the latter as associate members. In 2012, the terms of co-operation were spelled out in more detail by the 'High-Level Principles and Objectives for FATF and FATF-style regional bodies' ('High Principles').[23]

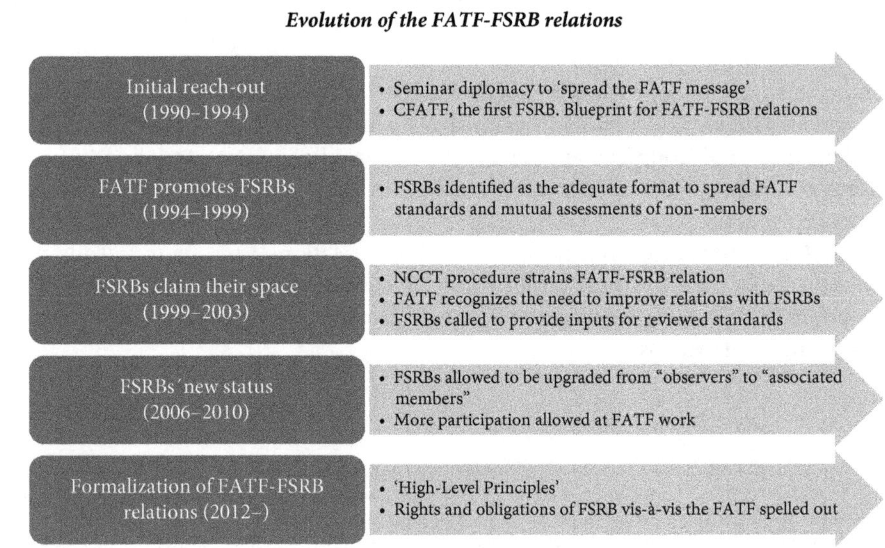

Figure 12.1 Evolution of FATF–FSRB Relations

[18] FATF (n 17), 11 and FATF, *Annual Report 2003–2004*, 1.

[19] It is true, nonetheless, that the FSRBs were not the only external actors consulted in the process of reviewing the standards, see FATF, *Annual Report 2000–2001* (n 17), 17.

[20] FATF, *Annual Report 2005–2006*, 4.

[21] FATF, *2005–2006* (n 20), Foreword by the President.

[22] FATF, *2005–2006* (n 20), 5.

[23] FATF, *High-Level Principles and Objectives for FATF and FATF-style regional bodies*, October 2012.

12.2.2 Assessing the FSRBs' Role in Ensuring Participation to Non-Members

At least nominally, the FSRBs are presently granted an unprecedented amount of participatory capacities in the work of the FATF. It is not clear, though, whether all FSRBs are equipped with resources to take *equal* advantage of the enhanced capacity to influence the FATF decision-making. In fact, the indication is that there are variations in the effectiveness with which FSRBs see their input reflected into the FATF decisions.

As far as standard setting is concerned, for example, MONEYVAL,[24] the FSRB that gathers members of the Council of Europe, seems to retain sufficient expertise and influence to be an active participant in the FATF. For example, it reports having actively participated in the review process that led to the 2012 version of the FATF standards, as well as in the drafting of the methodologies to assess the implementation of these standards.[25] This is unsurprising, since MONEYVAL is predominantly a forum of developed countries. Conversely, it may be reasonable to expect that, for some other members, in particular developing countries, membership in an FSRB does not translate into the same degree of influence in the FATF decision-making process.

Be that as it may, membership in an FSRB can empower a given country with capacities it would not otherwise have. The experience of the Asia and Pacific Group (APG) with respect to the ICRG (International Cooperation Review Group) procedures suggests that FSRBs may offer their members tools to better navigate the FATF network. The ICRG is the forum in charge of countries non-compliant with the Recommendations, in replacement to the previous 'blacklisting' of NCCTs. Countries considered by the ICRG procedure to be uncompliant with FATF standards may still be subject to countermeasures.

The APG offers '*priority assistance*'[26] to its members involved in the FATF's ICRG procedure. This includes assistance to develop strategies to meet the recommendations of the ICRG, capacity building to implement these recommendations, as well as support to 'ensure that [...] reports accurately represent our members' AML/CFT systems'.[27] It means that APG members can tap into resources possibly otherwise unavailable, were they not participating in this FSRB.

A number of caveats arguably apply to the APG example. First, although most members of the APG are developing countries—especially those receiving 'priority assistance'—the tools provided by this FSRB certainly owe their existence to its influential and well-resourced members. Second, it could also be argued that the provision of assistance to implement the FATF standards has little relation with influence in the FATF standard-setting or decision-making process in general.

Both points are plausible and highlight that FSRBs *may* give each of its individual members a stronger influence than they would otherwise have.

[24] Committee of Experts on the Evaluation of Anti-Money Laundering Measures and the Financing of Terrorism.

[25] MONEYVAL, '33rd Plenary Meeting of MONEYVAL (Strasbourg, 27 September–1 October 2010)', Meeting Report, paras. 17, 19. See also MONEYVAL, *Annual Report 2012*, 37.

[26] APG, *Annual Report 2014–2015*, 38.

[27] APG, *Annual Report 2010–2011*, 22.

This is illustrated by the participation of GAFISUD (now GAFILAT, gathering mostly South American countries) at another stage of the ICRG procedure. During a Plenary session in June 2010, the FATF discussed the situation of Ecuador, which had previously been 'blacklisted'. GAFISUD was one of the members advocating for the improvement of Ecuador's status in view of the commitment the country had expressed to implement the Recommendations—a 'dramatic change of attitude' on the part of Ecuador, GAFISUD claimed at the occasion. The Plenary later decided to improve the status of Ecuador to the 'grey list' of countries with regulatory deficiencies but showing willingness to address them.[28] The endorsement of Ecuador's case by GAFISUD certainly contributed to the decision to improve the country's status.

The reality of uneven contribution of FSRBs to the FATF was captured by the Mexican Presidency of the FATF (2010–2011), whose term placed emphasis on the promotion of more participation of FSRBs in the FATF network. Then Mexican President of the FATF unequivocally spelled out the reasons that led to choosing this topic as a priority: '... the FATF, in general, is not yet fully satisfied with the implementation of the Associate Membership status [granted to the FSRBs]'.[29]

All in all, the channels for increased participation of non-members in the FATF are present and are more numerous than ever. Nonetheless, it must be recognized that FSRBs are a function of the aggregate resources, including expertise, of their members—and these resources are, of course, irregularly distributed across the world.

12.3 The Regional Consultative Groups of the Financial Stability Board (FSB)

The FSB is a unique element in the landscape of transnational networks: not only does it possess a one-of-a-kind mix of members—from national regulators to Standard Setting Bodies (SSBs)—it also reaches a broad scope of issues under its purview. In addition, the FSB was tasked with the prerogative of pooling the resources of key global regulatory and supervisory institutions[30] towards policies prioritized outside of these institutions—suggesting a quasi-hierarchical position of the FSB vis-à-vis other networks. The FSB is entrusted, thus, to act as an 'umbrella organization'.[31]

Yet, in contrast to the FATF, the FSB is not so involved in disseminating standards to the rest of the world. At least in these initial years, the FSB has taken advantage of its mandate and of the *imprimatur* of the G20 to lead regulatory and supervisory

[28] As reported by a diplomatic cable from the Brazilian Ministry of Foreign Affairs to the Embassy in Paris (*Despacho telegráfico* number 658, 6 September 2010, declassified).

[29] 'Reinforcing the Global AML/CFT structure', Address by FATF President, Grand Cayman, 5 November 2010. Other parts of this address are more outspoken: 'Over the past years, FATF [...] has noted the absence of CFATF Chairs from FATF meetings. [...] Input to FATF is very limited. CFATF Members rarely comment on FATF papers, and the CFATF Secretariat is not present at all important meetings as would be expected ... ' <http://www.fatf-gafi.org/documents/documents/reinforcingtheglobalamlcftstructure.html>, last accessed 06/24/2017.

[30] FSB, *Charter*, Articles 2.1(e) and 2.2.

[31] Stavros Gadinis, 'The Financial Stability Board: The New Politics of International Financial Regulation' *48 Texas International Law Journal* (2013) 163-176.

initiatives, in particular in those areas that are perceived as falling in the interstices of mandates of existing SSBs.[32]

12.3.1 Assessing the performance of the Regional Consultative Groups (RCGs)

Differently from the FSRBs, which have evolved over time with the regime structured around the FATF, the RCGs have been established all at once by the FSB. They are now part of the permanent structure of the FSB.[33] There are six RCGs for the following regions: Americas, Asia, Commonwealth of Independent States, Europe, Middle East and North Africa and Sub-Saharan Africa.[34] They gather both members and non-members of the FSB and are chaired by both one FSB member and one non-member.

A 2014 review of the structure of representation of the FSB sought to increase the participation of RCG representatives at meetings of the FSB. Non-FSB member co-chairs of each of the six RCGs were granted a standing invitation to attend Plenary meetings. Also, the FSB committed to find ways to seek opportunities for non-members to be involved in the activities of Standing Committees or Working Groups.[35]

To what extent have the RCGs been able to express their views and concerns into the decision-making process taking place at the FSB? One of the reasons invoked for the establishment of the RCGs was the 'need to continue to bring issues of relevance for EMDEs [Emerging Market and Developing Economies] to the attention of the international community'.[36] Has this intention materialized?

The experience of the FSB with the RCGs so far has elicited a varied range of contributions coming from different regions. But, just as with the FSRBs, there are no reasons to believe that the inputs and the influence from the RCGs show no less variation across regions.[37]

12.3.1.1 RCGs' influence setting the FSB agenda

The evolution of the discussions on 'correspondent banking' reveals that some RCGs have played an important role in introducing this topic into the agenda of the FSB.

A correspondent banking 'allows a local bank to give its customers access to a faraway institution's services, such as currency exchange or sending money to an account abroad'—for many developing countries, this kind of service is 'an indispensable link

[32] Stefano Pagliari, 'The Financial Stability Board as the New Guardian of Financial Stability' in Manuela Moschella and Catherine Weaver (eds), *Handbook of Global Economic Governance* (Routledge 2014) 143-155, 147.

[33] FSB, *Charter*, Article 7(5).

[34] For the current composition of the RCGs, see <http://www.financialstabilityboard.org/wp-content/uploads/rcg.pdf>, last accessed 06/24/2017.

[35] FSB, *Report to the G20 Brisbane Summit on the FSB's Review of the Structure of Its Representation*, 6 November 2014, items 6 and 7.

[36] Financial Stability Board, International Monetary Fund and The World Bank, *Financial Stability Issues in Emerging Market and Developing Economies Report to the G-20 Finance Ministers and Central Bank Governors*, 20 October 2011, 6.

[37] Hyoung-kyu Chey, 'Changing Global Financial Governance International Financial Standards and Emerging Economies since the Global Financial Crisis' (Centre for International Governance Innovation 2015), 7.

to the international banking system.'[38] In recent years, though, a number of financial institutions discontinued the provision of the service to developing countries as a result of allegedly costly regulations on, among others, money laundering.

One of the links between the correspondent banking service and global financial stability is the idea of *financial inclusion*—that is, the notion that the formal financial system should be widespread in order to support growth. With a view to introducing the item in the FSB agenda, some RCGs seem to have been effective in sophisticating their case and framing it as a need to reconcile financial inclusion—and the financial stability it produces—with the requirements imposed by anti-money-laundering regulations.[39]

Soon afterwards, the FSB Plenary acknowledged the relevance of factoring this question into its workstream.[40] Subsequent discussions at the FSB and at some RCGs contributed to fine-tune the problem. It was then recognized that 'some financial institutions [...] have reduced their services to certain categories of customers or to certain countries/regions' and that '[p]ossible drivers of such behaviour include concerns about the legal risk of penalties in case of breach with Anti-Money Laundering and Counter-Terrorist Financing (AML/CFT) standards.'[41]

A number of insights emerge from the evolution of these debates. Firstly, it expresses a response to a concern raised by *some* regions. The RCGs Sub-Saharan Africa, Middle East and North Africa, and Asia placed a special emphasis on this debate. In contrast, no mention to this topic is found on the reports of the RCG-Americas in the same period. Secondly, the way the question was presented—financial stability/inclusion vs. anti-money-laundering/counter-terrorism financing—suggests an interesting way to use the FSB as a channel to influence the agenda not only of the FSB itself, but also of another international network—in this case, the FATF. One of the results is that the FSB was called to coordinate the work of, among others, the FATF. In this capacity, the FSB submitted to the 2015 G20 Summit a report on the actions being taken internationally to address the decline in correspondent banking.[42]

12.3.1.2 RCGs provide comments on standards being drafted

A second type of interaction is the possibility given to the RCGs to comment on draft standards under consideration by the FSB. The process of setting the standard on 'Total Loss-Absorbing Capacity' (TLAC), concluded in November 2015,[43] illustrates this interaction.

[38] Mark Carney and Bertrand Badré, 'Keep Finance Safe but Do Not Shut Out the Vulnerable' *Financial Times* (2 June 2015).

[39] FSB, 'FSB RCG SSA Meets in Cape Town', Press release 59/2014, 1 October 2014.

[40] FSB, 'FSB Plenary Meets in Frankfurt', Press release 18/2015, 26 March 2015.

[41] FSB, 'Ninth Meeting of the Financial Stability Board Regional Consultative Group for Asia', Press release 63/2015, 20 October 2015. See also, FSB, 'Eighth Meeting of the Financial Stability Board Regional Consultative Group for the Middle East and North Africa', Press release 64/2015, 26 October 2015; FSB, 'FSB RCG SSA Meets in Zanzibar', Press release 14/2015, 11 March 2015; FSB, 'FSB RCG MENA Meets in Bahrain', Press release 22/2015, 27 April 2015.

[42] FSB, 'Report to the G20 on Actions Taken to Assess and Address the Decline in Correspondent Banking' 6 November 2015.

[43] FSB, *Principles on Loss-Absorbing and Recapitalisation Capacity of G-SIBs in Resolution. Total Loss-Absorbing Capacity (TLAC) Term Sheet*, 9 November 2015.

The TLAC standard is part of the package of measures for 'ending too-big-to-fail', one of the 'core elements' of the international financial reforms the G20 entrusted the FSB to coordinate.[44] In a nutshell, the TLAC standard is meant to ensure that, in case of resolution, a global systemically important bank (G-SIB, in FSB parlance) 'has sufficient loss-absorbing and recapitalisation capacity available' in order to provide for 'an orderly resolution that minimises impacts on financial stability, ensures the continuity of critical functions, and avoids exposing public funds to loss'.[45]

The FSB worked in consultations with the Basel Committee on Banking Supervision (BCBS) to sketch an initial draft of the TLAC standard that was subsequently subject to public consultation.[46] At the same time the consultations were underway, meetings of RCGs also discussed the draft TLAC standard.[47] In the Asia RCG, in particular, the idea of exempting G-SIBs headquartered in an Emerging Market Economy (EME) was raised.[48]

The TLAC standard ultimately adopted did not stretch so far as proposed at the Asia RCG. Instead, it grants EMEs' G-SIBs an extended period to enforce the standard,[49] in a compromise between the Asia RCG proposal and the results of the consultations, when 'a majority of respondents' questioned the exemption for EMEs.[50]

This example illustrates that the standard-setting process at the FSB draws on inputs provided by RCGs as well as by public consultations. It unveils, in fact, a divergence of views between a position raised at an RCG and the views of many respondents. Yet, more than assessing whether respondents in consultations yield more influence over the FSB standard-setting process than the RCGs, the point is to underscore that RCGs are allowed some participation in standard-setting, an opportunity for influence that is offered in large part thanks to the existence of the RCGs.

12.3.1.3 RCGs provide regional inputs on topics on the FSB agenda

RCGs also contribute to refine discussions at the FSB with inputs that may shed light on regional peculiarities or nuances of a given topic. The discussions on 'shadow banking' provide an example of this interaction.

The FSB defines shadow banking as 'credit intermediation involving entities and activities (fully or partly) outside the regular banking system, or non-bank credit intermediation in short'.[51] The broad scope of the definition is itself evidence to the wide range of businesses that may be encompassed under shadow banking.

[44] FSB, *Implementation and Effects of the G20 Financial Regulatory Reforms*. Report of the Financial Stability Board to G20 Leaders, 9 November 2015, 6.

[45] FSB, *Total Loss-Absorbing Capacity* (n 43).

[46] FSB, 'FSB Consults on Proposal for a Common International Standard on Total Loss-Absorbing Capacity (TLAC) for Global Systemic Banks', Press release 76/2014, 10 November 2014.

[47] For example, the RCG-Americas ('FSB RCG Americas meets in Panama City', Press release 85/2014, 24 November 2014), RCG Europe ('FSB RCG Europe meets in Basel, Switzerland', Press release 68/2014, 24 October 2014), and the RCG CIS ('FSB RCG CIS meets in Moscow', Press release 92/2014, 12 December 2014).

[48] FSB, 'FSB RCG Asia meets in Bohol', Press release 10/2015, 4 March 2015.

[49] FSB, *Total Loss-Absorbing Capacity* (n 43), *Term Sheet*, item 21. According to the FSB's assessments, China is currently the only EME to headquarter a G-SIB.

[50] FSB, *Overview of the Post-Consultation Revisions to the TLAC Principles and Term Sheet*, 9 November 2015, 8.

[51] FSB, *Transforming Shadow Banking into Resilient Market-Based Finance* - An Overview of Progress, 12 November 2015, 1.

The input provided by the RCGs on this topic have proven instrumental to the work of the FSB, in the sense that they provide a more refined view of regional nuances of a topic being considered.

At least two types of input emerge from the RCGs' work on 'shadow banking'. The first are calls for an approach that takes into consideration the particularities of a given regional experience. The RCG Asia, for example, 'observed that shadow banking instruments and activities in Asia are somewhat different from those in other regions ... '.[52] It also 'noted that shadow banking activities differ across countries and hence the need for proportionality in the regulatory response, taking into account national circumstances and regulations in place'.[53]

The second type are studies organized by RCGs that monitor the reality of shadow banking in some regions. This has been done, for example, by the RCG Americas and its results have been factored into the FSB regular task of assessing global trends and risks in the global shadow banking system.[54]

12.4 Lessons from the FATF and FSB Experiences: Addressing Global-Level Legitimacy Challenges through Regional Branches?

In the view of former Brazilian Foreign Minister Antonio Patriota, once the G20 replaced the G7 as the leading global financial governance forum, the challenge becomes that of building better communication between the G20 and the 'G173'—that is, all the others that do not sit at the decision-making table.[55]

To what extent do regional branches of club-like governance institutions contribute to bridge the communication gap with non-members? The cases of the FSRBs and the RCGs provide elements to this discussion, many of which dovetail with points raised by Berman, Büthe, Maggetti, and Pauwelyn.[56]

Regional branches do not do away with the hierarchy that exists between members and non-members. Countries participating only in regional branches do not enjoy the same leeway as do the members of the central forum to make their views and interests expressed.

Nevertheless, examples presented in this chapter indicate that the existence of regional branches allows some room for exerting influence, in both decisional and non-decisional processes. In fact, they show that some regions are finding ways to take advantage of the status they enjoy as participants in a regional branch. The 'correspondent banking' case suggests that RCGs can effectively bring their concerns into the workstream of a global institution. This requires, of course, the capacity to design

[52] FSB, 'FSB RCG Asia meets in Kyoto', Press release 44/2014, 27 August 2014.

[53] FSB, 'FSB RCG Asia meets in Tokyo', Press release 79/2013, 30 October 2013.

[54] FSB, *Transforming Shadow Banking* (n 51), 4.

[55] Antonio Patriota, 'Brazil and the Shaping of a Cooperative Multipolar Order' Brookings Institution, 9 February 2015 <http://www.brookings.edu/~/media/events/2015/02/09-patriota-brazil/20150209_brazil_transcript.pdf>, last accessed 06/24/2017.

[56] Ayelet Berman, Tim Büthe, Martino Maggetti, and Joost Pauwelyn, 'Introduction: Rethinking Stakeholder Participation in Global Governance.' Chapter 1, this volume.

strategies, a point raised by DeMenno and Büthe.[57] As mentioned earlier, these capacities are unevenly distributed, and this has an obvious impact on the degree of influence regional branches can deliver.

Also, the extent to which regional branches can participate also depends on the setup established by the central institution, particularly on the arrangements that discipline the centre-branch interaction. The contrast between the FATF and FSB experiences also suggests some insights on this topic.

The contribution of the FSRBs seems to be disproportionately devoted to the task of monitoring and ensuring compliance with the FATF standards, rather than influencing the political work of the FATF, for example, standard- and agenda-setting. Exact measurements are of course hard to come by, but one indication of this state of things is that reports of the FSRBs heavily concentrate on informing results of peer-reviews. In contrast, RCGs seem to have more space for focusing on the political aspects of the FSB mandate.

All things considered, the picture that emerges is a complex one. The establishment of regional branches may prove an effective mechanism to engage excluded parties into the works of club-like global institutions. Irrespective of their possible shortcomings, the experience of the FSRBs and the RCGs shows that non-members are better served now than if these bodies did not exist. At the same time, there is plenty of room to increase the participatory capacity of non-members. The question is whether this increase would result from pressure from outside or from a deliberate decision by the centre institutions, such as the ones that led the FATF and the FSB to establish and promote the regional branches in the first place.

[57] DeMenno and Büthe, 'Voice and Influence' (n 10).

PART III
INSTITUTIONS AND REFORMS IN GLOBAL HEALTH GOVERNANCE

A. MAPPING THE REFORMS

13
Stakeholder Participation Reforms in Global Health Governance

Ayelet Berman

13.1 Introduction

This chapter surveys the main reforms granting stakeholder participation opportunities to previously marginalized stakeholders—notably developing countries and non-state actors (NSAs)—in several global health bodies. Building on this volume's analytical framework,[1] I examine the types of institutional reforms which have been introduced to improve the participation opportunities of marginalized stakeholders in institutions with different organizational forms: intergovernmental organizations (IOs) such as the World Health Organization (WHO) and the Codex Alimentarius Commission (Codex), multi-stakeholder partnerships (MSPs) such as the Global Fund to Fight AIDS, Tuberculosis and Malaria (Global Fund) and the GAVI Alliance, transgovernmental regulatory networks (TRNs) such as the International Council for Harmonization (ICH) and the International Medical Device Regulators Forum (IMDRF), and a private standard-setting body (SDOs) such as GlobalG.A.P.

To this end I lay out, for each organization, the main traditional governance structures which prevailed before the reforms. I then lay out the main participation reforms. As I explain, measures to increase stakeholder participation opportunities vary between global health bodies, yet include expanding membership, providing observer or other non-voting status, consultations or commenting opportunities, setting up outreach bodies, earmarked funding, expert consultations, and national consultation processes.

The trend that emerges from this survey is that global health bodies increasingly give developing countries an opportunity to participate—yet they do so to varying degrees and using different measures. Some bodies have strengthened participation of existing developing country members (for example, Codex), and others have integrated new members (for example, Global Fund, GAVI, ICH, IMDRF, and GlobalG.A.P.) or added observers (for example, WHO, ICH). With respect to NSAs, the trend that emerges is that global bodies also increasingly engage NSAs. While in IOs (WHO and Codex) states alone have decisional authority, in informal (non-treaty based) modes of governance, NSAs more often have decisional authority (Global Fund, GAVI, ICH, IMDRF, and the GlobalG.A.P.).

[1] See Ayelet Berman, Tim Büthe, Martino Maggetti and Joost Pauwelyn, 'Introduction: Rethinking Stakeholder Participation in Global Governance.' Chapter 1, this volume; Mercy De Menno and Tim Büthe, 'Voice and Influence in Global Governance: An Analytical Framework.' Chapter 2, this volume.

Ayelet Berman, *Stakeholder Participation Reforms in Global Health Governance* In: *Rethinking Participation in Global Governance.* Edited by: Joost Pauwelyn, Martino Maggetti, Tim Büthe, and Ayelet Berman, Oxford University Press.
DOI: 10.1093/oso/9780198852568.003.0013

Existing literature as well as this chapter's empirical inquiry suggest that despite reforms, inequalities persist. Regulatory networks (ICH and IMDRF) have formally opened up participation opportunities towards large-market economies (and business interests) yet have continued excluding or giving weaker or indirect access to small or low-income countries and public interest groups. Furthermore, business actors alone set the standards in private standard setting bodies (GlobalG.A.P.) Moreover, even when diverse stakeholders are formally given participation opportunities, stakeholders often lack the resources and capacity to take advantage thereof (for example, Global Fund). Business actors or developed countries are often de facto better represented (in comparison to actors representing the public interest) (for example, Codex).[2] These gaps in participation are examined in greater depth in the empirical country case studies[3] and the chapter which assesses the consequences of the reforms.[4]

To promote balanced participation or participation in the public interest, a few bodies (Global Fund, Codex, WHO) have reforms aimed at improving balanced participation among different stakeholder groups, or at safeguarding the public interest against special interests or conflicts of interest.[5]

Whether or not the reforms surveyed in this chapter have brought about changes in actual engagement of previously marginalized stakeholders and changes in their actual influence is addressed in the following country-specific chapters and the chapter assessing the consequences of the reforms.

Table 13.1: Main Global Health Governance Institutions Surveyed

World Health Organization (WHO)
Codex Alimentarius Commission
Global Fund to Fight AIDS, Tuberculosis and Malaria
GAVI Alliance
International Council for Harmonization (ICH)
International Medical Device Regulators Forum (IMDRF)
GlobalG.A.P.

[2] On the political dimensions of international standard setting, see Tim Büthe and Walter Mattli, *The New Global Rulers: The Privatization of Regulation in the World Economy* (Princeton University Press 2011); Walter Mattli and Tim Büthe, 'Setting International Standards: Technological Rationality or Primacy of Power?' 56(1) *World Politics* (2003) 1-42; Ayelet Berman, 'Industry, Regulatory Capture and Transnational Standard Setting' 111 *American Journal of International Law Unbound* (2017) 112-118; Tim Büthe and Walter Mattli, 'International Standards and Standard-Setting Bodies' in David Coen, Wyn Grant and Graham Wilson (eds), *The Oxford Handbook of Business and Government* (2010) 440-471.

[3] André de Mello e Souza and Facundo Pérez Aznar, 'Brazil and Argentina in Global Health Governance.' Chapter 15, this volume ; Cindy Cheng with Anh Do, 'China and Vietnam in Global Health Governance.' Chapter 16, this volume; Tim Büthe, Sachin Chaturvedi, Peter Payoyo and Krishna Ravi Srinivas, 'India and the Philippines in Global Health Governance.' Chapter 17, this volume.

[4] Ayelet Berman and Joost Pauwelyn, 'Assessing Stakeholder Participation Reforms in Global Health Governance.' Chapter 18, this volume.

[5] Relevant literature on the politics of global health governance includes: Tania Keefe, *The Politics of Global Health Governance* (Palgrave 2008); Anne Roemer-Mahler, 'The Rise of Companies from Emerging Markets in Global Health Governance' 40(5) *Review of International Studies* (2014) 897-918; Colin McInnes, Adam Kamradt-Scott, Kelley Lee, Anne Roemer-Mahler, Simon Rushton, and Owain Williams, *The Transformation of Global Health Governance* (Springer 2014).

13.2 Stakeholder Participation Reforms

Over the past decades, global health governance has transformed from a relatively limited, intergovernmental system to a global system with diverse actors.[6] After the Second World War, the WHO was the main global health agency, but then the World Bank (WB) emerged as a major actor, and for much of the second half of the twentieth century, these two IOs, sometimes acting jointly, were unquestionably the institutional focal point for the governance of global health.[7] In the 1990s, however, many NSAs began to crowd the space,[8] including organizations representing commercial interests, such as multinational corporations (for example, Coca Cola) or industry associations (for example, the International Food and Beverage Alliance), as well as organizations pursuing public interests (for example, Oxfam, Consumers International). Philanthropic foundations, notably the Bill and Melinda Gates Foundation, are also massively engaged. Moreover, alongside IOs, in the past two decades, MSPs have emerged. Health related standards are also increasingly set in TRNs[9] or SDOs.[10]

The following sections briefly survey the main participation opportunities of NSAs and developing countries, and important reforms of the past two decades to this end. I lay out the governance structure of each organization, followed by a description of the main participation reforms. I also address reforms aimed at improving balanced participation and safeguarding the public interest.

13.3 The World Health Organization

The WHO is an IO established in 1948,[11] and acts as the directing and coordinating international health authority in the United Nations system. It undertakes technical coordination, supports research, coordinates responses to international health emergencies, and produces standards. Its headquarters are in Geneva, and it has six regional offices.[12]

[6] Andrew Cooper and John Kirton, *Governing Global Health: Challenge, Response, Innovation* (Routledge 2016).

[7] Lawrence O Gostin, *Global Health Law* (Harvard University Press 2014).

[8] Joost Pauwelyn, Ramses A Wessel, and Jan Wouters (eds), *Informal International Lawmaking* (Oxford University Press 2012).

[9] Anne Marie Slaughter, *A New World Order* (Princeton University Press 2004).

[10] Kenneth W Abbott and Duncan Snidal, 'The Governance Triangle: Regulatory Standards Institutions and the Shadow of the State' in Walter Mattli and Ngaire Woods (eds), *The Politics of Global Regulation* (Princeton University Press 2008) 44-88.

[11] Chelsea Clinton and Devi Sridhar, *Governing Global Health: Who Runs the World and Why?* (Oxford University Press 2017) 34.

[12] Nick Drager and Laura Sunderland, 'Public Health in a Globalising World: The Perspective from the WHO' in Andrew Cooper and John Kirton (eds), *Governing Global Health: Challenge, Response, Innovation* (Routledge 2016) 67-78, 67.

13.3.1 Traditional Governance Structure

As the WHO is a universal organization, all 194 country members follow the one country–one vote rule, and all members may send delegates to the annual World Health Assembly.[13] The Executive Board (EB) with its thirty-four members is, however, exclusive, with members elected for a three-year term. The 1948 WHO Constitution also enables NSA engagement.[14] Nongovernmental organizations (NGOs) who have obtained 'official status' (following a burdensome admissions process[15]) may attend WHA and EB meetings.[16] They can attend without a vote, make statements, submit memorandums, and have access to nonconfidential information.[17] NSAs also participate 'indirectly' as members of government delegations. Further, on the basis of personal qualifications, technical experts participate in expert committees.

13.3.2 Main Reforms

A 2003 reform opened up the Executive Board to non-committee members, including developing countries, associate members, the UN, other IOs and NGOs in official relations, all who may attend as observers. Proposals made by such non-members will be considered by the board if endorsed by a member.[18] 'Open meetings' are open to member states and associate members, and 'public meetings' are open to non-EB member states, associate members, other organizations, and the public.[19] In exceptional cases, committees of limited membership may be established, yet these too must be structured in accordance with the principles of equitable geographical representation, and balanced representation of developed and developing countries.[20]

Furthermore, although decision-making remains a member state prerogative, since the 1990s, the WHO has been increasingly collaborating with NSAs, including those that do not have official relations status. The revised Principles Governing Relations with Nongovernmental Organizations enabled consultation with NSAs independently of official relations status.[21] Since the 2000s, the WHO has also been increasingly

[13] The Constitution of the World Health Organization, Article 9 <https://www.who.int/governance/eb/who_constitution_en.pdf?ua=1>, last accessed 05/10/2020.

[14] WHO Constitution (n 13), Articles 2(h), 18(h), 33, 71; World Health Organization, 'Principles Governing Relations Between the World Health Organization and NGOs', <https://www.who.int/governance/civilsociety/principles/en/>, last accessed 05/10/2020.

[15] Gostin, *Global Health Law* (n 7), 118.

[16] WHO, 'Principles' (n 14).

[17] WHO, 'Principles' (n 14), Article 6.

[18] World Health Organization, 'Rules of Procedure of the Executive Board of the World Health Organization', Rules 3 and 4, <https://www.who.int/governance/rules_of_procedure_of_eb_of_wha_en.pdf>, last accessed 05/15/2020.

[19] WHO, 'Rules of Procedure' (n 18), Rule 7.

[20] WHO, 'Rules of Procedure' (n 18), Rule 16.

[21] Nitsan Chorev, *The World Health Organization between North and South* (Cornell University Press 2012) 190-196. World Health Organization, WHA69.10 'WHO Framework of Engagement with Non-State Actors' (28 May 2016) <http://apps.who.int/gb/ebwha/pdf_files/WHA69/A69_R10-en.pdf?ua=1>, last accessed 05/16/2020. Since FENSA this policy is no longer in force.

collaborating with other stakeholders, such as through WHO collaborating centres.[22] Notably, in 2010 it adopted the Policy on WHO's Engagement with Global Health Partnerships and Hosting Arrangements which encourages WHO hosted (for example, Stop TB) or external multi-stakeholder partnerships (for example, Global Fund).[23] Moreover, the WHO sometimes carries out public consultations, as it did for the draft guideline on sugar intake.[24]

Further, whereas historically, member state contributions made up 80% of the budget, funding rules in the past two decades have changed and allow NSA donors to make contributions.[25] These voluntary contributions make now around 80% of total funding. Most voluntary donations are earmarked, and funds can only be spent on specific issues identified by the donor. Thus, voluntary donations like those from the Gates Foundation have effectively set the agenda.[26]

Moreover, efforts on the part of the tobacco industry,[27] the food industry,[28] and the pharmaceutical industry to unduly influence WHO normative action on tobacco, sugary drinks, and vaccines[29] strengthened long-standing concerns about improper commercial influence on the WHO. Previous policies for regulating engagement were deemed insufficiently robust for safeguarding the public interest.[30] In 2016, therefore, the WHO enacted the 'Framework of Engagement with Non-State Actors' (FENSA),[31] a reform whose purpose is to enable the WHO to engage more NSAs (with or without official relations), while managing the risks of NSA engagement. It identifies the following risks: conflicts of interest, exercise of undue influence, negative impacts on WHO's integrity or reputation, NSA acquisition of disproportionate benefits, competitive advantage, and whitewashing of the NSA's image by association with WHO.[32] To manage these risks, FENSA introduces several new tools.

[22] WHO, 'Collaborating centres' <https://www.who.int/about/who-we-are/structure/collaborating-centres>, last accessed 05/19/2020.

[23] WHO, 'Guidelines on Interaction with Commercial Enterprises to Achieve Health Outcomes' in EB107/20 *WHO 'Guidelines on working with the Private Sector to Achieve Health Outcomes* (30 November 2000) <https://apps.who.int/gb/archive/pdf_files/EB107/ee20.pdf?ua=1>, last accessed 05/15/2020.

[24] WHO, 'WHO Opens Public Consultation on Draft Sugars Guideline' (2014) <http://www.who.int/mediacentre/news/notes/2014/consultation-sugar-guideline/en/>, last accessed 05/19/2020.

[25] Erin R Graham, 'Follow the Money: How Trends in Financing Are Changing Governance at International Organizations' 8(5) *Global Policy* (2017) 15-25.

[26] Karolin Seitz and Jens Martens, 'Philanthrolateralism: Private Funding and Corporate Influence in the United Nations' 8(5) *Global Policy* (2017) 46-50; Sheri Fink, 'WHO Leader Describes the Agency's Ebola Operations' *The New York Times* (4 September 2014); Catriona Wellington, 'Does Earmarked Donor Funding Make it More or Less Likely that Developing Countries Will Allocate Their Resources Towards Programmes that Yield the Greatest Health Benefits?' 82(9) *Bulletin of the World Health Organization* (2004) 703-306.

[27] Kent Buse and Chris Naylor, 'Commercial Health Governance' in Kent Buse and Wolfgang Hein (eds), *Making Sense of Global Health Governance* (Palgrave MacMillan 2009) 187-208.

[28] Rema Nagarajan, 'How Food, Beverage Giants Influence WHO Rules' *The Times of India* (22 May 2015) <https://timesofindia.indiatimes.com/india/How-food-beverage-giants-influence-WHO-rules/articleshow/47378845.cms>, last accessed 05/17/2020.

[29] Deborah Cohen and Philip Carter, 'WHO and the Pandemic Flu 'Conspiracies'' 340 *British Medical Journal* (2010) 1274-1279.

[30] Judith Richter, 'Public Private Partnership and International Health Policy Making: How Can Public Interests Be Safeguarded?' 98(10) *Journal of Royal Society of Medicine* (2004) 476-477.

[31] WHO, 'Framework of Engagement' (n 21).

[32] WHO, 'Framework of Engagement' (n 21), Article 6.

FENSA distinguishes between four NSA types: non-profit NGOs, private sector entities, philanthropic foundations, and academic institutions. Previously, the WHO (as all UN organizations) identified any organization that is not governmental as an 'NGO'. Due to the inherent conflict of interest between commercial interests and the WHO, these new distinctions are critical.[33] Further, FENSA enables engagement with NSAs regardless of the official relations status. Thus, participation in WHO governing bodies is not conditional on having official status. Further, FENSA establishes a risk assessment process, whereby any NSA engagement is proceeded by due diligence and a risk assessment.[34] Annual reports on NSA engagement and a public NSA register are supposed to improve transparency.[35] FENSA's implementation so far has however been weak. Thus, critics have been concerned that it gives a resemblance of legitimacy while actually increasing the entanglement of the WHO with the business sector.[36]

13.4 Codex Alimentarius Commission

Codex was established in 1963 by the Food Agricultural Organization (FAO) and the WHO. Its mission is to develop food standards and guidelines to assure safety, quality, and fair practices in food trade.[37]

[33] Melissa J Durkee, 'Astroturf Activism' 69 *Standford Law Review* (2017) 201-268.

[34] WHO, 'Framework of Engagement' (n 21), Articles 27–31, 32, 8.

[35] WHO, 'Framework of Engagement' (n 21), Articles 37–41.

[36] Ayelet Berman, 'Between Participation and Capture: The WHO Framework of Engagement with Non-State Actors', 32(1) *European Journal of International Law* (2021) 227–254. Richter, 'Public Private Partnership' (n 30); Katherine Brown, Patti Rundall, Tim Lobstein, Modi Mwatsana, and Bill Jeffery, 'Open Letter to WHO DG Candidates: Keep Policy and Priority Setting Free of Commercial Influence' 389(10082) *The Lancet* (2017) 1879; Lida Lhotska and Arun Gupta, 'Whose Health? The Crucial Negotiations over the World Health Organization's Future,' Gifa, 19 May 2016 <https://www.gifa.org/whose-health-the-crucial-negotiations-for-the-world-health-organizations-future/>, last accessed 05/19/2020; Mirza Alas, 'WHO: Civil Society Protest Undermining of Current Negotiation on FENSA,' Third World Network, 2016 <https://www.twn.my/title2/health.info/2015/hi151017.htm>, last accessed 05/15/2020; Arun Gupta and Lida Lhotska, 'A Fox Building a Chicken Coop? WHO Reform: 'Health for All' or More Corporate Influence?' Centre for Science in Public Interest (2015) <https://www.policyforum.net/a-fox-building-a-chicken-coop/>, last accessed 05/15/2020; Amandine Garde, Bill Jeffery, and Neville Rigby, 'Implementing the WHO Recommendations Whilst Avoiding Real, Perceived or Potential Conflicts of Interest' 8 *European Journal of Risk Regulation* (2017) 237-250; Lauren Vogel, 'WHO Mulls Closer Ties to Private Sector?' 188(2) *Canadian Medical Association Journal* (2016) 106; 'WHO: Restructuring Fails to Address Conflict of Interest in FENSA Implementation,' Third World Network, 24 April 2019 <https://www.twn.my/title2/health.info/2019/hi190406.htm>, last accessed 05/15/2020; Danielle Hanna Rached and Deisy de Freitas Lima Ventura, 'World Health Organization and the Search for Accountability: a Critical Analysis of the New Framework of Engagement with Non-State Actors' 33(6) *Cad Saude Publica Reports in Public Health* (2017); Kent Buse and Sarah Hawkes, 'Sitting on the FENSA: WHO Engagement with Industry' 388(10043) *The Lancet* (2016) 446-447.

[37] Frode Veggeland and Svein Ole Borgen, 'Negotiating International Food Standards: The World Trade Organization's Impact on the Codex Alimentarius Commission' 18(4) *Governance* (2005) 675-708; Natalie Avery, Martin Drake and Tim Lang, *Cracking the Codex* (National Food Alliance 1993); David E Winickoff and Douglas M Bushey, 'Science and Power in Global Food Regulation: The Rise of Codex Alimentarius' 35(3) *Science, Technology & Human Values* (2009) 356-381.

13.4.1 Governance Structure

Codex consists of the Commission, the Executive Committee, and subsidiary bodies. The Commission is the supreme decision-making body at which member states discuss food standards matters. The Executive Committee includes six elected representatives from the six geographical regions. Subsidiary bodies include, inter alia, specific technical committees that develop draft standards.[38]

Codex engages NGOs with official 'observer' status. These may participate in committees, task forces, or working groups.[39] Observers may intervene and submit comments on draft standards (which are developed at the committee level, and adopted by the Commission), but only country members can make decisions.[40] NGOs do not participate in the Executive Committee. Automatically eligible NGOs are those with official FAO or WHO relations.[41] Others must (among others) be multilateral 'in scope or structure', representative of their specialized field.[42] In contrast to the WHO (following FENSA), Codex does not distinguish between NGO types, and in practice, out of the approximately 164 NGOs,[43] most represent industry interests[44] and outnumber consumer or patient interests.[45] Furthermore, being put on national delegations is another route by which NSAs participate in Codex. Business is typically over-represented there too. The long struggle over Genetically Modified Food labelling reflected this tension between business interests and the public interest.[46] Physical attendance also tends to be skewed towards business NGOs.[47]

[38] WHO, 'WHO and the Codex Alimentarius' <https://www.who.int/foodsafety/areas_work/food-standard/general_info/en/index3.html>, last accessed 05/19/2020.

[39] Food and Agricultural Organization, E-Learning Academy, 'Enhancing Participation in Codex Activities', Lesson 2.2 <https://elearning.fao.org/course/view.php?id=178>, last accessed 05/18/2020.

[40] FAO, E-Learning Academy (n 39), Lesson 2.2.

[41] Codex Alimentarius, 'Members' <http://www.fao.org/fao-who-codexalimentarius/about-codex/members/en/>, last accessed 05/19/2020; Codex Alimentarius, 'Codex Observers' <http://www.fao.org/fao-who-codexalimentarius/about-codex/observers/en/>, last accessed 05/19/2020; FAO, E-Learning Academy (n 39); Codex Alimentarius, 'The Principles Concerning the Participation of International Non-Governmental Organizations in the Work of the Codex Alimentarius Commission' (1999) Article 3 <http://www.fao.org/docrep/005/Y2200E/y2200e09.htm>, last accessed 05/19/2020.

[42] Codex, 'Principles Concerning Participation' (n 41), Article 2; See also Codex Alimentarius Commission, *Procedural Manual 24th Edition* (FAO and WHO 2015) http://www.fao.org/3/a-i5079e.pdf, last accessed 05/19/2020.

[43] Codex, 'Codex Observers' (n 41).

[44] Sanderijn Duquet and Dylan Geraets, 'Food Safety Standards and Informal International Lawmaking' in Ayelet Berman, Sanderijn Duquet, Joost Pauwelyn, Ramses A Wessel and Jan Wouters (eds), *Informal International Law-Making: Case Studies* (TOAEP 2012) 395-433, 409; Edward Scarbrough, 'Codex—What's All the Fuss?' 65 *Food and Drug Law Journal* (2010) 631-638,; Elizabeth Smythe, 'In Whose Interests? Transparency and Accountability in the Global Governance of Food: Agribusiness, the Codex Alimentarius, and the World Trade Organization' in Jennifer Clapp and Doris Fuchs (eds), *Corporate Power in Global Agriffod Governance* (MIT Press 2009) 93-123, 97–99; Consumers International, 'Codex Alimentarius' <https://www.consumersinternational.org/who-we-are/partners/codex-alimentarius/>, last accessed 05/19/2020.

[45] Tim Büthe and Nathaniel Harris, 'The Codex Alimentarius Commission: A Hybrid Public-Private Regulator' in Thomas Hale and David Held (eds), *Handbook of Transnational Governance: Institutions and Innovations* (Polity Press 2011) 219-228, 223.

[46] Smythe, 'In Whose Interests?' (n 44), 107; Consumers Union, 'US Ends Opposition to GM Labeling Guidelines' Consumers Reports (5 July 2011) <https://consumersunion.org/news/us-ends-opposition-to-gm-labeling-guidelines/>, last accessed 05/19/2020.

[47] Consumers International, 'Codex Alimentarius' (n 44), 20.

Further, scientific advice is the foundation of all Codex standards.[48] In developing standards, committees draw on input provided by experts (expert committees or ad hoc expert consultations). Experts are invited in their personal capacity to diverse expert committees. For established expert committees, there are rosters of experts. For ad hoc meetings, calls for experts are issued.[49] Occasionally, Codex issues public calls for data[50] (industry players frequently provide the data).[51] Scientific advice is supposed to be provided in accordance with principles of soundness, responsibility, objectivity, fairness, transparency, and inclusiveness,[52] and is subject to a risk assessment process.

Moreover, in elaborating standards, Codex follows an eight-step procedure. Observers and members are entitled to comment, but Codex does not carry out public consultations. Member state consultations includes sending the draft to its members national contact points for comments. Such national contact points link Codex with national stakeholders. Draft and final Codex documents are circulated to national stakeholders, such as ministries, national food industry, public health professionals, scientific experts, and consumer organizations.[53] On the basis of their input, a national position is developed.[54]

National Codex Committees provide an additional opportunity to participate. They are often multi-stakeholder bodies comprised of 'relevant government departments/ministries, consumer organizations, industry—food manufacturers and food producers, food importers and/or exporters, universities, professional bodies, leading research institutions, [and] notable national experts'.[55] Although the process used to form national delegations varies across countries, NSAs often sit on

[48] FAO, E-Learning Academy (n 39), Lesson 4.2.

[49] FAO, E-Learning Academy (n 39), Lesson 4.2.

[50] FAO, E-Learning Academy (n 39), Lesson 4.2.

[51] FAO, E-Learning Academy (n 39), Lesson 4.2.

[52] 'Inclusiveness' is 'considered to include group balance' and requires 'due respect and consideration' for 'minority scientific opinion'. When selecting participants, 'in addition to their expertise, due consideration should be given to geographical and socioeconomic balance, but not to the extent that it compromises scientific integrity. Particular emphasis should be placed on improving the participation of developing countries. Where participation is limited by skill or knowledge gap, appropriate capacity building activities should be undertaken.' FAO, E-Learning Academy (n 39), Lesson 4.2; Food and Agriculture Organization and World Health Organization, 'Provision of Scientific Advice to Codex and Member Countries - Report of a Joint FAO/WHO Workshop WHO Headquarters' (FAO and WHO 2004) <http://www.fao.org/3/y5388e/y5388e00.htm>, last accessed 05/19/2020; Dariush Mozaffarian, 'Role of Government Policy in Nutrition— Barriers to and Opportunities for Healthier Eating' 361 *BMJ* (2018) 1-11.

[53] FAO, E-Learning Academy (n 39), Lesson 3.1.

[54] FAO, E-Learning Academy (n 39), Lesson 3.1., 3.2.

[55] FAO, E-Learning Academy (n 39), Lesson 3.2.; Food and Agriculture Organization and World Health Organization, 'Appendix II: Draft Guidelines for Codex Contact Points and National Codex Committees (Asian Regional Guidelines)' <http://www.fao.org/docrep/meeting/005/w7974e/w7974e0n.htm#bm23.3.1>, last accessed 05/19/2020; Codex Alimentarius Commission, CAC/GL 58R-2005 'Regional Guidelines for Codex Contact Points and National Codex Committees (Near East)' <http://www.fao.org/fao-who-codexalimentarius/sh-proxy/en/?lnk=1&url=https%253A%252F%252Fworkspace.fao.org%252Fsites%252Fcodex%252FStandards%252FCXG%2B58R-2005%252FCXG_058Re.pdf>, last accessed 05/19/2020; Codex Alimentarius Commission, CAC/GL 43R-2003 'Regional Guidelines for Codex Contact Points and National Codex Committees (Africa)' <http://www.fao.org/fao-who-codexalimentarius/sh-proxy/en/?lnk=1&url=https%253A%252F%252Fworkspace.fao.org%252Fsites%252Fcodex%252FStandards%252FCXG%2B43R-2003%252FCXG_043Re.pdf>, last accessed 05/19/2020.

national delegations as 'advisors'.[56] They are included thanks to their effectiveness or expertise.[57] The food industry is more often on these delegations than consumer organizations.

13.4.2 Main Reforms

In the 1990s, with growing international trade in food, the public's growing concern with food safety, and following the WTO Sanitary and Phytosanitary (SPS) and Technical Barriers to Trade (TBT) Agreements, and the de facto binding nature of Codex standards under these agreements, Codex gained importance.[58] Therefore, although all WHO and FAO member states had always been entitled to become Codex members, it was only in the 1990s that developing country membership increased significantly, with Codex growing from 30 to 183 members. Currently, there are 189 members. The number of observers has increased, too. While around the year 2000 there were 196 observers (comprised of forty-one IOs, 139 NGOs, and sixteen UN organizations), in 2020, there are 238 observers (fifty-eight IOs, 164 NGOs, and sixteen UN organizations).[59]

Many new developing-country members, however, have not taken advantage of their participation rights[60] because they lack the resources, capacity, or expertise.[61] Many of these new members thus appeared to remain *de facto* marginalized.[62] To 'help developing countries and countries in transition to increase their participation in . . . the Commission', the FAO and WHO enacted the Codex Trust Fund (CTF). CTF I (2004–2015), which grants eligible members financial support, has funded the physical attendance of over 2300 representatives from regions such as Asia and Africa at

[56] FAO, E-Learning Academy (n 39), Lesson 3.3.

[57] FAO, E-Learning Academy (n 39), Lesson 3.3.

[58] Tim Büthe, 'The Codex Alimentarius Commission in the SPS Agreement of the WTO' in Cary Coglianese, Adam Finkel, and David Zaring (eds), *Import Safety, Regulatory Governance in the Global Economy* (University of Pennsylvania Press 2009) 88-109; Tim Büthe, 'The Globalization of Health and Safety Standards: Delegation of Regulatory Authority in the SPS Agreement of the 1994 Agreement Establishing the World Trade Organization' 71(1) *Law and Contemporary Problems* (2008) 219-255; David Victor, 'The Sanitary and Phytosanitary Agreement of the World Trade Organization: An Assessment After Five Years' 32 *New York University Journal of International Law and Politics* (2000) 865-937; Joost Pauwelyn, 'The WTO Agreement on SPS Measures as Applied in the First Three SPS Disputes' 2 *Journal of International Economic Law* (1999) 641-664.

[59] Codex, 'Observers' (n 41). Report of the Evaluation of the Codex Alimentarius and Other FAO and WHO Food Standards Work (2002), <https://www.who.int/foodsafety/codex/en/codex_eval_report_en.pdf>, last accessed 05/19/2020; Codex Alimentarius Commission, List of Governmental and Non-Governmental Organizations in Observer Status with the Codex Alimentarius Commission, CAC/LIM 4 (1999) <http://www.fao.org/tempref/codex/Reports/Alinorm99/lim99_04.pdf> , last accessed 05/19/2020.

[60] Codex Alimentarius, *Understanding Codex* (FAO and WHO, 2016) <http://www.fao.org/3/a-i5667e.pdf>, last accessed 05/19/2020; Bruce Traill, 'Report of the Evaluation of Codex Alimentarius and Other FAO and WHO Food Standards Work,' 15 November 2002 <https://www.who.int/foodsafety/codex/en/codex_eval_report_en.pdf>, last accessed 05/19/2020.

[61] Codex Alimentarius, 'Strategic Framework 2003–2007' (FAO and WHO, 2002) <http://www.fao.org/docrep/004/Y2361e/y2361e00.htm>, last accessed 05/19/2020; Michael A Livermore, 'Authority and Legitimacy in Global Governance: Deliberation, Institutional Differentiation, and the Codex Alimentarius' 81 *New York University Law Review* (2006) 766-801, 783.

[62] Büthe and Harris, 'The Codex Alimentarius Commission' (n 45), 223.

meetings.[63] By training over 1200 officials[64] on technical and scientific matters,[65] it has also sought to improve their capability to develop informed positions. Indeed, to 'facilitate ... effective participation',[66] CTF II (2016–2027)[67] aims at 'promot[ing] capacity development programs that assist countries in creating sustainable national Codex structures' and 'conduct[ing] educational and technical capacity building activities' largely through regional and sub-regional workshops.[68] It supports more than 100 eligible countries in enhancing their scientific and technical capacities so as to strengthen their participation.

Finally, WHO's FENSA is disconnected from Codex,[69] with Codex indicating that 'it is at the national level that consumers can make their most valuable and effective input.'[70]

13.5 The Global Fund to Fight AIDS, Tuberculosis and Malaria

The Global Fund, set up in 2002, disburses funding to eligible developing countries to support the fight against AIDS, Tuberculosis and Malaria.

13.5.1 Governance Structure

The Global Fund is an MSP, bringing together public and private actors. The Board has twenty voting members, which are divided into a donor bloc and recipient/implementer bloc. Governments form about three-quarters of the board (fifteen members), split almost evenly among developed country donors (eight countries) and developing country representatives of the six WHO regions, with one additional representative from Africa (seven countries). The remaining quarter of the voting board (five members) represent NSAs: three civil society organizations (NGO from a developing country, NGO from a developed country, and an NGO representing affected communities), one private sector representative, and one member representing private

[63] Codex, 'FAO/WHO Codex Trust Fund' <http://www.who.int/foodsafety/areas_work/food-standard/codextrustfund/en/>, last accessed 05/19/2020.

[64] Codex, 'Codex Trust Fund-2: Project Document' (December 2015) 6f <http://www.who.int/foodsafety/areas_work/food-standard/CTF2ProjectDocument.pdf?ua=1>, last accessed 05/19/2020; Codex Alimentarius Commission, CX/CAC 15/38/18-Add.3 'FAO/WHO Project and Fund for Enhanced Participation in Codex (Codex Trust Fund): Final Project Evaluation' (2015) <http://www.who.int/foodsafety/areas_work/food-standard/cac38_18_add3e.pdf>, last accessed 05/19/2020.

[65] Codex, *Understanding Codex* (n 60), 35.

[66] See Codex Alimentarius Commission, 'Strategic Plan 2014–2019' Strategic Goal 3 <http://www.fao.org/3/a-i3826e.pdf>, last accessed 05/19/2020.

[67] Codex, 'FAO/WHO Codex Trust Fund' (n 63).

[68] Codex, 'Strategic Plan 2014–2019' (n 66), Objective 3.2.

[69] World Health Organization, *Guide for Staff on Engagement with Non-State Actors* (WHO 2018), Art. 5.2. <http://www.who.int/about/collaborations/non-state-actors/FENSA_guide-for-staff.pdf>, last accessed 05/19/2020.

[70] Codex, *Understanding Codex* (n 60), 39.

foundations (held by the Gates Foundation). In addition, there are eight non-voting members, including the WHO, UNAIDS, and the WB.

Decision-making is organized along the principle of donor and implementer blocs. The donor bloc includes all governments and NSAs from developed countries and the implementer bloc includes governments and NSAs from developing countries. To ensure equality, decisions are reached by consensus, and by vote if consensus cannot be reached.[71] Each member has an equal amount of votes.[72] To ensure both blocs support the decision, a two-thirds majority of each bloc is required for a vote to pass.

Country ownership is a central principle of the Global Fund's governance, and the Global Fund relies on national structures to implement its programs. Every recipient country has a 'Country Coordinating Mechanism' (CCM) that submits grant applications to the Global Fund and oversees implementation of Global Fund programmes. CCMs must be MSPs,[73] including civil society, the private sector, technical partners, and representatives of people living with or affected by the three diseases.[74]

13.5.2 Main Reforms

Despite the MSP model, imbalances in participation persist, with the donor bloc *often de facto* setting the agenda, and the implementer bloc remaining relatively passive.[75] The Global Fund has sought to tackle the structural barriers to meaningful participation, such as language barriers, inadequate access to technology, and complexity of materials.[76] Declaring that 'work needs to be done to ensure that all stakeholders are heard equally on the Board, at committees, and in decisions and actions that taken across the Fund more generally,'[77] it introduced a 'Strategic Roadmap to Enhance Implementer Voice' that would proactively mitigate these barriers.[78] It

[71] The Global Fund, 'Bylaws of the Global Fund to Fight AIDS, Tuberculosis and Malaria', Article 7.6 <https://www.theglobalfund.org/media/6007/core_globalfund_bylaws_en.pdf>, last accessed 05/18/2020.

[72] Global Fund, 'Bylaws of the Global Fund' (n 71).

[73] Gostin, *Global Health Law* (n 7), 149.

[74] The Global Fund, 'Country Coordinating Mechanism Eligibility', Requirement 4 <https://www.theglobalfund.org/en/country-coordinating-mechanism/eligibility/>, last accessed 05/18/2020.

[75] Michel Kazatchkine, 'Reflections on the Global Fund, an Open Letter from Michel Kazatchkine' (Geneva, 16 March 2012) <http://www.michelkazatchkine.com/?p=1>, last accessed 05/19/2020; Garrett Wallace Brown, 'Safeguarding Deliberative Global Governance: The Case of the Global Fund' 36 *Review of International Studies* (2010) 511-530; Gostin, *Global Health Law* (n 7), 522–524; Sania Nishtar, 'Public—Private 'Partnerships' in Health—a Global Call to Action' 2(1) *Health Research Policy and Systems* (2004) 1-7.

[76] The Global Fund, GF/B26/11 'Continuing the Board's Strategic Governance Reform Program - Phase 2 (26th Board Meeting)' (2012) 3, <https://www.theglobalfund.org/en/board/decisions/>, last accessed 05/19/2020.

[77] The Global Fund, Office of the Inspector General, 'Governance Review' (2014) <https://www.theglobalfund.org/media/2605/oig_gf-oig-14-008_report_en.pdf?u=636637835180000000>, last accessed 05/19/2020.

[78] Global Fund, GF/B32/08 Revision 2 'Strategic Governance Reform' (n 76), 3; The Global Fund, 'The Global Fund Governance Plan for Impact - Ad-Hoc Working Group on Governance Report to the Board

sets guidance for improving board participation,[79] and funds coordination among constituencies.[80]

Likewise, to strengthen the participation of vulnerable populations in the CCM, the Global Fund introduced reforms for improving the participation of women,[81] 'key population' (those highly impacted by the diseases but with reduced access because they are criminalized or otherwise marginalized, such as gay men, transgender people, sex workers, drug addicts, etc.).[82] In 2014 the Fund introduced the 'New Funding Model' (NFM), which sets out guidelines on how CCMs should reach out to civil society, women, and other key populations, engage them in the country dialogues,[83] and include their priorities in the grants.[84] Moreover, by making funding eligibility conditional on proof of such inclusiveness,[85] the NFM has introduced an accountability mechanism that enforces inclusiveness.

In recent years, the Global Fund has also introduced financial support and capacity building reforms, such as the Community Systems Strengthening Framework, the Key Populations Action Plan, and the Technical Assistance Program on Community, Rights and Gender. These provide funds or technical assistance to overcome structural barriers to participation—such as gaps in knowledge, or 'participation literacy'.[86] A Human Rights Complaints Mechanism tackles human rights barriers to access. To further improve civil society engagement, the Global Fund has restructured its Secretariat, setting up a Community, Rights and Gender Department with the objective of supporting civil society and communities in participation, as well as a 'Civil Society Hub' that centralizes all civil society matters in the Global Fund.[87]

(The Global Fund 32nd Board Meeting)' (2014), 27 <http://www.theglobalfund.org/en/board/meetings/32/>, last accessed 05/19/2020.

[79] The Global Fund, Implementer Group, 'Consultancy of the Implementer Group Roadmap: Terms of Reference' <https://www.theglobalfund.org/en/documents-by-type/implementers/>, last accessed 05/19/2020.

[80] The Global Fund, GF/B35/08 '35th Board Meeting Final Report and Recommendations of the Transitional Governance Committee (TGC)' (2016), 14 <https://www.theglobalfund.org/media/4232/bm35_08-finalreport recommendationstransitionalgovernancecommittee_report_en.pdf>, last accessed 05/19/2020.

[81] The Global Fund, 'Gender Equality Strategy - Action Plan 2014-2016' <https://www.theglobalfund.org/media/1247/publication_genderequalitystrategy_actionplan_en.pdf>, last accessed 05/19/2020.

[82] The Global Fund, 'Engage! Practical Tips to Ensure the New Funding Model Delivers the Impact Communities Need' (2014), 9 <https://www.theglobalfund.org/media/5675/publication_engagecivilsociety_brochure_en.pdf?u=637233413350000000>, last accessed 05/19/2020.

[83] Global Fund, 'Engage!' (n 82), 9–14.

[84] Global Fund, 'Engage!' (n 82), 9.

[85] Global Fund, 'Country Coordinating Mechanism Eligibility' (n 74), Requirements 1 and 4.

[86] Examples include: The Community Systems Strengthening Framework—see The Global Fund, 'Key Populations Action Plan 2014-2017' <https://www.theglobalfund.org/media/1270/publication_keypopulations_actionplan_en.pdf>, last accessed 05/19/2020; The Community Rights and Gender Technical Assistance Program—see The Global Fund, 'Technical Cooperation: Community, Rights and Gender Technical Assistance Program' <https://www.theglobalfund.org/en/technical-cooperation/community-rights-gender-technical-assistance-program/>, last accessed 05/19/2020; The CRG Special Initiative, the Key Affected Population Country Coordinating Mechanism Pilot (2013) and the Special Initiative for Capacity Development and Technical Assistance (2014)—see The Global Fund, GF/B33/09 '33rd Board Meeting: Community, Rights and Gender Report' (2015), 3, 14, and 6f, respectively <http://www.theglobalfund.org/en/board/meetings/33/>, last accessed 05/19/2020; Women for the Global Fund movement—see The Global Fund, GF/B33/09 '33rd Board Meeting: Global Fund Secretariat Activities to Increase Community Engagement and Promote Human Rights and Gender Equality under the New Funding Model' (2015), and Annex 1, 11 <http://www.theglobalfund.org/en/board/meetings/33/>, last accessed 05/19/2020.

[87] Global Fund, '33rd Board Meeting' (n 86), 6f.

Finally, although MSPs embody an ideal of equality,[88] in reality, diversity gives rise to conflicts between the constituencies' interests or between constituency and Global Fund interests.[89] Board members have dual responsibilities to their constituencies and to the Global Fund which are not necessarily aligned.[90] Recognizing that egalitarianism 'in itself contains inevitable tensions between the interests of various constituencies and the overall best interest of the Global Fund',[91] the Global Fund launched the Ethics and Integrity Initiative, and in 2015 issued a Code of Ethical Conduct for Governance Officials.[92] The Code clarifies that board members are 'ultimately obligated to work in the best interests of the Global Fund,' notwithstanding constituency interests that 'are to be respected.'[93] Furthermore, members must understand that the Global Fund's direction is shaped by 'incorporating and balancing varying constituency interests.'[94] The Code sets out specific procedures for implementing and enforcing this obligation, and establishes an Ethics Officer for oversight.[95]

13.6 Global Alliance for Vaccines and Immunization (GAVI)

Established in 1999, GAVI's mission is to increase immunization of children in developing countries.[96]

13.6.1 Governance Structure

When set up in 1999, GAVI was a loosely structured, unincorporated partnership of major immunization stakeholders. It was not established by treaty and lacked legal personality.[97] The Bill and Melinda Gates Foundation made a USD 750 million donation and thus played a crucial role in GAVI's establishment; the foundation continues its role as an important influence.[98]

[88] Kent Buse and Andrew Harmer, 'Power to Partners?: The Politics of Public-Private Health Partnerships' 47 *Development* (2004) 49-56, 51.
[89] Global Fund, 'Governance Plan for Impact' (n 78), 27.
[90] Global Fund, Office of the Inspector General (n 77), 24.
[91] Global Fund, 'Governance Plan for Impact' (n 78), 27.
[92] The Global Fund, GF/B33/DP10 'Decision of the Global Fund Board at its Thirty-Third Meeting' (2015) <https://www.theglobalfund.org/en/board/meetings/33/>, last accessed 05/19/2020.
[93] The Global Fund, GF/B33/15-Revision 2 '33rd Board Meeting: Ethics and Integrity Initiative: Second Stage Proposals,' Section 18 <https://www.theglobalfund.org/media/4170/bm33_15-ethicsintegrityinitiativeincludingannexes_report_en.pdf>, last accessed 05/19/2020; The Global Fund, GF/B33/15- Revision 2 'Code of Ethical Conduct for Governance Officials' (2015), Article 3b, <https://www.theglobalfund.org/media/4293/core_codeofethicalconductforgovernanceofficials_policy_en.pdf?u=636488964300000000>, last accessed 05/19/2020.
[94] Global Fund, 'Code of Ethical Conduct' (n 93).
[95] Global Fund, 'Code of Ethical Conduct' (n 93), Section 4.
[96] GAVI, 'Gavi Alliance Statutes,' Article 2 <https://www.gavi.org/library/gavi-documents/legal/gavi-alliance-statutes/>, last accessed 12/06/2019.
[97] Eelco Szabo, 'Gavi, the Vaccine Alliance: A Unique Case Study in Partnership' 13(1) *International Organisations Law Review* (2016) 149-170.
[98] Desmond McNeill and Kristin Ingstad Sandberg, 'Trust in Global Health Governance: The GAVI Experience' 20 *Global Governance* (2014) 325-243, 325, 331; Kristin Sandberg, Steinar Andresen and

Board-adopted guiding principles governed the functioning of the Alliance,[99] and defined the partnership as 'a network of international organizations, industrialized and developing countries, technical agencies, research and development agencies, industry, foundations, non-governmental organizations and other entities which have expressed their interest in its mission and objectives … '. UNICEF hosted its Secretariat. Its board was composed of two developing country governments, three industrialized country governments, and one seat each for the WHO, WB, UNICEF, technical health institutes, the vaccine industry from developed countries, the vaccine industry from developing countries, NGOs, Foundations (Rockefeller), research institutes, and the Bill and Melinda Gates Foundation.[100]

Given that the Alliance did not have legal personality and could not receive funding, the GAVI Fund was established as a United States-based 501(c)(3) not-for-profit organization, and it received and managed the donations.[101]

13.6.2 Main Reforms

Following several years of operations, GAVI's activities expanded and the dual governance structure became too complex leading to a governance reform. Thus, in 2009 the GAVI Alliance and Fund established GAVI as a Swiss Foundation governed by Swiss law. Furthermore, it signed a Headquarters Agreement with the Government of Switzerland,[102] and was recognized as an international organization under the Swiss Host State Act,[103] bestowing upon it an internationally recognized legal personality as well as various privileges and immunities in Switzerland.[104]

GAVI also increased the size of the board to twenty-seven voting seats (or twenty-eight, including the non-voting GAVI CEO) and changed its structure. Developing country governments and developing countries now each hold five seats.[105] The WHO, WB, UNICEF, vaccine industry from developed countries, vaccine industry from developing countries, civil society, technical/research institutes, and the Gates Foundation each have one seat. Further, nine private individuals unaffiliated to

Gunnar Bjune, 'A New Approach to Global Health Institutions? A Case Study of New Vaccine Introduction and the Formation of the GAVI Alliance' 71 *Social Science & Medicine* (2010) 1349-1356.

[99] Third GAVI Board Meeting, June 2000. Report with the author.

[100] Szabo, 'Gavi, the Vaccine Alliance' (n 97), WHO, Report by the Secretariat: Global Alliance for Vaccines and Immunization, 55th World Health Assembly (A55/10, 23 March 2002) <https://apps.who.int/iris/bitstream/handle/10665/78464/ea5510.pdf?sequence=1&isAllowed=y>, last accessed 05/19/2020.

[101] Szabo, 'Gavi, the Vaccine Alliance' (n 97).

[102] Agreement between the GAVI Alliance and the Swiss Federal Council in order to determine the legal status of the GAVI Alliance in Switzerland ('HQ Agreement') <www.admin.ch/opc/fr/classified-compilation/20091983/index.html>, last accessed 05/19/2020.

[103] Federal Act on the Privileges, Immunities and Facilities and the Financial Subsidies Granted by Switzerland as a Host State of 22 June 2007 <https://www.admin.ch/opc/en/classified-compilation/20061778/index.html>, last accessed 05/19/2020.

[104] Article 1 of the HQ Agreement (n 102) provides that '[t]he Swiss Federal Council acknowledges, for the purpose of the present Agreement, the international legal personality and capacity of the GAVI Alliance within Switzerland'.

[105] GAVI, 'Board Composition' <https://www.gavi.org/governance/gavi-board/composition>, last accessed 05/19/2020.

any organization participate in their own capacity as experts on a range of relevant topics.[106]

The 2009 reform also strengthened the position of civil society in GAVI's governance.[107] It has a significant role implementing GAVI's immunization programmes, such as by delivering the programmes, or training local health workers,[108] and delivers up to 60% of vaccines.[109] It also serves as a bridge between GAVI and the local community. It represents local communities and works to influence policy formation.[110]

The reform established the Civil Society Organisations (CSO) Constituency, a network of over 250 CSOs from both developed and developing countries, the GAVI Steering Committee, a group of nineteen CSOs from fifteen different countries to guide the Constituency in its work,[111] and a Civil Society Forum that encompasses all CSOs and individuals with an interest in GAVI's mission. Members represent a diversity of perspectives, positions, and experiences. A Civil Society Constituency Charter has further bolstered civil society engagement.[112]

To support civil society partners implementing GAVI immunization projects, GAVI has been funding CSOs.[113] Disbursed funds strengthen capacity, including CSO coordination and representation.[114] Finally, the private sector is more heavily engaged than in the Global Fund,[115] giving cash donations and in-kind support. The vaccine industry also has two seats on the board. Although GAVI has a conflicts of interest policy, it has nevertheless come under criticism for potential conflicts of interest.[116]

13.7 International Council for Harmonization

Set up in 1991, the ICH's purpose is to harmonize the technical requirements for the registration of medicines.[117]

[106] GAVI, 'GAVI Alliance By-Laws', Article 2.4.3, <https://www.gavi.org/library/gavi-documents/legal/gavi-alliance-by-laws/>, last accessed 05/19/2020.

[107] GAVI, 'GAVI Alliance Progress Report' (2009) <https://www.gavi.org/sites/default/files/publications/progress-reports/Gavi-Progress-Report-2009.pdf>, last accessed 05/19/2020.

[108] GAVI, 'Progress Report' (n 107).

[109] Clinton and Sridhar, *Governing Global Health* (n 11), 129.

[110] GAVI, 'Civil Society Organisation Support' < https://www.gavi.org/programmes-impact/types-support/civil-society>, last accessed 05/19/2020.

[111] GAVI, 'Civil Society Organisations' <http://www.gavi.org/about/partners/cso/>, last accessed 05/19/2020; WHO, 'GAVI Alliance Civil Society Constituency Charter'<http://www.who.int/pmnch/media/news/2013/gavi_cso_charter.pdf>, last accessed 05/19/2020.

[112] GAVI, 'Civil Society Organisations' (n 111).

[113] Clinton and Sridhar, *Governing Global Health* (n 11), 130.

[114] GAVI, 'Implementation and Results Framework: GAVI Programmatic Support to Civil Society Organisations Implementation Framework' <https://www.gavi.org/library/gavi-documents/guidelines-and-forms/cso-implementation-and-results-framework/>, last accessed 05/18/2020; GAVI, 'Civil society organisation support' (n 110); GAVI, 'GAVI Alliance Progress Report 2007' < https://www.gavi.org/library/publications/gavi-progress-reports/gavi-alliance-progress-report-2007/>, last accessed 05/18/2020.

[115] Clinton and Sridhar, *Governing Global Health* (n 11), 130f.

[116] Clinton and Sridhar, *Governing Global Health* (n 11), 130–132.

[117] J A Molzon, A. Giaquinto, L Lindstrom, T Tominaga, M Ward, P Doerr, L Hunt, and L Rago, 'The Value and Benefits of ICH to Drug Regulatory Authorities: Advancing Harmonization for Better Health' 89(4) *Clinical Pharmacology & Therapeutics* (2010) 503-512.

13.7.1 Governance Structure

The US Food and Drug Administration (FDA), the European Commission/European Medicines Agency, and the Japan Ministry of Health, Labour and Welfare (JMHLW) are its founding regulatory authorities, alongside industry associations—the Pharmaceutical Researchers and Manufacturers of America (PhRMA), European Federation of Pharmaceutical Industries and Associations (EFPIA), and the Japan Pharmaceutical Manufacturers Association (JPMA). 'Interested parties' from related drug industries, such as the World Self-Medication Industry (WSMI) and the International Generic Pharmaceutics Alliance (IGPA)[118] were observers. The WHO, the Canadian drug regulatory authority (Health Canada), and EFTA countries[119] were also observers.[120] The International Federation of Pharmaceutical Manufacturers and Associations (IFPMA) hosted the ICH.[121]

13.7.2 Main Reforms

Since 2005, the ICH has gradually opened up towards regulators from other countries or regions of relevance for the pharmaceutical market. The 'Global Cooperation Group' (GCG) included regional harmonization initiatives such as Asia-Pacific Economic Cooperation (APEC), ASEAN, Pan American Network for Drug Regulatory Harmonization (PANDRH), Southern African Development Community (SADC), the Cooperation Council for the Arab States of the Gulf (GCC), and the East African Community (EAC).[122] In 2007, a 'Regulators Forum' brought regulators from Australia, Brazil, China, Chinese Taipei, India, Russia, Singapore, and South Korea. Members of the GCG and Regulators Forum could observe working group and steering committee meetings.

In view of becoming a 'genuinely global forum', in 2016 the ICH enacted a governance reform, intending to expand decision-making beyond the original members to GCG and Regulators Forum members.[123] It established itself as an association under Swiss law with an assembly (where guideline topics are selected and final guidelines

[118] Molzon *et al.*, *Value and Benefits* (n 117); see also the words of the Deputy FDA Commissioner for External Affairs Sharon Smith Holston in her Address at the 4th International Conference on Harmonisation, in Patrick Francis D'Arcy and Dean W G Harron (eds), *Proceedings of the 4th International Conference on Harmonization* (Queen's University at Belfast 1997) 26.

[119] EFTA's members are Norway, Switzerland, Iceland, and Liechtenstein.

[120] ICH, 'History', <https://www.ich.org/page/history>, last accessed 05/18/2020; Molzon *et al.*, *Value and Benefits* (n 117), 21.

[121] Ayelet Berman, 'The Role of Domestic Administrative Law in the Accountability of IN-LAW: The Case of the ICH' in Pauwelyn *et al.* (eds), *Informal International Lawmaking* (n 8) 468-499.

[122] The GCG's purpose was to act as the primary representative of ICH Steering Committee outside the ICH regions, and equally as such as a conduit for non-ICH parties to the ICH Steering Committee.

[123] Maureen Kenny, 'Finishing Line in Sight for ICH Reforms' (*SCRIP Regulatory Affairs*, 5 May 2015); ICH, 'ICH Announces Organisational Changes as it Marks 25 Years of Successful Harmonisation' *IFPMA News Releases* (Online, 26 October 2015) <https://www.ifpma.org/resource-centre/ich-announces-organisational-changes-as-it-marks-25-years-of-successful-harmonisation/>, last accessed 05/18/2020.

adopted), a management committee (which oversees all of the operational aspects of the ICH), and working groups (where draft guidelines are being developed). Under the new ICH association, there are five membership categories. On the governmental side, alongside Founding Regulatory Members,[124] there are Standing Regulatory Members and Regulatory Members. On the industry side, alongside Founding Industry Members, there are Industry Members.

So far, Switzerland and Canada have joined as 'Standing Regulatory Members', and Brazil, China, Singapore, and South Korea as 'Regulatory Members'.[125] They both have the right to vote in the assembly and in working groups, yet only standing members are represented in the management committee.[126]

In addition, the 2016 reform introduced three categories of observers (standing observers, observers, and ad hoc observers).[127] All previous GCG and Regulators Forum members may apply for membership or observer status,[128] and most of the regional initiatives (APEC, ASEAN, EAC, GHC, PANDRH, and SADC) and drug regulators (India, Cuba, Mexico, Colombia, Russia, South Africa, Kazakhstan, Chinese Taipei, and Australia) have opted to become observers.[129] The WHO and IFPMA are 'standing observers'. Both standing and regular observers may observe assembly meetings and working groups, but only the standing observers may attend the management committee.[130]

Thus, while the assembly and working groups have opened up to developing countries, the managing committee remains insular. It remains limited to the founding regulatory members (US, EU, and Japan) the standing regulatory members (Switzerland and Canada) and standing observers (WHO and IFPMA),[131] as well as certain NSAs (below).

As for the ICH's relation with NSAs, for two decades, industry associations and drug regulatory authorities had been equal members. Yet, that too has gradually changed. In reinforcing what they considered their 'ultimate responsibility to public health',[132] the ICH reformed in 2012 to strengthen regulators' voice and remove industry's decision-making rights. Working groups (developing guidelines) could only be chaired by a regulator 'who will be responsible for ensuring regulatory oversight as well as integrity of the entire process.'[133]Furthermore, under the 2016 reform, Founding Industry Members were given a right to vote in the Assembly, but denied a

[124] ICH, 'Articles of Association', Article 8 <https://www.ich.org/page/articles-procedures>, last accessed 05/18/2019.

[125] ICH, 'Members and Observers: Current Members and Observers' <https://www.ich.org/page/members-observers>, last accessed 05/18/2020.

[126] ICH, 'Articles of Association' (n 124), Article 10.

[127] ICH, 'Articles of Association', Sections II and III (n 124).

[128] ICH, 'Articles of Association' (n 124), Article 17.

[129] ICH, 'Articles of Association' (n 124), Article 10; ICH, 'Members and Observers' (n 125).

[130] ICH, 'Articles of Association' (n 124), Article 27(4).

[131] ICH, 'Members and Observers' (n 125).

[132] Vibha Sharma, 'Regulators to Chair Future ICH Expert Working Groups to Ensure 'Integrity' of Guidelines (*SCRIP Regulatory Affairs*, 4 July 2012).

[133] ICH, 'ICH Parties Agree on New Principles of Governance' *ICH Press Release* (Fukuoka 3 July 2012) <https://www.ich.org/pressrelease/ich-steering-committee-fukuoka-japan-6-7-june-2012>, last accessed 05/18/2020.

vote on matters related to ICH guidelines.[134] However, since ICH relies on industry's expertise, whether industry's formally reduced role also reduces its influence behind the scenes in practice is a matter for further enquiry.

Further, although ICH guidelines regulate innovative medicines, in practice, regulators have required generic drug manufacturers to comply with certain ICH standards.[135] The generic industry has, in turn, sought to participate in the development of ICH standards which affect it.[136] The 2016 reform recognized their standing, and now enables the international generic pharmaceuticals association and other industry associations whose members 'are regulated or affected by all or some ICH guidelines' (and had previously been an 'observer or an interested party'),[137] to apply for Industry Member. So far, three pharmaceutical industry associations have joined as industry members.[138] As industry members, they can vote in the Assembly, although they are prohibited from voting on ICH guidelines, including their selection and adoption. They may appoint experts to working groups that are developing ICH guidelines 'which ... the Industry Members ... would be regulated or affected by'.[139] They may also appoint representatives to the management committee. Hence, the ICH has somewhat improved the participation rights of affected pharmaceutical industries. Further, as industry associations must 'represent members from several countries in at least three continents',[140] regional industry associations are barred from joining, in contrast to the founding industry members, which remain American, European, and Japanese.

Finally, allowing 'international organizations ... regulated or affected by ICH guidelines' to join as observers has enabled, among others, the Gates Foundation and Council for International Organizations of Medical Sciences (CIOMS), to join,[141] and the IFPMA has a 'standing observer' status.

13.8 International Medical Device Regulators Forum (IMDRF)

Set up in 1996, the IMDRF (originally, the Global Harmonization Task Force, or GHTF) seeks to converge medical device regulatory guidelines and practices.[142]

134 ICH, 'Articles of Association' (n 124).

135 Two examples: (1) ICH Q3A ('Impurities in New Drug Substances') and Q3C ('Impurities: guidelines for the residual solvents') were developed for new products but their application had been extended by European authorities to cover all products, including generics, registered in the EU; (2) ICH Q7A on GMP for APIs expands requirements for manufacturers of pharmaceutical active starting materials, and so creates increased rigidity in the starting material supply system, with consequent effects on starting material prices and availability.

136 Interview with IGPA official (August 2015).

137 ICH, 'Articles of Association' (n 124), Article 12.

138 ICH, 'Members and Observers' (n 125).

139 ICH, 'Articles of Association' (n 124), Article 12.

140 ICH, 'Articles of Association' (n 124), Article 12.

141 ICH, 'Articles of Association' (n 124), Article 17; ICH, 'Members and Observers' (n 125).

142 Global Harmonization Task Force, GHTF/SC/N1R8:2005 'GHTF Guiding Principles' (20 May 2005), Article 2.2(B) <http://www.imdrf.org/docs/ghtf/final/steering-committee/procedural-docs/ghtf-sc-n1r8-050520-ghtf-guiding-principles.pdf>, last accessed 05/19/2020.

13.8.1 Governance Structure

The original GHTF members were medical devices regulatory authorities from the US, EU, Japan, Australia, and Canada, and their medical device industries.[143] Regulatory authorities included the US FDA, the European Commission's Directorate General Health and Consumers (previously Directorate General Enterprise and Industry), the Japanese Pharmaceuticals and Medical Devices Agency/Ministry of Health, Labour and Welfare, Health Canada, and Australia's Therapeutic Goods Administration. Industry representatives included the Advanced Medical Technology Association, Philips Healthcare, the European Coordination Committee of the Radiological, Electromedical and Healthcare IT Industry, and others.[144] Under the GHTF, diverse organizations had been recognized as observers or liaison bodies with non-decisional access, including the WHO, international standard setting bodies such as the International Organization for Standardization (ISO), and regional harmonization initiatives such as the Pan American Health Organization (PAHO) and the Asian Harmonization Working Party (AHWP), and others.

13.8.2 Main Reforms

Seeing membership expansion as its 'future hallmark'[145] and committed 'increasingly [to] welcome nations and regions wishing to be more active participants' in its ongoing work,'[146] the IMDRF has since 2007 gradually expanded membership to include medical device regulators from countries of relevance for the global medical device market. Then, in 2011, the GHFT underwent reform to become the IMDRF and introduced a new membership and observership structure.[147]

First, the most significant change following this reform has been that medical device regulators from Brazil (ANVISA), China, Russia, South Korea, and Singapore have joined as members.[148] The IMDRF's Terms of Reference foresee additional expansion of membership provided 'the expansion to other regulatory

143 Berman, 'Informal International Law-Making in Medical Products Regulation' in (n 44).

144 Ayelet Berman, *Reining in the Regulators: Transnational Regulatory Networks and Accountability* (PhD Thesis, Graduate Institute of International and Development Studies 2014) <https://www.researchgate.net/publication/303246756_Reining_in_the_Regulators_Transnational_Regulatory_Networks_and_Accountability>, last accessed 05/19/2020.

145 GHTF, 'Action Plan for 2007–2010: Path Forward for the Global Harmonization Task Force' (24 May 2007), <http://www.elsevierbi.com/~/media/FB5E14D851EB4C539B471E2BAB87A35A>, last accessed 05/18/2020.

146 GHTF, 'Action Plan for 2007–2010' (n 145).

147 For overview of membership and observership, see IMDRF, Standing Operating Procedures (2020), <http://www.imdrf.org/docs/imdrf/final/procedural/imdrf-proc-n2-sop-200925.pdf> , last accessed 05/18/2020.

148 Vibha Sharma, 'GHTF Successor to IMDRF to Expand Membership; Shortlists Work Priorities at Inaugural Meeting' (*SCRIP Regulatory Affairs*, 23 March 2012); IMDRF, 'About IMDRF' <http://www.imdrf.org/about/about.asp>, last accessed 05/18/2020.

authorities contributes to the contemporary and foreseeable public health-missioned responsibilities.'[149]

The second most important change is with respect to industry membership. Industry had been GHTF members, yet in view of improving the IMDRFs' integrity, in 2011, under the IMDRF, they lost their membership status.[150] Thus, while industry remains an important source of scientific and technical expertise, and may be invited as observers, they are no longer members.

The IMDRF reform also changed some of the terminology and criteria for observers[151] and other non-decisional participants. Yet, in practice, these changes, at least on paper, do not appear to have been significant in terms of the type or amount of observers granted access.

For example, under the current rules, if regulatory authorities or the WHO are perceived as contributing or bringing value to the IMDRF, the Management Committee may designate them as 'Official Observers'.[152] So far, only the WHO has received such official observer status, although the WHO had already been an observer under the GHTF. The Management Committee may also invite a regulatory authority, global industry or stakeholder association to attend on a case-by-case basis a Management Committee meeting on the basis of perceived contribution or value to the IMDRF ('Invited Observers').[153] Further research is needed as to which observers have been invited.

Further, regional organizations who have an interest in medical device regulation and are 'directly related to … fostering global convergence',[154] may be invited to attend Management Committees as an observer.[155] Currently, such regional harmonization initiatives largely include those regional harmonization initiatives that had been involved under the GHTF: the Pan American Health Organization (PAHO), the Asian Harmonization Working Party (AHWP), and the APEC LSIF Regulatory Harmonization Steering Committee.[156]

Finally, as was the case under GHTF, draft guidelines continue being open to public consultation.[157]Yet, the IMDRF is more clearly open towards other stakeholders, saying that other medical device stakeholders may participate in working groups, open stakeholder forums, and if invited, at management committee meetings.[158]

[149] IMDRF, 'Terms of Reference' (2018) IMDRF/MC/N1FINAL:2018, Article 4 <http://www.imdrf.org/docs/imdrf/final/procedural/imdrf-proc-180727-terms-of-reference.pdf>, last accessed 05/18/2020.

[150] GHTF, 'Statement from GHTF Chair: Update on Future Directions of GHTF' (28 March 2011), <http://www.imdrf.org/docs/ghtf/final/media-releases/web-statement-re-future-of-ghtf-28-march-2011-final.pdf>, last accessed 05/18/2020; IMDRF, 'About IMDRF' (n 148).

[151] IMDRF, 'Terms of Reference' (n 149), Article II(B) (a) and (b).

[152] IMDRF, 'Terms of Reference' (n 149), 4f.

[153] IMDRF, 'Terms of Reference' (n 149), Article II(B)(b)9.

[154] IMDRF, 'Terms of Reference' (n 149), 4f.

[155] IMDRF, 'Terms of Reference' (n 149), Article II(D).

[156] IMDRF, 'About IMDRF' (n 148).

[157] IMDRF, 'Consultations' <http://www.imdrf.org/consultations/consultations.asp>, last accessed 05/18/2020.

[158] IMDRF, 'Stakeholders' <http://www.imdrf.org/stakeholders/stakeholders.asp>, last accessed 05/18/2020.

13.9 GlobalG.A.P

The GlobalG.A.P. sets Good Agricultural Practice (G.A.P) standards for safe and sustainable food production and certifies agricultural products (crops, livestock, agriculture). Although voluntary, consumers increasingly demand high-quality foods produced safely and sustainably, resulting in retailers demanding certification from their producers, leading, consequently, to significant adherence to G.A.P. standards.[159]

13.9.1 Governance Structure

Historically, European retailers established 'EuropG.A.P' as a business-to-business standard in response to consumers' growing concerns regarding food safety, environmental impact, and the welfare of workers and animals.[160]

13.9.2 Main Reforms

With growing international trade in food and the shifts in supply chains, EuropG.A.P.'s membership gradually evolved to include retailers, suppliers, and producers outside of Europe.[161] In 2007, it was renamed GlobalG.A.P.[162] Retail members are largely western companies such as the Coop, Migros, McDonalds, Tesco, Walmart, and Marks & Spencer. Companies from Africa, South America, Asia, and the Middle East have mostly joined as producer and supplier members.[163] The board, comprised of ten seats, has an equal number of producer and retailer seats.[164] Currently, most board

[159] Rebeka Tennent and Stewart Lockie, 'Production Relations under GLOBALG.A.P: The Relative Influence of Standards and Retail Market Structure' 52(1) *Sociologia Ruralis* (2012) 31-47; Yoshiko Naiki, 'The Dynamics of Private Food Safety Standards: A Case Study on the Regulatory Diffusion of GlobalG.A.P.' 63(1) *International and Comparative Law Quarterly* (2014) 137-166; Sam F Halabi and Ching Fu Lin, 'Assessing the Relative Influence and Efficacy of Public and Private Food Safety Regulation Regimes: Comparing Codex and GlobalG.A.P. Standards' 72 *Food and Drug Law Journal* (2017) 262-294.

[160] Nicolas Hachez and Jan Wouters, 'A Glimpse at the Democratic Legitimacy of Private Standards: Assessing the Public Accountability of GlobalG.A.P.' 14(3) *Journal of International Economic Law* (2011) 677-710, 695.

[161] GlobalG.A.P., 'Let's Become Partners' <https://www.globalgap.org/uk_en/who-we-are/members/become-a-member/>, last accessed 05/18/2020.

[162] Hachez and Wouters, 'A Glimpse' (n 160); Donald K Casey, 'Three Puzzles of Private Governance: GlobalG.A.P. and the Regulation of Food Safety and Quality' *UCD Working Papers in Law, Criminology & Socio-Legal Studies Research Paper* No. 22/2009 (2009) 3f; GlobalG.A.P., 'Technical Committees Terms of Reference' <https://www.globalgap.org/uk_en/who-we-are/governance/technical-committees/>, last accessed 05/18/2020; GlobalG.A.P., 'GlobalG.A.P. Board' <https://www.globalgap.org/uk_en/who-we-are/governance/board/>, last accessed 05/18/2020; GlobalG.A.P, 'GlobalG.A.P. History' <https://www.globalgap.org/uk_en/who-we-are/about-us/history/>, last accessed 05/18/2020; GlobalG.A.P., 'Producer & Supplier Members' <https://www.globalgap.org/uk_en/who-we-are/members/supplier/>, last accessed 05/18/2020; GlobalG.A.P., 'Retail & Food Service Members' <https://www.globalgap.org/uk_en/who-we-are/members/retailers-food-service/>, last accessed 05/18/2020.

[163] GlobalG.A.P., 'Producer & Supplier Members' (n 162).

[164] GlobalG.A.P., 'Terms of Reference for the GlobalG.A.P. Board', Section 3 <https://www.globalgap.org/uk_en/who-we-are/governance/board/board-elections-2019/board-terms-of-reference/index.html>, last accessed 05/18/2020.

seats are held by European members. Resolutions are made on a consensus basis where majority voting is applied if necessary.[165] Standards are elaborated in technical committees, which are similarly composed equally of retailer and supplier members. In practice, committees are dominated by western business.[166]

Further, 'National Technical Working Groups', present in almost fifty member countries, including Brazil, Kenya, Vietnam, India, and Thailand, obtain input from local stakeholders into GlobalG.A.P. standard setting.[167] They also adapt GlobalG.A.P. standards to local circumstances and support their implementation. Moreover, stakeholder input was previously drawn from eight stakeholder committees, whose membership consists of 'a wide range of industry experts, including GlobalG.A.P. members, non-members, NGOs, retailers and suppliers'. These have now been replaced by Focus Groups which work on specific issues.[168]

The GlobalG.A.P is more concerned with the producer/supplier–retailer equilibrium than with equal geographic representation. Thus, western business continues to dominate (as both retailer and producer/supplier members)[169] in the board[170] and in the technical committees, which develop standards.[171] Moreover, small farmers in developing countries have little or no capacity to comply with these requirements and lose access to western markets whose retailers require adherence.[172] To support such small farmers, GlobalG.A.P. has introduced 'LocalG.A.P.', a stepping-stone standard reflecting what the GlobalG.A.P. says is a cost effective solution for small producers in developing countries that lack the capacity to comply with the full standard.[173] By adapting 'northern' standards to 'southern' capacity, the GlobalG.A.P. has found a way to gradually integrate more producers from developing countries.[174] GlobalG.A.P. has also sought to include smallholders in standard setting through a smallholder ambassador and observer who participate in technical committee meetings.[175]

[165] GlobalG.A.P., 'Terms of Reference' (n 164), Section 4.

[166] Agni Kalfagianni and Philipp Pattberg, 'Participation and Inclusiveness in Private Rule Setting Organizations: Does it Matter for Effectiveness?' 26(3) *Innovation: The European Journal of Social Science Research* (2013) 231-250.

[167] GlobalG.A.P., 'The GlobalG.A.P. National Technical Working Groups' <http://www.globalgap.org/uk_en/who-we-are/ntwgs/>, last accessed 05/18/2020; GlobalG.A.P. 'NTWG Terms of Reference', <https://www.globalgap.org/uk_en/who-we-are/ntwgs/>, last accessed 05/18/2020; GlobalG.A.P., 'List of All GLOBALG.A.P. National Technical Working Groups' <http://www.globalgap.org/uk_en/who-we-are/ntwgs/list-of-ntwgs/index.html>, last accessed 05/18/2020.

[168] Anne McNaughton and Stewart Lockie, 'Private Actors in Multi-Level Governance: GlobalG.A.P. Standard Setting for Agricultural and Food Products' in Katherine Daniell and Adrian Kay (eds), *Multi-Level Governance: Conceptual Challenges and Case Studies from Australia* (ANU Press 2017) 385-402.

[169] Hachez and Wouters, 'A Glimpse' (n 160), 702.

[170] Hachez and Wouters, 'A Glimpse' (n 160), 698.

[171] Kalfagianni and Pattberg, 'Participation and Inclusiveness' (n 166), 12; Hachez and Wouters, 'A Glimpse' (n 160), 695.

[172] McNaughton and Lockie, 'Private Actors in Multi-Level Governance' (n 168), 399; Tetty Havinga, 'Actors in Private Food Regulation: Taking Responsibility or Passing the Buck to Someone Else?' 1 *Nijmegen Sociology of Law Working Papers Series* (2008).

[173] GlobalG.A.P., 'The LocalG.A.P. Brand—A Stepping Stone to Safe and Sustainable Agriculture', <https://www.globalgap.org/uk_en/for-producers/localg.a.p./> , last accessed 05/18/2020.

[174] McNaughton and Lockie, 'Private Actors' (n 168), 399.

[175] Alexia Herwig, 'The Application of the SPS Agreement to Transnational Private Food Standards' 7(3) *European Journal of Risk Regulation* (2016) 610-616, 612.

Further, strictly limited to business (retailers, producers, or suppliers), animal welfare,[176] consumer, or health groups, although affected, are not represented in GlobalG.A.P.[177] That said, they could likely participate in stakeholder consultations,[178] or public notice and comments.[179] Public interest stakeholders could also possibly access National Technical Working Groups, as these 'should consist of a pool of experts and stakeholders in the specific GlobalG.A.P. scope ... producers, retailers, representatives from the fields of certification, agribusiness, as well as stakeholders that have experiences in the sector regarding food safety, environment, social or animal welfare impacts ... .'[180] Thus, while it has opened up participation opportunities to retailers/producers from non-European countries, small producers from developing countries and consumers and other public interests remain excluded.[181]

13.10 Conclusion

Table 13.2 summarizes some of the main reforms regarding participation opportunities and regarding participation quality (such as reforms for promoting balanced or impartial participation) in each of the surveyed global health bodies. I then conclude regarding the emerging general trend.

Table 13.2 Summary of the Main Reforms

	Developing Countries		Non-state actors	
	Participation Opportunities	**Participation Quality**	**Participation Opportunities**	**Participation Quality**
WHO	Universal membership with voting rights (since 1948) in WHA EB reform (2003).	No policy to financially or technically support developing country participation	Non-decisional Increased participation of NSAs since 1980s: official relations, experts, donors, partnerships etc.	FENSA (2016) manages risks of NSA engagement.

(continued)

[176] Diane Ryland, 'Animal Welfare Governance: GLOBALG.A.P. and the Search for External Legitimacy' 30 *Journal of Environmental Law* (2018) 453-482.

[177] Ryland, 'Animal Welfare Governance' (n 176).

[178] GlobalG.A.P., 'GlobalG.A.P. Associate Members' <http://www.globalgap.org/uk_en/who-we-are/members/associates/>, last accessed 05/18/2020.

[179] GlobalG.A.P., 'Public Consultation' <http://www.globalgap.org/uk_en/what-we-do/globalg.a.p.-certification/public-consultation/>, last accessed 05/18/2020; Hachez and Wouters, 'A Glimpse' (n 160), 704.

[180] GlobalG.A.P., 'Terms of Reference' (n 164), Article 2.

[181] Hachez and Wouters, 'A Glimpse' (n 160); Kalfagianni and Pattberg, 'Participation and Inclusiveness' (n 166).

Table 13.2 Continued

	Developing Countries		Non-state actors	
	Participation Opportunities	**Participation Quality**	**Participation Opportunities**	**Participation Quality**
CODEX	Formal membership rights since 1963, de facto membership has been growing since the 1990's.	Codex Trust Fund I (2004) and II (2016)	Non-decisional Increased participation since 1990s: Observer status, experts, national contact points, national delegations etc.	--
Global Fund	Developing countries are equal voting members on the board (since establishment, 2002)	for example, Strategic Roadmap to Enhance Implementer Voice (2014)	Decisional NSAs are equal voting members on the board and in national Country Coordinating Mechanisms.	Ethics and Integrity Initiative (2015). New Funding Model (2014); Capacity building and financial aid.
GAVI	Developing countries are equal voting members (2009 reform)	--	NSAs are equal voting members; industry stronger representation than civil society.	Conflict of Interest Policy Civil society empowerment (for example, 2009 reform).
ICH	Gradually, since 2005, and mostly after 2016, several developing countries /regional organizations have been included as observers or members.	--	R&D industry had been included as equal voting member (1991); Membership of generic medicines industry (and other affected industries) in 2016; Public notice and comment	Limitation of industry voting rights (2012 and 2016).
IMDRF	Since 2007, several developing countries/ regional organizations have been included as observers or members.	--	Medical devices industry had been included as voting member (1999); observers; public notice and comment.	Removal of industry's voting rights (2011).
Global G.A.P	--	--	From European to Global Organization (2007) National Technical Working Groups, Focus Groups etc.	Conflicts of interest policy.

This chapter has reviewed institutional reforms to improve participation opportunities of previously marginalized stakeholders. The measures vary and include expanding membership, providing observer or other non-voting status, consultations or commenting opportunities, setting up outreach bodies, earmarked funding, expert consultations, and national consultation processes.

As regards developing countries, the WHO has reformed the Executive Board, while in Codex more countries have joined as members and are being financially supported. The Global Fund and GAVI include developing country members, and the Global Fund supports developing countries in overcoming capacity barriers to participation. And the ICH and IMDRF have integrated developing countries as members or observers. Despite this general trend, the extent to which developing countries have been integrated, varies. The Global Fund and GAVI have been relatively balanced, while the ICH and IMDRF have integrated economically strategic countries. The WHO and Codex remain the most inclusive.

As regards NSA participation, the WHO and Codex engage many NSAs, yet states retain decision-making authority. In informal (non-treaty based) bodies—the Global Fund, GAVI, ICH and IMDRF, and GlobalG.A.P.—NSAs have or have had decision-making authority.[182] NSA indirect engagement through national processes remains important, too.

Most NSA participation is selective,[183] and existing research suggests that business is often better represented in standard setting, such as in Codex, ICH, IMDRF, and GlobalG.A.P. While business dominance is formally mandated in some organizations (ICH, IMDRF, GlobalG.A.P.), in others, it is simply a fact (Codex).

Though hardly sufficient, several efforts for improving the quality of participation, such as by managing the risks of NSA participation or advancing balanced participation, have been made: WHO FENSA is the most prominent example. Further, the ICH and IMDRF have revoked industry voting rights, and GAVI and the Global Fund have bolstered participation of civil society and vulnerable populations.

Inasmuch as these reforms have been adopted, there are gaps in our knowledge regarding the actual involvement of those previously marginalized stakeholders following these reforms and whether these reforms have improved their actual influence. The following country-specific empirical chapters address these gaps.[184] Drawing from these case studies, we then assess the effects of these reforms on actual participation and whether they have brought about more influence.[185]

[182] Clinton and Sridhar, *Governing Global Health* (n 11), 40.

[183] See also OECD, *International Regulatory Cooperation: The Role of International Organizations in Fostering Better Rules of Globalization* (OECD Publishing 2016).

[184] Mello e Souza and Pérez Aznar, 'Brazil and Argentina' (n 3); Cheng with Do, 'China and Vietnam' (n 3); Büthe *et al.*, 'India and the Philippines' (n 3).

[185] Berman and Pauwelyn, 'Assessing' (n 4).

14
Global Health Governance and Stakeholder Participation

David Gartner

14.1 Introduction

Global health governance provides a unique lens on questions of stakeholder participation. Global health institutions encompass a wide range of mechanisms for including diverse stakeholders in governance. In recent decades, there has been a dramatic shift from models based on transparency and observer status for non-state actors to speaking rights, voting rights, and even veto rights for different stakeholders within the governance structure of global health institutions. The conceptualization of stakeholder participation has also shifted somewhat from one initially focused on individual stakeholders often selected by the institution itself to broader constituencies of stakeholders who select their own representatives and retain stronger accountability relationships with these representatives.

The amount of resources flowing in the global health sector has more than tripled over the past two decades. In 1997, total Overseas Development Assistance for health was just $8.54 billion but by 2016 it totalled more than $37.6 billion.[1] Global health financing and global health has traditionally been dominated by long-standing institutions such as the World Bank (WB) and the World Health Organization (WHO). Today, the scale of financing provided by the WB and WHO have been matched or exceeded in scale by two recent institutions which did not exist in 1997: the Global Alliance for Vaccines and Immunizations (GAVI) and the Global Fund to Fight AIDS, Tuberculosis, and Malaria (Global Fund).

Despite this dramatic transformation in global health financing, the WHO remains the leading technical institution and the only institution of this group with both a broad and exclusive focus on health issues ranging from infectious to non-communicable diseases. However, it now operates in a much more complex and challenging governance ecosystem in which non-state actors are playing an ever-growing role. In addition to the Global Fund and GAVI, the two largest newer institutions, many other smaller new institutions and innovative partnerships have been created in recent decades. Some of these have been nurtured within the WHO itself, such as the Roll Back Malaria Partnership and the Stop TB Partnership. Others were created

[1] Institute for Health Metrics and Evaluation (IHME), *Financing Global Health 2016: Development Assistance, Public and Private Health Spending for the Pursuit of Universal Health Coverage* (IHME 2017).

David Gartner, *Global Health Governance and Stakeholder Participation* In: *Rethinking Participation in Global Governance*.
Edited by: Joost Pauwelyn, Martino Maggetti, Tim Büthe, and Ayelet Berman, Oxford University Press. © David Gartner 2022.
DOI: 10.1093/oso/9780198852568.003.0014

within the United Nations (UN) system in response to weaknesses of the WHO, such as UNAIDS. Finally, a much larger universe of partnerships exist which are focused on particular diseases or focused on specific dimensions such as pharmaceuticals.

Within this increasingly fragmented universe of global health governance, there is a mostly consistent story with respect to stakeholder governance in term of an evolution over time towards wider forms of participation within newer institutions. While there are important distinctions between traditional and non-traditional institutions within global health and some evidence of change over time within each institution, the major shift in stakeholder participation is reflected in the differences between those institutions created in the twenty-first century and those created in the twentieth century. In terms of stakeholder participation, the contrast between the traditional institutions created after the Second World War, such as the WB and the WHO, and non-traditional twenty-first-century institutions, like the Global Fund and GAVI, could not be more striking. While the governance of the WB and the WHO remains essentially the province of states, despite reforms within both institutions to expand consultation with non-state actors, the twenty-first-century institutions are governed through a multi-stakeholder process in which non-state actors are co-equals with the representatives of states. The exact membership and processes of decision-making varies by institution, but the gap between the twenty-first-century model and the twentieth-century model remains the defining feature of the global health when it comes to the role of diverse stakeholders.

Traditional institutions, such as the WB, have over time sought to embrace consultation with non-state actors as informants in relation to its programmes and expanded overall transparency but remain fundamentally state-centric institutions. The WHO has recently modified its engagement with non-state actors but the overall model of incorporating these actors as observers within a structure of state-led governance remains essentially the same. The next generation of institutions, including GAVI and the Global Fund, incorporated non-state actors as co-governors and full-fledged participants in the governance of the institution. Yet while GAVI was launched on a model that highlighted the role of individuals and individual institutional partners the Global Fund embraced a constituency-based model and sought to extend this multi-stakeholder model to national-level decision-making processes. Stakeholders within both institutions hold voting rights but stakeholders within the Global Fund also have somewhat unique veto powers when acting in concert with others in the context of a bloc system requiring two-thirds support from each voting bloc for controversial decisions.

This chapter analyses the governance structure of each major institution, the evolution of stakeholder participation, and the impact of stakeholder participation on the institutional effectiveness of each. It seeks to draw broader lessons around the dynamic of stakeholder participation within the context of global health governance and explain how stakeholder participation might be structured in order to optimize engagement and also to foster institutional effectiveness by drawing on lessons from these leading global health institutions.

14.2 The WB: Stakeholders as Informants

At the end of the Second World War, the creation of the UN, the WB, and the WHO within a few short years reflected new faith in global cooperation to foster peace, prosperity, and health around the world. However, cooperation was generally conceived of in terms of relationships among states despite the important role of some non-state actors in facilitating the creation of many of these institutions. Over time, challenges to the effectiveness and the legitimacy of the WB catalysed reform at the same time as non-state actors were expanding their involvement in many international arenas. The WB responded by moving in the direction of greater openness in terms of transparency and expanded consultation with external stakeholders.

The governance structure of the WB consists exclusively of states with voting shares weighted based on a quota system that was meant to roughly reflect each country's share of the global economy.[2] Before 1981, there was no formal mechanism for the WB to consult with nongovernmental organizations (NGOs). Even after 1981, the formal consultation role for non-state actors remained quite limited in terms of its scope. In 1981, the WB developed a new policy which highlighted potential benefits from more direct engagement with civil society groups and suggested the possible involvement of NGOs in the design, implementation, and evaluation of WB projects. The initial WB–NGO Committee was established in 1981 and focused on engagement with individual NGO leaders. Within a decade, the WB issued a new directive that provided for consultation with NGOs on specific bank projects at different stages of development.[3]

Beginning in the 1990s, the WB took an active role in seeking civil society feedback on its work but this interest was focused primarily on the implementation of WB projects.[4] An important catalyst for this growing engagement with non-state actors were the recommendations of an independent commission that concluded that the WB should create an independent body to evaluate citizen complaints regarding ongoing projects.[5] The WB also launched a review of the role of participatory development practices, which found significant evidence that participation could 'enhance the quality, effectiveness, and sustainability of projects, and strengthen ownership and commitment of government and stakeholders.'[6] The report contributed to the subsequent expansion of the WB's formal engagement with non-state actors. Within just a few years, the WB–NGO Committee created six regional bodies and soon after the

[2] Ngaire Woods, *The Globalizers: The IMF, the World Bank, and Their Borrowers* (Cornell University Press 2006), 22f.

[3] Ibrahim F I Shihata, 'World Bank and Non-Governmental Organizations' 25(3) *Cornell International Law Journal* (1992) 623-641.

[4] *See generally* Jane G Covey, 'Is Critical Cooperation Possible? Influencing the World Bank Through Operational Collaboration and Policy Dialogue' in Jonathan A Fox and Lloyd David Brown (eds), *The Struggle for Accountability: The World Bank, NGOs, and Grassroots Movements* (MIT Press 1998) 81-119.

[5] Lori Udall, 'The World Bank and Public Accountability: Has Anything Changed?' in Fox and Brown (eds), *The Struggle for Accountability* (n 4) 391-436.

[6] Carolyn Reynolds Mandell, William Reuben, Jeff Thindwa, John Garrison, Cynthia Gears, and Carmen Monico, *Issues and Options for Improving Engagement Between the World Bank and Civil Society Organizations* (World Bank 2005), 6.

WB hired civil society liaison staff at all of its seventy-two country missions around the world.[7]

From this early engagement with individual NGO leaders, the WB in the twenty-first century significantly expanded its relationships with networks of non-state actors. In 2002, a Joint Facilitation Committee was established in cooperation with CIVICUS: World Alliance for Citizen Participation. After only a few years, the WB eliminated the Joint Facilitation Committee based on criticism from civil society groups excluded from the process. Subsequently, the WB came to rely more and more on its annual and spring meetings as the forum for engaging with external stakeholders. In 2012, for example, 550 civil society representatives participated in dialogue sessions involving WB officials.[8] However, despite the timing of these meetings to coincide with the convening of the WB's governing board, non-state actors had no role in the formal governance meetings.

Within the health sector, the WB established a WB–Civil Society Consultative Group on Health, Nutrition, and Population in 2011, which provides a forum for dialogue related to its strategy and programmes in the health sector. The most extensive consultation with non-state actors in the health sector is reflected in the activities of bank-financed projects. As of 2012, civil society actors participated in some form in 82% of 1,018 new projects financed by the WB and sometimes served direct recipients of funds for 'community-driven development projects.'[9]

Despite these steps towards greater engagement with non-state actors, the WB board does not include a formal role for broader stakeholders in its governance.[10] Stakeholder input remains discretionary and has been characterized by some scholars as being one-directional in that it is generally based on solicitations from the WB itself for input.[11] According to the WB's self- assessment, the engagement with civil society actors evolved beyond one-way information access and programmatic consultation to a model of equal decision-making through its partnerships.[12] While there is limited evidence for this role for diverse stakeholders as equals within the WB's formal structures, it is the case that some WB-housed partnerships are closer to the models of multi-stakeholder governance that have been adopted by other global health governance institutions.

14.3 The WHO: Stakeholders as Observers

The WHO was originally designed on a model similar to other major UN organizations in terms of stakeholder participation. While non-state actors could serve as

[7] Woods, *The Globalizers* (n 2), 170.

[8] Woods, *The Globalizers* (n 2).

[9] World Bank, *World Bank Civil Society Engagement: Review of Fiscal Years 2010-2012* (World Bank 2013).

[10] John Garrison, *World Bank-Civil Society Engagement: Review of Fiscal Years 2005 and 2006* (World Bank 2006), 67 (highlighting that, even though there is a growing trend in WB and civil society relations, it still needs to make changes to engage with civil society more effectively).

[11] Sabine Schlemmer-Schulte, 'The Impact of Civil Society on the World Bank, The International Monetary Fund and the World Trade Organization: The Case of the World Bank' 7(2) *ILSA Journal of International & Comparative Law* (2001) 399-428.

[12] World Bank, 'World Bank-Civil Society' (n 9).

registered observers in governance there was little room for actual participation in the decision-making processes of the WHO. Specifically, NGOs defined as 'any international organization which is not established by intergovernmental agreement' could be granted consultative status by the WHO. However, national NGOs could only be granted such status with the explicit authorization of their home governments.[13]

At several important junctures, the WHO has confronted the limits and possibility of its approach to engagement with non-state actors. Although the WHO initially was the lead agency in responding to HIV/AIDS, legitimacy challenges contributed to the creation of a new series of institutions outside of the WHO structure to respond to the pandemic. Fallout from the SARS crisis led to a major revision of the International Health Regulations and an expanded role for non-state actors in disease surveillance. The WHO is once again undergoing a process of reform and recently adopted a new framework for institutional engagement with non-state actors.

The AIDS crisis catalysed a rethinking of the role of non-state actors in global health governance and contributed to growing interest within the WHO in hosting multi-stakeholder partnerships. Although the WHO established a special program on HIV/AIDS, bureaucratic conflicts and frustrated external stakeholders contributed to the establishment of a new coordinating agency outside of the WHO. Ultimately UNAIDS was created because it was seen as a better vehicle for leading an effort which required a complex multi-sectoral response.[14] In contrast with the WHO, the UNAIDS Programme Coordinating Board provided seats for five civil society organizations to sit on its governing board.[15] Yet these representatives could not 'participate in any part of the formal decision-making process, including the right to vote which is reserved for representatives of Governments.'[16]

The creation of UNAIDS was the start of a shift to a new generation of multi-stakeholder institutions to respond to AIDS. One response by the WHO itself was to support the creation of a range of multi-stakeholder partnerships under its umbrella, such as Roll Back Malaria Partnership and the Stop TB Partnership, in order to leverage the contributions of various non-state actors.[17] These partnerships derive their legal personality from the WHO and are therefore subject to the rules and regulations prescribed by the WHO. However, they also have formal governance structures

[13] Steve Charnovitz, 'Two Centuries of Participation: NGOs and International Governance' 18(2) *Michigan Journal of International Law* (1997) 183-286.

[14] Jon Lidén, 'The World Health Organization and Global Health Governance: Post-1990' 128(2) *Public Health* (2014) 141-147.

[15] United Nations, 'Economic and Social Council: Resolution 1994/24' <http://data.unaids.org/pub/externaldocument/1994/19940726_ecosoc_resolutions_establishing_unaids_en.pdf>, last accessed 11/30/2019.

[16] The Joint United Nations Programme on HIV and AIDS (UNAIDS), 'A Stronger Civil Society Voice in the UNAIDS Work' <http://www.unaids.org/en/resources/presscentre/featurestories/2008/april/20080411astrongercivilsocietyvoiceunaidswo/>, last accessed 11/30/2019. According to the terms of reference for the CSO delegation, however, in practice CSO representatives 'fully participate' in deliberations. The Joint United Nations Programme on HIV and AIDS (UNAIDS), 'Terms of Reference of the UNAIDS PCB NGO Delegation' <http://www.unaids.org/en/aboutunaids/unaidsprogrammecoordinatingboard/ngocivilsocietyparticipationinpcb/>, last accessed 11/30/2019.

[17] Sophie Harman, 'Is Time Up For WHO? Reform, Resilience, and Global Health Governance', <https://www.futureun.org/media/archive1/briefings/FUNDSBriefing17-WHO-Harman.pdf>, last accessed 11/30/2019.

that are separate from those of the WHO and that generally involve a diverse range of stakeholders in governance. Among the most important of these partnerships are the International Drug Purchase Facility (UNITAID) and the Partnership for Maternal, Newborn, and Child Health, alongside the older initiatives. In each of these partnerships, NGOs and foundations are full governing member. In UNITAID, people living with HIV/AIDS are also board members, while in the other partnerships private-sector commercial entities are also board members.

SARS also led to major reforms within the WHO of formal engagement with non-state actors at the country level. The International Sanitary Regulations established by the WHO created a system in which the institution was entirely dependent on reporting by governments in order to act in response to a new outbreak.[18] In 2003, the SARS crisis revealed the inadequacy of this approach in the context of emerging pandemics. At the time, the WHO was not allowed to rely on independent sources other than the government for confirmation about the existence of a disease within its borders. The WHO also lacked the authority to compel sovereign nations to share information about the fast-spreading new disease.[19] In response to this crisis, new regulations allowed the WHO to rely on diverse sources of data, including information from non-state actors. Upon receiving information from non-governmental sources, the WHO can act even without confirmation by the relevant government. Non-state actors were integrated into the overall surveillance functions of the WHO as a counterweight to governments that might be reluctant to report outbreaks of disease.

In 2016, the WHO adopted a new framework for engagement with non-state actors. The framework provides that non-state actors may attend meetings of the governing bodies of the WHO as well as other consultations or hearings hosted by the WHO. In addition, non-state actors can be extended the privilege of 'official relations' based on a plan for collaboration on agreed objectives which could include research and advocacy in relation to WHO meetings and policies. For non-state actors, participating in WHO governance is contingent on approval by a committee of its Executive Board based on a formal application.[20] It requires all non-state actors to provide information on their legal status, governance structure, assets, annual income, and funding sources. Overall, the framework is unlikely to substantially expand the participation of non-state actors in the governance of the WHO; the new registration requirements—especially as they relate to financing—could discourage some actors from engaging with the WHO.

The evolving governance of the WHO also reflects a growing role for non-state actors as major funders of programmes in recent decades. Between 1998 and 2008 the biennial budget of the WHO doubled from USD 1.6 billion to USD 4.2 billion. Over the same period, voluntary funding expanded from less than half to more than three-quarters of all funds contributed to the WHO.[21] As a result, the influence and leverage

[18] Jeremy Youde, 'Mediating Risk Through the International Health Regulations and Bio-Political Surveillance' 59(4) *Political Studies* (2011) 813-830, 817.

[19] Youde, 'Mediating Risk' (n 18), 823.

[20] World Health Organization, 'WHA 69, Framework of Engagement with Non-State Actors' <http://apps.who.int/gb/ebwha/pdf_files/wha69/a69_r10-en.pdf>, last accessed 11/30/2019.

[21] Devi Sridhar and Lawrence O Gostin, 'Reforming the World Health Organization' 305(15) *Journal of the American Medical Association* (2011) 1585-1586.

of leading voluntary funders, including non-state actors, increased substantially. Voluntary contributions currently constitute 80% of the WHO's budget and the Bill and Melinda Gates Foundation is among the top three funders of the WHO.[22]

14.4 GAVI: Stakeholders as Equal Participants

Launched in 2000, the Global Alliance for Vaccines and Immunization (GAVI), initiated a new era for multi-stakeholder governance.[23] GAVI involved non-state actors beginning in the early design stage and ultimately included them in its formal governance structure. When GAVI was established it was unique among global health institutions in the significant role it provided for non-state actors, including partner foundations, the private sector, and technical experts.[24] GAVI's initial board structure primarily involved non-state actors as independent individuals along with a few representatives from the vaccine industry, research institutes, and NGOs.[25] One seat is designated for civil society groups, while others are allocated to research and technical institutes, the developing country vaccine industry, and the industrialized country vaccine industry.[26] In addition, the Bill and Melinda Gates Foundation holds one of four permanent seats on the GAVI Alliance Board.

In 2005, the GAVI Alliance Board determined that it needed to further strengthen the participation of civil society constituencies in its governance and programmes and allocated expanded resources to enhance civil society representation at the country level. The GAVI Partners forum created a GAVI Civil Society Constituency—a group of civil society representatives, to support members of GAVI's governance bodies in their responses related to governance functions.[27] GAVI's civil society constituency consists of several hundred organizations led by a steering committee of eighteen members. A GAVI board member and alternate are elected from within the constituency to serve on the GAVI board. In addition, the GAVI Civil Society Forum and Communications Focal Point provide mechanisms for participation by a broader range of non-state actors.[28]

The major initial expansion of funding for GAVI was closely tied to its expanding relationships with private sector actors. The rapid scale-up of financing for GAVI was largely a product of an initiative led by the United Kingdom to front-load development financing through bond issues on the financial markets: the International

[22] Devi Sridhar, J Frenk, L Gostin, and S Moon, 'Global Rules for Global Health: Why We Need an Independent, Impartial WHO' 108(June) *British Medical Journal* (2014) 1-3.

[23] Global Alliance for Vaccines and Immunization (GAVI), 'Innovative Partnership' <https://www.gavi.org/our-alliance/about>, last accessed 14 May 2020.

[24] GAVI, 'Innovative Partnership' (n 23).

[25] *See* Global Alliance for Vaccines and Immunization (GAVI), 'Board' <https://www.gavi.org/our-alliance/governance>, last accessed 12/06/2019; UNITAID, 'Executive Board' <https://unitaid.org/about-us/governance/#en>, last accessed 12/06/2019.

[26] GAVI, 'Board' (n 25).

[27] GAVI, 'Civil Society Organisations' <https://www.gavi.org/operating-model/gavis-partnership-model/civil-society>, last accessed 12/06/2019.

[28] World Health Organization, 'GAVI Alliance Civil Society Constituency Charter - Revised January 2013' <http://origin.who.int/pmnch/media/news/2013/gavi_cso_charter.pdf>, last accessed 12/06/2019.

Finance Facility for Immunisation (IFFim). The IFFim dramatically expands the role of the private sector in shaping GAVI's funding and programmes. In terms of its governance, the IFFim operates as a charitable company with a board made up of individuals with backgrounds in finance and financial regulation. The role of the board is to review funding requests by the GAVI immunization program, to oversee the IFFim's governance and policies, and to monitor its investment portfolio and efficacy.[29] IFFim rapidly scaled-up the capacity of GAVI and has allocated USD 2.5 billion to immunization programmes since its inception.[30]

GAVI has also entered into unique financial arrangements with vaccine manufacturers through its Advanced Market Commitments (AMC). The AMC was formally launched in February of 2007 as donors committed to provide USD 1.5 billion in order to guarantee a market for the pneumococcal vaccine in low-income countries.[31] The ultimate design of the AMC provided that each manufacturer would receive a share of the committed financing in proportion to their supply commitment. Two leading pharmaceutical manufacturers, Pfizer and GlaxoSmithKline, agreed to supply 60 million doses over ten years.[32] While the legally binding commitments on donor pledges were important to building confidence among manufacturers, these legal guarantees fell short of the resources needed to fully implement the AMC.[33] Despite these challenges, fifty-seven countries had introduced pneumococcal vaccines into the schedule for routine childhood immunization reaching a total of 109 million children.[34] In 2015, GAVI approved a more modest Advanced Purchase Commitment for the development of a candidate Ebola vaccine.[35]

GAVI's overall governance structure appears to be contributing to its effectiveness as reflected in recent evaluations of its work. The United Kingdom's Department for International Development (DFID) review rated GAVI in terms of its level of organizational effectiveness. A DFID review found that GAVI had a strong partnership with government, civil society, and the private sector, but also suggested that there was a lack of clarity on the roles and responsibilities of key partners and on the inclusion of civil society within GAVI's current structure.[36] According to GAVI's own strategic goal indicators, only 40% of countries are meeting its benchmarks for civil society engagement in national immunization programmes. These indicators include incorporating civil society organizations in national immunization plans, defining budget allocations for civil society activities, and documenting evidence of the implementation

[29] International Finance Facility for Immunisation (IFFim), 'Governance' <http://www.iffim.org/about/governance/>, last accessed 11/30/2019.

[30] Global Alliance for Vaccines and Immunization (GAVI), 'Annual Progress Report 2016' <https://www.gavi.org/sites/default/files/publications/progress-reports/Gavi-Progress-Report-2016.pdf>, last accessed 11/30/2019, 36.

[31] *See* Veronica Chau, Vicky Hausman, Wouter Deelder, Angela Rastegar, Mara De Monte, Ya'ir Aizenman, Patricia Pina, Cecilia Chen, and Liesl Goecker, 'The Advance Market Commitment for Pneumococcal Vaccines: Process and Design Evaluation' https://www.convergence.finance/resource/Ad8nCj7aGO4wu0QqCQ2Oi/view, last accessed 12/06/2019.

[32] Donald W Light, 'Saving Pneumococcal AMC and GAVI', 7(2) Human Vaccines (2011) 138–141.

[33] Chau *et al.*, 'The Advance Market' (n 31), 69.

[34] GAVI, 'Annual Report 2016' (n 30), 36.

[35] GAVI, 'Annual Report 2016' (n 30), 52.

[36] The United Kingdom's Department for International Development (DFID), *Multilateral Review 2013* (Department for International Development 2013).

of civil society activities. Nonetheless, a more recent update by DFID focused on organizational effectiveness once again gave GAVI its highest rating along with only two other development institutions.[37] GAVI's reported results include immunizing 640 million children, with a resulting 9 million lives saved.[38]

14.5 Global Fund: Stakeholders as Veto Holders

The Global Fund was initially conceived of in 2000 and its launch gained momentum after the G8 summit of the leading economies in Japan that year. Its formal establishment grew out of the UN Special Session on AIDS and the initial contribution was made by UN Secretary General Koffi Annan. Despite these close ties to longstanding institutions of global governance, the Global Fund embraced a very distinct model of governance in which non-state actors were not only equals in the formal structure, but also collectively held potential veto power within the governance of the institution.

Inspired by the collaborative model of its design group, the Transitional Working Group, the Global Fund adopted a governance structure in which NGOs, foundations, and the private sector were all represented on its board. The delegation of NGOs representing people affected by the three target diseases gained voting rights in 2004. Unlike prior institutions, the Global Fund also created a system of blocs designed to ensure that neither donor countries nor recipient counties could independently override the other. As a result of this structure, all major decisions require consensus, which effectively provides potential veto powers to groups who are entirely excluded from governance in many global health institutions. While in practice such a veto is extremely rare, it offers a distinct model of shared decision-making that extends beyond the mere power of casting the vote of a given constituency.

At the country level, the Global Fund's work is managed by multi-stakeholder Country Coordinating Mechanisms (CCMs). Recent examinations of the CCMs found that in many countries these institutions contributed to a redefinition of the relationship between civil society and government in the health sector. In Brazil, for example, the process contributed to the emergence of new civic movements and participatory institutions that increased domestic political commitment to respond to the challenge posed by tuberculosis.[39] However, a survey of civil society groups in Sub-Saharan Africa found that opportunities for civil society to participate meaningfully in priority setting remained limited in some countries and that the voices of civil society within many CCMs were still relatively weak.[40]

[37] The United Kingdom's Department for International Development (DFID), Raising the Standard: The Multilateral Development Review 2016 (Department for International Development 2016).

[38] GAVI, 'Annual Report 2016' (n 30), 5.

[39] Carlos Bruen, Ruairí Brugha, Angela Kageni, and Francis Wafula, 'A Concept in Flux: Questioning Accountability in the Context of Global Health Cooperation' 10(December) *Globalization and Health* (2014) 1-15.

[40] Jennifer Cohn, Asia Russell, Brook Baker, Alice Kayongo, Esther Wanjiku, and Paul Davis, 'Using Global Health Initiatives to Strengthen Health Systems: A Civil Society Perspective' 6(7) *Global Public Health* (2011) 687-702.

In 2011, the Global Fund responded to potential fraud claims by adopting a new strategy to guide the institution, including the adoption of a new funding model based on the recommendation of the high-level panel. Some accounts suggest that this shift reflected the informal power of a small number of states over the operations of the Global Fund.[41] The new strategy highlighted the importance of partnership and sought more extensive engagement with country level processes. Nonetheless, several stakeholder-related governance issues remained challenging for the Global Fund. A report by the Global Fund's independent Office of Inspector General highlighted the failure to hold a Partnership Forum in recent years, the lack of continuity among delegates to board meetings from implementer countries, and the fact that the voices of implementer country delegations account for just over one-quarter of interventions in the context of board meetings. Finally, the report questioned the way in which the bloc voting rules can empower minority interests over the overall interests of the organization.[42]

A working group established by the Global Fund responded to these challenges with specific recommendations for further governance reforms. Among these recommendations were that the Board reaffirm the importance of the Partnership Forum and that individual constituency votes be systematically recorded and publicly reported on the website of the institution.[43] While the Global Fund's strategy sought to strengthen engagement with diverse stakeholders at the country-level its ultimate impact remains to be seen. Some early evaluations suggest a positive impact in a number of countries.

A key feature of the country dialogue process is that broad participation be documented before any grant awards can be made. It is designed to be a process which is led by the CCM to foster 'strengthened multi-stakeholder involvement in the development of national disease strategies improved coordination, relevance, and effectiveness of the disease program response.'[44] A series of reforms to the CCM process, beginning in 2015, to strengthen stakeholder participation, include new stricter requirements that 40% of members be drawn from civil society, that non-governmental representatives must be selected from their own constituencies, that there be evidence of the involvement of people living with the three diseases, and that the funding recipient be nominated using transparent objective criteria.[45]

There is some evidence that expanded stakeholder participation has contributed to the organizational strength and effectiveness of the Global Fund; it received the highest ranking in terms of organizational strength in the most recent review of development institutions by the United Kingdom's development agency.[46] The diversity

[41] Bruen *et al.*, 'Concept in Flux' (n 39).

[42] Office of the Inspector General of The Global Fund to Fight AIDS, Tuberculosis, and Malaria, *Governance Review 2014* (The Global Fund 2014).

[43] Ad-Hoc Working Group on Governance of the Global Fund, *Governance Report to the Board 2014* (The Global Fund 2014), <https://www.theglobalfund.org/media/4126/bm32_08-thegovernanceplanforimpact_report_en.pdf?u=637066575430000000> , last accessed 05/14/2020.

[44] International Council of Aids Service Organizations (ICASO), *Civil Society and Key Populations in the Country Dialogue Process* (ICASO 2014).

[45] AIDSPAN, *New Minimum Standards 20153,* (AIDSPAN 2013), <http://www.aidspan.org/gfo_article/global-fund-introduces-new-minimum-standards-implementers>, last accessed 05/14/2020.

[46] DFID, 'Raising the Standard' (n 37).

of its implementers has also been a major strength in the Global Fund's efforts to scale up its activities. On average, civil society groups, the private sector, and multilateral recipients received higher evaluation scores than government implementers.[47]

Since its launch, the Global Fund's overall impact has been quite significant; it accounts for 65% of all international tuberculosis funding, 50% of all international malaria funding, and 20% of all international HIV funding. Financing from the Global Fund has resulted in 11 million people receiving HIV drugs, 17.4 million people receiving tuberculosis treatment, and the distribution of 668 people million receiving malaria treatment. According to its own estimates, these interventions contributed to a one-third decline in the number of people dying from AIDS, TB, and malaria since 2002, resulting in 22 million fewer deaths.[48]

14.6 Conclusion

Stakeholder participation has moved from the margins to the centre of global health governance. While the traditional institutions founded after the Second World War have expanded their engagement with diverse non-state actors, their governance remains fundamentally the province of states. Non-state actors generally remain informants in relation to the policies and programmes of the WB and are essentially excluded from its formal governance process. At the WHO, by contrast, non-state actors are increasingly important as both funders of core programmes and also as front-line agents of disease surveillance. Despite their growing importance, external stakeholders remain mostly observers in the formal governance process of the WHO. The gap between the role which non-state actors are playing in the global health sector in practice and the formal roles which the traditional institutions linked to the UN and Bretton Woods agreements provide for these actors remains quite substantial. This significant divide contributed to the rise of a new generation of global health institutions in the twenty-first century that have subsequently matched (or even exceeded) the scale of the WB and the WHO in terms of global health financing. It also catalysed new forms of engagement by traditional institutions through hosting arrangements with multi-stakeholder partnerships in which non-state actors participate as equals. However, the ongoing institutional tensions between these hosted multi-stakeholder partnerships and their respective state-centric sponsoring institution remains somewhat unresolved.

The most participatory global health institutions are those which are genuinely independent of the constraints that come with being a part of the UN or the WB. These non-traditional institutions also reflect the path dependence of expanding stakeholder participation within the context of global health. The spinoff of UNAIDS from the WHO represents an important turning point in terms of the emergence of a new model of multi-stakeholder governance independent of traditional institutions. The demand by those directly affected by AIDS and other diseases was central to the

[47] DFID, 'Raising the Standard' (n 37).

[48] The Global Fund, Results and Impact, https://www.theglobalfund.org/en/impact/, last accessed 12/06/2019.

emergence of this more participatory model, which is now reflected both among independent non-traditional institutions and among many of the multi-stakeholder partnerships hosted by the WB and the WHO.

Perhaps most strikingly, more participatory global health institutions have dramatically outpaced the traditional institutions in terms of the growth of their resources and disbursements. By 2012, the Global Fund overtook the WB as the leading global health financing institution in terms of its disbursements.[49] The Global Fund received nearly USD 30 billion from donors over its first thirteen years of existence. GAVI received nearly USD 10 billion from both donors and innovative financing mechanisms over the same period with pledges totalling over USD 15 billion by 2015. Since the year 2000, donors are increasingly shifting resources towards more participatory global health institutions. At the same time, institutions such as the WHO have actually become more dependent on donors who are increasingly earmarking or cherry-picking the programmes in which they wish to invest.

Even as global level stakeholder participation has expanded dramatically in global health governance, national level models of participation have been slower to take root. Traditional institutions, such as the WB, have sought to build formal consultation with civil society into most of its new programming. Yet this model of consultation is quite different from the cooperative model of decision-making required as part of the Global Fund's CCM process. Despite its role in expanding national level stakeholder participation and growing evidence that diverse stakeholders acting implementers contributes to improved performance, the Global Fund's CCM model remains very much a work in progress. It has yet to be adopted by leading peer global health institutions and is viewed in some quarters as undermining national strategies and planning. Yet it is this level of stakeholder engagement which is likely to be one of the biggest challenges for the future of global health governance.

At the same time, the introduction of diverse stakeholders into the formal process of global health governance generates risks and concerns that need to be addressed through improved models of participation. One of the core challenges for any model of expanded stakeholder participation in governance is to guard against non-state actors pursuing a narrow or self-interested agenda which does not reflect the concerns of the wider constituencies from which they emerge. Key dimensions include the breadth of the overall constituency, the relationships between representatives and the broader constituency, and the interaction between different constituencies.

Global health governance is at the forefront of innovation in models of stakeholder participation and governance. Expanded stakeholder participation is increasingly embraced by traditional and non-traditional institutions alike. The proper role for non-state actors in global health governance and in the governance of international institutions more generally remains quite contested. Yet global health governance offers a range of clear models from stakeholders as informants in the context of WB consultation processes, to stakeholders as observers of formal governance as the WHO provides, to stakeholders as equal voting participants in formal governance within GAVI, to stakeholders as veto holders in the governance of the Global

[49] Institute for Health Metrics and Evaluation (IHME), *Financing Global Health 2014* (IHME 2015), 122.

Fund. A clear and dramatic evolution towards greater participation in recent decades may become even more controversial as the Global Fund rethinks its bloc system and the WHO creates a new register for non-state actors. Nonetheless, the new normal in global health governance is robust multi-stakeholder participation in formal governance and there are growing signs that this model may offer distinct advantages that lead it to be embraced more widely.

B. DEVELOPING COUNTRIES' PARTICIPATION IN COMPARISON

15

Brazil and Argentina in Global Health Governance

*André de Mello e Souza and Facundo Pérez Aznar**

15.1 Introduction

This chapter investigates and compares changes in the engagement and influence of Brazilian and Argentine stakeholders in global health governance. It assesses whether and to what extent these changes are attributable to the institutional reforms carried out by global health organizations, particularly the World Health Organization (WHO), the Codex Alimentarius Commission (Codex), the Global Fund to Fight AIDS, Tuberculosis and Malaria (Global Fund), the International Council for Harmonization (ICH), and GlobalG.A.P. In attempting this assessment, we caution that, for some of these reforms, it may be too early to conclusively assess their effects.

Beyond the reforms, we focus on two factors that influence the extent to which stakeholders capitalize on participation opportunities: (i) the salience of the policy issue and the importance of the organization for the governments of Brazil and Argentina and key non-governmental stakeholders from those countries, as well as (ii) the stakeholders' preferences, resources, and capabilities. In addition, we analyse the influence of Brazil and Argentina in shaping those institutional reforms.

The participation of Argentina and especially Brazil in global health governance has generally increased over time, though the extent of such participation has varied considerably across institutions. This has not only been a result of institutional reforms but often is a consequence of the importance of the institution for the global role a country seeks to play and for addressing health problems that go beyond national borders. It is also a consequence of stakeholder capabilities and constraints, such as the availability of financial resources or technical knowledge. Moreover, with the increasing importance of health for the production and accumulation of wealth, private health corporations have become important global actors,[1] in turn impacting state behaviour.

* For interviews, we are grateful to José Roberto de Andrade Filho, Patrícia Oliveira Pereira, Renata Motta, Paulo Buss, Paulo Roberto Teixeira, Deisy Ventura, Ariel Martins, Ayelén Amigo, Gabriela Catalani, Valeria Garay, Marcelo Matto, Darío Magallanes, Enrique Kurincic and Sebastián Tobar, Patricio Grané Riera and interviewees who preferred to remain anonymous. We also thank Ayelet Berman, Tim Büthe, José Roberto de Andrade Filho, Patrícia Oliveira Pereira and participants of the SNIS Rethinking Participation workshops for comments and suggestions on earlier drafts of this chapter. This chapter covers developments through 2018.

[1] Tobar Sebastián, Buss Paulo, Coitiño Andrés, Kleiman Alberto, Fonseca Luiz Eduardo, Rigoli Félix, Karen Sealy, and Vanessa Victoria, 'Diplomacia de la salud: fortalecimiento de las oficinas de relaciones internacionales de los ministerios de salud en las Américas' 41 *Revista Panamericana de Salud Publica* (2017) e145.

André de Mello e Souza and Facundo Pérez Aznar, *Brazil and Argentina in Global Health Governance* In: *Rethinking Participation in Global Governance*. Edited by: Joost Pauwelyn, Martino Maggetti, Tim Büthe, and Ayelet Berman, Oxford University Press.
 DOI: 10.1093/oso/9780198852568.003.0015

Since the 1990s, when stakeholder participation reforms began taking place in global health institutions, Brazil and Argentina have had different ambitions in the international arena.[2] Brazil has experienced relatively high rates of income growth and has become internationally recognized as an emerging power, for instance, through its inclusion in the BRICS. Brazil has also adopted a deliberate foreign policy strategy of increasing its engagement and influence in global governance. Regionally, Brazil has attempted to unify and lead Latin American countries in global health governance negotiations.

Brazil's ability to shape structures and processes in global governance in general has derived from, and has been concentrated in, the pivotal role it has played in the health issue-area, especially in relation to HIV/AIDS policies and institutions.[3] In this issue-area more than any other, Brazil has interacted effectively on many fronts with other state and non-state actors, and thereby helped to shape international institutions. By and large, this can be attributed to its success in carrying out innovative and highly effective healthcare and HIV/AIDS policies domestically.[4]

Argentina has, in general, held very similar preferences regarding global health governance, and has pursued them in sometimes similar ways, such as joint regional initiatives in regional institutions.[5] At the same time, Argentina has exercised a less prominent voice than Brazil in global health governance. The political and economic crises which Argentina underwent in the past forty years led to an inward orientation and reduced the availability of resources, which in turn has resulted in a lower capacity to participate in international institutions. Between 2003 and 2011, as economic performance improved and healthcare was prioritized, Argentina's international engagement in health governance increased, particularly on specific issues it values and where it has high expertise and capabilities, such as universal and free access to medicines. However, it is difficult to see a coherent Argentine international policy on health matters across time.

15.2 World Health Organization (WHO)

15.2.1 Importance and Formal Participation

Given their foreign policy traditions of favouring multilateralism, Brazil and Argentina were among the founding member states of the WHO in 1946. And given

[2] For an overview of the stakeholder participation reforms, see Ayelet Berman, 'Stakeholder Participation Reforms in Global Health Governance.' Chapter 13, this volume.

[3] Marco Cepik and Rômulo Paes de Sousa, 'A Política Externa Brasileira e a Cooperação Internacional em Saúde no Começo do Governo Lula' 2(1) *Fórum Século XXI* (2011) 109-134.

[4] André de Mello e Souza, 'Saúde Pública, Patentes e Atores Não-Estatais: A Política Externa do Brasil ante a Epidemia de AIDS' in Leticia Pinheiro and Carlos R S Milani (eds), *Política Externa Brasileira: As Práticas da Política e a Política das Práticas* (Fundação Getúlio Vargas 2012) 203-240; Markus Fraundorfer, *Brazil's Emerging Role in Global Governance: Health, Food Security and Bioenergy* (Palgrave Macmillan 2015), 4.

[5] Notably, educational exchanges between Brazil and Argentina helped to reinforce similar views concerning global health governance (in-person interview with Paulo Marchiori Buss, Rio de Janeiro, 7 June 2017).

the central role that the WHO has come to play as the institutional focal point for many issues on the global health agenda, Brazil and Argentina have remained actively engaged in WHO-based global governance ever since.[6] Their important role can also be observed in the Pan-American Health Organization (PAHO). The one-country one-vote governance system in the World Health Assemblies (WHA) has helped to ensure that developing countries such as Brazil and Argentina have a say in setting the WHO's agenda. Notwithstanding formal institutional equality, Brazil's participation in the WHO has been more significant than Argentina's, mostly as result of the greater importance attributed by Brazil to public health issues, as well as greater resources devoted to this issue area, which have resulted in greater capacity and capability.

Especially since the late 1990s, Brazil has both increased its engagement and influence in the WHO. However, this was not the result of institutional reforms. Rather, it is explained by Brazil's shifting domestic political and policy priorities favouring health, by its enhanced capabilities, translated into greater technocratic expertise and political standing, and, finally, by Brazil's leadership of a regional bloc of supporting South American countries.

First, Brazil has, since the 2000s, increased the number of permanent diplomats to the WHO from one to three. Having more diplomats affords the country considerably greater political clout in the numerous and growing negotiation arenas of the WHO, where it is common to have three to four different negotiations and meetings occurring simultaneously.[7] Furthermore, experts from other Brazilian governmental bodies also take part in the WHO's negotiations more frequently than before the turn of the century. Additionally, Brazil was elected to three mandates in the Executive Board since 2000, for a total of nine years. Finally, Brazil has also increased its financial contributions: in 2013 the country became the tenth largest contributor to the WHO.[8] During the 2016–2017 period, Brazil's total contributions to the organization amounted to almost USD 32 million.[9]

Brazil's influence on the WHO has also been exercised through the mobilization of its neighbours. Notably, in 2008, Brazil spearheaded the creation of a regional institution—the South American Health Council (SAHC)—within the Union of South American Nations (UNASUR). The SAHC is composed of the UNASUR states' health ministers, and its Coordinating Committee is composed of representatives from the member states and the most important international organizations in the Americas.[10]

[6] Regarding the distinction between unitary vs. plural institutional structures of global governance, see Tim Büthe and Walter Mattli, *The New Global Rulers: The Privatization of Regulation in the World Economy* (Princeton University Press 2011); Mercy DeMenno and Tim Büthe, 'Voice and Influence in Global Governance: An Analytical Framework.' Chapter 2, this volume, Sections 2.2.3 and 2.5.1). The WHO is at the core of a unitary structure for many global health issues, making it a very important global health governance body for any issue that is salient for a given stakeholder.

[7] In-person interview with José Roberto de Andrade Filho (Brasília, 22 November 2016).

[8] Deisy Ventura, 'Saúde Pública e Política Externa Brasileira' 10(19) *SUR—Revista Internacional de Direitos Humanos* (2013) 99-117.

[9] WHO, 'Contributors' <http://open.who.int/2016-17/contributors>, last accessed 06/16/2017.

[10] These organizations include the Southern Common Market (Mercosur), the Andean Health Organization, Amazon Cooperation Treaty Organization and PAHO. Fraundorfer, *Brazil's Emerging Role* (n 4), 74f; Buss interview (n 5). The SAHC therefore is an instrument for mobilizing and coordinating the position of like-minded and less powerful South American countries rather than a competing alternative institution to the WHO.

The SAHC aims to promote the social determinants of health—in opposition to the US-backed agenda centred on disease control—and increase universal access to medicines, among other goals.

Argentina's level of participation in the WHO has been lower than Brazil's, and it has decreased in the past decade. First, as of 2016, the country's representation at the WHO amounts to only one diplomat. Second, the size of Argentine delegations and the frequency of their participation in WHO meetings have been declining. Third, Argentina's total contributions to the WHO, a little over USD 6 million in 2016–2017, are less than one-fifth of Brazil's.[11] Nevertheless, Argentina was a member of PAHO's Executive Committee (2009–2011) and has also been a member and vice president of the Executive Council.[12] In addition, Mirta Roses Periago, an Argentine, has been the Director of PAHO for two periods, between 2003 and 2012.

Argentina also played an important role in the creation of the SAHC. Notably, the Argentine Minister of Health proposed, with PAHO's support, the creation of the South American Vaccination Week, which was one of the main precursors of the SAHC. Similar to Brazil, Argentina relies on and uses regional institutions to advance its interests within the WHO.[13]

15.2.2 Influence and Major Achievements

Brazil's greater engagement has translated into greater influence in the WHO. The country has led some of the organization's most noteworthy achievements, such as the Framework Convention on Tobacco Control (FCTC 2003). With regard to formal representation, Vera Luiza da Costa e Silva, a Brazilian medical doctor and former coordinator of the National Tobacco Control Programme, was recruited to lead the WHO's Tobacco Free Initiative (TFI), and Brazilian diplomats Celso Amorim and Luiz Felipe de Seixas Correa were appointed to chair the Intergovernmental Negotiating Body (INB) for the FCTC. As the TFI sought to counter the claim of the industry that tobacco control was 'a first world issue', Brazil helped build support for the FCTC within the developing world. In particular, it helped to carefully select the six deputy chairs of the INB, led regional meetings and built consensus within such groups as the Group of Latin American and Caribbean Countries (GRULAC) and Mercosur (Southern Common Market).[14]

Furthermore, Brazil has spearheaded a shift in the organization's policy paradigm and directives regarding the global fight against HIV/AIDS. In particular, it successfully changed the focus of this policy from prevention to treatment. It also built

[11] WHO, 'Contributors' (n 9).

[12] While Brazil has prioritized the WHO over the PAHO, Argentina has been much more engaged in the latter institution (Buss interview (n 5)).

[13] Ministerio de Salud, Argentina, 'La salud no puede estar regulada por las reglas del mercado afirmó el ministro Gollan ante la OMS' <http://www.msal.gob.ar/prensa/index.php?option=com_content&view=article&id=2679:la-salud-no-puede-estar-regulada-por-las-reglas-del-mercado-afirmo-el-ministro-gollan-ante-la-oms&catid=1:noticias2679>, last accessed 02/17/2017.

[14] The six deputy chairs of the INB were the US, Australia, Iran, India, South Africa, and Turkey. See also Kelley Lee, Luiz Carlos Chagas and Thomas E Novotny, 'Brazil and the Framework Convention on Tobacco Control: Global Health Diplomacy as Soft Power' 7(4) *PLoS Medicine* (2010): e1000232.

coalitions in the WHAs to approve resolutions supporting changes in the global governance of pharmaceutical patent rights so as to expand access to essential drugs.[15] These changes refer primarily to the Agreement on Trade-Related Aspects of Intellectual Property Rights (TRIPS) and highlight the reinforcement of issue-linkages between health, trade, and property rights in global governance institutions. They were carried out despite opposition from the United States and other high-income countries, which claimed that the WHO did not have competence or a mandate to deal with issues of patent rights.

The SAHC has served as a significant additional channel of engagement and influence in the ambit of the WHO. For instance, it established a consultation process of the positions of member countries. Furthermore, it has held parallel meetings to the WHA with the purpose of promoting the adoption of joint positions by members, including in the WHO's Executive Board.[16] The SAHC also advocated 'a WHO reform broader than the review of forms of financing, as originally planned'.[17]

Moreover, in 2009, the SAHC agreed on the creation of the South American Institute of Health Governance (ISAGS), an intergovernmental institution located in Rio de Janeiro that became completely financed and coordinated by the Brazilian government.[18] ISAGS is mandated, among other things, 'to assist in the formulation of common UNASUR foreign policies to support the negotiation of health-related issues in global and regional international agendas'.[19] Brazil's key role in the creation of ISAGS bears testimony to 'its continuous insertion in both regional and global health governance'.[20]

Similarly to Brazil, Argentina has tried to promote successful national policies, some of which have served as models for WHO/PAHO policies. Notable examples include Argentina's Universal Child and Pregnancy Allowance,[21] the 2012 Right to Gender Identity Law[22] and the Law on the Protection of Mental Health. Furthermore, Argentina has had significant involvement in the WHO/PAHO programme 'Less salt, more life'[23] and, since 2008, in implementing the WHO's Global Health Care Waste

[15] Mello e Souza, 'Saúde Pública'(n 4), 224–226; Fraundorfer, *Brazil's Emerging Role* (n 4), 60–63; Buss interview (n 5).

[16] Ventura, 'Saúde Pública' (n 8); Buss interview (n 5).

[17] UNASUL/ISAGS, '65ª AMS Discutiu Reforma da OMS com Destacada Atuação da UNASUL' (Informe, 2012) 1, 3, < http://www.isags-unasul.org/uploads/eventos/ev[47]ling[1]anx[45].pdf>, last accessed 06/07/2018.

[18] Fraundorfer, *Brazil's Emerging Role* (n 4), 74f; Buss interview (n 5).

[19] ISAGS, 'Funções' <http://www.isags-unasur.org/isags.php?lg=1>, last accessed 06/16/2017.

[20] Fraundorfer, *Brazil's Emerging Role* (n 4), 75.

[21] WHO, 'Estrategia de cooperación de la OMS con Argentina 2012–2016' <http://iris.paho.org/xmlui/bitstream/handle/123456789/3604/2012-ARG-estrategia-cooperacion-argentina.pdf>, last accessed 06/16/2017.

[22] WHO, 'Sexual Health, Human Rights and the Law' <http://apps.who.int/iris/bitstream/10665/175556/1/9789241564984_eng.pdf>, last accessed 02/17/2017.

[23] WHO, 'Argentina: Less Salt More Life' <http://www.who.int/features/2014/argentina-less-salt-more-life/en/>, last accessed 02/14/2017; Ministerio de Salud, Argentina, 'Ministerio de Salud asesoró a Surinam en la estrategia para reducir la sal en alimentos elaborados' <http://www.msal.gob.ar/ent/index.php/home/6-destacados-slide/490-ministerio-de-salud-asesoro-a-surinam-en-la-estrategia-para-reducir-la-sal-en-alimentos-elaborados>, last accessed 02/14/2017; Ministerio de Salud, Argentina, 'Viceministro Kaski destacó que el Estado lidera iniciativas para reducir el consumo de sal' <http://www.msal.gob.ar/ent/index.php/component/content/article/1-noticias/489-viceministro-kaski-destaco-que-el-estado-lidera-iniciativas-para-reducir-consumo-de-sal->, last accessed 02/14/2017.

Project.[24] Lastly, in 2015 Argentina launched a WHO Framework of Engagement with Non-State Actors (FENSA) reform working group[25] on non-state actor collaboration guidelines.[26] This role allowed Argentina to lead other participating countries in claiming that financial contributions by non-state actors should be allowed, as long as the origin, provenance and transparency of the funds are determined.

Argentina's influence in the organization has also been reflected in the provision of technical assistance on a number of important matters within its expertise in different countries through PAHO/WHO supported projects. Examples include projects on integrated foodborne diseases surveillance, mental health primary care, vector-borne diseases, polio eradication, organ transplants, supply and quality control of medicines, training of human resources, and Ebola.[27]

15.2.3 WHO-Hosted Multi-Stakeholder Partnerships

Brazil and Argentina have also engaged with the WHO through multi-stakeholder partnerships. Although these partnerships are open to governmental and non-governmental actors alike, the participants from these countries have been largely governmental. For example, the Brazilian Ministry of Health has implemented several joint initiatives with UNAIDS, including the first International Centre for the Cooperation on HIV/AIDS, based in Brasilia,[28] and *Rede Laços Sul-Sul*. The objective of both initiatives is to replicate the Brazilian strategy against HIV/AIDS, or parts thereof, elsewhere in the developing world. Moreover, many of the founders and key figures of Brazil's National AIDS Programme have occupied important positions at UNAIDS, such as Pedro Chequer and Luiz Loures.[29]

In 2006, Brazil helped create UNITAID with the aim of reducing the price of medicines for pandemics like HIV/AIDS. The country is UNITAID's fifth largest donor.[30]

[24] WHO, 'Argentina Mercury-Free' <http://www.who.int/features/2013/argentina-mercury-free/en/>, last accessed 02/14/2017.

[25] Ministerio de Salud, Argentina, 'Argentina lidera grupo de trabajo de la OMS para garantizar transparencia de aportes privados a esa Organización' <http://www.msal.gob.ar/prensa/index.php?option=com_content&view=article&id=2507:argentina-lidera-grupo-de-trabajo-de-la-oms-para-garantizar-transparencia-de-aportes-privados-a-esa-organizacion&catid=1:noticias2507>, last accessed 02/17/2017.

[26] WHO, 'Collaborations', <http://www.who.int/about/collaborations/non-state-actors/en/> accessed 02/22/2017.

[27] PAHO, 'South-South Cooperation: Triangular Cooperation Experience Between the Government of the Argentine Republic and the Pan-American Health Organization/World Health Organization' (2009) <http://cooperacionarg.gob.ar/userfiles/publi_ss_ops_arg_en.pdf>, last accessed 05/30/2018; Ministerio de Salud, Argentina, 'Intensa agenda de trabajo del ministro Gollan en la primera jornada de la Asamblea Mundial de la Salud' <http://www.msal.gob.ar/prensa/index.php/noticias-de-la-semana/2677-intensa-agenda-de-trabajo-del-ministro-gollan-en-la-primera-jornada-de-la-asamblea-mundial-de-la-salud>, last accessed 02/22/2017; Nora Bär, 'Ébola: usarán una estrategia desarrollada en la Argentina', *La Nación* 22 October 2014 <http://www.lanacion.com.ar/1737546-ebola-usaran-una-estrategia-desarrollada-en-la-argentina>, last accessed 02/22/2017. WHO, 'Estrategia de cooperación' (n 21).

[28] Then-Executive Director of UNAIDS, Peter Piot, explained that Brazil's leadership in the fight against HIV/AIDS was critical in deciding to establish this International Centre in Brazil (see Fraundorfer, *Brazil's Emerging Role* (n 4), 69).

[29] Fraundorfer, *Brazil's Emerging Role* (n 4), 69.

[30] UNITAID, 'UNITAID: Innovation in Global Health 2016-2017 Report', 59 <https://unitaid.eu/unitaid-ar-1617/pdf/Annual-report2016-17.pdf>, last accessed 06/09/2018.

Notably, Brazil has been influential in all important decisions taken by the UNITAID Executive Board,[31] including the Medicines Patent Pool.[32] Moreover, Brazilian health professional Jorge Bermúdez became Executive Secretary of UNITAID from 2007 to 2011. Since 2016, the Executive Board, UNITAID's main decision-making body, has been chaired by Celso Amorim, a former Minister of Foreign Affairs of Brazil.[33] Significantly, the Executive Board chose the Brazilian Ministry of Foreign Affairs for their first-ever meeting outside Geneva in 2008.[34]

However, Brazil and Argentina have by no means participated in, let alone influenced, all important partnerships associated with the WHO. For example, neither country has been represented on the Board of the Partnership for Maternal, Newborn, and Child Health,[35] perhaps because of Brazil's achievements in reducing child mortality.[36] Similarly, they have no representation, governmental or otherwise, in the partnership board, management team, partner committees, or working groups of Roll Back Malaria.[37] The low and decreasing incidence of malaria in both Brazil and Argentina[38] and the powerlessness of malaria patients help to explain why the two countries have not been more engaged in this institution. Likewise, although both Brazil and Argentina are members of the Stop TB Partnership, their representation is limited to nineteen Brazilian partner institutions (of which eight are NGOs) and two Argentine partner institutions.[39]

Moreover, notwithstanding the multi-stakeholder nature of these partnerships, most Brazilian and Argentine participation in them has been governmental and rarely involved civil society organizations. For example, only four Brazilian and one Argentine civil society organizations have served on UNAIDS' Programme

[31] Fraundorfer, *Brazil's Emerging Role* (n 4), 79f.

[32] The patent pool offers 'licenses for patents to other manufacturers including generic producers, in return for royalty payments;' see UNITAID, 'Innovative Financing for Health: Increasing Access and Affordability of Medicines through Market Impact' (2010), 4 <http://www.unitaid.eu/images/Factsheets/unitaid_brochure_july_en.pdf>, last accessed 07/13/2017.

[33] The chair of the Executive Board presides over negotiations with the aim of facilitating consensus in UNITAID's decision-making processes; see Unitaid Constitution <https://unitaid.org/assets/UNITAID-Constitution-revised-version-15-June-2018.pdf>, last accessed 11/19/2019.

[34] Fraundorfer, *Brazil's Emerging Role* (n 4), 79f.

[35] Only four Argentine NGOs and one Brazilian university hold membership in the partnership, see PMNCH Online Database <http://www.who.int/pmnch/about/members/search/en/>, last accessed 06/16/2017.

[36] Songa Wa Songa, 'Brazil Wins World Cup Health Scorecard' *The Citizen* (June 30, 2014) <http://www.thecitizen.co.tz/News/Brazil-wins-world-cup-health-scorecard/1840340-2366624-a1akxbz/index.html>, accessed 06/16/2017; Cesar G Victora, Estela ML Aquino, Maria do Carmo Real, Carlos Auguste Monteiro, Fernanco C Barros, and Celia L Szwarcwald, 'Maternal and Child Health in Brazil: Progress and Challenges' 377(9780) *The Lancet* (2011) 1863-1876.

[37] Roll Back Malaria Partnership, 'Organizational Structure' <http://www.rollbackmalaria.org/organizational-structure/>, last accessed 06/16/2017.

[38] Roll Back Malaria Partnership, 'Brazil Sets Sights on Malaria Elimination' Press Release (30 November 2015) <http://www.rollbackmalaria.org/news-events/latest-news/2015/brazil-sets-sights-on-malaria-elimination-1>, last accessed 06/16/2017; Ministerio de Salud, Argentina, 'Argentina a un paso de ser declarada país libre de paludismo autóctono' (24 April 2014) <http://www.msal.gob.ar/prensa/index.php/noticias-de-la-semana/1949-argentina-a-un-paso-de-ser-declarada-pais-libre-de-paludismo-autoctono->, last accessed 02/22/2017.

[39] Stop TB Partnership, 'Our Partners' <http://www.stoptb.org/about/partners_landing.asp>, last accessed 11/19/2019.

Coordinating Board.[40] Likewise, despite the considerable and growing incidence of tuberculosis in Brazil,[41] particularly in its drug-resistant strains, and the increased susceptibility of AIDS patients to this opportunistic infection, Brazilian tuberculosis NGOs have not been engaged or influential in the WHO's Stop TB Partnership.

Hence, although multi-stakeholder partnerships were set up in response to the WHO's shortcomings in engaging with non-state actors, in Brazil's case some of them actually served to increase the engagement and influence of the national government. This is especially puzzling given that, in health more than in any other sector, Brazilian civil society organizations have thrived and become very engaged and influential ever since democratization in the early 80s.[42] How can this paradox be explained?

As Mello e Souza has argued elsewhere, Brazilian civil society organizations—unlike their counterparts in many other countries—have generally not become engaged in international health institutions because they usually have unrestricted access to the domestic governmental decision-making process. The Brazilian government supported many of the main demands and initiatives of Brazilian health NGOs, employed many of their most prominent representatives, and generally shared their views on health rights, policies, and institutions. For these reasons, NGOs tended to work domestically with governmental authorities rather than seeking their own independent stance in global health governance. The Brazilian government has largely represented NGO health positions at the international level.[43]

In sharp contrast to Brazil's experience with HIV/AIDS partnerships, however, during the 1990s no organized social movements or NGOs sought to work with the government in fighting tuberculosis, which helps to explain the low level of Brazilian civil society participation in the Stop TB Partnership. As was the case with Roll Back Malaria, the lack of influential local tuberculosis NGOs, as well as the disenfranchisement of their constituencies, account for this outcome. The level of Argentine civil society participation in the WHO generally has been lower than that of Brazilian civil society.

15.2.4 Barriers to Participation

The growing engagement of Brazil and Argentina in the WHO has encountered persistent as well as new challenges. First, Brazil and Argentina are constrained by their human and financial resources and technical expertise. As global health increasingly

[40] UNAIDS, 'NGO Delegation Membership to the UNAIDS Programme Coordinating Board 1995–2015' <http://www.unaidspcbngo.org/wp-content/uploads/2011/10/Delegation-Members-1995-2015.pdf>, last accessed 06/16/2017.

[41] Eduardo J Gómez, *Contested Epidemics: Policy Response in Brazil and the U.S. and What the BRICS Can Learn* (Imperial College Press 2015), 260-262.

[42] Kurt Weyland, 'Social Movements and the State: The Politics of Healthcare Reform in Brazil' 23 *World Development* (1995) 1699-1712; Madel T Luz 'Políticas de Descentralização e Cidadania: Novas Práticas de Saúde no Brasil Atual' in Roseni Pinheiro and Ruben Araujo de Mattos (eds), *Os Sentidos da Integralidade na Atenção e no Cuidado à Saúde* (UERJ, IMS, ABRASCO 2001), 17f; André de Mello e Souza, 'Defying Globalization: Effective Self-Reliance in Brazil' in Paul G Harris and Patricia Siplon (eds), *The Global Politics of AIDS* (Lynne Rienner 2007), 38-40.

[43] Mello e Souza, 'Defying Globalization' (n 42); 'Saúde Pública'(n 4).

addresses cross-cutting issues, such as food quality and security and pharmaceutical patent rights, member engagement demands a larger number of permanent diplomatic staff assigned to the WHO, and it requires experts for all of these issues. Both countries are still unable to match the engagement of high-income countries in this regard.

Second, the WHO's growing dependency on private donors has undermined Brazil and Argentina's relative influence on agenda and priority setting.[44] Most notably, the contribution of the Bill and Melinda Gates Foundation to the WHO is double the combined contribution of Brazil and Argentina.[45] Since donation funding is earmarked, allowing the private donors to set the agenda through their donations, the relative agenda-setting power of governments (and most non-governmental stakeholders) from countries such as Brazil and Argentina has been diminished, even while the total resources available for global health might have increased. Indeed, private donations are directed towards specific projects, initiatives, or goals, and may 'distort the priorities defined by countries in the WHA'.[46]

Furthermore, Brazil's and Argentina's influence in the WHO has also been undercut by the for-profit private sector, capable of pressing forward several anti-counterfeiting WHA resolutions and of launching the International Medical Products Anti-Counterfeiting Taskforce in 2006, which deliberately ties the quality, efficacy, and safety of medicines to drug brands. All such initiatives involve pharmaceutical patenting contentions and go against the preferences of Brazil and Argentina.

Finally, the permanent employees of the WHO's secretariat are still largely from high-income countries, which volunteer most expert members of task forces who subsequently are incorporated in the organization. This is significant given the relative autonomy of the secretariat and its capacity to shape the dynamics of negotiations and to control access to key documents and information. For instance, among the duties incumbent upon the secretariat are the distribution of resolution drafts and reports, the divulgence of session programmes and agendas and generally the determination of decision-making arrangements, settings, and procedural details. Hence, diplomats need to stay in touch and maintain good working relations with secretariat members, something much more easily achieved if they share the same nationality and views on health policies and governance.[47]

15.2.5 Conclusion

The WHO is a very important global health institution for both Brazil and Argentina. These two countries have not only prioritized the WHO as the adequate venue for negotiations on wide ranging health-related issues, but have also defended the role of the

[44] In the 2014–2015 WHO budget proposal, only 23% of the financing came from member states; the remaining 77% came from voluntary private donations; see Sebastián Tobar, 'Governança da Saúde Global e Regional: OMS/OPAS' in Paulo Marchiori Buss and Sebastián Tobar (eds), *Diplomacia em Saúde e Saúde Global* (Editora Fiocruz 2017), 385-420, 395.

[45] WHO, 'Contributors' (n 9); the Gates Foundation also delivers the opening speech at the WHA.

[46] Tobar, 'Governança da Saúde' (n 44), 395.

[47] Andrade Filho interview (n 7).

organization in relation to other more recent global health institutions. For instance, they have supported the role of the WHO in setting the norms used by the Global Fund. They have also previously defended the WHO's mandate to harmonize pharmaceutical standards in opposition to the ICH. Finally, they have used the WHO to promote issue-linkages between public health, intellectual property rights and international trade, issues beforehand treated as pertaining exclusively to the WTO.

Brazil's growing participation in the WHO has manifested itself both through formal channels—such as increasing the monetary value of its contributions and the size of its delegation—as well as through informal means, such as Brazil's political and regional leadership in support of some noteworthy resolutions and initiatives, especially but not only with regard to HIV/AIDS. This participation has been conducted primarily by the government. It has resulted from Brazil's deliberate strategy to become a global player as well as from the higher volume of resources at its disposal, rather than from institutional reforms in the WHO. In terms of this book's analytical framework,[48] Brazil's participation in the WHO has been driven primarily by its growing capabilities and the importance it attributes to the organization, rather than by new opportunities to participate.

Generally, Brazil's level of actual participation and its influence on WHO decision-making has been higher than Argentina's, though this difference appears more pronounced in the WHO than in any of the other global health bodies discussed in this chapter. This may be attributable to the globalist orientation of Brazil's foreign policy, as well as its superior economic performance, at least from 2004 to 2011.

Even so, the two countries have very similar preferences, and there has been a high degree of cooperation and coordination between Brazil and Argentina in the WHO. Unlike Brazil, however, Argentina's international health policy appears to be less coherent and highly affected by political changes in the government.

Brazil and Argentina have also faced similar barriers to participation in the WHO. These countries still fall behind in terms of human and financial resources, and on some issues they face opposition, not just from the economically more powerful countries, but increasingly also from the private sector. Finally, the WHO secretariat is a significant, though informal and generally unnoticed, means through which high-income countries still retain negotiating influence. These considerations indicate how influence in the WHO is not just a function of formal representation, but also of the availability of resources and the occupation of certain key organizational positions.

15.3 Codex Alimentarius Commission (Codex)

15.3.1 Importance and Domestic Politics

The standards set by the Codex are of great importance to both Brazil and Argentina, not just because of their health impact but also because these countries are major

[48] DeMenno and Büthe, 'Voice and Influence' (n 6).

food producers and exporters. As of May 2017, the agricultural sector accounted for 49% of Brazilian exports and 23% of Brazil's GDP.[49] At the same time, agriculture accounted for 49% of Argentina's exports and 13% of Argentina's GDP.[50] As a result, these countries must respond to rapidly changing standards and certifications governing global agricultural markets, often developed by the Codex and the GlobalG.A.P., including quality requirements, packaging, safety, and even process attributes such as socially or environmentally friendly production methods.[51] The commercial implications of Codex (and GlobalG.A.P.) rulemaking and decision-making has therefore become a source of concern in Brazil and Argentina, especially because the standards they set can be applied in a discriminatory or protectionist manner.[52]

Argentina has been a member of the Codex since it was founded in 1963.[53] In 1949, the country had already proposed a Latin American food code.[54] Argentina actively participates in the Codex through the National Food Safety and Quality Service (SENASA), an independent agency of the government charged with surveillance, regulation, and certification of products of animal and plant origin and the prevention, eradication, and control of diseases and plagues that affect them.[55] At the national level, the National Directorate of International Agrifood Relations of the Ministry of

[49] MAPA, 'Soja Representa Quase 50% das Exportações Brasileiras do Agronegócio em Maio' <http://www.agricultura.gov.br/noticias/soja-representa-quase-50-das-exportacoes-brasileiras-do-agronegocio-em-maio>, last accessed 06/16/2017.

[50] TELAM 'El 46% de las exportaciones argentinas son granos, harinas, aceites y subproductos' <http://www.telam.com.ar/notas/201701/178197-exportaciones-granos-harinas-aceites-bolsa-rosario.html>, last accessed 07/03/2017; Codex Alimentarius Commission (Codex), *Codex Trust Fund Mid-Term Review: Final Report*, 30 April 2010, CX/CAC 10/33/14 Add.1, <http://www.who.int/foodsafety/codex/cac33_14_Add1e.pdf> last accessed 11/19/2019.

[51] Tim Büthe and Nathaniel Harris. 'The Codex Alimentarius Commission: A Hybrid Public-Private Regulator' in Thomas Hale and David Held (eds), *Handbook of Transnational Governance* (Polity Press 2011), 219-228.

[52] Notably, Brazil is among the developing countries with the largest number of agricultural imports rejections in the United States and the EU. From 2011 until April 2018, food exports of Brazil and Argentina to the United States have been detained twenty-eight and fourteen times, respectively. From January to October 2019 alone, Brazil and Argentina have been notified to the WTO SPS Committee fourteen and twelve times, respectively. Challenges to these rejections based on agricultural standards are also reflected in WTO complaints. USFDA, 'Import Refusal Report' <www.fda.gov/ora/oasis/ora_oasis_ref.html>, last accessed 06/16/2017; USFDA, 'Import Alerts for a Country/Area' <https://www.accessdata.fda.gov/cms_ia/country_br.html> and <https://www.accessdata.fda.gov/cms_ia/country_ar.html>, last accessed 11/19/2019; WTO, 'Sanitary and Phytosanitary Information Management System', <http://spsims.wto.org/en/PredefinedReports/NotificationSummary>, last accessed 10/30/2019. See also Steven Jaffee and Spencer Henson, 'Standards and Agro-Food Exports from Developing Countries Rebalancing the Debate' *World Bank Policy Research Working Paper* No. 3348 (2004), 19, 23; Tim Büthe, 'The Politics of Food Safety in the Age of Global Trade: The Codex Alimentarius Commission in the SPS-Agreement of the WTO' in Cary Coglianese, Adam Finkel, and David Zaring (eds), *Import Safety: Regulatory Governance in the Global Economy* (University of Pennsylvania Press 2009) 88-109.

[53] 'List of Codex Members' <http://www.fao.org/fao-who-codexalimentarius/about-codex/members/en/>, last accessed 03/30/2016.

[54] FAO, 'Understanding the Codex Alimentarius' <http://www.fao.org/3/a-i5667e.pdf>, last accessed 05/30/2018.

[55] SENASA, 'Relaciones Internacionales' <http://www.senasa.gov.ar/institucional/relaciones-internacionales>, last accessed 05/30/2018.

Agroindustry is the Codex Contact Point in the country.[56] This Codex Contact Point has strong political backing and close links to the food and agroindustry confederations and many research centres in the country.[57]

Brazil became a Codex member state in 1968. It is represented by the Ministry of Foreign Affairs, the national drug regulatory and health surveillance agency ANVISA, the Ministry of Agriculture, Livestock and Food Supply (MAPA) and the governmental standards setting and enforcing institute, the National Institute of Metrology, Quality and Technology (INMETRO). INMETRO leads the Brazilian Committee of the Codex Alimentarius (CCAB), founded in 1980, in which industry associations and universities are also represented.

Historically, technical food regulations have been a source of tensions and disputes between Brazilian government bodies that are primarily concerned with promoting agricultural exports, especially MAPA, and regulatory bodies that prioritize safety and public health concerns, most notably ANVISA. While ANVISA tends to adopt a more precautionary position regarding food additives, contaminants, growth promoting substances and the like, MAPA claims that, unless conclusively proven to represent a threat to human health, these should not be proscribed.[58] Because of this dispute within the Brazilian government, INMETRO, which deals with general standards and regulations, and is considered more impartial, has been selected as the head of the CCAB.[59]

Notwithstanding INMETRO's de jure leadership, MAPA has generally prevailed because it has been better able to organize itself and allocate resources, both financial and human, for the purpose of shaping Brazil's position in the Codex. Notably, unlike ANVISA, MAPA also benefits from the support of the Brazilian private agricultural sector and acts on its behest. As a consequence, Brazil has generally favoured less stringent standards in the Codex.

Both Brazil and Argentina have generally supported permissive standards regarding genetically modified food products, since they are the second and third most important growers of biotechnology-intensive, transgenic crops.[60]

Brazilian representatives also note that they view the Codex Alimentarius General Subject Committees as much more politicized than its Commodity Committees, which tend to be more technical.[61]

[56] FAO, 'Codex Alimentarius' <http://www.fao.org/fao-who-codexalimentarius/about-codex/members/detail/en/c/15588/>, last accessed 05/30/2018.

[57] Codex, *Codex Trust Fund Mid-Term Review* (n 50).

[58] In-person interviews with Renata Motta (Berlin, 21 May 2016) and with Patricia Oliveira Pereira (Brasilia, 24 October 2016).

[59] Oliveira Pereira interview (n 58).

[60] Elisabetta Piqué 'La Argentina se pronunció a favor de los alimentos transgénicos' *La Nación* (12 June 2002) <http://www.lanacion.com.ar/404600-la-argentina-se-pronuncio-a-favor-de-los-alimentos-transgenicos>, last accessed 04/14/2020; Moises Burachik, 'Regulation of GM Crops in Argentina' 3(1) *GM Crops & Food* (2012) 48-51.

[61] Motta interview (n 58) and Oliveira Pereira interview (n 58).

15.3.2 Institutional Reforms

The Codex Trust Funds (CTF) aimed to remove barriers to participation of developing countries by granting 'financial support that enabled such countries to physically attend Codex meetings' (CTF 1) and by 'improv[ing] their technical capacity' (CTF 2), thereby enabling a meaningful participation in the standards development process.

Although Brazil was eligible to apply for support from the CTF 1, it opted not to do so. ANVISA and MAPA usually send two representatives to Codex Committee meetings; when there are budget cuts, they send only one representative; but very rarely do financial constraints prevent Brazil's Codex participation. For this reason, Brazil prefers to let other Latin American members that possess fewer resources and hold similar positions in the Codex benefit from CTF 1. Since the most contentious decisions are taken by majority vote of the members, Brazil considers the participation of like-minded Latin American neighbours in its best interest.[62]

Argentina has had three participants financed in Codex meetings, but it belonged to group 3b of upper-middle-income countries and graduated very early.[63] Hence, the CTF has had no meaningful impact on Argentina's Codex participation.[64] Had the CTF used more of its funds for research, Argentina could have benefited and offered more meaningful Codex participation.[65]

With respect to CTF 2, neither Brazil nor Argentina has been eligible to apply for funding because the countries were neither classified as 'low & medium' on the Human Development Index (HDI), nor are they small island or landlocked developing countries.[66]

15.3.3 Barriers to Participation

Notwithstanding Argentina's long-existing (albeit stagnant) and Brazil's increasing interest and involvement in Codex, both countries still face two sets of mutually reinforcing barriers to participation. The first of these is related to institutional features of Codex, and the second to their own resource and capacity constraints. Both countries' inability to occupy the chairmanship of Codex committees is the most important institutional barrier, whereas resource and capacity constraints curtail their ability to produce data and research based on which these committees' recommendations are made.

[62] Oliveira Pereira interview (n 58).
[63] Codex, *Codex Trust Fund Mid-Term Review* (n 50).
[64] Codex, *Codex Trust Fund Mid-Term Review* (n 50).
[65] Codex, *Codex Trust Fund Mid-Term Review* (n 50).
[66] Codex, 'Codex Trust Fund-2 (CTF2) Table of Eligible Countries' <http://www.who.int/foodsafety/areas_work/food-standard/CTF-EligibilityTable.pdf>, accessed 05/30/2018.

Both Brazil and Argentina view committee chairs as holding much power regarding procedural rules, agenda setting, and decision-making processes. By the time the Commission considers a certain issue, the substantive discussions have already taken place in the technical committee to which the issue was assigned—and the Commission usually only takes an up or down vote on the committee's proposal.[67]

Yet, committee chairs are for the most part from high-income countries. Nominating them is no simple matter since it requires financial and human resources to set up a secretariat and organize the meetings.[68] Currently, of all Latin American and Caribbean members, only Mexico chairs one permanent committee. Brazil and Argentina have, however, co-hosted several meetings.[69]

This problem is compounded by the fact that there is very low rotation in committee chairs. Indeed, some committee chairmanships are in effect held indefinitely by high-income countries, such as that of the Committee on Milk and Milk Products, held by New Zealand, and that of the Committee on Natural Mineral Waters held by Switzerland, purportedly due to the influence of Nestlé. While in theory committee chairs can be replaced, in practice this has never happened.[70]

Furthermore, technical discussions within Codex Committees require data and research, usually financed by the food industry of high-income countries, and used to promote its interests.[71] Brazil and Argentina do not have sufficient resources to regularly conduct studies necessary to support their positions in the Codex. Consequently, the three FAO/WHO expert committees that support the work of the Codex [72] conduct studies based almost exclusively on data from the US, Europe, and Japan. The results of these studies are not always applicable to populations from other countries and regions. Indeed, the Brazilian population has different eating habits, in terms of proportion of protein and carbohydrate intake, for example, than those of the high-income member countries that hold entrenched positions within this global health governance body.[73]

In a deliberate response to these shortcomings, ANVISA in 2010 led Brazilian universities in an initiative to generate data on the safe use of aflatoxin, based on which a proposal concerning the limits of this contaminant in Brazil nuts was submitted to, and endorsed by, the Joint FAO/WHO Meeting on Pesticide Residues, leading to the approval of a new standard in the Codex.[74] This decision benefited Brazilian Brazil nut producers.[75]

[67] A Brazilian diplomat reported in a not-for-attribution interview that he knows of no other international organization amenable to as much manipulation by its chairmanship as the Codex. Not-for-attribution interview, Brasilia, 21 November 2016.

[68] Gerald G Sander, 'Codex Alimentarius Commission (CAC)' in *Max Planck Encyclopedia of Public International Law* (MPEPIL 2016), par. 10 <https://opil.ouplaw.com/view/10.1093/law:epil/9780199231690/law-9780199231690-e1857?prd=OPIL>, accessed 05/30/2018.

[69] Ricardo Molins (ed), *Codex Alimentarius: Handbook of Best Practices in Negotiations* (Inter-American Institute for Cooperation on Agriculture 2009) 34.

[70] Oliveira Pereira interview (n 58).

[71] Motta interview (n 58) and Oliveira Pereira interview (n 58).

[72] The committees are the Joint FAO/WHO Expert Committee on Food Additives (JECFA), the Joint FAO/WHO Meeting on Pesticide Residues (JMPR), and the Joint FAO/WHO Expert Meetings on Microbiological Risk Assessment (JEMRA).

[73] Motta interview (n 58) and Oliveira Pereira interview (n 58).

[74] Motta interview (n 58) and Oliveira Pereira interview (n 58).

[75] In 2002, non-compliance with the European aflatoxin standards accounted for fifty-one cases of import rejections of Brazilian Brazil nuts; see Jaffee and Henson, 'Standards and Agro-Food Exports' (n 52), 31.

Similarly, MAPA played an important role in the 2012 decision to increase a residue limit for ractopamine hydrochloride, a controversial drug used in the feed of cattle and swine, after years of political deadlock. It made it easier for Brazil, the world's largest meat exporter, to challenge the EU, China, and other countries that have zero tolerance policies for ractopamine residues in meat products, including in the ambit of the WTO.[76]

While Brazil's participation and influence in Codex has in recent years increased, Argentina's participation in the Codex has been undermined by a lack of resources, though it has found ways to overcome some of those constraints. Generally, Argentina has sought to address the information asymmetries in technical knowledge by mobilizing other developing countries. In the period from 1990 to 2010, it did so by commenting on the documents, giving a very thorough follow-up to the discussions, translating negotiations into simple language, and demonstrating the impact that negotiations would have on these countries.

A strategy to overcome barriers to participation adopted by both Brazil and Argentina was the creation of the Codex Coordinating Committee for Latin America and the Caribbean (CCLAC). Through the CCLAC, delegates meet yearly to determine strategies and identify subjects of mutual interest in order to coordinate joint positions and thereby exert greater influence over international food standards. Argentina was Coordinator of the CCLAC and regional representative in the Codex Executive Committee, for which it was elected.[77]

15.3.4 Conclusions and Final Considerations

The Codex is very important for Brazil and Argentina, as its technical, negotiated norms significantly impact their agricultural export earnings and opportunities. Nonetheless, the participation of these countries in the Codex has been undermined both by institutional barriers and by lack of resources and expertise. Crucially, the two trust funds have benefited Brazil and Argentina very little and only indirectly. As was the case in the WHO, Brazil and Argentina have resorted to a regional institution, CCLAC, as a means of overcoming barriers to participation in the Codex and of enhancing collective action capacity. In terms of the analytical framework offered by DeMenno and Büthe,[78] participation in Codex has high salience for both Brazil and Argentina, but the reforms Codex adopted in recent years have offered these countries no new institutional opportunities for participation, and they are still lacking in capabilities due to a shortage of material and scientific resources.

[76] Alberto Alemanno and Giuseppe Capodieci, 'Testing the Limits of Global Food Governance: The Case of Ractopamine' 3(3) *European Journal of Risk Regulation* (2012) 400-407.

[77] Gabriela A Catalani, 'Argentina y las negociaciones internacionales en el Codex Alimentarius: Integración y principios' (2008) <http://www.alimentosargentinos.gob.ar/contenido/revista/ediciones/42/articulos/r42_16_Codex.pdf>, last accessed 11/19/2019.

[78] DeMenno and Büthe, Voice and Influence' (n 6)

15.4 International Council for Harmonization (ICH)

15.4.1 Importance, Preferences and Participation: Membership Has (Some) Privileges

Both Brazil and Argentina have a growing stake in the export of pharmaceuticals. While pharmaceuticals accounted for only 0.58% and 0.89%, respectively, of Brazilian and Argentine exports in 2017, they are seen as a growth industry,[79] making the ICH important for both countries insofar as its standards govern manufacturers' access to international markets.

At the same time, Brazil and Argentina have long seen the ICH as a body inimical to their interests. Ever since it was set up in 1990, both countries have harshly criticized the ICH for promoting standards for the production of medicines which, under the pretext of ensuring drug safety, quality, and efficacy, can only be met by the pharmaceutical industry of its founding members. Considering the ICH was created to keep developing countries' pharmaceutical manufacturers out of global markets, Brazil and Argentina preferred discussing drug guideline harmonization within the ambit of the WHO.

As Brazilian pharmaceutical firms expanded and began to compete in the global economy, however, their product portfolios have increasingly become geared towards the more stringently regulated markets of industrialized countries.[80] This industrial transformation eventually prompted Brazil to join the ICH; for similar reasons, Argentina is considering applying for membership.

In 2009 Brazil's ANVISA became a member of the ICH's Global Cooperation Group (GCG), which gave it access to the working groups. It then joined the ICH as an observer in 2015—a step enabled by the recent ICH institutional reforms aimed at integrating emerging countries. In 2016, ANVISA became a full regulatory member, which entitled it to nominate a representative to each working group.[81]

Brazil expects its ICH membership to enable ANVISA to participate in the formulation of new ICH guidelines and to influence the revision of existing guidelines, as well as to more effectively oppose norms that are merely veiled market barriers to Brazilian pharmaceutical exports. Additionally, ANVISA seeks to inform the national pharmaceutical industry about ICH guidelines, their elaboration process, and their impact.[82] Brazil thus hopes to make the transition from rule-taker to rule-maker and to increase Brazilian companies' share of the largest pharmaceutical markets.

[79] For instance, pharmaceutical exports of Argentina have increased 147% from 2003 to 2009, see Alexander Simões, The Observatory: Designing Data-Driven Decision-Making Tools (Masters Thesis, MIT 2012), see also The Observatory of Economic Complexity <https://oec.world/en/resources/about>, last accessed 08/11/2021.

[80] Carlos Cezar Flores Vidotti, Lia Lusitana Cardozo de Castro, and Simone Saad Calil, 'New Drugs in Brazil: Do They Meet Brazilian Public Health Needs?' 24 *Revista Panamericana de Salud Publica* (2008) 36-45; UNCTAD, *Local Production of Pharmaceuticals and Related Technology Transfer in Developing Countries: A Series of Case Studies by the UNCTAD Secretariat.* (UNCTAD 2011), 6 <http://unctad.org/en/PublicationsLibrary/diaepcb2011d7_en.pdf>, last accessed 06/16/2017.

[81] UNCTAD, *Local Production* (n 80).

[82] Oliveira Pereira interview (n 58).

At the same time, ICH membership is economically and potentially politically costly for Brazil. As a member, Brazil must implement existing ICH standards which diverge substantially from its own regulatory framework. Although it has complied with the first three set of guidelines, certain testing requirements are still outstanding, and the next phases of membership require Brazil's compliance with five additional guidelines in five years, and subsequently a commitment to comply with the remainder of the over sixty guidelines which the ICH seeks to harmonize.[83] This process largely lacks enforcement mechanisms, relying mostly on trust; while monitoring could be carried out by the private pharmaceutical sector, it is not at this time—at least not in Brazil.

Argentina, by contrast, has so far remained more of a rule taker. Its *Administración Nacional de Medicamentos, Alimentos y Tecnología Médica* (ANMAT)[84] has been an ICH 'invited regulatory authority', but has participated primarily through the Regional Harmonisation Initiative of the Pan American Network for Drug Regulatory Harmonization (PANDRH), an ICH-linked regional forum to foster the use of ICH standards. In 2019, ANMAT became an ICH observer, but Argentina is still developing a strategy for joining the ICH. Like Brazil, it hopes to influence ICH standards which create technical and commercial barriers to pharmaceutical production and export, and impact medicine prices, but does not want ICH to impose costly constraints on its domestic health policy.

15.4.2 Participation and Influence in the Aftermath of the Reforms

ICH institutional reforms have facilitated membership and hence—for Brazil, though not (yet) for Argentina—involvement in discussions and decisions. However, Brazilian representatives are finding membership insufficient for achieving equality with the founding members in ICH decision-making (via the input or throughput channel) or even just inclusivity (in the spirit of greater output legitimacy). Crucially, the US, Japan, and Europe, and their pharmaceutical industry associations retain decision-making control thanks to their veto power and permanent membership in the ICH Management Committee. In contrast, new country members such as Brazil have no veto power, have fixed mandates in the Management Committee, and need to be re-elected to retain committee membership.[85]

The Management Committee is important because its members negotiate among themselves the themes to be addressed, define the ICH's work plan and what should be included in new guidelines, make recommendations to the Assembly, and generally exercise wide-ranging agenda-setting power. In practice, it is difficult to oppose or reject Management Committee recommendations because most Assembly members have not taken part in this preceding negotiation process, have not had access to all the relevant information, and have not been adequately prepared to present

[83] Oliveira Pereira interview (n 58).

[84] Administración Nacional de Medicatentos, Alimentos y Tecnología Médica, Argentina <http://www.anmat.gov.ar/principal.asp>, last accessed 02/22/2017.

[85] However, to date ANVISA has not applied for Management Committee membership (*ICH Articles of Association*, 9 November 2016, <http://www.ich.org/fileadmin/Public_Web_Site/ABOUT_ICH/Articles_Procedures/ICH_Articles_of_Association_for_Assembly_final_9Nov2016.pdf>, last accessed 06/16/2017.

counter-proposals. Hence, though presented as an essentially managerial body by the founding members, the Committee exerts much influence over the substance of the guidelines to be harmonized.[86]

During the ICH reform process, ANVISA called for greater inclusiveness and representativeness of the Management Committee. The only concession made in this regard was that new members may now submit their candidacy after two years of membership and, if elected by Assembly members, they will be granted Management Committee membership for a four-year term.[87] It remains to be seen how applications under these new rules will fare.

Finally, ICH's rules require that pharmaceutical industry associations be represented in the three regions of the founding country members in order to be eligible for ICH membership. In practice, these requirements prevent Brazil's pharmaceutical associations from becoming ICH members. Such membership would be important for Brazil not just because it would allow its industry to directly have a say in the elaboration of guidelines and to defend norms that are more applicable in the country, but also because it would represent an opportunity for this industry to build technical capacity.[88]

15.4.3 Conclusions

Of all the global health institutions examined in this chapter, the ICH undoubtedly has implemented the most consequential reforms. By enabling the membership of developing countries, these reforms are expected to significantly boost to unprecedented levels the participation of Brazil—and possibly Argentina. As a consequence of providing countries such as Brazil with a chance to have more of a voice, the input received by the ICH working groups now reflects a greater diversity of perspectives and positions. Hence, in terms of the analytical framework adopted in this volume, the ICH allowed Brazil (and possibly Argentina in the near future) to join as a member in order to enable the choice or design of better policies. ICH reforms may also ensure support for implementation of its standards in key emerging markets.

The reforms did not go far enough, however, to afford even a large emerging power such as Brazil real influence, as decision-making power remains concentrated on the founding member countries and their industry associations. It also has been the experience of the Brazilian representative in ICH that having a larger number of participants increases the time taken to reach decisions in working groups as well as the costs of their meetings. For instance, the Expert Working Group on Pharmaceutical Lifecycle Management has about fifty participants.[89] These efficiency shortcomings

[86] Oliveira Pereira interview (n 58).

[87] Oliveira Pereira interview (n 58); ICH, International Council for Harmonization of Technical Requirements for Pharmaceuticals for Human Use Articles of Association (9 November 2016). <http://www.ich.org/fileadmin/Public_Web_Site/ABOUT_ICH/Articles_Procedures/ICH_Articles_of_Association_for_Assembly_final_9Nov2016.pdf>, last accessed 06/16/2017.

[88] Interview with Oliveira Pereira (n 58).

[89] Interview with Oliveira Pereira (n 58).

are bound to increase as ICH membership expands and may undermine the greater influence of new members such as Brazil.

15.5 Global Fund to Fight AIDS, Tuberculosis and Malaria (Global Fund)

15.5.1 Importance, Preferences, and Participation

Argentina has had a representative serving on the Global Fund Board, Mirta Roses Periago; the Brazilian Ministry of Health had been a Board member until the 6th Meeting in 2004.[90] Despite initially strong interest, engagement and even influence in the Global Fund (and continued participation via the board member in the case of Argentina), both Brazil and Argentina have ceased to depend on Global Fund's resources or to be involved in its operations as donors or recipients during the last five years. As was the case with the CTF, funding and other institutional reforms have not, for these reasons, significantly impacted the participation of these countries in the Global Fund.

Brazil is one of the Global Fund's founding members and played an active and influential role in its creation. Brazilian government representatives participated in the G-8 meeting in Okinawa in June 2000, when the French government originally proposed the Global Fund. The first meetings for the design of the Global Fund took place in parallel with the UN General Assembly Special Session in July 2001 and involved potential high-income donor countries, as well as Brazil. In order to structure the Global Fund, a transitional group was created consisting of technicians assigned by several countries, including Brazil.[91]

Brazil endorsed the Global Fund as a vehicle for promoting the expansion of the international market for antiretroviral drugs. At the same time, the global recognition of Brazil's model as a blueprint for fighting HIV/AIDS increased its legitimacy and bargaining power in shaping the governance of the Global Fund.[92] Hence, Brazil's objectives and strategies in the Global Fund were very similar to those in UNAIDS and UNITAID, as previously discussed in Section 15.2.

Argentina likewise initially played an active role in the Global Fund, also with the primary goal of gaining support for its position on universal and free access to antiretroviral drugs. The Global Fund considers Argentina a high-income country that has transitioned from Global Fund support to government-supported programmes.

Brazil likewise is considered no longer eligible for Global Fund support. It received approximately USD 48 million from the Global Fund until its last disbursement in July 2014.

[90] Global Fund, 'Global Fund Board Members' <https://www.theglobalfund.org/en/board/members/>, last accessed 10/16/2021.

[91] Lindinalva Laurindo Teodorescu and Paulo Roberto Teixeira, *Histórias da AIDS no Brasil 1983—2003 - Volume I: As Respostas Governamentais à Epidemia de AIDS* (Ministério da Saúde 2015), 447–449.

[92] Mello e Souza, 'Saúde Pública'(n 4).

The Global Fund has sought further participation and support from all the BRICS both as donors and as partners in fighting the three infectious diseases, especially after 2012. Not only were the BRICS increasingly seen as potential donors due to their substantial share of global economic growth, they also were countries with a high incidence of HIV/AIDS, tuberculosis, and malaria. However, neither Brazil nor Argentina became Global Fund funders—partly due to governmental budgetary, legal, and administrative structures that do not allow for making donations to international public-private partnerships, as Brazil's experience failing to donate to the Global Alliance for Vaccines and Immunization also illustrates.[93]

Global Fund grants to Brazil were used to implement projects that decentralized the control and management of tuberculosis and malaria; strengthened advocacy, social mobilization, and training regarding these epidemics; and provided much needed visibility to tuberculosis.[94] In the case of Argentina, the Global Fund's grants assigned to that country were limited in number and were directed mainly to expand access to drug therapies.

Although the WHO defines most technical standards and procedures in policies to fight AIDS, tuberculosis, and malaria, and despite formal rules ensuring equality and transparency in decision-making among board members, Brazilian representatives believe that major donors of the Global Fund have disproportionate influence over the allocation of funds and over which kinds of projects will benefit from them. They also believe that the Global Fund's model should be more flexible and adapt its operations to the complexities and multiple challenges that require emerging countries to deal with serious internal health problems while having rapidly increasing know-how and still very limited financial resources to contribute to actions at the global level.[95]

15.5.2 Impact on Domestic Governance

Despite being relatively small and short-lived, Global Fund funding has helped to positively transform health governance in Brazil by increasing political attention and commitment to tuberculosis. Notably, the grant requirement that tuberculosis–HIV/AIDS co-infection be addressed created incentives for greater collaboration between previously uncooperative national tuberculosis and HIV/AIDS programmes. Global Fund financial support also allowed the National Tuberculosis Programme (NTP) to hire more staff, mostly from the National HIV/AIDS Programme, reinforcing cooperation between the two programmes.[96]

[93] Brazil has, however, partly reimbursed the Global Fund; see Jamil Chade, 'Fundo Global de Luta Contra a Aids Quer Brasil como Doador' *O Estado de São Paulo* 3 May 2011, <http://www.estadao.com.br/noticias/geral,fundo-global-de-luta-contra-a-aids-quer-brasil-como-doador-imp-,714133>, last accessed 04/17/2018; Andrade Filho interview (n 7).

[94] Maureen Lewis, Pedro Chequer and Anna Bonfert, *Sustainability of Global Fund Supported Programs: What Happened Before and After the Global Fund Left Brazil? Brazil Country Case Study* (Acesoglobal July 2015) <https://static1.squarespace.com/static/56116c1ce4b0890ee92cf835/t/57e41d10197aea3f4edafc42/1474567443615/Brazil+Country+Study.pdf>, last accessed 06/16/2017.

[95] Andrade Filho interview (n 7).

[96] In 2005 a special division was created within the NTP to strengthen its partnership with the National HIV/AIDS Programme.

In addition, the Global Fund's periodic evaluation of the Country Coordinating Mechanism performance for grant renewal has improved inter-governmental relations by encouraging the Ministry of Health to strengthen its ties with state and municipal health departments and NGOs. This is particularly important given the financial and administrative challenges of devolution in health policy implementation in a country as large and populous as Brazil.[97] Finally, at the community level, the Global Fund's requirement of civil society involvement in funded projects led to the emergence of new movements, networks and the creation of new municipal participatory institutions intended to monitor its financing, fostering 'a greater commitment to civil engagement, empowerment and accountability'.[98] Argentina, having only received very small, highly targeted grants, did not experience such effects.

15.5.3 Conclusions and Final Considerations

As a recent and highly innovative health governance body, the Global Fund has from the outset provided a much greater degree of inclusivity and equality in decision-making than the other institutions addressed in this chapter. Indeed, Brazil and Argentina helped to bring forth the Global Fund. However, given that these countries were neither sufficiently deprived to be eligible for substantial Global Fund funding nor sufficiently well-off to donate to the fund, they subsequently became unengaged and renounced any influence in Global Fund-based health governance. Given this fading importance of the Global Fund for Brazil and Argentina, the analytical framework adopted in this book would lead us to expect, as actually happened, lower incentives and desires for these countries' participation in this global health institution. Moreover, the reforms undertaken by the Global Fund to increase stakeholder participation, regardless of their merit as such, had no impact whatsoever on the participation of Brazil and Argentina. Nevertheless, within Brazil, the Global Fund produced a significant offshoot in strengthening the NTP, promoting inter-governmental cooperation and empowering community-level participatory institutions.

15.6 Global Good Agricultural Practices (GlobalG.A.P.)

15.6.1 Importance and Preferences Regarding GlobalG.A.P. Certification

The GlobalG.A.P. is commercially important for both Brazil and Argentina. Meeting its standards facilitates agricultural goods' access to foreign markets and creates better business opportunities. Conversely, non-compliance is increasingly used to keep imports out of these markets. Although the GlobalG.A.P.'s food standards are in principle

[97] Eduardo J Gómez and Rifat Atun, 'The Effects of Global Fund Financing on Health Governance in Brazil' 8 *Globalization and Health* (16 July 2012) <http://www.globalizationandhealth.com/content/8/1/25>, accessed 06/24/2017, 7; Lewis *et al.*, *Sustainability* (n 94), 3.

[98] Gómez and Atun, 'Effects of Global Fund Financing' (n 97), 8.

voluntary, they have in practice become mandatory since meeting the standards is a pre-requisite for access to the European market.[99] Argentina and Brazil—along with a handful of other emerging economies—account for most WTO complaints against the EU related to the adoption of private food standards by EU retailers.[100] Here and in other contexts, they take the position that GlobalG.A.P. standards are more stringent than Codex standards, and argue that, in case of conflict, Codex standards should prevail.[101]

In addition, the dramatic growth in supermarket shares of food retail in both Brazil and Argentina in the 1990s[102] meant the emergence of demanding new procurement channels and the decline of smaller informal markets that would more willingly agree to take both small quantities and varying qualities of food from farmers and distributors. Yet, small producers in Brazil and Argentina often lack the technical and administrative capacities needed for compliance with the newly required standards.

There is a plethora of agricultural certification schemes available for Brazilian producers and retailers. In a few agricultural sectors, they have attempted to use alternative standards, instead of or in combination with the ones set by the GlobalG.A.P. In some sectors, such as coffee and fruit production, Brazil even created its own certification schemes.[103] Yet, there is generally much overlap between different agricultural certifications, and the GlobalG.A.P. has become the largest private certification institution in terms of geographical reach and commercial significance, especially geared towards global markets.

GlobalG.A.P. standards affect the earnings of large and small producers differently, as, for example, revealed by case studies of fruit production in Brazil.[104] In particular, only the large and integrated enterprises can afford to install and invest in new systems of monitoring, both of labour and of production and processing activities.[105] This forces small independent producers to engage with the large export-oriented businesses, creating dependencies. Furthermore, the expansion of GlobalG.A.P. certification exacerbates the intense competition for export markets, making it more difficult for small independent producers—which often lack the technical and administrative capacities needed for compliance with more stringent standards—to maintain their export markets outlets and the necessary relationships with the export and packing

[99] Ana Cristina Carrera, 'GlobalG.A.P. and Agricultural Producers: Bridging Latin America and the European Union' 21 *Drake Journal of Agricultural Law* (2016) 155-176, 163.

[100] Spencer Henson and Steven Jaffee, 'Understanding Developing Country Strategic Responses to the Enhancement of Food Safety Standards' 31(4) *World Economy* (2008) 548-568, 556.

[101] Sam F Halabi and Ching-Fu Lin, 'Assessing the Relative Influence and Efficacy of Public and Private Food Safety Regulation Regimes: Comparing Codex and GlobalG.A.P. Standards' 72(2) *Food and Drug Law Journal* (2017) 262-294.

[102] Thomas Reardon, Peter Timmer and Julio Berdegue, 'The Rapid Rise of Supermarkets in Developing Countries: Induced Organizational, Institutional, and Technological Change in Agrifood Systems' 1(2) *Journal of Agricultural and Development Economics* (2004) 168-183.

[103] Andrea Cristina Dorr and Ulrike Grote, 'The Role of Certification in the Brazilian Fruit Sector' 13(3) *Revista de Economia Contemporânea* (2009) 539-571; Hely Corrêa de Rezende, *Modelos de Certificação de Produtos e Propriedades Cafeeiras no Brasil* (Honours thesis, Universidade Federal de Lavras 2011).

[104] Nicolien M Van Der Grijp, Terry Marsden, and Josefa Salete Barbosa Cavalcanti, 'European Retailers as Agents of Change Towards Sustainability: The Case of Fruit Production in Brazil' 2(1) *Environmental Sciences* (2005) 31-46.

[105] Berman, 'Stakeholder Participation Reforms' (n 2).

house firms. As a result, many such producers are turning to the secondary domestic market, which is free from such regulations but, due to lower prices, also limits the producers' gains.[106]

15.6.2 Membership, Participation, and Influence

Participation of Brazilian and Argentine stakeholders in GlobalG.A.P. rule-making and decision-making is a direct consequence of institutional reforms aimed at expanding the membership of what was previously EuropG.A.P. Their actual participation is, however, still limited to a few stakeholders,[107] which is at least in part because the membership categories most accessible for Brazilian and Argentine firms confer only non-decisional rights.[108]

Within the two membership categories that grant decision-making powers in the GlobalG.A.P., neither country has a representative in the retailers and food service category (*Arcos Dourados*—McDonald's Latin America Brazil—was a member for several years); Brazil has four representatives in the producers and supplier category (*Agrivale Agricultura do Vale*, *Seara Alimentos*, *Sweet Fruits*, and *Terra Viva*), as does Argentina: *Citromax S.A.C.I.*, *COPEXEU*, *Patagonian Fruits Trade*, and *S.A. San Miguel*.[109]

The Brazilian members are all large exporting firms from the meat and fruits sectors, which target the global market and source in the region. Their efforts to increase producer compliance with GlobalG.A.P. standards are, hence, a direct consequence of their global commercial realities. *Arcos Dourados*, for example, as the largest restaurant operator in Latin America and the most important McDonald's franchise in the world, has a stake in GlobalG.A.P.: it is a key component of McDonald's Quality Systems and allegedly harmonizes the best global practices in agriculture. Accordingly, in 2014 GlobalG.A.P. introduced, in cooperation with *Arcos Dourados*, the G.A.P. in Action Project, an initiative to promote these practices in Peru, Brazil, and Argentina. Although formally a representative of Brazil, *Arcos Dourados* has close links with its US franchisor and transfers part of its earnings abroad to this franchisor.[110]

Similarly, Seara is a unit of JBS, the world's largest meat processing company, specializing in poultry, pork, turkeys, and processed foods. Its compliance with GlobalG.A.P. standards has been particularly important in allowing it to expand poultry exports to the EU. Seara is a member of the 'Livestock Technical Committee' at GlobalG.A.P., which discusses global animal welfare parameters.[111]

[106] Van Der Grijp *et al.*, 'European Retailers' (n 104).

[107] Argentina has six associate members, Brazil has five; see Instituto Argentino de Normalizacion y Certificacion <www.iram.com.ar> and GlobalG.A.P. 'Associate Members' <http://www.globalgap.org/uk_en/who-we-are/members/associates/>, last accessed 10/22/2021.

[108] Berman, 'Stakeholder Participation Reforms' (n 2); DeMenno and Büthe (n 6).

[109] GlobalG.A.P. 'Producer & Supplier Members' <http://www.globalgap.org/uk_en/who-we-are/members/supplier/>, last accessed 10/16/2021.

[110] GlobalG.A.P. 'Producer & Supplier Members' (n 109).

[111] JBS, *Annual Sustainability Report 2016* <http://jbss.infoinvest.com.br/enu/4070/JBS%20RAS%202016%20EN%20170502%20Final.pdf>, last accessed 02/22/2017.

The Argentine members are also large exporting firms, mostly from the fruit sector. COPEXEU is an association of agricultural producers focused on exporting fresh fruits and vegetables to the United State and Mexico; *Citromax* is one of the world's leading producers of lemons and its derivatives, such as juices and oils.[112] *Patagonian Fruits* is a leading export company of apples, pears, kiwi, and grapes, both in traditional and organic production markets; San Miguel a major exporter of fresh lemons, oranges, mandarins, and grapefruits, as well as various citrus fruit products.[113]

Brazil and Argentina's participation in the National Technical Working Groups (NTWG) is similarly low, with only one Argentine and four Brazilian participants.[114]

The Global GAP Risk-Assessment on Social Practice (GRASP) National Interpretation Guidelines has developed specific guidelines for Argentina[115] and for Brazil.[116] These were created to assess social practices on the farm, addressing specific aspects of workers' health, safety, and welfare, with national regulations as a basis.

Argentine stakeholders have indicated that a significant obstacle to their participation in GlobalG.A.P. are the costs of full participation, not only in terms of membership but also the cost of travel and accommodations for participation in the meetings. To encourage or at least facilitate input from domestic stakeholders, Argentina, Brazil, and other Latin American countries have organized national and regional groups. They also brought their concerns regarding this issue to GlobalG.A.P., but so far to no avail, demonstrating their limited influence at the international level.

15.6.3 Conclusions and Final Considerations

Similarly to the ICH, applying the DeMenno and Büthe's analytical framework to the GlobalG.A.P. institutional reforms suggests that extended membership rights to Brazilian and Argentine stakeholders aimed at improving policy choice or design and at allowing support for implementation of its standards in key emerging markets.

Yet, despite efforts to globalize its membership base beyond Europe, the GlobalG.A.P. is still dominated by European producers and retailers, which in practice lead the standard setting processes.[117] Indeed, European firms account for 93% of all retailer members, and 72% of all producer/supplier members.[118]

Unlike European members, which tend to be already in compliance with most of the norms established by the GlobalG.A.P., Brazilian and Argentine current or potential

[112] Citromax, 'Cirtromax' <https://www.citromax.com>, last accessed 10/20/2021.

[113] Patagonian Fruits, 'Frutas De Excelencia' <http://patagonianfruits.com> and S.A. SAN MIGUEL A.G.I.C.I. y F., 'About Us' https://www.sanmiguelglobal.com/desde-el-hemisferio-sur-al-mundo, last accessed 10/20/2021.

[114] GLOBALG.A.P. *List of all GLOBALG.A.P. National Technical Working Groups.* <https://www.globalgap.org/uk_en/who-we-are/ntwgs/list-of-ntwgs/index.html>, last accessed 12/20/2021.

[115] GLOBALG.A.P., *Evaluación de Riesgos en Prácticas Sociales (GRASP) GRASP Módulo—Interpretación para Argentina, Versión 1.3, Agosto de 2016.* <http://www.globalgap.org/export/sites/default/.content/.galleries/documents/161013_GG_GRASP_NIG_ARGENTINA-V1_3_es.pdf>, last accessed 05/30/2018.

[116] GLOBALG.A.P., *Risk-Assessment on Social Practice (GRASP) GRASP Module—Interpretation for Brazil Version 1.3, July 2015.* <http://globalgap.org/es/documents/?fq=gg.standard.ga:(%22grasp%22)&fq=gg.document.type:(%22guidelines%22)>, last accessed 05/30/2018.

[117] See Berman, 'Stakeholder Participation Reforms' (n 2).

[118] Halabi and Lin, 'Assessing the Relative Influence' (n 101), 274.

members incur often substantial additional costs to adapt to them.[119] Setting international standards for agricultural products is especially difficult because of the variety of conditions that exist worldwide regarding climate, soils, and ecosystems; and because agricultural practices are an integral part of cultural diversity.[120] Moreover and particularly problematic for output legitimacy is the participation of Brazilian small producers which do not hold membership in but are nonetheless affected by GlobalG.A.P. standards in their efforts to compete and export. Notably, membership in both Brazilian and Argentine stakeholders is highly concentrated among large firms that already compete in the global market.

15.7 Chapter Conclusions

Brazil and Argentina have historically favoured the WHO as the traditional multilateral venue for global health governance, which offers equal decision-making rights to all country members. Codex, GlobalG.A.P., and the ICH are also and increasingly important to Brazil and Argentina as major developing country exporters of agricultural, livestock and, to a lesser but increasing extent, pharmaceutical products. By contrast, although the two countries were influential in the creation of the Global Fund, they subsequently lost interest and reduced their level of participation in this global health governance institution, partly because they dispose of sufficient domestic funding sources to fight HIV/AIDS, tuberculosis, and malaria.[121]

Brazil has generally increased its presence and voice in global health governance. It has also been more engaged and influential than Argentina in the WHO and in multistakeholder institutions, in the ICH and arguably also in the Codex. However, both countries' participation in the Global Fund and GlobalG.A.P. is low. The contrasting patterns of economic growth (and the resulting increasing versus decreasing availability of material, analytical and political resources) as well as the foreign policy positions and priorities of Brazil and Argentina help to explain the differences in their engagement and influence in global health governance.

At the same time, Brazil and Argentina share some of the main challenges in levelling the playing field with high income countries in global health institutions. Their engagement and especially their influence in these institutions are still undermined by lack or insufficiency of institutional reforms as well as constrained by (substantial yet) limited human and material resources. From the perspective of both countries, while the relatively deeper and more comprehensive reforms of the ICH and the GlobalG.A.P. were significant, most notably by granting them membership eligibility, the reforms did not go far enough. Many inequities in access to key negotiations and decision-making processes, voting rights, veto rights, agenda-setting, private-sector membership and participation, and in distribution of information still undermine

[119] Carrera, 'GlobalG.A.P. and Agricultural Producers' (n 99), 163.

[120] Cora Dankers, *Environmental and Social Standards, Certification and Labeling for Cash Crops* (FAO 2003), 120.

[121] The World Bank has also provided alternative funding for the prevention of HIV infection in Brazil, see Lewis *et al.*, *Sustainability* (n 94), 21.

the engagement and influence of Brazil and Argentina in these institutions. Codex reforms were much more limited and simply did not address any of the barriers faced by Brazil and Argentina, because they were targeted towards low-income countries.

In addition, the human and financial resources required for leading working groups, proposing new norms, standards, or regulations and, above all, conducting technical and scientific studies which can support negotiating positions in these institutions are obstacles to Brazilian and Argentine participation and influence, particularly in the ICH and Codex. This is problematic because technical norms always have political, commercial, or distributive implications, and hence are never entirely neutral.[122] Different perspectives related to climate, ecosystems, agricultural technologies and modes of production, population eating habits, drug stability and temperature, and the like also tend to be neglected (or at least not adequately appreciated) because Brazil and Argentina are less capable of investing in research.

[122] Büthe and Mattli, *New Global Rulers* (n 6); Tim Büthe, 'Distributional Consequences of Transnational Private Regulation: Institutional Complementarity as a Structural Source of Power in Global Product and Financial Markets' (2013) *Duke University Rethinking Regulation Working Paper* no.6 <https://ssrn.com/abstract=2238100>, last accessed 10/30/2019.

16
China and Vietnam in Global Health Governance

Cindy Cheng and Anh Do[*]

16.1 Introduction

We explore how China and Vietnam have responded to institutional reforms designed to increase participation of previously marginalized stakeholders in the following international health governance bodies: Vaccine Alliance (GAVI), Global Fund to Fight AIDS, Tuberculosis and Malaria (Global Fund), International Council for Harmonisation of Technical Requirements for Pharmaceuticals for Human Use (ICH), International Medical Device Regulators Forum (IMDRF), Global Good Agricultural Practice (GlobalG.A.P.), and the Codex Alimentarius Commission (Codex).[1]

Whether institutional change leads to greater involvement and potentially even influence of previously marginalized actors is heavily conditioned by several factors, including *issue salience*, *participant resources*, and *institutional specificity*. Although issue salience is high for both countries across the global health bodies examined here, China's engagement is generally more substantive than Vietnam's, in part due to China's greater economic and political resources.

With regards to institutional specificity, for organizations that set very precise rules with wide geographic consequences, for example, standard-developing organizations (SDOs) such as ICH, IMDRF, GlobalG.A.P., and Codex, the relevant institutional organs for participation are often situated at or near the heart of the organization in various inter- and transnational (sub)committees where rules and standards are developed, debated, and approved. For other organizations, whose work has consequences of greater country-level specificity (GAVI and the Global Fund), there is less of a necessity to sit on executive-level committees to exert influence. Often of greater consequence is participating in initiatives aimed at addressing specific national-level issues. Participants in institutions with national-level specificity are more likely than participants in SDOs to use policy learning as a lever of influence. Sometimes, this allows them to influence the institutions of the international organization (IO) itself.[2]

* For constructive criticisms and feedback on previous versions of our analysis, we thank the editors of this volume as well as attendees of presentations at the SNIS authors' workshops of the Rethinking Participation Project at the Graduate Institute Geneva and the Technical University of Munich.

[1] We do not examine here China's and Vietnam's involvement and influence in the World Health Organization (WHO) given constraints on the chapter length. Instead, we chose to focus on China and Vietnam's engagement with the remaining HGBs.

[2] Mercy DeMenno and Tim Büthe, 'Voice and Influence in Global Governance: An Analytical Framework.' Chapter 2, this volume.

Cindy Cheng and Anh Do, *China and Vietnam in Global Health Governance* In: *Rethinking Participation in Global Governance*. Edited by: Joost Pauwelyn, Martino Maggetti, Tim Büthe, and Ayelet Berman, Oxford University Press. © Cindy Cheng and Anh Do 2022. DOI: 10.1093/oso/9780198852568.003.0016

In this chapter, we first compare and contrast China and Vietnam's respective engagement with each of the above-mentioned organizations. Then, we present an analytical discussion of the factors driving the divergence between China's and Vietnam's engagement in global health governance.

16.2 International Health Funding Agencies

16.2.1 GAVI

We first discuss how China and Vietnam have responded to GAVI's governing board expansion before exploring each country's engagement with GAVI, vis-à-vis funding, programme implementation, and vaccine production.

16.2.1.1 GAVI governing board reforms

China and Vietnam's varying modes of participation in the GAVI governing board, which ultimately decides GAVI's funding allocation, is reflective of their respective and changing roles in aid allocation. Though their differing modes of participation have predated institutional changes undertaken by GAVI to expand participation,[3] they have also been reinforced by them.

At first glance, Vietnam's governing board participation appears to be more vigorous than China's. Figure 16.1 shows that Vietnam was a voting developing country board member from 2008 through 2011[4] while China has been absent from the board, at least as an aid recipient.[5]

Vietnam further deepened its involvement with GAVI by hosting two important GAVI meetings in 2009: a GAVI board meeting and the 4th GAVI Partners' Forum. Its selection as a host was in part predicated on its successful implementation of the GAVI-funded Expanded Programme of Immunisation.[6] At the 4th GAVI Partners' Forum, Vietnam (with Nepal) was given an award for achieving the highest average annual rate of reduction of child mortality since 1990 (highest among the seventy-two GAVI countries). Vietnam took advantage of this opportunity to ask for more funding to support its immunization efforts.[7]

China, by contrast, has not hosted a GAVI board meeting.[8] Its involvement with GAVI and its governing board instead has been more indirect, reflecting its status as a rising power and its shift from aid recipient to donor. For instance, Dr. Margaret Chan, the first Chinese WHO Director-General, was appointed as Chair of the GAVI

[3] Ayelet Berman, 'Stakeholder Participation Reforms in Global Health Governance,' Chapter 13, this volume.

[4] Vietnam was not a board member prior to 2008. However, from available GAVI documentation, it is unclear whether its induction took place before or after the October 2008 board reforms because documentation on pre-2009 GAVI board meetings is only incompletely publicly available.

[5] One exception was the November 2013 GAVI board meeting where China sent three non-voting observers. See GAVI, 'GAVI Alliance Board Meeting 21–22 November 2013, Phnom Penh, Cambodia Final Minutes' <https://www.gavi.org/governance/gavi-board/minutes/21-november-2013>, last accessed 12/05/2019.

[6] VietnamPlus, 'Vietnam Asks for GAVI's Continued Support for Immunisations' <https://en.vietnamplus.vn/vietnam-asks-for-gavis-continued-support-for-immunisations/14526.vnp>, last accessed 12/04/2019.

[7] VietnamPlus, 'Vietnam Asks for GAVI's' (n 6).

[8] According to publicly available records, China has not done so after 2009, nor is there evidence it did so before 2009, although documentation for pre-2009 GAVI board meetings is incomplete.

Alliance Board (its programmatic board prior to GAVI's 2008 reforms) in 2006 and 2007. Though Dr. Chan's role was not to represent Chinese interests per se, her leadership reflected China's rising international profile.

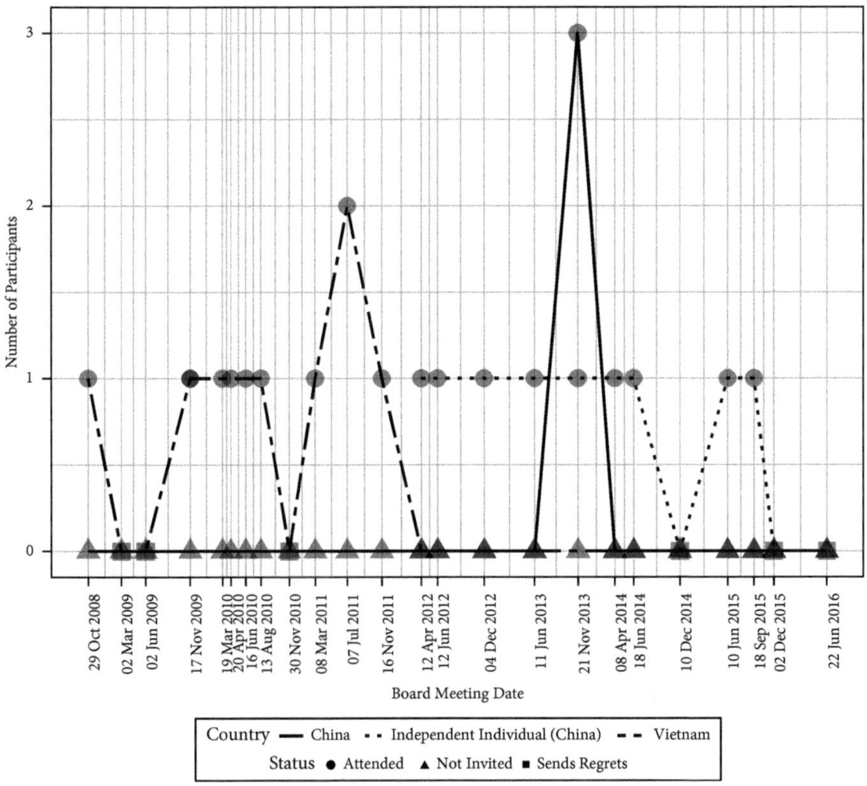

Figure 16.1 Chinese and Vietnamese Participants at GAVI Alliance Board Meetings after the 2009 Reforms

Source: http://www.theglobalfund.org/en/board/meetings/. Data before 2009 not available.

China has also been represented by Yifei Li since April 2012,[9] whose membership as an independent individual on the GAVI board was only possible because of GAVI's 2008 reforms. Her status as 'one of China's most powerful and well-connected businesswomen'[10] makes her a valuable asset, given GAVI's push to expand its donor base to emerging economies. These efforts coincided with China making its first contribution of USD 5 million for the 2016–2020 period at the 2015 Berlin Pledging conference.[11]

[9] GAVI, 'GAVI Alliance Board Meeting 12 April 2012, Teleconference Final Minutes' <https://www.gavi.org/sites/default/files/board/minutes/2012/12-june/01c%20-%20Minutes%20from%2012%20April%202012.pdf>, last accessed 12/04/2019.

[10] Lisa Du, 'Meet Yifei Li—A Martial Arts Champion, Former MTV Exec and Now Man Group's Frontwoman for China' *Business Insider* <https://www.businessinsider.com/meet-yifei-li-man-groups-china-frontwoman-2011-11>, last accessed 11/29/2019.

[11] GAVI, 'Contributions and Pledges from China' <https://www.gavi.org/investing-gavi/funding/donor-profiles/china>, last accessed 11/29/2019.

16.2.1.2 Funding arrangements

GAVI's financial commitments to Vietnam from 2002–2017 have been far more expansive than to China in terms of both the amount and the scope of the associated programmes. At USD 182 million, GAVI commitments to Vietnam is more than quadruple its commitments to China (Figure 16.2).[12] Moreover, unlike its China partnership, the GAVI–Vietnam partnership includes grants for numerous diseases (i.e. rotavirus, measles-rubella, and those covered by the pentavalent vaccine). The discrepancy between Vietnam's and China's respective GAVI funding is unlikely due to divergent capacities for dealing with these diseases. In fact, since the late 1970s, both countries have had great success in vaccinating children for polio, measles, diphtheria, and DPT.[13]

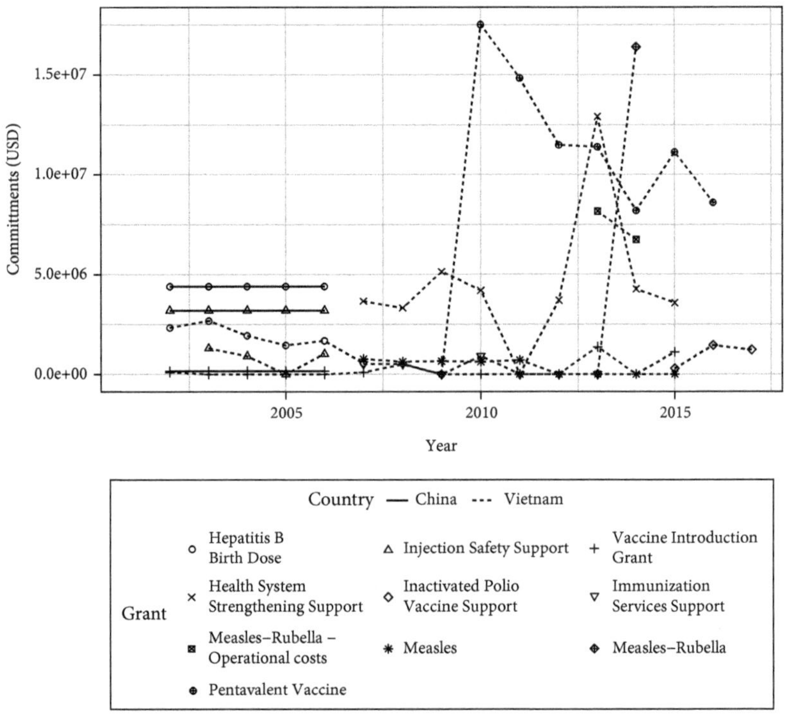

Figure 16.2 GAVI Grant Commitments to China and Vietnam, 2002–2017

Sources: GAVI, 'Vaccine Introduction Grants and Operational Support for Campaigns Policy' <https://www.gavi.org/sites/default/files/document/gavi-alliance-vaccine-introduction-grants-and-operational-support-for-campaigns-policypdf.pdf>, last accessed 11/29/2019; GAVI, 'Health System and Immunization Strengthening' <https://www.gavi.org/programmes-impact/types-support/health-system-and-immunisation-strengthening>, last accessed 11/29/2019; GAVI, 'Immunisation Services Support'<https://www.gavi.org/programmes-impact/types-support/sustainability>, last accessed 11/29/2019.

[12] Voice of Vietnam, 'Vietnam Needs More Support from GAVI' <http://english.vov.vn/society/vietnam-needs-more-support-from-gavi-109927.vov>, last accessed 12/04/2019.

[13] Jingshan Zheng, Yuqing Zhou, Huaqing Wang, and Xiaofeng Liang, 'The Role of the China Experts Advisory Committee on Immunization Program' (2010) 28 *Vaccine* A84-A87; Yezhou Liu, Rebecca Ling Ling, and Xinwei Yu, 'The National Immunization Plan: China - Australasian' 3(7) *Australasian Medical Journal* (2010) 375-375; Trung Dac Nguyen, Anh Duc Dang, Pierre Van Damme, Cuong Van Nguyen, Hong Thi Duong, Herman Goossens, Heidi Theeten, and Elke Leuridan, 'Coverage of the Expanded Program on Immunization in Vietnam: Results from 2 Cluster Surveys and Routine Reports' 11(6) *Human Vaccines & Immunotherapeutics* (2015) 1526-1533.

Instead, China's relatively meagre funding can be explained by the combination of China's large population and GAVI funding constraints. Because the GAVI Board had decided not to make financial commitments beyond firmly committed funds, it was unable to provide free hepatitis vaccines or grants to China, India, or Indonesia. Instead, these countries were eligible for special grants, up to USD 40 million each, and given autonomy for their use, subject to GAVI approval. To that end, China chose to address its hepatitis B virus (HBV) burden with a USD 76 million project equally co-funded between China and GAVI.

The interaction between GAVI funding constraints and China's large population meant that other domestic diseases could not be given similar attention, even if they represented a significant proportion of the global disease burden. For example, despite China's success in lowering its measles incidence rate,[14] it was still reporting 100,000 measles cases annually from 2005–2008—constituting over 90% of cases in the Western Pacific.[15] Nevertheless, China received no GAVI measles funding while GAVI helped finance Vietnam's largest-ever measles–rubella campaign.[16] Though measles affected 5,000 Vietnamese children in 2014, this was a fraction of China's measles burden.[17]

As emerging economies grow, parsing out how to finance strategies to address global public health problems has become increasingly fraught. Since economic growth has generally been accompanied by economic inequality, although many countries reach middle-income status they still shoulder large burdens of vaccine-preventable disease. As GAVI continues to tie eligibility for funding to GDP per capita, the health outcomes in such countries, including China, may become adversely affected. Although China's burden for many diseases is still high, it became ineligible for GAVI support when its GDP per capita exceeded USD 1500.[18]

16.2.1.3 Programme implementation

While China's relatively large disease burden and tremendous economic growth might have impeded its chances of receiving substantial GAVI funds, those same characteristics have proven advantageous in terms of programme implementation. Seeing itself purely as a funding agency, GAVI generally relies on the partner country's existing bureaucracy to implement proposed programmes. Though few

[14] See Table 1 from Chao Ma, Lixin Hao, Yan Zhang, Qiru Su, Lance Rodelwald, Zhijie An, Wenzhou Yu, Jing Ma, Ning Wen, Huiling Wang, Ziaofeng Liang, Huaqing Wang, Weizhong Yang, Li Li, and Huiming Luo, 'Monitoring Progress Towards the Elimination of Measles in China: An Analysis of Measles Surveillance Data' 92 *Bulletin of the World Health Organization* (2014) 340-347.

[15] Ying Hu, Peishan Lu, Xiuying Deng, Hongxiong Guo, and Minghao Zhou, 'The Declining Antibody Level of Measles Virus in China Population, 2009-2015' 18 *BMC Public Health* (2018) Art.906.

[16] WHO, 'Viet Nam Launches Largest Measles-Rubella Immunization Campaign with United Nations Support' <https://www.who.int/vietnam/news/detail/11-10-2014-viet-nam-launches-largest-measles-rubella-immunization-campaign-with-united-nations-support>, last accessed 11/29/2019.

[17] Mark Kane, Stephen Hadler, Lisa Lee, Craig Shapiro, Fuqiang Cui, Xiaojun Wang, and Rajnish Kumar, 'The Inception, Achievements, and Implications of the China GAVI Alliance Project on Hepatitis B Immunization' 31 *Vaccine* (2013) J15-J20.

[18] Note that, given both GAVI's funding constraints and the astronomical rise in China's GDP per capita (from under 1000 GDP per capita in 2000 to 1700 GDP per capita in 2005 and 4500 GDP per capita in 2010), it is unlikely that GAVI could have raised its eligibility threshold to accommodate China and the other countries that would have met a higher threshold; G Chee, X Zheng and S Nakhimovsky, *Evaluation of GAVI-Government of China Hepatitis B Vaccination Program* (Abt Associates 2012); Kane *et al.*, 'Inception' (n 17).

countries have the requisite infrastructure and expertise at the local level, China does. In fact, when the Chinese Ministry of Health (MoH) and GAVI set up a project office within China's Center for Disease Control and Prevention (CDC) National Immunization Program, it was the first (and so far, only) GAVI country or project office.

The MoH and GAVI established its China office in large part due to the partnership's scale.[19] Despite great strides, China's HBV burden (65% of the world's) has long posed a significant public health problem domestically and globally—HBV afflicts around 100 million Chinese people, with 300,000 dying each year from HBV-related liver disease.[20]

Indeed, the establishment of the project office 'proved to be critical to implementation of this [HBV] project for such a large population over such a short time'.[21] Having an international co-manager helped increase knowledge transfer and governance capacity while also lending credibility to the initiative. Meanwhile, situating the project office within the CDC also improved access to other players in the Chinese health system.

16.2.1.4 Vaccine provision

Another unusual feature of the China–GAVI collaboration was its local procurement of vaccines and injection safety equipment.[22] GAVI policy dictates that its partnerships use WHO-prequalified vaccines, which obligates many partner countries to import vaccines. The policy's rationale is to guarantee vaccine safety and effectiveness, although many partner countries argue that it hinders development and technology transfer.

Before the China–GAVI partnership, China was already procuring HBV vaccines and auto-disable syringes domestically.[23] The Chinese government overcame GAVI objections against using locally sourced vaccines by working with the WHO to increase its regulatory capacity.[24] As such, the partnership used domestic Chinese vaccines without WHO prequalification, conditional on the Chinese Food and Drug Administration (CFDA) working towards one.

[19] Chee *et al.*, 'Evaluation of GAVI-Government of China' (n 18).

[20] WHO, 'At Last a Global Response to Viral Hepatitis' 88(11) *Bulletin of the World Health Organization* (2010) 801-802.

[21] Chee *et al.*, 'Evaluation of GAVI-Government of China' (n 18), 12; Xiaofeng Liang, Fuqiang Cui, Stephen Hadler, Xiaojun Wang, Huiming Luo, Yuansheng Chen, Mark Kane, Craig Shapiro, Weizhong Yang, and Yu Wang, 'Origins, Design and Implementation of the China GAVI project' 31 *Vaccine* (2013) J8-J14.

[22] Liang *et al.*, 'Origins, Design and Implementation' (n 21), J10.

[23] Liang *et al.*, 'Origins, Design and Implementation' (n 21), J10. Auto-disable syringes are disposable syringes used to administer vaccines; they are designed to minimize the amount of vaccine lost to dead space in the syringe, eliminate the risk of air bubble, and prevent the re-use of syringes.

[24] Amanda Glassman and Miriam Temin, *Millions Saved: New Cases of Proven Success in Global Health* (Brookings Institution Press 2016), Section: The Keys to Lasting Success.

While China has indeed strengthened its regulatory capacity for vaccines,[25] its HBV vaccines have yet to be prequalified. However, the use of the domestically produced vaccines contributed to cost savings for the China–GAVI partnership, enabling it to extend past 2007 through the end of 2010.[26]

Though Vietnam has also made rapid strides in the research and mass production of vaccines, it did not receive a similar boost from a WHO prequalification exemption. While the WHO's 2015 certification of Vietnam's regulatory system[27] means that Vietnam is now eligible to apply for WHO prequalification for specific products, Vietnam has yet to receive WHO prequalification, though it is actively making efforts to do so.[28]

16.2.2 Global Fund

Before investigating and comparing how Chinese and Vietnamese Global Fund participation has been affected by the Global Fund's institutional proclivities towards inclusiveness, we first contextualize China and Vietnam's domestic health governance, particularly vis-à-vis HIV/AIDS.

China's involvement with the Global Fund represents a drastic change from its previous handling of HIV/AIDS. Although its first AIDS-related death occurred in 1985, the government's response was characterized by denial and inaction until 2002. Indeed, despite its greater population, the Chinese HIV/AIDS budget was less than Vietnam's until 2000.[29]

The lack of public discourse and government funding for HIV/AIDS was hardly reflective of the diseases' severity. Although China's HIV/AIDS incidence was comparatively low, it was found in all thirty-one provinces by 1998.[30] More than half of the people who had contracted HIV by 2001 did so from 1999 to 2001.[31] The 2002 UN assessment of China's HIV/AIDS situation represented a breaking point. It estimated

[25] One major breakthrough was when its Japanese encephalitis vaccine obtained prequalification. See WHO, 'China Enters the Global Vaccine Market' 92 *Bulletin of the World Health Organization* (2014) 626-627.

[26] Liang *et al.*, 'Origins, Design and Implementation' (n 21), J13.

[27] WHO, 'National Regulatory Authority of Viet Nam Meets International Standards for Vaccine Regulation' <https://www.who.int/vietnam/news/detail/22-06-2015-national-regulatory-authority-of-viet-nam-meets-international-standards-for-vaccine-regulation>, last accessed 12/01/2019.

[28] WHO, 'Promoting Quality and Safety to Increase Access' <https://www.who.int/medicines/about/country-stories/promo-increase-qas/en/>, last accessed 11/25/2020.

[29] Elisabeth Rosenthal, 'Scientists Warn of Inaction as AIDS Spreads in China' *New York Times* <http://www.nytimes.com/2000/08/02/world/scientists-warn-of-inaction-as-aids-spreads-in-china.html>, last accessed 12/04/2019; Associated Press, 'Chinese Government Urged to Admit Responsibility for HIV cases' *The Guardian* <https://www.theguardian.com/world/2010/dec/01/china-blood-selling-scandal-hiv>, last accessed 12/04/2019.

[30] Zunyou Wu, Sheena G Sullivan, Yu Wang, Mary Jane Rotheram-Borus, and Roger Detels, 'Evolution of China's Response to HIV/AIDS' 369(9562) *The Lancet* (2007) 679-690, 680.

[31] See Chart 1 in UNAIDS, 'HIV/AIDS: China's Titanic Peril: 2001 Update of the AIDS Situation and Needs Assessment Report' *United Nations* (2002).

that there were anywhere from 800,000 to 1.5 million Chinese people living with HIV/AIDS (PLWHA) in 2001. It further warned that continued inaction might mean there could be as many as 10 million PLWHA by 2010, serving as a wake-up call for the Chinese government.[32]

As part of the government's new political will, in 2002 China applied for HIV/AIDS funding from the newly created Global Fund, thus conferring legitimacy on Global Fund policies and by extension, the Global Fund itself. As the head of AIDSPAN, an NGO which monitors the Global Fund notes, 'Honestly, they don't really need the money . . . but . . . it is important because China's decision to apply to the . . . Fund for money was . . . its way of saying it wanted to join the developing world in fighting AIDS.'[33]

The evolution of China's Global Fund applications further illustrates a remarkable degree of policy learning. While its first and second proposals were rejected by the Global Fund because they failed to provide harm reduction policies and were unwilling to bear the financial cost of anti-retroviral treatment programmes,[34] its subsequent proposals were accepted for including both provisions. This turnaround was possible due to China's efforts to improve their applications by: 1) creating a forum for harm reduction advocates to organize and 2) inviting international advisers for help writing proposals. The application process proved central to encouraging greater engagement and learning between domestic and international actors.[35]

This policy learning also spilled over to domestic policy. China's first HIV/AIDS control legislation, effective March 2006, included the same harm reduction measures China proposed to the Global Fund. Similarly, China's 'Action Plan for Reducing and Preventing the Spread of HIV/AIDS' for 2006–2010 set goals for scaling up needle/syringe provision, methadone maintenance treatment (MMT), and condom distribution.[36] Overall then, given China's previous refusal to recognize HIV/AIDS as a serious public health issue, that China applied for Global Fund money at all, and even more so, that it subsequently adapted some of its HIV/AIDS policies to be in greater alignment with Global Fund priorities, a priori, represents a surprising turnaround in China's health policy.

Meanwhile, although there were misperceptions about HIV transmission and exaggerated fears of HIV infection in Vietnam, there is no evidence of similar initial denial. Increased engagement with global bodies such as the Global Fund, however, also led to a major shift in Vietnam's policy towards HIV/AIDS.

[32] Yanzhong Huang, 'The Politics of HIV/AIDS in China' *Asian Perspective* (2006) 95-125.

[33] Voice of America, 'Global Fund Fights AIDS in 131 Nations' <http://www.voanews.com/a/a-13-2006-12-01-voa73/311868.html>, last accessed 12/01/2019.

[34] Yanzhong Huang and Jia Ping, 'The Global Fund's China Legacy' *Council on Foreign Relations Working Paper* (2014) 1–24.

[35] Lorrae Van Kerkhoff and Nicole Szlezák, 'Linking Local Knowledge with Global Action: Examining the Global Fund to Fight AIDS, Tuberculosis and Malaria through a Knowledge System Lens' 84 *Bulletin of the World Health Organization* (2006) 629-635.

[36] State Council of the People Republic of China, *Action Plan on HIV/AIDS Prevention and Containment, 2006–2010* (Beijing 2006).

For example, in 2006, Vietnam's National Assembly enacted the National HIV/AIDS Law and promulgated the 'National Action Program on HIV/AIDS Harm Reduction Intervention and Transmission Prevention for 2007–2010'. Both documents focus on harm reduction measures for affected peoples. However, support for substitution treatment in Vietnam has been weaker than in China, in part because of the Vietnamese government's concern over the high dropout rate in China's government-supported MMT programme. Despite this, passage of Vietnam's HIV/AIDS Law provided significant momentum towards the use of MMT programmes,[37] with pilot programmes launched in eleven (out of sixty-three) provinces in 2008. Due to its success, the Ministry of Health has decided to expand it to at least thirty provinces to provide treatment for more than 80,000 drug users by 2015.[38]

Notwithstanding their by now long-standing engagement with the international health expert community, both Vietnam and China continue to view drug use as a 'social evil' and have subsequently adopted consonant law and enforcement strategies, contrary to international best practices. In 2005, China's 'People's War on Drugs' imposed arrest quotas, and used paid informants and bounties to identify dealers and users. Similarly, Vietnam cracked down on drug users, expanded compulsory detoxification centres, and re-education through labour camps.[39] While the Global Fund has been successful in conditioning its aid against such practices in Vietnam,[40] China continues to run compulsory drug detention centres unabated.[41]

Note, the Global Fund is by no means the only international organization through which China and Vietnam have engaged the issue of HIV/AIDs. Indeed, China and Vietnam's participation in the Global Fund vis-à-vis HIV/AIDS is better characterized as part of a *general* push to address HIV/AIDS, with significant partnerships with many other international actors.[42] For China, these include partnerships with United Kingdom's Department of International Development (DfID), the United States Agency for International Development (USAID), the Australian Agency for International Development, and the Clinton Foundation,

[37] Theodore M Hammett, Zunyou Wu, Tran Tien Duc, David Stephens, Sheena Sullivan, Wei Liu, Yi Chen, Doan Ngu, and Don C Des Jarlais, 'Social Evils' and Harm Reduction: The Evolving Policy Environment for Human Immunodeficiency Virus Prevention among Injection Drug Users in China and Vietnam' 103(1) *Addiction* (2008) 137-145.

[38] Tam Nguyen, Long T Nguyen, Manh D Pham, Hoang H Vu, and Kevin P Mulvey, 'Methadone Maintenance Therapy in Vietnam: An Overview and Scaling-Up Plan' *Advances in Preventive Medicine* [2012]: Art. 732484.

[39] Hammett *et al.*, 'Social Evils' (n 37).

[40] David Garmaise, 'Global Fund to End Funding for HIV Services in Drug Treatment Centres in Viet Nam' *Aidspan* <https://www.aidspan.org/fr/c/article/2028>, last accessed 12/18/2021.

[41] Richard Pearshouse and Joseph J Amon, 'Human Rights and HIV Interventions in Chinese Labour Camps' 91(5) *Sexually Transmitted Infections* (2015) 337-337; Adeeba Kamarulzaman and John L McBrayer, 'Compulsory Drug Detention Centers in East and Southeast Asia' 26 *International Journal of Drug Policy* (2015) S33-S27.

[42] Bates Gill, 'Assessing HIV/AIDS Initiatives in China Persistent Challenges and Promising Ways Forward' *Center for Strategic and International Studies* (2006) 1–53.

among others, to address HIV/AIDS.[43] Similarly, Vietnam has received a significant amount of support from the US Presidents Emergency Plan for AIDS Relief (PEPFAR), USAID, and DfID.

Though the focus of this volume is to identify how and whether *specific institutional innovations* undertaken by global governance bodies has affected participation, and potentially, influence, by previously marginalized stakeholders, we note that like GAVI, the Global Fund's very existence represents a new model for global health governance and it is worthwhile investigating how Chinese and Vietnamese participation in the Global Fund has differed in response to its institutional features which encourage participation of previously marginalized stakeholders. As identified by Newton,[44] these features of the Global Fund include: (i) the creation of an inclusive and diverse governing board that mandates membership of developing countries and non-governmental entities; (ii) the creation of Country Coordinating Mechanisms (CCM) in each implementing country to encourage greater local ownership and participation in decision-making and implementation processes; and (iii) emphasis on NGO inclusion in decision-making and implementation. We also discuss differences between China's and Vietnam's engagement with the Global Fund in terms of funding.

16.2.2.1 More inclusive and diverse governing membership

While the structure of the governing board has institutionalized *representativeness* of previously marginalized actors, not all such actors are guaranteed an equal chance of *participation*. With this in mind, China has clearly been a much more active participant. It was a board member from the Global Fund's 2002 inception to its 2015 34th Board meeting and also hosted its 16th Board meeting. Meanwhile, Vietnam has never been a board member and has yet to host a board meeting. While, as board member, China speaks for the interests of the wider Western Pacific region rather than its own domestic interests, China's ability to retain that responsibility for more than a decade speaks to its regional power status.

Global Fund Board meetings are also attended by alternate board members, focal points, delegates, and observers.[45] Figure 16.3 show how, even on this score, China continues to be more active than Vietnam. Though the number of Chinese participants has waned over time, and Vietnamese participation has creeped up, Vietnam still sends fewer participants than China.

[43] Gill, 'Assessing HIV/AIDS Initiatives' (n 42).

[44] Gülen Atay Newton, 'The Global Fund to Fight AIDS, Tuberculosis and Malaria: An Innovation in the Form of International Organization' 3 *IRPA Research Paper* (2012) 1–14.

[45] Note there are twenty voting members on the Global Fund Board, with each member representing a particular constituency. See Berman, 'Stakeholder Participation Reforms' (n 3) for more details about the various constituencies. There is one non-voting alternate board member for each member and a focal point that coordinates the information for each constituency, see Global Fund, 'Members' <https://www.theglobalfund.org/en/board/members/>, last accessed 12/04/2019.

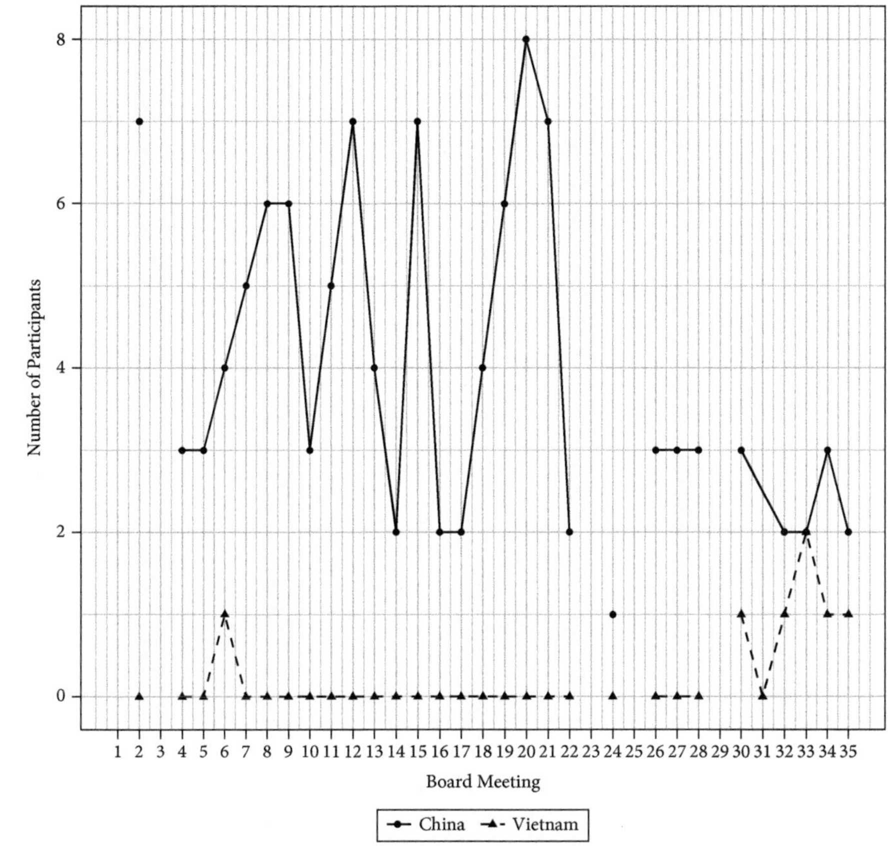

Figure 16.3 Chinese and Vietnamese Participants at Global Fund Board Meetings

Data on participants for the 1st, 3rd, 23rd, 25th, and 29th meetings is missing from the Fund website and could not be included.

16.2.2.2 Funding

Receiving more than USD 805 million from 2003–2012, China was the Global Fund's fourth-largest grant recipient before it became ineligible in 2014.[46] The Global Fund was also one of China's largest international partners—Global Fund money reached more than two-thirds of China's counties and districts.[47] Global Fund commitments

[46] The Global Fund's eligibility criteria are based on a country's economic status and disease burden. Funding constraints have played a role in the use of these criterion. A country becomes ineligible for Global Fund grants if it: (1) moves to a high income status; (2) moves to upper-middle income (UMI) status and their disease burden is low or moderate; (3) has a disease burden for a component which decrease to low or moderate and has UMI status; (4) is a G20 member and moves to UMI status and the disease burden for a component is less than extreme; or (5) it becomes a member of the Organization for Economic Co-operation and Development's (OECD) Development Assistance Committee (DAC).

[47] Huang and Ping, 'Fund's China Legacy' (n 34).

to Vietnam have also been substantial, totalling USD 370 million from 2003 to 2017 (see Table 16.1). Overall, China has received more funding than Vietnam based on their per capita disease burdens.

Table 16.1 Global Fund Commitments, 2016 (USD)

	China	Vietnam
HIV/AIDS	323,824, 956	137,669,336
Tuberculosis	368,143,053	73,939,497
Malaria	113,924,895	54,603,190
Other	0	58,626,754

Source: 'Global Fund Data Explorer' (*https://data.theglobalfund.org)*

Given Global Fund grants' competitive nature, the discrepancy between China's and Vietnam's grant sizes is likely a function of each country's relative grant-writing capacity, rather than demonstrable need. Although technical assistance and support for Global Fund grant proposal development is available in Vietnam, it faces some difficulty taking advantage of it, including: (i) an inability to articulate its needs; (ii) confusion over knowledge or mechanisms to access it; and (iii) a mismatch between the accepted proposal and Vietnam's actual needs.[48]

Meanwhile, China's first round application for TB and malaria were accepted, largely because of its proposal quality as opposed to its disease burden.[49] More generally, in addition to receiving far more funding than not only Vietnam but most countries, China has been subject to a good deal of criticism for its larger grants.[50]

Despite this criticism, China's large population means that its relatively greater funding for some diseases compared to Vietnam can be justified in absolute terms. Indeed, with regards to HIV/AIDS (Table 16.2) and tuberculosis (Figures 16.4 and 16.5), China's absolute disease burden is much larger than Vietnam's.

Table 16.2 Incidence of HIV/AIDS

	Total	HIV/AIDS (% domestic population)	HIV/AIDS (% Asia Pacific)	HIV/AIDS (% Global)
China	501,000 (2014)[P]	0.037%	17%	2%
Vietnam	256,000 (2014)[T]	0.28%	5%	0.7%

P: 2015 China AIDS Response Progress Report (National Health and Family Planning Commission of the People's Republic of China 2015).

T: Vietnam AIDS Response Progress Report (UNAIDS 2014).

48 Coordinating A.I.D.S. Technical Support Group, 'Study on Technical Assistance and Technical Support to Global Fund Grant Implementation at Country Level: Summary Report' (2009) <https://www.theglobalfund.org/media/2967/terg_01meeting_report_en.pdf?u=637066527960000000>, last accessed 12/01/2019.

49 Huang and Ping, 'Fund's China Legacy' (n 34), 11.

50 Jack Chow, 'Foreign Policy: China's Billion-Dollar Aid Appetite' *NPR* <http://www.npr.org/templates/story/story.php?storyId=128664027>, last accessed 12/01/2019.

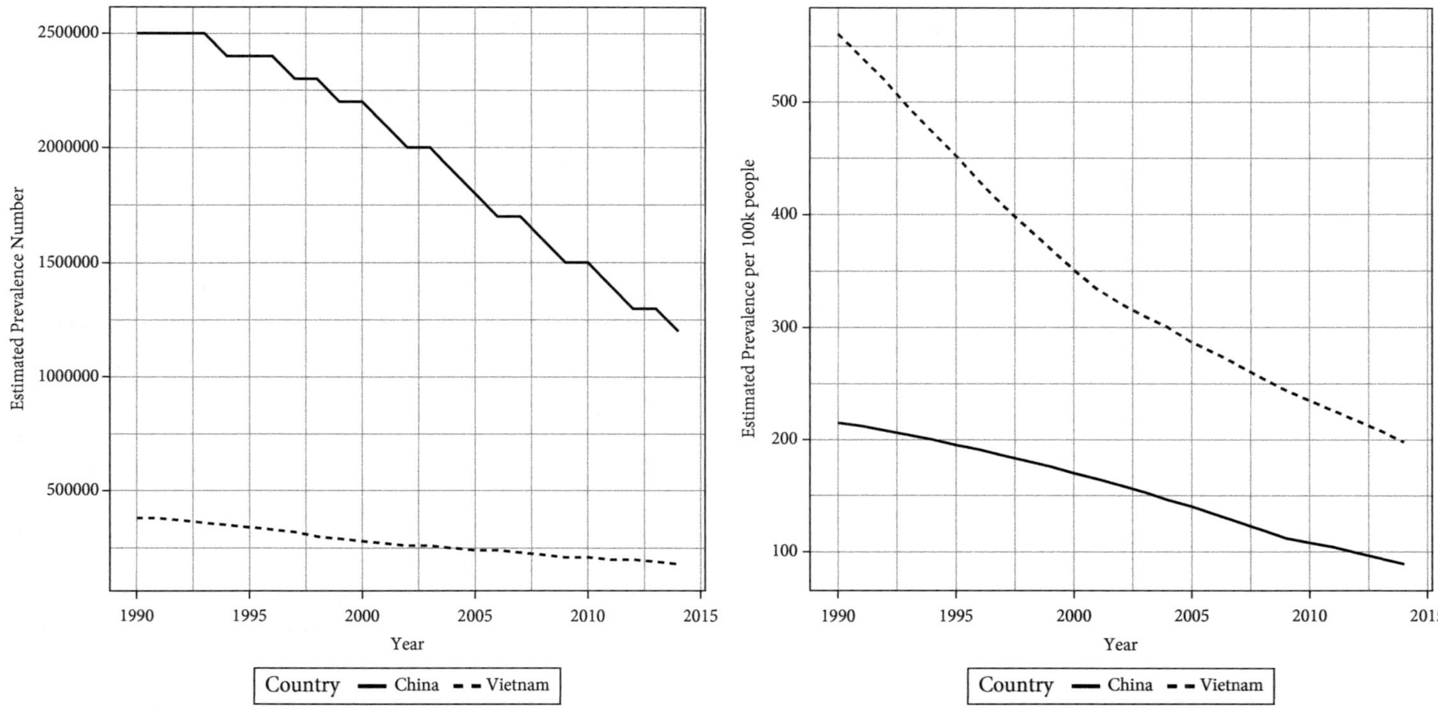

Figure 16.4 Prevalence of Tuberculosis (number of persons with a new or pre-existing tuberculosis infection), 1990–2014

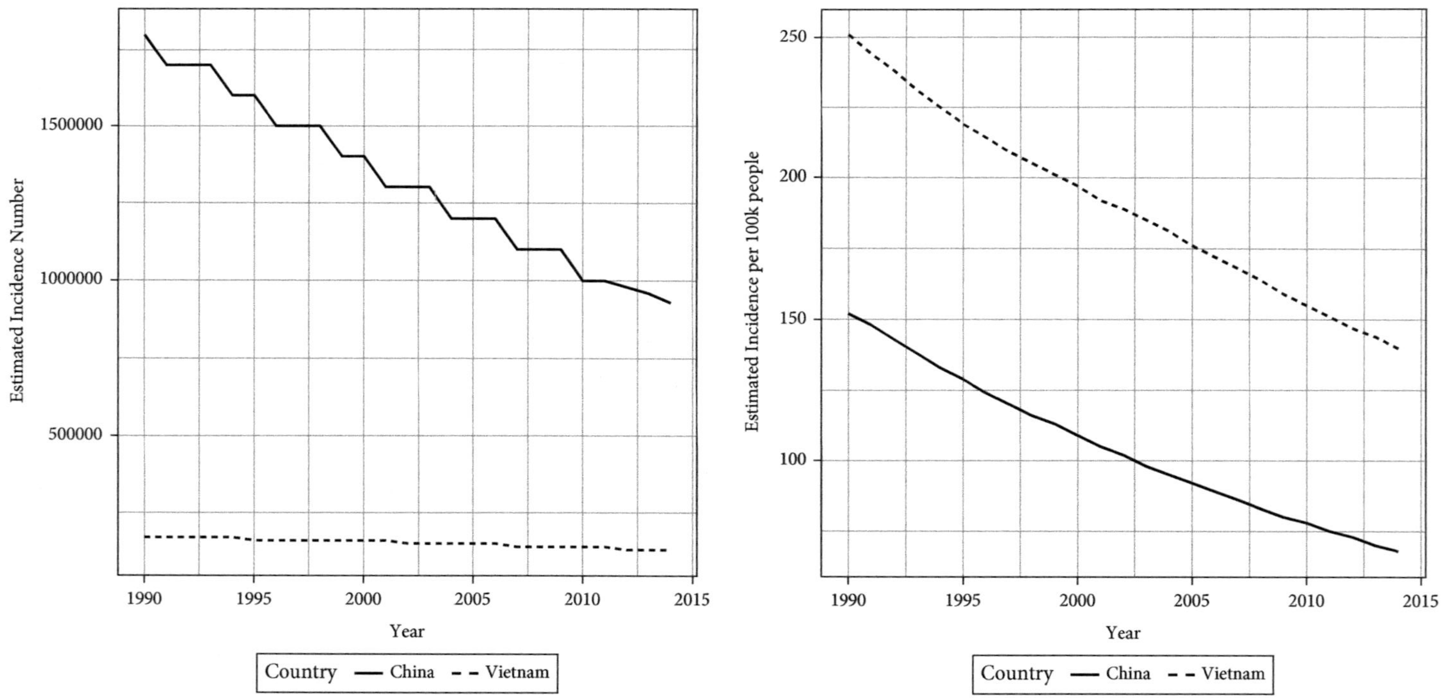

Figure 16.5 Incidence of Tuberculosis (number of persons newly infected each year), 1990–2014

Global Fund grants for malaria constitute an exception. While China reported 25,520 malaria cases and forty-two malarial deaths in 2002, around 11.9 million Vietnamese people are infected with malaria (Figure 16.6).[51] Nevertheless, China received 9.2% of Round 1 funding for malaria control. Although China reduced malaria-related deaths by 55%, as Huang and Ping note, ' … even if we attribute the drop entirely to the … Fund, it remains unclear whether it was wise … to spend $115.7 million in China just to reduce the malaria deaths from forty-two to nineteen when the money might have been spent more effectively in other areas or in other countries'.[52] Indeed, it may have been better spent in Vietnam, where the Global Fund is currently the only major donor for malaria control.

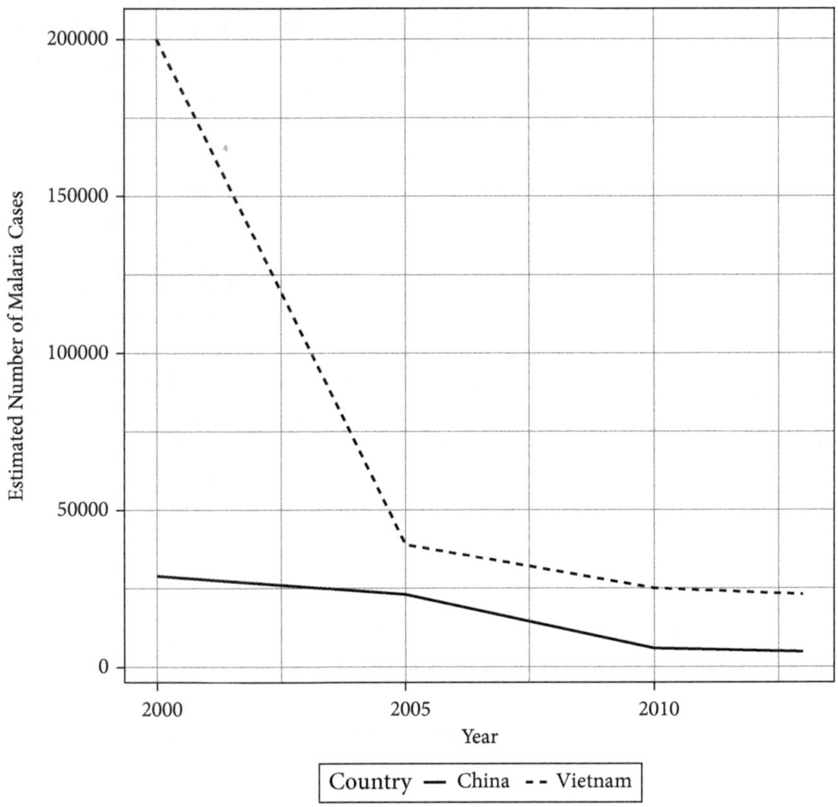

Figure 16.6 Incidence of Malaria, 2000–2010

16.2.2.3 Decentralizing responsibility to target actors

CCMs are the multi-stakeholder partnerships through which the Global Fund realizes its vision of local ownership of, and local participation in, funded grants. They

[51] Global Fund, 'Viet Nam' <https://www.theglobalfund.org/en/portfolio/country/?loc=VNM&k=90fb7820-b2f0-4401-bc77-067270585a9b>, last accessed 12/04/2019.

[52] Huang and Ping, 'Fund's China Legacy' (n 34), 12.

replicate the norm of inclusiveness and participation at the governing board level down to the country level where projects are actually implemented.

However, while CCMs supposedly encourage greater dialogue and learning among stakeholders, China's CCM 'worked more as a rubber stamp for applications developed and executed by China's Ministry of Health and CDC'.[53] According to a prominent HIV/AIDS advocate, the Chinese government never internalized the idea of a CCM and even after many years of Global Fund experience, China still prefers a top-down state-controlled model for disease prevention.[54]

This top-down mentality was reflected in how Chinese projects were implemented. CCMs must designate a principal recipient (PR) to implement and manage programmes[55] and the China CCM designated the China CDC as its PR. The central China CDC in turn designated its provincial and county level CDC offices as sub-recipients (SR) to implement programmes at the local level and distribute funds to community organizations. This 'filter model' gave the government significant power over which community organizations received financial support and influence over which would survive.[56] As such, while the Chinese CCM has sought to increase greater grassroots participation, it has done so on its own terms, while minimizing threats to the central government's power.

Meanwhile, the long chain of actors needed to distribute funds locally also increases corruption opportunities. Because local CDC offices are usually weak local political players, their success in implementing policy goals often depends on 'interdepartmental or inter-unit cooperation'—often bribery—to grease the wheels.[57] Moreover, while central government officials signal their support of Global Fund efforts, some local government officials have expressed discomfort with even acknowledging the reality of HIV/AIDS, much less implementing programmes to address it.[58]

This dynamic may help explain why corruption and fund misuse has been documented more extensively in the China– Global Fund partnership than in the China–GAVI partnership.[59] On average, a mediocre 60–89% of its original targets have been achieved and of the 140 countries receiving Global Fund support, forty-five have received ratings higher than China.

Meanwhile, in 2012, as part of the Global Fund's audit of seven Global Fund grants to Vietnam totalling USD 144 million,[60] the Office of Inspector General (OIG) noted that Vietnam's CCM changed its membership composition in compliance with new Global Fund guidelines. Moreover, Vietnam's CCM agreed to

[53] Joan Kaufman, *State and Society Response to Social Needs in China: Serving the People* (Routledge 2009).

[54] Huang and Ping, 'Fund's China Legacy' (n 34), 16.

[55] Global Fund, 'Implementing Partners' <https://www.theglobalfund.org/en/implementing-partners/>, last accessed 12/01/2019.

[56] Timothy Hildebrandt, 'The Political Economy of Social Organization Registration in China' 208 *The China Quarterly* (2011) 970-989.

[57] Huang and Ping, 'Fund's China Legacy' (n 34), 11.

[58] Huang and Ping, 'Fund's China Legacy' (n 34).

[59] Huang and Ping, 'Fund's China Legacy' (n 34).

[60] Global Fund, Office of Inspector General, 'Audit of Global Fund Grants to the Socialist Republic of Viet Nam' <https://www.theglobalfund.org/media/2750/oig_gfoig13001auditvietnam_report_en.pdf?u=637001820350000000>, last accessed 12/01/2019.

strengthen its oversight role through field visits and other monitoring tools and make provisions for a full-time secretariat to ensure Global Fund programme objectives are achieved.

Moreover, before 2015, the PR for all grants to Vietnam was its MoH. In September 2015, Vietnam appointed its first non-governmental PR, the Vietnam Union of Science and Technology Associations, which had served for four years as SR under the Vietnam Authority on AIDS Control. In 2017, Vietnam's CCM continued to expand its engagement with NGOs and CSOs by issuing a call for expression of interest from NGOs and CSOs to be considered as SRs for the implementation of the Regional Artemisinin Initiative. These steps signal Vietnam's willingness to involve previously marginalized actors in the health policy process.

16.2.2.4 Encouraging greater participation of NGOs

The Global Fund has sought to emphasize inclusiveness by mandating the participation of domestic NGOs in implementing policy through its 2006 Round 6 requirement. While Chinese government leaders have publicly acknowledged the benefits of grassroots NGO involvement in tackling HIV/AIDS, they are sensitive to any action that could threaten its hegemony over policy implementation and weaken political control.

Nevertheless, the Global Fund's emphasis on promoting domestic civil society involvement *has* led to a greater role for NGOs in domestic health governance. This emphasis led to 'open, transparent, and independent election of a CCM NGO representative in April 2006', the first time the Chinese government allowed non-Communist Party members to organize elections. While one cannot discount the symbolic value of this act, because China's CCM is not truly a collaborative multi-stakeholder partnership, increased NGO participation had little real bite.[61]

Further, while Global Fund encouragement of civil society led to a greater number of NGOs, the quality of many was wanting, leading to situations where NGOs with the least technical capacity received the most resources.[62] Following the Round 6 requirement that an NGO be appointed as PR, the China Association for STD and AIDS Prevention and Control (CASAPC), a government-organized NGO, took on this role in 2006. However, CASAPC was removed following a 2007 Global Fund review, which found that CASAPC did not have the necessary capacity to act as PR.[63] Consequently, the PR role reverted back to the CDC and 'China was the only country among the Fund-recipient countries that saw the domination of government health authorities at CCM, PR, and SR levels.'[64]

[61] Huang and Ping, 'Fund's China Legacy' (n 34), 8.

[62] Yanzhong Huang, 'The Global Fund, China, and Civil Society' *Council on Foreign Relations* <https://www.cfr.org/blog/global-fund-china-and-civil-society>, last accessed 12/01/2019; Andrew Wells-Dang, *Civil Society Networks in China and Vietnam: Informal Pathbreakers in Health and the Environment* (Palgrave Macmillan 2012).

[63] Bernard Rivers, 'China Changes Course on Using NGOs as Grant Implementers' *Aidspan* <http://69.175.39.170/web/gfo-newsletter-articles/china-changes-course-using-ngos-grant-implementers>, last accessed 12/01/2019.

[64] Huang and Ping, 'Fund's China Legacy' (n 34), 14.

Meanwhile, in May 2011, the Global Fund froze hundreds of millions of dollars to China[65] when a 2010 audit revealed that China failed to give 35% of its USD 283 million AIDS grant to community-based organizations. When questioned, officials stated that civil society groups could not be trusted with Global Fund money. By May 2011, China and the Global Fund reached an agreement in which China pledged to ensure civil society involvement and better bookkeeping for Global Fund projects.[66]

While this episode suggests that China still has a long way to go in creating a vibrant civil society, it is worth noting that the Global Fund was alerted to this problem because a Chinese NGO took it upon itself to do so.[67] While NGOs have suffered from the funding freeze and many expressed concerns about their future after the Global Fund, the Global Fund requirement for inclusiveness has pushed China to take a small, if halting, step towards greater civil society engagement.

Meanwhile, civil society is still a relatively new phenomenon in Vietnam, leading to a catch-22 situation: without funds and an established presence, it is hard for NGOs and CSOs to qualify for registration, yet they need to register to raise funds and set up offices.[68] Other obstacles include limited organizational capacity and accountability, and the lack of a clear legal framework for NGOs and CSOs.[69]

Global Fund pressure to include more civil society representatives prompted Vietnam to increase NGO involvement in the health policy process. For example, while drafting the HIV/AIDS Law, the National Assembly of Vietnam consulted often with local and international NGOs and invited draft comments. NGO participation resulted in stronger language for protecting PLWHA rights, in particular, for HIV testing, education, employment, marriage, and reproduction. Such participation also led to the inclusion of substitution therapy, which was advocated by policymakers, local activists, and IOs. As part of the process, a local NGO, working closely with the WHO and the Vietnamese government, organized seminars on harm reduction interventions and substitution therapy with journalists and high-ranking officials. This advocacy process took more than two years but contributed to the law's successful passage.[70]

Moreover, Vietnam appointed two PLWHA to serve on its CCM. However, one representative said his role was mostly symbolic and that he lacked the economic resources and technical knowledge to meaningfully participate:

> All other CCM members ... have a job ... they have a salary. I have no job and no income, but they keep asking me to participate in meetings, and so many meetings! ... Before each meeting, they send us a lot of documents. Who can read all of them? And even when I try to read them, I don't understand.[71]

[65] Sharon LaFraniere, 'In Grant Dispute, AIDS Funds Frozen for China' *New York Times* <http://www.nytimes.com/2011/05/21/world/asia/21china.html>, last accessed 12/01/2019.

[66] Huang and Ping, 'Fund's China Legacy' (n 34), 7.

[67] Huang and Ping, 'Fund's China Legacy' (n 34), 6.

[68] Nathalie Abejero, 'Marking a Progression in its HIV Landscape, Vietnam Chooses a Civil Society PR' *Aidspan* <https://www.aidspan.org/en/c/article/3431>, last accessed 12/18/2021.

[69] Abejero, 'Marking a Progression' (n 68).

[70] Thi Hai Oanh Khuat, 'HIV/AIDS Policy in Vietnam: A Civil Society Perspective' *Open Society Institute* (2007) 24.

[71] Khuat, 'HIV/AIDS Policy in Vietnam' (n 70), 55f.

In general, activists from other NGOs expressed concern over the lack of CCM outreach to the larger constituency they were representing.

Overall, while Global Fund participation has pushed both the Chinese and Vietnamese governments towards greater NGO engagement in policy-making, monitoring, and evaluation, the nature of this participation is often of poor quality due to government ambivalence and a continued lack of NGO resources (which are not unrelated).

16.3 Pharmaceutical and Medical Device SDOs

16.3.1 ICH

16.3.1.1 Relevance of ICH

Both Chinese and Vietnamese pharmaceutical markets are expanding rapidly, making ICH standards increasingly relevant to both countries. The main drivers of both markets include expanding populations, increasing life expectancy, higher levels of health awareness, and increased investments in health-care infrastructure.[72]

Indeed, the number of Chinese pharmaceutical manufacturers increased by 44.6%, from 2004 to 2009, reaching 6,807 in 2009.[73] Because of this rapid growth, China's pharmaceutical market became the world's second largest at the end of 2018, behind the US.[74] China has also become the biggest emerging market for pharmaceuticals, and is slated to grow to USD 145 to USD 175 billion by 2022.[75]

Although Vietnam's pharmaceutical industry is smaller, it has shown strong growth, even when the global economic crisis was derailing other sectors: it expanded 18.8% annually from 2009 to 2013.[76] It is forecast to reach a net worth of USD 8 billion by 2020.[77] As a consequence, the importance of the ICH for China and Vietnam—and vice versa—has greatly increased.

Both countries have much to gain from complying with ICH standards. Though China is a large drug manufacturer, Chinese-made drugs constitute only a fraction of the global market due to the mismatch between domestic and international technical and quality standards.[78] Similarly, Vietnam's domestic producers focus mostly on generic medicines, and imported drugs still dominate the market. One reason is

[72] Sean Milmo, 'ICH Prepares for Major Reform' 39(5) *Pharmaceutical Technology* (2015) n.p. <http://www.pharmtech.com/ich-prepares-major-reform>, last accessed 12/01/2019.

[73] Censere, 'An Overview of China's Pharmaceutical Industry' <https://www.censere.com/index.php/en/articles-publications/articles/an-overview-of-china-s-pharmaceutical-industry>, last accessed 12/04/2019.

[74] Xinhua, 'Fast Growth in China's Pharmaceutical Market to Benefit Foreign Firms: Report' China Daily <https://www.chinadaily.com.cn/a/201909/29/WS5d901f4ca310cf3e3556e1cc.html>, last accessed 12/01/2019.

[75] Huileng Tan, 'China's Pharmaceutical Industry is Poised for Major Growth. '*CNBC* <https://www.cnbc.com/2018/04/19/chinas-pharmaceutical-industry-is-poised-for-major-growth.html>, last accessed 12/01/2019.

[76] VietinbankSC, 'Vietnam Pharmaceutical Industry' <http://vietinbanksc.com.vn>, last accessed 03/01/2016.

[77] VietinbankSC, 'Vietnam Pharmaceutical Industry' (n 76).

[78] Ren Minghui and Lu Guoping, 'China's Global Health Strategy' 384(9945) *The Lancet* (2014) 719-721.

that Vietnamese medical practitioners equate expense with higher quality, so they prescribe only 18–20% domestic medicines for their patients.[79] To counter these perceptions, domestic companies intend to increase their investments in R&D to produce drugs that meet international standards.

However, both China and Vietnam's pharmaceutical markets face significant regulatory hurdles in becoming internationally competitive. In both countries, enforcement of many minimum-quality regulatory standards is suboptimal. There is often insufficient information on product use and safety—drugs are frequently dispensed by unqualified staff, and health care workers are rarely held accountable for drug prescription errors. Counterfeit, unsafe, and illegal pharmaceuticals are also a problem and have been implicated in a number of product scandals in China.[80] Domestic Chinese and Vietnamese firms that are able to comply with ICH standards are the exception, not the rule.

To address its regulatory shortcomings, the Chinese government has taken numerous steps to improve its regulatory capacity and the industry's ability to create innovative, high-end drugs.[81] Similarly, Vietnam has updated certain aspects of its legal framework to be more in line with international practices. For example, its 2017 pharmaceutical law provides quicker access to drugs for patients, increases consumer protection, and creates more incentives for local drug manufacturing.

16.3.1.2 Engagement with ICH

Today, China is an ICH member—made possible by the ICH's October 2015 reforms—whereas Vietnam is not. Yet, even though those reforms were specifically motivated by the desire to admit China and India as members, China did not become a member until 2017,[82] in large part because of its uneven geographic regulatory capacity.[83] It hosted a joint MedDRA/WHODrug meeting in September 2017.[84]

Even before the opportunity for formal membership was—for China—created through the 2015 institutional reforms, the ICH provided numerous alternative avenues of stakeholder engagement, though several of these opportunities for

[79] VietinbankSC, 'Vietnam Pharmaceutical Industry' (n 76).

[80] Samuel S Lieberman, Joseph J Capuno and Hoang Van Minh, 'Decentralizing Health: Lessons from Indonesia, the Philippines, and Vietnam' *East Asia Decentralizes: Making Local Government Work* (2005) 155-178; Melanie Lee and Ben Hirschler, 'Special Report: China's Wild East Drug Store' *Reuters* <http://www.reuters.com/article/us-china-pharmaceuticals-idUSBRE87R0OD20120828>, last accessed 12/01/2019.

[81] David Deere, 'China's Zhixiang - A Global Pharmaceutical Industry' *Paiza Bio* <http://paizabio.com/blog/chinas-zhixiang-a-global-pharmaceutical-industry/>, last accessed 12/01/2019.

[82] Milmo 'ICH Prepares' (n 73); ICH, 'Final Minutes ICH Assembly, May 31 & June 1, 2017, Montreal, Canada' <https://admin.ich.org/sites/default/files/2019-05/Assembly_report_Montreal_2017.pdf>, last accessed 12/01/2019.

[83] Waikeung Tam and Dali Yang, 'Food Safety and the Development of Regulatory Institutions in China' *Asian Perspective* (2005) 5-36; PharmaCompass, 'India, China Absent as Countries Align on Global Pharma Quality Standards' <https://www.pharmacompass.com/radio-compass-blog/india-china-absent-as-countries-align-on-global-pharma-quality-standards>, last accessed 12/01/2019; Zachary Brennan, 'ICH and Pharmaceutical Inspection Co-operation Scheme: No Expectations for China or India to Join' *Regulatory Affairs Professionals Society* <http://raps.org/ichpicsnoexpectations/>, last accessed 12/01/2019.

[84] ICH, 'MedDRA Management Committee, Geneva, Switzerland' <https://www.meddra.org/news-and-events/news/meddra-management-committee-geneva-switzerland-november-2017>, last accessed 11/30/2019.

participation were de jure or de facto only open to select very large developing countries, that is, the ICH provided such opportunities to China, but not to Vietnam. For example, in recognition of the potential far-reaching consequences of ICH's 2000 Good Manufacturing Practices (GMP) for Active Pharmaceutical Products guidelines, the ICH invited a number of non-members, including China, to participate in the deliberations, which was then emerging as a large active pharmaceutical ingredients (API) manufacturer.[85] The ad hoc nature of this participation was formalized in the ICH's 2003 invitation of other regional harmonization initiatives to its Global Cooperation Group (GCG).[86] As a result, the APEC Quality Guideline Workshop was held in 2008 in China.[87] In 2007, the ICH also invited individual non-members, including China, to participate in the GCG.[88] More significantly, in 2008, the ICH created the Regulators Forum specifically to help China, India, and Brazil implement ICH guidelines.[89]

The ICH Steering Committee's 2010 decision to open its ICH technical working group to 'active participation from experts from non-ICH member regions and countries'[90] further increased ICH non-members' involvement and potential influence. China quickly made use of this opportunity and by 2011, the ICH had nominated Chinese technical experts to some quality efficacy expert working groups.[91]

China has also paid close attention to ICH developments and has taken the initiative to participate in meetings and adopt various ICH guidelines[92]—actions that have required concerted effort to improve domestic technical and scientific capacity. This effort is manifested in China's ICH Study Group, established in July 2009. Its goals are to:[93]

- Translate and publish ICH guidelines and related documents in Chinese;
- Compare ICH guidelines to Chinese guidelines, with an eye towards revising and improving Chinese guidelines as needed;
- Provide training to use ICH guidelines;
- Disseminate its findings; [and]
- Increase contact and cooperation with the ICH.

[85] Achema Worldwide News, 'Trend Report: China's Pharmaceutical Industry' (2004); ICH, 'Good Manufacturing Practice Guide for Active Pharmaceutical Ingredients'<http://www.ich.org/products/guidelines/quality/quality-single/article/ good-manufacturing-practice-guide-for-active-pharmaceutical-ingredients.html>, last accessed 08/01/2017.

[86] The GCG is a sub-body of the ICH with a mission to promote mutual understanding and increase capacity to adhere to ICH guidelines, both regionally and globally.

[87] Pierre-Louis Lezotre, *International Cooperation, Convergence and Harmonization of Pharmaceutical Regulations: A Global Perspective* (Academic Press 2013).

[88] Lezotre, *International Cooperation* (n 87).

[89] Justina Molzon, 'ICH - Its History, Evolution, Achievements and Challenges' *Biomed/Biotech SIG* <http://www.asq509.org/ht/a/GetDocumentAction/i/101605>, last accessed 12/02/2019.

[90] ICH, 'Further Opening to Non-ICH Regions' <https://www.ich.org/news/further-opening-non-ich-regions>, last accessed 12/02/2019.

[91] ICH, 'Press Release from the ICH Steering Committee meeting in Cincinnati' <https://www.ich.org/pressrelease/ich-steering-committee-cincinnati-oh-us-15-16-june-2011>, last accessed 12/01/2019.

[92] IBP, *China Medical and Pharmaceutical Industry Handbook Volume 1 Strategic Information and Regulations* (IBP, Inc 2015)

[93] Jianhua Ding, 'Introduction of ICH China Research WG' PowerPoint Presentation to the ICH Global Cooperation Group, Estonia June 2010.

The working group is highly organized[94] and, as of April 2015, had translated around '150 FDA, EMA and ICH guidelines and published ... [them] to the CFDA website for industry reference'.[95] Furthermore, ICH training sessions have been held in China at the request of the CFDA and its predecessor, the SFDA, including two in 2012[96] and one in 2013.[97]

To date, there is no evidence of a similarly protracted relationship between Vietnam and ICH. Vietnam has engaged with the ICH to a very limited extent via its ASEAN membership. Efforts towards harmonization were initiated in 1992 by a Malaysian proposal to the ASEAN Consultative Committee for Standards and Quality. Consequently, the Pharmaceutical Product Working Group (PPWG), which established consultation procedures similar to the Formal ICH Procedure and applied ICH procedures of drafting, consultation, and adoption of final guidelines,[98] was founded in 1999. In December 2015, ASEAN was invited as an ICH observer.[99] Thus, while China has been able to engage with the ICH directly, Vietnam's ICH engagement has been mediated by the interests of other ASEAN members.

Though both the Chinese and Vietnamese domestic pharmaceutical markets are growing rapidly, China's relatively large drug (in particular, API) market, seems to play an important role in explaining both ICH's attention towards China and China's greater effort to participate relative to Vietnam's.

16.3.2 IMDRF

16.3.2.1 Relevance of the IMDRF

IMDRF standards have increasing relevance for China and Vietnam's growing medical device markets. At USD 34.68 billion in 2013,[100] China is the world's second-largest medical device market, growing on average 20% annually since 2009. However, although there were 17,800 Chinese medical device manufacturers in 2013, most of them supplied low- to mid-range products.[101] According to the Chinese government,

[94] ICH, 'The Value and Benefits of ICH to Drug Regulatory Authorities' <https://www.ich.org/publication/value-and-benefits-ich-drug-regulatory-authorities>, last accessed 12/02/2019.

[95] Brian Bollwage, 'Regularizing Regulatory Requirements in Clinical Research: 25 Years of Harmonization and the Path Forward' *Clinical Leader* <https://www.clinicalleader.com/doc/regularizing-regulatory-requirements-in-clinical-research-years-of-harmonization-and-the-path-forward-0001>, last accessed 12/02/2019.

[96] ICH, 'ICH Guidelines in China' <http://www.ich.org/trainings/ich-trainings/ich-m-guidelines-in-china.html>; ICH, 'ICH E2 Pharmacovigilance Training in China' <https://admin.ich.org/sites/default/files/inline-files/DIA_ICH_PGM_China_Final_0.pdf>, last accessed 12/02/2019.

[97] ICH, 'ICH E11 Guideline in China' <http://www.ich.org/trainings/ich-trainings/ich-e11-guideline-in-china.html?print=1>, last accessed 12/04/2019.

[98] Maha M Lakkis, 'The ASEAN Harmonization Scheme: Another CTD-Another Challenge to the Industry' *Regulatory Focus* (2008) 39-43.

[99] Zachary Brennan, 'ICH Adds 14 New Observers, Adopts New Guidelines at Lisbon Meeting' *Regulatory Affairs Professionals Society* <https://www.raps.org/regulatory-focus™/news-articles/2016/7/ich-adds-14-new-observers,-adopts-new-guidelines-at-lisbon-meeting>, last accessed 12/01/2019.

[100] Adam Jourdan, 'China Calls for Greater use of Homegrown Medical Devices' *Reuters* <http://www.reuters.com/article/us-china-medicaldevices-idUSKBN0GI0UU20140818>, last accessed 12/02/2019.

[101] Maine International Trade Center (MITC), *Medical Devices Industry Opportunities in Japan & China* (MITC 2015), 10.

China still needs to raise the level and quality of its domestic medical devices and create incentives for medical institutions to buy them.[102]

Vietnam's medical device market is much smaller than China's, but it has been expanding rapidly. The market—valued at USD 634 million in 2012—has been growing rapidly, and was valued at USD 1.3 billion in 2020.[103] Contrary to China, until 2009, only domestic companies were permitted to distribute medical devices in Vietnam; before 2009, foreign medical device companies had to sell their products to Vietnamese distributors to bring them to market.[104]

16.3.2.2 National medical regulatory capacity

The regulatory landscape for China's medical devices has undergone profound change over the course of its development. While China's first medical device regulation, created in 1994, merely required companies to register medical devices before putting them to market,[105] by 2000 they were obligated to substantiate product quality and effectiveness.

By 2011, the Chinese government had adopted the international Good Manufacturing Practices (GMP) of Medical Devices and GMP of Medical Device Inspection. As Sun[106] argues, the eleven-year delay between 2000 and the GMP regulations cannot be attributed to a lack of resources or knowledge but rather: bureaucratic lag and reliance on imports which limited need for domestic regulation. The adoption of GMP standards reflects a shift in government focus towards promoting the production of domestic high quality medical devices. Evidence suggests that China's IMDRF engagement is also motivated by the desire to further develop its domestic medical device industry. To that end, China has continued to take steps to bolster its regulatory capacity with its 2014 'Five Rectifications Campaign', which pushes for greater alignment with ISO and US regulatory standards.[107]

Meanwhile, Vietnam has also been gradually increasing its regulatory capacity in medical devices. In 2016, Vietnam issued Decree No. 36/2016/ND-CP, introducing new regulatory guidelines harmonized to ASEAN's to evaluate risk and unify the registration processes for domestic and imported medical devices. Before 2016, there were two separate systems of legislation for domestically manufactured and imported medical devices. While foreign medical devices were not required to comply with domestic regulatory protocols, they were subject to onerous import license requirements.

[102] Miriam Dabrowa, 'Medical Device Market in China: Opportunities and Challenges' *Med Device Online* <https://www.meddeviceonline.com/doc/medical-device-market-in-china-opportunities-and-challenges-0001>, last accessed 12/04/2019.

[103] Pacific Bridge Medical (PBM), 'Vietnam's Medical Device Market 2013' <http://www.pacificbridgemedical.com/publication/vietnams-medical-device-market-2013/>, last accessed 12/02/2019. United States International Trade Administration, 'Vietnam Healthcare Sector' < https://www.trade.gov/market-intelligence/vietnam-healthcare-sector>, last accessed 16/10/2021.

[104] PBM, 'Vietnam's Medical' (n 103).

[105] Pulin Sun, 'Medical Device Regulation in China and the US: A Comparison and a Look Forward' 5 *Intersect: The Stanford Journal of Science, Technology and Society* (2012) 1–16.

[106] Sun, 'Medical Device Regulation in China' (n 105).

[107] Boston Biomedical, 'Changes to Medical Device Regulations in China' <https://bbacro.com/changes-to-medical-device-regulations-in-china/>, last accessed 12/02/2019.

16.3.2.3 Country IMDRF engagement

Overall, China has taken greater initiative than Vietnam in participating in the IMDRF. Prior to becoming a member, China had observed a number of GHTF[108] and IMDRF meetings.[109] It also engaged with the GHTF as chair of the Asian Harmonization Working Party (AHWP), a regional harmonization group that includes both China and Vietnam, from 2009 to 2012.[110] However, the path towards membership has been long. While China submitted its membership application to the IMDRF's predecessor, the GHTF, in November 2009,[111] membership was not extended until 2013,[112] after the 2011 creation of the IMDRF.[113]

China's IMDRF membership has given it greater opportunities for engagement relative to Vietnam: as a member, China provides regular updates on its domestic regulatory reforms. China is also part of the Medical Device Single Audit Program (MDSAP)'s working group, contributing to its goal of developing a single audit to cover Australia, Brazil, Canada, Japan, and the US. Finally, in 2018, China assumed the rotating chairmanship of the IMDRF for the first time.[114]

Meanwhile, Vietnam's more limited involvement with the IMDRF has occurred at the IMDRF's initiative and has been mediated through ASEAN. In the IMDRF's previous life as the GHTF, it sought to produce guidance documents for countries with under-developed regulatory systems to promote standards harmonization. To that end, it cooperated with ASEAN as well as the AHWP. This IMDRF guidance forms the basis of the ASEAN Medical Device Directive (AMDD) which Vietnam, and other ASEAN countries, signed in 2014. The AMDD aims to establish a consistent path to market for foreign medical device manufacturers registering their products in ASEAN countries.[115]

Overall, China's participation in IMDRF is much deeper than Vietnam's. As with the ICH, this participation seems to be predicated in part on the relative size of their

108 IMDRF, 'Outcome Statement of the IMDRF Management Committee' <http://www.imdrf.org/docs/imdrf/final/meetings/imdrf-meet-120228-singapore-outcome-statement.pdf>, last accessed 12/02/2019.

109 IMDRF, 'IMDRF Media Statement. Successful Launch to IMDRF' <http://www.imdrf.org/docs/imdrf/final/media-releases/imdrf-media-120228-successful-launch.pdf>, last accessed 12/02/2019.

110 IMDRF, 'Report of the SG1 Meeting Held from 20th to 23rd January 2009 in Sydney, Australia' <http://www.imdrf.org/docs/ghtf/final/sg1/meetings/ghtf-sg1-n074-meeting-minutes-090120-australia-sydney.pdf>, last accessed 12/02/2019.

111 GHTF, 'Meeting Minutes, Hong-Kong, November 2009' <http://www.imdrf.org/docs/ghtf/final/sg2/meetings/ghtf-sg2-n121-meeting-minutes-091103-kowloon-bay-hong-kong.pdf>, last accessed 12/02/2019.

112 Arthur Brandwood, 'China Rolls Out Devices International Audit Program' *Brandwood CKC* <http://brandwoodbiomedical.com/china-rolls-out-devices-international-audit-program/>, last accessed 12/02/2019.

113 GHTF, 'Meeting Minutes, Canberra, Australia, November 2011' <http://www.imdrf.org/docs/ghtf/final/sg2/meetings/ghtf-sg2-n129-meeting-minutes-111114-australia-canberra.pdf>, last accessed 12/02/2019.

114 China Association for Medical Device Industry, 'Association attended the 14th Meeting of International Medical Devices Regulations Research Group' <http://en.camdi.org/news/4397>, last accessed 12/02/2019.

115 Stewart Eisenhart, 'Progress Reported on ASEAN Medical Device Directive in Southeast Asia' *Emergo* <https://www.emergobyul.com/blog/2014/09/progress-reported-asean-medical-device-directive-southeast-asia>, last accessed 12/02/2019; Erik Swain, 'Global Harmonization is Here to Stay' *Medical Device and Diagnostic Industry* <https://www.mddionline.com/global-harmonization-here-stay>, last accessed 02/01/2015.

respective markets for medical devices and China's drive to reform its medical device regulatory regime to be more internationally competitive.

16.4 Food Safety SDOs

16.4.1 Relevance of GlobalG.A.P. and Codex

Both China and Vietnam have experienced a spate of food safety crises over the past decade, elevating the importance of engaging with international food safety SDOs.

Aside from the threat compromised food safety poses to public health, such occurrences also have economic implications. China's agricultural production capacity is much larger than Vietnam's, due to its large population, although China's trade in agricultural goods (Figure 16.8) is only a fraction of its domestic production (Figure 16.7). As Chinese agricultural producers seek to access higher-valued export markets, conforming to international food safety standards will become increasingly important.

Meanwhile, Vietnam's export revenue from the agricultural sector has increased significantly over the last decade. It is expected to hit USD 41 billion by the end of 2021[116] Thus, meeting importers' quality standards by adopting international food safety standards will be beneficial to the Vietnamese economy.

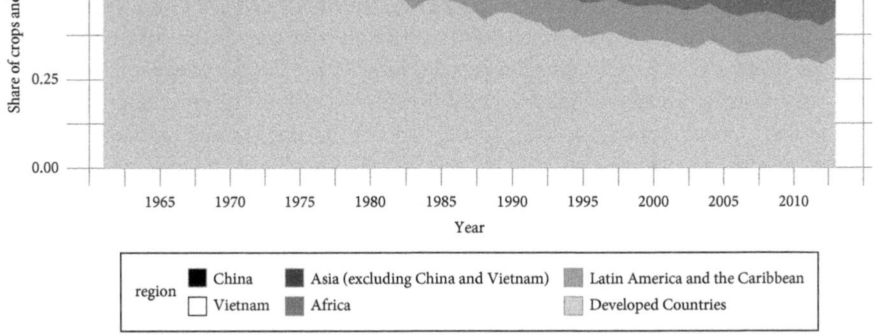

Figure 16.7 Agricultural Production as a Share of the Total Global Production

[116] Viet Nam News, 'Viet Nam targets $41b agriculture export in 2021' < https://vietnamnews.vn/economy/977045/viet-nam-targets-41b-agriculture-export-in-2021.html >, last accessed 16/10/2021.

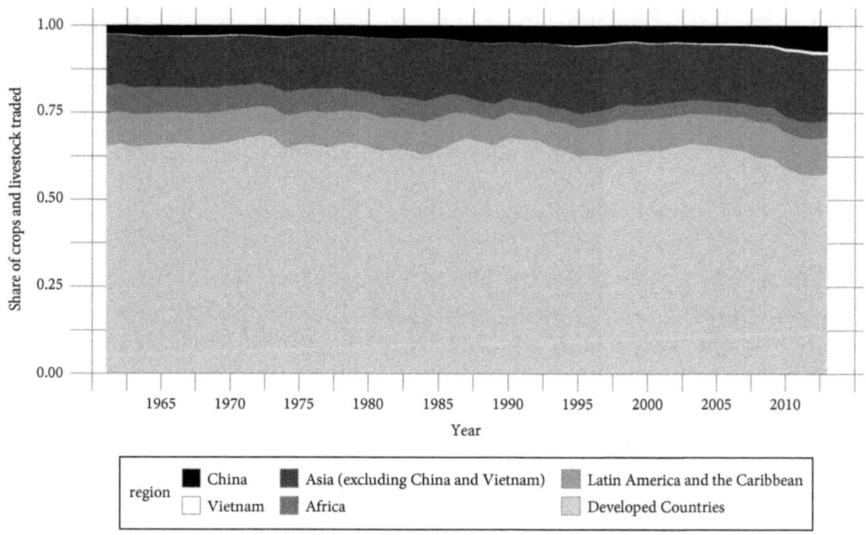

Figure 16.8 Agricultural Trade as a Share of the Total Global Trade

16.4.1 GlobalG.A.P.

16.4.1.1 Country engagement with GlobalG.A.P.

To promote greater international participation, GlobalG.A.P. has encouraged the establishment of 'National Technical Working Groups' (NTWGs) to help countries implement and act as a source of local expertise and development for GlobalG.A.P. standards.[117] In this respect, China has been the more active participant, establishing an NTWG covering aquaculture, crops, and livestock, while Vietnam has not.

GlobalG.A.P. itself has also made a greater effort to engage with China relative to Vietnam. While its 2013 tour stopped in Harbin, China,[118] it did not give Vietnam similar attention. This is perhaps a function of Vietnam's relatively lower domestic capacity. Although GlobalG.A.P. accreditation successfully boosts agricultural exports, many small-scale farmers find its certification costs too high and its requirements almost impossible to satisfy. For example, according to a survey of thirteen provinces in the Vietnamese citrus industry, the average family income is VND 50 million—GlobalG.A.P. certification costs about VND 30 million annually and requires satisfying more than 200 criteria, which only a few large enterprises in Vietnam can accomplish.[119]

[117] GlobalG.A.P., 'The GlobalG.A.P. National Technical Working Groups' <https://www.globalgap.org/uk_en/who-we-are/ntwgs/>, last accessed 12/04/2019.

[118] A GlobalG.A.P. Tour is a one- to two-day conference between GlobalG.A.P. representatives and local, national, or regional hosts to exchange information and experiences about the GlobalG.A.P. certification process. See GlobalG.A.P., 'GlobalG.A.P. Tour 2018/2019' <https://www.globalgap.org/uk_en/media-events/tour/>, last accessed 12/05/2019; GlobalG.A.P., 'Tour 2013 Stop–China' <http://www.globalgap.org/uk_en/media/TOUR-2013-Stop-China/>, last accessed 12/04/2019.

[119] Kaoru Nabeshima, Etsuyo Michida, Hoang Nam Vu, and Aya Suzuki, 'Emergence of Asian GAPs and its relationship to Global G.A.P.' 507 *IDE Discussion Papers* (2015) Institute of Developing Economies, Japan External Trade Organization (JETRO).

Chinese farmers face similar problems, though to a lesser extent. These mismatches in resources and capacity have led to the creation of various 'country' GAPs, such as ChinaG.A.P. and VietG.A.P. Though country GAPs heavily reference GlobalG.A.P. standards and FAO principles, they also take into consideration countries' unique national laws and regulations. Rather than the partnership model pursued by GAVI or the Global Fund or a SDO's hub and spoke model, country GAPs have enabled developing countries to exercise greater control over the standard-making process.

To that end, in 2003, the Certification and Accreditation Administration of the People's Republic of China (CNCA) commenced drafting ChinaG.A.P., and its codes, rules and training documents were officially approved and published in 2005.[120] ChinaG.A.P. refers to two certifications: one for individual producers and one for producer groups, each with separate requirements and certification procedures.[121] The cost of acquiring ChinaG.A.P. certification is around CNY 20,000 (USD 3,000) per year for a medium-sized enterprise, relatively cheaper than GlobalG.A.P. and other international standards.[122]

Reflecting China's ambitions to expand its agricultural export ability,[123] the Chinese government signed a memorandum of understanding with GlobalG.A.P. in 2005 to promote technical cooperation[124] and another in 2006[125] to initiate the formal benchmarking procedure for the ChinaG.A.P.. Since 2009, the first class ChinaG.A.P. certification has been benchmarked to GlobalG.A.P.,[126] and is now fully recognized by GlobalG.A.P.. Companies holding such certifications now have full access to the world market.[127] Exceptionally, GlobalG.A.P. has allowed ChinaG.A.P. to be self-managed by the CNCA.[128]

Meanwhile, in 2008, the Vietnamese Ministry of Agriculture and Rural Development established VietG.A.P. as the main standard for fruit and vegetable production.[129] Covering fisheries, farming, and livestock, VietG.A.P. is expected to replace other standards such as GlobalG.A.P., Marine Stewardship Council and Aquaculture Stewardship Council. Though VietG.A.P. incorporates some GlobalG.A.P. requirements, it is currently not benchmarked to GlobalG.A.P..

Despite government support, the diffusion of both ChinaG.A.P. and VietG.A.P. has been relatively slow due to legitimacy concerns. ChinaG.A.P.'s slow uptake is mostly due to consumers' and exporters' unfamiliarity, though alternative standards and accreditations have also encumbered its diffusion. Local governments within China

[120] Lei Lei, 'A Closer Look at the Diffusion of ChinaG.A.P.' 501 *IDE Discussion Papers* (2015) Institute of Developing Economies, Japan External Trade Organization (JETRO).

[121] Lei, 'A Closer Look' (n 120).

[122] Lei, 'A Closer Look' (n 120), 6–7.

[123] Teruaki Nanseki and Min Song, *Food Safety and the Agro-Environment in China: The Perceptions and Behaviors of Farmers and Consumers* (Intech 2013).

[124] Lei, 'A Closer Look' (n 120).

[125] Pascal Liu, Sibhan Casey, Jean-Joseph Cadilhon, Peter Sousa Hoejskov, and Nancy Morgan, 'A Practical Manual for Producers and Exporters from Asia. Regulations, Standards and Certification for Agricultural Exports' *RAP Publication* (FAO 2007).

[126] Liu *et al.*, 'Practical Manual' (n 125).

[127] Lei, 'A Closer Look' (n 120).

[128] Mark Godfrey, 'GlobalG.A.P. Goes Big in China' *SeafoodSource* <https://www.seafoodsource.com/news/aquaculture/globalgap-goes-big-in-china>, last accessed 12/03/2019.

[129] Nabeshima *et al.*, 'Emergence of Asian GAPS' (n 119).

have attempted to address these obstacles by introducing pilot programmes, training sessions, and even subsidies to leading firms that successfully achieve certification.[130]

Meanwhile, producers also hesitate to switch to VietG.A.P. for fear of lowering product credibility because VietG.A.P. lacks international recognition. Moreover, though the Vietnamese government has promised financial support to farmers who wish to obtain VietG.A.P. accreditation, the support comes with two demanding conditions: 1) VietG.A.P. must be applied in the production process and 2) the farmers must already have sales contracts and a sales plan.[131]

With regards to participation in GlobalG.A.P. and the creation of their respective country GAPs, China has pushed further to learn from and align itself with international standards. Such efforts are a function of the relative ability of Chinese domestic producers to meet such standards, though on an absolute level, both Chinese and Vietnamese producers face challenges in adhering to GAP standards.

16.4.2 Codex

Following China and Vietnam's respective economic openings (beginning with China's 1978 Open Door policy and Vietnam's 1986 Doi Moi), China and Vietnam both became Codex members: China in 1984, Vietnam in 1989.

Both China and Vietnam have national committees to study Codex standards and established Codex Contact Points to engage with Codex. These national committees coordinate and delegate tasks to relevant government ministries and provide advisory and training functions regarding Codex standards.[132]

China in particular has evolved from a 'silent observer' to an increasingly active participant. Examples include hosting or participating in Codex working groups, providing scientific data to help Codex assess food safety risks and contributing to FAO/WHO expert committees (which, in turn, provide independent scientific advice to Codex).[133] Moreover, it was elected as the Geographical Representative for Asia in the Executive Committee of the Codex Alimentarius Commission (CAC) from 2011 to 2015. According to Chinese health officials, building domestic capacity has been key to increasing involvement in Codex meetings. Meanwhile, China's domestic food safety standards are also increasingly in line with Codex.[134]

Vietnam has also become more actively involved with Codex particularly vis-à-vis participation in the Codex meetings, submission of new work proposals, and the provision of scientific data to Codex committees. For example, Vietnam co-hosted the

[130] Lei, 'A Closer Look' (n 120).

[131] Nabeshima *et al.*, 'Emergence of Asian GAPS' (n 119).

[132] Junshi Chen, 'China National Food Safety Standards & Codex' <http://studylib.net/doc/5419384/china-national-food-safety-standards-and-codex>, last accessed 12/03/2019; Keirin Association, 'Study on Strengthening Food Standards and the Certification System in the Socialist Republic of Vietnam' *Engineering and Consulting Firms Association* (2006).

[133] Junshi Chen, 'China's Contribution to Codex Standard Setting' 4 *International Food Risk Analysis Journal* (2014), 17-18.

[134] Chen, 'China's Contribution' (n 133).

45th session of the Codex Committee on Food Hygiene (CCFH) with the US[135] and hosted the 2012 FAO Regional Conference for the Asia and the Pacific in relation to food safety. Collaborating with Thailand, Vietnam developed the draft standard for fish sauce, which was later adopted.[136] However, according to an FAO/WHO evaluation, Vietnam showed minimal participation in e-working groups and no participation in physical working groups.[137] Overall, in recent years, Vietnam has showed 'comparatively moderate participation' in Codex activities—to a lesser extent than China.[138]

Meanwhile, Codex has also sought to increase participation through its 2004 Codex Trust Fund. As we find in our analysis in Section 16.4.2.2, the establishment of the Trust Fund does not appear to have had a significant further effect on participation or influence of these two countries.

16.4.2.1 Data

We use Codex sub-committee meeting reports to measure country participation and influence. Generally, each report documents delegation comments, whether there was consensus among participants, and the committee's overall progress in the standard-making process.

Such reports represent an official, comprehensive, and valid record of the meeting's proceedings. Before a report's adoption, the Codex Secretariat prepares a draft report for review on the session's final day—it is not possible to re-open discussions or insert comments that were not stated during the actual meeting session and all delegations are requested to participate.[139]

There are 802 English-language reports from 1963 to 2015, available on the Codex website, of which 786 were used in this analysis.[140] The proportion of meetings attended by China and Vietnam respectively is shown in Figure 16.9. Using a customized text algorithm, we extracted information on whether China and Vietnam were participants in each subcommittee meeting.

To extract the number of comments that China and Vietnam made at each subcommittee meeting, we first sampled six reports from 1981, 1985, 1991, 1995, 2001, and 2005 to obtain a broad cross-section of possible language used to describe delegation comments. We then used these phrases (see Appendix A) to extract comments each country made in each meeting.

135 This is the first time the CCFH held its meeting in Vietnam. See Vietnam Breaking News, 'Vietnam to Host Codex Committee on Food Hygiene' <https://www.vietnambreakingnews.com/2013/10/vn-to-host-codex-committee-on-food-hygiene/>, last accessed 12/03/2019.

136 Ministry of Agriculture and Rural Development, 'The 33rd Session of Codex Alimentarius Commission was Held in Geneva' <https://www.mard.gov.vn/en/Pages/the-33rd-session-of-codex-alimentarius-commission-was-held-in-geneva-347.aspx>, last accessed 12/03/2019.

137 FAO/WHO Coordinating Committee for Asia, Twentieth Session, 'Agenda Item 6: Codex Work Relevant to the Region' New Delhi, India, 26–30 September 2016.

138 FAO/WHO 'Agenda Item 6' (n 137), 3.

139 Codex Alimentarius Commission, 'Information for New Delegates—Report of the Session' <http://www.fao.org/fao-who-codexalimentarius/meetings/information-for-new-delegates/en/>, last accessed 12/03/2019.

140 The sixteen reports not included in the analysis contained insufficient information about participants.

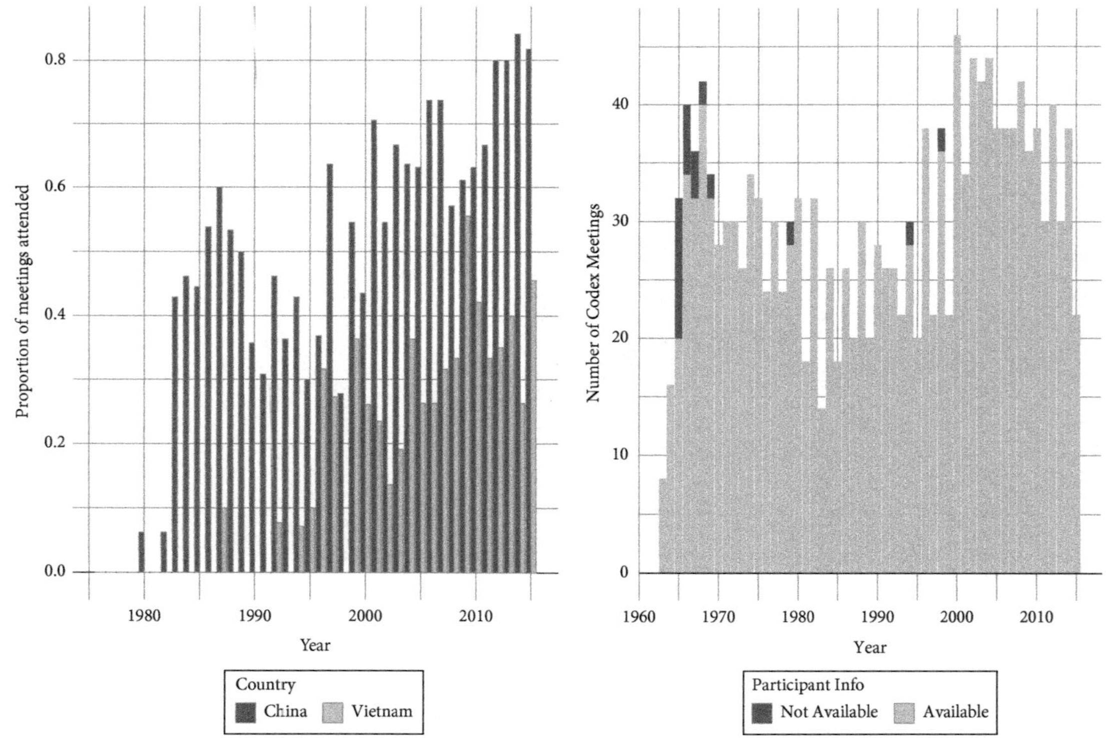

Figure 16.9 Proportion of Codex Committee Meetings Attended by Chinese and Vietnamese Participants

16.4.2.2 Analysis

We use two measures of participation (the number of participants and the number of meetings in which China and Vietnam participated) as well as two measures of influence (the number of comments per year and the number of comments per meeting) to assess differences in Chinese and Vietnamese Codex participation as well as the effect of the Codex Trust Fund on participation.[141] Note that only one representative is allowed to comment for each delegation; thus the number of comments is not a function of the number of participants. Figure 16.10 shows that China and Vietnam have increased participation and Fig. 16.11 shows that China consistently provides more comments than Vietnam, and that the difference persists or even increases over time.

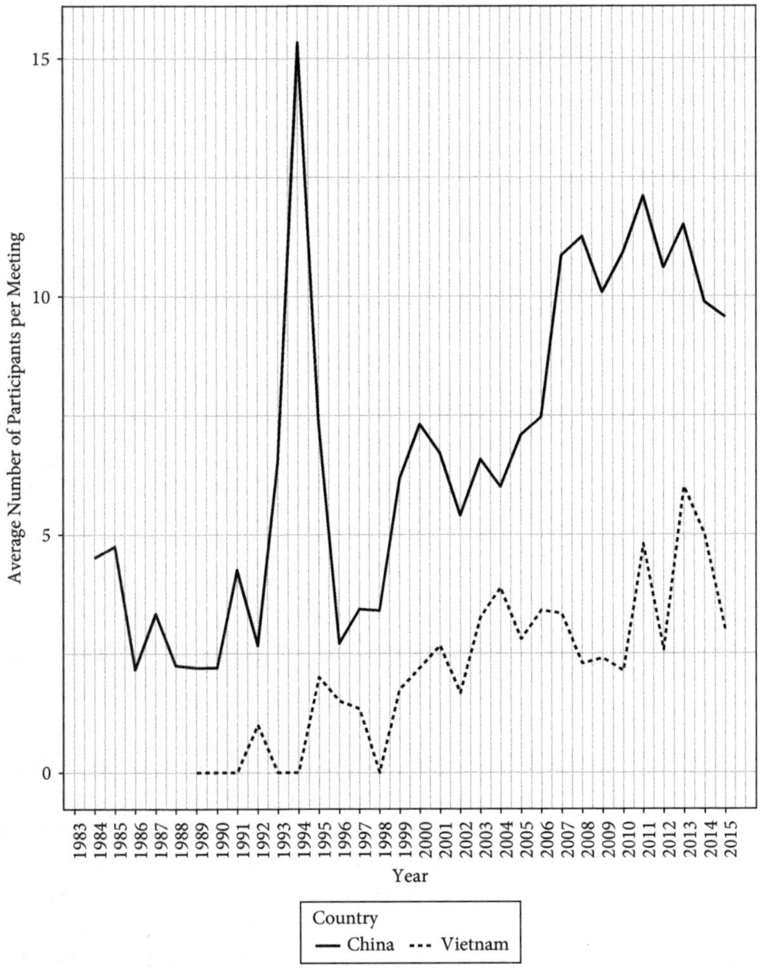

Figure 16.10 Average Number of Codex Committee Meetings attended by Chinese and Vietnamese Participants by Year

[141] Note that the crudeness of these measures means that we are unable to assess how much meaningful impact these comments had on the meeting's proceedings. However, making comments does represent a necessary condition for influence in a formal setting.

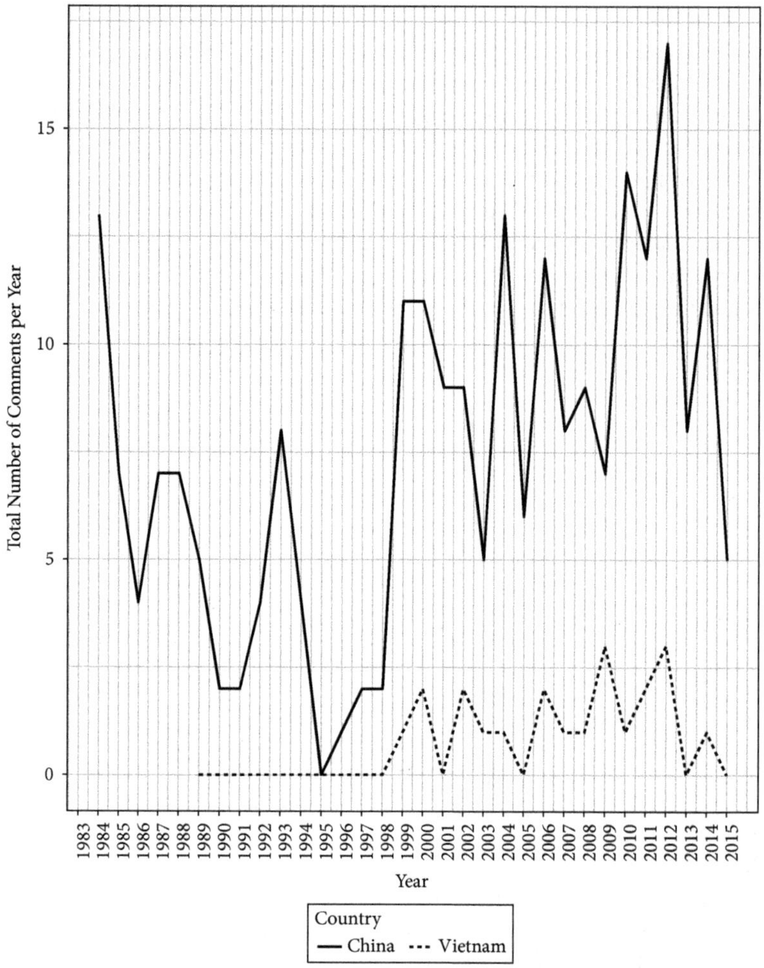

Figure 16.11 Total Number of Comments by China and Vietnam in Codex Committee Meetings

To assess whether the Codex 2004 Trust Fund increased Chinese and Vietnamese participation in Codex Meetings, we take the first difference of these measures to control for the overall trend towards greater participation among all members over time.[142] Using data both at the meeting-year level and at the aggregated year level, there is no statistically significant change in these measures after 2004 when we use a simple t-test. There is also no evidence of a substantive effect of the Codex Trust Fund on participation or influence levels when using OLS regression, where the

[142] We applied Augmented Dicky–Fuller and KPSS tests to test for unit-root and trend stationarity. Virtually all of our measures of participation were of unit root 1, suggesting the appropriateness of first differencing our measures.

dependent variable is the detrended measure of participation or influence, the main independent variable of interest is a dummy variable for the year 2004, and covariates include a continuous year variable and dummy variables for meeting types.[143]

While overall, the Codex Trust Fund has supported 2,300 more participants from developing countries,[144] our analysis suggests that for at least two countries, China and Vietnam, such efforts did not lead to a substantial increase in participation over their baseline trends. Note that had we found that the Trust Fund boosted Chinese and Vietnamese participation in excess of the prior trend, this would have provided strong evidence for its efficacy. However, given that Chinese and Vietnamese participation in Codex was already exhibiting an upward participation prior to the establishment of the Trust Fund, we consider this finding inconclusive as to the Trust Fund's efficacy in fulfilling its stated objective to increase participation.

16.5 Discussion

16.5.1 Country Participation and Influence in International Health Organizations

As the cases analysed in this chapter illustrate, China's and Vietnam's participation in different global health bodies might be explained by many factors. While institutional reforms to increase participation often provide a necessary opening, they are insufficient to explain whether and how China and Vietnam subsequently engaged. In what follows, we discuss how other factors may affect stakeholder participation, including incentives to participate, participant resources, and institutional specificity.

16.5.1.1 Incentives to participate

While increasing external stakeholder participation has been a common stated goal among international institutions, any investigation as to their success must account for stakeholder's own incentives to participate.[145]

For instance, given China and Vietnam's disease burden across a range of diseases, greater engagement with GAVI and the Global Fund is highly attractive. Meanwhile, the growing market for Chinese and Vietnamese drug and medical device exports make membership in both the ICH and the IMDRF desirable. Likewise, given the importance of agricultural export markets to China and Vietnam's economies, they have strong incentives to participate in the GlobalG.A.P. and Codex.

However, issue salience can only incentivize participation if the country is *aware* of its saliency. In DeMenno and Buthe's[146] framework, the recognition of an issue's

[143] Models available upon request.

[144] Codex Alimentarius Commission, 'FAO/WHO Codex Trust Fund' <http://www.fao.org/fao-who-codexalimentarius/about-codex/faowho-codex-trust-fund/en/>, last accessed 12/03/2019.

[145] DeMenno and Büthe, 'Voice and Influence' (n 2), esp. Section 2.5.

[146] DeMenno and Büthe, 'Voice and Influence' (n 2).

salience is assumed, but China's HIV/AIDS history shows that such recognition may be suppressed it if is socio-politically not expedient. China's experience with international pharmaceutical market standards underscores this point in a less politicized context. Only when government officials could see the potential benefits of competing on the international pharmaceutical market did they begin to take steps to bring regulation of the domestic pharmaceutical market up to speed.

Issue salience can also run up against hard budget constraints. For instance, though the majority of people who have HBV live in China, GAVI did not have sufficient resources to fulfil its stated desire to reduce the prevalence of HBV in China and provide assistance to other countries.

16.5.1.2 The importance of participant resources

While issue salience is high for both countries across these different HGBs, China's participation has generally been more substantive than Vietnam's. Stakeholder resources can play a substantial role in explaining this divergence.[147]

Indeed, the rationale for focusing on China and Vietnam to begin with is that while they are similar in many respects, their differences in economy, population and power allows us to explore whether any conclusions we draw about the efficacy of increasing external stakeholder participation is ultimately a function of differences in stakeholder material and political resources. In terms of their similarities, China and Vietnam are both Asian countries with nominally Communist authoritarian governments which have undertaken significant capitalist market reforms in the past thirty years. Such reforms have been remarkably successful in raising income levels and living standards in both countries.

However, China is a famously populous country, with 1.39 billion people in 2017. Vietnam's relatively smaller population of 95.54 million says less about Vietnam—it is the fifteenth most populous country in the world—than it does about China's outlier status. Meanwhile, China's extraordinary economic growth and military aspirations have also marked it as a rising political and economic power. As such, China arguably has greater ability to participate and shape global governance. In contrast, while Vietnam has been one of the world's fastest growing economies, its more modest market size and political clout has limited its participation in global governance.

These differences in economic and political resources can have a substantial impact on China and Vietnam's engagement in global health governance. For instance, whereas Vietnam's smaller population and economy means that it must rely on ASEAN to engage with the ICH and IMDRF, because these bodies generally do not offer membership to individual countries except for the largest ones, China faces no such collective action problem. China's resources have limits of course as its inability to immediately secure membership with the ICH and IMDRF attests to. Yet, its greater resources compared to Vietnam means that China still is more readily able to participate in global health bodies.

Meanwhile, stakeholder resources can do more than just enable participation—they can shape its very nature. When a global health body has economic leverage over

[147] Berman, 'Stakeholder Participation Reforms' (n 3); DeMenno and Büthe, 'Voice and Influence' (n 2).

participants, such leverage is less compelling as the stakeholder's economic status improves, as illustrated by China's transition from aid recipient to donor. This status confers more negotiating room for China compared to Vietnam, which firmly remains an aid recipient, at least as evidenced in their respective experiences with GAVI and the Global Fund show.

Lastly, though global bodies have taken steps to increase participation of previously marginalized stakeholders,[148] we find that overall, SDOs have made a greater effort to direct such efforts towards China than towards Vietnam. Indeed, the ICH, the IMDRF, and the GlobalG.A.P. have all made entreaties for greater Chinese participation via invitations to meetings and training sessions. These efforts likely reflect China's relatively larger market power. Meanwhile, engagement with stakeholders is a prerequisite for dealing with disease burdens, which may explain the GAVI and the Global Fund's more equitable, if still skewed, engagement with both countries.

16.5.1.3 Participation, influence, and institutional specificity

Less discussed than the themes covered earlier in either DeMenno and Buthe[149] and Berman[150] is how the nature of the international organization can also play an important role in shaping stakeholder participation and influence. Here we observe a substantive difference in both China and Vietnam's engagement with global bodies whose actions have consequences of greater specificity to individual countries, as exemplified by funding agencies, versus those which set very precise rules with far-reaching global consequences, as exemplified by SDOs.

With regards to the former, an external stakeholder's disease burden creates its own leverage, which affects how it engages with the funder. The more a global health burden is produced in a particular country, the more realizing the mission is contingent on that country's participation. For example, one of GAVI's first stated goals was to reduce the incidence of hepatitis B.[151] Given that a substantial proportion of people afflicted with hepatitis B live in China, GAVI's ability to reach its goal was largely contingent on collaboration with China.

The particulars of the institutional design are also pertinent because they can privilege different mechanisms of influence. For instance, stakeholder influence over policy outcomes appears be more heavily driven by policy learning in funding agencies compared to SSOs. In funding agencies, the technical and political information that stakeholders can provide is often of greater significance as the relevant policy outcomes directly affect the stakeholder's domestic population. Meanwhile, policy outcomes produced by SDOs generally have broader international consequences, reducing the relevance of the country-specific technical and political information national governments as stakeholders can offer. While policy learning can certainly play a substantial role in the relationship between the stakeholder and the SDO, in the case of China and Vietnam, the dynamic between the two is often driven more by the stakeholder's desire to learn

[148] Berman, 'Stakeholder Participation Reforms' (n 3).
[149] DeMenno and Büthe, 'Voice and Influence' (n 2).
[150] Berman, 'Stakeholder Participation Reforms' (n 3).
[151] GAVI, 'Hepatitis B Vaccine Support—GAVI's response' <http://www.gavi.org/support/nvs/hepb/>, last accessed 12/03/2019.

technical and political information from the SDO. Consequently, the international SDOs generally plays a bigger role in influencing the stakeholders' policy than vice-versa.

Meanwhile, the nature of the issue area and institutional design further encourages adaptation in how the international health funding agency subsequently operates in a way that is not true of international SDOs. For instance, though GAVI originally only envisioned itself as a funding mechanism, it was pushed to change its operating procedures and set up a country office in China, an adaptation which proved integral to the partnership's subsequent success.

China and Vietnam's participation in international health SDOs like the ICH, the IMDRF, and Codex have not prompted any comparable adaption likely in part due to the centralized, rather than locale-specific, nature of the standard-setting process. Although SDOs clearly have made institutional adaptations to encourage greater participation from previously marginalized stakeholders, these adaptations are primarily aimed at expanding participation, not changing the nature of participation itself.

The creation of country GAPs within the GlobalG.A.P. framework at first glance appears to contradict this assessment. Yet, while the creation of ChinaG.A.P. and VietG.A.P. show that standards can be increasingly localized, their creation can better be understood as an attempt to replicate the GlobalG.A.P. within specific countries rather than attempting to change the GlobalG.A.P. itself.

16.5.2 NGO Participation and Influence in International Health Organizations

Finally, a goal of this volume is to explore to what extent and under what conditions reforms to increase participation affect not just previously marginalized countries but previously marginalized civil society members. This chapter has thus far discussed civil society participation only to a very limited extent. This omission is no accident. China's and Vietnam's authoritarian governments' attitude towards civil society can be described at best as tolerant, with an ever-present wariness of civil society's potential to disturb political stability. As such, civil society's interactions with HGBs are highly mediated by the state, limiting the extent to which it can take advantage of reforms to increase participation of external stakeholders. For instance, the Global Funds' efforts to increase the participatory engagement and influence of NGOs were ultimately limited by the Chinese government.

Meanwhile, for SDOs, where participation is more centralized, civil society engagement has been even less prominent. To date we have found no evidence of non-governmental Chinese or Vietnamese participation in the ICH. To the extent that non-governmental voices are heard in the IMDRF, the Global Diagnostic Imaging, Healthcare IT, and Radiation Therapy Trade Association (DITTA), a global trade organization which counts domestic industry trade organizations as members, has actively participated in IMDRF working groups and forums.[152] The Chinese

[152] Nicole Denjoy, 'IMDRF Stakeholders Meeting' *Global Diagnostics Imaging, Healthcare IT & Radiation Therapy Trade Association* <http://www.imdrf.org/docs/imdrf/final/meetings/imdrf-meet-130319-france-presentation-ditta.pdf>, last accessed 12/03/2019.

Association for Medical Devices Industry (CAMDI), is a member of DITTA, while DITTA has no Vietnamese representation. Established in 1991,[153] CAMDI is a trade association for medical device companies (to date forty-nine) and includes both Chinese and foreign companies as members. Meanwhile, through the AHWP's industry representative, Johnson and Johnson's China division has participated in IMDRF/GHTF Meetings, though the AHWP's IMDRF status is only: observer affiliate organization.[154]

Meanwhile, while the GlobalG.A.P. is dominated by European producers and retailers, ChinaG.A.P. and VietG.A.P. were spearheaded by state agencies, with limited initiative or input from industry actors.

Finally, although Codex has generally been characterized as a government-industry affair,[155] most of the listed Chinese and Vietnamese participants are government officials. In Codex meetings from 1987 to 2015, there were 2,162 Chinese participants, among which 133 were from industry (6.2%), twenty-eight from academia (1.3%), and the rest from the government (92.6%), though industry representation has been growing over time. In the same time period, there were only 314 total Vietnamese participants. Similarly, there were only twenty-one representatives from industry (6.6%), seven from academia and CSOs (2.2%); all others were government officials (91.2%).

While these is some contact between Chinese and Vietnamese NGOs and global health bodies, our investigation suggests that such engagement is sporadic and shallow at best—government engagement is overwhelmingly dominant.

16.6 Conclusion

This chapter has provided an overview of how China and Vietnam engage with major global health organizations including GAVI, the Global Fund, the ICH, the IMDRF, GlobalG.A.P., and Codex, and their respective attempts to increase participation through institutional reforms.

We find evidence to suggest that stakeholder resources are an important factor in explaining China's and Vietnam's relative engagement across a variety of inter-related policy areas, public health, drug safety, and food safety. China's actual engagement is greater than Vietnam's on most counts. Where this engagement takes place differs according to the overall aims of the institution. For international health IOs, there is a greater emphasis on engagement at the level of domestic health project implementation while for international SDOs, the emphasis is on engagement with the IOs themselves as this is where the rules that affect access to access markets are set.

[153] China Association for Medical Devices Industry, 'Introduction' <http://en.camdi.org/about.html>, last accessed 12/03/2019.

[154] GHTF, 'Meeting Minutes, Santa Rosa, USA October 2010' <http://www.imdrf.org/docs/ghtf/final/sg1/meetings/ghtf-sg1-n081-meeting-minutes-101005-usa-santa-rosa.pdf>, last accessed 12/03/2019.

[155] See, e.g. Tim Büthe and Nathaniel Harris, 'The Codex Alimentarius Commission: A Hybrid Public-Private Regulator' in Thomas Hale and David Held (eds), *Handbook of Transnational Governance: Institutions and Innovations* (Polity Press 2011) 219-228.

Appendix

We used all combinations of the following nouns (Table 16.3) and verbs (Table 16.4) to extract the number of comments China or Vietnam made during a Codex committee meeting.

Table 16.3 Nouns used to refer to China and Vietnam in Codex Meetings

Viet Nam	China
Vietnam	the Peoples Republic of China
the delegation of Vietnam	the People's Republic of China
the delegation of Viet Nam	the Chinese delegation
the Vietnamese delegation	the delegation of China
	the delegation of the Peoples Republic of China
	the delegation of the People s Republic of China

Table 16.4 Verbs used by China and Vietnam when making comments in Codex Meetings

proposed	supported	posed
pointed	indicated	requested
noted	emphasized	presented
disagreed	drew attention to	underlined
introduced	felt	was the opinion of
informed	considered	proposal by
had reservations	reserved	proposal of
stressed	opposed	proposal from
stated	suggested	comments of
expressed	questioned	working group led by

17
India and the Philippines in Global Health Governance

Tim Büthe, Sachin Chaturvedi, Peter B Payoyo, and Krishna Ravi Srinivas *

17.1 Introduction

This chapter examines and compares changes in the engagement and influence of Indian and Philippine stakeholders in global health governance. We particularly try to assess whether—and to what extent—the institutional reforms, introduced in recent decades by global health bodies with the supposed purpose of increasing stakeholder participation,[1] have changed the magnitude and character of their participation in the World Health Organization (WHO), the Codex Alimentarius Commission (Codex), the International Council for Harmonisation (ICH), and the Global Fund to Fight AIDS, Tuberculosis and Malaria (Global Fund). In keeping with this volume's analytical framework by DeMenno and Büthe,[2] and following the comparative country pair analysis for Brazil and Argentina,[3] we also consider the role of other factors that may have influenced the extent to which stakeholders make use of participation opportunities. In particular, we discuss (i) the importance of the global body for the governments and key non-governmental stakeholders from India and the Philippines, as well as (ii) stakeholders' resources, most importantly their access to the required material means, expertise, and collective action capacity.

We compare India and the Philippines, following the matched country-pair research design explained in the chapter by Büthe and Cheng.[4] We thus examine two

* [This paper is based on detailed single-country case studies of India in Global Health Governance, written by Sachin Chaturvedi and Krishna Ravi Srinivas, and of the Philippines in Global Health Governance, written by Peter B. Payoyo, both published separately as Graduate Institute working papers. Tim Büthe's primary contribution has been to draw together the information from the two case studies, preceded by a common introduction and to supplement the empirical sections—in some parts substantially—with additional original research, to allow for the consistently structured comparative analysis presented here. Chaturvedi, Payoyo, and Srinivas thank Ayelet Berman for guidance, comments and suggestions, which helped to improve the underlying country case studies. Chaturvei and Srinivas also thank Dr. Namrata Pathak and Ms. Nimita Pandey for excellent research assistance for the India case study. They write in a personal capacity; any opinions or assessments in this paper do not necessarily reflect the views of RIS or any other institution/organization.]

[1] For an overview of those reforms, see Ayelet Berman, 'Stakeholder Participation Reforms in Global Health Governance.' Chapter 13, this volume.

[2] Mercy B DeMenno and Tim Büthe, 'Voice and Influence in Global Governance: An Analytical Framework,' Chapter 2, this volume.

[3] André de Mello e Souza and Facundo Pérez Aznar, 'Brazil and Argentina in Global Health Governance,' Chapter 15, this volume.

[4] Tim Büthe and Cindy Cheng, 'Analysing the Consequences of Institutional Reforms Using Country Pairs: A Note on the (Coarsened Exact) Matched-Country-Pairs Methodology of the Rethinking Stakeholder Participation Project.' Chapter 3, this volume.

Tim Büthe, Sachin Chaturvedi, Peter B Payoyo, and Krishna Ravi Srinivas, *India and the Philippines in Global Health Governance* In: *Rethinking Participation in Global Governance.* Edited by: Joost Pauwelyn, Martino Maggetti, Tim Büthe, and Ayelet Berman, Oxford University Press.
 DOI: 10.1093/oso/9780198852568.003.0017

lower-middle-income countries in South/East Asia (the Indo-Pacific region), which have much in common. Both have democratic political regimes, strengthened by several decades of strong economic growth (even if more unevenly in the most recent years), thanks in substantial part to their increasing integration into the world economy, but both also face many challenges related to rapid development and residual poverty. Both countries, moreover, have high stakes in global health governance, since both are characterized by a very high disease burden, including high incidences of key communicable diseases and rising rates of non-communicable diseases. India has the world's largest absolute burden of at least eleven of the seventeen WHO-recognized major neglected tropical diseases;[5] in the Philippines, thirteen out of the seventeen WHO-recognized neglected tropical diseases remain endemic.[6] Both countries exhibit a high prevalence of numerous risk factors, as well as pervasive health inequities.

At the same time, India and the Philippines also differ, most notably in size and consequently the power resources they might be able to bring to global governance of any issue. India is an emerging superpower. It occupies most of a subcontinent and, with 1.34 billion inhabitants, is on the verge of surpassing China as the most populous country. By contrast, some 100 million inhabitants, spread densely over an archipelago of more than seven thousand islands to the east of the South China Sea, make the Philippines not a small, but a much smaller, country—with regional, rather than global, ambitions. This difference in size and political ambition is a major motivation for the comparison.[7] Moreover and especially important for *some* fields of global health, only India is a major supplier of generic medicines and vaccines, an increasingly important source of pharmaceutical innovations, and a vocal proponent of greater international recognition for 'traditional systems of medicine'.

To assess whether Indian and/or Philippine stakeholders' actual participation has increased in the aftermath of the reforms, we examine membership status, attendance of meetings (of the major decision-making bodies and more specialized committees and working groups where draft standards, policy proposals and various details of global rules are often developed). We also analyze actual speaking roles at such meetings, as well as indications of more indirect forms of exercising voice, such as the submission of position papers, funding proposals, and other forms of input into a given health governance body's process of deliberation and decision-making. We draw on public and internal documents from the four global health bodies, including meeting minutes, archives of submissions received, etc., supplemented by press reports, direct communications by the authors with representatives of the global bodies or Indian or Philippine stakeholders, and secondary literature.

Whether a particular country or any other sub- or transnational stakeholder has exerted influence in the course of often complex multilateral negotiating and decision-making processes is much harder to ascertain. As noted in the concluding chapter of this volume,[8] establishing influence requires the consideration of non-decisions, such as

[5] 'WHO Country Cooperation Strategy at a Glance: India' <https://apps.who.int/iris/handle/10665/136895>, last accessed 04/18/2020; Peter J Hotez and Ashish Damania, 'India's Neglected Tropical Diseases' 12(3) *PLOS Neglected Tropical Diseases* (2018), e0006038.

[6] 'WHO Country Cooperation Strategy at a Glance: Philippines 2011–2016', updated May 2014 and May 2015, and for 2017–2022 updated May 2018 <http://apps.who.int/iris/bitstream/10665/136828/1/ccsbrief_phl_en.pdf>, last accessed 04/18/2020.

[7] See Büthe and Cheng, 'Note on the Matched-Country-Pairs Methodology' (n 4).

[8] Tim Büthe, Joost Pauwelyn, Martino Maggetti and Ayelet Berman, 'Conclusion: The Participation of Marginalized Stakeholders in Global Governance.' Chapter 25, this volume.

preventing (or even just delaying) the adoption of an unwanted policy, rule, or standard, as well as possible changes in the terms of the debate, through which intellectual hegemony might be established or challenged. Generally speaking, we build on Dahl's notion of power to assess possible influence. A determination that a stakeholder exerted influence thus requires indications that outcomes differed from what they 'would have been' in the absence of the stakeholder's participation, and we generally expect the divergence to change the outcome in the direction of the stakeholder's preferences.

17.2 World Health Organization (WHO)

The WHO is the global health governance body with the broadest portfolio. Established after the Second World War in the context of the founding of the United Nations, it is a traditional international—that is, inter-governmental—organization. Headquartered in Geneva, it recognizes only states as members. However, the WHO has long acknowledged a wide range of stakeholders.[9] This section examines the participation of India and the Philippines in the WHO prior to and after the stakeholder participation reforms of recent years.[10]

17.2.1 Importance, Incentives, and Constraints

Both India and the Philippines have a close, long-standing relationship with the WHO. India was one of the founding members of the WHO, having ratified the founding documents on 12 January 1948, less than five months after gaining independence, and Delhi became the host for the first WHO Regional Office (for South-East Asia) later that month.[11] Over the ensuing decades, the WHO played an important role in enabling India to address various public health challenges. In 1967, the WHO launched its 'Intensified Smallpox Eradication Programme', with India as a special focus since India at that point accounted for nearly two-thirds of all recorded cases and more than 26,000 deaths in that year alone. The ensuing ten-year close coordination between the Indian government and the WHO resulted in the eradication of smallpox in India by 1977, three years before the campaign was considered successful worldwide.[12] Polio eradication is another public health achievement that would not have been possible without cooperation with the WHO: after decades-long efforts, India was declared polio-free in 2014.[13] In addition

[9] For overviews of the WHO and its work, see Kelley Lee, *The World Health Organization (WHO)* (Routledge 2008); Yves Beigbeder, *The World Health Organization: Achievements and Failures* (Routledge 2018).

[10] For the antecedents of the WHO reforms, see Derek Yach, 'World Health Organization Reform' 106(11) *American Journal of Public Health* (2016) 1904-1906; Jon Lidén, 'The World Health Organization and Global Health Governance: Post-1990' 128(2) *Public Health* (February 2014) 141-147. For an overview, see the extensive and very informative 'WHO reform'- pages on the WHO website and Berman (n 1), esp. Section 13.3.2.

[11] Milton I Roemer, 'The World Health Organization and Its Work' (Excerpt from 'Internationalism in Medicine and Public Health') in W F Bynum and R Porter (eds), *Companion Encyclopedia of the History of Medicine* (Routledge 1993) 1417-1435.) Milton I Roemer, 'The World Health Organization and Its Work' 98(9) American Journal of Public Health (2008) 1594–1597.

[12] Sanjoy Bhattacharya, *Expunging Variola: The Control and Eradication of Smallpox in India, 1947–1977* (Longman and Sangam Books 2006).

[13] WHO Regional Office for South-East Asia, 'WHO South-East Asia Region certified polio-free', Press release 27 March 2014 <http://www.searo.who.int/mediacentre/releases/2016/1629/en/>, last accessed 06/07/2018.

to being considered important for contributing funding and expertise to the achievement of better health outcomes, the WHO is seen by India as having enhanced its capacity for (participating in global) health governance.

The Philippines similarly was a 1948 founding member state of the WHO and since 1951 has been the host for the WHO Western Pacific Regional Office. While the Philippines has not played a similarly prominent role in major WHO campaigns as India did with smallpox and polio, the WHO is seen as also having been an effective and important contributor to health care capacity building and improving health outcomes in the Philippines. From major improvements in maternal and child health[14] to tobacco control (anti-smoking campaign),[15] to the achievement of limited but near-universal health coverage (a long-standing ambition for successive Philippine governments),[16] the Philippines has leveraged its WHO membership to advance national health goals. The WHO remains important for the Philippines, above all for what may be said to have been one of the WHO's core functions from the beginning: 'strengthening national health services',[17] but also for its other core functions, like providing early warnings of impending new health risks and emergency assistance—a critical concern for what is considered the third-most disaster-prone country in the world.[18]

Some have suggested that the WHO's role in global health has diminished, while developing countries' participation in global health governance has increased.[19] And indeed, new actors and institutions have emerged, including private ones such as the Gates Foundation. For some specific issues, these new players provide alternative sources of funding, as well as capacity-building and networking opportunities, reducing the centrality of the WHO as a global governance body for Indian and Philippine stakeholders. And India, in particular, pursues its global health agenda not just via the WHO but also in various other international bodies, including organizations with a much broader agenda, such as the BRICS, IBSA, and the G77. Yet, the WHO remains for both countries the single most important international health governance body, affirming India's and the Philippines' achievements and facilitating

[14] Xerxes Seposo, 'Developmental Changes in the Philippine Health System: Accomplishments, Successes and Challenges' 7(4) *Healthcare* (2019), Art.116.

[15] Lee, *World Health Organization* (n 9), 71ff; Beigbeder, *The World Health Organization* (n 9), 157–165; WHO, *WHO in the Philippines* (WHO Western Pacific Region Office (WHO-WPRO) 2017), 5, 7.

[16] A G Romualdez, J F E dela Rosa, J D Flavier, S L A Quimbo, K Y Hartigan-Go, L P Lagrada, and L C David, *The Philippines Health System Review* (WHO-WPRO 2011); WHO, *WHO in the Philippines* (n 15), 9; *The UHC Act in the Philippines: A New Dawn for Health Care* (WHO, 14 March 2019) <http://www.who.int/philippines/news/feature-stories/detail/uhc-act-in-the-philippines-a-new-dawn-for-health-care >, last accessed 04/25/2020.

[17] Beigbeder, *World Health Organization* (n 9), 5. Sustained support from and organic cooperation with WHO in key areas of Philippines' health sector reform has made WHO the leading technical partner of the Philippine Department of Health.

[18] According to the United Nations University Institute for Environment and Human Security (UNU-EHS) and Alliance Development Works/*Bündnis Entwicklung Hilft* (BEH) World Risk Index, a ranking of 173 countries by their risk of experiencing disasters due to natural hazards such as earthquakes, volcanic eruptions, storms, floods, droughts, and sea level rise—and related vulnerabilities.

[19] Matthias Helble, Zulfiqar Ali, and Jera Lego, 'A Comparison of Global Governance Across Sectors: Global Health, Trade, and Multilateral Development Finance' (2018) 806 *Asian Development Bank Institute Working Paper* 7 <https://www.adb.org/publications/comparison-global-governance-across-sectors-health-trade-development-finance>, last accessed 06/07/2018.

continued improvements in Indian and Philippine public health (as different as the specific achievement and sought-after improvements may be).

In recent years, India's incentives to seek voice and influence in the WHO have further increased, for several reasons. India has sought international recognition of the commercial and medical potential and importance of Indian traditional medicines, and the WHO is an ideal forum for gaining such recognition. The WHO plays a central role in shaping global discourses around health and medicine, making it an important forum for India to defend its position on access to medicine[20] and to defend its stance on the use of terms like 'substandard drugs' and 'counterfeit drugs' against generics and drugs from the developing world[21]—an issue on which India has long held a principled position but increasingly also has a substantial commercial stake, given its by now very large pharma industry. India's ability to participate has also increased thanks to reduced constraints. Years of rapid economic growth have eased resource limitations, and Indian government representatives' experience with regional and international governance have increased their capabilities for effective participation in global health governance.

Last but not least, as the sole UN body focused on health, the WHO also allows the Indian government to form networks and alliances to support its leadership role in global institutions on behalf of developing countries. Consequently, greater assertiveness of the Indian government's foreign policy stance has further increased the importance of the WHO for India. As Amrita Narlikar writes:

> India may ... be at a turning point under the leadership of Prime Minister Modi. Never before has the commitment to growth and development been so clearly mandated; nor has it been manifest in such a clear set of second-generation economic reforms. As a government committed to economic growth, the Modi regime is more heavily invested in the existing rules and structures of global economic governance than most previous administrations ... translating into a growing ability to take on a more constructive role in global governance.[22]

The Philippines do not share India's global leadership ambitions, but also see the WHO as valuable in that it 'provide[s] a platform for the Philippines to engage in regional and global health initiatives'.[23]

17.2.2 Governmental Participation and Influence

India's relationship with, and participation in, the WHO has evolved over seven decades. Initially, the relationship was skewed towards the WHO offering expert advice,

[20] See Mello e Souza and Pérez Aznar, 'Brazil and Argentina' (n 3) for a brief discussion of the important role played by BRICS coordination on this topic.

[21] Amrita Narlikar, 'India's Role in Global Governance: A Modification?' 93(1) *International Affairs* (2017) 93-111.

[22] Narlikar, 'India's Role' (n 21), 110.

[23] WHO, *Philippines WHO Country Cooperation Strategy 2017-2022* (WHO-WPRO 2017), vii <https://apps.who.int/iris/handle/10665/259907>, last accessed 04/17/2020.

as well as financial and in-kind support, mostly for disease eradication efforts in India. During those early decades, the WHO often set the agenda. Over time, the relationship has developed into much more of a partnership, especially between the WHO and the Indian Ministry of Health and Family Welfare. Philippine participation in the WHO has similarly evolved, becoming more even over time. These long-term trends in the two countries' relationships with the WHO have accelerated and shifted in recent years, with at least some of the changes attributable to the WHO's stakeholder participation reforms.

17.2.2.1 Post-reform participation and influence

India still benefits from WHO expertise (particularly when new diseases emerge) and from WHO capacity-building support, but increasingly, India is not only a beneficiary, but also a donor of financial contributions to the WHO[24] and, especially, a donor of medical and public health expertise. The WHO continues to conduct and publish numerous studies concerning health (policy) issues in India every year, and it is involved in numerous projects and programmes aimed at improving health and healthcare in India. However, the projects that are focused on public health *in India* have, in recent years, increasingly become genuine joint projects of the WHO and Indian public institutions, for which Indian government officials join forces with WHO officials—from agenda-setting to implementation. The jointly developed WHO India Country Cooperation Strategy (CCS) for 2012–2017[25] and the new WHO India Country Cooperation Strategy 2019–2023 with its four 'strategic priorities', which reflect long-standing Indian domestic priorities,[26] illustrate this new, increasingly equal cooperation. And when it comes to shaping the public health agenda *beyond India*, India plays a role in setting the agenda, setting standards (for instance for the Millennium Development and Sustainable Development Goals on healthcare), and participating in decisions in ways that also suggest that India is at least sometimes able to leverage its participation into influence.

India's ability to exert real influence in the WHO is nicely illustrated by the anti-smoking ('tobacco control') issue. Beginning in 2004, under the leadership of Indian Minister for Health Anbumani Ramadoss, the government made an intensified push to reduce smoking as a growing cause of deadly cancer, combining advocacy campaigns that mobilized civil society and parts of the media with tobacco control legislation at the national level.[27] To advance its policy preference, India—as the country

[24] India's increasing voluntary financial contributions to the WHO budget illustrate this point well; see, e.g. WHO (65th World Health Assembly) 'Annex: Voluntary Contributions by Fund and by Donor for the Financial Period 2010 to 2011' A/65/29 Add.1 vs. WHO (71st World Health Assembly) 'Voluntary Contributions by Fund and by Contributor, 2017' (19 April 2018) A71/INF./2. This role is particularly notable on specific priority items: In 2014, for instance, India was the fifth-largest financial contributor to the WHO Ebola crisis response (after the US, the EU, Canada, and the Netherlands); see Madhurima Nundy, 'The Ebola Crisis: Responses from India and China' 23 *Institute of China Studies Analysis* (2014) 1–9.

[25] See https://www.who.int/india/our-work and Ministry of Health & Family Welfare, *Annual Report 2011–2012*, 172 <https://mohfw.gov.in/documents/publication1/publication-archives>, last accessed 06/07/2018.

[26] See <https://www.who.int/india/country-cooperation-strategy-2019-2023>, last accessed 04/16/2020.

[27] Jagdish Kaur and D C Jain, 'Tobacco Control Policies in India: Implementation and Challenges', 55(3) *Indian Journal of Public Health* (2011) 220-227.

with the second-largest number of tobacco users in the world—also pushed the issue internationally; a key part of that strategy was to foster a breakthrough on the long-stalled issue at the WHO. The Indian delegation played a key role during the 2005 negotiations for the Framework Convention on Tobacco Control (FCTC), especially on key components such as Article 13.[28] Further, during the intersession periods of the intergovernmental negotiations, India chaired four regional consultations and forged consensus on a draft text of the FCTC.[29] The Indian skill and success in these negotiations was later rewarded by being unanimously elected as the regional coordinator for the South-East Asian members of the WHO in the negotiations. India's participation and support were also beneficial to the FCTC by enhancing the legitimacy of this attempt to regulate and reduce tobacco use internationally.[30] In turn, the FCTC legitimated Indian efforts to strengthen its domestic laws and regulations concerning the production, sale, and consumption of tobacco products. In addition, participation in the FCTC enabled India to showcase its commitment to solving a major global public health concern.

Similarly, India has pushed to put and keep 'neglected tropical diseases' on the WHO agenda, resulting in an intensified effort known as the 2012 WHO Neglected Tropical Diseases Roadmap. Thanks to this effort, the campaign to eliminate yaws in India (one such tropical disease), which started as the first disease eradication programme launched with WHO support in 1952, succeeded in 2016, when India became the first country under the 2012 Roadmap to eliminate yaws.[31]

Philippine participation in the WHO similarly now involves much more of a give-and-take relationship, where the Philippines does not just benefit from its engagement with the WHO but also contributes substantial technical, as well as political information to the WHO's policy learning process[32]—and as a consequence appears to be able to exercise influence. Today, the Philippines participates in WHO decision-making at all three levels of WHO health governance: at the global/HQ level (both via the World Health Assembly and the Executive Board), at the regional level (not least thanks to the regional office for the Western Pacific, which has remained in Manila ever since it was set up there in 1951) and at the national level.[33]

At the national level, the Philippines continues to benefit from a range of WHO programmes, adapted to the needs and priorities of the Philippine government and society via the WHO Philippines Country Cooperation Strategy, developed jointly by

[28] Article 13 covers tobacco advertising, promotion, and sponsorship.

[29] Kelley Lee, Adam Kamradt-Scott, Sungwon Yoon, and Jingying Xu, 'Asian Contributions to Three Instruments of Global Health Governance' 3(3) *Global Policy* (2012) 348-361, 351.

[30] Gauravi A Mishra, Sharmila A Pimple, and Surendra S Shastri, 'An Overview of the Tobacco Problem in India' 33(3) *Indian Journal of Medical and Paediatric Oncology* (2012) 139-145.

[31] WHO Regional Office for South-East Asia, 'WHO Felicitates India for Yaws, Maternal and Neonatal Tetanus Elimination' *Press Release* (14 July 2016) <http://www.searo.who.int/mediacentre/releases/2016/1629/en/>, last accessed 06/07/2018.

[32] See DeMenno and Büthe, 'Voice and Influence' (n 2), esp. Section 2.6.1.

[33] Recently, the Philippines has also engaged the WHO at the subnational level, endorsing the WHO working directly with local governments to define and execute public health missions; see, e.g. 'WHO Subnational Initiative: Accelerating Convergence Efforts Through Systems Strengthening for Maternal and Newborn Health (AcCESS for MNH)' in WHO Media Centre, 21 April 2016 <http://www.wpro.who.int/philippines/mediacentre/features/sni_access_mnh_davao/en/>, last accessed 11/01/2018.

the WHO and the Republic of the Philippines' Department of Health.[34] This strategy includes financial support for the Philippine health sector—from the assessed and voluntary contributions in the WHO budget, as well as from other funds mobilized through the WHO—in accordance with the Biennium Country Budget, planned and programmed every two years by the WHO together with the Department of Health of the Philippines. And it allows the Philippines to draw upon WHO medical and technical expertise for the pursuit of Philippine health policy priorities—with notable potential for positively reinforcing feedback between the Philippines and the WHO.

'Universal health coverage' (UHC) provides an illustrative example.[35] UHC, more comprehensively denominated as 'universal health care' in the Philippines, has long been at the heart and centre of Philippine health policy. Successive governments have pursued this elusive objective ever since the country embarked on its systemic health sector reform and development in the 1990s—in the hopes that it might allow the country to overcome the vast and persistent inequity in access to health care, exacerbated by demographic, geographic, and structural challenges and barriers.[36] In a series of programmes over the years, the WHO has worked with the Philippines to move towards that goal, culminating in the adoption of the landmark Philippine UHC Act in February 2019. In the context of the 2030 Agenda for Sustainable Development, the WHO itself has now adopted 'universal health coverage' as a high-level goal, which it pursues with a Philippine co-chair of the global SDG Interagency Expert Group on Sustainable Development Indicators.[37] Among the thirteen specific commitments and targets indicated for Sustainable Development Goal 3 ('ensure healthy lives and promoting the well-being at all ages is essential to sustainable development'), the WHO has determined that target item 3.8—'achieving universal health coverage'—underpins all other targets and as a consequence will be given top priority in future WHO strategic action.[38] The WHO's adoption of the UHC goal, in turn, has strengthened the Philippines' calls for more active engagement in WHO decision-making at all levels so as to ensure that more WHO resources are devoted to this goal—which, of course, also serves its own national health needs and priorities.[39]

At the international level, decision-making and norm creation in the governing bodies of the WHO predominantly follows the traditional intergovernmental process of deliberation and voting by state parties. For example, the system for electing members to the Executive Board is based on representation from WHO regional groupings.

[34] WHO, *Philippines CCS 2017-2022* (n 23).

[35] While the Indian examples and this case from the Philippines seem quite clear, we note as a caveat that, in any ongoing discursive exchange, it can be very difficult to discern any one party's 'true' preference, particularly when one party is in many ways intellectually hegemonic; see Antonio Gramsci, *The Prison Notebooks* (Columbia University Press 1992); Steven Lukes, *Power: A Radical View*, 2nd ed. (Palgrave 2004).

[36] On the 'fragmented' system of the public health governance, see WHO, *The Philippines Health System Review* (n 16).

[37] WHO, *Philippines CCS 2017-2022* (n 23), 8ff.

[38] M Chan and G H Bruntland, 'Universal Health Coverage: An Affordable Goal for All' *Commentary* (12 December 2016) <http://www.who.int/mediacentre/commentaries/2016/universal-health-coverage/en/>; WHO Doc. WHA 69.11/28 May 2016 <http://apps.who.int/gb/ebwha/pdf_files/WHA69/A69_R11-en.pdf>, both last accessed 04/22/2020.

[39] Philippine Department of Health, *National Objectives for Health 2011–2016*, (2012), 130 <http://www.doh.gov.ph/sites/default/files/publications/noh2016.pdf, last accessed 04/09/2018.

This has assured the Philippines of a seat on the Executive Board several times.[40] Membership in the WHO Executive Board allows the Philippines to provide direct input into WHO decision-making. The Philippines thus sees the Executive Board as an important platform to advance its views and priorities and to stay close to the core processes of WHO decision-making.

17.2.2.2 Other barriers to participation and influence

Notwithstanding years of rapid economic growth, India's participation in the WHO is still constrained by its own limited material resources. In addition, institutional fragmentation and bureaucratic politics undermine what DeMenno and Büthe call collective action capacity, further constraining Indian participation (and its effectiveness). For instance, India in recent years has sent as few as nine delegates to the World Health Assembly, the WHO's annual, most important meeting of delegates from all 194 member states and thousands of non-governmental stakeholders.[41] Given that the delegates must engage in multiple simultaneous negotiations, the lack of sufficient personnel has hindered Indian participation in negotiations, the finalization of key resolutions and the decision-making process. Further, delegates also get little time for preparation, due to the fragmentation of responsibility for Development Cooperation[42] and the domestic bureaucratic politics of selecting delegates, which delays the confirmation of the Indian participant list. Consequently, India is not a prominent voice in many of the discussions in the WHO Assembly, despite the election of Dr Soumya Swaminathan, the former head of the Indian Council of Medical Research (ICMR), as Deputy Director General of the WHO from 2017 to 2019 and then as Chief Scientist in 2019.[43]

Despite having less than 10% of the population of India and just over 10% of its GDP, the Philippines seems to face no greater constraints to its participation—and maybe even to its influence. One important factor here is the Philippines' willingness to commit similar (or even greater) resources than India to its participation in

[40] An early mention of the Philippines in the archival records of the WHO is the election of the Philippines to the WHO Executive Board in 1949. UN Doc. WHO/A2/88, 24 June 1949 <http://apps.who.int/iris/bitstream/10665/99064/1/WHA2_88_eng.pdf>, last accessed 04/16/2020. The Philippines most recently held a seat in the Executive Board from 2015 to 2018. The WHO regional office for the Western Pacific is headquartered in Manila.

[41] See, e.g. WHO (65th World Health Assembly) 'List of Delegates and Other Participants' (24 May 2012) A65/DIV/1 Rev.1 25. In 2014, India sent a delegation of sixteen and by 2017 a delegation of twenty-four—notably larger but still no larger (or even smaller) than the delegations of numerous much smaller countries; see WHO (67th World Health Assembly) 'List of Delegates and Other Participants' (23 May 2014) A67/DIV/1 Rev.1 <https://apps.who.int/iris/handle/10665/162733>, last accessed 04/17/2020, 24f; WHO (70th World Health Assembly) 'List of Delegates and Other Participants' (26 May 2017) A70/DIV/1 Rev.1, <https://apps.who.int/gb/ebwha/pdf_files/WHA70/WHA70_DIV1REV1-en.pdf>, last accessed 04/17/2020, 23f.

[42] Aravinda Meera Guntupalli and Karthik Nachiappan, 'India and Global Health Governance: Past, Present, and Future' in Kelley Lee, Tikki Pang, and Yeling Tan (eds), *Asia's Role in Governing Global Health* (Routledge 2013). In recent years, however, India has revamped institutional arrangements for development cooperation with the formation of a new agency, aiming at more coordination and less fragmentation; see Milindo Chakraborti, 'Development Compact—The Cornerstone of India's Development Cooperation: An Externalities Perspective' 53(1) *International Studies* (2016) 2-14.

[43] Amit Sengupta, 'WHO Has a New Chief: Will India Now Find Its Voice at the Global Health Organisation?' *Scroll.in: Pulse* (26 May 2017) <https://scroll.in/pulse/838722/the-who-has-a-new-chief-will-india-now-find-its-voice-at-the-global-health-organisation>, last accessed 06/07/2018.

WHO-based global health governance. World Health Assembly delegations of approximately equal size or even larger than India's illustrate this point.[44] In terms of other remaining barriers due to WHO institutions and procedures, the Philippines considers overly 'donor-centric' budgeting a major issue and hence sees a need for improved 'allocation, utilization, and accountability' vis-à-vis the assistance-receiving countries.[45] Compared to its Indian counterpart, however, the government of the Philippines appears remarkably content with its opportunities to have a voice and exert actual influence in WHO-based global health governance, though this might be partly a function of its more modest global ambitions.

17.2.3 Participation and Influence of Non-Governmental Stakeholders

As a traditional intergovernmental organization, the WHO has long focused on its member *states*, and engagement with the WHO has for both India and the Philippines mostly taken place at the governmental level. Beginning in the 1990s, though, the WHO explicitly sought to increase its engagement with non-governmental stakeholders. And it has sought not just engagement with funders (usually from the Global North) but also with implementers and representatives of affected groups from the Global South—in recognition of the important role they play across the broad range of health policies.[46] It may be too early to assess these efforts, especially its new 'Framework of Engagement with Non-State Actors' (FENSA), adopted by the WHO World Health Assembly in 2016,[47] but so far the resulting changes have been modest for Indian and Philippine non-governmental stakeholders.

In recent years, India has encouraged greater participation of the Indian civil society and NGOs in global health governance, at least on select issues, such as tobacco control and access to medicines, and the WHO has sought to involve them, working closely with some Indian NGOs. However, Indian NGOs continue to face often severe resource constraints, restricting their ability to make use of participation opportunities. Those constraints have become even more severe in recent years due to the new restrictions on foreign funding as well as government actions against some NGOs, such as the Public Health Foundation of India, a prominent Indian civil society organization for health issues. As Gutupalli and Nachiappan point out, Indian non-state actors have traditionally been marginalized in both domestic and international health governance, which they attribute to India's state-centric, often paternalistic approach to health policy-making.[48]

[44] WHO, 'List of Delegates': 13 vs. 9 in 2012) (n 41), 41; 17 vs. 16 in 2014 (n 41), 40; 22 vs. 24 in 2017 (n 41), 39f.

[45] Statement of the Philippines regarding the WHO programme budget 2016–2017, delivered during the 138th Session of the 69th World Health Assembly and the recent 67th Session of the Regional Committee for the Western Pacific. Text supplied by Department of Health in the survey questionnaire used for the Payoyo case study of the Philippines.

[46] For details, see Berman, 'Stakeholder Participation Reforms' (n 1), esp. Section 13.3.2.

[47] See also K M Gopakumar, 'The World Health Organization's Engagement with Non-State Actors: The Risk of Corporate Influence.' Chapter 22, this volume.

[48] Guntupalli and Nachiappan, 'India and Global Health Governance' (n 42).

While Philippine health NGOs have long been numerous as well as exceptionally active and innovative in comparison with their counterparts from other South-East Asian countries,[49] their (and other non-state actors') participation in WHO-based global health governance has been modest, though it has not suffered from the domestic push-back experienced by their Indian counterparts in recent years. In 2015, the WHO country office in the Philippines reportedly interacted with 76 NGOs, sixteen private sector entities, sixteen philanthropic foundations, and twenty-five academic institutions, with engagement ranging from resource sharing to advocacy to technical cooperation in WHO activities in the country.[50] The Philippine government has generally endorsed the WHO FENSA reforms, but has taken the position that the burden of its implementation belongs to the WHO and its Secretariat.[51] With no major funding support for more participation forthcoming, it remains to be seen whether FENSA will lead to a sustained quantitative or qualitative increase in Philippine non-state actors' participation in WHO health governance.

17.2.5 Summary and Concluding Reflections

The WHO has long been and remains a very important global health governance body for both India and the Philippines. India's governmental participation and influence in the WHO has increased, as evidenced by examples such as tobacco control and access to medicines. India's engagement with the WHO has, moreover, been well aligned with its domestic policy priorities, including capacity building, which has resulted in positive feedback loops, where India contributes both expertise and legitimacy to WHO policy-making, and alignment with the WHO in turn strengthens Indian policy effectiveness and legitimacy domestically. On a number of specific topics, India—i.e. its government—has exerted influence within the WHO both by putting issues such as traditional medicines on the agenda and by bringing about specific WHO policy positions closer to India's preferences than the status quo, reinforcing the mutually beneficial relationship. The Philippines' governmental participation in, and engagement with, the WHO has clearly increased, too—and there are numerous indications that it, too, at least occasionally, has been able to exert real influence, most notably in putting 'universal health coverage' on the WHO agenda and shaping the WHO's position on Sustainable Development Goal 3, making UHC a priority.

We cautioned at the outset that establishing a causal effect (as implied by claims of influence) is much more difficult than establishing increased participation in the sense of attending meetings, providing information, and generally exercising 'voice'

[49] Michael L Tan, 'The Development of Health NGOs in the Philippines' 41(1/4) *Philippine Sociological Review* (1993) 111-122.

[50] *Philippines FENSA Survey Response*. The WHO database identifies two scientific/university-based technical 'collaborating partners' from the Philippines working on WPRO region-wide projects, see <http://apps.who.int/whocc/List.aspx?cc_code=PHL>, last accessed 06/01/2018.

[51] WHO country office (Philippines) response to the FENSA survey, para 14 <http://www.who.int/about/collaborations/non-state-actors/questionnaire-philippines.pdf>, last accessed 04/15/2020. See also *External audit report on the implications for the World Health Organization of the implementation of the framework of engagement with Non-State actors (FENSA) March 2016* <http://www.who.int/about/collaborations/non-state-actors/A_FENSA_OEIGM_4-en.pdf>, last accessed 04/15/2020.

opportunities, which doubtlessly has increased for both India and the Philippines. That said, evidence of influence is not limited to the singular examples discussed in some detail in Section 17.2.2 above. The DOTS strategy to control tuberculosis, for instance, is an innovation of the Indian National Institute for TB Research Chennai, which was adopted by the WHO in the 1990s.[52] Indian research institutes (most of them governmental/public) regularly supply information to WHO global strategy and working groups tasked with developing guidelines and tools about surgical care delivery in low and middle income countries (Bhabha Atomic Research Centre, BARC), viral hepatitis (Sanjay Gandhi Postgraduate Institute of Medical Sciences), and palliative care (Institute of Palliative Medicine). The current Centre for Chronic Disease Control (CCDC) evolved from the WHO Initiative for Cardiovascular Health Research in Developing Countries into an independent research organization now providing critical research support to the WHO. In the particular cases noted above, providing such expert input appears to have contributed substantially to actual influence, but conclusive evidence whether or not such expertise allows India or the Philippines to influence outcomes requires case-by-case analysis.

Reflecting on the reasons for the increased participation and influence—as well as the persistent obstacles to participation and influence—WHO institutional reforms to boost stakeholder participation appear to have helped. And persistent institutional barriers to participation and influence are perceived as obstacles. As the Indian delegation observed: 'WHO needs a transformation through an ongoing reform process to meet new and emerging global health challenges. We need a more participative and equitable Executive Board. Non-members should have an equal stake in determining the agenda and resolutions for the W[orld] H[ealth] A[ssembly].'[53]

Returning to the hypotheses laid out in the analytical framework,[54] the Philippines' ability to use participation opportunities to exert actual influence appears to be based on the expertise mechanism more than the legitimacy mechanism, consistent with the Philippine understanding of the WHO as a 'learning organization'.[55] The WHO benefits from its partnership with the Philippines by obtaining inputs to its institutional knowledge base. WHO projects on the ground in the Philippines and the day-to-day cooperation with the government at the national and subnational level, provide opportunities to gain experiences and insights of practical value for WHO missions in other countries. For instance, crucial lessons about how to handle emergencies have been drawn from the collaborative WHO-Philippines response to Typhoon Haiyan—the first ever 'level 3 emergency' event that was registered in the WHO Emergency Response Framework. Another example is the WHO's push for (more) universal health coverage, where the WHO explicitly seeks to learn from the Philippines' experience.

India's increased participation and its ability to leverage that participation into influence, also is clearly helped by India's rapidly increasing ability (over the last couple

[52] Sujata Rao, *Do We Care* (Oxford University Press 2017), 189.

[53] Permanent Mission of India, 'Statement by India at the 142nd Session of the Executive Board (EB) of the World Health Organization' Geneva, 22 January 2018 <http://pmindiaun.org/pages.php?id=1578>, last accessed 06/07/2018.

[54] DeMenno and Büthe, 'Voice and Influence' (n 2), esp. Section 2.6.

[55] WHO, *Philippines CCS 2017–2022* (n 23), vii, 22, 24–26.

of decades) to provide valuable expert input—and arguably legitimacy, though we have seen no explicit articulation of the legitimacy mechanism for the WHO. Factors beyond institutional barriers at the international level also clearly mattered. Where reforms have made participation and influence easier, India has only partly been able to take advantage of them due to domestic material resource constraints, as well as domestic institutional constraints resulting in the lack of a coherent strategy for engaging with the WHO, despite its clearly recognized importance for India.

17.3 Codex Alimentarius Commission (Codex)

As the main governance body of the Food and Agriculture Organization's and WHO's Joint Food Standards Program, the Codex develops standards for food commodities, for the labelling and hygienic handling of food, and for the assessment of food-related safety risks.[56] Both India and the Philippines have substantially increased their participation in this comparatively specialized global health governance body in the aftermath of institutional reforms that were supposed to boost stakeholder participation, exerting influence over Codex decisions on at least some occasions in recent years.[57] Non-governmental Indian and Philippine stakeholders, however, remain, almost completely marginalized in Codex.

17.3.1 Importance, Incentives, and Constraints

Founded in 1963, Codex was for decades one of at least four international bodies developing food safety standards.[58] While a few of its explicit technical norms were well known beyond a narrow circle of experts—especially its standards specifying 'safe' levels of pesticide residues on fruits and vegetables[59]—Codex for decades lived in relative obscurity and essentially free of conflicts or controversies, because its standards were no more than recommendations. Governments remained at liberty to decide independently of each other whether to make market access for agricultural goods conditional on compliance with Codex's or any other food safety standards. Given the low cost of membership for countries that already were members of both the FAO and the WHO, India became a member of Codex in 1964; the Philippines followed in 1968.[60]

[56] Tim Büthe and Nathaniel Harris, 'The Codex Alimentarius Commission: A Hybrid Public-Private Regulator' in Thomas Hale and David Held (eds), *Handbook of Transnational Governance: Institutions and Innovations* (Polity Press 2011) 219-228; Cindy Cheng, 'Codex Alimentarius Commission' in Elliot Berry, Pasquale Ferranti, and Jock Anderson (eds), *Encyclopedia of Food Security and Sustainability* (Elsevier 2019) 50-55.

[57] For an overview of the reforms, see Berman, 'Stakeholder Participation Reforms' (n 1), esp. Section 13.4.

[58] Tim Büthe, 'The Codex Alimentarius Commission in the SPS Agreement of the WTO', in Cary Coglianese, Adam Finkel, and David Zaring (eds), *Import Safety, Regulatory Governance in the Global Economy* (University of Pennsylvania Press 2009) 88-109, esp. 96–99.

[59] David A Kay, *The International Regulation of Pesticide Residues in Food* (West Publishing for the American Society of International Law 1976); David M Leive, *International Regulatory Regimes: Case Studies in Health, Meteorology, and Food* (Lexington Books 1976).

[60] Codex, 'Members' <http://www.fao.org/fao-who-codexalimentarius/about-codex/members/en/>, last accessed 04/11/2020.

However, reflecting the modest importance of Codex, both countries rarely devoted much attention to Codex-based global health governance during the early decades of their Codex membership.

This all changed in 1994, when the Agreement on the Application of Sanitary and Phytosanitary Measures (the 'SPS-Agreement'), an integral part of the treaty establishing the World Trade Organization (WTO), obligated all member states to base their domestic regulations on 'international standards' for whenever such standards can achieve the desired level of consumer protection[61]—and defined international standards, for food safety, as the standards 'established by the Codex Alimentarius Commission'.[62] This development substantially raised the stakes in Codex-based global health governance for both India and the Philippines, at a time when both countries sought to increase their agricultural exports.[63]

For India, in particular, an additional consideration has been food safety in the domestic market. Due to India's embrace of economic globalization—a major change after decades of having largely closed its domestic markets—Indians have become exposed to a much greater diversity of food products, some of which have no equivalent in India. Under these circumstances, the ability to rely upon Codex standards has come to be seen by Indian government officials as helping them protect Indian consumers.

17.3.2 Governmental Participation and Influence

Prior to the 1990s, India participated in Codex only very selectively. India, for instance, encouraged—and got involved in—the development of Codex standards for buffalo milk and buffalo milk products, which were important both for domestic consumption and exports. Further, as the production of buffalo milk involves millions of small-scale farmers and others engaged in rearing cattle, the production, collection,

[61] Joost Pauwelyn, 'An Overview of the WTO Agreements on Health and Technical Standards' Zeitschrift für das gesamte Lebensmittelrecht (2000) 843–858; Tim Büthe, 'The Globalization of Health and Safety Standards: Delegation of Regulatory Authority in the SPS Agreement of the 1994 Agreement Establishing the World Trade Organization' 71(1) *Law and Contemporary Problems* (2008) 219-255.

[62] SPS-Agreement, Annex 3A.

[63] David Victor, 'The Sanitary and Phytosanitary Agreement of the World Trade Organization: An Assessment after Five Years' 32 *N.Y.U. Journal of International Law and Politics* (2000) 865-937; Frode Veggeland and Svein Ole Borgen, 'Negotiating International Food Standards: The World Trade Organization's Impact on the Codex Alimentarius Commission' 18(4) *Governance* (2005) 675-708; Büthe and Harris, 'The Codex Alimentarius Commission' (n 56), 221–224. The importance of Codex standards for opening up foreign markets is nicely illustrated by India's transition from a small-scale exporter of agricultural products in the 1990s to a major exporter after the Directorate of Health Services, under the Ministry of Health and Family Welfare, and the Agricultural and Processed Food Products Export Development Authority (APEDA) got Indian producers to adhere to Codex norms; see Harish K Sharma, Uma Partap, and Min B Gurung, 'Policy and Processes that Enable Honey Export: A Case Study from India' *Centre for Integrated Mountain Development Working Paper* 1/2012 <http://www.indiaenvironmentportal.org.in/files/file/icimod-policy_and_processes_that_enable_honey_export.pdf>, last accessed 06/11/2018. However, ensuring and documenting compliance with quality and safety standards remains a challenge for Indian exporters, resulting in their products being denied access to foreign markets; see Tanu M Goyal, Arpita Mukherjee, and Avantika Kapoor, 'India's Exports of Food Products: Food Safety Related Issues and Way Forward' ICRIER Working Paper 345/2017 <http://icrier.org/pdf/Working_Paper_345.pdf>, last accessed 06/11/2018.

and transportation are decentralized though processing is centralized. Having good, clear, and practical standards could facilitate coordination along the value chain, increase consumer safety (and confidence), and foster the development of market exchange.[64] Hence, India engaged with Codex on setting a standard for the collection, safe handling, and transportation and processing of buffalo milk products, which it sought both for domestic use and to foster the export of Indian buffalo milk products. The Philippines were virtually entirely absent from the Codex-based governance of food safety prior to the 1990s.[65]

For India and the Philippines, as for most other developing countries, the primary impediments to participation in Codex have not been formal institutional barriers. The key impediments, rather, were weak positive incentives (low perceived importance prior to 1994) as well as strong negative incentives, that is, a shortage of requisite capabilities—above all, the lack of financial resources, given the cost of attending numerous Codex meetings a year all over the world as well as (often related to material resource constraints) the lack of the required technical expertise. These barriers applied to virtually all Codex activities, so few developing countries actually participated in Codex-based governance until the 1990s.

When the 1994 'upgrading' of Codex quite suddenly rendered Codex standards much more important, these constraints came into much more prominent view, prompting vocal criticisms of Codex, questioning the legitimacy of its governance on account of the pervasive marginalization of developing countries. The most important stakeholder participation reform for Codex therefore was the establishment of the Codex Trust Fund (CTF) in 2004 to provide resources to member state governments from the Global South to help them pay for sending delegations to Codex meetings and to help them build technical–analytical expertise and related governmental bureaucratic capacity.[66]

17.3.2.1 Post-reform participation

India and the Philippines both benefitted from CTF support to enhance their domestic capabilities for food safety regulation and participation in global governance at Codex. With regard to participation, the initial twelve-year CTF (2004–2015) was supposed to: (1) increase participation; (2) strengthen participation; and (3) enhance scientific/technical participation in Codex. According to Codex's own assessment at the end of the programme, for developing countries in general, progress regarding objectives 1 and 2 had been 'fully' and 'partially demonstrated', respectively, given that the CTF had funded the participation of 2,359 individuals in Codex meetings and more than 1,100 in training courses and workshops.[67] This assessment is consistent

[64] Regarding the importance of standards and regulations for markets with information asymmetries, see generally: George A Akerloff, 'The Market for Lemons: Quality Uncertainty and the Market Mechanism' 84(3) *Quarterly Journal of Economics* (1970) 488-500; Edward J Balleisen and David A Moss (eds), *Government and Markets: Toward a New Theory of Regulation* (Cambridge University Press 2010).

[65] In the 1980s, the government of the Philippines sent delegations of 1–3 persons to the main biennial meetings of 1981, 1983, and 1987; in 1985 and 1989, it did not even send a single delegate to the main CAC meeting.

[66] See Berman, 'Stakeholder Participation Reforms' (n 1).

[67] Codex, 'FAO/WHO Project and Fund for Enhanced Participation in Codex: Final Project Evaluation' Codex Doc. CX/CAC15/38/18-Add.3 (2015) <http://www.who.int/foodsafety/areas_work/food-standard/cac38_18_add3e.pdf>, last accessed 04/18/2020. See also WHO, 'Codex Trust Fund: Building Codex

with observations by others about the increasing number of developing countries actually sending representatives to Codex annual and committee meetings.[68] Progress regarding objective 3 'could not be evaluated' as yet in 2015.[69]

With regard to the three objectives of the CTF, India and the Philippines may be said to both have done better than developing countries in general. Between 1964 and 2000, India attended rarely and almost never provided substantive comments on Codex projects; from 2000 to 2004, Indian representatives provided comments on one to two sessions/year, which, however, were seen as having 'no prioritization and no consistency'; from 2005 onward, India actively participated in four to five sessions/year and was perceived as being increasingly well informed about its economic and consumer interests; from 2008 onwards it started to co-host and chair working group meetings; from 2011 onwards, it began to make focused presentations based on data from Indian scientific institutes.[70] The Philippines, according to its Department of Agriculture, participated in Codex technical work for the first time in the 1990s, when carrageenan, an important Philippine export, was on the agenda in the Codex Committee of Food Additives and Contaminants. It was only after the CTF was launched that the Philippines set up a national Codex committee and began to regularly send delegations to the Codex annual meetings as well as, soon thereafter, to commodity committees and standards-setting working groups.[71]

In 2010, the Philippines 'graduated' from the CTF funding support eligibility,[72] but it has continued to participate regularly (enabled by years of strong economic growth), especially after enactment of the 2013 Food Safety Act (see Section 17.3.2.2). And according to the Philippine Codex Contact Point, the current Codex agenda contains several issues of great interest to the Philippines, creating a strong incentive for ongoing Codex engagement, including: antimicrobial resistance (preventing such resistance in the food chain); food handling (sanitation/hygiene of food preparation at home and in food establishments); acceptable levels of residues for pesticides, veterinary drugs, and other production chemicals; safety of animal feeds and health of food plant and animals; and preventing the growth of zoonotic pathogens such as salmonella and campylobacter in animal plant food under aerial conditions.

Globally' (2016) <http://www.who.int/foodsafety/areas_work/food-standard/CTF_EN.pdf>, last accessed 04/18/2020.

[68] See, e.g. Büthe and Harris, 'The Codex Alimentarius Commission' (n 56), 223, 225f.

[69] Codex, 'FAO/WHO Project and Fund for Enhanced Participation' and WHO, 'Codex Trust Fund' (n 67).

[70] Sanjay Dave, 'A Story of Change: India and Codex.' Presentation given at the Codex Trust Fund Call to Action, Geneva 18 November 2015 <https://www.who.int/foodsafety/areas_work/food-standard/Dave.pdf>, last accessed 04/18/2020. See also Rohin Kaul, 'WTO Agreement on the Application of Sanitary and Phytosanitary Measures and the Indian Experience' (Winter) *Indian Law Institute Law Review* (2016) 78-109; Shashi Sareen, 'India Responds to International Food Safety Requirements' in Laurian J Unnevehr, *Food Safety in Food Security and Food Trade. International Food Policy Research Institute 2020 Vision Focus Brief* no.10(1) (International Food Policy Research Institute 2003) <http://ebrary.ifpri.org/cdm/ref/collection/p15738coll2/id/95132>, last accessed 06/11/2018.

[71] Information provided by Philippines' Department of Agriculture in the survey questionnaire used for the Payoyo case study of the Philippines, February 2017.

[72] 'Codex Trust Fund Mid-Term Review: Final Report, 30 April 2010' Codex Doc. CX/CAC 10/33/14 Add.1, 30 <http://www.who.int/foodsafety/codex/cac33_14_Add1e.pdf?ua=1>, last accessed 08/12/2021.

In sum, the CTF, without doubt, intensified the participation of India and the Philippines in Codex deliberations and decision-making, and the increased participation appears to have been largely sustained even after the end of the subsidies for participants.

17.3.2.2 Other barriers to participation

For India, an important additional barrier to effective governmental participation in Codex was for a long time its domestic institutional fragmentation of food safety regulation. As of the late 1990s, food safety (and closely related issues like sanitation in agricultural and industrial food production) were regulated by at least ten different pieces of legislation, passed between 1937 and 1998, which assigned often-overlapping responsibilities to numerous different ministries and agencies—with no coordinating mechanisms for ensuring cohesion of domestic rules nor for deciding who would speak for India at the international level.[73] To overcome the resulting collective action problems, the Indian government in 1998 launched an institutional reform process that culminated in the adoption of the Food Safety and Standards Authority Act of 2006. The Act rationalized Indian food safety legislation and centralized implementation and enforcement in the new Authority, FSSAI (operational in 2011), which became the institutional focal point for food safety and the Indian 'national contact point' for Codex.[74] As a consequence (and thanks to its improved technical expertise), India has participated in a growing number of different Codex committees, putting forth its position in statements that represent a consensus, or at least have broad support, among Indian food safety stakeholders.[75]

For the Philippines, the domestic barriers to participation in global food safety governance were not so much contradictory laws and fragmented institutions, but rather the pervasive lack of capabilities in the food safety realm, which were exacerbated by the lack of a legal framework and a national-level infrastructure for building such capabilities in the public sector. The government began to address these barriers with the passage of the 2013 Food Safety Act, the first overall legislative framework for food safety in the Philippines, which provides the basis for incorporating the entirety of Codex 'standards, guidelines and codes of practice' into the Philippines' legal system as national regulatory norms. Reflecting the common practice of the Philippines to model its law after other countries' (often US) legislation, the 2013 Food Safety Act prescribes the structure of domestic food safety governance exactly as envisioned in the Codex Procedural Manual, including the scope and process of Philippine

[73] Shyam Narayan Jha, *Rapid Detection of Food Adulterants and Contaminants: Theory and Practice* (Academic Press 2016), part 3.1.5. For a general discussion of the problem of domestic institutional fragmentation when the institutional structure of governance at the international level requires taking a unified national position, see Tim Büthe and Walter Mattli, The *New Global Rulers: The Privatization of Regulation the World Economy* (Princeton University Press 2011), esp. ch.3.

[74] Codex requires every member state to have such a National Contact Point as the 'link' and 'coordinator of all relevant Codex activities at the national level': WHO and FAO, Understanding the Codex Alimentarius 5th ed. (FAO 2018), 19.

[75] FSSAI, 'National Codex Committee (India)' <http://www.fssai.gov.in/home/codex-committee.html> last accessed 06/11/2018; FSSAI, 'About Codex' <http://www.fssai.gov.in/home/fss-legislation/about-codex.html> last accessed 06/11/2018.

participation as well as the level of involvement that the Philippines should maintain in the Codex Commission.[76] The Act also calls for public financing of Philippine participation in Codex going forward.[77]

17.3.2.3 Influence of governmental stakeholders

The influence of individual countries in multilateral governance is difficult to determine with precision, but there are indications for both India and the Philippines that increased actual participation in Codex has, at least occasionally, translated into real influence over outcomes.

Spurred by the liberalization of the Indian economy, which had started in 1991, and the WTO SPS-Agreement, which had raised the stakes in Codex standard setting, India, in the aftermath of the Codex stakeholder participation reforms, increased its participation in several Codex committees to ensure that Codex standards would facilitate the acceptance of Indian products in global markets.[78] One example is India's push for Codex to develop standards for spices and herbs—an important export for India. Here, India clearly was able to exert influence as a direct consequence of institutional reforms that led to India's 2014 election as the Regional Coordinator for Asia, which made India a member of the Codex Executive Committee and allowed the FSSAI to organize meetings of the Codex Committee on Spices and Culinary Herbs in 2014, 2015 and 2017, through which it eventually succeeded in forging a consensus.[79] India has also successfully pushed for Codex to develop standards for street vendor food and hygiene practices, adopted in 2017.[80] This was an issue of no concern to developed countries, but important for developing countries.

The Philippines, too, can point to examples of voice resulting in apparent influence, such as when the Committee on Food Additives and Contaminants put forth the Philippines' scientific contribution as its proposal for a standard for the 'maximum level for lead in fish', for adoption at the 29th Session of Codex (2006)—a matter that had been lingering on the Codex agenda unresolved for several years.[81] Compared to India, however, the Philippines' level of influence appears more selective and less institutionalized.

[76] Republic Act No. 10611 (2013): 'An Act to Strengthen the Food Safety Regulatory System in the Country to Protect Consumer Health and Facilitate Market Access of Local Foods and Food Products, and for Other Purposes' (RA 10611 & IRR), Sec. 9c. Online at <http://www.wipo.int/wipolex/en/details.jsp?id=14075>, last accessed 04/18/2020.

[77] RA 10611 & IRR, Sec. 9d.

[78] Sareen, 'India Responds' (n 70). India also proposed that Codex risk assessment studies be conducted in developing countries and that the resulting data be taken into consideration in the development of Codex standards.

[79] K T Jagannathan, 'CAC adopts Codex norms for three spices' *The Hindu* (26 July 2017) <http://www.thehindu.com/business/cac-adopts-codex-norms-for-three-spices/article19365587.ece>, last accessed 06/11/2018. See also: Codex, 'Joint FAO/WHO Food Standards Programme: [...] Report of the 3rd Session of the Codex Committee on Spices and Culinary Herbs' (6–10 February 2017) REP17/SCH.

[80] Codex, 'Regional Code of Hygienic Practice for Street-Vended Foods in Asia' (2017) CRC 76R-2017.

[81] Robert J Connor, *Initiative to Explore Linkages Between Increased Participation in Codex and Enhanced International Food Trade Opportunities: Final Report* (WHO CTF Secretariat 2007), 17, 19, 40 <http://www.who.int/foodsafety/codex/Connor_report.pdf>, last accessed 04/20/2020.

17.3.3 Participation and Influence of Non-Governmental Stakeholders

Even though Codex is a joint venture of two traditional intergovernmental organizations—strictly speaking the 'organizational progeny'[82] of the Food and Agriculture Organization and the WHO—it has long been unusually open to the participation of non-governmental stakeholders. National delegations to the Codex meetings, including to the standards committees, where most of the governance work takes place, are appointed by the member states. They are usually led by a public official but can (and for a long time have) include(d) non-governmental experts from the private sector, academia, and civil society. In addition, Codex has from the beginning recognized other international organizations (from the UN and beyond, upon request) as 'observer' members,[83] a category that was later expanded to also recognize domestic and transnational non-governmental bodies. Observer members have no voting rights but have 'voice' opportunities during meetings, as well as the right to make written submissions,[84] and Codex sees them as very important to its legitimacy:

> Codex would have little authority in the field of international standard-setting if it did not welcome and acknowledge the valuable contribution made by observers. Governmental, non-governmental, public, and private organizations alike play a vital role in ensuring Codex texts are of the highest quality and based on sound science. Expert technical bodies, industry and consumer associations contribute . . . .[85]

Approximately two-thirds to three-quarters of the more than two hundred accredited observer members in the last two decades have been non-governmental,[86] but closer inspection reveals that the vast majority of them are representative of commercial stakeholders, mostly food industry multinationals, major retailers, and national as well as transnational industry associations.[87] On national delegations, too, industry and commercial interests are far more commonly represented than consumer representatives or civil society groups,[88] including on the Indian and Philippine delegations on the rare occasions when they have included non-governmental members.

[82] Tana L Johnson, *Organizational Progeny: Why Governments Are Losing Control over the Proliferating Structures of Global Governance* (Oxford University Press 2014).

[83] Franklin M Depew, 'The Second Session of the Codex Alimentarius Commission' 20(3) *Food, Drug, Cosmetic Law Journal* (1965) 136-148.

[84] David Victor, 'The Operation and Effectiveness of the Codex Alimentarius Commission' in *Effective Multilateral Regulation of Industrial Activity* (PhD dissertation, Massachusetts Institute of Technology 1997).

[85] WHO and FAO, *Understanding the Codex* (n 74), 17.

[86] The proportion has remained remarkably stable; currently, it is 163 out of 236, see Codex, 'Observers: About' <http://www.fao.org/fao-who-codexalimentarius/about-codex/observers/observers/about/en/>, last accessed 04/18/2020.

[87] Victor, ' Operation and Effectiveness' (n 84); Diane McCrea, 'A View from Consumers' in Naomi Rees and David Watson (eds), *International Standards for Food Safety* (Aspen Publishers 2000) 149-167.

[88] Natalie Avery, Martine Drake, and Tim Lang, *Cracking the Codex: An Analysis of Who Sets World Food Standards* (National Food Alliance 1993); Lewis Rosman, 'Public Participation in International Pesticide Regulation' 12 *Virginia Environmental Law Journal* (1993) 329-365; John Braithwaite and Peter Drahos, *Global Business Regulation* (Cambridge University Press 2000), 401; Diahanna L Post, 'Standards and Regulatory Capitalism: The Diffusion of Food Safety Standards in Developing Countries' 598 *Annals of*

On the whole, non-governmental stakeholders from India and the Philippines have been virtually entirely absent from Codex health governance so far, despite low formal barriers to participation. There is not a single Indian nor Philippine NGO among the Codex observer members.[89] In recognition of this deficiency, the Food Safety and Standards Authority of India (FSSAI), the Indian Codex contact point, made 'enhancing the participation of all [Indian] stakeholders in Codex-related activities' the first of the five goals for its 2015–2019 Strategic Plan.[90] And Codex, in 2016, launched CTF-2, which unlike the original, government participation-focused CTF (2004–2015), is supposed to help 'build strong, solid and sustainable national capacity to engage in Codex' including through increased involvement of a broad range of stakeholders at the national level.[91] Yet, even though both countries are eligible for CTF-2 funding, only India has so far submitted a proposal for CTF-2 funding (for a joint project with Bhutan and Nepal, which initially was unsuccessful but in revised form was in 2018 accepted for support for three years, 2019–2022).[92]

The current state of non-governmental participation from India and the Philippines is summed up well by the September 2019 assessment of the FAO/WHO Coordinating Committee for Asia, meeting in Goa, India, which could still only 'acknowledge the ongoing challenges with participation in Codex meetings' for both physical meetings and the 'electronic working group' (established in the hopes to eliminating travel expenses as an impediment to participation). It called for 'innovative solutions to address the barriers to participation'.[93] While the report was not accompanied by an analysis of those barriers, it appears clear that the key obstacles at this point are insufficient stakeholder capabilities and insufficient incentives.[94]

17.3.4 Summary and Concluding Reflections

Focused on setting (as such voluntary) standards for food safety and related issues for the trade in agricultural goods, the Codex addresses a specialized piece of the broad realm of global health governance. India and the Philippines both became members

the American Academy of Political and Social Science (2005) 168-183; Büthe and Harris, 'The Codex Alimentarius Commission' (n 56), 224f.

[89] <http://www.fao.org/fao-who-codexalimentarius/about-codex/observers/observers/obs-list/en/>, last accessed 04/18/2020.

[90] USDA Foreign Agricultural Service, 'India: Codex India Publishes a Strategic Plan for 2015–2019' *Attache Reports*, 16 January 2015 <https://www.fas.usda.gov/data/india-codex-india-publishes-strategic-plan-2015-19>, last accessed 06/11/2018.

[91] FAO and WHO, 'Codex Trust Fund-2: Project Document' (December 2015), sections 1 and 4.3.1 <https://www.who.int/foodsafety/areas_work/food-standard/CTF2ProjectDocument.pdf>, last accessed 04/18/2020.

[92] FAO and WHO, 'List of countries eligible for support from CTF (as at 1 August 2019)' <https://www.who.int/foodsafety/areas_work/food-standard/CTF-eligible-countries-Round4.pdf>; FSSAI, online notification regarding the FAO/WHO Codex Trust Fund <https://fssai.gov.in/cms/fao-who-codex-trust-fund.php> , last accessed 10/24/2021.

[93] Codex, *Report of the 21st Session of the FAO/WHO Coordinating Committee for Asia, 27–29 Sep 2019, for the CAC Meeting, Rome, July 2020* (REP20/ASIA), 7–10, iv.

[94] See DeMenno and Büthe, 'Voice and Influence' (n 2), esp. Section 2.5.

of Codex in the 1960s but given that their trade in agricultural goods was concentrated in only a few products and the use of Codex standards was voluntary and not widespread, Codex was—for a long time and for both countries—of little importance. Accordingly, both countries participated in Codex standard setting and decision-making only very occasionally and selectively, despite low barriers to participation compared to some of the other global governance bodies analyzed in this volume.

Then, in the mid-1990s, the WTO's SPS-Agreement bestowed a special role upon Codex, making it the institutional focal point for food safety governance in the international trade regime,[95] which raised the stakes for India and the Philippines. With rapid economic growth in the 2000s yielding greater material resources, an increase in food safety-related expertise yielding greater analytical resources, and domestic institutional development, India and the Philippines gained capabilities for participation, at the same time as increased opportunities for agricultural exports (increasingly governed by Codex standards), as well as increased imported food supplies, further increased the importance of Codex, especially for India. India, in particular, but also the Philippines responded to these increased incentives with increased engagement in Codex, especially when institutional reforms, such as the introduction of the Codex Trust Fund, lowered the barriers to participation, creating new voice opportunities.

With regard to several specific issues and standards, the increased engagement appears also to have resulted in increased influence over policy choices in Codex. The changes, however, are still ongoing and in that sense may be considered still tentative. Increased Indian and Philippine participation in Codex, moreover, has so far been limited to government representatives (public officials). Non-governmental stakeholders from India and the Philippines, even commercial ones, still appear to play virtually no role in Codex-based global health governance—though efforts are underway attempting to increase the direct or even indirect participation of Indian and Philippine civil society stakeholders.

17.4 The International Council for Harmonisation (ICH)

Turning to the ICH, our analysis shifts from traditional international organizations to a transgovernmental network (though the 2016 reform transformed it into an entity much more like a traditional international organization).[96] Launched in 1990, it was established with the objective of bringing together the drug regulatory authorities and pharmaceutical producers of Europe, Japan, and the United States to facilitate discussions on scientific and technical aspects of pharmaceutical product registration.[97] A key objective of ICH is to enhance harmonization of technical requirements so that

[95] Büthe, 'Globalization of Health and Safety Standards' (n 61); Büthe, 'Codex in the SPS' (n 58); Tim Büthe, 'Institutionalization and Its Consequences: The TLO(s) for Food Safety' in Terence C Halliday and Gregory Shaffer (eds), *Transnational Legal Orders* (Cambridge University Press 2015) 258-286.

[96] See Berman, 'Stakeholder Participation Reforms' (n 1), esp. Section 13.7.2.

[97] ICH, The Value and Benefits of ICH to Drug Regulatory Authorities: Advancing Harmonization for Better Health (ICH 2010) <http://www.ich.org/ichnews/publications/browse/article/the-value-and-benefits-of-ich-to-drug-regulatory-authorities.html> last accessed 06/05/2018. The ICH released this publication at the time of the 2010 Steering Committee meeting in Fukuoka.

effective, high quality and safe medicines are developed and registered in an efficient and cost-effective way.[98]

17.4.1 Importance, Incentives, and Constraints

For ICH member regulatory agencies, the ICH 'guidelines' constitute de facto binding standards for the registration of medicines. Consequently, they affect the development and production of pharmaceuticals in large parts of the world directly—and in most of the rest of the world indirectly, not least because of their effect on market access and hence trade. Both India and the Philippines therefore have a stake in ICH-based global health governance, particularly since there is no readily available alternative way of influencing these aspects of the production and trade in medicines, though the stakes may be said to be notably higher for India with its large pharmaceuticals sector.

ICH guidelines have been governing parts of Indian pharmaceuticals development for years, especially clinical trials. Many (but not all) Indian pharmaceuticals producers, moreover, are internationally highly competitive (their products account for about 40% of Indian exports[99]). Due to the economies of scale logic of the 'California effect',[100] these Indian pharmaceuticals manufacturers already must comply with ICH guidelines if they produce for export to almost any country other than poor developing countries. To safeguard and increase their export opportunities, those firms have supported Indian ICH membership. Other Indian pharmaceuticals producers, however, have pushed back, arguing that ICH puts at risk the traditional policy priority of successive Indian governments to maximize access to medicines. They have also prevented the wholesale adoption of ICH guidelines as domestic regulatory requirements for India.

The possibility of ICH membership has additionally been controversial in India because ICH is focused on rapid 'harmonization' whereas many in India prefer the more gradual, less comprehensive 'regulatory convergence', consistent with the approach taken by the Asia-Pacific Economic Cooperation (APEC) forum and the International Generic Drug Regulators' Programme (IGDRP), which allow for greater capacity building in pharmaceutical regulation before engaging internationally.

The Philippines also has a stake in ICH-based global health governance, most prominently thanks to the harmonization initiative undertaken by ASEAN. ASEAN launched its pharmaceuticals regulation harmonization project for its ten member countries in 1999 when it established its Pharmaceutical Product Working Group (PPWG)—part of a broader effort to harmonize technical standards and regulations whenever their divergence impedes the realization of the ASEAN Free Trade

[98] ICH, *Value and Benefits* (n 97). ICH also envisions that harmonization reduces the amount of testing required to meet specific regional regulatory requirements, and that patients benefit from faster testing times.

[99] Export-Import Bank of India, 'Study on Indian Pharmaceutical Industry' (2015) EXIM Bank Working Paper 37-33 <https://www.eximbankindia.in/Assets/Dynamic/PDF/Publication-Resources/ResearchPapers/39file.pdf> accessed 06/08/2018.

[100] David Vogel, *Trading Up: Consumer and Environmental Regulation in a Global Economy* (Harvard University Press 1995), 248ff.

Area—'without compromising on drug quality, efficacy, and safety'.[101] The result has been the regional adoption of ICH 'guidelines' (with few adaptations or omissions) for all ASEAN member states.[102] As a consequence, ICH guidelines have become part of the national regulatory environment with legal effects for market participants. ICH standards thus impact Philippine stakeholders directly and significantly.[103]

17.4.2 Governmental Participation and Influence

Neither India nor the Philippines (nor pharmaceutical manufacturers from either country) had any role in ICH when it was first set up in the 1990s. The Philippines indirectly gained observer status in 2005, when ASEAN was invited to join the ICH's Global Cooperation Group (which has become a permanent feature of the structure of ICH).[104] The Indian pharmaceuticals regulator was first invited to the ICH's new Regulators' Forum in 2007, which similarly (but directly) gave it observer status.

The stakeholder reforms of ICH mostly made observer status official and permanent. As an observer,[105] India has voice opportunities in the ICH Assembly and Working Groups, but those opportunities are limited, and observers have no decision-making (voting) rights in ICH bodies, not even the right to attend the ICH Management Committee meetings. The Philippines as such has never been (directly) involved in the deliberations or the decision-making of the ICH, nor has it sought or aspired to such participation, unlike fellow ASEAN partners Singapore (which is a voting member of ICH) or Malaysia (which maintains ICH observer status). To this day, the Philippines has no direct participation opportunities at all; instead, the country is represented by ASEAN, which has the same rights and restrictions as national observer members (i.e. just like India). Formal participation opportunities thus remain very limited for both countries—though India (but not the Philippines) could under the rules of the 2016 reforms become a regular 'regulatory' member if it were willing to bear the costs and obligations of such membership. Since India has opted not to pursue membership, its only option—as an observer with restricted voice and no voting rights—appears to be to rely upon the power of persuasion vis-à-vis the ICH's full members. Neither country's government (or

[101] Yuppadee Javroongrit, 'ASEAN Harmonization', Presentation, 12–13 October 2006 <https://www.pmda.go.jp/files/000151267.pdf>, last accessed 4/20/2020, 24.

[102] Yuppadee Javroongrit, 'Development of ICH Global Cooperation Group: A Non-ICH Regional Harmonization and Country Perspective' (Thailand), Presentation 18 September 2008, <http://www.who.int/medicines/areas/quality_safety/regulation_legislation/icdra/1_Thailand_DevelopmentICHGlobalCooperationGroup.pdf>, last accessed 04/20/2020; Javroongrit, 'ASEAN Harmonization' (n 101).

[103] The consequences of the de facto harmonized ASEAN guidelines might not yet be fully visible at this early stage, given the weakness and wide variation in regulatory capacity to implement the guidelines; see Achin Jain, M P Venkatesh, G Raja Mohan Reddy, and Pramod T M Kumar, 'Regulatory Requirements and Marketing Authorization of Generic Drugs in Singapore and Thailand' 3(1) *International Journal of Drug Regulatory Affairs* (2015), 62-74, at 63.

[104] M Ward, 'The Global Cooperation Group: A Bridge from ICH to the World Beyond' 3(2) *Global Forum* (2011) 18-19.

[105] ICH, 'Members and Observers: Current Members and Observers' <https://www.ich.org/page/members-observers>, last accessed 04/20/2020.

pharmaceuticals regulator) is in a position to exert influence over the agenda or the contents of the guidelines of the ICH, at least not through the formal institutional mechanisms of the ICH.

Actual decision-making practices in international organizations can, at least when the stakes for powerful countries are high, diverge substantially from the formally prescribed processes.[106] Might India and/or the Philippines exercise at least some influence in ICH 'informally'? Note that the ICH is not completely impervious to outside influence. In 2004/05, when the ASEAN started drafting its own minimum adequacy standard for pharmaceuticals quality maintenance under the hot and humid climatic conditions found in many ASEAN member states, it prompted the WHO-based development of such a standard, to which ICH then deferred.[107] We have found no indications, however, that this turn of events can be attributed to the preferences or actions of Indian or Philippine stakeholders specifically, nor have we identified any other instance where India or the Philippines has discretely exercised influence in ICH through informal or indirect means.

17.4.3 Participation and Influence of Non-Governmental Stakeholders

As noted above, parts of the Indian pharmaceutical industry would like to see India join (and then actively shape) ICH guidelines as a way to boost their market access abroad. Indeed, joining the ICH as a member has been advocated by numerous think tanks, academics, and consultants, too. Unlike the governments or regulators of China and Brazil, however, the Indian government has so far consistently decided against ICH membership (and the Philippines does not even seek observer status).

The only other opportunity for Indian pharma companies to participate in ICH governance would be to get involved indirectly through one of the 'Founding Industry Members' (unlikely, since only the main pharmaceutical industry associations of the EU, Japan and the United States are in this category) or through one of the other three 'Industry Members', among which only the International Generic and Biosimilar Medicines Association[108] would seem a credible candidate. There is no indication, however, that Indian firms have in any substantive, sustained way even attempted to exercise voice and/or influence in ICH through this channel. Non-commercial non-governmental stakeholders from India or the Philippines appear to be entirely excluded from ICH governance.

Indian (and Philippine) non-governmental stakeholders still lack formal opportunities for (direct) participation in ICH-based global health governance, and they

[106] Randall W Stone, *Informal Governance: International Organizations and the Limits of U.S. Power* (Cambridge University Press 2009).

[107] Ruth Lätzel, *Development of the ASEAN Pharmaceutical Harmonisation Scheme: An Example of Regional Integration* (Master's thesis, Bonn University 2007) 24–28 <http://dgra.de/media/pdf/studium/masterthesis/master_laetzel_r.pdf>, last accessed 04/21/2020.

[108] See <https://www.igbamedicines.org>, last accessed 04/20/2020.

appear not to have found alternative, indirect, or de facto means of exercising voice or influence in ICH.

17.4.4 Summary and Concluding Reflections

ICH standards have affected the production, trade and hence the availability of pharmaceuticals in both India and the Philippines, giving both countries a stake in ICH-based global health governance. The stakeholder participation reforms in this transgovernmental body, however, have left both countries with only very limited voice opportunities and no real influence.

Philippine participation in ICH, even post-reform, has been mediated by ASEAN and exclusively governmental.[109] The government of the Philippines has considered this form of indirect engagement acceptable in order to achieve the removal of technical barriers to trade through intra-regional regulatory harmonization. Such 'participation', however, provides no perceptible gain in legitimacy for ICH and very little, if any, ICH learning opportunities—consistent with the minimal, voice-only participation opportunity gained by the Philippines.

Indian participation in ICH is more direct, given its observer status, but also very limited and exclusively governmental, though in India's case, its limited voice opportunities (and lack of any real influence) may be considered more a matter of choice in that the Indian government has opted not to seek ICH membership, given domestic opposition and the preference for gradual converge rather than instantaneous 'harmonization'.

17.5 The Global Fund

The Global Fund was created as a funding mechanism to mobilize and disburse aid for AIDS, TB, and malaria prevention and treatment to developing countries.[110] The guiding principles of the Global Fund are performance-based funding and local ownership of programmes and action plans by the implementing countries. Envisaged as a multi-stakeholder partnership between (donor and implementer) governments, the private sector, civil society, and especially the patients who are the supposed beneficiaries, the Global Fund was meant to be a new mechanism, rather than a new actor, on the global health stage. It has, however, evolved into a global actor in health policy and governance—in part precisely because it has become an important source of funding.

[109] Whereas ICH was initially a partnership between regulatory authorities and (mostly private sector) industry (with industry often driving the process; see Ankit Gupta, Raghav Goel, Suresh Jain, and Vipin Saini, 'A Review on Impact of ICH and Its Harmonisation on Human Health Care and Pharmaceuticals' 4(2) *Journal of Pharmaceutical Research & Clinical Practice* (2014) 41-49), and ICH later was transformed into a transgovernmental network with special recognition for industry stakeholders, ASEAN has been strictly inter-governmental throughout.

[110] Global Fund, 'Impact' <https://www.theglobalfund.org/en/impact/>, last accessed 06/08/2018.

17.5.1 Importance, Incentives, and Constraints

The Global Fund has from its beginning been very important for India, and vice versa. The Global Fund came to India in 2003, and it soon became one of the largest sources of funding for improving health outcomes in India. The Global Fund has for years supported the Indian government's national programmes for the control of the three major diseases that are the Global Fund's focus (the Indian National AIDS Control Programme, the Revised National TB Control Programme and the National Vector Borne Disease Control Programme for Malaria),[111] as well as NGO programmes throughout India.[112] Moreover, 70% of the antiretroviral drugs procured by the Global Fund to treat HIV/AIDS come from Indian suppliers; a smaller but still substantial portion of its other medicines have come from India, too.[113] This makes the Global Fund an important customer of the Indian pharmaceuticals industry—and India an important source of critical supplies for the Global Fund.

The Philippines, too, has been a beneficiary of Global Fund financial support for its programmes dealing with HIV/AIDS, tuberculosis, and malaria—even if somewhat more hesitatingly than India, as the Philippines takes pride in being increasingly financially self-reliant with regard to important health outcomes, such as universal access to quality vaccines for the prevention of the most common vaccine-preventable diseases.[114] Since 2003, the Philippines has received substantial funding from the Global Fund. Of cumulative disbursements totalling some USD 360 million up to 2017, about 62% went to the tuberculosis programme, 26% to Malaria, and 12% to HIV/AIDS.[115] In fact, given the initially relatively modest government funding for the fight against these three diseases, the Global Fund grants have without a doubt been indispensable in meeting government commitments under the Millennium Development Goals.[116] Following the adoption of the 'sin tax' in 2012, which redirected substantial tax

[111] Global Fund, 'Global Fund Grants to the Republic of India', Audit Report, 2016 and 2018 editions <https://www.theglobalfund.org/media/2664/oig_gf-oig-16-023_report_en.pdf>, last accessed 06/08/2018; <http://www.india-ccm.in/global-fund-grant-india-HIV.php>, last accessed 06/02/2018.

[112] Krishna Dipankar Rao *et al.*, 'Exploring How Disease-Specific Programmes in TB and HIV/AIDS Interact with Health Systems' in *Interactions Between Global Health Initiatives and Health Systems: Evidence from Countries* (WHO Maximizing Positive Synergies Academic Consortium 2009) 88-96.

[113] Monirul Azam, *Intellectual Property and Public Health in the Developing World* (Open Book Publishers 2016) 121; Cipla 'CIPLA Wins USD 188.95 million of a Global Fund ARV Tender' (CIPLA Press releases, 13 February 2015) <http://www.cipla.com/uploads/mediakit/1443699782_Press-Release-Global-Fund-ARV-Tender.pdf> last accessed 06/08/2018; 'Ipca Labs Says The Global Fund Selected Co as Panel Supplier of Anti-Malarial Medicines' *Reuters*, 10 November 2017 <https://www.reuters.com/article/brief-ipca-labs-says-the-global-fund-sel/brief-ipca-labs-says-the-global-fund-selected-co-as-panel-supplier-of-anti-malarial-medicines-idUSFWN1NG12C>, last accessed 06/08/2018.

[114] Republic of the Philippines Department of Health, 'Expanded Program on Immunization' <http://www.doh.gov.ph/expanded-program-on-immunization>, last accessed 04/19/2020.

[115] Global Fund, <http://www.theglobalfund.org/en/portfolio/country/?loc=PHL&k=7b433a8d-92ac-4557-beab-13ceee659690>, last accessed 11/01/2018. For the 2017–2019 allocation period, the total for the Philippines amounts to USD 97.7 million, with 80% earmarked for the TB component, 11% for malaria, and 9% for HIV/AIDS; Global Fund, <http://www.theglobalfund.org/en/fundingmodel/process/allocations/>, last accessed 11/01/2018.

[116] Philippine National Economic and Development Authority, 'Infographic: The Philippines' progress in attaining the UN Millennium Development Goals', 2014 <http://www.neda.gov.ph/2014/08/26/infographic-philippines-progress-attaining-un-millennium-development-goals/>, last accessed 04/09/2018.

revenues from tobacco and alcohol products to the health sector,[117] the Philippines' national budgetary allotments for HIV/AIDS, TB, and malaria increased, but given the disease burden of these three communicable diseases in the Philippines, Global Fund funding is still very much needed.

17.5.2 Governmental Participation and Influence

The stakeholder participation reforms undertaken by the Global Fund had two main goals: First, the reforms were supposed to encourage more active 'meaningful'[118] participation by the representatives of implementers on the Global Fund Board. The second objective was to strengthen the multi-stakeholder representativeness and inclusiveness of the Country Coordinating Mechanism for each implementing country, which implied increasing participation, especially non-governmental participation, in Global Fund governance at the national and local level.[119]

In the most immediate sense, Global Fund reforms may be said to have been unsuccessful—with regard to both India and the Philippines—in boosting governmental participation from implementing countries. Even though the WHO region of South-East Asia is recognized for governmental representation on the Global Fund Board, we have found no record of post-reform Indian nor Philippine participation in any meetings of the Global Fund Board—not as a governmental, nor as a non-governmental participant—not even as an observer.[120] Consequently, the Global Fund governance reforms launched in 2011, which by all indications led to major shifts in the working methods and decision-making processes of the Global Fund Board,[121] cannot be said to have had any effect on direct Indian or Philippine participation and influence in the highest level of formal Global Fund decision-making. Given the short history of the Global Fund, though, and given that the Global Fund Board has only twenty members with multi-year memberships from across all the world's 193 (UN-recognized) states, we probably should not expect meaningful trends (neither country had a representative on the board prior to the reforms).[122]

[117] Republic Act no. 10351, the Philippines 'Sin Tax' law of 2012. *Sin Tax Incremental Revenue for Health: Annual Report CY 2015*, DOH 2015.

[118] The Global Fund, 'Continuing the Board's Strategic Governance Reform Program—Phase 2 (26th Board Meeting) GF/B26/11' (2012).

[119] See Berman, 'Stakeholder Participation Reforms' (n 1).

[120] Indian-born US businessman Rajat Gupta chaired the Board from 2007 to 2012, but he did so as a US private sector participant.

[121] For historical highlights of Global Fund governance reforms, see J Stephen Morrison and Todd Summers, Righting the Global Fund (CSIS 2012) <http://www.hst.org.za/publications/NonHST%20Publications/120227_Morrison_RightingGlobalFund_Web.pdf>, last accessed 04/20/2020. See also Gülen Atay Newton, 'Evolving Norms and Objectives Regarding Stakeholder Participation: The Global Fund to Fight AIDS, Tuberculosis and Malaria.' Chapter 21, this volume.

[122] To complicate matters further, India, which as a very populous implementing country has been one of the recipients of a very large amount of aid, has also become a Global Fund donor which might boost its claim to a seat on the Board, but such a dual status goes against the logic of Board membership separated by donor and implementer countries <https://www.theglobalfund.org/en/government/profiles/india/>, last accessed 04/19/2020.

Other GF reforms, however, have had a significant impact on Indian and Philippine participation in Global Fund operations. In 2012, India and the Philippines were both re-classified by the Global Fund as 'high impact' countries that should receive larger volumes of funding for having a particularly high burden of the three diseases.[123]

17.5.3 Participation and Influence of Non-Governmental Stakeholders

The Global Fund reforms may have had their greatest effect with respect to the participation of non-governmental stakeholders at the national level. This effect is most notable in the Philippines, which reorganized its Country Coordinating Mechanism (CCM) in response to the Global Fund's greater emphasis on multi-stakeholder participation as an indispensable element of health sector reform.[124] In particular, the Global Fund's 'new funding model' since 2013 has led to structural reforms in the Philippine CCM, which have entrenched the inclusion of 'key affected populations' and increased involvement of civil society NGOs. These changes in the Philippine CCM were recognized by the Global Fund as a best-practice case of mainstreaming key population involvement in the CCM.[125] India also increased the involvement of non-governmental stakeholders in its CCM. Given the central role of the CCMs in developing funding proposals for Global Fund programming and assessing programme implementation, this can be considered a substantial increase of *indirect* non-governmental participation from India and the Philippines in Global Fund-based global health governance.

It is too early to assess any lasting impact of these changes, but Global Fund-supported NGO programme implementation sites have increased throughout India,[126] as has private sector collaboration with the Global Fund. Most notably, Tata Trusts and the Global Fund started to collaborate in 2016 in fundraising and the recruitment of private sector expertise for the development of the India Health Fund to combat AIDS, TB and Malaria.[127] In the Philippines, too, there is a strong sense that participation in the Global Fund's operational architecture through the CCM has brought about new ways of addressing national health priorities and delivering health outcomes.

[123] 'How Grants Will Be Managed in the Restructured Secretariat' 184 *AIDSPAN News*, 14 May 2012 <http://www.aidspan.org/gfo_article/how-grants-will-be-managed-restructured-secretariat>; 'Report of the General Manager' to the 27th GF Board Meeting, 13–14 September 2012, Doc. GF/B27/02, para. 2.3–2.5 <https://www.theglobalfund.org/media/2545/bm27_02generalmanager_report_en.pdf>, both last accessed 04/19/2020.

[124] Ruthy C D Libatique, *Global Fund Proposal Development: A Philippines Experience* (International HIV/AIDS Alliance 2004).

[125] Global Fund, *Involvement of Key Populations and People Living with the Diseases: Achieving Inclusiveness of Country Coordinating Mechanisms* (GF, June 2016), 8–11 <https://www.theglobalfund.org/media/1269/publication_keypopulations_casestudy_en.pdf>, last accessed 04/20/2020.

[126] This increase has occurred alongside increased Indian public spending on health care; see Kiran Sharma, 'India's Ambitious 'Modicare' Raises Hopes and Doubts' *Nikkei* (22 February 2018) <https://asia.nikkei.com/Politics/India-s-ambitious-Modicare-raises-hopes-and-doubts2>, last accessed 06/08/2018.

[127] Global Fund, <https://www.theglobalfund.org/en/private-ngo-partners/resource-mobilization/tata-trusts/>, last accessed 04/19/2020.

17.5.4 Summary and Concluding Reflections

The Global Fund has, despite its narrow focus, become an important actor in global health governance for both India and the Philippines, since the three diseases are quite widespread in both countries. Even in the aftermath of the reforms, neither country has a seat on the Global Fund Board, the highest decision-making body. This persistent structural barrier deprives both countries of a direct decisional role. At the same time, the central role of the CCM provides India and the Philippines with regular opportunities for having a voice in Global Fund governance: These multi-stakeholder bodies, set up separately for each implementing country, must deliberate and ideally are supposed to jointly develop the projects proposed for the country; at a minimum the members of the CCM must support each project proposal. And clearly the Global Fund Board has been responsive to the proposals coming out of the CCMs for India and the Philippines, respectively, as evidenced by its repeated and increasing funding allocations for the two countries.

With regard to India, it is clear that the Global Fund gains legitimacy from funding programmes that benefit its still in large parts very poor population of more than 1.3 billion people. The Global Fund's need for greater legitimacy as a global health governance body may suffice to explain the voice opportunities and real influence afforded to India by the Global Fund, since legitimacy can be gained by welcoming inputs and being responsive to them with procedural fairness.[128] At the same time, India's participation in Global Fund programming also provides learning opportunities, especially given the growing Indian expertise in the health policy realm. The expert mechanism therefore might also explain the Global Fund's responsiveness towards India, though we have not found any prominent examples of the Global Fund explicitly drawing on its experience in India to motivate projects and practices elsewhere. More generally, it is difficult to ascertain to what extent, if any, working in India has had an impact on the Global Fund's mission, processes, or practices beyond the portfolio of Global Fund projects in India. In the end, the most important consequence of the Global Fund's work in India might have been elevating the role of Indian non-governmental stakeholder in (certain areas of) global health governance by empowering the Indian CCM and insisting on its inclusiveness and deliberative character.

17.6 Conclusion

For India and the Philippines, the stakeholder participation reforms of the global health governance bodies examined in this chapter have clearly resulted in increases in voice opportunities, in actual engagement, as well as gains in real influence—but quite unevenly across the four global health bodies examined in this chapter. Generally, governmental participation has increased to a much greater extent than non-governmental participation. Non-commercial stakeholders in particular, such as

[128] See DeMenno and Büthe, 'Voice and Influence' (n 2), esp. Section 2.6.2.

civil society organizations, from these large lower-middle income democracies, continue to be quite marginalized in the WHO, Codex, and the ICH. The particular governance structure of the Global Fund, with its (post-reform) insistence on an inclusive multi-stakeholder CCM within each country, seems to have resulted in non-trivial increases of participation and influence for non-governmental stakeholders from both India and the Philippines, including traditionally marginalized and excluded ones, albeit only via the CCM.

In contrast to some of the other country pair comparisons in this volume, the experience of India and the Philippines in global health governance has been strikingly similar. While India's much greater population and size often gives it somewhat greater weight (e.g. via observer status in the ICH where the Philippines participates only very indirectly via the ASEAN representative), the Philippines has frequently been able to compensate by devoting greater resources to global health governance, resulting in often equal or even slightly greater use of the voice opportunities offered to them. The special focus on India—which we have observed in the WHO and the Global Fund—is consistent with a utilitarian attribution of legitimacy, though such a norm has not been articulated in any of the documents we have reviewed or interviews we have conducted. We have found rather few clear indications of greater Indian than Philippine influence when both countries had comparable stakes (with the possible exception of the greater number of instances where India appears to have succeeded in shaping the Codex agenda or outcomes). With regard to the (limited but increasing) participation of non-governmental stakeholders, the Philippines generally started out with more voice opportunities for such stakeholders, as well as greater actual engagement and influence by them. Here, India has experienced greater change, resulting in recent years in more similar outcomes across the two countries, albeit still quite unevenly across the different global governance bodies.

C. CONSEQUENCES OF AND RESPONSES TO THE REFORMS

18

Assessing Stakeholder Participation Reforms in Global Health Governance

Ayelet Berman and Joost Pauwelyn

18.1 Introduction

Have the participation reforms in global health bodies improved the *actual* level of participation of previously marginalized stakeholders? Have they improved their influence on outcomes? These are the main questions asked in this chapter.[1]

Chapter 13 and Chapter 14 reviewed participation reforms in a diverse group of global health bodies: the World Health Organization (WHO), the Codex Alimentarius Commission (Codex), the International Council for Harmonisation (ICH), the International Medical Devices Regulators Forum (IMDRF), the Global Fund to Fight AIDS, Tuberculosis and Malaria (Global Fund), GAVI the Vaccine Alliance (GAVI), and GlobalG.A.P.[2]

Further, hypothesizing that the size of a country and the sustained strength of its economic growth impacts whether and to what extent developing countries take advantage of participation opportunities in global governance, the chapter compares, using a series of paired-country case studies, the experiences of the three largest emerging powers (Brazil, China, and India) and their smaller and/or less strongly economically rising regional counterparts (Argentina, Vietnam, and the Philippines, respectively—see Chapters 15–17).[3]

The purpose of this chapter is to synthesize the main lessons we can draw from these case studies as to the consequences of the supposedly participation-boosting reforms.

We find that although global health bodies are introducing participation reforms, they vary in the extent of their inclusiveness towards large emerging (Brazil, China, India) and smaller and/or lower-income (Argentina, Vietnam, Philippines) developing countries (henceforth, 'large' and 'small' developing countries, respectively).

[1] See Ayelet Berman, Tim Büthe, Martino Maggetti and Joost Pauwelyn, 'Introduction: Rethinking Stakeholder Participation in Global Governance.' Chapter 1, this volume; Mercy De Menno and Tim Büthe, 'Voice and Influence in Global Governance: An Analytical Framework.' Chapter 2, this volume.

[2] For an overview of the main reforms, see Ayelet Berman, 'Stakeholder Participation Reforms in Global Health Governance.' Chapter 13, this volume.

[3] Tim Büthe and Cindy Cheng, 'Analysing the Consequences of Institutional Reforms Using Country Pairs: A Note on the (Coarsened Exact) Matched-Country-Pairs Methodology of the Rethinking Stakeholder Participation Project.' Chapter 3, this volume; André de Mello e Souza and Facundo Pérez Aznar, 'Brazil and Argentina in Global Health Governance.' Chapter 15, this volume; Cindy Cheng with Anh Do, 'China and Vietnam in Global Health Governance.' Chapter 16, this volume; Tim Büthe, Sachin Chaturvedi, Peter Payoyo and Krishna Ravi Srinivas, 'India and the Philippines in Global Health Governance.' Chapter 17, this volume.

Ayelet Berman and Joost Pauwelyn, *Assessing Stakeholder Participation Reforms in Global Health Governance* In: *Rethinking Participation in Global Governance.* Edited by: Joost Pauwelyn, Martino Maggetti, Tim Büthe, and Ayelet Berman, Oxford University Press. © Ayelet Berman and Joost Pauwelyn 2022. DOI: 10.1093/oso/9780198852568.003.0018

An analysis of the case studies suggests that two main factors affect the participation of developing countries, and the relative access of large and small developing countries: institutional participation opportunities, and stakeholder preferences and constraints. We find that meaningful participation of marginalized stakeholders depends not only on institutional design, but also on stakeholders' preferences and constraints. Thus, institutional participation reforms that do not address such stakeholder constraints are unlikely to be successful in improving the participation of marginalized stakeholders.

In what follows, we address institutional participation opportunities (Section 18.2) and stakeholder factors (Section 18.3). Section 18.4 concludes.

18.2 Institutional Participation Opportunities

Global bodies set out institutional rules or procedures regarding the opportunity to participate—who is allowed to participate, by what means, and when. In what follows we lay out the general trends in institutional participation opportunities which emerge from the case studies.[4] We find that institutional participation opportunities of small and large countries largely depend on the kind and purpose of the global health body:

(1) *Transgovernmental and private standard-setting bodies* (ICH, IMDRF, and GlobalG.A.P.)
(2) *Multi-stakeholder partnerships* (Global Fund, GAVI)
(3) *Intergovernmental organizations* (WHO, Codex).

18.2.1 Transgovernmental and Private Standard-Setting Bodies

International standard-setting bodies set or harmonize standards among different countries or actors. Standards prescribe behaviour or characteristics of products or services and play a central role in product, service, and financial markets. Divergent national or industry standards create non-tariff barriers to trade. Thus, since the 1980s, with the rising global integration of markets and as interdependence has increased, there has been a growing demand to remove or harmonize standards, leading in turn to the emergence of international standard-setting bodies.[5] While some standards are developed in IOs (Codex, WHO), many are developed by transgovernmental regulatory networks (ICH, IMDRF), or in private standard setting bodies (GlobalG.A.P.).

[4] Berman, 'Stakeholder Participation Reforms' (n 2); Ayelet Berman, 'The Stakeholder Participation Triangle: Trusteeship, Functionality, and Efficiency.' Chapter 23, this volume; Mello e Souza and Pérez Aznar, 'Brazil and Argentina' (n 3); Büthe *et al.*, 'India and the Philippines' (n 3); Cheng with Do, 'China and Vietnam' (n 3).

[5] Tim Büthe and Walter Mattli, 'International Standards and Standard Setting Bodies' in David Coen, Wyn Grant and Graham Wilson (eds), *The Oxford Handbook of Business and Government* (Oxford University Press 2010) 440-471; Ayelet Berman, 'Industry, Capture and Transnational Standard Setting' 111 *American Journal of International Law Unbound* (2017) 112-118.

The ICH and IMDRF harmonize pharmaceutical and medical device standards, respectively, and the GlobalG.A.P. sets agricultural food standards.

The case studies exemplify that participation opportunities in standard-setting bodies tend to be skewed towards developed countries, large emerging countries, and business stakeholders.

For example, large developing countries—Brazil and China—have become ICH members. Although Brazil is not on an entirely equal footing with the US and the EU (who continue to enjoy 'founding regulatory member status'), it now has a vote.[6] Similarly, China's role in the ICH has increased over the years, leading to membership. India, too, has been invited but has not yet decided whether to join (see Section 18.3). In contrast, Argentina, Vietnam, and the Philippines, do not fulfil ICH membership criteria. They have some indirect access through regional organizations such as ASEAN or PANDRH. With the integration of Brazil, China, and India (but the exclusion of Argentina, Vietnam, and the Philippines (and their representation through regional organizations such as ASEAN), the IMDRF shares a similar dynamic. Furthermore, in both the ICH and IMDRF, the pharmaceutical or medical devices industry participates as a member or observer, yet public interest NSAs (patient or consumer organizations) remain excluded.

Similarly, compliance with GlobalG.A.P. standards is a precondition for membership. While export-oriented companies seek to comply with such standards, implementing them is costly, creating a barrier to participation by small- and medium-sized companies and companies from small developing countries. As a result, European firms continue to dominate GlobalG.A.P.. For example, although Brazilian and Argentine firms have joined GlobalG.A.P., they still have much fewer representatives than from European countries.[7] GlobalG.A.P. also makes more efforts to engage larger markets like China while paying smaller markets like Vietnam less attention.[8] Further, businesses make up GlobalG.A.P.'s membership, whereas public-interest NSAs (consumer or environmental organizations) remain excluded.

Some standard-setting bodies preserve *de iure* inequality between the founding members and the new, large, developing country members, such as, by giving founders veto rights. For example, in the ICH's management committee, which sets the agenda, decides on matters of membership, and has the final say on the approval of standards, the US, the EU, and Japan as 'founding regulatory members' have veto power, whereas new members Brazil and China do not. Furthermore, some standard-setting bodies limit new members' decisional rights. For example, GlobalG.A.P. has included new Brazilian and Argentinian firms in an affiliate membership category without decisional rights.[9]

But why have standard-setting bodies granted more or better participation opportunities to large developing countries and business interests?

With most economic interdependence between developed countries, trans-governmental or private standard-setting bodies had traditionally been 'clubs' of

[6] Mello e Souza and Pérez Aznar, 'Brazil and Argentina' (n 3).
[7] Mello e Souza and Pérez Aznar, 'Brazil and Argentina' (n 3).
[8] Cheng with Do, 'China and Vietnam' (n 3).
[9] Mello e Souza and Pérez Aznar, 'Brazil and Argentina' (n 3).

regulators or business actors from the US, Europe, and several other developed countries. This had been the case in the ICH, IMDRF, and GlobalG.A.P.. Yet, since the 1990s and the emergence of new economies, there has been growing demand to harmonize or set common standards with emerging markets, too.

It is this demand for internationally harmonized standards that best explains the nature of the more recent membership expansion in standard-setting bodies. Their expansion has been functional and driven by a desire to diffuse the standards among the main global market actors. This clarifies why standard-setting bodies have integrated strategic emerging economies, but continue to exclude (or give lesser, non-decisional opportunities) to smaller developing countries who are not important market players.[10]

Further, NSA inclusion in standard-setting bodies has also been driven by functional concerns. Notably, standards are technical and increasingly complex, requiring expertise that governmental actors lack, yet businesses possess.[11] The dependency on business expertise has driven business inclusion, yet they exclude or giver fewer participation opportunities to groups representing diffused interests (e.g. patient or consumer groups) who have little or less to contribute on technical or scientific matters. As a result, the participation opportunities in standard-setting bodies are skewed towards developed countries, emerging economies, and business interests.

18.2.2 Multi-Stakeholder Partnerships

In contrast to standard-setting bodies, the Global Fund and GAVI include developed, large, and small developing countries as well as business and civil society.[12] Their multi-stakeholder model was adopted as a response to the ineffectiveness of the traditional WHO model. Having all relevant stakeholders at the table was perceived as the most effective way of achieving their purpose.[13] Moreover, in contrast to the transgovernmental and private standard-setting bodies, whose main purpose is to harmonize and diffuse standards among the main *market* actors (thus expanding towards large emerging economies), the Global Fund and GAVI are mechanisms for funding health projects in developing countries. Thus, their mission and target audience are of a different nature—to supply a public good to developing countries and marginalized populations (rather than coordinating among market players). In this

[10] Ayelet Berman, 'Accordion Governance' 13(3) *Vienna Journal of International Constitutional Law* (2020) 203–236; Berman, 'Industry, Capture and Transnational Standard Setting' (n 5); Berman, 'Stakeholder Participation Triangle' (n 4); Frank Dobbin, B Simmons and G Garrett, 'The Global Diffusion of Public Policies: Social Construction, Coercion, Competition, or Learning?' 33 *Annual Review of Sociology* (2007) 449-472, 449; Beth A Simmons and Zachary Elkins, 'Globalization and Policy Diffusion: Explaining Three Decades of Liberalization' in Miles Kahler and David A Lake (eds), *Governance in a Global Economy: Political Authority in Transition* (Princeton University Press 2003) 275-304.

[11] Berman, 'Accordion Governance' (n 10); Berman, 'Industry, Capture and Transnational Standard Setting' (n 5); Berman, 'Stakeholder Participation Triangle' (n 4).

[12] Berman, 'Stakeholder Participation Triangle' (n 4); Berman, 'Stakeholder Participation Reforms' (n 2).

[13] Ayelet Berman, 'The Rise of Multistakeholder Partnerships' (2017) *American Society of International Law Annual Meeting Proceedings* <https://www.cambridge.org/core/journals/proceedings-of-the-asil-annual-meeting/article/rise-of-multistakeholder-partnerships/3B66B33B0D1A0E1BFF724D0412DFAFBF> , last accessed 05/10/2020.

case, including marginalized stakeholders alongside the donors has been considered necessary for achieving effective outcomes.[14]

In both partnerships, both the large and the small countries began as recipients. That said, since recipient status depends on the partnership's *eligibility criteria*, over time, participation of large and small developing countries has changed. In GAVI, to be eligible, countries need to be below a certain economic threshold (GDP per capita). Large developing countries have, therefore, 'graduated' and can no longer be recipients. China graduated once it reached a USD 1500 per capita, whereas Vietnam remains a recipient and GAVI board member. Likewise, both Brazil and Argentina no longer qualify for recipient status and are not board members. Accordingly, in partnerships whose eligibility criteria depend on an economic threshold, low-income countries remain recipients, whereas countries that have emerged to middle-income status are ousted. As Brazil and China are reluctant to donate, they also do not participate as donors.[15]

In contrast to GAVI, Global Fund eligibility depends not on an economic threshold, but on the *competitiveness of the grant application*. Hence, thanks to its grant writing capacity, China receives much more funding than does Vietnam, although Vietnam is poorer.

Finally, notwithstanding the inclusive model of multi-stakeholder partnerships, major developed country donors continue to significantly influence the agenda.[16] Thus, it is unlikely that multi-stakeholder partnerships have successfully eliminated underlying power asymmetries between developed and developing countries.[17] We address some of the reasons for this continued asymmetry in Section 18.3.

18.2.3 Intergovernmental Organizations

Thanks to their universal nature, IOs—such as the WHO and Codex—include developed and developing countries, both large and small. Participation of countries, at least formally, is thus universal. Such IOs have also significantly opened up to NSAs.[18]

Nevertheless, in practice, imbalances between large and small developing countries (and developed countries) often persist: China participates more than Vietnam in Codex.[19] Seeking to overcome de facto participation gaps, Codex has introduced the Codex Trust Fund (CTF), which funds poor members' participation. Yet inequalities also persist through key organizational positions: employees from high-income countries dominate the WHO's secretariat, which is autonomous and powerful in shaping negotiations. Additionally, holding a Codex committee chair requires financial and organizational resources; thus, developed countries hold most chairs.[20] Imbalances

[14] Berman, 'The Rise of Multistakeholder Partnerships' (n 13).
[15] Cheng with Do, 'Vietnam and China' (n 3); Mello e Souza and Pérez Aznar, 'Brazil and Argentina' (n 3).
[16] Mello e Souza and Pérez Aznar, Brazil and Argentina' (n 3); Berman, 'Stakeholder Participation Reforms' (n 2).
[17] Berman, 'The Rise of Multistakeholder Governance' (n 13).
[18] Berman, 'Stakeholder Participation Reforms' (n 2).
[19] Cheng with Do, 'China and Vietnam' (n 3).
[20] Mello e Souza and Pérez Aznar, 'Brazil and Argentina' (n 3).

between commercial and public interest groups, as in the case of Codex, also persist.[21] We address some of the reasons for these imbalances in Section 18.3.

18.2.4 Conclusion

Driven by their desire to globally diffuse their standards, transgovernmental and private standard-setting bodies have expanded to include large emerging countries (and selected commercial NSAs), leaving smaller countries (and public interest NSAs) out, or giving them lesser, non-decisional participation opportunities. In contrast, multistakeholder partnerships (at least those examined), seeking to tackle diseases in developing countries, have been more balanced, including developed, small, and big developing countries (as well as business and public interest groups) though they, too, have evolved over time, depending on eligibility criteria. IOs are formally universal and inclusive (also increasingly towards NSAs) with some efforts made in Codex to also achieve de facto inclusiveness, especially for the poorest participants.

Despite these formal reforms, gaps between participation opportunities and actual participation often remain. In practice, developed countries often continue dominating the process (or business stakeholders, as in the case of Codex). Thus, despite the important improvements in the institutional opportunities of developed countries (and NSAs), gaps in practice remain.

What explains this gap? Our analysis of the studies suggest that stakeholder preferences and constraints determine these gaps. We address these next.

18.3 Stakeholder Factors

While stakeholders may have the opportunity to participate, these opportunities vary. These sometimes are due to different institutional opportunities (discussed earlier, e.g. ICH grants membership to China but not to Vietnam), and sometimes—as predicted by liberal international theory[22]—they are a consequence of stakeholder preferences and constraints. Such stakeholder factors critically influence the ability or desire of stakeholders to take advantage of institutional opportunities.

Building on the country case studies in Brazil, Argentina, India, the Philippines, China, and Vietnam, we next lay out the main stakeholder factors that we have found to influence whether, how, and the extent to which stakeholders take advantage of their opportunity to participate in global health governance.

We cover six main factors: salience, resources, capacity, expertise, policy learning, and foreign policy orientation.[23] These factors often overlap or reinforce each other.

[21] Berman, 'Stakeholder Participation Reforms' (n 2); Berman, 'Stakeholder Participation Triangle' (n 4).

[22] Andrew Moravcsik, 'Taking Preferences Seriously: Liberalism and International Relations Theory' 51(4) *International Organization* (1997) 513-553.

[23] De Menno and Büthe's chapter in this volume subsumes several of these factors (financial resources, expertise, capacity) under the common constraint category of 'resources'. They also identify a 'collective action capacity' factor. In this chapter we differentiate between these factors. See De Menno and Büthe, 'Voice and Influence' (n 1).

18.3.1 Salience

Salience of the particular issues governed by a global governance body is an important factor in determining whether a country takes advantage of its participation opportunities. With the agricultural export sector accounting for much of their exports, and with the de facto binding nature of Codex standards through the WTO TBT and SPS Agreements,[24] Codex's importance has grown for Brazil, Argentina,[25] China, Vietnam,[26] the Philippines,[27] and India, which explains why these countries have actively pursued the opportunities for greater participation. Thanks to their greater involvement, these countries also have had a greater influence on pertinent standards, such as on Codex' adoption of a standard on fish sauce—a staple of South East Asian cuisine—which had been developed by Thailand and Vietnam.[28] Likewise, India, with a stake in traditional Ayurveda medicine, has sought to influence the development of WHO policies on traditional medicines.[29] Similarly, while countries with exports to Europe (like Brazil) have joined the GlobalG.A.P., countries (like the Philippines) with relatively few European exports have not.

Furthermore, as the world's second-largest medical devices market, China has sought to join the IMDRF. In contrast, not only have IMDRF's institutional reforms not allowed for Vietnam's inclusion, but it also has a smaller (though growing) medical devices market, leading to lower issue salience (in comparison to China).[30] Vietnam thus only has indirect access, through ASEAN. Similarly, with domestically produced medical devices accounting for only 2% of the Philippines medical device market, the issues addressed by the IMDRF are far removed from more pressing health-related issues for the Philippines. Consequently, the Philippines are largely absent from this specialized global health body.[31]

Given the importance of HIV/AIDS policies, Brazil and Argentina have sought to participate in the relevant global health bodies.[32] Seeking to spread its position on universal and free access to antiretroviral drugs, Argentina sought to participate in the Global Fund. Similarly, Brazil sought to participate in the Global Fund in order to disseminate the country's novel treatment model and to internationally promote its approach to reducing drug prices. Likewise, China's and Vietnam's hepatitis B, measles, AIDS, tuberculosis, and malaria disease burden have driven their participation in the Global Fund and GAVI. In contrast, high achievements in reducing child mortality and the decreasing incidence of malaria explain Brazil's lack of engagement with the

[24] Tim Büthe, 'The Globalization of Health and Safety Standards: Delegation of Regulatory Authority in the SPS Agreement of the 1994 Agreement Establishing the World Trade Organization' 71 *Law and Contemporary Problems* (2008) 219-256.
[25] Mello e Souza and Pérez Aznar, 'Brazil and Argentina' (n 3).
[26] Cheng with Do, 'China and Vietnam' (n 3).
[27] Büthe *et al.*, 'India and the Philippines' (n 3).
[28] Cheng with Do, 'China and Vietnam' (n 3).
[29] Büthe *et al.*, 'India and the Philippines' (n 3).
[30] Cheng and Do (n 3).
[31] Büthe *et al.*, 'India and the Philippines' (n 3)
[32] Mello e Souza and Pérez Aznar, 'Brazil and Argentina' (n 3).

Partnership for Maternal, Newborn and Child Health, and the Roll Back Malaria partnership, even when they had the opportunity.[33]

Although certain topics are important to both large and small developing countries, resource and capacity constraints often undermine participation, especially for smaller developing countries, since participation often carries significant initial fixed costs, regardless of country size.

18.3.2 Resources

The availability of financial resources is crucial in order for stakeholders to take advantage of their participation opportunities. Physical attendance at meetings is only possible if a country has the funds available. Thanks to improved resources, Brazil has increased the number of permanent diplomats and Brazilian ministers attending WHO meetings. However, the recent economic recession in Brazil has led to budgetary cuts, which have undermined its ability to effectively promote its position in Codex.[34] Similarly, Argentina's attendance at the WHO, since 2016 in particular, has been meagre, in large part due to resource constraints.[35] India, too, has not been able to send sufficient delegates to WHO meetings to be effectively involved.[36]

For the same reason, and despite Codex' importance for most developing countries, Argentina has been unable to send representatives,[37] and Vietnam has participated less than China.[38] Indeed, to overcome resource and capacity gaps so as to strengthen participation by low-income members, Codex has introduced the CTF. Thanks to the CTF, overall participation by developing countries has increased. For example, in the 1990s CTF support allowed the Philippines' first active involvement in the technical work of Codex. That said, the eligibility criteria of the CTF are so restrictive, that, with the exception of the Philippines,[39] all of the countries examined have not qualified or are no longer eligible.[40]

Furthermore, organizational leadership positions are also often only open, in practice, to countries with the resources to service them. In Codex, for instance, most of the operational work is done in specialized committees, and committee chairs mostly come from high-income countries; Brazil and Argentina lack the financial and operational resources required for setting up a committee secretariat and organizing meetings.[41]

Financial shortages have consequences that run deeper than reduced physical attendance—they also impact the capacity to develop an informed position. Technical discussions require data and research, and such information cannot be developed

[33] Mello e Souza and Pérez Aznar, 'Brazil and Argentina' (n 3).
[34] Mello e Souza and Pérez Aznar, 'Brazil and Argentina' (n 3).
[35] Mello e Souza and Pérez Aznar, 'Brazil and Argentina' (n 3).
[36] Büthe *et al.*, India and the Philippines' (n 3).
[37] Mello e Souza and Pérez Aznar, 'Brazil and Argentina' (n 3).
[38] Cheng with Do, 'China and Vietnam' (n 3).
[39] Büthe *et al.*, 'India and the Philippines' (n 3).
[40] Mello e Souza and Pérez Aznar, 'Brazil and Argentina' (n 3).
[41] Mello e Souza and Pérez Aznar, 'Brazil and Argentina' (n 3).

without sufficient resources. As a result, developed country industries present much of the data, as has been the case in Codex.[42] Mello e Souza and Pérez Aznar illustrate this point in the case of Brazil and Argentina in Codex.[43] Consequently, those with the resources to develop data and knowledge are also more likely to influence the outcome of the decision.[44]

Finally, resources are needed for implementation—and making a credible commitment to implementation is often a precondition for joining standards-developing organizations such as the ICH or GlobalG.A.P.. Yet, given their Western industry origins, these standards are often too costly for developing countries or their firms to implement. As a result, Vietnamese farmers—despite being affected by the GlobalG.A.P.—do not have the financial resources to comply with GlobalG.A.P. standards, which in turn leads to less participation by Vietnamese firms.[45] Likewise, Argentinian producers have indicated that the compliance costs and attendance costs are barriers to their participation in GlobalG.A.P.[46]

18.3.3 Capacity

To take advantage of participation opportunities and make meaningful contributions, countries must have the organizational, human, regulatory, scientific, and technical capacity to contribute substantively to the discussion. Yet such capacity is often lacking. For example, Argentina's economic crisis has had a significant impact on the scientific research and capacity needed to effectively participate in Codex. Recent economic improvements have enhanced its scientific and institutional capacity and strengthened its national infrastructure, which is comprised of comprehensive national policies, a Codex Contact Point, political backing, and close links with the food industry and research centres. All this, in turn, has led to better participation.[47] Likewise, Brazil's improved participation in the WHO is the result, since the 1990s, of its greater resources and foreign policy interests, which have translated into greater technical expertise and capacity to act as a regional leader.[48]

Building domestic capacity has also been key in China's, Vietnam's, and India's more active Codex participation, although, thanks to China's greater capacity, China participates more than Vietnam in the IMDRF and the Global Fund (Vietnam still lacks the necessary capacity for completing high-quality proposals).[49] Likewise, thanks to the CTF, the Philippines has been able to launch its national Codex committee, enabling the Philippines to attend meetings and develop country positions on technical matters, such as its scientific contribution in 2006 to the proposal for the maximum

[42] Mello e Souza and Pérez Aznar, 'Brazil and Argentina' (n 3).
[43] Mello e Souza and Pérez Aznar, 'Brazil and Argentina' (n 3).
[44] Berman, 'Industry, Capture and Transnational Standard Setting' (n 5).
[45] Cheng with Do, 'China and Vietnam' (n 3).
[46] Mello e Souza and Pérez Aznar, 'Brazil and Argentina' (n 3).
[47] Mello e Souza and Pérez Aznar, 'Brazil and Argentina' (n 3).
[48] Mello e Souza and Pérez Aznar, 'Brazil and Argentina' (n 3).
[49] Cheng with Do, 'China and Vietnam' (n 3).

level of lead in fish, a food safety standard developed by the Codex Committee on Food Additives and Contaminants.[50]

Notwithstanding the greatly increased resources of the large emerging countries (Brazil, China, India) and their increased participation opportunities, on balance they still have fewer human and financial resources than high-income countries, preventing them to match, for example, the number of staff and experts the countries from developed countries can send to global bodies. Such a (at least relative) lack of capacity is, of course, not written in stone. As Lavenex, Serrano, and Büthe argue and show, building state capacity in any issue is a matter of political priorities. At the same time, such capacity can rarely be built overnight, and it is for this reason that we analytically take as given the level of capacity for a given country in the short run.[51] Developing countries also often have fewer resources and less capacity than large private-sector firms and foundations, which in turn not only affects their capacity to develop data and research but also reduces their relative voice in comparison to business interests and bodies such as the Gates Foundation.[52]

To overcome resource and capacity constraints, smaller states have resorted to two main strategies. One has been to act collectively through regional organizations. For example, Brazil and Argentina have mobilized South American countries through the South American Health Council or resorted to the Codex Coordinating Committee for Latin America and the Caribbean.[53] The ICH has also admitted several regional organizations, including PANDRH, APEC, and ASEAN, which represent Argentina, Vietnam, or the Philippines. Similarly, ASEAN, as a regional organization, provides Vietnam indirect access to IMDRF.[54]

A second strategy, given the mismatch between global standards and developing country resources and capacities, has been to set up domestic bodies, which adapt the international standards to local capacities and needs. For example, Vietnam and China have created national VietG.A.P. and ChinaG.A.P., both of which indirectly build on the GlobalG.A.P..[55]

18.3.4 Expertise

Expertise in a specific policy area has also driven participation. Although resources or capacity often restrict low-income countries, such countries often do participate on matters that are within their field of expertise (and of high saliency). For example, thanks to its expertise on universal access to medicines and free access to antiretroviral drugs, Argentina has participated in several relevant international processes and successfully influenced the outcome.[56] Likewise, the Philippines has actively participated

[50] Büthe *et al.*, 'India and the Philippines' (n 3).

[51] Sandra Lavenex, Omar Serrano and Tim Büthe, 'Power Transitions and the Rise of the Regulatory State: Global Market Governance in Flux' 15(3) *Regulation and Governance* (2021) 445–471.

[52] Büthe *et al.*, 'India and the Philippines' (n 3).

[53] Mello e Souza and Pérez Aznar, 'Brazil and Argentina' (n 3).

[54] Cheng with Do, 'China and Vietnam' (n 3).

[55] Cheng with Do, 'China and Vietnam' (n 3).

[56] Mello e Souza and Pérez Aznar, 'Brazil and Argentina' (n 3).

in the WHO on matters of financing universal health coverage and typhoon management, and India has contributed its expertise on controlling polio, TB, and tobacco use.[57] Expertise has also been an important driver behind the inclusion of business groups.[58]

18.3.5 Policy Learning

Policy learning drives participation, too, as developing countries seek to learn from more experienced peers. Indeed, large developing countries have joined standard-setting bodies to improve their regulatory capacity—as reflected in China's, Vietnam's, and the Philippines' participation in ICH, IMDRF, or GlobalG.A.P., developing their regulatory capacity in medicines, medical devices, and agricultural goods, respectively. China's participation in the Global Fund has also largely been driven by the country's desire to learn from other countries about their fight against AIDS.[59] The ASEAN Medical Device Directive (based on IMDRF guidance) and its spill-overs to domestic law and policy in both China and Vietnam reflect this process.[60]

18.3.6 Foreign Policy Orientation

Foreign policy—a country's policy regarding engagement with global bodies in general or in certain policy areas—preconditions participation, and also explains variations in participation. Brazil, for example, has adopted a deliberate strategy to increase its participation in international institutions. Due to the HIV/AIDS crisis, global health is an important part of its foreign policy, and it has prioritized the WHO as a venue for negotiations on many health-related issues. Argentina, in contrast, due to its internal woes, has taken a less globalist approach .[61] Likewise, China's and Vietnam's participation in the Global Fund has been part of a general policy to address HIV/AIDS matters with international partners. Additionally, following the introduction of reforms to liberalize their economies and open to the global economy, both China and Vietnam have become more active Codex participants, joining Codex in 1984 and 1989, respectively. Finally, China's decision to apply for Global Fund backing has been mostly driven by its desire to be perceived as a member in the global fight against AIDS.[62]

Lastly, the protection of national policy autonomy may play a role in a country's decision to refuse an invitation to join as a member. India's reluctance to join the ICH—and its preference to stay an observer—reflects this ambivalence. As a member, India would have to implement ICH standards. Yet, within India, due to conflicting industry

[57] Büthe *et al.*, 'India and the Philippines' (n 3).
[58] Berman, 'Stakeholder Participation Triangle (n 4); Berman, 'Industry, Capture and Transnational Standard Setting' (n 5).
[59] Cheng with Do, 'China and Vietnam' (n 3).
[60] Cheng with Do, 'China and Vietnam' (n 3).
[61] Mello e Souza and Pérez Aznar, 'Brazil and Argentina' (n 3).
[62] Cheng with Do, 'China and Vietnam' (n 3).

and public health interests there has been reluctance to harmonize national standards with international standards.[63]

18.4 Conclusion

Building on our reading of the case studies, we have tried to determine if the institutional participation reforms improved the participation of developing countries in global health bodies, and if they have improved their influence.

At the institutional level, we have found that, overall, global health bodies have introduced participation opportunities towards developing countries, yet participation reforms towards large and small developing countries have varied.

Seeking to remove regulatory barriers through international standardization, transgovernmental and private standard setting bodies (ICH, IMDRF, GlobalG.A.P.) have provided participation opportunities to large, emerging markets. Yet, they have largely left smaller countries out or given them lesser, non-decisional participation opportunities. Driven by the standard-setting bodies' dependency on industry for expertise on technical matters, they also tend to provide business participation opportunities while excluding (or giving fewer participation opportunities) to civil society groups.

In contrast, seeking to fund health projects for tackling health crises in developing countries and among marginalized groups, multi-stakeholder partnerships (Global Fund and GAVI) have provided participation opportunities to large and small developing countries, and have made efforts to include both business and non-commercial, civil society groups.

Finally, IOs such as the WHO and Codex are officially universal and are equally open (at least formally) to developed and developing countries. They have also opened up towards NSAs. That said, a gap between formal opportunities and actual participation often persists.

An analysis of the country studies suggests that, although institutional opportunities are a necessary precondition for participation, whether a stakeholder takes advantage of this opportunity ultimately depends on stakeholder preferences and constraints.

We have identified several main stakeholder factors: issue salience, resources, capacity, expertise, policy learning, and foreign policy orientation. These factors affect the extent to which developing countries have taken advantage of their participation opportunities. Variations in participation among large and smaller developing countries are often a result of these stakeholder factors, with saliency, resources, and capacity playing a critical role. However, a specific expertise, for example, might explain small country participation even in the general absence of resources.

Thus, to return to our central question: have institutional reforms improved the participation of previously marginalized developing countries in global health governance? Have they improved influence? For global health governance bodies, the

[63] Büthe *et al.*, 'India and the Philippines' (n 3).

answer is that not all marginalized developing countries have equally been given opportunities to participate. Moreover, even when opportunities for participation are granted, stakeholder factors affect the extent to which stakeholders can or want to take advantage of the opportunities.

Effective participation in international rule-making depends, therefore, not only on institutional design, but also depends on stakeholders' preferences and constraints. As a consequence, institutional participation reforms that do not also address stakeholder constraints—especially resources and capacity—will be ineffective in improving the participation of marginalized stakeholders.

19

The Effects of Stakeholder Reforms on Global Health Governance

A Response

Gian Luca Burci

19.1 Introduction

I am broadly in agreement with the conclusions reached by Ayelet Berman and Joost Pauwelyn with regard to the effect of institutional reforms in global health governance on both the opening of global health institutions to participation by previously neglected stakeholders as well as to the effectiveness of their participation.[1] I agree in particular with their two main findings. First, different types of international institutions have opened up differently to certain groups of states and non-state actors (NSAs). Standard-setting organizations, in particular, have been especially welcoming towards larger industrialized countries and industry associations that represent the interests of the corporate sector. Second, other things being equal, endogenous national factors play a significant role in explaining the intensity, level, and form of participation by the countries reviewed in this volume. In this short response, therefore, I focus on a number of points that may not be sufficiently fleshed out in the preceding chapters or which in my view need to be qualified. I rely in part on my professional experience as a former Legal Counsel of the World Health Organization (WHO) to bring some less-analysed perspectives, although I acknowledge that some of them may sound anecdotal.

At the outset, I offer a few methodological considerations that, in my view, may limit the comparability of the national case studies. First, even though the emphasis in this volume is on institutional reform as a tool for stakeholder participation, 'reform' has manifested itself in different ways in global health governance. In some cases (e.g. the WHO, the ICH, GlobalG.A.P., and the Codex Alimentarius), existing institutions have introduced reforms to promote broader and effective participation by developing countries and NSAs. In other cases, the need to achieve meaningful participation as a governance principle in global health has led to the establishment of new institutions based on a horizontal model of governance and a broad notion of stakeholders; this is notably the case of GAVI and the Global Fund. In turn, the latter institutions have introduced at times governance reforms to address perceived shortcomings in

[1] Ayelet Berman and Joost Pauwelyn, 'Assessing Stakeholder Participation Reforms in Global Health Governance.' Chapter 18, this volume.

Gian Luca Burci, *The Effects of Stakeholder Reforms on Global Health Governance* In: *Rethinking Participation in Global Governance*. Edited by: Joost Pauwelyn, Martino Maggetti, Tim Büthe, and Ayelet Berman, Oxford University Press.
 DOI: 10.1093/oso/9780198852568.003.0019

effective and representative participation, for example, through the distribution of seats in the GAVI Board, as well as the regulation of constituencies and the reform of the funding model in the Global Fund.[2] Second, the scope of national case studies is not always the same, with that on China and Vietnam, for example, not covering the WHO; such differences make a meaningful comparison more difficult.

19.2 The World Health Organization: Assumptions and Omissions

It is striking that the WHO does not seem to attract much attention in most of the case studies to the point, as noted earlier, that the case study on China and Vietnam does not even mention it. Is that because, as graphically put by Berman and Pauwelyn,[3] the WHO is an unproblematic 'watermelon' open to neglected stakeholders in view of its universal nature, the strength in numbers of developing countries, and its sweeping mandate that does not automatically favour powerful member states and corporate interests? Or is it because of its decreasing relevance that leads developing countries to prioritize limited political and financial resources for gaining better access to organizations of more immediate importance for their national public health and economic interests? Even though this question merits consideration, the example of Brazil shows that the WHO can still be an important agent to amplify at international level national policies such as access to antiretrovirals and other essential medicines. Brazil's political activism also points to the use of the WHO as a political resource to be used in other settings, for example, the WTO with regard to the challenges against pharmaceutical patents as a barrier to access essential medicines.

In this connection, the case studies (in particular comparative case study of Brazil and Argentina[4]) could have emphasized more the specific impact of some of the countries under review—such as Argentina, Brazil, China, and India—on the policy setting and normative activities of the WHO. As further elaborated later, the professional qualities of the representatives of those countries and their ability in using tactically the procedures and practices of the WHO (e.g. its attachment to consensus decision-making), as well as in building alliances of like-minded states, have given them an influence in negotiating processes sometimes disproportionate to their overall political and economic importance. The influence of Brazil in the revision of the International Health Regulations in 2004–2005, the negotiation of the 2009 Global Strategy and Plan of Action on Public Health, Innovation and Intellectual Property, and the successful challenge against the International Medical Products Anti-Counterfeiting Taskforce established by the WHO Secretariat are cases in point.

None of the case studies mentions the 2003 reform of the procedures of the WHO's Executive Board (Board) as an important factor in increasing participation

[2] Ayelet Berman, 'Stakeholder Participation Reforms in Global Health Governance.' Chapter 13, this volume.

[3] Berman and Pauwelyn, 'Assessing' (n 1).

[4] André de Mello e Souza and Facundo Pérez Aznar, 'Brazil and Argentina in Global Health Governance.' Chapter 15, this volume.

of developing countries in the governance of the WHO. The revision of the Board's rules of procedure opened up its work to broad participation by non-members of the Board and turned it into a 'mini-World Health Assembly'. In particular, non-members may participate in meetings much more easily than was previously the case and make proposals that will be considered by the Board if endorsed by a Board member. Given the strong regional discipline characterizing WHO, such endorsement is most of the times automatic, thus giving non-members an almost equal weight in negotiations. Moreover, and in stark difference from previous practice, all member states participate with equal rights in the work of drafting and working groups that often negotiate during Board's sessions draft resolutions to be submitted to the World Health Assembly for adoption. While this form of institutional openness does not ensure effective participation of developing countries that still suffer from power and resource differentials compared to developed countries, it has certainly amplified the opportunities to influence WHO's policy setting, in particular, in the case of better resourced middle-income countries with strong political interests in particular issues.

A final comment with regard to the WHO: having worked for eighteen years in the Secretariat, I disagree with its characterization as biased and largely populated by officials from high-income countries. Even though certainly not immune from the pressure of the most powerful countries, the WHO's secretariat is highly representative of its membership both at headquarters and, even more, in regional and country offices. If there is pressure on the secretariat, this is brought not only by high-income countries but often by large middle-income countries such as China, India, and Brazil. The criticism contained, for example, in Argentina's and Brazil's case study is disingenuous in this respect. It is interesting, however, that Cheng and Do speculate whether the fact that the former WHO Director-General was a Chinese national facilitated the increasingly assertive role of China in the organization.[5] A similar speculation is made in the case study on India with regard to the appointment in 2017 of an Indian national as a Deputy Director-General. It is not mentioned in the case study, but a similar consideration could be raised with regard to the fact that the current WHO Regional Director for South-East Asia is an Indian national and that the WHO Regional Office is located in New Delhi. This could arguably increase the opportunities for India to increase its influence on the WHO through unofficial channels.

It is also a fact that the secretariat makes good faith efforts to ensure that expert committees and other technical advisory bodies—very influential in the WHO's normative activities—are as regionally representative as possible. However, in highly technical fields such as virology and biotechnology, the need to retain the best experts militates in favour of an over-representation of the most scientifically developed countries.

19.3 Meaning and Scope of Participation

Problems in comparability arise also because the scope and meaning of 'participation' has been interpreted differently in the case studies; while the case study on Argentina

[5] Cindy Cheng with Anh Do, 'China and Vietnam in Global Health Governance.' Chapter 16, this volume.

and Brazil, for example, focuses on participation by the governments concerned or national NSAs in the governance of global health institutions, other cases (e.g. the Philippines) show how the concept of 'participation' has been extended to the impact of those institutions on the national health systems or regulatory capacities of the states concerned. In the case study on the Philippines, moreover, the author seems to consider the use by the WHO of lessons learned by the country (e.g. in the management of the health consequences of Typhoon Haiyan) as one of the benefits of the 'partnership' between the two and somehow a form of engagement.[6] This approach, focusing on the mutual influences between international institutions and countries from a technical, financial, and policy perspective, is also very visible in the case study on India. With regard to the WHO, for example, the case study highlights the contributions that Indian research institutions gave to the development of WHO's flagship programmes, for example, those on viral hepatitis and palliative care. Conversely, Chaturvedi and Srinivas acknowledge the impact of Codex Alimentarius standards on the rationalization of India's food regulation after the establishment of the WTO and the exposure of the Indian food market to global standards through the operation of the Agreement on Sanitary and Phytosanitary Measures.[7] The realization of Indian food exports' vulnerability to global harmonization of food safety standards in turn has led the Indian government to increase its engagement in Codex governance, culminating in its election in 2014 as Regional Coordinator for Asia. The case studies, in synthesis, reveal a broad interpretation of 'participation' that extends beyond engagement in the governance of the institutions under review. It includes their impact on national governance as well as the contributions by the countries concerned and their research institutions to the technical programmes of the organizations.

The case studies define 'participation' in a broad and holistic manner that involves interactions going in both directions between state and international institution. It is evident, for example, that direct and effective participation in the meetings and the governance of standard-setting organizations such as the Codex Alimentarius Commission and ICH is a priority for developing countries with strong market potentials such as Brazil, India, and China. Only through direct engagement in the decision-making processes of those institutions could those countries try to counterbalance their bias in favour of the corporate interests of high-income countries and influence their standard-setting activities. Conversely, given the importance of China as a manufacturer of active pharmaceutical products and the growth of Brazil's pharmaceutical capacities, as well as the increasing global reach of ICH itself, it became important for the latter to adapt and then reform its governance structure so as to make their direct participation possible.

However, the analysis of the relationship of the countries concerned with funding institutions such as the Global Fund and GAVI clearly points out their significant impact and influence on the development of national health governance and policies. Cindy Cheng and Anh Do, for example, point out how China's applications for Global Fund's support of its HIV-AIDS programmes induced 'a remarkable degree of policy

[6] See Tim Büthe, Sachin Chaturvedi, Peter Payoyo, and Krishna Ravi Srinivas, 'India and the Philippines in Global Health Governance.' Chapter 17, this volume.

[7] Büthe *et al.*, 'India and the Philippines' (n 6).

learning' including in exposing China's policy makers to foreign experts and international actors. The particular approach of both the Global Fund and GAVI required a measure of adaptation and reform of local models of health policies, with particular regard to the role played by NGOs and other NSAs. Cheng and Do again bring the example of the different ways in which China and Vietnam, respectively, implemented the Global Fund's requirement to establish Country Coordinating Mechanisms (CCM) and involve domestic NGOs.[8]

19.4 The Importance of Power

The case studies show that the extent and manner in which global health institutions have opened to participation by neglected stakeholders is influenced by complex power dynamics between the actors involved. This can consist of the absolute power of a government in political and economic terms (arguably the case of China), its relative market position as a supplier of strategic commodities that makes it particularly relevant for certain institutions (as again in the case of China as a supplier of active pharmaceutical ingredients), or the particular interest of the institution in being active in a particular country to secure the legitimacy of its functions and role.

While the foregoing can be self-intuitive, the case studies show some remarkable manifestations of how power considerations have shaped participation in global health institutions; this is particularly visible again in the case of China. Cheng and Do's study shows, for example, how GAVI relaxed its policy against opening peripheral offices through the establishment of a project office at China's CDC due to the scale of programme implementation.[9] GAVI also exceptionally agreed to let China use locally produced vaccines to implement its grants, even though those vaccines were not pre-qualified by the WHO as normally required by GAVI as an absolute condition. Similarly, it is striking that the Global Fund has apparently acquiesced to China's top-down handling of its CCM in order to secure political control over what should have instead been a tool to empower civil society and other stakeholders and to strengthen their participation in the implementation of the Global Fund's grants. It is evident that the sheer power and size of China has enabled it—in various ways—to shape the policies and operational practices of some of the institutions under review.

An aspect that may be difficult to conceptualize but empirically may have a significant effect on the perception of a country's power and leverage in international governance frameworks is the personal and professional qualities of key individuals in both governments and international institutions. In the case of Brazil, for example, two outstanding diplomats effectively and successfully led the negotiations of the Framework Convention on Tobacco Control and boosted the image of Brazil as a leader in the WHO. Similarly, an Argentinian diplomat chaired, with remarkable skills and credibility, the negotiations that led to the adoption in 2016 of the WHO Framework for Engagement with Non-State Actors (FENSA). Along similar lines, the

[8] Cheng with Do,' China and Vietnam' (n 5).
[9] Cheng with Do, 'China and Vietnam' (n 5).

professional abilities of governmental representative at both a strategic and tactical level are an important driver to amplify the perception of a country's power in order to fully exploit the participation space opened by global health institutions. This consideration is only partly related to the amount of financial and human resources at the disposal of government agencies and arguably has to do more with professional and sociological traditions within particular governments. Brazil's role in the WHO's governance is again a case in point: the ability and skills of Brazilian representatives, their occasional ruthlessness when confronting tactical difficulties, and their capacity to form and lead alliances of like-minded states have projected Brazil's leadership and influence probably beyond its power in absolute terms. It has also allowed Brazil and other middle-income developing countries to use the WHO's normative and policy-setting functions in an antagonistic manner against the promotion of pharmaceutical patents through TRIPS and regional free-trade agreements. In other words, participation in the WHO has been used as a tool to increase their influence over policy setting in different institutions such as the WTO.

A less evident form of political leverage to achieve better terms of participation in certain global health institutions is through the sheer burden of the diseases targeted, in particular, by funding institutions like GAVI and the Global Fund. The legitimacy and the perception of relevance and effectiveness of those institutions could be questioned if they did not play a significant role in countries with a high incidence of covered diseases, both in absolute terms and relative to other diseases or other countries with a similar epidemiological profile. This consideration was made, for example, in the case study on India, where the authors note the need for the Global Fund to support India's health programmes to maintain its credibility and underline the mutually beneficial effects of such involvement thanks to the closer connections built with Indian civil society organizations and pharmaceutical companies.

19.5 Direct vs. Indirect Participation

It is striking from the findings of several case studies how participation (in the broad sense noted) is sometimes exercised indirectly through the role and functions of regional organizations and groupings. Regional structures seem to serve two distinct purposes. The first is to increase the power of participating countries through regional coordination and a stronger leverage in negotiations. The second is as a 'filter' or a 'buffer' to soften the impact of some of the institutions reviewed on national policies and norms and adapt international standards to local circumstances.

I previously mentioned the ability of countries like Brazil and India in mobilizing tactical groups of like-minded countries around specific issues in the WHO. Besides such occasional and largely opportunistic initiatives, the case studies concentrate on the role played by formal international organizations or organs. The first instance, for example, is in the role played by the regional Codex coordinating committees in the governance of the Codex and the outcome of its standard-setting process. The comparative case analysis of Argentina and Brazil highlights how both countries have invested in improving the cohesion of the Codex Coordinating

Committee for Latin America and the Caribbean as a tool to strengthen participation and influence.[10]

The second instance is exemplified by the role of the ASEAN in guiding the progressive implementation of ICH guidelines in its region. The progressive expansion of the ICH's governance through the establishment in 1999 of the Global Cooperation Group allowed the ASEAN to provide the immediate interface with the ICH for the purpose of exchange of information and experiences, as well as for the reception of finalized ICH guidelines and their translation into instruments more adapted to the absorption capacities of ASEAN members and their companies. One important observation is that, while ICH guidelines are the outcome of a partnership between drug regulators and industry, the ASEAN took over harmonization in pharmaceutical requirements as government-driven with the principal aim of reducing trade barriers within the regional bloc. Therefore, indirect participation through regional organizations not only provided a reassuring regulatory buffer for a low-income country like the Philippines, but also constituted a device to ensure a more immediate control by the governments concerned and the translation of the harmonization project into a political tool to pursue common policy priority goals.

19.6 Conclusions

The brief considerations in this contribution aimed at highlighting a number of interesting aspects of the analysis contained in the case studies and at offering some additional elements of reflection. As noted at the outset, they do not contradict the conclusions drawn by Berman and Pauwelyn regarding the main drivers of participation in global health governance. If anything, they underline that a thorough analysis of the relationship between governance reform and participation by neglected government and non-government stakeholders must take into account a wide variety of endogenous and exogenous factors that have to be considered in their own mutual interactions. The ensuing level of complexity will definitely benefit from additional research both for the purpose of conceptual clarity as well as of policy recommendations.

[10] Mello e Souza and Pérez Aznar, 'Brazil and Argentina' (n 4).

20
How Much do Health Actors from the Global South Influence Global Health Governance?
A Response

Suerie Moon

20.1 Introduction

This book takes up a critical yet under-studied question in global governance in general, and global health governance in particular: how have institutional reforms shaped the participation of previously marginalized stakeholders in global governance, and what influence have they subsequently wielded? The case studies examine the participation of state and non-state actors across six middle-income countries (MICs) and seven global governance institutions relating to health. They offer rich empirical data across a breadth of issue areas, geographies, and national political systems. The overall picture that emerges is not of a definitive power shift from developed to emerging powers, nor of a steady expansion of power and influence to a broader range of actors. Rather, what appears is a somewhat idiosyncratic set of instances in which a particular developing country government wields a degree of influence in a particular issue area, such as Brazil on global approaches to combating HIV/AIDS, China's exceptional role in GAVI's approach to Hepatitis B, or India's influence on traditional medicines at the WHO. The evidence in this volume suggests that a global shift to a more multi-polar system will take place in fits and starts, driven by particular episodes of leadership and entrepreneurialism rather than inexorable historical forces.

In response to these case studies and supporting analyses, the next four sections present my observations drawing on the broader study of global health.

20.2 What Does 'Global Health Governance' Encompass, and What Difference Does It Make?

First, the choice of which global governance institutions to include or exclude within the scope of 'global health governance' has important implications for the conclusions we may draw. The field of global governance is relatively new, and global health governance as a specialized sub-field even more so. As such, the boundaries of the field are

Suerie Moon, *How Much do Health Actors from the Global South Influence Global Health Governance?* In: *Rethinking Participation in Global Governance.* Edited by: Joost Pauwelyn, Martino Maggetti, Tim Büthe, and Ayelet Berman, Oxford University Press. © Suerie Moon 2022. DOI: 10.1093/oso/9780198852568.003.0020

not clearly defined. Much of the literature in the sub-field has focused on governance among actors in the health sector—those whose primary intent is the protection or promotion of health; this group of actors and the institutions that govern their interactions has been conceptualized as the 'global health system',[1] and the WHO, GAVI, and the Global Fund would fall squarely within it, with the other cases perhaps on the borderline. Frenk and Moon have argued for a more expansive conceptualization of the field to include both the global health system, and the many other arenas of global governance that *impact health* such as trade and investment—using the terminology global governance for/and health.[2] The approach taken in this book has, interestingly, taken a middle road: it includes actors primarily concerned with health (the WHO, GAVI, the Global Fund) and those with dual objectives relating to health and the economy (Codex, the ICH, the IMDRF, GlobalG.A.P.), but excludes consideration of non-health sectors (e.g. trade, environment).

A remarkable finding of the case studies of institutions with a dual health and economic mission is that developing country engagement in them seems rarely to be driven by health considerations, but rather by economic incentives. For example, the logic for China, Vietnam, the Philippines, Brazil, or Argentina to seek to influence GlobalG.A.P. or to develop national versions of the GlobalG.A.P. standards is to protect domestic producers' access to high-income export markets, not to ensure safe domestic food supplies. Similarly, it seems the rationale to engage in Codex was to prevent protectionist barriers to exports of food products from developing countries, not to protect health within them. In other words, it is the health of consumers in the Global North that seems to be prioritized, not necessarily public health in the South. Indeed, the extent to which Codex or GlobalG.A.P. (or national versions) standards have contributed to—or, through the promulgation of inappropriate rules, harmed—public health in the six developing countries examined here is not clear. Similarly, for the ICH and the IMDRF, developing country governments have found reason to engage when the standards set by these bodies may touch on the interests of domestic firms such as manufacturers of medical devices, active pharmaceutical ingredients (API), and/or generic medicines producers in India and China. But these governments seem to have put far less emphasis on ensuring that global ICH or IMDRF standards reflect national public health needs or are adapted to national contexts. Berman has highlighted how ICH standards may restrict the supply of low-cost generic medicines on which many developing countries rely, and unnecessarily raise the regulatory hurdle for neglected disease drug development.[3] Yet neither ICH participation reforms nor developing country government engagement seems to address these types of risks. And, as the case study authors have pointed out, their capacity to change global standards is quite limited.

The limited engagement of health actors in *rulemaking* institutions (vs. the financing institutions GAVI and Global Fund) is troubling precisely because rulemaking is likely to be where the future of global health governance lies. That is, as more and more

[1] Nicole A Szlezák, Barry R Bloom, Dean T Jamison, Gerald T Keusch, Catherine M Michaud, Suerie Moon, and William C Clark, 'The Global Health System: Actors, Norms, and Expectations in Transition' 7(1) *PLOS Medicine* (2010): e1000183.

[2] Julio Frenk and Suerie Moon, 'Governance Challenges in Global Health' 368 *New England Journal of Medicine* (2013) 936-942.

[3] Ayelet Berman, 'Industry, Regulatory Capture and Transnational Standard Setting' 111 *American Journal of International Law Unbound* (2017) 112-118.

countries develop economically, they will either stop relying on development aid to finance their health systems, and/or will lose eligibility for such financing,[4] making GAVI and Global Fund policies relatively less consequential for health in MICs.

Yet it seems to be precisely in these rulemaking arenas that health actors, such as Ministries of Health or health-focused CSOs from middle income countries, have either not participated at all or with very limited influence. Developing country health actors appear to be engaging in far fewer global governance institutions than the many (e.g. trade, investment, security, migration, environment) that have important health implications. This leads to my second main observation:

20.3 Public and Private Economic Interests vs. Health

Compared to health actors, both public and private economic actors seem to exhibit much greater capacity to make use of existing and new channels for participation in global governance institutions with health implications. For example, as noted, the governments that engaged in Codex, the ICH, the IMDRF, and GlobalG.A.P. did so largely out of economic interests, not domestic health interests.

In their chapter, Berman and Pauwelyn rightly characterize 'stronger' actors in global governance as developed country governments and the private (for-profit) sector. However, in their characterization of developing country governments they did not distinguish between the various interests within a single government.[5] Yet, economic actors within government (e.g. Ministries of Trade, Economy, Industry, Finance) have often been portrayed as holding greater sway than health interests (e.g. Ministries of Health or Social Welfare), with important implications for government policy positions in global negotiations.[6] Similarly, it is useful to distinguish between stronger and weaker private sector actors—as the case studies show, developing country firms and industries exert less influence than multinational industries based in the North, with their well-developed global networks of operations and lobbying capacities. Nevertheless, the case studies suggest that private firms in developing countries still have greater capacity to participate and influence global governance processes as compared to CSOs and other (non-state) public interest organizations from the same countries, which seem nearly absent.[7]

Have recent reforms to expand stakeholder participation in rulemaking bodies (excluding the financing bodies) largely resulted in greater participation by public and private *economic* interests, but not health interests? If so, how much of this outcome

[4] Chatham House Report, *Shared Responsibilities for Health: A Coherent Global Framework for Health Financing—Final Report of the Centre on Global Health Security Working Group on Health Financing* (Chatham House 2014).

[5] Ayelet Berman and Joost Pauwelyn, 'Assessing Stakeholder Participation Reforms in Global Health Governance.' Chapter 18, this volume.

[6] Chantal Blouin, Nick Drager, and Richard Smith, *International Trade in Health Services and the GATS: Current Issues and Debates* (The World Bank 2006); David P Fidler, Nick Drager, and Kelley Lee, 'Managing the Pursuit of Health and Wealth: The Key Challenges' 373 *The Lancet* (2009) 325-331; Deborah Gleeson and Sharon Friel, 'Emerging Threats to Public Health from Regional Trade Agreements' 381 *The Lancet* (2013) 1507-1509; Kelley Lee, Devi Sridhar, and Mayur Patel, 'Bridging the Divide: Global Governance of Trade and Health' 373 *The Lancet* (2009) 416-422.

[7] Berman and Pauwelyn, 'Assessing' (n 5).

can be attributed to national factors (salience, capacities, political structures) vs the institutional reform?

At the same time, it is quite noteworthy that the WHO, the ICH, and the IMDRF have each recently formalized policy changes to restrict the participation of businesses in governance processes and to limit the perception of their undue influence on rulemaking. While critics have argued that FENSA risks legitimizing inappropriate business participation in WHO governance processes, FENSA also goes further than any other IGO's policy by differentiating and more tightly regulating for-profit actors as compared to other non-state actors such as NGOs, academic researchers, or philanthropic foundations. These developments echo Andonova's finding that states have continued to jealously guard their rulemaking power in global governance institutions.[8] They also raise the risk, however, that private actors seek less formal and less visible ways of wielding influence, such as funding research, NGOs, or academic experts; such pathways of influence can be more difficult to govern *precisely because* they are less obvious.[9]

Are businesses widely considered legitimate actors in global governance, and if so, on what basis? De Menno and Buthe's conceptual framework usefully highlights many of the rationales that justify private sector participation—namely, the provision of useful technical and political information, a greater likelihood of compliance, and enhanced input legitimacy.[10] Yet, the extent to which business participation and influence enhances democratic accountability remains highly debatable. Indeed, the cases suggest that the democratic accountability of global governance institutions continues to be the weakest link, which leads to my third observation:

20.4 Still-Marginalized Public Interest Voices

As Berman points out, public interest non-state actors from the Global South remain absent in several of the institutions examined.[11] The reasons vary across countries and global governance institutions. In China and Vietnam, domestic civil society is relatively weak and/or has been suppressed by non-democratic national political systems. In Brazil, despite robust civil society mobilization around HIV/AIDS, CSOs seemed uninterested in engaging in other health-related global governance institutions. Similarly, in Argentina, a strong HIV/AIDS movement is likely to have shaped its government's foreign policy positions on HIV-related policies, but such engagement did not extend to other health issues.

[8] Liliana B Andonova, *Governance Entrepreneurs: International Organizations and the Rise of Global Public-Private Partnerships* (Cambridge University Press 2017).

[9] Eliza Suzuki and Suerie Moon, 'Informal Channels of Influence on Global Health Policy Making: A Mapping of Strategies across Four Industries' in Nora J Kenworthy, Ross MacKenzie and Kelley Lee (eds), *Case Studies on Corporations and Global Health Governance: Impacts, Influence and Accountability* (Rowman & Littlefield 2016).

[10] Mercy B DeMenno and Tim Büthe, 'Voice and Influence in Global Governance: An Analytical Framework.' Chapter 2, this volume.

[11] Ayelet Berman, 'Stakeholder Participation Reforms in Global Health Governance.' Chapter 13, this volume.

Global health governance has not yet evolved to become truly democratic nor democratically accountable, and more concerted efforts to support meaningful engagement by public interest CSOs is needed. Berman has pointed out the significant variation in stakeholder reforms[12]—yet even the most extensive efforts to support participation (i.e. Global Fund and Codex) have not been adequate to allow some marginalized voices to be heard and to exert influence. This is a striking finding to which I return in the conclusion.

Furthermore, it seems that the exceptional transnational political mobilization of HIV activists remains just that—exceptional. Historian Allan Brandt has argued that HIV/AIDS 'invented global health'[13] and UNAIDS has highlighted how AIDS 'changed everything'.[14] Indeed, the creation of the Global Fund and the unprecedented weight given to CSO representatives in its governance structure can largely be credited to politically savvy AIDS activists.[15] However, while there has been some institutional isomorphism—UNITAID's board also includes a seat for populations directly affected by its diseases of focus, as does the Drugs for Neglected Diseases initiative (a non-profit product development organization)—these governance innovations do not seem to have extended beyond the field of development aid. Indeed, AIDS may have changed many aspects of how the global health system functions, but it had far less impact in other governance arenas, as the studies of the ICH, the IMDRF, Codex, and GlobalG.A.P. underscore.

20.5 Who Punches Above Their Weight?

Finally, with few exceptions, the case studies support the conclusion that the larger countries—Brazil, China, and India—hold greater sway across a range of global governance institutions than their smaller counterparts, Argentina, Vietnam, and the Philippines, respectively. The choice of countries for the case studies was well designed and scientifically justified for addressing the central questions of the book.[16] Yet, case study methodology necessarily provides a partial picture, and it may be useful to examine the actors that have exerted more influence than would be expected based on their size or material resources. What if we also examined countries or NGOs that had 'punched above their weight' in the global arena? What other insights might emerge?

Among developing countries, the country that most often seems to wield influence beyond its size, and therefore merits further study, is arguably Thailand, and perhaps also South Africa or Colombia (among high-income countries, Norway might claim this place.) Evidence of Thailand's outsize influence in health governance processes

[12] Berman, 'Stakeholder Participation Reforms' (n 11).

[13] Allan M Brandt, 'How AIDS Invented Global Health' 368 *New England Journal of Medicine* (2013) 2149-2152.

[14] UNAIDS, *How AIDS Changed Everything. MDG 6: 15 Years, 15 Lessons of Hope from the AIDS Response* (2015) <http://www.unaids.org/sites/default/files/media_asset/MDG6Report_en.pdf>, last accessed 08/13/2021.

[15] Jon Lidén, *The Grand Decade for Global Health, 1998–2008* (Chatham House 2013); Raymond A Smith and Patricia D Siplon, *Drugs into Bodies: Global AIDS Treatment Activism* (Praeger 2006).

[16] De Menno and Büthe, 'Voice and Influence' (n 10).

includes chairing many sensitive negotiations at the WHO such as those relating to intellectual property; authorship of many health policy studies in the international peer-reviewed literature; hosting the most prominent global health conference outside the West, the annual Prince Mahidol Awards Conference; sending a large delegation to the WHO governing bodies each year; a strong network with Northern NGOs and academics; participation of its experts in many advisory committees and commissions; and an exceptionally sophisticated health technology assessment body, among other factors.[17]

Similarly, illustrating Margaret Mead's oft-cited adage that 'a small group of thoughtful, committed citizens' is the only thing that has ever changed the world, relatively small NGOs have also been very influential. For example, Knowledge Ecology International is well known among diplomats, journalists, and CSOs for its role in intellectual property and health debates.[18] The Third World Network was arguably the main civil society voice shaping negotiations on the Pandemic Influenza Preparedness Framework.[19] Outside the health arena, Global Witness helped craft the Kimberley Process to govern conflict diamonds[20] (from which it later dissociated itself). Each of these NGOs operated with a mere handful of professional staff.[21]

In line with the book's analysis, this degree of participation and influence seems largely driven by factors specific to a government or organization (e.g. charismatic or highly skilled leadership), rather than due to participation reforms enacted in global institutions. Thus, examining these 'outsize influencers' does not undermine the overall conclusions of the book. However, it does counterbalance the emphasis of the case studies on the influence wielded by the largest middle income countries and highlights the possibility of smaller countries and non-state actors having both voice and influence in global health governance.

20.6 Conclusions

Recent reforms across a broad range of global governance institutions to broaden and deepen meaningful participation by previously marginalized stakeholders have been significant. Yet the studies in this book underscore that there is a long way to go. The rise of emerging powers is real, but slow.[22] MIC governments and non-state actors

[17] This list is based on the author's knowledge and is necessarily somewhat impressionistic. See also: Joseph Harris, *Achieving Access: Professional Movements and the Politics of Health Universalism* (Cornell University Press 2017); Suriwan Thaiprayoon and Richard Smith, 'Capacity Building for Global Health Diplomacy: Thailand's Experience of Trade and Health', 30(9) *Health Policy and Planning* (November 2015) 1118–1128..

[18] Wolfgang Hein and Suerie Moon, *Informal Norms in Global Governance: Human Rights, Intellectual Property Rules and Access to Medicines* (Ashgate 2013); Susan K Sell, 'TRIPS and the Access to Medicines Campaign' 20 *Wisconsin International Law Journal* (2002) 481.

[19] David P Fidler, 'Negotiating Equitable Access to Influenza Vaccines: Global Health Diplomacy and the Controversies Surrounding Avian Influenza H5N1 and Pandemic Influenza H1N1' 7 *PLOS Medicine* (2010): e1000247.

[20] Virginia Haufler, 'The Kimberley Process Certification Scheme: An Innovation in Global Governance and Conflict Prevention' 89(4) *Journal of Business Ethics* (2009) 403-416.

[21] This paragraph is based on both cited sources and the author's knowledge of these organizations.

[22] Miles Kahler, 'Rising Powers and Global Governance: Negotiating Change in a Resilient Status Quo' 89 *International Affairs* (2013) 711-729.

can wield significant influence, and have done so, in various global health governance processes—but such influence appears to be sporadic rather than systematic or inexorable. At the same time, the case studies illustrate that countries are profoundly affected by these global governance institutions.

The rapid growth of national income that characterizes many of the countries studied here has not yet translated into the full-fledged diplomatic, advocacy, or sophisticated research capacity needed to shape global rulemaking. In other words, there is a long lag between growing economic power and commensurate policy influence. Notably, there is also little evidence of developing countries going around existing global governance institutions by creating alternative global arenas. While the creation of the Asian Infrastructure Investment Bank and New Development Bank as alternatives to the World Bank has raised the possibility of such workaround approaches, this does not appear to be a general phenomenon.

'Multi-stakeholderism', the norm of including business, civil society, philanthropies, academics, and other non-state actors in governance processes, seems to have firmly taken hold at the core of the global health system—that is, at the WHO, GAVI, the Global Fund, and a host of other organizations (tellingly, often described as 'partnerships') with the primary intent to protect and promote health. However, this norm is less widely or deeply accepted elsewhere. As the weight of global governance processes affecting health shifts away from development assistance and towards global rulemaking, limits on opportunities for voice and influence may prompt greater scrutiny and pressure on rulemaking bodies.

This volume provides important answers to its motivating questions regarding the nature and impact of participation reforms, and also opens up many directions for future research, three of which I highlight here. First, it would be useful to examine through in-depth case studies the voice and influence exercised by African countries, with South Africa an important player in many health policy issues, and Kenya, Rwanda, Egypt and others also frequently seen as influential depending on the specific issue. Since all the country case studies in this volume were of middle income countries, it would also be useful to examine whether and how low-income countries (most of which are African) are able to take advantage of participation reforms—particularly since some reforms target such countries, such as the Codex Trust Fund. As with the Asian and Latin American countries studied in this volume, African regional bodies may also play an important role in facilitating collective action at the global level.

A second area of further research could focus on transnational civil society networks, which have attracted attention from other global governance scholars.[23] Because the case studies focused on specific countries, they may not have fully captured the influence of transnational civil society networks or large international advocacy NGOs such as Oxfam, Médecins Sans Frontières, or the International Baby Food Action Network. International NGOs often work with developing country stakeholders through national branch offices, or networks with local individual activists or academics, which would not be captured under the category of 'national NGO'.

[23] Margaret E Keck and Kathryn Sikkink, *Activists Beyond Borders* (Cornell University Press 1998); Sanjeev Khagram, James V Riker, and Kathryn Sikkink, *Restructuring World Politics: Transnational Social Movements, Networks and Norms* (University of Minnesota Press 2002).

Influential CSOs also are able to exert influence through multiple channels, as the case studies suggest, not only through formal means such as CSO-designated board seats, but also by lobbying national government representatives (as highlighted in the Brazil case study), through traditional media, and increasingly, through social media. By bringing complementary types of power and resources (such as expertise or networks) to bear, international NGOs can amplify the influence of developing country governments in a given global policy negotiation.[24] These influential actors merit additional study.

Finally, further research on business engagement in health-related global governance institutions is needed. While several institutions have taken measures to ensure both business participation and limitations on undue influence, the extent to which private interests influence global governance processes remains unclear. With new formal restrictions on their participation, influence may become even more difficult to discern, but not necessarily less important in impact. For example, the Brazil, Argentina, and the Philippines case studies highlighted that MICs governments are not yet funding or generating the kind of research that can sway global technical standards (e.g. in Codex or the ICH), and that this remains the purview of high-income countries and businesses. This is but one area in which business influence may be exerted, though not necessarily easily discerned. Further research in this area would provide important insights for both scholarship and policy.

A final conclusion from these case studies is that ensuring the protection of public health in developing countries—about three-quarters of the world's population and disease burden—in global governance remains a daunting challenge, despite important participation reforms. The reforms have been uneven, and even where most extensive, they were not sufficient to ensure widespread, regular, and meaningful influence from these previously marginalized actors.

[24] Hein and Moon, 'Informal Norms' (n 18). See also Suerie Moon, '"Power in Global Governance: An Expanded Typology from Global Health' 15(1) *Globalization and Health* (2019): 1–9.

21

Evolving Norms and Objectives Regarding Stakeholder Participation

The Global Fund to Fight AIDS, Tuberculosis and Malaria

Gülen Atay Newton

21.1 Introduction

Over the past decade, the development community has witnessed an unprecedented growth of innovative mechanisms designed to fund international humanitarian initiatives through partnerships among governments, intergovernmental organizations, and civil society. Among these partnership initiatives, the Global Fund to Fight AIDS, Tuberculosis and Malaria (the Global Fund) has taken a prominent role in a development sphere traditionally dominated by international organizations such as the UN and the World Bank. Since its founding in 2002, the Global Fund has made disbursements of about USD 34 billion,[1] making it a principal financier in global health, channelling two-thirds of the international financing provided to fight TB and malaria, and a fifth of the international financing against AIDS.

The Global Fund entered the international development landscape as a very different kind of actor. Though the institution was established pursuant to a UN resolution and receives most of its resources from national governments, it was formed as a multi-stakeholder partnership. Rather than being established and governed by treaty among governments, it brought together donor and implementer governments, civil society, the private sector, philanthropic foundations, representatives of communities living with the three diseases, the UN, and other technical partners. These partners, united by a common stake in public health, are involved at all levels of the Global Fund model, from membership of the Board through to country coordination and implementation of programmes in communities.

In this way, the Global Fund reflects changing norms regarding stakeholder participation and inclusion of affected and often marginalized groups. Partnership forms the very basis of its model, and this is exhibited across its operations, its governance, and its funding approach. The Global Fund represents a novel form of cooperation among governments, international development institutions (including UN agencies and the World Bank), civil society, philanthropists, the private sector, and communities.

[1] The Global Fund to Fight AIDS, Tuberculosis and Malaria: Financials <http://theglobalfund.org/en/financials>, last accessed 05/13/2020.

Gülen Atay Newton, *Evolving Norms and Objectives Regarding Stakeholder Participation* In: *Rethinking Participation in Global Governance.* Edited by: Joost Pauwelyn, Martino Maggetti, Tim Büthe, and Ayelet Berman, Oxford University Press.
 DOI: 10.1093/oso/9780198852568.003.0021

The Global Fund has embraced three major innovations in facilitating stakeholder participation: (i) an inclusive and diverse governing Board, with voting procedures designed to ensure equity between donor and implementing blocs; (ii) local ownership and participatory decision-making in programme implementation through the Country Coordinating Mechanism (CCM); and (iii) a novel legal arrangement to accommodate inclusion of NGOs while advancing its status as an international organization. Despite these innovations—or because of them—the Global Fund faced new challenges and has had to refine its stakeholder model, specifically as it relates to methods for ensuring collaborative decision-making within a stakeholder system, as well as its funding model.

21.2 Background: The Context and Rationale Leading to Establishment of Global Fund

By the end of the 1990s, the escalating HIV/AIDS crisis had yielded a tremendous increase in international awareness of the pressing public health needs in the developing world.[2] The HIV/AIDS epidemic had already infected 40 million people.[3] By 2010, life expectancy in South Africa was projected to drop to thirty years.[4] This appreciation of the potential devastation resulting from an HIV/AIDS epidemic fuelled global momentum to create a fund to channel resources into public health initiatives.[5] The Group of 8 (G8) nations subsequently acknowledged this need in their 2000 meeting in Okinawa,[6] and in June 2001, the UN General Assembly called for the creation of 'a global HIV/AIDS health fund to finance an urgent and expanded response to the epidemic' mobilizing contributions 'from public and private sources, with a special appeal to donor countries, foundations, the business community, including pharmaceutical companies, private sector, philanthropists and wealthy individuals'.[7] As a reflection of the understanding that global public health, as a public good, demanded engagement of a wide cross-section of stakeholders, the negotiations that led to the creation of the organization involved representatives of developing countries, donor countries, NGOs, the private sector, and the UN system.[8] In January 2002, a Secretariat was established[9] to be the Global Fund's permanent standing body and manage its day-to-day operations.[10]

Despite its catalysis by UN resolution[11] and the substantial role of national governments in its planning and formation, there was a consensus that the Global Fund

[2] See *The Global Fund to Fight AIDS, Tuberculosis and Malaria: History of the Global Fund*, <http://www.theglobalfund.org/en/history/>, last accessed 01/25/2011.

[3] UNAIDS, *Report on the Global AIDS Epidemic*, July 2004 <http://data.unaids.org/Global-Reports/Bangkok-2004/unaidsbangkokpress/gar2004html/gar2004_00_en.htm>, last accessed 05/13/2020.

[4] UNAIDS, *Report* (n 3).

[5] Global Fund, *History* (n 2).

[6] Global Fund, *History* (n 2).

[7] G.A. Res. S-26/2, ¶ 90, U.N. Doc. A/RES/S-26/2 (2001/08/02).

[8] The Global Fund to Fight AIDS, Tuberculosis, and Malaria, Transitional Working Group, <http://www.theglobalfund.org/en/twg/>, last accessed 01/25/2011.

[9] Global Fund, Transitional Working Group (n 8).

[10] Press Release, G.A. Res. S-26/2 (n 7).

[11] Resolution, (n 7), para 90.

should differ from and operate more efficiently than existing bilateral and multilateral aid mechanisms.[12] The World Health Organization (WHO) hosted the Global Fund during its early stages, through an administrative services agreement.[13] On 1 January 2009, the Global Fund became an autonomous international financing institution.[14]

21.3 Innovations in Governance: Ensuring Inclusive and Equitable Participation

The main governing body of the Global Fund is its Board, which approves funding proposals. Before they come before the Board, proposals must have been developed and put forth by the recipients, reviewed and endorsed by an independent Technical Review Panel ('TRP'), and recommended by the Grant Approval Committee of the Secretariat.[15]

The Global Fund Board (the Board) reflects the innovative, stakeholder-driven partnership model upon which it was founded. The structure and composition of its Board was established with an overarching goal of ensuring both inclusive and equitable stakeholder participation.

21.3.1 Inclusiveness: Broadening Beyond Traditional Actors

The extent of participation by affected groups, especially affected stakeholders who are often marginalized or excluded, may be considered the key test of inclusive governance. In the Global Fund's case, inclusiveness was ensured through a Board that not only includes representatives from donors and implementer governments, but also affected communities and civil society organizations from both the developing and developed worlds.

This feature is accomplished through the Board's constituency system. All Board Members represent 'constituencies', that is, a group of communities, networks, countries, or institutions. Even Board Members that represent a single agency or country must represent and communicate to multiple interested parties within their respective institutions. As such, constituencies are the 'building blocks' of Global Fund's governance system.

[12] 'While the Global Fund's *purpose* was driven by the imperative of fighting the three diseases, its particular *structure* resulted from the strong belief held by some of its founders that it should differ from and operate more effectively than existing bilateral and multilateral aid mechanisms.' See Steven Radelet, *The Global Fund to Fight AIDS, Tuberculosis and Malaria: Progress, Potential, and Challenges for the Future* (Center for Global Development 2004), <http://portal.unesco.org/education/es/file_download.php/689078c299513623b161bf53d5a14cb9GFATM+full+report.pdf>, last accessed 08/13/2021.

[13] Anna Triponel, 'Global Fund to Fight AIDS, Tuberculosis and Malaria: A New Legal and Conceptual Framework for Providing International Development Aid', 35 *North Carolina Journal of International Law & Comparative Regulation* (2009) 175-232, 185.

[14] Global Fund, Nineteenth Board Meeting: *Executive Director's Report to the Board*, 27 (2009), <http://www.theglobalfund.org/documents/board/19/GF-B19-03_EDReport.pdf>, last accessed 08/13/2021.

[15] Global Fund, *Executive Director's Report* (n 14).

Constituencies are granted ownership over their processes and decision-making, within the parameters of set guidelines. Each constituency decides for itself on a process to select which countries/organizations will represent it as Board members, alternate Board members, Focal Points, and committee members.[16] Some constituencies have formal processes, some informal; the process itself is dependent on what is practical for that constituency and is not influenced by Global Fund.

The Board consists of twenty voting members, representing developing countries, donors, civil society, and private sector.[17] In addition, international organizations such as the WHO, UNAIDS, and the World Bank play a role in its governance through representation on the Board as non-voting members.[18] International organizations play a significant role in the administration and implementation of Global Fund programmes, as well. The World Bank acts as its Trustee, receiving, holding, and disbursing donor contributions on its behalf. Moreover, the UNDP, UNICEF, the UNHCR, and UNOPS have supported the implementation of a number of programmes financed by the Global Fund, particularly in countries with relatively limited public health infrastructure and capacity.

The Board is therefore a setting in which representatives of country governments sit alongside representatives of civil society organizations, philanthropic foundations, communities, and the private sector. This innovation significantly expanded beyond the traditionally state-centric approach of international financing institutions, whose governing bodies are dominated by or entirely composed of national governments.

Despite this twenty-first-century set-up to foster participation and inclusiveness, progress in achieving an effective engagement by all stakeholders has been uneven. In particular, participation of the stakeholders from developing countries remained unequal, which prompted the second-generation reforms mentioned in the overview of Global Health Reforms.[19] The Board adopted a Strategic Roadmap to Enhance Implementer Voice to increase the incentives and opportunities for meaningful participation of implementers and facilitate implementers' exercise of real influence as opposed to nominal participation,[20] and enable them to contribute to outcomes. More funds were allocated to support better engagement, organization, and participation at the level of constituencies as well as the Country Coordinating Mechanisms (discussed in detail in Section 21.4). More meaningful participation of key populations was guaranteed through changes made to the funding requirements. Capacity building was prioritized through several programmes and mechanisms adopted by the Global Fund Secretariat.[21] In addition, prior to the meetings of the Board or its Committees, in preparation of the agendas, policies, and strategies, the Secretariat

[16] Global Fund Board and Committee Operating Procedures, Section A(1).

[17] Global Fund Bylaws, Section 7.1.

[18] Global Fund Bylaws, Section 7.1. The board's composition is: eight donor countries, one private sector, one private foundation, seven developing countries, and three NGOs.

[19] Ayelet Berman, 'Stakeholder Participation Reforms in Global Health Governance.' Chapter 13, this volume.

[20] See the discussion of this distinction in Mercy B DeMenno and Tim Büthe, 'Voice and Influence in Global Governance: An Analytical Framework.' Chapter 2, this volume.

[21] For details, see Berman, 'Stakeholder Participation Reforms' (n 19).

held more frequent and targeted contacts and consultations with the Board members, the constituencies they represent, and their larger support groups in order to increase awareness and ensure meaningful input. The commitment to effective engagement has been strengthened, in a dedicated manner, both inside and outside the Global Fund.

Increasing inclusiveness also means enabling presence of diverse views and voices around the table at Board and Committee meetings. The governance rules ensure equal participation of donor and implementer blocs in the Board, as well as its Committees, with leadership in these bodies to be alternated between these two blocs every two years in order to prevent dominance of views of one particular group.

In the country case study on China and Vietnam,[22] the authors discuss representation in the Board, in particular perceived insufficient representation of Vietnam in governance. The Western Pacific Region (WPR) constituency, which includes China and Vietnam, was represented by China in the Board for many years, directly selected by the countries in that constituency (including Vietnam). Moreover, due to the declining engagement on the part of China, which is now neither a major recipient nor (yet) a sizable donor, there is more scope for increased engagement by other countries in the WPR. That said, should Vietnam seek a more direct representation in Global Fund's Board, it is able to do so only through the WPR constituency.

A direct correlation between membership in the Board and the impact on a country's national health governance outcomes is difficult to establish. Much depends on the profile of the individual Board Member and their ability to exercise influence in country contexts. Should the Board Member be a health minister of a country or other high ranking official well integrated in the national decision-making processes, such impact can be expected, but it is not guaranteed.

21.3.2 Equity: Making Governance Participation Meaningful

To ensure meaningful participation by all stakeholders, particularly those representing affected populations, inclusiveness must be coupled with equity. The Board operates on an equity principle. The voting members of the Board are split into implementer and donor blocs to ensure their concerns and priorities are addressed equally.[23] There is no distinction between the blocs in terms of roles and responsibilities. The blocs are used when the Board cannot reach consensus and must decide by vote; a two-thirds majority of each bloc is required for a vote to pass.[24]

As a consequence of this voting system, all decisions of the Board require majority support from both donors and implementers. This rule has the effect of 'hard-wiring' equitable participation into Global Fund decision-making and addresses the historical marginalization of affected groups in global health governance.

[22] Cindy Cheng with Anh Do, 'China and Vietnam in Global Health Governance.' Chapter 16, this volume.

[23] Global Fund Bylaws, Section 7.6.

[24] Global Fund Bylaws, Section 7.6.

In the Brazil–Argentina country case study, the authors convey the Brazilian representatives' view that:

> ... major donors of Global Fund have influence over the allocation of funds and over which kind of projects will benefit from them. In particular, these donors have the power to determine which countries or regions will receive which portion of the available funds, as well as whether projects favoring prevention of treatment strategies will be selected.[25]

The Global Fund seeks to safeguard against such disproportionate influence procedurally through its allocation model: the funding envelope to be made available to each implementing country is decided by its Board, which includes donors and implementers alike, with equal voting structure. Similarly, each grant proposal is developed by the implementing country in a multi-stakeholder participatory manner. Given the manner of decision-making at the Board, any particular group's disproportionate influence over funding decisions or the nature of projects to be funded is largely mitigated through the equity-based voting structure.

However, prospects of undue influence in decision-making cannot be mitigated by administrative measures alone. The scope of each constituency's influence is primarily dependent on the strength of its respective participation; its awareness and preparation on the discussion topics, its knowledge of issues and capacity to develop and defend views, as noted in the analytical framework.[26] The implementer bloc's ability to participate and exercise influence has been largely dependent on its access to enabling resources. When such resources are provided for effective functioning in participatory settings such as the Global Fund, the profile of participants and the quality of discussions have tended to improve. For multi-stakeholder partnerships to function effectively, access to resources and capacity building for historically marginalized groups cannot be neglected.

21.4 Innovations in Country Operations: Promoting Country-Led Solutions and Participatory Decision-Making through Inclusive Country Coordinating Mechanisms (CCMs)

A founding principle of the Global Fund is country ownership. As noted within its Framework Document, establishing its operating model and core principles, the 'Global Fund will base its work on programmes that reflect national ownership and respect country-led formulation and implementation processes'.[27]

To implement the concept of country ownership, the Global Fund created the innovation of the CCM. The Global Fund's Governance Handbook states: '[t]he founding

[25] André de Mello e Souza and Facundo Pérez Aznar, 'Brazil and Argentina in Global Health Governance.' Chapter 15, this volume.

[26] DeMenno and Büthe, 'Voice and Influence' (n 20).

[27] Global Fund Framework Document, Section VI(A)(2).

principles of CCMs are in line with those of the Global Fund: they are intended to promote country ownership, foster innovative partnerships to fight the three diseases, encourage in-country formulation and implementation, build upon national policies, priorities and partnerships, and promote accountability and transparency.'[28]

An inclusive CCM is the foundation of Global Fund grant operations. Each recipient country is to maintain a CCM, which develops and submits grant proposals, nominates the principal recipients, and (following grant approval) oversees progress during implementation. With its emphasis on cross-sectoral participation, especially from affected communities, CCMs very much mirror the Board. In addition to being open to government representatives, civil society, and the private sector, guidelines require that all CCMs must include membership by: (i) people that are both living with and representing people living with HIV; (ii) people affected by and representing people affected by tuberculosis and malaria; and (iii) people from and representing key affected populations.[29]

In view of the key role of CCM in the Global Fund's funding model, a separate pool of funds was established to fund their operation. While CCMs are responsible for establishing their own processes, the Global Fund employs eligibility requirements and standards for CCMs, including requirements to ensure good governance, transparency, and the avoidance of conflict of interest, which are reviewed on a yearly basis and with every application for funding.

The CCM is a vehicle for inclusive multi-stakeholder governance, opening the way for active civil society and private sector participation, and is as such one of the major legacies of the Global Fund. Through the CCM, country priorities are identified at the country level, through dialogue including affected, vulnerable, and marginalized key populations, within a platform where various sectors work together—in many cases for the first time—in a structured way. The CCM has therefore offered the opportunity to bring government, charitable groups, the private sector, donors, UN agencies, and affected populations to the same table in the service of a common cause. A 2011 independent assessment of the Global Fund noted the following examples of stakeholder participation achieved through the CCM model:[30]

- HIV-positive people meet regularly and openly with Ministers and Presidents and appear in the media.
- Governments must account for spending that previously would have been off-the-books, including by submitting to monitoring through unannounced visits.
- Faith-based organizations coordinate the delivery of health care with State-operated institutions.
- NGOs bid for funds in transparent tenders.
- Donors engage recipients on their terms.
- Ordinary citizens stand to represent their peers in competitive elections.

[28] Global Fund Governance Handbook, Section II.

[29] Global Fund Guidelines and Requirements for Country Coordinating Mechanisms, Requirement 4.

[30] *The Final Report of the High-Level Independent Review Panel on Fiduciary Controls and Oversight Mechanisms of the Global Fund to Fight AIDS, Tuberculosis and Malaria*; Section 1.2.

This assessment also noted: '[o]ften, the governance model of a CCM breaks the traditional dynamics of power in certain countries where the state, politics and economy are run by the same cliques. The Panel has concluded a unique and invaluable outcome of the Global Fund's system in many places has been a boost to democratization and good governance.'[31]

In the China–Vietnam country case study,[32] the authors detail how the Global Fund has influenced these countries' public health policies and practices, particularly with respect to compulsory drug detoxification and re-education centres. The Global Fund's requirements for inclusiveness in developing funding proposals have very definitely altered the way these governments interacted with their respective civil society sectors, facilitating greater engagement of the latter (more limited in the case of China than Vietnam). Increased engagement of marginalized stakeholders has not only resulted in development of more successful proposals but has also improved general awareness on public health issues stemming particularly from HIV/AIDS and tuberculosis and thus helped improve relevant domestic policies.

In the country case study of the Philippines, the author discusses convincingly the impact Global Fund's business model has had on how the Philippines currently addresses its national health priorities and delivers health outcomes, and pronounces the Global Fund's contribution as 'impactful' particularly due to the institution building process accomplished through the CCM setup.[33] Working through multi-stakeholder CCMs has had a similar effect on the majority of countries that receive funding from the Global Fund and represents a twenty-first-century approach to making global health policy or funding decisions. Public health, as a global public good, must include all the public and private stakeholders concerned in order to ensure that health strategies and interventions reflect the real priorities on the ground and deliver relevant, effective, and *durable* solutions. CCMs have proven to be highly successful conduits in establishing such a participatory and inclusive approach, not only with respect to tackling local public health issues, but also for adopting global health governance policies, triggering crucial health sector reforms.

Given the serious burden of tuberculosis and increasing levels of new HIV infections in the Philippines, these diseases must continue receiving commensurate attention in the local context in preparation of the national plans and specific grant proposals. The funding decisions taken by the Board are largely consistent with the country proposals, having been endorsed by the TRP and negotiated with the principal recipients. Although the author laments inadequate funding for HIV/AIDS, funding decisions for diseases are influenced mostly by health priorities of the country and how they are worked into the national strategic plans and funding proposals, as opposed to the views of the Global Fund, as a consequence of the country ownership principle it embraces.

[31] *Final Report* (n 25), section 1.2.

[32] Cheng with Do, 'China and Vietnam' (n 22).

[33] Tim Büthe, Sachin Chaturvedi, Peter Payoyo, and Krishna Ravi Srinivas, 'India and the Philippines in Global Health Governance.' Chapter 17, this volume. See also: Peter B Payoyo, *Philippine Participation in International Health Governance Institutions* (unpublished manuscript, The Graduate Institute Geneva, 2019).

In the comparative case study of Brazil and Argentina,[34] the authors state that, despite initial interest and engagement, both countries have, to a large extent, ceased their involvement in the Global Fund. These countries are currently neither recipients of Global Fund grants nor donors to it.

However, the authors also attest that, in the case of Brazil, despite its short-lived engagement with the Global Fund as a grant recipient, working with the Global Fund increased awareness and political commitment, particularly regarding tuberculosis and its co-infection with HIV/AIDS. Furthermore, such engagement has helped to positively transform national health governance in Brazil by influencing inter-governmental relations, facilitating strengthened ties between the Ministry of Health and the state and municipal health departments, as well as the NGOs.

Moreover, at the community level, new movements, networks, and municipal monitoring institutions have emerged as a result of Global Fund's influence, fostering 'a greater commitment to civil engagement, empowerment and accountability'.[35]

21.5 Innovations in Legal Arrangements of International Organizations: The Hybrid Approach of Global Fund

The Global Fund, as a multi-stakeholder partnership, with its inclusive and diverse Board represented an innovation in the governance of international organizations. Its novel governance structure demanded a novel legal arrangement to accommodate it—one that differed significantly from that used for the international organizations established in earlier eras. In particular, it demanded an expansion of the traditionally state-centric conception of the international organization, typified by establishment through a multilateral treaty among states. In order to ensure equal standing of the public and private sectors, as well as civil society in the governance of the organization, the Global Fund was not established through a treaty, but as a non-profit foundation under Swiss law. Simultaneously, the status of the Global Fund as an international organization has been elaborated through a gradual process of legal recognition by national governments.

This legal arrangement has provided the Global Fund with an architecture that facilitates full participation by both public and private sectors, and the civil society in its governance and operation. On a broader level, this arrangement, which has been recognized in the academic literature as a 'groundbreaking legal status that is unique to the international legal arena',[36] has also moved forward the traditional understanding of the international organization as a state-centred concept to one that encompasses a broader array of stakeholders. Taken as a whole, the approach undertaken by the Global Fund to establish its legal status represents a new pathway in the design of international organizations.

[34] Mello e Souza and Aznar, 'Brazil and Argentina' (n 25).

[35] Eduardo J Gómez and Rifat Atun, 'The Effects of Global Fund Financing on Health in Brazil' 8 *Globalization and Health* (2012), art. 25.

[36] Triponel, 'Global Fund' (n 13), 193.

21.6 Meeting New Challenges: Refining the Board's Stakeholder System and Funding Model

21.6.1 Stakeholder System

The Global Fund's governance system represents an achievement in the larger project of advancing inclusive and equitable participation by marginalized groups in global health governance. However, as the Global Fund has matured, new challenges have arisen requiring further reform. Within the context of governance operations, the observation is that a purely stakeholder-oriented approach can create a barrier to consensus. A model under which Board Members view their role as purely advocating for their specific stakeholder interests can reinforce differences and interfere with the advancement of the organization's best interests in achieving its mission.

As noted earlier, the Global Fund employs a voting bloc system and passage of a decision requires a two-thirds majority of both donor and implementer blocs. While this is a crucial step towards equity, it also can lead to challenges. Under this voting system, objection to a motion by a minority of members in either bloc can place the Board in deadlock. As such, a recent challenge faced by the Global Fund concerned encouraging collaboration within a stakeholder-based system, so as to ensure the Board ultimately works towards the best interests of the organization as a whole.

In 2013, the Board Leadership launched the Ethics and Integrity Initiative (the Initiative), a comprehensive reform of Global Fund's ethical foundations. A major component of this initiative was clarifying Board Member responsibilities by addressing the tension between constituency interests and the best interests of Global Fund, through a new Code of Ethical Conduct for Governance Officials (the Code).

The Code was adopted in April 2015,[37] obligating Board Members to balance their constituency responsibilities with the organization's best interest, which is understood as working in a way that is aligned with the Global Fund's mission, objectives, priorities, and values. This Code also acknowledges that best interests of the organization can differ from constituency interests, and in such instances, the organization's interests should take precedence. The guidance contained in the Code highlights that governance officials should demonstrate transparency regarding their interests by disclosing them.

21.6.2 New Funding Model

The initial funding model of the Global Fund was built on a rounds-based system, which called on the countries to submit their funding proposals during a specific funding period and compete for funds. Successful proposals, as evaluated by the

[37] Decision of the Global Fund Board at its Thirty-Third Meeting (GF/B33/DP10).

TRP, ended up securing funding, while unsuccessful proposals were simply rejected. This system worked in favour of those countries with improved technical capacity to prepare grant proposals, for example, China, while it punished those who did not have such capacity, irrespective of the disease burden they carried and the needs they demonstrated. This anomaly was rectified when the Global Fund adopted a new funding model in 2013, allocating (pursuant to a formula) pre-determined funding packages to individual countries, largely based on their disease burden and economic capacity. The new funding model brought about a much-needed predictability and a fairer distribution of funds. In 2016, the Global Fund further refined the allocation methodology to increase the impact of country programmes that prevent, treat, and care for people affected by HIV, TB, and malaria and build resilient and sustainable systems for health.

The Global Fund's 2017–2019 allocation methodology drives an increased proportion of funding to higher-burden, lower-income countries, specifically accounts for HIV epidemics among key populations, the threat of multidrug-resistant TB, and for malaria elimination efforts, while providing sustainable and paced reductions where funding is decreasing.[38] The success of the new allocation methodology in delivering the mission of the organization can be expected to be seen after the end of the pandemic-induced halt of field operations, when data for the funding period 2017–2019 will be made available by the implementers, hopefully in a well-documented manner.

China successfully built one of the largest grant portfolios during the rounds-based funding model, based largely, as authors of that study suggest, on its relative capacity to write acceptable proposals. The authors' reference to the 'competitive nature of Fund grants' would be accurate with respect to the time period till 2012, when this model was replaced in 2013, making funding less of a competition but more of a function of the disease burden and economic capacity of the countries concerned. Under the current model, Vietnam, along with other grant-implementing countries, receives a pre-determined funding package for a certain funding period and how much of that package can actually be utilized depends on Vietnam's own needs and its implementation capacity.

The reforms and refinements undertaken by Global Fund, in particular those concerning its funding model and eligibility requirements, have considerably strengthened inclusion and engagement of key affected populations in the decision-making process of CCMs, ensuring that the grant proposals reflected the voices of these groups, and the progress made by the Philippines in this respect was noteworthy. It is hoped that such inclusion will increase the precision and relevance of the country's national plans, particularly with respect to key populations, and lead to preparation of more robust grant proposals, having facilitated more inclusive and thorough discussions on the main drivers behind disease trajectories (in particular HIV/AIDS), with strategies to be adopted and interventions to be employed.

[38] The Global Fund to Fight AIDS, Tuberculosis and Malaria: Allocations, <https://www.theglobalfund.org/en/funding-model/before-applying/allocation/>, last accessed 05/13/2020.

21.7 Conclusion

The Global Fund is a ground-breaking and successful experiment of conducting global health governance through a participatory, all-inclusive model, whereby all stakeholders could converge around the same body, carrying equal status, at least structurally, bringing their unique perspectives, expertise, and experiences, and contributing to its mission. This model provides an excellent and a very rich learning opportunity for all concerned and offers the perfect stage to enable the most effective outcomes and relevant solutions. In tackling global public health issues, where diseases don't recognize boundaries or sectors, a healthy and ongoing dialogue among all those concerned and discipline in finding collective solutions have to be sustained perpetually. It is thus incumbent on all the players, donors, and implementers alike, to ensure maximum integration and meaningful contribution by all. The Global Fund experiment is, and will be, as strong as its weakest contributor. When some of the stakeholders remain less engaged and do not take advantage of this shared stage, be it capacity-related or due to lack of interest and/or funds (and which has been observed in the Global Fund's governance), the whole experiment will suffer and the institution's ability to achieve its mission will be compromised. So, for the Global Fund to realize its mission, any power asymmetry must be reduced, and eliminated, and weaker participants must be empowered accordingly. Despite ongoing measures to that end, as described in various chapters of this book, achieving an optimum equilibrium is a work in progress, as the Global Fund's governance continues to need dedicated attention. Like any capacity-building effort, however, enduring effects are likely to materialize over the medium to long term, with sustained and/or increased allocation of resources. The effort will be worth it.

22
The World Health Organization's Engagement with Non-State Actors
The Risk of Corporate Influence

K M Gopakumar

22.1 Introduction

The World Health Assembly (WHA), the highest decision-making body of the World Health Organization (WHO), adopted the 'Framework of Engagement with Non-State Actors' (FENSA) in its 69th session held in Geneva in May 2016.[1] FENSA sets norms for WHO's engagement with non-state actors (NSAs), that is, non-governmental organizations (NGOs), private sector entities, philanthropic foundations and academic institutions. Its objective is to promote 'good participation'; that is, to manage the risks of NSA engagement and prevent such engagement from undermining public interests in healthcare.[2] FENSA succeeds two WHO documents, namely the Principles Governing Relations between the World Health Organization and Nongovernmental Organizations (the 'Principles Governing Relations') and the Guidelines on Interaction with Commercial Enterprises to Achieve Health Outcomes.[3] The former was adopted by the WHA in 1987, the latter was never adopted by the WHO. Although FENSA is not the first attempt to regulate WHO's engagements with NSAs, its normative value is high.

22.2 FENSA: Inception and Processes

Although the exact origin of FENSA is unknown, it can be traced to the WHO reform programme launched at the 64th session of the WHA in 2011. Proactive WHO engagement with the private sector was initiated earlier during the tenure of Director-General Gro Harlem Brundtland (1998–2003). Proposals for such global health governance were put forth scholars,[4] and the World Economic Forum Global

[1] Ayelet Berman, 'Stakeholder Participation Reforms in Global Health Governance.' Chapter 13, this volume.

[2] Berman, 'Stakeholder Participation Reforms' (n 1).

[3] WHO, 'Framework of Engagement with Non-State Actors', Resolution of the World Health Assembly, 28 May 2016.

[4] Gaudenz Silberschmidt, Don Matheson, and Ilona Kickbusch, 'Creating a Committee C of the World Health Assembly', 371(9623) *The Lancet* (2008): 1483-1486.

K M Gopakumar, *The World Health Organization's Engagement with Non-State Actors* In: *Rethinking Participation in Global Governance*. Edited by: Joost Pauwelyn, Martino Maggetti, Tim Büthe, and Ayelet Berman, Oxford University Press.
 DOI: 10.1093/oso/9780198852568.003.0022

Redesign Initiative (GRI) called for such engagements in a 2010 report. The GRI report argued that the realities of an 'emerging' health paradigm consisted of 'stronger community and patient involvement with new international governance including NGO and business involvement, the drafting of binding health treaties, and the recognition that social sector spending is essential for development'.[5] However, the 2011 WHO reform programme was a key step towards FENSA. In recognition of the coordination and coherence challenges arising from the increasing role of stakeholders in shaping global and national health agendas,[6] the WHO Secretariat proposed a multi-stakeholder forum for global health called the World Health Forum. This forum was intended to shape decisions and agendas of the governing bodies of the WHO without usurping the intergovernmental nature of its decision-making.[7]

The Secretariat proposed three methods to improve stakeholder engagement for consideration at the Executive Board Special Session on WHO Reform (EBSS).[8] However, these proposals were rejected by the November 2011 special session of the WHO Executive Board (EB), which instructed the Secretariat to refine them further based on the following principles:[9]

i) the intergovernmental nature of WHO's decision-making remains paramount.
ii) the development of norms, standards, policies, and strategies lies at the heart of WHO Executive Board Special Session on WHO Reform (EBSS).
iii) any new initiative must have clear benefits and add value in terms of enriching policy or increasing national capacity from a public health perspective.
iv) existing mechanisms should take precedence over creating new forums, meetings or structures, and a clear analysis should provide how any additional costs would lead to better outcomes.

Subsequently, the proposal for a multi-stakeholder forum was replaced with FENSA. In January 2012, the EB agreed that:

> Further discussion would be required on WHO's engagement with other stakeholders, including non-governmental organisations and industry, and the proposals to review and update principles governing WHO relations with non-governmental organisations. Further work is also needed on comprehensive policy frameworks to guide interaction with the private-for-profit sector and not-for-profit philanthropic organisations.[10]

[5] World Economic Forum (2010), 'Everybody's Business: Strengthening International Cooperation in a More Interdependent World' Report of the Global Redesign Initiative, <http://www20.iadb.org/intal/catalogo/PE/2012/12191.pdf>, last accessed 06/28/2018.

[6] WHO, 'The Future of Financing for WHO', *Report of the Director General to the World Health Assembly*, 5 May 2011.

[7] WHO, 'The Future of Financing' (n 6), par. 86.

[8] The three proposals were: the creation of a multi-stakeholder platform for key issues on global health; individual consultations with different stakeholder groups to provide input on specific issues under consideration by member states; and the limiting of a stakeholder's role to commenting on specific aspects of issues where it has particular expertise or experience. See WHO (2011), 'WHO Reforms for a Healthy Future' *Report by the Director-General to the Special Session of the Executive Board*, 15 October 2011.

[9] WHO, 'Decisions of the Executive Board Special Session on WHO Reform', 7 November 2011.

[10] WHO, 'Executive Board Summary Records 130th Session', 16–23 January 2012.

Subsequent negotiations merged the mandate to develop separate policies for NGOs, private sector, philanthropic foundations, and academic institutions under the umbrella of FENSA, which treats these four actors on equal footing and bears the threat of undermining the influence of the private sector.

FENSA contains five sets of documents. First is its overarching framework, which governs WHO's engagements with the four categories of NSAs. It regulates forms of engagements such as participation in meetings, advocacy, knowledge management, capacity building and technical collaboration. Further, the overarching framework sets the rules for the management of conflict of interest, due diligence and risk assessment, risk management, transparency, official relations, and oversight. The other documents set out policy and operational procedures on engagements.

22.3 Risk of Private Sector Influence

WHO has the mandate to 'act as the directing and coordinating authority on international health work'.[11] Article 2 of its constitution also allows it to establish and maintain effective collaboration with any organizations as may be appropriate. Further, Article 71 provides the mandate to the Secretariat to 'make suitable arrangements for consultation and co-operation with non-governmental international organizations' and, with the consent of the Government concerned, with national organizations, governmental or non-governmental'.[12] These provisions provide the Secretariat with the necessary flexibility to achieve its objectives. Hence, engagements with NSAs have been legitimized by the WHO since its inception.

In general, NSA participation in WHO processes occurs either in policy-making processes or/and norms and standard-setting processes. While matters of policy require the approval of the governing bodies (WHA and EB), norms and standard-setting processes are considered technical work and are undertaken in expert committees such as the WHO Expert Committee on Biological Standardization (ECBS). However, there are no clear guidelines to determine which category a matter falls into, and it is up to the Secretariat to consider whether a matter is technical or is policy (or both). Before FENSA, NSA participation in WHO governing body meetings had been regulated through the Principles Governing Relations,[13] which allowed NGOs in official relation to participate as observers. Unlike FENSA's categorization of NSAs, the Principles Governing Relations used the term NGOs as an umbrella term and did not distinguish between different types of organizations.[14] As a result, many international business associations were allowed to establish official relations, enabling private sector participation in the WHO through business associations and NGO delegates.[15]

[11] WHO, *WHO Constitution Basic Documents*, 48th ed, 31 December 2014.

[12] WHO, *Basic Documents* (n 11).

[13] WHO, 'Principles Governing Relations between the World Health Organization and Nongovernmental Organizations' in *Basic Documents* (n 11).

[14] Official relation status was not extended to philanthropic foundations under the Principles of Governing Relations.

[15] WHO, 'Principles Governing Relations' (n 13).

The private sector may seek to exert influence on the WHO mainly for the following purposes. First, it could use engagement with the WHO to whitewash its unethical business practices. For instance, pharmaceutical companies may donate medicines while engaging in unethical promotion of their products or lobbying against the use of intellectual property (IP) flexibilities.[16] Second, such engagement could be exploited for commercial and competitive advantages by influencing WHO policies, norms, and standards, including by creating entry barriers into a particular market and to protect commercial interests by preventing tighter regulations.

The following examples illustrate clearly how the private sector and industry try to influence norms, standard-setting, and policy formulations of the WHO for furthering their commercial interests. For example, the Secretariat sets up a public-private partnership (PPP) called the International Medical Products Anti-Counterfeiting Taskforce (IMPACT) to combat counterfeit medicines in developing countries.[17] The International Federation of Pharmaceutical Manufacturers & Associations (IFPMA) was one of the vice chairs of IMPACT. The IFPMA, which headed the working group on track and trace technologies on counterfeit medical products, essentially sought to promote its IP agenda and targeted generic medicines. The IFPMA–WHO collaboration resulted in terming quality compromised products as counterfeit medicines. While counterfeit refers to a particular type of trademark infringement, the conflation of quality with IP helped the enforcement of IP rights in the name of enforcing quality. IFPMA's misuse of a platform aimed at solving the counterfeit problem led to criticism. Eventually, the active intervention of many developing countries like Brazil, Egypt, and India forced WHO to informally disassociate itself from IMPACT.[18]

Similarly, the WHO's association with the International Conference on Harmonisation of Technical Requirements for Registration of Pharmaceuticals for Human Use (ICH) has raised concerns. ICH is a regulatory network of drug regulatory authorities and pharmaceutical industry associations that harmonizes pharmaceutical standards. The association has resulted in the incorporation of industry-captured standards as WHO standards. ICH standards embody the interests of pharmaceutical companies, which have the resources to comply with the standards (typically, the multinational patent drug industry), disregarding the interests of developing countries. Consequently, they generated distributional effects and undermined generic drug manufacture, creating barriers to development of drugs for neglected diseases.[19]

There was also an attempt to establish ICH guidelines as the conventional standards through a draft WHA resolution on Regulatory System Strengthening in 2014. For example, the resolution recommended the implementation of 'relevant guidance and science-based outputs of international regulatory harmonization and convergence efforts such as, where applicable, the Conference on Harmonisation of Technical

[16] These flexibilities limit the abuse of patent monopoly.

[17] WHO, 'Counterfeit Medical Products', *Report by the Secretariat, Executive Board 124th Session*, 18 December 2009) EB124/14 6.

[18] K M Gopakumar and Sangeeta Shahshikant, *Unpacking the Issue of Counterfeit Medicines* (Third World Network 2010).

[19] Ayelet Berman, 'Industry, Regulatory Capture and Transnational Standard Setting' 111 *AJIL Unbound* (2017) 112-118, 117.

Requirements for Registration of Pharmaceuticals for Human Use'.[20] Although the resolution eventually adopted removed references to the ICH, an indirect reference remains. In the resolution, the Director-General is requested to 'continue to develop appropriate norms, standards and guidelines, taking into account national, regional and international needs and initiatives, in accordance with WHO principles'.[21] Arguably, 'international needs and initiatives' encompass the ICH. Thus, the WHO's engagement with ICH is indirectly legitimized.

WHO's Strategic Advisory Group of Experts (SAGE) on Immunization is free of scandal, either. SAGE recommends the types and quantities of vaccines member countries should purchase for pandemic contingencies. An investigation by the Danish newspaper *Information* in 2009 revealed that the National Institute for Health and Welfare (THI) in Finland received almost EUR 6.3 million for vaccine research from pharmaceutical heavyweight GlaxoSmithKline. SAGE member Professor Juhani Eskola was the then Deputy Director-General at THI. GlaxoSmithKline produces the H1N1 vaccine Pandemrix, which the Finnish government—following recommendations from THL and WHO—purchased as national pandemic reserve stockpile.[22] An investigation by the Social, Health and Family Affairs Committee of the Parliamentary Assembly of the Council of Europe described WHO advisory bodies as 'particularly exposed to the risk of conflicts of interest concerning scientific experts', naming SAGE among them.[23]

These examples are suggestive of influence of the private sector on WHO. With such diverse private sector influence, concerns that corporate influence would threaten the credibility and independence of the WHO have increased, especially in the absence of robust safeguards. FENSA emerged in this context, and it has been hoped that it would be a mechanism to prevent or manage the risk of engagement of WHO with NSAs, including the private sector.

22.4 Regulation of the Private Sector

FENSA's policy provides specific norms for WHO engagement with the private sector in participation, resources, evidence gathering, advocacy, and technical collaboration.[24] The private sector is broadly defined as 'businesses that are intended to make a profit for their owners' and 'entities that represent, or are governed or controlled by, private sector entities'. FENSA recognizes that private sector organizations may exercise influence through other NSAs. Hence, 'business associations representing

[20] WHO, 'Regulatory System Strengthening for Medical Products', Executive Board 134th Session Resolutions (2014), EB134.R17 34.

[21] WHO, 'Regulatory System Strengthening for Medical Products', 67th World Health Assembly Resolutions and Decisions (2014), WHA67.20 45.

[22] Louise Voller and Kristian Villesen, 'WHO-rådgiver skjuler millionbidrag fra medicinalindustrien' (11 December 2009) <https://www.information.dk/indland/2009/12/who-raadgiver-skjuler-millionbidrag-medicinalindustrien>, last accessed 06/29/2018.

[23] Council of Europe (Parliamentary Assembly Social, Health and Family Affairs Committee), 'The Handling of the H1N1 Pandemic: More Transparency Needed', 23 March 2010.

[24] WHO, 'Policy and Operational Procedures on Engagement with Private Sector Entities', in WHO, 'Framework of Engagement' (n 3).

commercial enterprises, entities not 'at arm's length' from their commercial sponsors, and partially or fully State-owned commercial enterprises acting like private sector entities' are included in its definition.[25] Further, the Secretariat has discretion to identify other NSAs as private sector entities through 'due diligence'. If an NSA is subject to private sector influence, WHO may categorize it as a non-private sector entity, but 'apply relevant provisions of policy and operational procedures on engagement with private sector entities, such as not accepting financial and in-kind contributions for use in the normative work'.[26] An analysis carried out by the author on the disclosures and declarations made in the WHO NSA Registry of 119 NSAs listed in the participants' list at the 71st WHA shows eighty-one declared engagements with industries such as alcohol, food and beverages, healthcare and pharmaceuticals. With a few exceptions, the majority of these engagements are in the nature of accepting financial resources from the industries.

Although FENSA prohibits any engagement with the tobacco and weapon industries,[27] the efficacy of WHO's policy on non-engagement with the arms industry is doubtful. For instance, General Electric (GE) has significant stakes in both the arms industry and in medical technologies. In 2016 the Stockholm International Peace Research Institute (SIPRI) ranked GE as the thirty-sixth largest arms-producing and military service company.[28] Yet GE participates in WHO meetings through the Global Diagnostic Imaging Healthcare IT and Radiation Therapy Trade Association (DITTA), which has official relations with WHO and is also a member of WHO Global Coordination Mechanism on Non-Communicable Diseases (GCMNCD).[29] GE's executive director also chairs the DITTA working group in WHO.[30]

Paragraph 45 of FENSA requires WHO to 'exercise particular caution when engaging with private sector entities and other non-State actors whose policies or activities are negatively affecting human health and are not in line with WHO's policies, norms and standards in particular those related to noncommunicable diseases and their determinants'. However, there is no clarity on the term 'particular caution'. It is left to the Secretariat to determine the meaning and content of this term. The engagement of the food and beverage industry does not contravene WHO requirements in their current scope. And the absence of clarity on the term 'particular caution' allows the Secretariat to change its approaches towards the food and beverages industry.

FENSA allows the WHO to engage with the private sector in evidence gathering, advocacy and technical collaboration. The private sector is allowed to provide 'up-to-date information and knowledge on technical issues and share their experience with WHO'.[31] However, the engagement on evidence gathering is governed through

[25] WHO 'Policy and Operational Procedures' (n 24).

[26] WHO 'Policy and Operational Procedures' (n 24), 7.

[27] WHO, 'Framework of Engagement' (n 3), 13 para 44.

[28] SIPRI, 'Data for the SIPRI Top 100 for 2002—2016' (SIPRI Arms Industry Database), <https://www.sipri.org/databases/armsindustry>, last accessed 06/17/2018.

[29] WHO, 'WHO Global Coordination Mechanism on the Prevention and Control of Noncommunicable Diseases: Progress Report 2014—2016' (2017), WHO/NMH/NMA/GCM/17.03 61.

[30] National Academies of Sciences, Engineering, and Medicine (NASEM), *Global Health and Future Role of the United States* (National Academies Press 2017) 353.

[31] WHO, 'Framework of Engagement' (n 3), Article 18.

the provisions of the overarching framework, and specific policy and operational procedures, and other applicable WHO rules, policies, and procedures. Further, the contribution of the private sector should be made public as appropriate.[32] Similarly, 'wherever possible scientific evidence generated should be made publicly available'.[33] These qualifications like 'as appropriate' and 'wherever possible' gives enough flexibility to the Secretariat to decide whether the contribution from the private sector should be made public.

Private sector entities are allowed to engage with the WHO for advocacy.[34] However, these engagements are limited to 'implement and advocate for the implementation of the WHO's policies, norms, and standards'.[35] Furthermore, the private sector entities working with the WHO are expected 'to conform to WHO's public health policies in areas such as food safety, chemical safety, ethical promotion of medicinal drug products, tobacco control, noncommunicable diseases, as well as health and safety at work'.[36] This provision would reduce the scope of whitewashing the private sector entities image through engaging with WHO on advocacy activities.

The WHO can also engage the private sector in technical collaboration for activities falling within the General Programme of Work, including product development, capacity building, operational collaboration in emergencies, and contributing to the implementation of WHO's policies. However, the 'technical collaboration must be in the interest of WHO and managed in accordance with the overarching framework and this policy to protect WHO, and in particular, its normative work, from any undue influence or conflict of interest and to ensure there is no interference with WHO's advisory function to Member States'.[37]

22.4.1. Financial Resources

The WHO's reliance on voluntary contributions has made it more donor-driven rather than a membership-driven organization. Ostensibly, the private sector's contribution to the WHO is quite low (for instance, around 0.99% in 2016–2017). However, its influence is immense, primarily due to political patronage from large donor countries like the US, the UK, and Germany, as well as patronage from philanthropic foundations (such as the Gates Foundation) and various professional bodies which receive private sector funding. Funding, whether direct or indirect, is the traditional means deployed by the private sector to influence an international organization's activities.

FENSA has imposed strict conditions on accepting financial resources from the private sector. The WHO may accept financial contributions from private sector entities only when their activities are unrelated to it and they are not engaged in activities with, or have close ties to, other entities incompatible with its mandate and work. Furthermore, it should not accept financial contributions from an entity that

[32] WHO, 'Framework of Engagement' (n 3), Article 18.
[33] WHO, 'Framework of Engagement' (n 3), Article 18.
[34] WHO, 'Framework of Engagement' (n 3), Article 19.
[35] WHO Policy and Operational Procedures on Engagement with Private Sector Entities, Article 31.
[36] WHO Policy and Operational Procedures (n 35), fn 2.
[37] WHO Policy and Operational Procedures (n 35), Article 34.

has, either directly or through its affiliates, a direct commercial interest in the project to be financed. The Secretariat is also to exercise caution while accepting contributions from an entity with indirect commercial interests. In such cases, other entities with similar indirect interest are to be invited to contribute to 'avoid the possibility of a conflict of interest or appearance of an inappropriate association with one contributor'.[38]

FENSA's private sector policy details the following conditions for accepting financial contributions:[39]

a) No use of the contribution for normative work;
b) Public health benefit of the engagement needs to clearly outweigh its potential risks if a contribution is used for activities other than normative work;
c) Proportion of funding for any activity coming from the private sector cannot be such that the programme's continuation would become dependent on this support;
d) Acceptance of the contribution does not constitute an endorsement by WHO of the private sector entity, or its activities, products or services;
e) Contributor may not use the results of WHO's work for commercial purposes or use the fact of its contribution in its promotional material;
f) Acceptance of the contribution does not afford the contributor any privilege or advantage;
g) Acceptance of the contribution does not offer the contributor any possibility for advising, influencing, participating in, or being in command of the management or implementation of operational activities; and
h) WHO keeps its discretionary right to decline a contribution, without any further explanation.

Crucially, a financial contribution should not be used for normative work. However, FENSA does not define normative work, though it does state that policy-, norm-, and standard-setting include information gathering, preparation for, elaboration of and the decision on the normative text.[40] Therefore, financial or in-kind contributions from the private sector cannot be used for a range of activities related to the finalization of norms.

22.4.2 Conflict of Interest

FENSA identifies conflict of interest as one of the key risks involved in engagement with NSAs. Avoiding or managing it is considered as a key principle of FENSA. A conflict of interest is defined as 'circumstances where there is potential for a secondary interest (a vested interest in the outcome of WHO's work in a given area) to unduly influence, or where it may be reasonably perceived to unduly influence, either the independence or objectivity of professional judgement or actions regarding a primary interest (WHO's work)'. Although improper action may not necessarily have occurred,

[38] WHO, 'Policy and Operational Procedures' (n 24), 24.
[39] WHO, 'Policy and Operational Procedures' (n 24), 25.
[40] WHO, 'Framework of Engagement' (n 3), 5 par. 5(e).

the risk of its occurring is to be guarded against. It should be noted that the conflict does not necessarily have to be financial.[41]

FENSA distinguishes between two types of conflicts of interest: individual and institutional. The former occurs when staff, experts or consultants working for WHO abuse their professional position to influence its decisions,[42] while the latter results when the primary public health interest of WHO is unduly influenced by the conflicting interest of an NSA. Institutional conflict of interest encapsulates all situations 'where WHO's primary interest as reflected in its Constitution may be unduly influenced by the conflicting interest of a non-State actor in a way that affects, or may reasonably be perceived to affect, the independence and objectivity of WHO's work'.[43] The expansion of the scope of the definition of conflict of interests to include non-financial interests might create problems in applying the concept of institutional conflict of interest in real situations because all types of conflicting interests of NSAs do not constitute a conflict of interest. For instance, the public interest bias of a CSO could be termed as a conflict of interest under the broad definition.[44] However, Para 26 of FENSA provides a clear direction to this issue. It states:

> For WHO, the potential risk of institutional conflicts of interest could be the highest in situations where the interest of non-State actors, in particular economic, commercial or financial, are in conflict with WHO's public health policies, constitutional mandate and interests, in particular, the Organization's independence and impartiality in setting policies, norms and standards.[45]

22.4.2.1 Rules for managing conflict of interest

FENSA does not give any clear indication of what constitutes an individual or institutional conflict of interest. Hence, the concrete steps to be taken to avoid or manage such conflicts are not provided. This gives ample scope for the Secretariat to interpret and implement the provisions related to conflict of interest in a non-transparent and ineffective manner. The WHA Resolution 69.10 requests the WHO Director-General 'to include in the guide to staff, measures that pertain to the application of the relevant provisions contained in the existing WHO policies on conflict of interest, with a view to facilitating the implementation of the Framework of Engagement with Non-State Actors'. However, this guide, published in January 2018, is silent on the conflict of interest policy.[46] When it comes to the institutional conflict of interest, there is also a transparency deficit. FENSA does not make the due diligence and risk assessment report public. Only Member States have 'electronic access to a summary report on due diligence of each non-State actor and their respective risk assessment and risk management on engagement. Member States also have access, on demand, to the

41 WHO, 'Framework of Engagement' (n 3), 10 par. 23.
42 WHO, 'Framework of Engagement' (n 3), 10 par. 23.
43 WHO, 'Framework of Engagement' (n 3), 10 par. 24.
44 Marc A Rodwin, 'Attempts to Redefine Conflicts of Interest', *Suffolk University Law School Research Paper* No. 17-18 (December 2017) <https://ssrn.com/abstract_id=3084307, last accessed 06/28/2018.
45 WHO, 'Framework of Engagement' (n 3), para 26.
46 WHO, *Guide for Staff on Engagement with Non-State Actors* (2018) <http://www.who.int/about/collaborations/non-state-actors/FENSA_guide-for-staff.pdf>, last accessed 06/19/2018.

associated full report through a remote secure access platform'.[47] As a result, public scrutiny of the risk assessment, including the conflict of interest in NSA engagements, is difficult, if not impossible.

22.5 Implementation of FENSA

FENSA was implemented following the adoption of Resolution 69.10 by the 69th WHA in 2016.[48] As per the resolution, the WHO Director-General is to submit an annual report to the governing bodies with regard to the engagements with NSAs.[49] However, the two annual reports did not contain any details about WHO–NSA engagement.[50] Apart from the annual report, the Secretariat is also expected to take a series of steps, including the categorization of NSAs, as part of FENSA's implementation.[51] FENSA implementation is slow even after two and a half years, and its provisions are often bypassed. The following two examples illustrate the gaps in the implementation of FENSA. The first relates to the extension of official relations status to the Foundation, while the second concerns the development of criteria to regulate secondments from NSAs.

22.5.1 Official Relations with the Gates Foundation

On the basis of Programme, Budget and Administration Committee's (PBAC) recommendation, the EB approved official relations between WHO and five NSAs, including the Gates Foundation (the Foundation), at its 140th meeting in early 2017. Official relations status enables NSAs to attend and make statements during meetings of WHO governing bodies, including the EB and the WHA. Arguably, engagement with the Foundation could potentially give rise to a conflict of interest that undermines the public health objectives of WHO due to its investment in private sector. The investments of the Foundation are managed by a different legal entity known as the Bill & Melinda Gates Foundation Trust (the Trust), which has huge investments in many food and pharmaceutical companies as well as companies whose products and services are linked with physical inactivity. The Trust's 2015 tax returns reveal that it holds shares and corporate bonds in pharmaceutical companies such as Pfizer, Novartis AG REG, Gilead Sciences, GlaxoSmithKline, BASF, Abbott Laboratories, Roche, Novo Nordisk A/SB, and Merck. Its tax returns also show investments in major insurance companies.[52]

[47] WHO, 'Framework of Engagement' (n 3), 42.
[48] WHO, 'Framework of Engagement' (n 3), 42.
[49] WHO, 'Framework of Engagement' (n 3), 42.
[50] WHO, 'Engagement with Non-State Actors', *Report by the Director-General*, Executive Board 140th Session, 21 (November 2016), EB140/41.
[51] WHO, 'Engagement with Non-State Actors' (n 50).
[52] The Bill & Melinda Gates Foundation Trust 2015 Annual Tax Return, Form 990-PF: Return of Private Foundation can be found at Bill and Melinda Gates Foundation, 'Who We Are: Financials' <https://www.gatesfoundation.org/Who-We-Are/General-Information/Financials>, last accessed 06/29/2018.

Since the Foundation is financed by corporate investments and its decision-making authorities are the same as the Trust's, it is arguably caught by FENSA's definition of an NSA 'subject to the influence of private sector entities'.[53] As previously noted, private sector influence 'can be exerted through financing, participation in decision-making or otherwise'.[54] However, the possible conflicts of interest were not considered; rather, the Foundation is considered a philanthropic foundation under FENSA. On the relationship between the two entities, the Foundation website states that there are two entities: the Foundation distributes grant money, and the Trust (managed by a team of outside investment managers) manages the asset investment. The Gates are co-chairs and trustees of the Foundation.[55] Hence, despite the theoretical split between programme work and asset investment, an 'arm's length relationship'[56] as defined by FENSA has not quite been achieved. Further, the Gates 'do guide the managers of the foundation's endowment in voting proxies consistent with the principles of good governance and good management'.[57] Moreover, in deriving its revenue from share and bond holdings in various private sector entities through Trust investments, the Foundation could be classified as a private sector entity.

22.5.2 Secondment to 'Sensitive Posts'

A 'secondment' to the WHO is the assignment of an individual already employed by an entity for a fixed period to WHO under a tripartite secondment agreement concluded by WHO, the releasing entity and the employee. A document produced by the Secretariat during FENSA negotiations in 2015 states:

> Secondees return to the releasing entity at the end of their secondment. While on secondment, secondees are WHO staff members, subject to WHO staff rules and regulations, except as otherwise agreed in the secondment agreement. Secondees are subject to WHO's declarations of interest for staff. The acceptance of a secondment from a non-State actor would be covered by the Framework of engagement with non-state actors.[58]

The data released during FENSA negotiations reveal that the following foundations identified as 'philanthropic' seconded their staff during the period 2012–2015: CDC Foundation (US), Fiocruz Foundation (Brazil), Gates Foundation (US), Korea Foundation for International Healthcare (Republic of Korea), IMPACT Foundation (UK), Thai Health Promotion Foundation (Thailand), Wellcome Trust

[53] WHO, 'Framework of Engagement' (n 3).
[54] WHO, 'Framework of Engagement' (n 3).
[55] Bill & Melinda Gates Foundation, 'Who We Are: Foundation Trust', <https://www.gatesfoundation.org/Who-We-Are/General-Information/Financials/Foundation-Trust>, last accessed 06/29/2018.
[56] WHO, 'Policy and Operational Procedures' (n 24).
[57] Bill & Melinda Gates Foundation, 'Foundation Trust' (n 55).
[58] 'Resources as referred to in the Framework of Engagement with Non-State Actors: Non-paper by the WHO Secretariat for consideration by the open-ended intergovernmental meeting of 7 to 9 December 2015' <http://www.who.int/about/collaborations/non-state-actors/fensa-nonpaper-resources.pdf?ua=1>, last accessed 06/29/2018.

(UK), and UN Foundation (US).[59] The remaining four are private philanthropic foundations from the US and the UK.

22.5.2.1. Regulating secondments

FENSA excludes secondments from the private sector.[60] However, with regard to secondments from the other types of NSAs, such as academia, philanthropic foundations, or NGOs, no consensus was reached during the FENSA negotiations. As a way forward, the 2016 WHA Resolution 69.10 requested the Director-General to develop and submit criteria and principles for secondment from these NSAs for the consideration of the 2017 WHA. Accordingly, the Secretariat prepared the document titled 'Criteria and principles for secondments from nongovernmental organisations, philanthropic foundations and academic institutions' for the consideration of the 70th WHA. However, this document deviates from the issues identified in WHA 69.10 as deserving of attention in drawing up the criteria. Notably, a requirement identified in the resolution was that secondments should adhere to 'specific technical expertise needed . . . *excluding managerial and/or sensitive positions*'.[61]

The Secretariat's criteria and principles for secondment document amended and limited this to read: 'Managerial and/or positions that involve the validation or approval of WHO's norms and standards are excluded.' The issue of whether the Secretariat could amend the mandate set by the 69th WHA regarding the criteria was not considered. At the 70th WHA, the Assembly merely noted the document. This has resulted in a lacuna: what regulation is there for posts where the staffer does not have the authority to validate or approve WHO norms and standards, but the position remains a sensitive one? However, the amended criterion arguably legitimizes secondment from NSAs for sensitive posts provided the position did not place the staffer in a position where he or she had authority to validate or approve WHO norms and standards. Sensitive posts should require more attention; for instance, a staffer from the UN Foundation was holding a sensitive post as a strategic advisor in the Director-General's office during the 2012–2015 period. Generally, there has been little transparency thus far with regard to secondments to the WHO. As per WHA 69.10, the Director-General is requested to make reference to secondments from NSAs in the annual report on engagement with NSAs to be submitted, including the justification behind secondments. However, no such information was provided in the annual report presented to the EB in January 2018.[62]

22.6 Conclusion

FENSA emerged as an instrument to regulate WHO's engagements with NSAs. It recognizes the risks involved in such engagements and provides mechanisms to avoid

[59] TWN, 'WHO: Unease over seconded philanthropic foundation staff to top management' <https://twn.my/title2/health.info/2015/hi151202.htm>, last accessed 05/13/2020.

[60] WHO, 'Framework of Engagement' (n 3).

[61] WHO 'Framework of Engagement' (n 3), section 3(8)(a), emphasis added.

[62] WHO, 'Engagement with Non-State Actors', *Report by the Director-General*, Executive Board, 142nd Session, 27 November 2017.

or manage these risks. One important way in which it seeks to address the risks is through transparency by establishing a register of NSAs. However, transparency alone cannot fully avoid or manage the risks of engagement. FENSA also contains provisions to prevent influence by the private sector and entities controlled by it. As a result, there are prohibitions against accepting financial resources from the private sector for the normative work of the WHO. Similarly, it prohibits secondment from the private sector to the WHO. It also imposes the condition that joint work plans between the WHO and NSAs in official relations should be 'free from concerns which are primarily of a commercial or profit-making nature'. FENSA covers WHO engagements through partnerships as well.

However, FENSA leaves the details of implementation to the Secretariat, which has considerable degree of discretionary powers, and the Member States expect it to exercise its discretion in good faith. These discretionary powers, however, increase its vulnerability to pressure to accommodate other interests. Thus far, it appears that the Secretariat's approach to implementation compromises the intentions guiding FENSA. The two case studies on implementation discussed earlier—on the official relations status of the Gates Foundation and on the development of criteria for secondments from NSAs—provide instances where the provisions of FENSA and Resolution WHA 69.10 have effectively been diluted. Without oversight by Member States and civil society organizations, implementation of FENSA may, in fact, result in the very risks of WHO engagement with NSAs, which FENSA was intended to prevent.

PART IV
STAKEHOLDER PARTICIPATION IN GLOBAL GOVERNANCE: CROSS-CUTTING ISSUES

23

The Stakeholder Participation Triangle

Trusteeship, Functionality, and Efficiency

Ayelet Berman

23.1 Introduction

In our globalized economy, global governance bodies increasingly set policies, rules, or standards. Traditionally, global bodies were of an intergovernmental nature, yet in recent decades, and as has been widely documented, non-state actors (NSAs; understood to include NGOs, private sector entities, philanthropic bodies, academic institutions—or the individuals or entities they represent) have become important global actors, and global bodies increasingly engage such NSAs alongside governments in the rule-making process.[1]

Against this background, I ask two questions. *Conceptually*, who, or which NSAs (stakeholders), should global bodies engage in rule-making? And *in practice*, to what extent have these conceptual approaches driven stakeholder participation, that is, how powerful are they in explaining who gets to participate?

To this end, I submit that trusteeship and functionality are the two main approaches that justify *with whom global bodies* should engage. Eyal Benvenisti's work on trusteeship[2] asserts that states are trustees of humanity, and as such, in their rule-making processes, should give a voice to stakeholders they *affect*. Building on this earlier work, by extension, global bodies, to which states delegate authority, are likewise trustees of humanity, which should give a voice to affected stakeholders. In contrast, functionality is a utilitarian approach, which contends that global bodies should engage stakeholders that *contribute* to the achievement of their mission. In other words, while a desire to be fair and just towards others drives trusteeship, functionality is driven by the advancement of self-interest. While in the long term, being fair and just towards others serves the enlightened self-interest of a body, this distinction is helpful in thinking about the immediate motivations behind stakeholder engagement.

Stakeholder engagement also has trade-offs. By increasing the number of participants, burdens on time, resources, or costs are introduced. In other words, more

[1] Ayelet Berman, Tim Büthe, Martino Maggetti, and Joost Pauwelyn, 'Introduction: Rethinking Stakeholder Participation in Global Governance.' Chapter 1, this volume; Ayelet Berman, 'Stakeholder Participation Reforms in Global Health Governance.' Chapter 13, this volume.

[2] Eyal Benvenisti, 'Sovereigns as Trustees of Humanity: On the Accountability of States to Foreign Stakeholders' 107(2) *American Journal of International Law* (2013) 295-333.

Ayelet Berman, *The Stakeholder Participation Triangle* In: *Rethinking Participation in Global Governance.*
Edited by: Joost Pauwelyn, Martino Maggetti, Tim Büthe, and Ayelet Berman, Oxford University Press.
DOI: 10.1093/oso/9780198852568.003.0023

participation introduces *efficiency* concerns. Thus, while trusteeship or functionality justify engaging stakeholders, concerns over efficiency act as a counterforce, which curbs where, when, and how global bodies engage entitled stakeholders.

To visualize these forces, I introduce the idea of the stakeholder participation triangle. The triangle has three apexes: trusteeship, functionality, and efficiency. It visualizes the two forces (trusteeship, functionality) justifying *who* should participate, against the forces curbing their participation (efficiency).

To test these concepts in practice, I examine whether or how they explain participation in four global health organizations: the World Health Organization (WHO), Codex Alimentarius Commission (Codex), the Global Fund to Fight AIDS, Tuberculosis and Malaria (Global Fund), and the Global Vaccine Alliance (GAVI). Although I focus on global health, I believe that these findings prove relevant to the study of participation in global governance more generally.

I find that, although the prevailing literature stresses functionality as the main driver of stakeholder engagement, the existing legal infrastructure of global bodies (at the very least those examined here) could be used for applying a trusteeship approach in at least some decision-making processes. By restricting participation to specific stakeholders, which organizations identify on the basis of their anticipated contribution, functionality indeed tends to drive governing bodies. Yet other decision-making processes are not as selective of stakeholders, allowing for broader participation. Broad participation processes allow all affected stakeholders to voice their concerns (trusteeship) while also enabling the organization to get all the information it needs to develop robust policies (functionality).

Moreover, most of the literature stressing the role of functionality has done so by examining traditional intergovernmental organizations (IOs). Here, I have broadened the scope and examine multi-stakeholder partnerships (MSPs). I find that they include both affected and contributing stakeholders. Indeed, in MSPs whose mission is to help those most marginalized, trusteeship and functionality overlap.

That said, while formal provisions may theoretically allow affected stakeholders to participate, global bodies would have to proactively embrace their role as a trustee of humanity so as to actually bring about inclusive participation. Indeed, one of the main problems with trusteeship is its application in practice. While provisions for the participation of affected stakeholders exist, resource or capacity barriers often prevent stakeholders from taking advantage of their rights.[3] Only very few bodies have introduced measures for overcoming these barriers.

Finally, efficiency concerns continue to play an important role. To be efficient, most participation is representative (rather than public and direct), and to contain global governance's scale, national stakeholder participation (rather than international) remains an important mode of collecting input.

[3] Ayelet Berman and Joost Pauwelyn, 'Assessing Stakeholder Participation Reforms in Global Health Governance.' Chapter 18, this volume.

23.2 The Stakeholder Participation Triangle: Trusteeship, Functionality, and Efficiency

Which stakeholders should global bodies engage in their rule-making? Traditional international law envisioned rule-making by member governments, yet in this chapter, and building on Eyal Benvenisti's earlier work,[4] I set out two justifications for engaging NSAs in the rule-making process: trusteeship and functionality. While these justify or drive *who* should participate, a third element—efficiency—acts as a counterforce and curbs the manner by which entitled stakeholders are engaged.

23.2.1 Trusteeship

The concept of trusteeship asserts that states are trustees of humanity, and as such, in their rule-making process, should give a voice to *affected* stakeholders. Today's global interconnectedness calls for a more encompassing vision of state sovereignty, which demands of states to be trustees of all humanity, that is, to be accountable towards all those affected by their policies. By extension, global bodies, to which states delegate authority, are likewise trustees of humanity, which should give a voice to affected stakeholders. As such, they are accountable not only towards their member states, but also towards those whom they have affected, or might affect. Trusteeship is a *deontological* approach to stakeholder participation: Irrespective of the benefits or consequences to the global body, the body invites those *affected* to participate (in contrast to those *contributing* as is the case under the functional approach, Section 23.2.2). It gives a voice because, *intrinsically*, that is the right or the fair thing to do.

Trusteeship sees all as having equal moral worth, and as such is motivated by being just and fair towards the other, whereas functionality (as discussed later) is driven by self-interest. To be sure, being fair and just towards affected stakeholders is in the organization's *long-term* self-interest. In that sense, also a trusteeship approach is in the organization's enlightened self-interest. Nevertheless, this distinction is helpful in thinking about the immediate justifications or drivers behind stakeholder participation.

23.2.2 Functionality

The functionality approach asserts that global bodies should hear stakeholders when it is instrumental for achieving the body's mission or for achieving better policy outcomes. An inclusive approach to policy-making, says the OECD, 'offers a way for governments to improve their policy performance by working with citizens, civil society organizations ... business and other stakeholders to deliver concrete improvements in policy outcomes'. Functionality is a *utilitarian* approach to stakeholder engagement.

[4] Benvenisti, 'Sovereigns as Trustees' (n 2).

Notwithstanding the effects the global body's rules have or might have on stakeholders, it only invites stakeholders who *contribute* to the work of the body. They are given a voice as it serves the body's self-interest. While trusteeship is about being fair or just towards the outsider (and gives a voice to all *affected*), functionality seeks to advance the self-interest of the organization or its members (and gives a voice to those *contributing*).

In the past two decades, global bodies in diverse policy fields have been opening up towards NSAs.[5] Most of the scholarship analysing this trend points to functionality as the main driver. Jonas Tallberg and colleagues find that '... when decisions have been taken to open-up IOs, these have primarily reflected functional benefits to states'.[6] Likewise, Wattli and Seddon find that 'IGO leaders have come to realize that they often lack the technical expertise and resources to expeditiously deal with ever more complex and urgent action challenges in the global economy' and that 'in response, IGOs ... have coopted a wide range of NSAs to help achieve their goals [...] Such cooption has become a strategy of choice, enabling IGOs to efficiently and effectively deliver regional or global public goods and services'.[7]

Next, I identify four main ways by which stakeholders contribute to the organization.

23.2.2.1 Expertise and knowledge

Given the complexity and the information asymmetry between stakeholders and governments, global bodies increasingly depend on stakeholders' expertise to strengthen the evidence base of rule-making. The OECD declares that governments do not have a 'monopoly of expertise ... other stakeholders (citizens, civil society, private sector, etc.) have valuable information', and stakeholder engagement 'increases the information available to governments on which they base policy decisions'.[8] Stakeholder engagement contributes to 'improving the quality of the rule-making process by providing policy makers with the evidence needed for their decision'. The Open Government Declaration similarly states that 'Public engagement ... increases the efficiency of governments, which benefit from people's knowledge, ideas ...'.[9]

23.2.2.2 Resources

Short on funds, global bodies benefit from in-kind or financial contributions made by the private sector or philanthropic organizations, such as the Bill and Melinda Gates Foundation, which donates to the WHO.

[5] Jonas Tallberg, Thomas Sommerer, Theresa Squatrito and Christer Jönsson, *The Opening Up of International Organizations: Transnational Access* (Cambridge University Press 2013); Klaus Dingwerth and Patricia Nanz, 'Participation' in Jacob Katz Cogan, Ian Hurd and Ian Johnstone (eds), *Oxford Handbook of International Organizations* (Oxford University Press 2016) 1127-1146; OECD, *International Regulatory Co-Operation: The Role of International Organisations in Fostering Better Rules of Globalisation* (OECD Publishing 2016), 85.

[6] Tallberg *et al.*, *The Opening Up* (n 5), 259–260.

[7] Walter Mattli and Jack Seddon, 'New Organizational Leadership: Nonstate Actors in Global Economic Governance' 6(3) *Global Policy* (2015) 266-276.

[8] OECD, *Focus on Citizens: Public Engagement for Better Policy and Services* (OECD Publishing 2009).

[9] Open Government Partnership, 'Open Government Declaration' <https://www.opengovpartnership.org/open-government-declaration> last accessed 11/05/2021.

23.2.2.3 Implementation and Compliance

Many global bodies lack the infrastructure to implement their policies,[10] and rely on the local knowledge and networks of NSAs. GAVI, for example, relies on local NGOs to implement its vaccination programmes.[11] Furthermore, engaging the targets of regulation improves compliance by giving a sense of ownership, and by taking the interests of the regulated into account, improving the likelihood of compliance. The International Conference on Harmonization (ICH), for example, engages the regulated pharmaceutical industry in its standard setting.[12]

23.2.2.4 Perceived Legitimacy

Stakeholder engagement, as the OECD points out, is a 'fundamental determinant of ownership and trust in [IOs]'. An 'increased openness and transparency of the decision-making process should help ... increase legitimacy of government's decisions and regain trust of society'.[13]

23.2.3 'Affected' vs. 'Contributing' Stakeholders

Applying trusteeship and functionality in practice means that a global body gives a voice to 'affected' stakeholders and 'contributing' stakeholders, respectively (Figure 23.1).

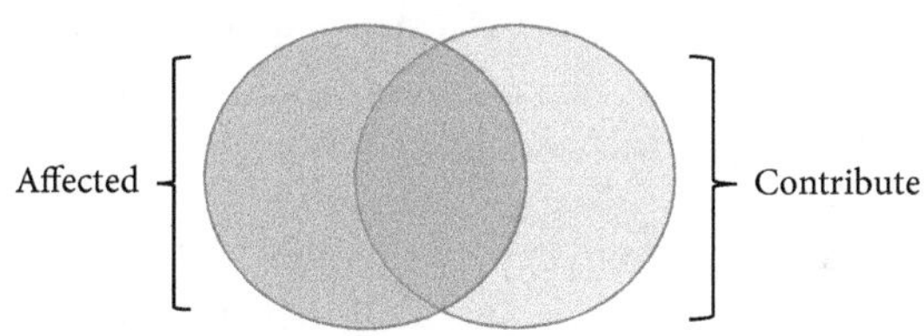

Figure 23.1 Affected and Contributing Stakeholders

Examples of affected stakeholders are gluten-intolerant patients who are affected by food labelling standards (are labelling requirements reliable?), and agriculture production standards (do permitted herbicides trigger gluten intolerance?). Food standards affect their situation, yet they lack expertise that could contribute to technical standard setting (e.g. standards on the use of herbicides). Examples of purely contributing stakeholders are scientists with technical expertise (on whether herbicides trigger gluten intolerance) who are not affected by the standard (are not intolerant).

Despite this distinction, these two approaches may overlap as some stakeholders are both affected and contributing. For example, an NGO representing gluten-intolerant patients may also have contributing insights as to labelling solutions that would work

[10] OECD, *International Regulatory Co-Operation* (n 5).
[11] Berman, 'Stakeholder Participation Reforms' (n 1).
[12] Berman, 'Stakeholder Participation Reforms' (n 1).
[13] OECD, *International Regulatory Co-Operation* (n 5), 85.

effectively with this group. Alternatively, think of the agricultural industry which will ultimately needs to comply with the standard (and as such is affected by it), but also contributes its scientific expertise in its development.

Moreover, public participation (that is, participation that is not selective but open to the entire public), could promote both trusteeship and functionality. Seeking to give all affected stakeholders a voice, a trusteeship approach opens participation to the public. At the same time, a functionalist approach, seeking to maximize information sources for making policy decisions, may encourage public participation. In other words, public participation may be justified, depending on the circumstances, by both approaches.

23.2.4 Efficiency

Trusteeship and/or functionality justify *who* participates. Participation, however, also introduces fears regarding the burden stakeholders will create on costs, time, and resources, undermining the ability of global bodies to get things done.[14]

These efficiency concerns are the third dimension of stakeholder participation, and are a counterforce, which curbs participation. Whereas trusteeship or functionality drive inclusion, global bodies concerned with efficiency can and will set limits to participation of entitled stakeholders along several sites. They can curb participation, be it by limiting *how* (notice and comment/consultations etc.), *when* (at what stage along the policy cycle), or *where* (which organ/process, national/international, etc.) stakeholders participate. This chapter focuses on two ways.

23.2.4.1 How? Representative vs. direct participation

Participation can be direct or by representation. When direct, any affected stakeholder has a voice (e.g. all millions of gluten-intolerant patients in the world). When representative, an organization represents affected stakeholders, such as an NGO or industry association (e.g. the Celiac Disease Foundation, which represents patients). Due to the scale of global governance, the representative approach is much more common,[15] with a 2015 OECD Survey of over fifty global bodies finding that most global bodies 'rely more heavily on organized groups than individuals'.[16]

23.2.4.2 Where? Domestic vs. international participation

Domestic (rather than international) consultations carried out by national governments who serve as a transmission belt between citizens and the global body also

[14] Kal Raustiala, 'Governing the Internet' 110(3) *American Journal of International Law* (2016) 491-503; Kal Raustiala, 'States, NGOs, and International Environmental Institutions' 41(4) *International Studies Quarterly* (1997) 719-740; Jonas Tallberg, Thomas Sommerer, Theresa Squatrito and Christer Jönsson, 'Explaining the Transnational Design of International Organizations' 68(4) *International Organization* (2014) 741–774.

[15] Patrizia Nanz and Jens Steffek, 'Global Governance, Participation and the Public Sphere' 39(2) *Government and Opposition* (2004) 314-335; OECD, *International Regulatory Co-Operation* (n 5), 85 (figure 5.1 demonstrates that, of the fifty IOs surveyed, the opportunity for the public to comment is rare).

[16] OECD, *International Regulatory Co-Operation* (n 5), 86.

balance between participation benefits and costs. Indeed, most organizations 'leave the responsibility of engaging stakeholders to their Members'.[17]

23.2.5 The Stakeholder Participation Triangle

In line with the above, the question who gets to participate has, accordingly, three dimensions: *trusteeship* and *functionality* justify *whom* to engage, and *efficiency* acts as a counterforce and curbs participation of entitled stakeholders by setting limitations on the manner whereby (how, when, where) stakeholders participate. The stakeholder participation triangle (Figure 23.2) visualizes this.

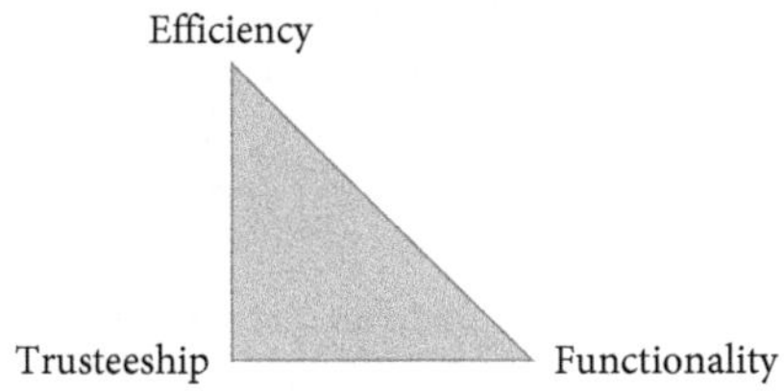

Figure 23.2 The Stakeholder Participation Triangle

The right-angled triangle reflects that while efficiency functions as a balancing factor vis-à-vis trusteeship and functionality, the costs and burdens of participation are likely felt more strongly on the trusteeship end where an 'all affected' principle could swamp the system with participants if not limited at a certain threshold (e.g. millions of patients). In contrast, those potentially contributing on a specific topic will likely be less (e.g. medical experts).

In what follows, I assess the extent to which these dimensions explain existing patterns of participation in global health governance.

23.3 The Case Studies

I analyse four global health bodies which have extensive stakeholder participation practices through the lens of trusteeship, functionality, and efficiency: the WHO, Codex, the Global Fund, and GAVI. To this end I examine statements made by these bodies, their participation criteria, and (whenever the information is available) the actual practice of the body.

23.3.1 The WHO

The WHO, traditionally the main international authority in public health, issues norms, policies, and standards. Its decisions potentially affect a broad range of

[17] OECD, *International Regulatory Co-Operation* (n 5), 85.

stakeholders: all people have an interest in health, and many of its decisions affect the pharmaceutical, food, and medical devices industries. What approach has dictated stakeholder engagement in the WHO?

I find that functionality has been the WHO's main driver. Established as an IO, it has traditionally been a member-driven organization, mostly responsive towards member states. That is not to say that the WHO had not envisioned some interaction with NSAs. The WHO Constitution states that the WHO may 'make suitable arrangements for consultation and cooperation with INGOs and … with national organizations, governmental or non-governmental'.[18] Although the constitution is neutral as to the intent of such collaboration, other official documents suggest that the WHO would engage stakeholders as long as they promoted its work. This functional purpose is reflected, for example, in the 1987 Principles Governing Relations Between the WHO and NGOs, which states that 'The objectives of WHO's collaboration with NGOs are *to promote* the policies, strategies and programmes derived from the decisions of the Organization's governing bodies; to collaborate with regard to various WHO programmes in jointly agreed activities *to implement* these strategies … ' (italics added).[19]

With the increase in the number of NSAs in the global health landscape, the WHO has recently adopted the Framework on Engagement with Non-State Actors (FENSA), where the functional rationale remains dominant. The rationale behind NSA engagement is that it 'supports *implementation* of the Organization's policies and recommendations … as well as the *application* of WHO's technical norms and standards'.[20] Likewise, the WHO's engagement with NSAs can *bring important benefits* to global public health and to the Organization itself in fulfilment of its constitutional principles and objectives'. The benefits are the '*contribution* of non-State actors to the work of WHO', the 'additional *resources* non-state actors can contribute to WHO's work', the 'influence that WHO can have on non-State actors' *compliance* with WHO's policies, norms and standards', and the 'wider *dissemination* of and adherence by non-State actors to WHO's policies, norms and standards'[21] (italics added).

23.3.1.1 Governing bodies

More specifically, functionality clearly drives participation in the WHO's governing bodies' main organs (World Health Assembly, Executive Board, and the six regional committees).[22] Only NSAs (NGOs, the private sector, academic institutions, or philanthropic organizations) with 'official relations' may participate. Requirements for meeting the criteria for official relations have somewhat changed, yet the gist is that it is an international entity with *competence* in public health and that 'the major part of

[18] The Constitution of the World Health Organization, Article 71 <https://www.who.int/governance/eb/who_constitution_en.pdf?ua=1>, last accessed 11/05/2021.

[19] World Health Organization, 'Principles Governing Relations Between the World Health Organization and NGOs', Article 1.3 <https://www.who.int/governance/civilsociety/principles/en/>, last accessed 11/05/2021.

[20] World Health Organization, 'WHO Framework of Engagement with Non-State Actors' WHA69.10 (28 May 2016) <http://apps.who.int/gb/ebwha/pdf_files/WHA69/A69_R10-en.pdf?ua=1>, last accessed 11//05/2021.

[21] WHO, 'Framework of Engagement' (n 20), Article 6.

[22] Constitution of the WHO (n 18), Article 9.

its activities shall be *relevant* to and *have a bearing on the implementation* of the health for all strategies as envisaged in [WHO strategies and work programmes][23] (italics added). The new FENSA has somewhat amended the definition of 'official relations' and it is more neutral, yet its functional undertone remains. To receive official status, the entities in question must have and must continue having 'a *sustained and systematic engagement* in the WHO' (understood as 'at least two years of systemic engagement as documented in the WHO Register of NSAs, assessed by both parties to be mutually *beneficial*'),[24] and that the 'aims and activities of all these entities shall *be in conformity* with the spirit, purpose and principles of WHO's Constitution', and they shall '*contribute significantly* to the advancement of public health' (italics added).[25] Such entities must also have, going forward, a joint working plan with the WHO.[26] Currently there are about 202 entities with official relations status.[27]

23.3.1.2 Consultations and hearings

While participation in governing bodies is largely limited to contributing stakeholders, 'consultations', and 'hearings' could be interpreted as allowing participation by affected stakeholders.[28] The WHO Secretariat or governing bodies will decide on a 'case-by-case basis' who to invite to consultations.[29] These criteria are flexible enough to allow the WHO in the future—were it to embrace its role as trustee—to identify and invite affected stakeholders. Online consultations, which the WHO undertakes from time to time, tend to be open before *all interested* to comment on draft policies[30] and the WHO says such comments 'will be taken into consideration in finalizing the document'[31] (italics added). Finally, '*all interested* parties should be invited on the same basis' to hearings[32] (italics added).

In the context of consultations and hearings, accordingly, were the WHO to embrace its role as trustee, the legal framework in place allows following a trusteeship approach and inviting affected stakeholders. That said, this legal framework is quite thin. While the WHO *may* hear affected stakeholders, there is no obligation to hear them *or*

[23] WHO, 'Principles' (n 19), Article 3.
[24] WHO, 'Framework of Engagement' (n 20), Article 50.
[25] WHO, 'Framework of Engagement' (n 20), Article 50.
[26] WHO, 'Framework of Engagement' (n 20), Article 52.
[27] World Health Organization, 'List of 202 Nongovernmental Organizations in Official Relations with WHO Reflecting Decisions of EB136, January 2015' <http://www.who.int/governance/NGO_list_rev_May2015.pdf?ua=1>, last accessed 11/05/2021).
[28] WHO, 'Framework of Engagement' (n 20), Article 15.
[29] WHO, 'Policy and Operational Procedures on Engagement with NGOs' WHA69.10 (2016) Article 4, <http://apps.who.int/gb/ebwha/pdf_files/WHA69/A69_R10-en.pdf?ua=1>, last accessed 11/05/2021.
[30] For example, World Health Organization, 'Public Consultation on the Draft of the Document: Protection, Promotion, and Support of Breastfeeding in Facilities Providing Maternity and Newborn Services: The Revised Baby-Friendly Hospital Initiative 2017' <http://www.who.int/nutrition/events/consultation-protection-promotion-support-breastfeeding/en/>, last accessed 11/05/2021; World Health Organization, 'WHO Opens Public Consultation on Draft Sugars Guideline' <http://www.who.int/mediacentre/news/notes/2014/consultation-sugar-guideline/en/>, last accessed 11/05/2021; 'WHO First Round Public Consultation: Recommendations to Assure the Quality, Safety and Efficacy of Hepatitis E Vaccines' <http://prais.paho.org/en/first-round-public-consultation-recommendations-to-assure-the-quality-safety-and-efficacy-of-hepatitis-e-vaccines-deadline-12-february-2018/>, last accessed 11/05/2021.
[31] WHO, 'Public Consultation' (n 30).
[32] WHO, 'Framework of Engagement' (n 20), Article 15.

to consider their input. Moreover, further research is needed into actual practice and what considerations the WHO takes when deciding whom to invite to consultations and hearings, and whether and how it considers their interests.

Ultimately, functionality and efficiency constraints determine and limit participation in the WHO. According to FENSA, all engagement is subject to 'risk management', which demands a cost-benefit analysis of engagement. The WHO may only engage a non-state actor when the '*benefits* in terms of direct or indirect *contributions* to *public health* and the fulfilment of the *Organization's mandate* ... outweigh any residual risks ... as well as the *time and expense involved* in establishing and maintaining the engagement'.[33] This speaks to functionality and efficiency, respectively.

23.3.2 Codex

Codex develops food standards, whose purpose is to assure the safety and quality of food. With the increase of international food trade and agricultural exports by developing countries, a lot is at stake for food producers, exporters, and consumers. The recent glyphosate debate exemplifies this. In 2016, Codex's expert body on safety of pesticides residues in food concluded that the highly controversial pesticide glyphosate (commonly known as Monsanto's Roundup®) was 'unlikely to pose a carcinogenic risk to humans via exposure from the diet'.[34] This recommendation contradicts other findings, notably the WHO's International Agency for Research on Cancer's classification of glyphosate as 'probably carcinogenic to humans', and its listing as carcinogenic in the State of California,[35] as well as recent findings of a US court. Countries that adopt Codex standards enjoy a presumption of compliance with the World Trade Organization Sanitary and Phytosanitary Agreement and the Technical Barriers to Trade Agreements. Therefore, Codex standards are authoritative and de facto binding. Thus, its recommendations on glyphosate—or any other substance for that matter—have without a doubt a potentially significant effect on the global public interest.

Against this background, what has driven stakeholder engagement in Codex?

Officially, both functionality and trusteeship drive Codex's stakeholder engagement. In its Principles Concerning the Participation of International Non-Governmental Organizations in the Work of the Codex Alimentarius Commission, Codex says that

> ... the purpose of collaboration with International NGOs is to secure for the Codex Alimentarius Commission, *expert information, advice and assistance* from

[33] WHO, 'Framework of Engagement' (n 20), Article 36.

[34] Food and Agriculture Organization and World Health Organization, 'Pesticide Residues in Food 2016 - Joint FAO/WHO Meeting on Pesticide Residues: Report 2016' (WHO and FAO 2016) <http://www.fao.org/fileadmin/templates/agphome/documents/Pests_Pesticides/JMPR/Report2016/JMPR_2016_Report_full.pdf>, last accessed 11/05/2021.

[35] International Agency for Research on Cancer, 'IARC Monographs: Glyphosate' (2016) <http://monographs.iarc.fr/ENG/Monographs/vol112/mono112-10.pdf>, last accessed 05/11/2021; Alessandra Arcuri, 'Glyphosate' in Jessie Homan and Daniel Joyce (eds), *International Law's Objects* (Oxford University Press 2018) 235-247.

> international non-governmental organizations and to enable organizations which *represent important sections of public opinion* and are authorities in their fields of professional and technical competence to *express the views of their members* ... (italics added).[36]

Thus, the formal criteria are broad enough for Codex to follow a trusteeship and functionality approach and to engage both affected and contributing stakeholders. In practice, however, most of its participating stakeholders have been business groups, suggesting that Codex has been driven in practice by a functionality approach.[37] Due to increased scientific complexity, governments increasingly depend on industry expertise. In contrast, global bodies often perceive public interest groups as lacking technical expertise and merely representing a social or political voice. Thus, the dominance of business suggests the dominant role in practice of functionality in stakeholder engagement.[38]

23.3.2.1 Governing and other bodies

Further, to participate, NSAs must have official 'observer status'.[39] The criteria for receiving such status are rather neutral. Both affected and contributing stakeholders could receive official status, as long as they fulfil certain prerequisites. The organization must either have a formal status in the FAO and the WHO, or be 'international in structure and scope of activity' and 'representative of the specialized field of interest in which they operate'; they must further be concerned with matters that are in Codex's field, have aims that conform to those of Codex, and have an institutionalized structure.[40]

Despite this apparent neutrality, in practice, most observers represent commercial interests, with insufficient representation of the public interest.[41] In practice, therefore, there is a gap between Codex's neutral formal criteria and their practical application. Being a standard-setting organization, Codex has been most concerned about getting scientific expertise, which in turn explains its tendency to include industry. If it followed a trusteeship approach, the expectation is that Codex would engage more affected groups, that is, groups representing consumers or other health or environmental concerns.

[36] Codex, 'Principles Concerning the Participation of International Non-Governmental Organizations in the Work of the Codex Alimentarius Commission' (1999) <http://www.fao.org/3/Y2200E/y2200e09.htm>, last accessed 11/05/2021.

[37] Berman, 'Stakeholder Participation Reforms' (n 1); Tim Büthe and Nathaniel Harris, 'Codex Alimentarius Commission: A Hybrid Public-Private Regulator' in Thomas Hale and David Held (eds), *Handbook of Transnational Governance: Institutions and Innovations* (Wiley 2011) 219-228; Elizabeth Smythe, 'In Whose Interests? Transparency and Accountability in the Global Governance of Food: Agribusiness, the Codex Alimentarius, and the World Trade Organization ' in Jennifer Clapp and Doris Fuchs (eds), *Corporate Power in Global Agrifood Governance* (MIT Press 2009) 93-124.

[38] Ayelet Berman, 'Industry, Capture and Transnational Standard Setting' 111 *American Journal of International Law Unbound* (2017) 112-118.

[39] Food and Agricultural Organization, E-Learning Academy, 'Enhancing Participation in Codex Activities', Lesson 2.2 <https://elearning.fao.org/course/view.php?id=178> , last accessed 11/05/2021.

[40] Codex Alimentarius Commission, *Procedural Manual 25th Edition* (FAO and WHO 2016).

[41] Berman, 'Stakeholder Participation Reforms' (n 1).

23.3.2.2 Expert committees and data

NSAs participate as scientific experts advising on Codex's expert committees, consultations, and meetings. Codex selects experts in their personal capacity.[42] Dependent on their scientific knowledge, Codex's inclusion of experts is evidently functional. Providing the essential foundation for the development of recommendations and guidelines, such scientific expertise is influential.[43]

By being open towards affected stakeholders, the process of gathering scientific expertise and data has several trusteeship characteristics. First, Codex issues public calls for data,[44] opening-up, in turn, at least potentially, the process to a broad set of stakeholders. In practice, industry frequently provides the data, yet in other cases, governmental regulatory agencies and other scientific research institutes have provided data.[45] Second, scientific advice must be carried out in accordance with core principles of soundness, responsibility, objectivity, fairness, transparency, and inclusiveness. To be 'inclusive', is:

> considered to include group balance [. . .] Inclusiveness requires that due respect and consideration be given to *minority* scientific opinion. In the selection of participants, in addition to their expertise, due consideration should be given to *geographical and socioeconomic balance*, but not to the extent that it compromise scientific integrity. Particular emphasis should be placed on improving the participation of *developing countries*. Where participation is limited by skill or knowledge gap, appropriate *capacity building* activities should be undertaken'. (italics added). Further, 'fairness' requires that 'participants should be given adequate and equal opportunities to express their views. Minority views should be properly considered . . . The selection of participants should be objective and inclusive to the extent possible . . . ' (italics added). [46]

To conclude, functionality drives expert participation, yet Codex has introduced trusteeship characteristics into the process. That said, further research is required as to the actual practices on the scientific committees and data collection.

23.3.2.3 National delegations

National delegations attend Codex sessions and working groups. Typically, the head delegate is a governmental official, yet it is common to include non-governmental advisors.[47] The process used to form national delegations varies from country to country,

[42] FAO, E-Learning Academy (n 39), Lesson 4.2.
[43] FAO, E-Learning Academy (n 39), Lesson 4.2.
[44] FAO, E-Learning Academy (n 39), Lesson 4.2.
[45] FAO, E-Learning Academy (n 39), Lesson 4.2.
[46] FAO, E-Learning Academy (n 39), Lesson 4.2, 'Provision of Scientific Advice'; Food and Agriculture Organization and World Health Organization, 'Provision of Scientific Advice to Codex and Member Countries—Report of a Joint FAO/WHO Workshop WHO Headquarters, Geneva, Switzerland 27–29 January 2004' (FAO and WHO 2004) <http://www.fao.org/3/y5388e/y5388e00.htm>, last accessed 05/15/2020; Food and Agriculture Organization and World Health Organization, 'FAO/WHO Framework for the Provision of Scientific Advice on Food Safety and Nutrition' (FAO and WHO 2007) <http://www.fao.org/3/a-a1296e.pdf>, last accessed 05/16/2021).
[47] FAO, E-Learning Academy (n 39), Lesson 3.3.

though Codex encourages functionality and efficiency, such as by encouraging to include an NSA who:

> has particular *expertise* that the government requires [and that] [p]reference should be given to organizations that have … indicated an interest in a broad spectrum of issues … or have *expertise* in the subject matter … or *recognized credentials* in the area of work related to the mandate of the Codex meeting in which their participation is being considered … '[48] (italics added).

In practice, due to their technical expertise, most advisors are from industry. Although whom to include on a national delegation is within each country's prerogative, were Codex to embrace its role as trustee, it could encourage countries to not only include contributing stakeholders (as it does), but also affected stakeholders.

23.3.2.4 Consultations

Standard elaboration is subject to a national consultation process, which could potentially allow participation by affected and contributing stakeholders: In its elaboration of standards, Codex sends drafts to each member's national 'Codex Contact Point', the focal point for all Codex-related activities within a state. Codex expects the national contact points to solicit input from a broad range of stakeholders—other ministries, industry, experts, public health professionals, academia, and consumer organizations.[49] In view of efficiency, Codex encourages national contact points to identify which groups are interested in what issues, and to facilitate comments from them.[50]

Furthermore, to facilitate the consultation process, many countries have a National Codex Committee (NCC) or an equivalent structure. Codex advocates a broad multi-stakeholder structure:

> Ideally, all government departments and organizations concerned with food safety, food production and trade in food should be included in the National Codex Committee. Further, some scientific organizations (such as public universities and research institutions) and any other notable experts in the relevant field could be co-opted to the NCC.[51]

A typical NCC could include 'relevant government departments/ministries, consumer organizations, industry—food manufacturers and food producers, food importers and/or exporters, universities, professional bodies, leading research institutions, notable national experts'.[52] Regional guidelines in Asia, Africa, and the Near East stress the inclusion of representatives from relevant government ministries,

[48] FAO, E-Learning Academy (n 39), Lesson 3.3, 'Selecting National Delegations: Additional Considerations to be Taken into Account When Selecting Non-Governmental Advisors'.

[49] FAO, E-Learning Academy (n 39), Lesson 3.1.

[50] FAO, E-Learning Academy (n 39), Lesson 3.2.

[51] Codex, Basics of National Codex Activities, Section 3, Module 3.2 (How to Develop national positions on Codex issues), p. 115, https://www.fao.org/3/y5884e/y5884e03.pdf, last accessed 11/5/2021.

[52] FAO, E-Learning Academy (n 39), Lesson 3.2.

scientific organizations, food industry, trading sector, consumers, and individual experts.[53] Aware of efficiency, 'The NCC should, however, not be so large as to make it unmanageable.'[54]

With more trusteeship awareness these structures could improve responsiveness towards affected stakeholders. As such national consultations are within each state's prerogative, in practice, different countries will likely have taken different approaches. This is an area for further research.

23.3.3 The Global Fund and GAVI

The Global Fund and GAVI are MSPs that bring governmental and non-governmental actors together to fund and implement programmes in the fight against three communicable diseases, and for increasing childhood immunization, respectively. Their MSP structure is a progressive attempt at integrating functionality and trusteeship into a global governance model.

23.3.3.1 The Global Fund

The board is composed of a 'donor' and 'implementer' bloc. NSAs participate within each of these blocs. On the donor bloc (alongside developed countries), the private sector and private foundations have a seat. On the implementers bloc (alongside developing countries), there is one NGO representative from a developing country, one NGO from a developed country, and NGOs representing persons living with the three diseases. NSAs are included for two main reasons.

23.3.3.1.1 Functionality

Private sector inclusion serves functional purposes: They 'have a number of ways to *contribute*—their *finances*, their *knowledge*, their participation in governance, their abilities as *implementers*, and through advocacy'[55] (italics added). Private-sector partners (including private foundations such as the Bill and Melinda Gates Foundation) donate funds and also 'help Global Fund-supported programs to *work better* through sharing *knowledge* and technical *expertise*. Coca Cola SAP ... and others have used their skills and capacities to strengthen health systems and improve program *implementation*'[56] (italics added).

The private sector contributes to the Global Fund's work not only at the international level but also at the national level. The Global Fund relies on elaborate national mechanisms, or Country Coordinating Mechanisms (CCMs), which constitute a central pillar of its governance. Such CCMs are responsible for creating requests for funding and overseeing the implementation of programmes, and have a multi-stakeholder

[53] Codex Alimentarius Commission, 'Regional Guidelines for Codex Contact Points and National Codex Committees (Near East)' CAC/GL 58R-2005; Codex Alimentarius Commission, 'Regional Guidelines for Codex Contact Points and National Codex Committees (Africa)' CAC/GL 43R-2003.

[54] FAO, E-Learning Academy (n 39), Lesson 3.2.

[55] The Global Fund, 'Private and Nongovernment Partners' <https://www.theglobalfund.org/en/private-ngo-partners/>, last accessed 05/16/2020.

[56] Global Fund, 'Private and Nongovernment Partners' (n 55).

structure, including, alongside governments, civil society, the private sector, technical partners, and representatives of people living or affected by the three diseases.[57] As the Global Fund indicates, 'as part of their sustainability efforts, private sector companies also participate on the ground ... *implementing* interventions to serve the men, women and children living with the diseases'. They also have a role in supporting the Global Fund's awareness and advocacy efforts: '[b]ecause the Global Fund does not have a presence in country, it relies on partners—including private sector companies—to help raise awareness of the work of the Global Fund ... '.[58] Civil society engagement has a functional role too: '[c]ivil society organizations also play a key role at the local level. Community-based organizations serve as *implementers* of Global Fund grants ... They also play a useful role in ... their capacity as watchdogs, to ensure that programs are implemented as intended'[59] (italics added).

23.3.3.1.2 Trusteeship

The Global Fund proactively integrates affected and marginalized communities in the decision-making process.

First, at the *board level, affected, marginalized stakeholders are represented.* Civil society (understood in the context of the Global Fund as 'all those stakeholders who are neither governmental bodies nor private sector enterprises: groups such as NGOs, advocacy groups, faith based organizations, networks of people living with the diseases etc.') has three seats.[60] Of these three seats, one seat represents NGOs from the developed world, one represents NGOs from the developing world, and one seat represents the Communities *living with and affected by HIV, Tuberculosis and Malaria*.[61] By giving a voice to the people living with or affected by these diseases—an obviously weak and marginalized group—the Global Fund takes a trusteeship approach.

Second, the Global Fund *sanctions the national bodies if they do not include affected marginalized stakeholders*. Not only are people with the disease represented at the board level, but also the Global Fund promises their inclusion in the CCMs by demanding a multi-stakeholder structure, which must include, alongside government officials, civil society, the private sector, technical partners, and representatives of people living or affected by the three diseases.[62] Notably, as the participation of the most vulnerable populations—that is, people who are impacted by the diseases yet have reduced access because they are criminalized or otherwise marginalized, such as gay men, drug addicts, and sex workers—has not been satisfactory in practice, the Global Fund has now conditioned financing on the engagement of such key populations.[63]

[57] The Global Fund, 'Country Coordinating Mechanism Policy Including Principles and Requirements', Requirement 4 <https://www.theglobalfund.org/media/7421/ccm_countrycoordinatingmechanism_policy_en.pdf?u=637244532480000000>, last accessed 05/16/2020.

[58] Global Fund, 'Private and Nongovernment Partners' (n 55).

[59] The Global Fund, 'Civil Society' <https://www.theglobalfund.org/en/civil-society/>, last accessed 05/16/2020.

[60] Global Fund, 'Civil Society' (n 59).

[61] Global Fund, 'Civil Society' (n 59).

[62] Global Fund, 'Principles and Requirements' (n 57), Requirement 4.

[63] Global Fund, 'Principles and Requirements' (n 57), Requirement 4.

Third, the Global Fund *proactively supports participation of affected stakeholders through financial, capacity building, and institutional mechanisms*. The Global Fund has introduced financial support, capacity building reforms and a human rights complaints mechanism—all geared at supporting communities and key populations to engage in the national mechanisms.[64]

23.3.3.2 GAVI

GAVI also follows a multi-stakeholder model, and the private sector (vaccine industry from developed and developing countries), civil society, research institutes, and individual experts all have seats.[65]

At the outset, functionality and a desire to be effective at its mission of improving access to immunization in poor countries largely drove GAVIs multi-stakeholder model. Following the WHO's failure to increase access to vaccines in developing countries, and after having reached the conclusion that a multi-stakeholder model was necessary to achieving effective results, the Bill and Melinda Gates Foundation initiated the establishment of GAVI as a multi-stakeholder partnership and the functional rationale was the main driving force for stakeholder inclusion. In its statements, GAVI underlines this functional rationale, saying:

> By bringing the key stakeholders in global immunization together around one mission, GAVI combines the technical expertise of the development community with the business know-how of the private sector . . . As a public private partnership, GAVI represents the sum of its partners individual strengths, from WHO's scientific expertise and UNICEF's procurement system to the financial know how of the World Bank and the market knowledge of the vaccine industry.[66]

As Dr Gro Harlem Bruntland, the former Director General of the WHO and GAVI's first chair puts it: 'GAVI is a merger of our comparative advantages that aims to deliver more than each of us can do if we go it alone.'[67]

Functionality underlies GAVI's collaboration with the vaccine industry, the scientific community, and civil society. Vaccine companies provide knowledge and expertise—they harness 'the research and technical *expertise* to supply vaccines that address the needs of developing countries'.[68] They also develop technologies that facilitate the distribution of vaccines, or by educating public health officials. Vaccine companies also provide actual resources by supplying vaccines to key GAVI supported programmes.[69] Likewise, GAVI indicates that

[64] Berman, 'Stakeholder Participation Reforms' (n 1).

[65] For more details on GAVI's model, see Berman (n 1).

[66] GAVI, 'Operating Model' <https://www.gavi.org/our-alliance/operating-model>, last accessed 11/05/2021

[67] GAVI, 'Gavi's Partnership Model' <http://www.gavi.org/about/partners/the-partnership-model/>, last accessed 11/05/2020.

[68] GAVI, 'Industrialised Country Pharmaceutical Industry' <http://www.gavi.org/about/partners/industrialised-country-vaccine-industry/>, last accessed 05/16/2020.

[69] GAVI, 'Industrialised Country Pharmaceutical Industry' (n 69).

> partnering with the research community allows us to *tap into the latest information* and thinking from the scientific, medical and product delivery communities ... The relationship has repeatedly enabled us to *deliver on our mission* by generating and communicating the evidence base required by global and national decision makers to argue in favor of introducing new and underused vaccines ... [70] (italics added).

Civil society organizations also provide knowledge and support implementation: they 'provide input to ensure that the Vaccine Alliance's programmes and *policies are robust* ... '.[71] They 'play a key role in *implementing* immunization programmes ... they deliver [most] immunization services, as well as strengthening health systems ... Civil society is vital in delivering health services and immunization to those who need them most'.[72] They do so 'by delivering the programs, training local health workers, supporting local logistics and so forth'[73] (italics added).

Finally, several years ago, GAVI reformed its membership structure and set up a significant infrastructure for the inclusion of a broad range of civil society organizations in its decision-making.[74] GAVI now stresses the importance of civil society organizations as they 'represent local communities',[75] and provide input to ensure that the Vaccine Alliance maintains a high level of 'accountability and responsiveness' to the needs of communities.[76] While the growing responsiveness towards affected and marginalized communities advances trusteeship, for an organization such as GAVI, whose mission is to help those most vulnerable, the broader and more effective representation of affected, marginalized stakeholders ultimately serves functional goals.

To conclude, functionality initially drove GAVI's multi-stakeholder model, yet in recent years, GAVI has introduced features, which strengthen its responsiveness towards civil society, and as such, has strengthened its trustee role. Nevertheless, in an organization such as GAVI, whose mission is to help the most vulnerable, trusteeship and functionality may significantly overlap, or be the same.

23.4 Conclusion

The prevailing literature on stakeholder participation has stressed the role of functionality in explaining stakeholder participation. This chapter introduced the stakeholder participation triangle as a model for thinking about stakeholder participation. Trusteeship and functionality justify or drive *who* should participate, while

[70] GAVI, 'Research and Technical Health Institutes' < https://www.gavi.org/operating-model/gavis-partnership-model/research-and-technical-institutes >, last accessed 05/16/2021.

[71] GAVI understands civil society organizations as including NGOs, advocacy organizations, professional and community associations, and faith-based organizations.

[72] GAVI, 'Civil Society Organisations' <http://www.gavi.org/about/partners/cso/>, last accessed 05/16/2021.

[73] GAVI, 'Civil Society Organisation Support' <https://www.gavi.org/programmes-impact/types-support/civil-society>, last accessed 05/16/2021.

[74] Berman (n 1).

[75] GAVI, 'Civil Society Support' (n 74).

[76] GAVI, 'Civil Society Organisations' (n 73).

efficiency acts as a counterforce and restricts the modalities of their engagement (*how, when, where*).

Applying this framework to case studies, I have further sought to understand the role of these factors in explaining existing stakeholder participation practice. Although this analysis focuses on global health bodies, I believe that these findings and insights are of relevance to our thinking about stakeholder engagement in general.

23.4.1 Functionality or Trusteeship? Fragmentation within Organizations

The prevailing approach regarding stakeholder participation in the literature explains stakeholder engagement by way of functionality. This literature, however, focuses on IOs governing bodies. This chapter opened up the black box and examined other decision-making bodies or processes, such as consultations, hearings, expert bodies, and national processes. I find that governing bodies indeed tend to be dominated by functionality (formally, as in the WHO, or in practice, as in Codex) and efficiency (participation open only to those who have fulfilled the strict criteria of having been recognized as being in 'official relations' or 'observers'). However, in some cases, such as the WHO's consultations and hearings, or in Codex's expert committees, national delegations, and national consultations, the rules are flexible enough to allow more inclusive participation. Such inclusiveness may serve functional goals (in certain cases, hearing all or most affected stakeholders ensures better information and more robust and implementable policies), but, notably, if these organizations chose to embrace a trustee role, the legal infrastructure is in place for them to invite all significantly affected stakeholders. An OECD that surveyed fifty IOs similarly found that while stakeholder engagement tends to be restricted in governing bodies, it tends to be much broader in committees and working groups.[77] Thus, in thinking about the role of trusteeship and functionality, we need to take a more nuanced and fragmented approach to stakeholder engagement in any respective IO.

23.4.2 Functionality or Trusteeship? Fragmentation between Organizations

The existing literature, which stresses the role of functionality, has focused on IOs. This chapter expanded the analysis to include two MSPs. In contrast to the IOs (whose governing bodies are dominated by functionality), these partnerships have embraced functionality and trusteeship in their governance. By proactively working towards the inclusion of affected and marginalized groups, the Global Fund takes a progressive trusteeship approach. While other organizations, including the WHO and Codex, may have openings for the public, the Global Fund stands out because it goes beyond lip service to actively reach out to affected and marginalized stakeholders. The

[77] OECD, *International Regulatory Co-Operation* (n 5), 85.

Global Fund also insists on a balanced trusteeship and functionality approach along the entire governance chain—all through to the national CCMs. By sanctioning those CCMs who do not engage key populations, it has introduced accountability mechanisms, which incentivize the CCMs to include marginalized populations. Furthermore, by supporting capacity building, it strengthens the capability of marginalized yet affected stakeholders to take advantage of their participation rights. Moreover, in GAVI, features for strengthening trusteeship have improved over time. In fact, in the case of partnerships whose mission is to support marginalized and vulnerable populations, the inclusion of marginalized populations serves trusteeship and functionalism simultaneously.

23.4.3 Strengthening the Trusteeship Legal Framework

Throughout this chapter I have relied on the notion of trusteeship. IOs have not used this term, certainly not as a source of their legal obligation to engage affected stakeholders. However, by opening up certain decision-making processes to affected stakeholders, they have essentially followed what the notion of trusteeship tries to achieve, that is, being responsive towards affected stakeholders. That said, most of the provisions are quite thin. They say little about how the IO should consider interests of affected stakeholders and do not set out any guarantees that they would be considered at all, let alone any proactive mechanisms for encouraging participation.

23.4.4 Trusteeship Gaps in Practice

Notwithstanding formal participation rights of affected stakeholders, applying them in practice encounters real-life problems. Quite often, there is a gap between formal provisions, which allow affected stakeholders to participate, and actual participation. In Codex, for example, the official criteria suggest that participation would be available to both affected stakeholders and contributing stakeholders, yet we know that in practice industry dominates Codex. Likewise, in the Global Fund, although the provisions demand balanced stakeholder participation, this has been difficult to achieve in practice.

23.4.5 Overcoming Barriers to Trusteeship

As mentioned, notwithstanding a formal right to participate, trusteeship is difficult to achieve in practice because many parts of society lack the capacity or resources to take advantage of the participation opportunities provided to them.[78] Moreover, rarely are stakeholders organized at the international level. The OECD made similar findings in its survey of about fifty IOs.[79] Thus, to achieve effective trusteeship, it is

[78] Berman and Pauwelyn, 'Assessing' (n 3).
[79] OECD, *International Regulatory Co-Operation* (n 5), 86.

not enough to have institutional participation opportunities in place. Organizations should take a proactive effort to support participation of affected stakeholders through institutional-, financial-, and capacity-building measures. Except for the Global Fund and GAVI, which have introduced certain measures to this end (accountability mechanisms, capacity building, etc.), Codex and the WHO (let alone other international institutions) still have much to improve. However, while Codex has introduced measures to improve participation by marginalized developing countries,[80] it has not done so regarding NSAs.

With states being the members of IOs, most consultation between the IOs and the public has traditionally been through the state, acting as an intermediary. Our study of Codex and the Global Fund demonstrates how these organizations rely on national consultation mechanisms for getting local input. Likewise, the OECD's survey of fifty IOs finds that most intergovernmental organizations 'leave the responsibility of engaging stakeholders to their Members'.[81] Furthermore, most participation—in the WHO, the Global Fund, GAVI, and Codex—is representative rather than direct. Thus, while stakeholder engagement has increased, these mechanisms (aimed at maintaining the efficiency of stakeholder engagement) continue curbing direct participation at the international level.

[80] Berman, 'Stakeholder Participation Reforms' (n 1).
[81] OECD, *International Regulatory Co-Operation* (n 5), 85.

24
Public Power and Private Stakeholders

*Kal Raustiala**

24.1 Introduction

The guiding principle of post-war global governance was multilateralism. As John Ruggie famously defined it, multilateralism 'is an institutional form which coordinates relations among three or more states on the basis of 'generalized' principles of conduct'.[1] From the grandest multilateral project—the United Nations—to the many international organizations created in the years following the end of the Second World War, global governance followed a familiar template. States, which stood at the centre, negotiated a multilateral treaty. This in turn created a formal international organization to govern a specified issue-area. These organizations had buildings, staff, and letterhead, and they exhibited many of the features of mid-century governance in the advanced industrial world generally: the belief in expertise, in scale, in centralized bureaucracy, and in legal foundations and process. While some states clearly had more power than others within erstwhile multilateral institutions—whether the Permanent Five of the Security Council or the skewed voting allocations in the World Bank and International Monetary Fund (IMF)—the equality of sovereigns and the central role of states remained core guiding principles.

Twenty-first-century global governance continues to reflect multilateral principles. But it is increasingly characterized by flexible structures, greater tolerance for informality, and, most strikingly, an openness to public–private partnerships and an increasingly active role for a wide range of non-state actors.[2] While the embrace of non-state actors is not uniform (e.g. the governance of global health differs markedly on this score from the governance of global finance), many international regimes now feature substantial participation by private actors.[3] Traditional multilateralism remains alive and well. But multilateral governance is increasingly supplemented, and in some cases even supplanted, by *multi-stakeholder* governance. Civil society, corporations, social and political groups, religious organizations, and indigenous peoples are all potential stakeholders in many issue areas, and the move to directly include them

* I thank Sydney Sherman, Ariel Cohen, and Patrick Hulme of UCLA School of Law for research assistance with this draft, and participants at the SNIS workshops at the Graduate Institute in Geneva in 2016 and at the Technical University of Munich in 2017 for their feedback.

[1] John Gerard Ruggie, 'Multilateralism: The Anatomy of an Institution' 46 *International Organization* (1992) 561-598, esp. 574. See also John Gerard Ruggie (ed), *Multilateralism Matters* (Columbia University Press 1993); Robert Z Lawrence, *Regionalism, Multilateralism, and Deeper Integration* (Brookings Institution Press 1996).

[2] Ayelet Berman, Tim Büthe, Martino Maggetti, and Joost Pauwelyn, 'Introduction: Rethinking Stakeholder Participation in Global Governance.' Chapter 1, this volume.

[3] Berman *et al.*, 'Introduction' (n 2).

Kal Raustiala, *Public Power and Private Stakeholders* In: *Rethinking Participation in Global Governance.* Edited by: Joost Pauwelyn, Martino Maggetti, Tim Büthe, and Ayelet Berman, Oxford University Press.
DOI: 10.1093/oso/9780198852568.003.0024

alongside governments in the sharing of power is one of the most striking contemporary trends in global governance.[4]

This ongoing embrace of multi-stakeholder governance raises a host of important questions for world politics today. Is 'multi-stakeholderism' more effective at achieving its ends than 'mere' multilateralism? Is it perceived as more legitimate by relevant actors? Is more inclusive governance more efficient? Regardless, how can multi-stakeholder governance be improved?[5]

At a more fundamental level, however, is a very basic question. Why is the shift to greater inclusion occurring? States remain the most powerful actors in world politics, and as organizations like the WTO and the UN Security Council show, they can readily cabin the role of private actors when they choose to. Moreover, even in the most novel examples of the new global governance, such as the Global Fund for AIDS, Tuberculosis and Malaria, public funding dominates private resources; indeed, some 95% of funding in the Global Fund comes from sovereigns. Nonetheless, it is undeniable that in a range of important global issues *public* entities are increasingly granting access and influence to *private* entities. Why this is happening is the focus of this chapter.

My core argument is that public power can be and often is strengthened by private power. The rise of private actors has not come at the expense of public actors, but instead often works to the political benefit of those public actors. This symbiotic relationship between public and private actors is insufficiently appreciated and helps to explain the striking rise of multi-stakeholderism in global governance.

In what follows I sketch out the basis of this claim, and, drawing on the role of private actors in domestic governance, suggest some concrete benefits that public actors gain from the inclusion of private actors. These benefits help explain the rising commitment to stakeholder participation in global governance, although there is no reason to believe that they are the only force propelling this trend forward. There is surely some degree of mimicry across regimes that takes place, as well as a growing sense that the inclusion of diverse stakeholders is more just, fair, and appropriate. But the concrete benefits inclusion provides are widespread and important to recognize, and the broad patterns of inclusion are consistent with an interests-based understanding of this transformation. I bolster my argument with examples drawn from the core areas of focus in this volume—global health and finance—as well as others, such as environment, intellectual property, and Internet governance.

The commitment to multi-stakeholderism varies markedly across issue areas. While more research is needed to move beyond the impressionistic, the overall pattern is broadly consistent. The inclusion of private power, far from threatening public power, often helps it to thrive.

[4] For other recent treatments see Jonas Tallberg, Thomas Sommerer, Theresa Squatrito and Christer Jönsson, *The Opening Up of International Organizations: Transnational Access in Global Governance* (Cambridge University Press 2013); Kal Raustiala, 'NGOs in International Treatymaking' in Duncan B Hollis (ed), *The Oxford Guide to Treaties* (Oxford University Press 2012); Deborah D Avant, Martha Finnemore and Susan K Sell, 'Who Governs the Globe?' in Deborah D Avant, Martha Finnemore and Susan K Sell (eds), *Who Governs the Globe?* (Cambridge University Press 2010) 1-32.

[5] Berman *et al.*, 'Introduction' (n 2) raise many important questions in this regard.

24.2 States and Non-State Actors in Global Governance

A century ago at the Paris peace talks of 1919, leading states hammered out some truly novel governance arrangements, including the landmark League of Nations. Woodrow Wilson had famously campaigned against secret agreements and sought to ensure that, after the First World War, covenants between nations would be openly arrived at and publicly available. Indeed, it was not a coincidence that he made this Point 1 of his Fourteen Points.[6] Yet there was still substantial secrecy in Paris, and while several NGOs—then still a novel concept—sent delegations, their level of participation was minimal. Indeed, all working sessions were closed to the public.[7] Still, the Paris peace talks were a high point for inclusion compared to the diplomatic practices of the past, and in their own way they augured a new form of global governance in which non-state actors and governments would begin to work together more closely.

As this suggests, private actors have been a part of the international landscape for some time. Corporations likewise existed a century ago and sometimes had interests in the emerging international structures. Diverse stakeholders have existed as long as leaders have sought to govern. But in the past, at the global level, these stakeholders were often not organized, not present for negotiations or debates, and, above all, not welcome as peer governors to states.[8] The first noteworthy exception was the International Labour Organization (ILO), which from its inception in 1919 has employed a unique tripartite structure of government, business, and labour representatives. The ILO's corporatist origins are unusual and reflected the prevailing politics of the time, in which socialism was ascendant in many nations. Powerful unions were often pitted against employers, and economic life between capital and labour was understood as a form of cooperation structurally laced with conflict. The ILO system embedded that complex and often antagonistic relationship quite directly by including all the major relevant parties. As the ILO itself describes the approach:

> The ILO aims to ensure that it serves the needs of working women and men by bringing together governments, employers and workers to set labour standards, develop policies and devise programmes. The structure of the ILO, where workers and employers together have an equal voice with governments in its deliberations, attempts to create a social dialogue. It ensures that the views of the social partners are closely reflected in ILO labour standards, policies and programmes.[9]

As ground-breaking as the ILO was, structurally it was largely a dead end. For decades there was no real parallel to it, and today's existing multi-stakeholder governance systems are more pluralistic and flexible in their approach. After 1945 the UN

[6] 'President Woodrow Wilson's Fourteen Points' (8 January 1918) <https://avalon.law.yale.edu/20th_century/wilson14.asp>, last accessed 05/15/2020.

[7] Steve Charnovitz, 'The Emergence of Democratic Participation in Global Governance (Paris, 1919)' 10 *Indiana Journal of Global Legal Studies* (2003) 45-77, 62.

[8] On the concept of 'global governors' see Avant *et al.*, *Who Governs the Globe?* (n 4), 2.

[9] International Labour Organization, 'How the ILO Works' <www.ilo.org/global/about-the-ilo/how-the-ilo-works/lang--en/index.htm>, last accessed 05/15/2020.

quickly became an important, if not the central, forum for treaty-making as well as for the creation of new international organizations. The UN Charter was and remains quite state-centric. It says relatively little about non-state actors and never uses the term stakeholder. But in practice, in the post-war era the UN soon began accrediting NGOs for participation in its governance processes.[10] By the 1980s and 1990s civil society groups of various kinds had become central to many UN-led governance efforts. Huge conferences filled with private as well as public actors became the norm.

The environment is one of the chief exemplars of this trend. At the final meeting of the 2015 Paris Accord on climate change, for example, there were 198 states in attendance, but over 1,000 NGOs.[11] This is typical for many global environmental efforts, which have tended to draw ever-larger numbers of private actors into the fold over time.[12] Running alongside the increasing presence of NGOs were a few more explicitly multi-stakeholder governance processes. For example, after a series of failed efforts at the creation of a legally binding forests regime, efforts moved towards a less state-centric approach. The Forest Stewardship Council was created in 1993 by 130 representatives from twenty-six countries, none of whom were government representatives. The Council has an ILO-like structure with a tripartite General Assembly divided into Environment, Social, or Economic chambers. These are further divided into Northern and Southern sub-chambers.[13]

This arrangement is noteworthy, but it reflects a broader tendency in global environmental governance. Inclusive governance is widely seen today as both necessary and appropriate. As the UN Development Programme argues, 'the development of a multi-stakeholder governance framework at the national, regional, and/or municipal levels is crucial for creating ownership, capacity, and consensus about long-term sustainable development objectives and results, and is similarly critical for effective action to combat climate change'.[14]

This evolution in participation can be seen in other arenas as well. The World Bank (WB) is emblematic. The early WB was decidedly not inclusive. Yet as a WB staff member noted:

> The World Bank Group has significant knowledge and experience of working with non-state stakeholders, including MSIs [(multi-stakeholder initiatives)]. This has not always been the case, though. Historically, our core expertise has been in working directly with governments. But this changed more than 20 years ago, spurred by the

[10] Pursuant to Article 71 of the UN Charter.

[11] UN Framework Convention on Climate Change, 'List of Participants' (11 December 2015) FCCC/CP/2015/INF.3 <http://unfccc.int/resource/docs/2015/cop21/eng/inf03p01.pdf>, last accessed 05/15/2020.

[12] See Kal Raustiala, 'States, NGOs, and International Environmental Institutions' 41(4) *International Studies Quarterly* (1997) 719-740.

[13] Forest Stewardship Council, 'Strategic Plan and Governance Structure' <https://fsc.org/en/governance-strategy>, last accessed 05/15/2020.

[14] UN Development Programme, 'Multi-Stakeholder Decision-Making' (2012), 8 <https://www.undp.org/content/undp/en/home/librarypage/environment-energy/low_emission_climateresilientdevelopment/MultiStakeholder.html>, last accessed 05/15/2020. Much the same can be said of environment, see European Environment Agency, *Global Governance—The Rise of Non-State Actors* (2011) <https://www.eea.europa.eu/publications/global-governance>, last accessed 05/15/2020.

World Bank's work on participation, and subsequently by the Poverty Reduction Strategies, which mandated broader engagement.[15]

At the annual WB/IMF meetings, private actors now play a large role and are officially incorporated via the Civil Society Policy Forum, 'a program of events to promote policy dialogue between Civil Society Organizations (CSOs), the IMF and the World Bank Group, their peers, and government delegations on a wide range of topics'.[16] In short, while private stakeholders may have had some modicum of participation in the early decades of the Bretton Woods institutions, today far greater inclusion is structured, formalized, and lauded.

For newer global governance bodies, the embrace of multi-stakeholder participation is even greater. Founded in 2000, the Global Alliance for Vaccines and Immunization (GAVI), for example:

> ... is somewhat unique in the significant role that it gives to non-state actors including partner foundations, the private sector and technical experts. The GAVI Alliance Board sets overall policies and monitors programs. The Bill and Melinda Gates Foundation holds one of four 'renewable' seats on the GAVI Alliance Board. In addition, there are several other seats for non-state actors among the 12 rotating seats on the board. Of these, one is designated for civil society groups while the others are allocated to research and technical health institutes, the developing country vaccine industry and the industrialized country vaccine industry. In 2005, the GAVI Alliance Board determined that it needed to strengthen the participation of civil society constituencies in its governance and programs and allocated expanded resources to enhance civil society representation at the country level. In 2010, the GAVI Partners forum created the GAVI Alliance Civil Society Constituency, a group of civil society representatives to support members of GAVI's governance bodies.[17]

Similarly, the Global Fund employs a multi-stakeholder model that includes states, private industries, and civil society. To be sure, the organization remains largely state-centric: governments control fifteen of the twenty of the seats on the Global Fund board. But the five remaining seats are set aside for, respectively, an NGO from a developing country, an NGO from a developed country, an NGO representing persons living with the diseases, the private sector, and private foundations. As Berman argues, this structure was 'groundbreaking, deviating from the traditional intergovernmental model at the time, embodied by the WHO and World Bank'.[18] Not only does

[15] Jeff Thindwa, 'Multi Stakeholder Initiatives: Platforms of Collective Governance for Development' (*World Bank Blogs*, 7 July 2015) <https://blogs.worldbank.org/governance/multi-stakeholder-initiatives-platforms-collective-governance-development>, last accessed 05/15/2020.

[16] International Monetary Fund, 'Participants' (under the sub-heading of 'Civil Society Representatives) <www.imf.org/external/am/2016/participants.htm>, last accessed 05/15/2020.

[17] David Gartner, 'Beyond Consultation: Civil Society and the Governance of International Institutions' (2010) *Center for Universal Education at Brookings*, 10 <www.brookings.edu/wp-content/uploads/2016/06/09_civil_society_gartner.pdf>, last accessed 05/15/2020.

[18] Ayelet Berman, 'Stakeholder Participation Reforms in Global Health Governance.' Chapter 13, this volume.

the Global Fund include private actors in its central governance, but it also requires it in the national structures that implement Global Fund programs on the ground:

> Every recipient country has 'Country Coordinating Mechanisms' which submit grant applications to the Global Fund and oversee implementation of Global Fund programs. Such [mechanisms] must, as a condition of funding, be a partnership. Rather than being a purely governmental structure, they must include civil society, the private sector, technical partners, and representatives of people living with or affected by the three diseases.[19]

Governance of the Internet is likewise premised on the broad participation of private actors. Internet governance from its inception was multi-stakeholder.[20] As the Internet grew dramatically in the 1990s the original and often ad hoc governance structures fell under strain. The US government, which had helped create the original Internet, sought a more formalized structure. The International Corporation for Assigned Names and Numbers, or ICANN, established in 1998, created a finely wrought structure of multi-stakeholder governance.[21] States are present in ICANN via a Governmental Advisory Committee, yet this is only one of several stakeholder deliberative bodies that can offer recommendations to the ICANN board, the ultimate decision-maker.

There are many other examples of inclusive, participatory global governance one could canvas. Multi-stakeholder governance is arguably the aspirational standard for legitimate global governance in many contexts.[22] Indeed, many international organizations describe their own engagement with incorporating private actors as an evolution. As the IMF recently stated:

> Over the years, the IMF has become more transparent and accountable—not only to member countries but also to the broader public. When the IMF began to engage with CSOs [civil society organizations] in the 1980s, it was usually at a global level, in response to advocacy by groups concerned with economic and social justice.[23]

Still, it is important to underscore that the movement towards more inclusive governance is not uniform. This is important empirically but also theoretically, as it makes clear the important ways states continue to control the terms of engagement and to meter out—and block—non-state actor participation when they choose to. The two chief areas of focus in this volume provide a useful contrast. While global health

[19] Berman, 'Stakeholder Participation Reforms.' (n 18).

[20] Kal Raustiala, 'Governing the Internet' 110(3) *American Journal of International Law* (2016) 491-503.

[21] Kal Raustiala, 'An Internet Whole and Free: Why Obama Was Right to Give Up Control' 96(2) *Foreign Affairs* (2017) 140.

[22] See Luc Fransen, 'Multi-Stakeholder Governance and Voluntary Programme Interactions: Legitimation Politics in the Institutional Design of Corporate Social Responsibility' 10 *Socio-Economic Review* (2012) 163-192.

[23] International Monetary Fund, 'Factsheet: The IMF and Civil Society Organizations' (5 April 2016) <www.imf.org/external/np/exr/facts/civ.htm>, last accessed 05/15/2020.

governance is increasingly inclusive and often avowedly multi-stakeholder in structure, global finance is far more closed. For example, Margetti and Kovarzina note with regard to the Basel Committee on Banking Supervision:

> The preparation of so-called Basel I (1988) was a closed meeting with limited transparency and no public input. Basel II (2004), on the other hand, was developed with the use of notice-and-comment procedure allowing for public input. The procedure consisted of the Basel Committee publishing a number of papers on their website for the public to be able to consult. It also allowed the public to make comments which were then collected and given feedback.[24]

These are useful steps, but a far cry from the sort of direct decisional roles for non-state actors we see in the Global Fund or GAVI. Likewise, the Financial Action Task Force, created in 1989, has incorporated some non-state actors, but almost none are private: participants include Interpol, the Organization for Security and Cooperation in Europe, and the UN Office on Drugs and Crime. IOSCO, the International Organization of Securities Commission, similarly has only government regulators as members and little opportunity for engagement with private actors.[25] The contrast with global health is striking and highlights that states continue to control access and participation in varied ways. Still, even in a very state-centric arena such as global financial regulation there has been change over time—sometimes marked, as in the IMF—and that change is generally in one direction: towards greater inclusion of private actors.

The core argument of this chapter is that this evolution in approach broadly reflects political incentives that governments face. Public power is often enhanced by private actors, and states thus have sought to incorporate diverse stakeholders because their wider participation serves their interests. But before turning to the political imperatives of governments, it is important to note that many other variables are at play in this evolution, and these also help explain why multi-stakeholder governance is more prominent today. At least four broad factors can be identified that have facilitated greater stakeholder engagement.[26]

First, and at a very basic level, technological change has made inclusion easier by making travel and communication easier. Phones and faxes and eventually the Internet and mobile connections have made it feasible for small groups and even individuals to participate in global governance. Jet travel has had a similar, and maybe even more profound, effect, enabling frequent meetings that, in turn, opened up the door to greater stakeholder participation. These developments have varied impact; stakeholders in wealthy societies obviously can leverage them more effectively. But the overall effect remains: technological change has dramatically enhanced the possibility of inclusion.

[24] Olga Kovarzina and Martino Margetti, 'Stakeholder Participation Reforms in Global Finance Governance.' Chapter 4, this volume.

[25] Kovarzina and Margetti, 'Stakeholder Participation Reforms' (n 24).

[26] This section draws on Raustiala, 'NGOs in International Treatymaking' (n 4).

A second factor, already noted, was the creation of the UN itself and the entrenchment of multilateralism as the default form for post-war cooperation. Multilateralism established a profound principle: participation in international affairs should not rest simply on power. By moving to a system grounded in notions of (sovereign) equality and broad participation, which entailed some quite small and weak states sitting nominally as equals with the great powers, it became easier to argue that other, non-sovereign, actors might also have something to offer.

The UN itself provided a focal point and a formalized means of access—NGO accreditation—that spurred significant civil society involvement. And in a broad sense, the twentieth century proliferation of international organizations was conducive to widening participation in global governance. As José Alvarez writes:

> Matters of interstate diplomacy were, at least in the 19th century, regarded as confidential interstate matters. Modern treaty-making under IO auspices, by contrast, is characterized by a much greater openness to the accumulated wisdom, shared experiences, and institutional biases and blind spots, of a variety of actors beyond the government representatives set to negotiate ... Certain structural aspects of IOs, including provision for access to documents and for 'observer' or other forms of non-voting status, have provided entry points for NGOs' growing participation in various forms of inter-state diplomacy, including treaty-making.[27]

A third factor promoting multi-stakeholder participation was the post-war growth in democratic states, which, thanks to their more open domestic civil societies, often birth domestic organizations that in turn may address international issues. Democratic states also unsurprisingly tend to be comfortable with the active involvement of a wide array of stakeholders in governance. And in practice, many democracies are wealthy, with well-developed administrative states. These domestic regulatory processes often incorporate wide participation via notice and comment processes, advisory committees, legislative hearings, and the like. This broad model is easily replicable at the global level, and directly relates to the next factor.

Fourth is the increasing tendency to govern globally those arenas that were traditionally governed nationally or even locally. Many issues, such as tobacco regulation, banking, and transboundary air pollution, were long thought of as subjects for national, not international, policy. Over the course of the last several decades, however, global governance has embraced these topics, and more. A much wider concept of regulation has blurred the lines between traditionally 'domestic' and 'international' topics. Consequently, many private actors have moved from a purely domestic orientation to an embrace of international forums, as global governance itself has expanded its ambit.

[27] José E Alvarez, *International Organizations as Law-Makers* (Oxford University Press 2005) 277–284. This may be because NGOs help provide an alternative power and legitimacy base to IOs. On this point see Kenneth Anderson, 'What NGO Accountability Means—And Does Not Mean' 103(1) *American Journal of International Law* (2009) 170-178, reviewing Lisa Jordan and Peter van Tuijl (eds), *NGO Accountability: Politics, Principles & Innovations* (Earthscan 2006).

Multinational firms and trade associations that traditionally lobby parliaments and executives, for example, are now more active in treaty negotiations, which often produce rules that in turn determine national regulatory policies. This is even true for issues of international security: once the UN began negotiations on a small arms treaty, for example, the powerful American NGO the National Rifle Association became an active player.[28] The shift to greater global governance of traditionally domestic issues has led to more extensive demands by domestic actors for inclusion. Arguably it has also led to a change in the style of global processes, as these stakeholders bring expectations and tactics forged in domestic settings into the diplomatic arena.

The confluence of all these factors (and surely others) yielded a very large increase in the post-war era in the number and range of stakeholders engaged in global governance. Many terms are used to capture this change, and indeed this broad rise is visible via some telling changes in the nomenclature used to discuss global governance. According to a Google Ngram search of over five million published books in English (Figure 24.1), the term 'stakeholder' was uncommon in the immediate post-war era and surged in use in the 1990s and 2000s.[29] By contrast, the term 'NGO' has a much longer pedigree, and indeed had an early peak of usage in the 1960s which was not surpassed till the end of the Cold War. Strikingly, as of about 2008 stakeholder had become a more common phrase than NGO.

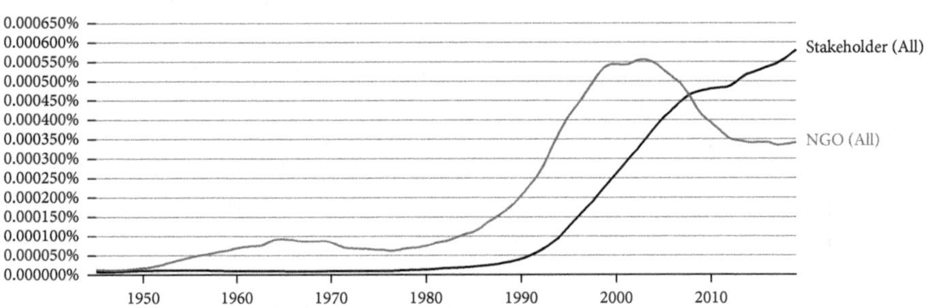

Figure 24.1 Google Ngram Search using Terms 'Stakeholder' and 'NGO'

The term 'multistakeholder' (or in the alternative spelling 'multi-stakeholder') is even more novel (Figure 24.2). In English the term first appears in the mid-1970s. By 1988 multi-stakeholder was used in 0.0000000460% of the sources searched. Twenty years later, the frequency had grown to 0.0000061487%—a remarkable increase of well over 10,000%.

[28] See Clifford Bob, 'Packing Heat: Pro Gun Groups and the Governance of Small Arms' in Avant *et al.* (eds) 183-201 (n 4).

[29] Unfortunately, I cannot limit the results to those relevant for global governance only.

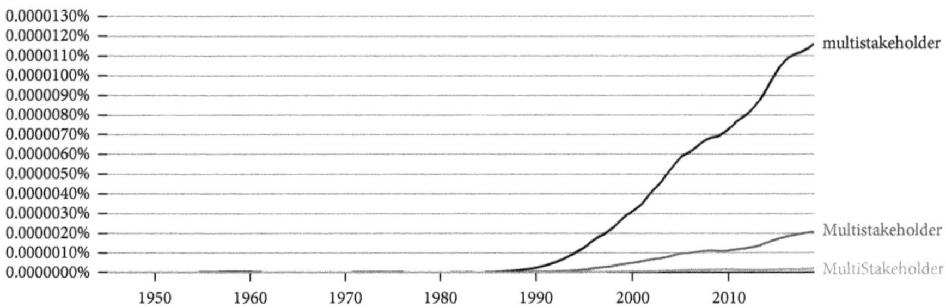

Figure 24.2 Google Ngram Search using Three Versions of the Term 'Multistakeholder'

It is hard to draw precise inferences from this data. But it is clear—and interesting—that the way we talk about global governance has changed, in many ways dramatically. The more inclusive and broader concept of global governance was simply unknown in the early post-war years, though the state-centric term multilateral was common (and remains so.) NGOs were well known, 'stakeholders' less so; 'multi-stakeholder' not at all. Today, all these terms are in wide use and, indeed, stakeholder has overtaken NGO as the preferred phrase in many settings.

24.3 Explaining the Inclusion of Private Actors

The wide participation that private actors now enjoy is not a hijacking of the process of international organization. Nor is it a major displacement of the central role traditionally played by governments. Rather, patterns of private participation are shaped by public actors and this participation is often beneficial to those public actors. The background factors just discussed are largely permissive factors. It is the political incentives modern governments face that frequently compel them to work with a wide array of stakeholders, especially those that possess specialized and useful resources and political power. That private stakeholders often (intentionally or not) serve the interests of governments is one reason—and I argue the most important one—that multi-stakeholder governance has become so pervasive.

Consequently, the relationship between public and private actors is in many respects mutually reinforcing. Private actors bring much to the governance process. Yet the sovereign state remains the leading actor in the international system, and private actors generally need the coercive power of governments to realize the changes they seek. Because states remain the core of the international order and multilateralism the default approach to cooperation, governments still largely control the terms of the relationship, even if in some newer governance processes—such as GAVI or ICANN—multi-stakeholderism is built in from the start.

Why then do governments permit private actors to participate so extensively? There are several distinct benefits for governments in doing so. Although not all governments enjoy or value these benefits, and some oppose wider participation, in the aggregate governments benefit often enough that broad, general rules and practices that include varied stakeholders make sense. I divide these benefits in two broad categories: those related to information provision, and those related to political incentives.

24.4 Information Provision

Perhaps the chief benefit for governments of broad-based participation is the provision of information. This information can come in several forms. Most centrally, private actors can provide important information about policy options and outcomes. This is especially valuable in issue-areas with high levels of uncertainty and technical or scientific complexity.

Consider the challenge of climate change. There are many large, expertly staffed private groups that devote considerable resources to climate policy research and development—research that can help governments (and others) develop and evaluate often-complex regulatory options. NGOs, academic institutions, and think tanks commonly provide such information to policy makers freely. Indeed, they typically compete to do so. Many such groups exist, and the competition among them provides not only a varied array of options and analyses, but also a check on accuracy, analytic quality, and the like. The result is that governments can gain useful and creative policy advice from many independent sources—and typically at no cost.

To be sure, a substantial portion of the world's policy expertise on climate change rests within governments or is funded by them. States have also created the Intergovernmental Panel on Climate Change (IPCC) as a way to gather and channel the best scientific advice. But private policy research provides perspectives that may not have emerged from a bureaucratic review process. Like lobbyists or experts testifying in domestic rule-making, private actors act as conduits for ideas and information.

Global health provides another excellent example of this dynamic. Global health policy was traditionally viewed as a virtual monopoly of specialists in the health sciences. Over time, however, the important role of local governments, of cultural and social practices, and of the experience of individuals living with specific diseases and conditions were recognized as critical to the creation and implementation of any effective policy. The inclusion of non-state actors reflected the ascendance of this view: that effective intervention could not rely on conventional expertise alone, and that a wide array of information sources would lead to better policy.

While civil society often receives the bulk of attention, the same logic applies to private firms. The pharmaceutical industry has a seat on GAVI thanks to its technical expertise.[30] Likewise, the International Conference on Harmonisation (ICH) relies on the scientific expertise of the pharmaceutical industry in the development of pharmaceutical standards. The World Health Organization (WHO) also cites 'the contribution of non-state actors to the Work of the WHO', and 'the additional resources non-state actors can contribute to the WHO's work' among the reasons it engages with a wide range of private actors.[31] Including a more varied array of stakeholders

[30] GAVI, 'Industrialised Country Pharmaceutical Industry' <www.gavi.org/about/partners/industrialised-country-vaccine-industry/>, last accessed 05/15/2020.

[31] World Health Organization, 'WHO Framework of Engagement with Non-State Actors' WHA69.10 (28 May 2016), Article 6 <http://apps.who.int/gb/ebwha/pdf_files/WHA69/A69_R10-en.pdf?ua=1>, last accessed 05/15/2020.

in decision-making is politically and morally appealing to many, to be sure; but it also provides a broader and sounder basis for decision-making.

Other global governance bodies similarly tap into private information by involving private actors directly. Codex Alimentarius, a standard-setting body, expressly states that the '... purpose of collaboration with International NGOs is to secure for the Codex Alimentarius Commission expert information, advice, and assistance from international NGOs ... '.[32] The IMF proclaims that it 'recognizes the benefits of a transparent and wide engagement with [civil society organizations], as a means for improving its policy advice and analysis'.[33] Likewise, the OECD Business and Industry Advisory Committee conveys 'business perspectives and expertise to policymakers on a broad range of global economic governance and policy issues'.[34] The World Intellectual Property Organization has incorporated private actors widely for many years, relying on them to critique and improve treaty proposals.

In sum, a wide array of governance bodies includes private actors; these private actors provide substantial and specialized expertise; and it is certainly plausible—and consistent with many stated rationales—that the provision of information that private actors possess is an important reason for this pattern of incorporation. The incorporation of expertise and information goes furthest in avowedly multi-stakeholder processes, in which private actors are not merely participants but also decision makers. For example, groups such as the Internet Engineering Task Force play a key (and legally defined) role in the Internet governance process precisely because they possess so much information about critical technical expertise. Likewise, the Global Fund and GAVI are partnerships in which private actors—the pharmaceutical industry and civil society—are not only participants but important decision makers.

Broader participation is not always normatively preferable, however. There is no reason to think that governance processes are necessarily better when more inclusive. While inclusion may improve governance—and plausibly does in many settings—more voices may simply lead to more deadlock. More participation may yield more capture. In the domestic administrative law context, these dynamics are well known.[35] A substantial literature exists on how and why regulatory capture occurs.[36]

Codex, for example, is formally open to both commercial and public interest NGOs. But in practice it is dominated by commercial NGOs. Likewise, the ICH is widely perceived as being strongly influenced by pharmaceutical industry interests.[37]

[32] Food and Agriculture Organization and World Health Organization (Codex Alimentarius Commission), 'Proposed Draft Principles Concerning the Participation of International Non-Governmental Organizations in the Work of the Codex Alimentarius Commission' (September 1998) CL 1998/31-GP <www.fao.org/tempref/codex/Meetings/CCGP/CCGP14/cl98_31e.pdf>, last accessed 05/15/2020.

[33] International Monetary Fund, '2015 Guidelines on IMF Staff Engagement with Civil Society Organizations' (2015) <www.imf.org/external/np/exr/consult/2015/civilsociety/pdf/CSOs_Guidelines.pdf>, last accessed 05/15/2020.

[34] The Business and Industry Advisory Committee to the OECD, 'Business at OECD (BIAC)' <http://biac.org/quick-facts/>, last accessed 05/15/2020.

[35] The classic cite is Samuel Huntington, 'The Marasmus of the ICC: The Commission, the Railroads, and the Public Interest' 61(4) *Yale Law Journal* (1952) 467-509.

[36] See Daniel Carpenter and David Moss (eds), *Preventing Regulatory Capture: Special Interest Influence and How to Limit It* (Cambridge University Press 2013).

[37] See Robert Gatter, 'Conflicts of Interest in International Human Drug Research and the Insufficiency of International Protections' 32 *American Journal of Law and Medicine* (2006) 351-364, 362; John Abraham

This pattern exists in other fields as well. Many comments submitted in the context of the Basel Committee's public consultation in the development of its accords were from the banking industry, suggesting that even when procedures are formally open to the public, commercial interests dominate them.[38] And even the Global Fund, whose multi-stakeholder model suggests equality among participants, has been criticized for the de facto power imbalances between the commercial and public interest sector in its consultative processes.[39] Despite the risk of capture by regulated industries or particularistic interests, very few global bodies have enacted regulatory frameworks for managing participation.[40]

In short, inclusive processes do not necessarily mean balanced or fair processes. Often participation will be skewed towards those private actors with the greatest resources, the greatest interest, or both. Often, they are one and the same: as substantial domestic experience shows, regulated actors will have the greatest incentive to shape regulation, and these actors may also have the greatest resources to do so. My argument does not depend on stakeholder participation yielding better governance, although that can be a happy and desirable by-product. It only depends on it being valuable to governments when they govern globally.[41]

In addition to providing valuable information about policy options, private actors also may provide useful information on compliance with international rules. Many NGOs have a worldwide reach and expend significant resources documenting problems in their area of focus around the world. Much of this effort uses a legal frame and often identifies specific global commitments that are being violated or improperly implemented. These reports can be influential and may garner significant media attention (and given that many international accords lack meaningful review of implementation or rely merely on self-reporting by parties about their compliance, private monitoring can be an important addition to what little occurs via more official channels.)[42]

The role of private stakeholders in monitoring implementation is clearly contentious, and governments differ on how much of a role, even informal, they are comfortable with private actors playing. But it also reflects some political realities that make private monitoring of commitments attractive to many governments. Principles of

and Rachel Ballinger, 'The Neoliberal Regulatory State, Industry Interests, and the Ideological Penetration of Scientific Knowledge: Deconstructing the Redefinition of Carcinogens in Pharmaceuticals' 37(5) *Science, Technology & Human Values* (2012) 443-477.

[38] Joseph J Norton, 'A Perceived Trend in Modern International Financial Regulation: Increasing Reliance on a Public-Private Partnership' 37 *The International Lawyer* (2003) 43-59, 54.

[39] Berman, 'Stakeholder Participation Reforms' (n 18).

[40] The WHO is the rare exception. The WHO straightforwardly addresses these risks of capture in its 'Framework of Engagement' (n 31) adopted in 2016.

[41] It is not always necessary to admit private actors into negotiating sessions or decision processes to convey the kind of information I have described earlier in the chapter. But it seems likely that inclusive processes foster a broader portfolio of arguments than do exclusive processes. Expertise transcends official position papers, and private actors can and do speak informally with decision makers to flesh out details and provide commentary on other ideas.

[42] On this phenomenon see Kal Raustiala, *Reporting and Review Institutions in Ten Multilateral Environmental Agreements* (UNEP 2001) <https://www.peacepalacelibrary.nl/ebooks/files/C08-0025-Raustiala-Reporting.pdf>, last accessed 05/15/2020.

sovereignty and general political disinterest in monitoring in some states make it relatively costly to create direct, formal evaluation by other parties or by international organizations. Due to their informal, decentralized nature, private efforts are less readily blocked; private actors would have to be kept out of the process altogether, for even formal bans on compliance discussions or papers can be circumvented around the fringes of meetings and negotiations. In short, in many instances private actors 'supply the personnel and resources for managing compliance that States have become increasingly reluctant to provide'.[43] Again, not all governments welcome this role. But once private stakeholders are actively participating in global governance, even if they are initially welcomed for other reasons, such as technical expertise, they may gravitate towards monitoring, implementation, and enforcement.

Private stakeholders may also provide information about the behaviour of government delegations. Governments want to control the decisions of their national delegations and appointed officials. Treaty negotiations in particular often create tensions between branches of government, where important aspects of foreign affairs may not be directly controlled by legislatures, for instance. Governments may fear that delegates will exceed their mandates or create political headaches through their positions. Direct participation by private actors is one means by which other officials can enable outside parties to alert them to undesired actions—what I have elsewhere called a form of 'fire alarm'.[44] In other words, private actors can help minimize a principal–agent problem. As interested parties, at least some private stakeholders have an incentive to both monitor delegates' actions and inform governmental principals of their findings. Because groups of many persuasions exist, movement in many directions can be covered. This decentralized process is both effective and low cost. Delegates that move too far away from the preferences of their principals are more likely to be identified and checked.[45]

24.5 Political Incentives

Bringing private stakeholders directly into the process also has political benefits. Private actors get a closer look at the positions of the relevant parties with regard to decision-making—especially the positions and preferences of other states. Specific areas of controversy are more apparent, as are the areas where compromise is possible. Problems are more readily identified and, perhaps, addressed.

Negotiating positions have sometimes been described by scholars in spatial terms, with various positions corresponding to points in a multidimensional 'policy space'. The set of points acceptable to all parties is the bargaining zone. As active participants, private actors become more aware of the shape of the bargaining zone. Revealing the

[43] Abram Chayes and Antonia Handler Chayes, *The New Sovereignty: Compliance with International Regulatory Agreements* (Harvard University Press 1995) 251.

[44] On this analogy, drawn from work in American politics, see Kal Raustiala, 'Police Patrols and Fire Alarms in the NAAEC' 26 *Loyola of Los Angeles International and Comparative Law Review* (2004) 389-413.

[45] Unless the NGOs present agree more with the delegates than their principals. But from the principal's point of view, creating a fire alarm of this kind that is only occasionally pulled in the presence of a fire is still superior to having no alarm at all.

bargaining structure in this way may help to diffuse criticism and placate at least some unsatisfied interests, as stakeholders become more knowledgeable about obstacles—and perhaps more invested in the success of the process. As with many bureaucracies, outsiders often go native—internalizing dominant views and prevailing assumptions. This is most powerful when the private actors involved in global governance are also powerful actors domestically. Bringing in a more diverse set of stakeholders may also lead to new ideas about how to reach desirable points in that bargaining space, since private actors have many incentives to provide practical proposals that overcome apparent deadlocks. These effects are probably most pronounced in negotiations over new rules. But they can also appear in other settings; virtually any decision about implementation, for example, will contain some degree of bargaining.

Private party participation may also facilitate the approval and implementation of international rules at the domestic level. Most states have some constitutionally-mandated process of review and consent that is required prior to treaty ratification. In many cases this involves the legislature. Legislatures (and other domestic actors who are veto players) may well reject an agreement that has been painstakingly negotiated—think of the famous rejection by the US Senate of the Treaty of Versailles. To use Robert Putnam's famous concept, there are two levels of the negotiating game, and successful cooperation requires alignment between the two.[46] One way to secure alignment is to bring some of the important domestic players directly to the international table, thereby effectively 'bridging' the levels. Problems can be rectified early, during the negotiation process, rather than late, when renegotiation may be extremely difficult.

This is especially valuable when private actors are powerful domestically. Global governance regimes typically must have some domestic support to succeed. Private-interest groups can provide this support, or they can withhold it. Thus, bridging the two-level game is an attractive strategy for minimizing ratification risk and improving implementation. By bringing these important societal actors into the negotiations process directly, information flow is enhanced, and more importantly, potential opponents may be turned into supporters—or at least abstainers. This logic is one reason Franklin Delano Roosevelt, cognizant of the bitter experience of the League in the US Senate, included Republican senators in his delegation to negotiate the UN Charter in San Francisco.

Global governance bodies are not unaware of this process. For example, in explaining its commitment to working with civil society organizations, or CSOs, the IMF argues that 'Engagement with CSOs can, especially over time, enhance and help translate IMF policy advice to member countries into successful policy.'[47] The WHO's Framework of Engagement justifies engagement with non-state actors on the basis of the benefits it brings to the work of the WHO, including 'the influence that WHO can have on non-state actors' compliance with WHO's policies, norms and standards' and 'the wider dissemination of and adherence by non-State actors to WHO's policies, norms and standards'.[48] The inclusion of the pharmaceutical industry—the target of

[46] Robert D Putnam, 'Diplomacy and Domestic Politics: The Logic of Two-Level Games' 42(3) *International Organization* (1988) 427-460.

[47] IMF, 'Guidelines on IMF Staff Engagement' (n 33).

[48] WHO, 'Framework of Engagement' (n 31).

ICH regulation—as ICH members, likewise counters potential resistance at the implementation stage.

This in turn may help explain why participation is often unequally distributed amongst private actors. Berman and colleagues note that, while 'new forms of global governance are often *de jure* broadly open to participation by a broad range of stakeholders, most are de facto inaccessible to non-commercial, diffuse interests'.[49] The latter type of stakeholder is typically less politically potent than concentrated commercial interests.

Similar dynamics exist in financial regulatory bodies. Bradlow argues that:

> [T]he Basel Committee is likely to consult, directly or indirectly, with large private banks and organisations representing banks and other entities that it sees as relevant to its work. Thus, informally these consultations are likely to create opportunities for participation by certain entities from outside the Basel Committee member countries in the work of the Basel Committee. However, since the Basel Committee has the discretion in deciding with whom to consult, it is less likely to consult with consumer groups and other civil society groups that may have in interest in the Committee's work. This will be true for civil society groups both from Basel Committee member countries and from elsewhere.[50]

Private actors may also have a direct role in implementation. For example, civil society organizations, thanks to their local knowledge and networks, play a key role in implementing Global Fund and GAVI policies and projects. Civil society organizations deliver most of GAVI's immunization services, its support logistics, and train its health workers.[51]

In earlier research focused on treaty negotiations I argued that if the skills, resources, and political power private actors wield are useful to state actors, demand for these resources should increase when the scope, complexity, and obligations of a treaty regime grow.[52] The major new governance initiatives of the 1990s, 2000s, and 2010s—such as the International Criminal Court, chemical weapons control, climate change, tobacco control, and disability rights—are generally more complex and more technically demanding than earlier treaties. And indeed the rules and practices governing participation by private actors in global governance have generally become more inclusive—sometimes much more so.

Moreover, the ways in which non-state actors have been included in treaty processes are broadly consistent with a symbiotic understanding of public and private power. Private actors possess many resources, but those resources and skills are not uniformly useful over time. Policy expertise is most useful at the early stages of negotiations, monitoring most useful in the implementation phase. When governments

[49] Berman *et al.*, 'Introduction' (n 2).

[50] Daniel Bradlow, 'Assessing International Financial Reform' in Julio Faundez and Celine Tan (eds), *International Economic Law, Globalization and Developing Countries* (Edward Elgar 2010) 67-93, 87.

[51] GAVI, 'Civil Society Organisations' <https://www.gavi.org/operating-model/gavis-partnership-model/civil-society>, last accessed 05/10/2020.

[52] Raustiala, 'NGOs in International Treatymaking' (n 4); Kal Raustiala, 'The 'Participatory Revolution' in International Environmental Law' 21(2) *Harvard Environmental Law Review* (1997) 537-586.

desire secrecy to air possible compromises or are at the stage of political horse-trading once positions have solidified, they may find participation undesirable or not useful. And when implementation becomes essential private actors may again prove useful. In short, governments face incentives to keep private actors out at some times and bring them in at others. By this logic, they ought to attempt to meter or calibrate participation.

In practice, states have achieved this calibration through the proliferation of working groups and informal meetings that occur in global governance. The negotiation process of the WHO's 2003 Framework Convention on Tobacco Control is representative. This was a major health treaty initiative, one of the most important advances of the era. As one close observer notes, a group of stakeholders called the Framework Convention Alliance 'encompassed more than 180 NGOs from over 70 countries and had established itself as an important lobbying alliance'. However, its impact in the final negotiations was 'hampered by the imposition of restrictions on NGO access to the negotiating sessions. Most sessions of the final INB [the chief negotiating body] were designated as informal, thus providing a pretext for the exclusion of NGO participants'.[53]

This general pattern is not atypical. As in many negotiations, the Tobacco Convention featured wider access and participation early on—as the basic structure of the regime was being defined and core policy prescriptions debated—and less access later, when the details of essentially fixed positions were being hammered out. This pattern is consistent with the basic claim that private participation does not come at the expense of public power, but instead is often symbiotic with it. Inclusive governance is often—though not always—helpful to governments, even if some actors may oppose the interests of some governments.

24.6 Conclusion

States have traditionally been the central players in global governance. Despite a host of changes that have brought in both new modes of organization and new players, they remain central today. Governments retain substantial power and when they chose, they can often wield that power to ensure that governance is multilateral, not multistakeholder, in nature. Still, global governance in the twenty-first century has distinctive features when compared to the past. Most noteworthy is the tremendous increase in private actors' participation and the rise of multi-stakeholderism. To understand what this change towards more inclusive governance means we must understand why it is has occurred.

I have argued that some fundamental exogeneous trends—such as the rise of cheap air travel and the increase in the number of democracies—have encouraged greater participation by private actors in global governance. But a deeper cause of the increase has been the benefits that accrue to governments themselves from a more inclusive process. This is particularly true for highly complex and technical issues, where

[53] Jeff Collin, 'Tobacco Politics' 47(2) *Development* (2004) 91-96, 93.

governance is especially challenging and expertise especially valuable. By bringing valuable resources, networks, and information to the table, multi-stakeholder processes have allowed for more effective—and sometimes more efficient—regulation of a host of critical global issues. Private power, in short, has often served public power.

This apparently symbiotic relationship should not be a surprise. We observe it often in domestic regulatory settings. In domestic law, detailed procedures exist to give private actors notice and the ability to comment on proposed regulations. Legislative hearings and other mechanisms allow even greater engagement. Private actors often play important roles in domestic regulation, and they provide extensive input to decision-making—and at times even act as direct decision makers. Yet the rise of powerful regulatory states has gone hand-in-hand with greater inclusivity. Wider participation enabled more and often more effective domestic regulation; wider participation also reflected that the regulatory power of the state was growing.

The army of lobbyists and private associations in London, Washington, and other major national capitals reflects not the weakness of the modern administrative state, but its power. As global governance increasingly tackles a wider array of complex regulatory challenges, there is no reason to think the international domain will be any different.

25
Conclusion
The Participation of Marginalized Stakeholders in Global Governance

*Tim Büthe, Joost Pauwelyn, Martino Maggetti, and Ayelet Berman**

25.1 Voice and Influence in the Aftermath of Reforms

As global governance has become more authoritative in recent decades, questions about its accountability and legitimacy have become ever more prominent. One key concern is the marginalization or even outright exclusion of many of the governed (and other affected 'stakeholders') from rule-making or operational decision-making in global governance bodies.[1] To be sure, actual voice and influence in global governance have *de facto* long been highly unequal, even in universal-membership organizations that *de jure* and explicitly espouse sovereign equality. Inclusiveness and providing equal opportunities to all stakeholders has not generally been a core concern of global governance.[2] Yet, many global governance bodies have taken up this issue in recent years. They have undertaken various institutional reforms with the declared objective to boost the participation of traditionally 'disregarded'[3] or 'external'[4] stakeholders[5]—often in response to legitimacy challenges from those marginalized

* We are grateful for the input of all contributors to this volume, especially the authors of the comparative case study analyses, which constitute the empirical core of this project, as well as the discussants at conference presentations and at the three workshops for the project. We also gratefully acknowledge funding support from the Swiss Network for International Studies (SNIS), supplemented by various forms of support from the Graduate Institute Geneva, Duke University, and the *Hochschule für Politik* at the Technical University of Munich.

[1] The legitimacy of governance, if the governance arrangement does not closely coincide with a well-established community, is open to challenges for a host of reasons, but the problem of marginalized and excluded stakeholders is surely one of the key issues; see Michael Zürn, 'Global Governance and Legitimacy Problems' 39(2) *Governance and Opposition* (2004) 260-287.

[2] See Mercy DeMenno and Tim Büthe, 'Voice and Influence in Global Governance: An Analytical Framework.' Chapter 2, this volume.

[3] Richard Stewart, 'Remedying Disregard in Global Regulatory Governance: Accountability, Participation, and Responsiveness' 108(2) *American Journal of International Law* (2014) 211-270.

[4] Joost Pauwelyn, Ramses Wessel and Jan Wouters (eds), *Informal International Lawmaking* (Oxford University Press 2012).

[5] See, e.g. Benedict Kingsbury *et al.* (eds), 'Symposium: The Emergence of Global Administrative Law' 68(3–4) *Law and Contemporary Problems* (2005) 1–377; Jan Klabbers, Anne Peters and Geir Ulfstein (eds), *The Constitutionalization of International Law* (Oxford University Press 2009); Jonas Tallberg, Thomas Sommerer, Theresa Squatrito and Christer Jönsson, *The Opening Up of International Organizations: Transnational Access in Global Governance* (Cambridge University Press 2013); Andrea Bianchi and Anne Peters (eds), *Transparency in International Law* (Cambridge University Press 2013); Alexandru Grigorescu, *Democratic International Organizations? Normative Pressures and Decision-Making Rules* (Cambridge University Press 2015).

Tim Büthe, Joost Pauwelyn, Martino Maggetti, and Ayelet Berman, *Conclusion* In: *Rethinking Participation in Global Governance.* Edited by: Joost Pauwelyn, Martino Maggetti, Tim Büthe, and Ayelet Berman, Oxford University Press. DOI: 10.1093/oso/9780198852568.003.0025

stakeholders and others, including governments, legislatures, scholars, and civil society organizations.[6]

We launched the *Rethinking Participation* project in 2015 to better understand the *consequences* of those reforms. A key objective in doing so was to challenge the still-common presumption that increased 'participation' is sufficiently achieved by broadening eligibility criteria for membership, creating new categories of (often lower status) membership, re-arranging the 'deck chairs' of highly unequal weighted votes on the ship of global governance, or offering stakeholders a range of opportunities to provide 'input' without any guarantee that such input would be taken into consideration in rule- or decision-making. We sought instead to problematize participation, distinguishing between mere voice opportunities and actual influence, that is, the exercise of power. We also sought to theorize the micro-foundations of participation in global governance. Specifically, we therefore asked:

- Have the stakeholder participation reforms, adopted by global bodies in recent years, increased the *actual engagement* of the previously disregarded stakeholders in global governance? Under what conditions do those stakeholders make use of the expanded *voice* opportunities?
- Have the reforms increased previously disregarded stakeholders' *influence* in global bodies' rule- and decision-making? To what extent have they gained any real influence—and why?

In an interdisciplinary (law and international relations) collaboration with emerging and established scholars—and several practitioners—from the global North and South, from across the Americas, Asia, and Europe, we have examined the consequences of varied institutional reforms. Following Richard Stewart, we have distinguished—and separately analysed—reforms that created decisional and non-decisional participation opportunities[7] in a variety of global governance bodies, ranging from traditional treaty-based international organizations to transnational private standard-setting bodies.

We have examined stakeholder participation reforms and their consequences across two major policy fields: finance and health. Within each of these policy fields, we have employed paired comparisons, comparing each of the three largest 'rising powers' in the world economy with a smaller (and arguably less powerful) but otherwise maximally comparable developing country from the same region, resulting in matched pairs of country case studies: China and Vietnam; Brazil and Argentina; India and Bangladesh/the Philippines.[8]

As explained in Section 25.2, this book has focused, first and foremost, on the consequences for governments of developing countries. Yet, seeking to go beyond

[6] Ngaire Woods, 'Multilateralism and Building Stronger International Institutions' in Alnoor Ebrahim and Edward Weisband (eds), *Global Accountabilities: Participation, Pluralism, and Public Ethics* (Cambridge University Press 2007) 27-44.

[7] Stewart, 'Remedying Disregard' (n 3).

[8] Tim Büthe and Cindy Cheng, 'Analysing the Consequences of Institutional Reforms Using Country Pairs.' Chapter 3, this volume.

state-centric analyses, we have also examined the consequences of the reforms for the similarly pervasively disregarded non-commercial and diffuse societal interests.

Returning to our project's title of 'Rethinking Participation', this concluding chapter begins with a few reflections about participation and legitimacy in global governance. We then summarize the findings of the empirical parts of this volume and, to put them in a larger context, discuss what the findings imply for the hypotheses developed in the analytical framework for the book.[9] Specifically, Section 25.3 summarizes the variation in new or expanded stakeholder voice opportunities in the key bodies for governing global finance and global health, with a special focus on changes that have been most pertinent for the stakeholders from our matched country pairs. Section 25.4 first summarizes the findings from the country case studies regarding the actual engagement of previously marginalized or excluded stakeholders in global finance or health governance in the aftermath of reforms. The section then discusses the implications of our findings for the possible explanations of actual stakeholder voice, hypothesised in chapter 2. Section 25.5 addresses the issue of stakeholder *influence* in the aftermath of reforms. The section thus seeks to answer the final set of questions that motivated our project. Section 25.6 highlights five interesting and important findings that are beyond our analytical framework, which we highlight as fruitful avenues for future research. Finally, Section 25.7 offers concluding reflections on the status of marginalized stakeholders' participation in global governance as of 2020—including a comparative reflection on the two policy fields of finance and health, which we have heretofore mostly examined separately.

25.2 Participation and Legitimacy in Global Governance

In domestic politics, political participation has been defined as 'all voluntary activities by citizens intended to influence, either directly or indirectly, political choices at various levels of the political system'.[10] The opportunity to participate in this sense is considered an essential requirement of a democratic political system, underpinning its legitimacy.[11]

Extrapolating insights from political theory and philosophy regarding political systems, in which individuals are the units, to political systems, in which the operational units are larger aggregates, is perilous under the best of circumstance, but necessary for advancing our understanding of global governance. Much of the global governance literature on participation and legitimacy has done so by substituting 'civil society [groups]' for 'citizens' in the above conceptualization of participation.[12] From the international law perspective, this focus on civil society is a welcome departure from

[9] DeMenno and Büthe, 'Voice and Influence' (n 2).

[10] Klaus Dingwerth and Patrizia Nanz, 'Participation' in Jacob Katz Cogan, Ian Hurd, and Ian Johnstone (eds), *The Oxford Handbook of International Organizations* (Oxford University Press 2015) 1126-1145, 1126.

[11] Robert A Dahl, *Polyarchy: Participation and Opposition* (Yale University Press 1971).

[12] See e.g. Jens Steffek, Claudia Kissling, and Patrizia Nanz (eds), *Civil Society Participation in European and Global Governance* (Palgrave Macmillan 2008); Lisa M Dellmuth and Elizabeth A Bloodgood, eds., Special Issue on 'Advocacy Group Effects in Global Governance' 8(3) *Interest Groups and Advocacy* (2019) 255-498; Marcel Hanegraaff, Jorik Vergauwen, and Jan Beyers, 'Should I Stay or Should I Go? Explaining Variation in Nonstate Actor Advocacy over Time in Global Governance' 33(2) *Governance* (2019) 287-304; and the literature discussed in Ayelet Berman, Tim Büthe, Martino Maggetti and Joost Pauwelyn,

the overly state-centric tradition, and it has yielded some highly original suggestions for improving global governance.[13] It might, however, be getting ahead of the reality of global governance, much of which is—for better or worse—still predominantly inter- and transgovernmental.

In his deliberate provocation, entitled *A Preface to Economic Democracy*, Robert Dahl sought to generalize the notion of democratic participation to governance institutions beyond the public institutions of the nation state, suggesting that genuinely *democratic* legitimacy requires that all who are affected by a decision ought to have the opportunity to have a voice in the decision-making.[14] Our conceptualization of 'stakeholders' draws on this understanding of participation and democratic legitimacy, extending it to global governance.[15] And although participation is no panacea for the legitimacy of global governance,[16] a growing, methodologically and substantively diverse body of literature suggest that (opportunities for) diverse stakeholder participation indeed boost the perceived legitimacy of global governance.[17]

Who, then, are the stakeholders of the global governance bodies in finance and health? Who, in particular, are the traditionally marginalized and excluded stakeholders? Strikingly, even after 20+ years of reforms, which supposedly aimed to boost the participation of just these stakeholders, global bodies engaged in the governance of finance or health have barely begun to address this issue in a systematic way. As noted in a recent study by the OECD about traditional IOs: 'Despite [the] recognized importance [of greater stakeholder engagement], so far, few IOs have developed a[n...] organization[al] policy or strategy for stakeholder engagement, mapping their stakeholders and defining objectives and key steps to engage them and manage risks ... They [lack] a framework of systematic practices and tools.'[18]

Providing a framework for identifying and delineating the stakeholders, for each of the global finance and health governance bodies considered here, is clearly beyond the scope of this book. Yet, the empirical chapters confirm our priors: The governments and public agencies of many or even most developing countries are amongst the key stakeholders of many global governance bodies. Many of them have also long been marginalized or even outright excluded. Our country case experts therefore focused

'Introduction: Rethinking Stakeholder Participation in Global Governance.' Chapter 1, this volume and DeMenno and Büthe, 'Voice and Influence' (n 2).

[13] See, e.g. John S Dryzek, Quinlan Bowman, Jonathan Kuyper, Jonathan Pickering, Jensen Sass and Hayley Stevenson (eds), *Deliberative Global Governance* (Cambridge University Press 2019).

[14] Robert A Dahl, *A Preface to Economic Democracy* (University of California Press 1985).

[15] See also the recent collection of essays in Jonas Tallberg and Michael Zürn (eds), special issue: The Legitimacy and Legitimation of International Organizations 14(4) *Review of International Organizations* (2019) 581-743.

[16] Ingi Iusmen and John Boswell, 'The Dilemmas of Pursuing 'Throughput Legitimacy' through Participatory Mechanisms' 40(2) *West European Politics* (2017) 459-478.

[17] Anna Ernst, 'How Participation Influences the Perception of Fairness, Efficiency and Effectiveness in Environmental Governance: An Empirical Analysis' 238 *Journal of Environmental Management* (2019) 368-381; Soetkin Verhaegen, Jan Aart Scholte and Jonas Tallberg, 'Explaining Elite Perceptions of Legitimacy in Global Governance' Paper presented at the 12th Annual Conference on the Political Economy of International Organizations (PEIO), Salzburg 2019); Jan Beyers and Sarah Arras, 'Stakeholder Consultations and the Legitimacy of Regulatory Decision-Making: A Survey Experiment in Belgium' 15(3) *Regulation and Governance* (2021) 877–893.

[18] OECD, *The Contribution of International Organisations to a Rule-Based International System* (OECD 2019), 15.

first and foremost on the consequences of the reforms for *governments* of developing countries. Where warranted and feasible, they have complemented those analyses by examining the consequences of the reforms for the disregarded non-commercial and diffuse societal interests from within those countries.

The pre-reform marginalization and exclusion of many stakeholders was hardly a secret. It was often based on restrictive formal requirements for membership, heavily skewed weighted voting based on publicly known quotas privileging a small group of Northern countries, and restricted access to meetings, documents, and other information about meetings and negotiations until after rules or decision had already been adopted. Early analyses of the stakeholder participation reforms have therefore very appropriately focused on the institutional reforms themselves, that is, the creation or expansion of opportunities for stakeholders to participate in a decisional or non-decisional role. We *started* our analysis of finance and health governance in the introductory chapters of Part II and Part III of the book with an overview of those reforms.[19] And since it is important to clarify at the outset to what extent those reforms in fact changed the formal opportunities for stakeholders from our case study countries, we briefly summarize the findings in the next section.

Our primary goal, however, is to push beyond an analysis of the reforms as such. We seek to problematize the notion of 'participation' by differentiating between (i) voice *opportunities*, (ii) making use of such opportunities (we also refer to such *exercising 'voice'* when given the opportunity as *involvement* in—or *engagement* with—a given global governance body) and (iii) exerting *influence* over the rules and decisions taken by a given global governance body. As we hypothesized at the outset and as the empirical chapters have shown, it should not be expected that institutional changes automatically result in increased engagement of traditionally disregarded stakeholders, nor that their engagement (that is, their exercise of 'actual stakeholder voice') automatically allows them to influence rules and decisions.

25.3 Decisional and Non-Decisional Stakeholder Participation Opportunities

Stakeholder voice and influence are most immediately a function of participation opportunities made available to stakeholders by a given global governance body. And even though all of the global governance bodies covered in this volume have undertaken some kind of stakeholder reforms in recent years, the kind and extent of those reforms have differed greatly. In many cases, participation opportunities for the governments of developing countries or their issue area-specific public regulators, have increased to a far greater extent than (and quite differently from) opportunities for non-governmental stakeholders from those countries.

Before reviewing what we have learned about stakeholder use of these voice opportunities and their actual influence in global governance bodies, we therefore briefly review the observed changes in opportunities.

[19] Olga Kovarzina and Martino Maggetti, 'Stakeholder Participation Reforms in Global Finance Governance' Chapter 4; Kern Alexander, 'Global Financial Governance and Banking Regulation' Chapter 5; Ayelet Berman, 'Stakeholder Participation Reforms in Global Health Governance' Chapter 13; David Gartner, 'Global Health Governance and Stakeholder Participation.' Chapter 14, all this volume.

25.3.1 Voice+ Opportunities for Developing Countries

Vis-à-vis developing countries, key reforms have been related to membership. Global governance bodies have broadened the eligibility criteria or requirements for formal 'full' membership (or lowered the direct financial cost of membership); created new forms of membership; or changed the distribution of the weights used in weighted voting towards a more equitable distribution. Although power in international organizations cannot always be discerned from an analysis of the formal rules,[20] many of these changes constitute decisional opportunities, because rule-making and decision-making are—subject to the caveat below—usually tied to membership. These reforms open up at least the possibility of voice and influence for traditionally disregarded stakeholders.

In addition or instead, many global governance bodies have created or extended a range of strictly non-decisional opportunities: they established consultative or advisory committees, introduced notice-and-comment procedures, etc. Such opportunities are by design voice-only opportunities, which provide stakeholders with no direct leverage over rule-making or decision-making (though possibly with indirect opportunities for influence).

Since the reforms have been discussed in detail in the introductions and preliminary conclusions to Part II and Part III of this book,[21] we only summarize them here, highlighting the main changes between the pre-reform situation (1/1/2000 for membership) and the situation as of the end of 2020. We note, in particular, the implications of these changes for the country pairs covered in the case studies.

Table 25.1 shows how both global finance and global health bodies have opened up towards developing countries—through membership, redistribution of voting rights or non-decisional participation opportunities. Amidst the specifics of the various institutional reforms, most of which have been particular to the history, the interests involved, and the type and the subject matter focus of each global governance body, a few developments come into clearer focus from this condensed summary presentation of the reforms. Global governance bodies that are membership-based virtually all have over the course of the last twenty years offered regular full membership to Brazil, China, and India (in some cases actively seeking them out). But only the global bodies that already had near-universal membership or sought to become (near)universal membership bodies have included Vietnam and Bangladesh or the Philippines, respectively, among their new members. We also note that Argentina does not fit this pattern, maybe due to being something of a legacy case: still included in numerous finance governance bodies, even though in several cases it did not in fact fully meet the

[20] Robert W Cox and Harold K Jacobson (eds), *The Anatomy of Influence: Decision-Making in International Organizations* (Yale University Press 1973); Timothy J McKeown, 'How U.S. Decision-Makers Assessed their Control of Multilateral Organizations, 1957-1982' 4(3) *Review of International Organizations* (2009) 269-291; Randall W Stone, *Controlling Institutions: International Organizations and the Global Economy* (Cambridge University Press 2011); Tim Büthe, 'Review of Randall Stone, *Controlling Institutions*' 11(1) *Perspectives on Politics* (2013): 282-284.

[21] Kovarzina and Maggetti, 'Stakeholder Participation Reforms' and Berman, 'Stakeholder Participation Reforms' (both n 19); Martino Maggetti and Olga Kovarzina, 'Assessing Stakeholder Participation Reforms in Global Finance Governance' Chapter 9 and Ayelet Berman and Joost Pauwelyn, 'Assessing Stakeholder Participation Reforms in Global Health Governance.' Chapter 18, both this volume.

Table 25.1 Voice opportunities for governmental stakeholders, changes through 2020

	Expansion of membership (regular full members)	New membership categories	Weighted voting changes	Voice-only (non-decisional) opportunities for case study country pairs
Treaty-based IGOs				
IMF	183 → 190 member states[a]	None	Voting based on quotas (capital committed to the IMF). Results of 1999–2016 quota reviews reforms: BRA: ↑ CHN: ↑ IND: ↑ ARG: ↓ VNM: slight ↑ BGD: unchanged	None/insignificant
World Bank	Same as IMF	None	Quota and voting power reforms similar to IMF[b]	None/insignificant
WHO	191 → 194 member states[c]	Associate membership (Puerto Rico and Tokelau) unchanged	n/a	2003 reforms opened WHO Exec. Board meetings to associate members, IOs, and recognized NGOs for non-voting participation
Codex Alimentarius	163 → 188 member states[d] + EU (since 2003)	None	n/a	In observer status: 41 → 58 Intergovernmental organizations; 139 → 164 NGOs; no change in UN organizations (16)[e]

(continued)

Table 25.1 Continued

	Expansion of membership (regular full members)	New membership categories	Weighted voting changes	Voice-only (non-decisional) opportunities for case study country pairs
Transgovernmental Regulatory Networks				
G20 (founded in 1998/99 as extension of the G7)	20 members incl. BRA, CHN, IND, and ARG, (not BGD, PHL, VNM)	None, but …	n/a	… G20 leaders have invited a number of 'guests' to each meeting, including some countries/governments;[f] among them VNM has since 2017 been a non-member participant (also on behalf of APEC and ASEAN)
Basel Committee on Banking Supervision (BCBS)	2009 + 2013/14 Reforms: 12 → 28 full members, including BRA, CHN, IND, ARG (not BGD, PHL, VNM)	Observer membership created (3 observers: Chile, Malaysia, UAE); decisional role	n/a	BCBS-affiliated bodies (International Conference of Banking Supervisors and the Financial Stability Institute) provide more inclusive fora for discussions and information sharing among banking supervisors from many countries
Financial Action Task Force	28 → 37 member jurisdictions, incl. BRA, CHN, IND, ARG (not BGD, PHL, VNM)[g] + two Regional Bodies (EU + GCC)	Observer jurisdiction status (Indonesia) + Associate and Observer member status created for international and transgovernmental bodies	n/a	Regional banks from less developed regions, as well as the African Development Bank and the Asian Development Bank take part as observer members
Financial Stability Forum → Financial Stability Board (2009)	7 → 25 member jurisdictions (24 countries + EU), FSB (but not previously FSF) includes BRA, CHN, IND, ARG (not BGD, PHL, VNM)	4 international organizations (BIS, IBRD, IMF, OECD) and 6 transnat'l bodies have also been FSB members since the beginning (2009)	n/a	Informal engagement with finance regulators or ministries from non-member jurisdictions
IOSCO	87 → 129 Ordinary members from now 123 countries and jurisdictions	Associate and Affiliate Membership created[h]	n/a	Associate and affiliate membership are non-decisional (= voice-only) roles

International Council for Harmonization (ICH)	3 'founding' regulatory members → +2 'standing regulatory' and +6 'regulatory' members, including BRA, CHN; (not ARG, BGD, IND, PHL, VNM)	'Standing Regulatory' and 'Regulatory' membership categories created for governmental stakeholders	n/a	Various institutional outreach bodies, such as 'Regulators Form', to allow select non-members to participate → several observer categories with non-decisional participation, including non-member 'Legislative or Administrative Authorities' from 17 countries, incl. IND (but not ARG, BGD, PHL, or VNM)[i]
Int'l Medical Devices Regulators Forum (since 2011)	5 [GHTF members] → 8 → 10 regulatory agency members, including BRA, CHN from the start of IMDRF; IND invited; (not ARG, BGD, PHL, VNM)	'Invited' and 'Affiliated Organizations' had observer status from the start	n/a	WHO has gained official observer status; three Regional Harmonization Initiatives from Asia and Latin America continue in observer status. They may provide additional indirect opportunities for input for countries from those regions. IMDRF Working Groups are free to draw on input from non-members[j]
Multi-Stakeholder Partnerships (not common in finance)				
Global Fund	No change; the 20 voting members include 8 donor and 7 developing country governmental representatives	None[k]	n/a	Eight non-voting members include representatives of international organizations (WHO, UNAIDS, and WB) and thus provide additional indirect opportunity for participation by non-member governments; Country Coordinating Mechanisms (CCMs), required for every grant-receiving country, provides indirect voice opportunities for the country's government along with other stakeholders

(continued)

Table 25.1 Continued

	Expansion of membership (regular full members)	New membership categories	Weighted voting changes	Voice-only (non-decisional) opportunities for case study country pairs
GAVI	2009 Reform (15 → 27 Board members) incl. 3 → 5 seats for donor and 2 → 5 seats for implementing country governments	One → 2 vaccine industry seats (1 developed, 1 developing); 4 research institute seats → 9 independent experts seats	n/a	WB, WHO, and UNICEF representation on GAVI Board provides indirect opportunity for governments without seat on the Board (e.g. 2012 WHO Assembly discussion of Global Vaccine Action Plan)
Private Standard-Setting Bodies				
International Accounting Standards Board (IASB)	Establishment of new groups, boards, and offices, such as the emerging economies group and, the Asia-Oceanic office	None	n/a	Establishment and development of several consultative bodies
Global G.A.P.	10 → 14 Board members (1/2 'producers / suppliers, 1/2 retailers) are *not supposed to represent countries or governments* through often seen as mostly representing developed countries' interests	None	Unchanged (vote only taken if consensus cannot be reached; chair's vote counts double in the event of a tie)	As a non-governmental body, GlobalG.A.P. is in principle open to wide range of interests. European stakeholders are still said to predominate[l]

[a] The IMF already had near universal membership by the end of the 1990s. East Timor (2002), Montenegro (2007), Kosovo (2009), Tuvalu (2010), South Sudan (2012), Nauru (2016), and Andorra (2020) were the only new member states in the 2000s; see <https://www.imf.org/external/np/sec/memdir/memdate.htm>; for quotas, see <https://www.imf.org/external/np/sec/memdir/members.aspx>; both last accessed 11/15/2020.

[b] For a discussion, including of small differences between the IMF and the IBRD (the main WB body), see Rob Clark, 'Quotas Operandi: Examining the Distribution of Voting Power at the IMF and World Bank' 58(4) *The Sociological Quarterly* (2017) 595-621.

[c] The WHO already had near-universal membership from all UN member states plus the Cook Islands (since 1984) and Niue (since 1994) except Liechtenstein. Since 01/01/2000, Serbia (2000) and Montenegro (2006) have gained separate membership status, and East Timor (2002) and South Sudan (2012) have joined.

[d] The twenty-five new members comprised three Asian countries (Afghanistan, Maldives, and Timor Leste), twelve European countries (plus the EU), seven African countries, and one country from the South West Pacific; see <http://www.fao.org/fao-who-codexalimentarius/about-codex/members/en/>, last accessed 11/20/2020.

[e] See List of Codex Observers and various Reports <http://www.fao.org/fao-who-codexalimentarius/about-codex/observers/observers/obs-list/en/>; <http://www.fao.org/tempref/codex/Reports/Alinorm99/lim99_04.pdf>, and <https://www.who.int/foodsafety/codex/en/codex_eval_report_en.pdf>, last accessed 12/15/2020. Codex baseline numbers are for 2001, not 01/01/2000.

[f] See Mike Callaghan, Daniela Strube, Emmanuel Nnadozie, and Azamat Abdymomunov, *G20 Outreach and Non-G20 Member Views* (Lowy Institute Reports 2014) <https://www.lowyinstitute.org/publications/g20-outreach-and-non-g20-member-views-g20>, last accessed 11/20/2020.

[g] FATF in 1991/92 already expanded from sixteen to twenty-eight member jurisdictions, see Kovarzina and Maggetti, 'Stakeholder Participation Reforms' (n 19). For current membership, see <http://www.fatf-gafi.org/about/membersandobservers/>, last accessed 11/21/2020.

[h] As part of a series of reforms, the IOSCO in 2011 adopted a differentiated fee structure to facilitate membership for developing countries.

[i] The other ICH observer categories include 'Standing Observers' (the WHO participates in this status) and 'Regional Harmonization Initiatives' (from six regions, including ASEAN, APEC, and PANDRH); <https://www.ich.org/page/members-observers>, last accessed 05/25/2021.

[j] See http://www.imdrf.org/about/about.asp—the Asian Harmonization Working Party (AHWP) and APEC's Regulatory Harmonization Steering Committee have been observers all along; the Pan-American Health Organization replaced the original observer Latin American Harmonization Working Party.

[k] However, the CCM is supposed to ensure inclusive, participatory local ownership of Global Fund projects; see Gülen Atay Newton, 'Evolving Norms and Objectives Regarding Stakeholder Participation: The Global Fund to Fight AIDS, Tuberculosis and Malaria.' Chapter 21, this volume, and case study chapters in Part III.

[l] Nicolas Hachez and Jan Wouters, 'A Glimpse at the Democratic Legitimacy of Private Standards: Assessing the Public Accountability of GlobalG.A.P.' 14(3) *Journal of International Economic Law* (2011): 677-710; Sam F Halabi and Ching-Fu Lin, 'Assessing the Relative Influence and Efficacy of Public and Private Food Safety Regulation Regimes: Comparing Codex and GlobalG.A.P. Standards' 72(2) *Food and Drug Law Journal* (2017): 262-294.

membership criteria. Often, it was considered the strongest contender when exclusive global finance bodies sought—a bit—greater geographic diversity.

The creation of new membership categories appears to have been a common element of stakeholder reforms—though in several cases geared towards non-state stakeholders rather than the governments of previously marginalized countries. Associate, affiliate, or observer membership also can be double-edged for the stakeholders who join in that status. These new membership categories may lower the barriers to entry, but they also may blunt demands for fully equal participation by offering a second-class and/or non-decisional trajectory. This issue surely warrants closer scrutiny—though it may be beyond this volume. Vietnam in the G20 (for finance governance) and India in the ICH (for global health governance) appear to be the only cases of such secondary memberships for governmental stakeholders among our paired country case studies.

25.3.2 Voice Opportunities for CSOs and Other Non-State Stakeholders

Stakeholder reforms have not just sought to open up global governance to the governments of previously marginalized developing countries. In the past three decades, international bodies in a broad range of fields, have also formally opened up to non-state actors.[22] They have done so by conducting consultations,[23] providing notice and inviting comments online,[24] holding public meetings,[25] establishing advisory or expert committees,[26] etc. This tendency to open up applies even to traditionally strictly intergovernmental international organizations, virtually all of which have transformed themselves from exclusive member state organizations to organizations that engage non-state actors in some form, as carefully documented in recent surveys by Tallberg and colleagues and by the OECD.[27]

Table 25.2 summarizes the voice opportunity reforms for non-governmental stakeholders in the global finance and global health governance bodies examined in the case studies in Part II and Part III of the book. As in Table 25.1, we use the pre-reform status quo ante at the end of the 1990s as the baseline for this overview (01/01/2000 for membership).

[22] E.g. Anne Peters, Lucy Koechlin, Till Förster, and Gretta Fenner Zinkernagel, *Non-State Actors as Standard Setters* (Cambridge University Press 2009); Kenneth W Abbott, Jessica F Green, and Robert O Keohane, 'Organizational Ecology and Institutional Change in Global Governance', 70 *International Organization* (2015) 247-277.

[23] E.g. World Bank, *Consultations with Civil Society Organizations: General Guidelines for World Bank Staff* (World Bank Group 2000); FATF, *Consultation and Dialogue with Non-Profit Organizations* <http://www.fatf-gafi.org/publications/fatfrecommendations/documents/npo-consultation-march-2015.html>, last accessed 08/23/2020.

[24] E.g. OECD, 'Guidelines for Online Public Consultation' <http://www.oecd.org/about/civil-society/guidelinesforonlinepublicconsultation.htm>, last accessed 08/23/2020.

[25] E.g. World Bank and IMF Civil Society Policy Forum, 'The International Monetary Fund, Factsheet: The IMF and Civil Society Organizations', 5 April 2016 <http://www.imf.org/external/np/exr/facts/civ.htm>, last accessed 08/23/2020.

[26] E.g. the Business and Industry Advisory Committee to the OECD (BIAC) and the Trade Union Advisory committee to the OECD <http://www.oecd.org/about/civil-society/the-oecd-and-civil-society.htm>, last accessed 08/23/2020.

[27] Tallberg *et al.*, *The Opening Up* (n 5); OECD, *International Regulatory Co-Operation: The Role of International Organisations in Fostering Better Rules of Globalisation* (OECD Publishing 2016), esp. 85.

Table 25.2 Voice Opportunities for Non-Governmental Stakeholders, Changes through 2020

	Membership options for non-state stakeholders	Other direct voice opportunities provided	Other indirect voice opportunities
Treaty-based IGOs			
IMF	None	None/insignificant	Since the early 2000s, civil society representatives are increasingly involved via communication with the IMF management, in meetings and forums. The public is more and more allowed to participate in consultations[a]
World Bank	None	Establishment of the Civil Society Team (2002/03)	Since the early 2000s, civil society participates informally and has been increasingly involved in discussions, consultations, and information exchanges. Participation also includes monitoring the Bank's activities and collaborating in operational activities[b]
WHO	None	Non-state actors participate as experts on expert committees; engagement of diverse non-state actors under the Framework of Engagement of Non-State Actors	Non-governmental actors can be members of national delegations; non-state actors with 'official status' may attend WHA and EB meetings; 'open' EB meetings are open to the public; WHO public consultations; WHO Collaborating centres; WHO partnerships; earmarked funding by non-state actors
Codex Alimentarius	None, but non-governmental actors may be members of national delegations	139 → 164 non-governmental organizations with observer status.[c] Non-governmental actors can be members of expert committees members, or of national Codex committees; may provide input in public calls for data	National stakeholders may participate as members on National Codex Committees; national non-governmental actors may comment on Codex drafts circulated by Codex national contact points

(continued)

Table 25.2 Continued

	Membership options for non-state stakeholders	Other direct voice opportunities provided	Other indirect voice opportunities
Transgovernmental Regulatory Networks			
G20	None	None	External collaboration with official engagement groups, which include non-state actors
Basel Committee	None	Insignificant	Development of notice-and-comment procedure allowing for public input
Fin. Action Task Force	None	Insignificant	Consultation and dialogue meetings with non-profit organizations
Fin. Stability Board	None	Insignificant	Informal engagement with NGOs.
IOSCO	None	Insignificant	Very indirect voice opportunities through consultation during Assessment Committee reviews
Int'l Council for Harmonization (ICH)	Three 'founding' industry members → 3 'founding industry members' +3 'industry members'	Standing observers including one industry assoc. (IFPMA), 'observers' incl. one industry association (APIC) and NGOs (e.g. Gates Foundation)	Notice and comment processes carried out by members and observers among their constituents; public consultations
Int'l Medical Devices Regulators Forum	The industry members of the predecessor body (GHTF) lost membership status when the IMDRF was founded as a strictly transgovernmental organization	Non-state actors, if recognized as stakeholders, may provide input at open meetings of working groups stakeholder forum, and management committee	Notice and comment processes carried out by members and observers among their constituents; public consultations
Multi-Stakeholder Partnerships (not common in finance)			
Global Fund	Voting members represent different constituencies, incl. five defined as strictly non-governmental: communities, developed countries NGOs, developing countries NGO, private foundations, private sector	The 'alternates' for several of the geographically defined constituencies are non-governmental	The Country Coordinating Mechanism (CCM), required for grant receiving countries, provides indirect voice opportunities for the country's stakeholders; constituencies expected to provide input via their representatives[d]

Table 25.2 Continued

	Membership options for non-state stakeholders	Other direct voice opportunities provided	Other indirect voice opportunities
GAVI	2009 Reform: 1→ 2 pharmaceutical industry seats (1 developing, 1 developed); 2→1 seats for foundations; 4→1 seats for research institutes[e]	+9 seats for 'independent experts' on the GAVI Board (experts need not be 'stakeholders' in any conventional sense)	Member's constituents may provide input to their representatives (e.g. civil society organizations constituency)
Private Standard-Setting Bodies			
International Accounting Standards Board (IASB)	Insignificant	Establishment of a monitoring board	Global public consultations (strictly non-decisional)
Global G.A.P.	Expansion of membership from western European industry to industry from Africa, Asia Pacific, Americas, and Eastern Europe	Experts and industry on technical committees; focus groups	Input through national technical working groups; input through stakeholder consultations, notice and comment

[a] For an overview of the status quo in the beginning of the 2000s, see Thomas C Dawson and Gita Bhatt, *The IMF and Civil Society: Striking a Balance* (International Monetary Fund 2001).

[b] See esp. World Bank, *Issues and Options for Improving Engagement between the World Bank and Civil Society Organizations* (The World Bank 2005).

[c] See Codex, List of Observers <http://www.fao.org/fao-who-codexalimentarius/about-codex/observers/observers/obs-list/en/>, last accessed 12/15/2020. 139 is the number of NGOs with observer status as of the 2001 report noted here; 164 is the number as of the end of 2020; Codex does not make information about individual NGOs' attainment of observer status publicly available.

[d] See Newton, 'Evolving Norms and Objectives' (Table 25.1, note k) and case study chapters in Part III.

[e] In addition, governmental membership increased (see Table 25.1); the vaccine industry retained its two seats (one for the developed, one for the developing countries industry); and the GAVI CEO was given an ex officio (non-voting) seat. The original NGO seat was renamed the 'civil society organizations' seat (otherwise no change). Among foundations, the Gates Foundation retained its designated seat, whereas Rockefeller lost its designated seat. See <https://www.gavi.org/our-alliance/governance/gavi-board/members>, last accessed 05/24/2021.

As noted in Section 25.2, both the identification of stakeholders and attempts to engage them have been remarkably unsystematic. The traditional IOs in finance, the IMF and World Bank, have introduced various non-decisional ('voice-only') opportunities for civil society organizations (CSOs), that is, 'business forums, faith-based associations, labor unions, local community groups, nongovernmental organizations […], philanthropic foundations, and think tanks'.[28] These stakeholders now have

[28] International Monetary Fund, 'Civil Society and the IMF' <http://www.imf.org/external/np/exr/facts/civ.htm>, last accessed 05/25/2021, and 5 April 2016 Factsheet (n 37).

(passive) access to meetings, forums, and policy decision; they are invited to provide comments and even participate in consultations about specific policy decisions. The IMF and the World Bank jointly organize a Civil Society Policy Forum alongside the Annual and Spring Meetings of the organizations, in which CSOs can participate and even organize their own sessions. There is also a CSO Fellowship Program to facilitate participation during those meetings.

On the whole, however, non-state actors' opportunities for non-decisional participation are much more restricted in global finance than in global health. The contrast appears particularly pronounced in transgovernmental regulatory networks, where most influence remains at the state level. Even though some global finance bodies have made efforts to include non-state actors (for instance via the FATF's consultations, IASB and IOSCO's improved transparency towards the general public, or the Basel Committee notice-and-comment procedure),[29] in most cases increases in voice opportunities have been marginal and very indirect.

In global health, by contrast, numerous, often quite varied opportunities for participation by various non-state actors have opened up. We caution that this observation does not yet allow us to draw the conclusion that CSOs or other non-state actors exert more influence in global health governance, but we certainly find a richer menu of *opportunities* for trying.

25.3.3 Assessing the Hypotheses

Our analytical framework identified two possible explanations for what might prompt global governance bodies to create or expand stakeholder voice opportunities[30]—beyond a normative commitment to increased stakeholder participation,[31] which might of course suffice as a motivation but surely is not universally shared or might by itself be too weak. Specifically, DeMenno and Büthe stipulated that we should expect a global governance body to increase voice opportunities if uncertainty about the effects of alternative policy choices is high (e.g. due to the complexity of the issue or due to resource or analytical constraints of the global body), such that input from previously disregarded stakeholders may help it choose or design better policies. Alternatively, DeMenno and Büthe stipulated that we should expect a global governance body to increase voice opportunities if it expects implementation challenges that can be mitigated through participation-enhanced democratic legitimacy.

The Rethinking Participation project was designed primarily to better understand the *consequences* of the existing stakeholder participation reforms. We have theorized and empirically examined the origins of, and variation in, those reforms, only to the extent that 'understanding the drivers of the expanded opportunities for stakeholder participation is necessary for understanding the likelihood of actual engagement and

[29] Maggetti and Kovarzina, 'Assessing' (n 21).
[30] DeMenno and Büthe, 'Voice and Influence' (n 2), Section 2.4.3, H_{1A} and H_{1B}.
[31] See Ayelet Berman, 'Stakeholder Participation Triangle.' Chapter 23, this volume.

influence in the aftermath of these reforms'.[32] It is worth noting, however, that our overarching review of the reforms as well as the matched pairs of country case studies support the initial hypotheses about the reasons for the reforms.

Global governance bodies appear to have expanded voice(+) opportunities for developing country *governments* mostly for instrumental reasons, in many cases hoping to mitigate implementation challenges, but also sometimes in anticipation of gaining information that would allow them to choose or design better policies. For instance, China's growing role in global financial markets (as well as global markets for pharmaceuticals), made it imperative for the IMF, the Basel Committee, and the IASB alike (and for the ICH in global health) to increase China's legitimating 'buy-in' and thus raise the likelihood of consistent domestic implementation of the rules and decisions adopted by these bodies. At the same time, in these global governance bodies, even voice opportunities for governments are much more commonly discussed in terms of access to local knowledge for choosing better policies than in terms of increasing legitimacy.

When it comes to *non-governmental* stakeholders, the creation or expansion of voice opportunities has been driven primarily by the increasing reliance (of the global bodies and their member state governments) on private expertise and resources. The ICH, for example, engages the pharmaceutical industry because it needs the scientific expertise of industry to develop workable proposals for harmonization. Similarly, Codex admits food industry representatives as observers or via government delegations to gain access to the specialized expertise of these commercial actors. GAVI likewise provides opportunities for engagement primarily to those stakeholders who implement GAVI programmes on the ground. The WHO similarly appears to seek engagement of those observers who contribute to the implementation of its work.

25.4 Increases and Variation in Stakeholder Voice

In global bodies that created or expanded voice opportunities for traditionally disregarded stakeholders, the empirical analyses in this book have generally found that previously marginalized or excluded stakeholders have increased their actual engagement in global governance. And in many cases, these increases in stakeholder voice can quite clearly be attributed to the stakeholder reforms. This overarching finding applies to the global finance governance bodies and the global health governance bodies examined by the contributors to the *Rethinking Participation* project. Yet, we also have found much variation. As noted, global finance governance bodies have been much less willing to increase voice opportunities for traditionally disregarded stakeholders, though stakeholders appear to have largely made use of whatever opportunities arose. At the same time, we have found tremendous variation between health and finance governance, with regard to the

[32] DeMenno and Büthe, 'Voice and Influence' (n 2) 47.

extent of voice opportunities, especially for non-state stakeholders, the availability and use of decisional vs. non-decisional participation, and often also with regard to the experience of large/leading versus smaller/later-emerging economies (China vs. Vietnam; Brazil vs. Argentina; India vs. Bangladesh/the Philippines). This section highlights key similarities and differences for governments (summarized in Table 25.3) and for non-state stakeholders.

25.4.1 Exercise of Voice by Developing Countries (Governments)

Henrique Choer Moraes and Facundo Pérez Aznar, in their in-depth examination of Brazil's and Argentina's participation in the G20, IMF, FSB, and FATF, demonstrate that Brazil—and to some extent also Argentina—have taken advantage of the new opportunities to voice their preferences during the agenda-setting stage as well as during the substantive discussions. Their analysis illustrates the substantial increases in voice opportunities for both countries, especially thanks to the formation of the G20. Both countries' governments used these opportunities to push for more far-reaching reforms of the governance architecture for global finance. Yet, although both countries increased their actual participation, the change was more pronounced for Brazil, especially in the IMF (where Argentina's vote share overtly declined, leading the Argentinian government to focus more on the G20) and in the FSB.[33]

In her study of China's and Vietnam's participation in global finance, Weiwei Zhang shows that the increase in China's participation in the G20, FATF, and the Basel Committee has been limited, though accelerating over time.[34] Vietnam, as a non-member of the G20 and the Basel Committee, has not even had voice opportunities in these bodies; in the FATF, it has barely made use of the indirect opportunity provided by the associate membership for the Asia/Pacific Group on Money Laundering (APG). In the IMF, both countries' actual exercise of voice has been more substantial: moderate in the early 2000s, then increasing after the Asian financial crisis, albeit more slowly for Vietnam.

Rahul Mukherji and Himanshu Jha show in their chapter that India and Bangladesh became active participants in global negotiations and contributors to the elaboration of global norms. Only India, however, did so by participating more intensively in the main finance governance institutions; Bangladesh occasionally gained voice by making the most of its outsider position.[35] Unfortunately, though, the institutions for the governance of climate finance, on which the chapter focuses, differ from the finance governance institution examined in the rest of the book, limiting the opportunities for drawing comparative insights.

[33] Henrique Choer Moraes and Facundo Perez Aznar, 'Brazil and Argentina in Global Finance Governance.' Chapter 6, this volume.

[34] Weiwei Zhang, 'China and Vietnam in Global Finance Governance.' Chapter 7, this volume.

[35] Rahul Mukherji and Himanshu Jha, 'India and Bangladesh in Global Finance Governance: From Structural Conflict to Embedded Liberalism in the Climate Finance Regime.' Chapter 8, this volume.

In global health, André de Mello e Souza and Facundo Pérez Aznar find generally substantial and increasing participation by Brazil and unevenly continuing engagement by Argentina. The extent to which changes in participation are attributable to institutional reforms, however, varies by health governance body. In the WHO, for instance, they note that institutional reforms made little difference for Brazil and Argentina, whereas ICH reforms have allowed for more input and a greater diversity of perspectives, including by Brazil.[36] Mello e Souza and Pérez Aznar identify domestic politics—and the discretionary decision of successive governments to make health policy a priority issue area—as particularly important drivers of Brazil's growing voice across a range of health governance bodies. Facing stagnant or declining resources instead, Argentina's engagement in global health governance has been lower and uneven.[37]

Cindy Cheng and Anh Do's analysis of China and Vietnam in global health governance finds many examples of China—and to a lesser extent Vietnam—making increasing use of voice opportunities. In some global governance bodies, these opportunities opened up only towards the end of the first decade or even the beginning of the second decade of the 2000s, and in ICH and the IMDRF only for China but not Vietnam. In some fora (specifically: in the health funding bodies), China's role has in recent years shifted, because its strong economic growth has made it ineligible for new funding support from GAVI and the Global Fund, whereas Vietnam remains eligible). Even in Codex, where Chinese and Vietnamese membership goes back multiple decades, their level of engagement has increased—by virtually every metric examined by Cheng and Do—albeit here, too, much more strongly for China than for Vietnam.[38]

Büthe, Chaturvedi, Payoyo, and Srinivas find, moreover, that the Codex Trust Fund (CTF), which Cheng with Do found to have had little effect on Chinese and Vietnamese participation, appears to have allowed the Philippines to increase participation in Codex on matters of national salience. Thanks to the CTF, the Philippines' first active involvement in the technical work of Codex took place in the 1990s, concerning 'carrageenan', a leading export product. Moreover, thanks to the CTF, the national Codex committee in the Philippines was launched, building capacity and enabling the Philippines to attend meetings and develop country positions on technical matters.[39]

[36] Interview with Brazilian regulatory official, cited in Andre de Mello e Souza and Facundo Pérez Aznar, 'Brazil and Argentina in Global Health Governances.' Chapter 15, this volume.

[37] Mello e Souza and Pérez Aznar thus also confirm a central contention of the analytical framework of this book, as well as of the Power Transition Theory of Global Economic Governance: that participation in transnational and global regulatory governance is, even for rising powers such as Brazil, a *political choice*—one of the possible ways to invest the additional resources gained from strong economic growth (see Sandra Lavenex, Omar Serrano and Tim Büthe, 'Power Transitions and the Rise of the Regulatory State: Global Market Governance in Flux' 15(3) *Regulation and Governance* (2021) 445–471).

[38] Cindy Cheng with Anh Do, 'China and Vietnam in Global Health Governance.' Chapter 16, this volume.

[39] Tim Büthe, Sachin Chaturvedi, Peter Payoyo, and Krishna Ravi Srinivas, 'India and the Philippines in Global Health Governance.' Chapter 17, this volume.

Table 25.3 Stakeholder voice in global governance: post-reform changes in actual engagement by governments (bodies covered in the case studies only)

	Brazil	Argentina	China	Vietnam	India	Bangladesh
Finance Bodies						
IMF	Moderate, ↑	Moderate, ↓	Moderate, ↑	Moderate, slowly ↑		(Engagement avoided)
World Bank						(Engagement avoided)
G20	Persistently high	Persistently high	(High)	No voice		
Basel Committee			Low but ↑	Rule-taker; no voice as non-member		
IOSCO			Initially mostly passive; after 2009 ↑	mostly passive; slowly ↑		
Financial Action Task Force			Initially mostly passive; since 2014 ↑	Very limited indirect engagement via Associate Member APG		
Financial Stability Board	High, including three Board seats participating in multiple ways	Moderate, since 2014, two Board seats otherwise limited engagement	(Moderate)			
IASB						
	Brazil	**Argentina**	**China**	**Vietnam**	**India**	**Philippines**
Health Governance Bodies						
WHO	High, ↑	Moderate; uneven; high on select issues			Very high though still uneven; evolved from beneficiary to partner	High, ↑
Codex Alimentarius	Moderate to high, ↑; limited by internal divisions	Moderate to high, stagnant	Until 1990s mostly passive; then ↑ to moderate-high	Until 1990s mostly passive; then slowly ↑ to weakly moderate	Until late 1990s, very rarely; since then strongly ↑; high	Until late 1990s, absent; since then strongly ↑; moderate-high

International Council for Harmonisation (ICH)	Initially avoided; forum-shifting strategy undermined by domestic industry; member since 2015: ↑	Initially avoided; passive observer mostly via regional body PANDRH	2008–2015 ↑ via ad hoc arrangements; since 2015 high as new member	Only indirectly via ASEAN observer membership	Invited, declined	Only indirect (via regional body)
International Medical Devices Regulators Forum			Until 2013, participation as observer and indirectly through AHWP; member since 2013	Some ad hoc engagement; in recent years, only indirectly via ASEAN and AHWP		
Global Fund[a]	Initially high as recipient, incl. via CCM; after crossing ineligibility threshold, no participation as funder	Initially high; soon declined to low engagement except for Argentinian Board Member	High from 2002 until shortly after crossing ineligibility threshold in 2014; little or no effective participation via CCM	Low ↑ to moderate; strong grassroots participation via CCM	High as recipient, esp. after 2012 re-classification; no representation on Board but effective participation via CCM	High as recipient, esp. after 2012 re-classification; no representation on Board but effective participation via CCM
GAVI			Moderate in early 2000s; uneven after crossing ineligibility threshold	High, esp. while developing country GAVI Board member, 2008–2011		
Global G.A.P.	Variable, depending on working group; overall low	Variable, depending on working group; overall low	Moderate, incl. via National Technical Working Group, focused on recognition of ChinaG.A.P.	Low; no NTWG established to align VietG.A.P. with GlobalG.A.P.		

[a] Categorization of voice/engagement is based on participation in Global Fund governance as Board member (usually as part of the grant recipient group), attendee of Global Fund meetings or in other governance activities as noted in the text. A categorization based on receipt of grants might lead to different results, not least depending on whether it would be conditioned on population, GDP, or disease burden.

Source: Authors' distillation of finding from the paired country case studies. Entries in parentheses indicate that they are based on only a brief discussion rather than a full-fledged analysis of the global governance body in the corresponding paired country case study; grey shading indicates that the global governance body was not examined in the case study. Please note that these findings must be interpreted in conjunction with the findings about stakeholder *opportunities* (see Section 25.3).

25.4.2 Stakeholder Voice by CSOs/Non-State Interests

Reflecting the relative dearth of stakeholder voice opportunities for non-state interests in global finance, the paired case studies for finance governance find little evidence that these stakeholders have actually gained more of a voice in global finance. Where it has happened, it appears to have occurred indirectly, involving predominantly commercial interests. In her analysis of the increased role of Chinese stakeholders in global finance governance, for instance, Zhang notes that the China Banking Association (CBA) has actively provided input into the discussions of the Basel Committee regarding a reform of Basel III. The members of the CBA, however, are mostly state-owned commercially operating financial intermediaries; the Association is *not* a CSO as this term is usually understood.

Finding practically no participation of non-commercial stakeholders in global finance governance and exceedingly sparse de facto participation even by commercial non-governmental stakeholders from the Global South (including from Brazil, China, and India) is consistent with earlier analyses. For the International Accounting Standards Committee (IASC), the IASB's predecessor organization, repeated studies in the 1990s found that substantial efforts to ostensibly boost involvement by accounting experts from developing countries bore little fruit: their pervasive under-representation was highly persistent.[40]

Prospects for participation by civil society organizations and more broadly non-governmental, including non-commercial interests are generally much better in the realm of global health. As the country case studies demonstrate, opportunities for such stakeholders to have a prominent voice in global governance are most pronounced in the multi-stakeholder partnerships of the Global Fund and GAVI, which guarantee a role for these non-governmental interests. The Global Fund, in fact—through its insistence on the establishment of a multi-stakeholder country coordinating mechanism (CCM) for recipients of its funds—can boost the involvement of previously marginalized societal interests in health policy-making even at the domestic level, as occurred in India and the Philippines.[41] At the same time, as Cheng and Do show, political institutions matter: China nominally includes non-governmental stakeholders in its CCM, but tightly controls—or at least limits—their input. Such stakeholders are more prominent in Vietnam's CCM, though still not at the level observed in democratic countries. Similarly, China and Vietnam have tightly controlled access to global food safety governance via the very limited and selective inclusion of civil society interests in Codex delegations, which for many countries regularly include numerous representatives of non-governmental interests.[42]

[40] R S Olusegun Wallace, 'Development of Accounting Standards for Developing and Newly Industrialized Countries' *Research in Third World Accounting: A Research Annual* vol.2 (JAI Press 1993) 121-165; Robert K Larson and Sara York Kenny, 'Developing Countries' Involvement in the IASC's Standard-Setting Process' 11(S1) *Advances in International Accounting* (1998) 17-41. See also Jan Beyers and Sarah Arras, 'Who Feeds Information to Regulators? Stakeholder Diversity in European Union Regulatory Agency Consultations' 40(4) *Journal of Public Policy* (2020) 573-598.

[41] Büthe *et al.*, 'India and the Philippines' (n 39).

[42] Cheng with Do, 'China and Vietnam' (n 38), Section 16.5.2.

Even the flagship international organization for global health governance, the WHO, which as a UN organization is at its roots strongly intergovernmental, has by now many years' experience of working with genuine CSOs. As the country case studies show, however, the availability of such non-commercial non-governmental stakeholders for participation at the inter- or transnational level varies across countries. At the same time, the growing engagement of Brazilian NGOs in the WHO suggest that such participation might also be learned.

25.4.3 Assessing the Hypotheses: Stakeholder Incentives to Participate

To understand *why* stakeholder voice in global governance might vary even when global governance bodies and processes provide opportunities for it, the analytical framework emphasized stakeholders' incentives to make use of the voice opportunities they are facing. Specifically, DeMenno and Büthe theorized two overarching determinants of stakeholder incentives: the importance of the specific global governance body for the stakeholder and the resources available to the stakeholder, which enable (or constrain) its exercise of voice opportunities.[43]

The importance of the global governance bodies covered in this book should—for stakeholders from developing countries—generally be high, given that the bodies were selected for analysis due to their central role(s) in global finance and global health.[44] We nonetheless might expect importance to vary, given that DeMenno and Büthe stipulate that the importance of a given global body is a function of both the salience of the issue governed by that body, and the availability of alternative fora for influencing the issue. With respect to capabilities, the analytical framework distinguishes between material, analytical, and political resources.[45]

A review of the case studies allows us now to assess the five hypotheses put forth in Chapter 2. The case study chapters provide substantial support for the hypotheses, especially the first four. We briefly illustrate each of them.

25.4.3.1 Salience of the Issue

All six countries covered by the paired case studies of global health governance have in recent years considered trade-related food safety standards very important, given their large (and for several of them still growing) agricultural export sector. This has rendered it important to have voice and influence in the Codex Alimentarius Commission,[46] given Codex's success in establishing itself as the institutional focal point for setting such standards. Codex standards, moreover, were for trade purposes

[43] DeMenno and Büthe, 'Voice and Influence' (n 2), Section 2.5.1, and $H_{2i} - H_{2v}$.

[44] Kovarzina and Maggetti, 'Stakeholder Participation Reforms' (n 19); Berman, 'Stakeholder Participation Reforms' (n 19).

[45] DeMenno and Büthe, 'Voice and Influence' (n 2), Section 2.5.2.

[46] Mello e Souza and Pérez Aznar, 'Brazil and Argentina' (n 36); Cheng with Do, 'China and Vietnam' (n 38); Büthe *et al.*, 'India and the Philippines' (n 39).

rendered binding and enforceable by the WTO SPS Agreement.[47] The importance of agricultural exports also explains the incentives of China and Vietnam to participate in GlobalG.A.P., as well as the incentives of incumbents to welcome these new exporters as active participants.[48]

Similarly, Brazil, India, and China's growing domestic market for pharmaceuticals and especially their desire to compete on the global market, has raised the importance of the ICH for all three countries (though for India, this increased salience has, for unrelated reason, not been sufficient yet to want to seek a 'seat at the [ICH] table').[49] And as the world's second-largest medical devices market, China has sought to participate in IMDRF meetings to improve competitiveness and build regulatory capacity. By contrast, Vietnam and the Philippines have a much smaller medical devices market, leading to lower issue salience.[50]

Variation in issue salience may also help explain the uneven use of newly created or expanded voice opportunities by non-governmental interest: For commercial stakeholders, the salience of transnational regulatory measures is relatively clear and often high, since most commercial actors are engaged in only one industry or line of business (or a few closely related ones). A transnational body whose rules or decisions affect that line of business is clearly important (and commercial actors typically are, at least in advanced industrialized democracies, well-organized along industry line). By contrast, for civil society organizations with a typically broad portfolio of public interest concerns, the salience of the rules and decisions of a particular global body at a specific moment in time is less clear. The need to spread their attention and resources across a broad range of concerns even applies to civil society organizations concerned with commercial activities, such as organizations concerned with protecting the interests of consumers or small investors. In addition, the interests of non-commercial stakeholders are often much more diffuse, making aggregating their preferences and collective action more challenging (see Section 25.5.5).

25.4.3.2 Availability of Alternative Fora for Influencing the Issue Area

The availability of alternatives clearly seems to affect the perceived importance of exercising voice opportunities in any particular global body. In the realm of global

[47] Joost Pauwelyn, 'An Overview of the WTO Agreements on Health and Technical Standards and the Impact on Communication' 6 *Zeitschrift für das gesamte Lebensmittelrecht* (2000) 843-858; Tim Büthe, 'The Politics of Food Safety in the Age of Global Trade: The Codex Alimentarius Commission in the SPS Agreement of the WTO' in Cary Coglianese, Adam Finkel, and David Zaring (eds), *Import Safety: Regulatory Governance in the Global Economy* (University of Pennsylvania Press 2009) 88-109; Tim Büthe and Nathaniel Harris, 'The Codex Alimentarius Commission: A Hybrid Public-Private Regulator' in Thomas Hale and David Held (eds), *Handbook of Transnational Governance: Institutions and Innovations* (Polity Press 2011) 219-228; Cindy Cheng, 'Codex Alimentarius Commission' in Pasquale Ferranti, Elliot Berry, and Jock Anderson (eds), *Encyclopedia of Food Security and Sustainability* (Elsevier 2019) 50-55.

[48] Cheng with Do, 'China and Vietnam' (n 38).

[49] Cheng with Do, 'China and Vietnam' (n 38); Büthe *et al.*, 'India and the Philippines' (n 39).

[50] Büthe *et al.*, 'India and the Philippines' (n 39). In the realm of climate finance, the salience of the issue, which has driven Bangladesh's use of any available voice opportunities (see Mukherji and Jha, 'India and Bangladesh' (n 35)) appears to arise more from its exceptional vulnerability to climate change, given that 20% of the country and much of its most fertile river delta land is elevated less than 1 meter from the sea level; see Saleemul Huq, 'Climate Change and Bangladesh' 294(5597) *Science* (2001) 1617; J Chen and V Mueller, 'Coastal Climate Change, Soil Salinity and Human Migration in Bangladesh' 8 *Nature Climate Change* (2018) 981-985.

finance, for instance, Argentina lost a substantial part of its weighted votes in the IMF as part of the 2010 IMF reforms that increased the weighted votes of Brazil, India, and China. Choer Moraes and Pérez Aznar find that the Argentinian government's sense of loss was cushioned by having gotten a seat in the then-recently launched G20, which provided an alternative forum in which to pursue various Argentinian interests with regard to the global governance of finance. At the same time, Argentina could not simply abandon the IMF (as some in its government would have liked to do) since this Bretton Woods Institution still occupies a central place in the governance of global finance, that is, there is no comparably comprehensive alternative forum.[51]

In the realm of global health, the issue salience of pharmaceuticals and medical devices has translated into great importance of the ICH and the IMDRF because there is no alternative forum to achieve regulatory cooperation among the pharmaceuticals and medical devices regulators, respectively. Similarly, Codex is the institutional focal point for food safety standards precisely because there has been no credible alternative—at least not since the SPS Agreement entered into force.[52]

Note that in some areas, such as development finance, China is often said to have pursued a go-it-alone strategy of setting up alternative regional bodies, which it then dominates. As Zhang points out, setting up the Asian Infrastructure Development Bank was a conscious Chinese attempt to create an alternative forum for gaining influence in the global governance of development finance. As she shows, however, such an alternative forum need not be strictly competing, at least not in the sense that a particular (well-resourced) stakeholder's participation would necessarily be zero sum: in development finance, China has simultaneously increased its involvement in the traditional global governance bodies (most prominently the WB). It is worth noting that, beyond development finance, however, we have (in the realms of health and finance) found no evidence of China setting up alternative institutional arrangements,[53] though we note that many scholars and policy-makers are concerned about China's Belt-and-Road initiative precisely because they fear it is an attempt to be able to put pressure on national and multilateral bodies to adopt Chinese standards and rules.

25.4.3.3 Material Resources

Material (financial) resources are needed, most immediately, to be able to devote time and effort to ascertain how the country's (or non-state group's) interests would be affected by a proposed rule or decision and which changes or alternatives to push for. To have voice opportunities that can make a difference—that is, that provide a country or interest group with an opportunity to influence the content of the rules and decisions, rather than just to register misgivings—often requires not only participating in the meetings during which the final rules are adopted and decisions made, but also attending the meetings during which those rules (or standards, guidelines, or

[51] Choer Moraes and Pérez Aznar, 'Brazil and Argentina' (n 33).

[52] The SPS Agreement actually allows the WTO member states, in principle, to recognize other inter- or transnational standard-setting organizations and elevate them to equivalent status, but since such a change would require consensus, no additional bodies have ever even been proposed for recognition (Büthe, not-for-attribution interviews with WTO staff; see also Büthe, 'Politics of Food Safety' (n 47)).

[53] See also, more generally: Lavenex, Serrano, and Büthe, 'Power Transitions' (n 37).

recommendations) are drawn up and the proposals for decisions are prepared. This may mean attending multiple meetings, formal and informal, in various locations around the globe with institutional memory (on the part of the participants) required over several years. Successful participants therefore usually need dedicated staff, who make a career out of contributing to specific regulatory issues, which (again) requires material resources to recruit and keep.

Holding positions of (informal) power with global governance bodies often requires additional resources. The WHO Secretariat, for instance, enjoys a substantial degree of autonomy vis-à-vis the member states and is powerful in shaping negotiations among WHO members. It is dominated by employees from high-income countries, because these countries typically volunteer most of the expert members of task-forces, who subsequently are incorporated in the WHO.[54] In Codex, too, having a committee chair requires financial and organizational resources, resulting in most chairs being held by developed countries.[55]

Across both issue areas (health and finance), the case studies provide a wealth of illustrative support for the importance of material resources (and the political will to commit them to participation in global governance). Strong economic growth over the past twenty to thirty years has allowed China, Brazil, and India to devote increasing financial resources to advancing their countries' interests in global governance. At the same time, business cycles or exogenous economic downturns have resulted in sometimes very sudden reductions of voice participation by representatives of Brazil and India (less clearly China).

Vietnam and the Philippines exhibit a similar pattern of generally but unevenly increased participation, albeit in Vietnam's case subject to greater material constraints, which has forced it to rely on regional representation in the ICH and the IMDRF, through the Asian Harmonization Working Party (AHWP) and ASEAN (in contrast to China, which has more resources and has been able to act independently).[56] The Philippines' somewhat more ample resources have allowed it to prioritize global health governance to a greater extent, in some cases fully compensating for the country's smaller size (compared to India) with greater commitment, reflected in delegations that have often been as large or larger than India's (often sparsely staffed) delegations.[57]

In the more specialized field of climate finance, Bangladesh, too, appears to have used some of its increased financial means resulting from two decades of high economic growth to pursue Bangladeshi interests more actively in multilateral settings (as India has also done). Mukherji and Jha attribute India's and Bangladesh's increased engagement, including financial contributions (in Bangladesh's case through

[54] As André de Mello e Souza explains, intentionality is difficult to establish: 'This may happen because these countries have more experts to offer (i.e. greater human resources) or simply because they are better able to identify and seize this opportunity for exerting influence in WHO negotiations' (email exchange with the editors, 9/20/2020, based on not-for-attribution interviews he conducted with numerous Brazilian diplomats).

[55] Mello e Souza and Pérez Aznar (n 36).

[56] Cheng with Do, 'China and Vietnam' (n 38).

[57] Büthe *et al.*, 'India and the Philippines' (n 39).

co-financing), to the combination of increased material capabilities and the countries' changed understanding of their 'social purpose'.[58]

Reductions in material resources also affect the exercise of voice opportunities. For Argentina, economic stagnation (and its longer-term economic decline) has resulted in a reduction in its voice in global governance bodies such as WHO and Codex, due to an inability to regularly send representatives to the meetings of these global governance bodies.[59]

Material resource requirements may also be helpful for understanding the divergence between the generally substantial increases in governmental voice in global finance and health governance and the very limited and uneven increases in engagement by non-governmental stakeholders. Furthermore, it surely contributes to the predominance of commercial non-governmental interests vis-à-vis non-commercial civil society interests: the resources available and justifiable for private engagement in global governance have increased very unevenly. For companies, rules and decisions that affect business costs and opportunities in their particular industry affect the company's commercial performance, thus clearly justifying some financial expense to prevent higher costs or achieve more profitable business opportunities. Consumers, small investors, and individual members of civil society cannot equally compensate for (or write off) such expenses and have a harder time to overcome collective action problems.

Commercially weaker economic actors, whose marginalization may be perpetuated or exacerbated if new voice opportunities are not accompanied by measures to help them overcome the resource constraints, also include small businesses. Cheng and Do, for instance, show that Vietnamese farmers do not have the financial resources to comply with GlobalG.A.P. standards, which, in turn, is leading to less Vietnamese engagement.[60]

25.4.3.4 Analytical Resources

The ability to develop meaningful policy preferences depends upon technical and scientific data, research, and discussions. Many developing countries lack the resources for carrying out such preliminary work. Even basic information about the feasible options for global governance have often come from commercial stakeholders in developed countries, creating informational imbalances, which, in turn, lower the likelihood that the resulting rules and decisions will align with the interests of developing countries and their domestic stakeholders.[61]

Accordingly, improved analytical capabilities have led to substantial increases in voice and influence of (some) developing countries. In the realm of global health, for instance, Brazil has, since the 1990s, substantially increased its expertise in HIV/AIDS

[58] Mukherji and Jha, 'India and Bangladesh' (n 35), esp. Sections 8.6.2, 8.7, and 8.8.2.

[59] Mello e Souza and Perez Aznar, 'Brazil and Argentina' (n 36).

[60] Cheng with Do, 'China and Vietnam (n 38).

[61] For examples from Codex standard-setting, see Natalie Avery, Martin Drake and Tim Lang, *Cracking the Codex: An Analysis of Who Sets World Food Standards* (National Food Alliance 1993); Büthe and Harris, 'Codex' (n 47); Ayelet Berman, 'Industry, Regulatory Capture and Transnational Standard Setting' 111 *American Journal of International Law Unbound* (2017) 112–118.

treatments, pharmaceuticals manufacturing, etc., which has translated into greater voice in several global health bodies. For Argentina, its expertise on matters such as the Universal Child and Pregnancy Allowance, the promotion of low-sodium diets, and mental health has allowed it to become a recognized voice in the WHO.[62]

In many areas of global governance, analytical resources are still highly unevenly distributed, and a lack of such resources impedes effective stakeholder voice. Differences in such capabilities explain the differences in the participation of, for instance, China and Vietnam in the IMDRF.[63] Remarkably, Codex has explicitly recognized the importance of analytical capabilities (after many years of ignoring them). Since the launch of the second Trust Fund in 2016, Codex has sought to focus on helping developing countries gain such an ability to identify and pursue their self-interests. So far, however, this initiative is unique—and limited to governmental beneficiaries; non-governmental stakeholders do not have access to a comparable programme.

Limited expertise is a real constraint even in partnerships—often considered the most equal governance model. The Global Fund, for instance, provides equal participation opportunities to developed and developing country members of its board. Yet, language barriers, inadequate access to technology, and the complexity of the issues continue to form structural barriers. These barriers still impede the ability of developing countries to exercise equally effective voice and influence over the agenda, the choice of projects, and the allocation of funds as the major developed country donors.[64]

25.4.3.5 Political Resources

The analytical framework highlights collective action capacity, that is, the ability to work with others to share costs and form broad coalitions of stakeholders whose preferences will need to be taken seriously (and which might even be decisive) in rulemaking and decision-making. DeMenno and Büthe identify collective action capacity as arguably the most critical political resource, needed by all but the largest, most powerful actors to make their voices heard and exert influence.[65] The empirical chapters in this volume provide tentative support for the hypothesis that variation in collective action capacity explains variation in actual stakeholder engagement in global governance.

The continued marginalization of non-commercial interests and CSOs is a finding that is at least consistent with the hypothesis. Non-governmental stakeholders, especially non-commercial civil society stakeholders ultimately comprised of disaggregated individuals, have almost by definition more limited collective action capacity than governmental or state stakeholders—and less than most commercial stakeholders.[66]

62 Mello e Souza and Perez Aznar , 'Brazil and Argentina' (n 36).
63 Cheng with Do, 'China and Vietnam' (n 38).
64 Berman and Pauwelyn, 'Assessing' (n 21); Mello e Souza and Pérez Aznar, 'Brazil and Argentina' (n 36).
65 DeMenno and Büthe, 'Voice and Influence' (n 2).
66 Tim Büthe, *The State as Facilitator of Collective Action*; Unpublished manuscript (Columbia University 1998).

One way to overcome both collective action challenges and material resource constraints is to institutionalize the pooling of resources and inputs. Some of the global governance bodies examined in this volume (e.g. Codex, FATF, FSB) have established regional sub-organizations;[67] others have admitted existing (external) regional organizations as affiliate members or observers. ASEAN, for example, has observer status in the ICH; and three regional organizations, such as the AHWP, are affiliate organizations of the IMDRF, which provides the Philippines and Vietnam with an indirect voice. These arrangements might indeed be helpful for pooling resources and coordinating like-minded governmental stakeholders' demands vis-à-vis global bodies. However, whether such arrangements really provide otherwise still-excluded countries with voice and influence is, at best, an open question; the case studies in this volume provide no evidence thereof.

25.4.3.6 Explaining Actual Stakeholder Voice, Given Voice Opportunities

In sum, our case studies of global finance and global health governance show that, among the previously marginalized or excluded stakeholders, it is governments (or representatives of the state, e.g. regulatory agencies) of developing countries who have most visibly gained voice opportunities through institutional reforms undertaken by global governance bodies. Differences (across global bodies and across stakeholders) in the salience of the issues, as well as differences in the availability of alternative fora for the governance of those issue, help explain differences in the extent to which these stakeholders make use of the new or expanded voice opportunities. Differences in the availability or scarcity of material resources, analytical resources, and political resources, needed to effectively engage in global governance, also play a role. When resources are tight, salience is particularly important for the political will to spend resources on engaging in global governance rather than focus on domestic issues or actions.

Several global bodies for the governance of finance and health (e.g. the IMF, the Basel Committee, the IASB, the WHO) have also created or reinforced opportunities for the inclusion of non-governmental stakeholders, and in particular, civil society representatives. Differences in the salience of the issues and the availability of alternative fora also matter here, but material/financial, analytical, and political constraints appear to be even more important for explaining the variation in the extent to which non-governmental stakeholders make use of the voice opportunities offered to them. Without including measures to also address the capacity and capability constraints of such stakeholders, initiatives to provide voice opportunities to these stakeholders will remain declamatory politics; they will not amount to a significant increase in voice or influence for non-commercial, civil society stakeholders.[68]

[67] Henrique Choer Moraes, ' Can Regional Institutions Increase the Legitimacy of Global Governance?' Chapter 12, this volume.

[68] See also Abdel Alshadafan, 'Energy Efficiency Standards: The Struggle for Legitimacy' 18(1) *International Journal of Standardization Research* (2020), 1-23.

25.5 Stakeholder Influence

Global finance bodies and global health bodies have opened up towards developing countries and, in global health governance, also towards non-state actors, as summarized in Section 25.3. And these increases in voice *opportunities* have resulted in substantial, though variable increases in actual stakeholder voice, as summarized in Section 25.4. Yet, 'equal participation does not mean equal influence'.[69] Indeed, many of the 'new' voice opportunities are not accompanied by any guarantee that previous marginalized stakeholders' input will be considered or even heard. It is therefore crucial to examine separately the question: Are the previously marginalized or excluded stakeholders, in the aftermath of reforms and increases in actual voice, able to exert any real influence over policy-making and decision-making outcomes?

It is, unfortunately, quite difficult to answer this question conclusively, given that it implies a causal claim,[70] for which the counterfactual is difficult to establish, given the complexity of global governance.[71] Properly establishing influence in fact requires the consideration of non-decisions, such as preventing (or at least delaying) the adoption of a policy, regulation, or standard,[72] as well as possible changes in the terms of the debate, through which intellectual hegemony might be established or challenged.[73] Notwithstanding these challenges in establishing conclusively the extent to which stakeholder reforms have allowed previously marginalized stakeholders to gain influence, the empirical chapters in this volume provide numerous examples of reforms having indeed allowed previously excluded stakeholders to influence outcomes. This evidence is mostly circumstantial, but often quite strong.

25.5.1 Global Finance Governance

Choer Moraes and Pérez Aznar, in their analysis of Brazil and Argentina in global finance, see the increases in the two countries' actual voice as having resulted in greater—though still highly variable—influence. This increased influence appears most notable with respect to agenda setting. Argentina, for instance, succeeded in putting several

[69] Thomas Hale, 'Transnational Actors and Transnational Governance in Global Environmental Politics' 23 *Annual Review of Political Science* (2020) 203-220, 213.

[70] Robert A Dahl, *Modern Political Analysis*, 5th ed. (Prentice Hall, 1991), esp. 35ff.

[71] James D Fearon, 'Counterfactuals and Hypothesis Testing in Political Science' 43(2) *World Politics* (1991) 169-195; Philip E Tetlock and Aaron Belkin (eds), *Counterfactual Thought Experiments in World Politics: Logical, Methodological, and Psychological Perspectives* (Princeton University Press 1996); Steven Bernstein, Richard Ned Lebow, Janice Gross Stein and Steven Weber, 'God Gave Physics the Easy Problems: Adapting Social Science to an Unpredictable World' 6(1) *European Journal of International Relations* (2000) 43-76.

[72] Peter Bachrach and Morton S Baratz, 'Two Faces of Power' 56(4) *American Political Science Review* (1962) 947-952; Raymond E Wolfinger, 'Nondecisions and the Study of Local Politics' 65(4) *American Political Science Review* (1971) 1063-1080.

[73] Steven Lukes, *Power: A Radical View*, 2nd ed. (Palgrave 2004); Robert W Cox, 'Gramsci, Hegemony and International Relations: An Essay in Method' 12(2) *Millennium: Journal of International Studies* (1983) 162-175; Michael N Barnett and Raymond Duvall (eds), *Power in Global Governance* (Cambridge University Press 2006).

topics on the agenda of the G20, including tax avoidance by multinationals, 'holdout bondholders' and their role in preventing the settlement of sovereign debt defaults, and credit rating agencies and their role in prompting or exacerbating financial crises. Choer Moraes and Pérez Aznar are able to conclude that the new voice opportunities for Argentina in the G20 yielded real influence, because these agenda-setting attempts succeeded after the IMF and the World Bank had proven unreceptive to Argentinian attempts to put the same topics on their agenda for international discussions over global finance and its governance. Gauging the impact of Argentina on the very modest decisions and actions eventually taken on these topics is much more difficult, though, given the large number of stakeholders that have tried to influence discussions of these topics. Moreover, establishing the counterfactual of a world without the rising powers' voice in global finance requires a multitude of untestable assumptions.

In other cases, however, there is strong evidence to suggest increases in real influence beyond the agenda-setting stage. Brazil not only succeeded in putting IMF working methods on the agenda of the IMF after the Financial Crisis of 2007–2009 broke; Choer Moraes and Pérez Aznar also credit, for instance, Brazil's push for new lending instruments with having directly led to the creation of the Flexible Credit Line lending facility.[74]

Zhang also focuses initially on agenda setting when assessing China's and Vietnam's influence in the aftermath of institutional reforms that created new voice opportunities. China, she notes, has been able to 'influence the IMF and the World Bank agenda [not directly but by] increasing [its] voice in [the] G20'.[75] Beyond agenda-setting, the picture is mixed but, for China, the findings suggest a substantial increase in voice-based influence. Indications of actual influence are weakest in the BCBS, where the Basel III reforms were already far advanced by the time China became a member in 2009. In IOSCO, its seat on both the Executive Committee and (since 2009) on the Technical Committee puts China at the heart of the organization's rule-making and decision-making, suggesting that China has (when desired) real influence, though we lack illustrative examples. In the FATF, China similarly attained a key position beyond mere membership in 2013, when it became a member of the seven-country committee with power over both the rule-making agenda and membership, which China says has yielded real influence (though it appears very reserved about giving examples or explaining how it exercises influence). In sum, China appears selective and preferably exercises its influence quietly, but there is little doubt that actual participation (voice) in global finance governance bodies has given it real leverage.

The contrast between China's and Vietnam's experience could hardly be starker: vis-à-vis IOSCO, BCBS, and FATF, Vietnam remains a mostly passive rule-taker. In an immediate sense, its lack of influence can be attributed to the lack of voice opportunities, but Zhang's analysis hardly suggests that Vietnam would wield any influence if it had voice opportunities (even if it could overcome the resource constraints that would probably prevent its exercise of actual voice in these global governance bodies). Regarding IMF governance, Zhang finds Vietnam 'satisfied' that its interests are taken into account 'by the IMF management'—but here, too, there is no indication of any

[74] Choer Moraes and Pérez Aznar, 'Brazil and Argentina (n 33).
[75] Weiwei Zhang, 'China and Vietnam' (n 34).

direct influence (neither on its own, due to its 0.24% quota share, nor jointly with other Asian or other developing countries).[76] The IMF might effectively take (some of) Vietnam's interests into account in pursuit of output legitimacy, but there is no indication of any changes in input and throughout.

25.5.2 Global Health Governance

Turning to global health governance, Mello e Souza and Pérez Aznar specifically credit Brazil's and Argentina's increased engagement (actually exercising voice) with having enabled greater influence, especially in the WHO. Argentina succeeded in advocating for WHO policies on mental health, child and pregnancy allowance, and gender identity, modelled on Argentinian domestic policies that were considered innovative and successful. Similarly, Brazil succeeded in getting the WHO to embrace its approach to pharmaceutical patents for essential medicines—and it is credited with having played a major (influential) role in the change of the WHO's approach to HIV/AIDS. While both countries have thus had real influence, Mello e Souza and Pérez Aznar see Brazil as having been notably more influential, in part due to the greater financial resources available for Brazilian participation, but also very importantly due to its strategy of exercising influence by mobilizing like-minded countries, especially from Latin America. Brazil has demonstrated this high inter- and transnational collective action capacity both through formal channels, such as the South American Health Council (where Brazil has played a leadership role), as well as informally and ad hoc. Such strategies of regional coordination and mobilization also appear to have been important to the—occasional—Brazilian and Argentinian successes in Codex. At the same time, internal (domestic) divisions have repeatedly impeded both countries' ability to translate voice opportunities and even actual engagement in Codex into influence. In the ICH and GlobalG.A.P., Brazilian and Argentinian stakeholders have not been able to gain meaningful influence, even when they have tried to make use of improved voice opportunities. Mello e Souza and Pérez Aznar attribute this finding to remaining de facto and institutional barriers, such as the costs of regular involvement and implementation in the case of GlobalG.A.P. and the veto power of US, Japanese and European interests in the ICH.[77]

The comparison of China and Vietnam similarly yields several examples of greater engagement in global governance bodies having—by all indications—resulted in greater influence, such as when China worked with GAVI and the WHO to support Chinese domestic capacity-building for vaccine production (and its regulatory oversight to ensure high quality), so as to overcome GAVI objections to locally sourced vaccines.[78] At the same time, this matched-country-pair case study illustrates the consequences of the power differential between the two countries—much more clearly than the Brazil–Argentina comparison. For instance, the Global Fund was able to make its programmes in Vietnam conditional on Vietnam ending forced drug

[76] Weiwei Zhang, 'China and Vietnam' (n 34).
[77] Mello e Souza and Pérez Aznar, 'Brazil and Argentina' (n 36).
[78] Cheng with Do, 'China and Vietnam' (n 38).

treatment programmes in detoxification centres and labour camps. Similar attempts to get China to stop—or at least reduce—such practices were unsuccessful, implying greater Chinese influence vis-à-vis the Global Fund (although in this case exercised mostly through means other than direct engagement with the Global Fund). In the ICH, the IMDRF, and GlobalG.A.P., greater Chinese (than Vietnamese) influence more clearly appears to have been based on increased involvement in response to new voice opportunities. That said, similar to what we saw in some of the global finance governance bodies, the evidence is much stronger for China having attained institutional *positions* of power, such as appointments to technical and decision-making committees than for actual Chinese influence (partly due to the inherent challenge of establishing the exercise of influence). A clear example of actual influence seems to be China working with GlobalG.A.P. to establish the equivalence of 'first class' ChinaG.A.P. certifications, which has yielded global market access for Chinese agricultural products from companies that hold such certificates. In several of the global health bodies, including GlobalG.A.P., the continued lack of Vietnamese influence also reflects the continued dearth of voice opportunities, discussed earlier (see Section 25.3).[79]

The comparative case study of India and the Philippines in global health governance yields similar findings. Where the Indian government decided to devote increased financial and political resources to Indian participation in global governance, those resources (along with India's global political ambition) have played a major role in driving increased Indian engagement in global governance bodies. This increase in involvement appears also to have resulted in greater influence. Examples include India's success in forging a breakthrough on Tobacco Control within the WHO and its successful push for the eradication of yaws—long recognized as one of the 'neglected tropical diseases'. On numerous topics, India is said to have become an increasingly equal partner of global health bodies—'from agenda-setting to implementation'.[80] The Philippines similarly has repeatedly succeeded in leveraging its increased engagement into influence, at least at the agenda-setting stage (such as in the WHO campaign for universal health coverage). In doing so, it also was helped by having attained positions of power, such as repeatedly getting elected to a seat on the WHO Executive Board. Its arguably more modest ambitions make a direct comparison difficult, but the Philippines' government's willingness to prioritize actual engagement (in its allocation of financial and political resources)—and its success in gaining influence in global health governance as a consequence—further underscore the assessment that actual involvement can significantly contribute to influence. Both countries' experience in Codex largely mirrors their experience in the WHO: strong increases in involvement (from a very low baseline) resulted in at least some increases in real influence. The change was especially notable after efforts to build domestic scientific capacity and capability succeeded in putting both countries into a much stronger position to support their positions with scientific data, expert reports, etc. Such improvements in analytical resources allowed the Philippines, for instance, to make its scientific contribution in 2006 on the proposal on the 'maximum level of lead in fish' to the Committee

[79] Cheng with Do, 'China and Vietnam' (n 38).
[80] Büthe *et al.*, 'India and the Philippines' (n 39).

on Food Additives and Contaminants, which ended up being reflected in the Codex standard. In Codex, the Philippines' increased influence thus almost matches India's. The India-Philippines comparison thus also underscores: Increased voice opportunities may translate into influence *if and only if* a previously marginalized country makes the *domestic political* decision to devote resources to actual engagement in global governance.[81]

25.5.3 Assessing the Hypotheses: Policy Effectiveness and Greater Democratic Legitimacy

Our analytical framework identified two possible reasons for why and how stakeholders might—as a consequence of increased engagement—gain actual influence in global governance bodies.[82] Specifically, DeMenno and Büthe stipulated that (a) *if voice opportunities were opened to help choose or design better policies*, we should expect stakeholders who make use of those opportunity to gain actual influence if (and only if) they are able to provide technical and/or political information, needed by the global body to choose or design better, that is, more effective, policies. Alternatively, DeMenno and Büthe stipulated that (b) *if voice opportunities were opened to enhance democratic legitimacy*, participating stakeholder would gain influence if (and only if) they are able to enhance output or, most likely, 'input ∩ throughput legitimacy' through their participation.

The preceding review of the case studies allows us now to assess these hypotheses, put forth in Chapter 2. Overall, the willingness of global bodies to take new information into account—even when it is provided by traditionally disregarded stakeholders—and generally their willingness to allow long-marginalized stakeholders to influence rules and decision, appears to be to a large extent instrumental rather than driven by deeply internalized changes in the norms of democratic governance. In that sense, we find substantial support for the thrust of the theoretical framework, as well as the two hypotheses about the conditions under which stakeholders gain influence. We also note that the two causal mechanisms are rarely as neatly separable in practice as in theory. That said, the empirical support from the case study chapters appears to be notably stronger for the first hypothesis, emphasizing stakeholder-specific information and policy learning for choosing or designing better policies.

Choer Moraes and Pérez Aznar, for instance, note that an important element in Brazil's success in getting the IMF to include the Flexible Credit Line among its broadened portfolio of lending instruments, was Brazil's status as a former 'client of the system'. In other words, its experience as an IMF borrower and target of IMF 'programmes' provided Brazil with unique insights into the operation of those programmes—information that could help the IMF improve programme design, creating an incentive for the IMF not just to listen but act on the information (not necessarily

[81] Büthe *et al.*, 'India and the Philippines' (n 39). See also Lavenex *et al.*, 'Power Transitions and the Rise of the Regulatory State' (n 37).

[82] DeMenno and Büthe, 'Voice and Influence' (n 2), Section 2.6.3, H_{3A} and H_{3B}.

in every respect as Brazil might have wished, but having 'influence' does not require being completely successful).[83]

A similar dynamic appears to play out across the global health case studies. For global bodies that design or fund programmes for specific locations or populations, learning how to make those interventions work in the particular local context is critical to their effectiveness. Stakeholders who can uniquely provide technical and political information that is specific to those particular places can therefore wield considerable influence within or through such global governance bodies, provided that taking the information into account promises to contribute to the policy's effectiveness. For global health organizations devoted to addressing certain diseases (e.g. GAVI), this means high responsiveness to (and thus influence for) countries that might seem particularly disadvantaged and dependent upon the global governance body. Its high disease burden thus allows, for instance, Vietnam to wield considerable influence within or through such global governance bodies.

By contrast, as Cheng and Do point out, global governance bodies that are 'only' engaged in *general* rule-making, such as standards-developing organizations, are much less concerned with gaining local knowledge. Global bodies such as the ICH or the IMDRF or the rule-making operations of Codex are therefore less likely to be influenced by stakeholders whose potential contribution consists primarily of such knowledge.[84]

Interestingly, Mello e Souza and Pérez Aznar suggest that Brazil and Argentina *could* wield substantially greater influence in global health governance if they had the human and financial resources to turn their specialized expertise 'related to climate, ecosystems, agricultural technologies and modes of production, population eating habits, drug stability and temperature and the like' into inputs (i.e. technical and scientific studies) for leverage in global health governance bodies.[85] In other words, instances where traditionally marginalized stakeholders remain marginalized in fact provide additional support for hypothesis H_{3A}.

Opening up global governance and including traditionally excluded stakeholders, especially the governments or other stakeholders from such populous countries as China and India, may of course also boost a global governance body's democratic legitimacy. Indeed, in the Global Fund, for instance, India contributes both expertise and legitimacy.[86] Only rarely, however, have our case studies yielded direct evidence of global governance bodies letting a traditionally marginalized country (or stakeholders from within such a country) wield substantive influence in order to boost legitimacy. And where China and India have been permitted to exclusively wield influence, it is difficult to distinguish the pursuit of some notion of global democratic legitimacy (as a reason for such a change) from the basic IR–Realist rationale of recognizing them as rising (super)powers. Where legitimacy seems to have played a role is when stakeholders have overtly made legitimacy-based demands.

[83] Choer Moraes and Pérez Aznar, 'Brazil and Argentina' (n 33).
[84] Cheng with Do, 'China and Vietnam' (n 38).
[85] Mello e Souza and and Pérez Aznar, 'Brazil and Argentina' (n 36).
[86] Büthe *et al.*, 'India and the Philippines' (n 39).

25.6 Unexpected Findings: A Research Agenda

Our research has also yielded a number of interesting findings not anticipated by our analytical framework (or wholly outside of it), which we highlight as fruitful avenues for future research.

25.6.1 Second Image Reversed Stakeholder Participation Effects

An unanticipated—but by all indications important—effect of the push for increased stakeholder participation in global governance, which emerges from several of our case studies, is that these efforts appear to have boosted the participation of previously excluded stakeholders at the *national* (domestic) level. This effect is particularly notable for the Global Fund and GAVI. For a country to receive Global Fund grants, they must demonstrate that civil society and other traditionally disregarded societal group have been included in the country's domestic country coordinating mechanism (CCM).[87] According to Mello e Souza and Pérez Aznar's analysis, those CCMs have resulted in stronger, more extensive involvement of civil society organizations in domestic health policy in Brazil, as well as ultimately improved domestic health governance.[88] According to Cheng and Do's analysis, GAVI has supported the establishment of a Chinese office, thereby improving local health governance and increasing access of previously marginalized domestic groups to the Chinese health care system.[89]

25.6.2 The Primacy of Domestic Politics

Even when salience is high, alternative fora are not readily available, and resources are sufficient, a government of a traditionally disregarded stakeholder might nonetheless opt not to exercise newly established voice opportunities (nor exert influence) in order to safeguard its national policy autonomy. India's decision to decline (at least so far) the invitation to join the ICH is a good example of a preference for national policy autonomy winning out over an opportunity to gain voice and maybe even influence in global governance.[90] Insofar as such a decision reflects prioritizing domestic political needs (for flexibility), it is consistent with the liberal tradition in international relations scholarship,[91] as well as with the observation that some countries have on occasion pursued domestically important symbolic gains over macro-economic benefits

[87] Berman, 'Stakeholder Participation Reforms' (n 19).

[88] Mello e Souza and Pérez Aznar, 'Brazil and Argentina' (n 36).

[89] Cheng with Do, 'China and Vietnam' (n 38).

[90] See Büthe *et al.*, 'India and the Philippines' (n 39).

[91] Helen V Milner, *Resisting Protectionism: Global Industries and the Politics of International Trade* (Princeton University Press 1988) and *Interests, Institutions, and Information: Domestic Politics and International Relations* (Princeton University Press 1997); Andrew Moravcsik, 'Taking Preferences Seriously: A Liberal Theory of International Politics' 51(4) *International Organization* (1997): 513-553.

when negotiating international agreements.[92] A positive political economy model could in fact accommodate such preferences by making the salience of the global governance body a partial function of domestic political priorities—but in the end, a fuller theoretical treatment of such preferences for autonomy is warranted to really advance our understanding of such choices in the context of global governance.

25.6.3 The Importance of Political Coalitions

We have also found that inter- and transnational supporting coalitions can play a major role. Brazil, in particular, has on many occasions been able to amplify its position by mobilizing regional neighbours and occasional other coalitions of similarly situated stakeholders—especially in health governance. Less-powerful countries, such as Vietnam and Philippines, have, at least occasionally, been able to influence rules and decisions in global governance by working through regional bodies or utilizing other forms of institutionalized cooperation.

25.6.4 Overcoming Barriers to Disregarded Stakeholders' Participation through Technology?

One of the most pervasive impediments to more voice and influence for traditionally marginalized or excluded stakeholders of global governance is the cost of participation, especially for non-commercial, civil society stakeholders. The problem is well known and has been confirmed again in the empirical analyses in this volume. Technological innovation and change have often been noted as a possible solution. The digital distribution of documents promises to reduce delays for stakeholders in countries with weak postal infrastructures; it also makes it virtually costless to provide information about the agenda in a given global governance body to a broader range of stakeholders. Finally, it lowers the costs of taking on positions of power, such as committee secretariats, for stakeholders of limited means. Conducting (many) meetings by video conference rather than in person, moreover, reduces the direct costs of participation.[93] Online voting, furthermore, allows decisional participation even for those who cannot afford to travel to the meetings. It is an open question, however, to what extent technological changes really empower previously disadvantaged stakeholders or simply reinforce the existing distribution of power.[94] Theoretically,

[92] Tim Büthe, 'The Globalization of Health and Safety Standards: Delegation of Regulatory Authority in the SPS-Agreement of 1994 Agreement Establishing the World Trade Organization' 71(1) *Law and Contemporary Problems* (2008) 219-255.

[93] See Tim Büthe, The Power of Norms; the Norms of Power: Who Governs International Electrical and Electronic Technology?' in Deborah D Avant, Martha Finnemore and Susan K Sell (eds), *Who Governs the Globe?* (Cambridge University Press 2010) 292-332.

[94] Tim Büthe, 'Global Private Politics: A Research Agenda' 12(3) *Business and Politics* (2010) 1–24; see also Janice E Thomson and Stephen D Krasner, 'Global Transactions and the Consolidation of Sovereignty' in E-O Czempiel and James N Rosenau (eds), *Global Changes and Theoretical Challenges* (Lexington Books 1989) 195-219.

power-redistributing dynamics may well be counteracted by power-reinforcing dynamics: the technology and the time required to learn how to use it effectively, for instance, are generally more amply available in richer countries and to incumbent commercial stakeholders. Empirical research on this issue is scarce and difficult since technology adoption tends to be endogenous. The SARS-CoV2/COVID-10 pandemic provides an opportunity to gain new insights on this question, because it might be treated as a truly exogenous technology shock, which has forced many global governance bodies (along with governments, the private sector, and private individuals and group) suddenly into the digital age—but it is too early to draw definitive inferences about the consequences of this technology shock.[95]

25.6.5 Preventing Undue Influence and Managing Conflicts of Interest

Although participation by non-state actors has the potential to improve democratic legitimacy, the engagement of such stakeholders also introduces new risks to legitimacy, notably the risk of regulatory capture and conflicts of interest.[96] There is much evidence for this problem in international rule-making, e.g. in the efforts of the beverage,[97] tobacco,[98] or vaccine industry[99] to influence WHO policy-making, or in big banks' capture of the Basel committee standards.[100] This problem is well known in the national context,[101] and some countries have policies in place to address it (whether or

[95] For a longer-term account of the consequences of technological innovations and technology diffusion for international politics, see Helen V Milner and Sondre Ulvund Solstad, 'Technological Change and the International System' 73 *World Politics* (2021) 545–589.

[96] Tim Büthe, 'Distributional Consequences of Transnational Private Regulation' Duke University Rethinking Regulation Working Paper no.6 (2013) 1–49; Ayelet Berman, 'Between Participation and Capture in International Rule-Making: The WHO Framework of Engagement with Non-State Actors' 32(1) *European Journal of International Law* (2021) 227–254; Berman, 'Industry, Capture and Transnational Standard Setting' (n 61).

[97] Sandeep P Kishore and Kavitha Kolappa, Unlikely Allies (14 February 2014) <http://www.huffingtonpost.com/sandeep-p-kishore-phd/healthy-living-news_b_4781300.html >, last accessed 08/15/2021; Third World Network, *Keep a Strong FENSA: Safeguard WHO's Independence from Private Interests* <http://www.twn.my/title2/health.info/2015/hi150506.htm>, last accessed 08/15/2021.

[98] Heide Weishaar, Jeff Collin, Katherine Smith, Thilo Grüning, Sema Mandal, and Anna Gilmore, 'Global Health Governance and the Commercial Sector: A Documentary Analysis of Tobacco Company Strategies to Influence the WHO Framework Convention on Tobacco Control' *PLOS Medicine* (2012) e1001249, 8.

[99] Deborah Cohen and Philip Carter, 'Conflicts of Interest: WHO and the Pandemic Flu 'Conspiracies' 340 *BMJ* (2010) c2912; Zosia Kmietowicz, 'WHO Admits to "Inconsistencies" in Its Policy on Conflicts of Interest' 340 *BMJ* (2010) c3167.

[100] Michael S Barr and Geoffrey P Miller, 'Global Administrative Law: The View from Basel' 17(1) *European Journal of International Law* 15-46; Maurizia De Bellis, 'Global Financial Standards and Networks: The Global Administrative Law Perspective' 30(1) *Revista de derecho publico de l'Universidad de los Andes* (2013) 1-28, at 14f; Kevin L Young, 'Transnational Regulatory Capture? An Empirical Examination of the Transnational Lobbying of the Basel Committee on Banking Supervision' 19(4) *Review of International Political Economy* (2012) 663-688; Daniel Tarullo, *Banking on Basel: The Future of International Financial Regulation* (Peterson Institute for International Economics 2008), at 104; Duncan R Wood, *Governing Global Banking* (Ashgate 2005), at 150; Adam W Chalmer, 'When Banks Lobby: The Effects of Organizational Characteristics and Banking Regulations on International Bank Lobbying' 19(1) *Business and Politics* (2017) 107-134.

[101] Brian Libgober and Daniel Carpenter, 'Lobbying with Lawyers: Financial Market Evidence for Banks' Influence on Rulemaking', *Washington Center for Equitable Growth Working Paper* (1/2018) 1–72; Daniel P

not this is done effectively is another issue).[102] Despite the increasingly dominant position of business in international rule-making, very few global bodies have tried to regulate the associated risks.[103] The WHO has been an exception. To better manage non-state actor engagement, the WHO introduced its 'Framework for Engagement with Non-State Actors' (FENSA) in 2016.[104] The Framework's purpose is to manage the risks of engaging with non-state actors, such as conflicts of interest, undue influence on the WHO, negative impact on the WHO's integrity, and competitive advantages for certain non-state actors.[105] However, it is still too early to determine whether the FENSA framework will effectively manage these risks.

25.7 Participation in Global Governance: Similarities and Differences between Finance and Health

The research project summarized in this book has sought to advance our theoretical understanding of stakeholder participation in global governance and contribute to our empirical knowledge. We have tried to do so especially regarding the participation by traditionally marginalized and excluded stakeholders following institutional reforms undertaken by global governance bodies with the declared objective of boosting the participation of such stakeholders. This concluding chapter aims to bring together and compare the key insights we have gained about the reforms and, in particular, about participation in the aftermath of those reforms—across the two major issue areas of global finance and global health, which we initially analysed separately in Part II (Chapters 4–12) and Part III (Chapters 13–22), respectively.

In both finance and health, the overall trend in global governance has been towards more voice opportunities and—more tentatively—greater influence for traditionally disregarded stakeholders. At the same time, the empirical analyses of the reforms, including the in-depth paired country case studies, have revealed substantial differences in voice opportunities across global finance and global health.[106]

Carpenter and David A Moss, *Preventing Regulatory Capture: Special Interest Influence and How to Limit It* (Cambridge University Press 2014); George J Stigler, 'The Theory of Economic Regulation' 2(1) *Bell Journal of Economics and Management Science* (1971) 3-21.

[102] E.g. OECD, *Independence of Regulators and Protection against Undue Influence* <http://www.oecd.org/governance/regulatory-policy/independence-of-regulators.htm>, last accessed 05/16/2017.

[103] OECD, *International Regulatory Co-operation* (n 27); Alshadafan, 'The Struggle for Legitimacy' (n 68).

[104] K M Gopakumar, 'The World Health Organization's Engagement with Non-State Actors: The Risk of Corporate Influence.' Chapter 22, this volume; Berman, 'Between Participation and Capture' (n 96).

[105] 69th World Health Assembly Framework of Engagement with Non-State Actors 2016, Section 7.

[106] We also have identified numerous differences across the individual global bodies examined within each of the issue areas—consistent with the findings of other scholars of reforms in global governance (see, e.g. Tallberg *et al.*, *The Opening Up* (n 5); Grigorescu, *Democratic International Organizations?* (n 5); Phillip Y Lipscy, *Renegotiating the World Order* (Cambridge University Press 2017); Ranjit Lall, 'Making Global Governance Accountable: States, Society, and the Politics of Reform' (Paper presented at the TUM School of Governance Research Seminar, May 2021)). These differences have been the focus of many of the previous chapters; some have been highlighted in previous sections of this conclusion. Here, we seek to zoom out and focus on the commonalities within each issue area—and especially the similarities and differences across them.

Most new and expanded participation opportunities have been geared towards governments and other stakeholders from large emerging economies. Global finance IOs (the World Bank and the IMF), as well as transgovernmental regulatory networks in both finance (e.g. G20, Basel Committee) and health (ICH, IMDRF) have mostly added large emerging countries as members or strengthened their voting rights—benefiting Brazil, China, and India but few or no others. In contrast, global health partnerships (Global Fund, GAVI) and global health IOs (such as the WHO and Codex, which already had near universal membership) have also increased voice opportunities for small countries.

As regards non-governmental stakeholders, global health bodies of all kinds (IOs, transgovernmental regulatory networks, partnerships, and private standard-setting bodies) have substantially expanded voice opportunities for non-governmental actors—sometimes by inviting them as members, often by creating diverse non-decisional participation opportunities. Global bodies concerned with the governance of finance, by contrast, have not granted new voice opportunities to non-state actors, or have done so only very modestly—with few exceptions (e.g. the Basel Committee, which has developed new notice and comment procedures for input from private-sector financial interests). Even in global health, new voice opportunities for non-governmental stakeholders have benefitted those stakeholders highly unevenly. Regulatory networks (ICH, IMDRF) and standard-setting bodies (GlobalG.A.P.) have opened up predominantly towards commercial (business) actors. Only global health IOs (WHO) and partnerships (Global Fund, GAVI) have also opened up substantially towards non-profit civil society organizations, along with commercial groups.

Although calls for more democratic accountability and legitimacy have had a role to play in bringing about the stakeholder participation reforms, our findings—summarized in Section 25.3—support our initial hypotheses that instrumental reasons have been the main rationale for the creation or expansion of stakeholder participation opportunities in global finance and health.

We set out to answer two key questions about the aftermath of those stakeholder participation reforms, adopted by global bodies in recent years. *First, have the reforms increased the actual engagement or involvement of the previously disregarded stakeholders in global governance?* Across both health and finance, the findings from the case studies suggest that hitherto disregarded stakeholders often make use of new or expanded voice opportunities, resulting—on average—in increases in actual voice or involvement of traditionally marginalized stakeholders in global governance bodies where voice opportunities were indeed expanded. In many cases, these increases can be clearly attributed to participation reforms.[107]

Notwithstanding an overall increase in the actual involvement of traditionally marginalized and excluded stakeholders in global governance (conditional on global health or finance bodies having provided new voice opportunities), the case studies show that stakeholders' use of these opportunities varies. Individually and jointly, the case studies find strong support for the hypotheses developed in Chapter 2 to explain

[107] While this finding holds across both health and finance, reforms that introduced or increased voice opportunities—and especially reforms that introduced or increased opportunities for decisional participation—have been far more common in global health than in global finance, as noted earlier.

such variation.[108] The case studies indicate that four factors—the salience of the governed issue, the availability of an alternative fora, material resources, and analytical resources—play a key role in determining whether stakeholders take advantage of participation opportunities. The case studies also provide at least tentative support that the availability of political resources—especially variations in collective action capacity—play an important role, too.

These findings contribute not only to the scholarly literature, but they also have practical implications for policy-makers—and possibly others. Anyone who might want to foster increases in actual stakeholder participation surely ought to consider not just the supply but also the demand for participation, *including feasibility constraints and remaining, often structural, barriers*. Specifically, initiatives to provide voice or influence for non-commercial, civil society stakeholders (who are often unable to get involved due to their lack of financial, analytical, or political resources) need to include measures to also address the capacity and capability constraints of such stakeholders. Otherwise, such initiatives will amount to little more than declamatory politics.

Second, to what extent have those previously disregarded stakeholders gained any real influence in the rule- and decision-making by global bodies devoted to the governance of health and finance? We have emphasized that empirically establishing any particular stakeholder's influence in global governance is fraught with empirical and inferential challenges, but the case studies provide a substantial number of at least circumstantial, anecdotal evidence that previously marginalized stakeholders have indeed been able to exert real influence over rule- and decision-making. This finding generally applies in both global health and global finance—conditional on the previous findings that stakeholder participation reforms have generally gone much less far in global finance than in global health; that the reforms have, in finance, still largely excluded non-governmental stakeholders; and that non-commercial interests in both issue areas are still subject to substantial constraints, which restrict their de facto participation.

The case study chapters identify a few cases where traditionally marginalized stakeholders appear to have been able to exert influence due to the belief that this was necessary to enhance process legitimacy, which in turn was expected to facilitate implementation and more generally policy effectiveness. India's increasing influence in the WHO might be an example of this pattern. In most cases, however, where a previously marginalized stakeholder was able to gain real influence, it does not appear to have been due to the stakeholder's ability to enhance the global governance body's process legitimacy. Rather, the crucial factor in most instances appears to have been the stakeholder's 'private' technical or political information (not otherwise readily available to the global governance body), which enabled policy learning and thus affected policy choices. Argentina's and Brazil's experiences as former 'clients' of IMF programmes—as well as India's and the Philippines' experience with carrying a high burden of certain diseases before they became priorities for the WHO and/or the Global Fund—are examples of such highly pertinent and hence 'influential' information.

[108] DeMenno and Büthe, 'Voice and Influence' (n 2), esp. Section 2.5.

Most examples of previously disregarded stakeholders exercising real influence are—unsurprisingly—drawn from global governance bodies where these stakeholders attained opportunities for decisional participation. This finding, however, might reflect a common bias in empirical research[109] and should not prematurely lead us to infer that non-decisional participation cannot be influential. Several of the successful attempts to influence the agenda of global governance bodies, for instance (summarized in Section 25.5), do not appear to have been a function of China, India, Brazil, or Argentina having attained formal agenda-setting power in the particular body, but rather having attained a more prominent yet still non-decisional role. This finding is consistent with research on the 'Hawthorne' effect, which has been shown in many different settings: knowing that others are watching generally prompts decision-makers to exhibit what they believe observers consider normatively desirable behaviour, *even when the observers have no means to exert any direct leverage over the observed.* In other words, openness of governance processes to closer observation by previously marginalized or excluded stakeholders may well foster actions more in conformity with social norms. As long as there is a widely shared social norm that decision-making ought to take the interests of all affected stakeholders into account, the increased transparency and opportunities for scrutiny of the decision-making process, along with an open articulation of participating stakeholders' preferences, might lead to rules or decisions influenced by those stakeholders' preferences. More generally, it might lead to public interest-oriented policies—to a greater extent than if those policies were adopted through a less participatory process.[110]

Note that the instrumental account of stakeholder participation at the core of this volume assumes that more widespread participation provides rule- and decision-makers with more comprehensive and/or more accurate information, facilitating policy learning and allowing decision-makers to design or choose better policies. In addition, participation is assumed to increase the legitimacy of the rule-making and decision-making processes, increasing acceptance of the result of the process, consequently boosting voluntary implementation and compliance. These benefits may in fact be counterbalanced by detrimental consequences,[111] but our analytical framework assumes that the key actors in global governance bodies expect that participation yields such benefits.

The assumption is reasonable, given that participation is widely believed—and across a broad range of empirical contexts has been shown—to yield such benefits.[112]

[109] The effect of an influence attempt is much more readily tractable when it is undertaken by an actor with decisional authority.

[110] See, e.g. Jan Aart Scholte, 'Toward Greater Legitimacy in Global Governance' 18(1) *Review of International Political Economy* (February 2011) 110-120.

[111] Mark S Reed, 'Stakeholder Participation for Environmental Management: A Literature Review' 141(10) *Biological Conservation* (2008): 2417-2431; John Gaventa and Gregory Barrett, 'Mapping the Outcomes of Citizen Engagement' 40(12) *World Development* (2012) 2399-2410; Matthijs Hisschemöller and Eefje Cuppen, 'Participatory Assessment: Tools for Empowering, Learning, and Legitimating?' In Andrew J Jordan and John R Turnpenny (eds), *The Tools of Policy Formulation: Actors, Capacities, Venues and Effects* (Edward Elgar 2015), 33-51.

[112] Michael Fagence, *Citizen Participation in Planning* (Oxford-Pergamon 1977); E Allan Lind and Tom R Tyler, *The Social Psychology of Procedural Justice* (Springer 1988); Virginia Haufler, *The Public Role of the Private Sector* (Carnegie Endowment for International Peace 2001); Samuel D Brody, 'Measuring the

We note, however, that it remains an assumption, adopted above all for its analytic productiveness. We have, within this project, not examined to what extent participation in global governance actually yields these benefits. Such an examination is warranted not just because participatory governance has been the focus of general critique,[113] often but not only building on the public choice critique of regulation.[114] It is also warrnted because participatory governance has been critiqued for inconsistently

Effects of Stakeholder Participation on the Quality of Local Plans Based on the Principles of Collaborative Ecosystem Management' 22(4) *Journal of Planning Education and Research* (2003): 407-419; Archon Fung, 'Varieties of Participation in Complex Governance' 66(S1) *Public Administration Review* (2006) 66-75; Diana C Mutz, *Hearing the Other Side: Deliberative versus Participatory Democracy* (Cambridge University Press 2006); Susanne Stoll-Kleemann and Martin Welp, 'Participatory and Integrated Management of Biosphere Reserves: Lessons from Case Studies and a Global Survey' 17(S1) *GAIA: Ecological Perspectives for Science and Society* (2008) 161-168; Lisen Schultz, Andreas Duit, and Carl Folke, 'Participation, Adaptive Co-management, and Management Performance' 39(4) *World Development* (2011) 662-671; Claudia Pahl-Wostl, Gert Becker, Christian Knieper, and Jan Sendzimir, 'How Multilevel Societal Learning Processes Facilitate Transformative Change' 18(4) *Ecology & Society* (2013) 58:1–15; Juliette C Young, Andrew Jordan, Kate R Searle, Adam Butler, Daniel S Chapman, Peter Simmons, and Allan D Watt, 'Does Stakeholder Involvement Really Benefit Biodiversity Conservation?' 158 *Biological Conservation* (Feb 2013) 359-370; Robert A Dahl and Ian Shapiro, *On Democracy*, 2nd ed. (Yale University Press 2015); Dingwerth and Nanz, 'Participation' (n 10); Joris de Vente, Mark S Reed, Lindsay C Stringer, Sandra Valente, and Jens Newig, 'How Does the Context and Design of Participatory Decision Making Processes Affect Their Outcomes?' 21(2) *Ecology and Society* (2016) 468-491; James S Fishkin and Jane Mansbridge (eds), Special Issue: The Prospects & Limits of Deliberative Democracy 146(3) *Daedalus* (2017); Marc Fleurbaey and the International Panel on Social Progress, *Rethinking Society for the 21st Century*, 3 vols (Cambridge University Press 2018); André Bächtiger, John S Dryzek and Jane Mansbridge (eds), *Oxford Handbook of Deliberative Democracy* (Oxford University Press 2019); Anna Ernst, 'How Participation Influences the Perception of Fairness, Efficiency and Effectiveness in Environmental Governance' 238 *Journal of Environmental Management* (2019) 368-381; Elisa Kochskämper, Edward Challies, Nicolas W Jager, and Jens Newig (eds), *Participation for Effective Environmental Governance* (Routledge 2019); Ernesto Cruz Ruiz, 'Underrepresented Groups and Constitution-Making' 19(2) *Political Studies Review* (2021) 164-170; Alan M Jacobs and Tim Büthe with Ana Arjona, Leonardo R Arriola, Eva Bellin, Andrew Bennett, Lisa Björkman, Erik Bleich, Zachary Elkins, Tasha Fairfield, Nikhar Gaikwad, Sheena Chestnut Greitens, Mary Hawkesworth, Veronica Herrera, Yoshiko M Herrera, Kimberley S Johnson, Ekrem Karakoç, Kendra Koivu, Marcus Kreuzer, Milli Lake, Timothy W Luke, Lauren M MacLean, Samantha Majic, Rahsaan Maxwell, Zachariah Mampilly, Robert Mickey, Kimberly J Morgan, Sarah E Parkinson, Craig Parsons, Wendy Pearlman, Mark A Pollack, Elliot Posner, Rachel Beatty Riedl, Edward Schatz, Carsten Q Schneider, Jillian Schwedler, Anastasia Shesterinina, Erica S Simmons, Diane Singerman, Hillel David Soifer, Nicholas Rush Smith, Scott Spitzer, Jonas Tallberg, Susan Thomson, Antonio Y Vázquez-Arroyo, Barbara Vis, Lisa Wedeen, Juliet A Williams, Elisabeth Jean Wood, and Deborah J Yashar, 'The Qualitative Transparency Deliberations: Insights and Implications' 19(1) *Perspectives on Politics* (2021) 171-208.

[113] Sarah C White, 'Depoliticising Development: The Uses and Abuses of Participation' 6(1) *Development in Practice* (1996) 6-15; Cary Coglianese, 'Assessing Consensus: The Promise and Performance of Negotiated Rulemaking' 46(4) *Duke Law Journal* (1997) 1255-1349; Bill Cooke and Uma Kothari (eds), *Participation: The New Tyranny?* (Zed Books 2001); Bill Durodié, 'The True Costs of Precautionary Chemicals Regulations' 23(2) *Risk Analysis* (April 2003) 389-398; Samuel Hickey and Giles Mohan (eds), *Participation - From Tyranny to Transformation? Exploring New Approaches to Participation in Development* (Zed Books 2004).

[114] See, e.g. Bruce Yandle, 'Bootleggers and Baptists: The Education of a Regulatory Economist' 7(3) *Regulation* (May/June 1983) 12-16; Steve Charnovitz, 'Two Centuries of Participation: NGOs and International Governance' 18(2) *Michigan Journal of International Law* (1997) 183-286, esp. 274f; Roman Goldbach, 'Asymmetric Influence in Global Banking Regulation: Transnational Harmonization, the Competition State and Regulatory Failure' 22(6) *Review of International Political Economy* (2015) 1087-1127. See also Richard A Posner, 'The Concept of Regulatory Capture: A Short, Inglorious History' in Daniel P Carpenter and David A Moss (eds), *Preventing Regulatory Capture: Special Interest Influence and How to Limit It* (Cambridge University Press 2014) 49-56.

leading to sometimes better and sometimes worse outcomes[115] and for reinforcing power relations instead of empowering traditionally marginalized stakeholders.[116] While a systematic assessment of the rules and decisions resulting from more participatory governance is beyond the scope of this book, it is noteworthy that the case studies do not report any instances where broadening participation has resulted in what many observers have feared might be a consequence of stakeholder participation reforms:[117] deadlock or substantially slower, less efficient rule- and decision-making.

Finally, the research in this book has yielded several findings that were not anticipated by our analytical framework. They highlight at least three aspects of global governance previously rarely discussed in the literature on global governance. First, global governance reforms that require input to reflect a broad range of societal interests can effectively increase stakeholder voice and influence at the *domestic* level, thus democratizing policy-making in those issue areas. We have dubbed this 'second image reversed stakeholder participation effects' of global governance.[118] Second, there is a dearth of systematic frameworks for preventing undue influence and managing conflicts of interest in global governance. Without addressing conflicts-of-interest concerns, reforms that are supposed to boost the legitimacy of global governance, but often result only in quite selective increases in stakeholder participation, can result in capture and undue influence and thus may in the end further threaten rather than strengthen the legitimacy of global governance. While there is a wealth of literature warning of such pitfalls in participatory governance at both the domestic and the international or global levels,[119] the lack of safeguards against conflicts of interests in global governance, the resulting threats to its legitimacy, and the institutional design or improvements for safeguards have received hardly any attention. Lastly, whether or under what condition technological changes provide tools for overcoming barriers to participation—or might exacerbate unequal participation—is an increasingly important, yet largely unanswered question. All three of these findings identify promising avenues for future research.

[115] Martin Hirschnitz-Garbers and Susanne Stoll-Kleemann, 'Opportunities and Barriers in the Implementation of Protected Area Management' 177(4) *Geographical Journal* (2011) 321-334; Jens Newig, Edward Challies, Nicolas W Jager, Elisa Kochskaemper, and Ana Adzerse , 'The Environmental Performance of Participatory and Collaborative Governance: A Framework of Causal Mechanisms' 46(2) *Policy Studies Journal* (May 2018) 269-297.

[116] Sigrid Nagoda and Andrea J Nightingale, 'Participation and Power in Climate Change Adaptation Policies' 100 *World Development* (2017) 85-93.

[117] See, e.g. Cary Coglianese, 'Does Consensus Work? A Pragmatic Approach to Public Participation in the Regulatory Process' in Alfonso Morales (ed), *Renascent Pragmatism: Studies in Law and Social Science* (Routledge 2017) 180-195.

[118] Note that, empirically, we find such democratizing effects in global health but not in global finance governance.

[119] Beyond the studies already noted, see in particular Frederick W Mayer and Gary Gereffi, 'Regulation and Economic Globalization: Prospects and Limits of Private Governance' 12(3) *Business and Politics* (2010) 1-25; Tim Büthe, 'Global Private Politics: A Research Agenda' 12(3) *Business and Politics* (2010) 1–25.

Index

Tables and figures are indicated by *t* and *f* following the page number